HIDDEN
New England

HIDDEN
New England

FOURTH EDITION

Ulysses Press
BERKELEY, CALIFORNIA

Published by:
ULYSSES PRESS
3286 Adeline Street, Suite 1
Berkeley, CA 94703

Library of Congress Catalog Card Number 96-60082
ISBN 1-56975-056-4

Printed in the United States of America
by R.R. Donnelley & Sons

10 9 8 7 6 5

Editorial Director: Leslie Henriques
Managing Editor: Claire Chun
Project Director: Ellen Nidy
Contributing Editor: Kelly Spencer
Copy Editor: David Sweet
Editorial Associates: Joy Clark, Mark Rosen,
     Deema Khorsheed, Jennifer Wilkoff
Cartographer: Phil Gardner
Cover Design: Sarah Levin Designs
Indexer: Sayre Van Young
Cover Photography: Larry Ulrich (front cover),
     Robert Holmes (front cover circle and back cover)
Illustrator: Timothy Carroll

Distributed in the United States by Publishers
Group West, in Canada by Raincoast Books,
and in Great Britain and Europe by World
Leisure Marketing

The author and publisher have made every effort
to ensure the accuracy of information contained in
Hidden New England, but can accept no liability for any
loss, injury, or inconvenience sustained by any traveler as
a result of information or advice contained in this guide.

What's Hidden?

At different points throughout this book, you'll find special listings marked with a hidden symbol:

◄ HIDDEN

This means that you have come upon a place off the beaten tourist track, a spot that will carry you a step closer to the local people and natural environment of New England.

The goal of this guide is to lead you beyond the realm of everyday tourist facilities. While we include traditional sightseeing listings and popular attractions, we also offer alternative sights and adventure activities. Instead of filling this guide with reviews of standard hotels and chain restaurants, we concentrate on one-of-a-kind places and locally owned establishments.

Our authors seek out locales that are popular with residents but usually overlooked by visitors. Some are more hidden than others (and are marked accordingly), but all the listings in this book are intended to help you discover the true nature of New England and put you on the path of adventure.

Write to us!

If in your travels you discover a spot that captures the spirit of New England, or if you live in the region and have a favorite place to share, or if you just feel like expressing your views, write to us and we'll pass your note along to the author.

We can't guarantee that the author will add your personal find to the next edition, but if the writer does use the suggestion, we'll acknowledge you in the credits and send you a free autographed copy of the new edition.

ULYSSES PRESS
3286 Adeline Street, Suite 1
Berkeley, CA 94703
E mail: ulypress@aol.com

Contents

Maps

Special Features

OUTDOOR ADVENTURE SYMBOLS

The following symbols accompany national, state and regional park listings, as well as beach descriptions throughout the text.

 CAMPING

 HIKING

 BICYCLING

 RIDING STABLES

 DOWNHILL SKIING

 CROSS-COUNTRY SKIING

SWIMMING

SNORKELING OR SCUBA DIVING

 SURFING

 WATERSKIING

 WINDSURFING

 CANOEING OR KAYAKING

 BOATING

BOAT RAMPS

FISHING

ONE

New England Sojourn

There is no more instantly recognizable scenery in the American landscape—or the American mind—than the picture-postcard image of a New England village: the white-steepled church on an emerald green, ringed by white clapboard houses, the whole of it haloed by forests aflame with fall reds and golds.

No wonder people come hoping, wanting, expecting to find this metaphor for New England life. And this place of centuries past still exists, in many small towns scattered throughout the six states.

But New England is stunningly heterogeneous, possessed of countless rich dimensions. In one state, you find old textile and industrial cities, rivers and lakes, and towering spruce forests whose denizens are moose and black bear. Visitors will discover miles and miles of white sand beaches fringed with dunes and marsh grasses; thriving metropolises like Boston and Providence; mountain ranges with hiking and skiing trails; fishing villages hundreds of years old; Indian burial grounds; and coastal resorts where elegant yachts bob in the harbor. Standing fast before time, New England's old wooden saltbox houses have weathered into the colors of the very ground that made them.

Bounded on the north by Canada, on the east by the Atlantic Ocean, on the south by Long Island Sound, and on the west by New York, New England sits squarely in the northeastern corner of the United States. Five states border the ocean, which is never far from anyone's mind. Fishing blessed all who settled here, from the Indians and the Pilgrims to the 19th-century whalers and today's fishermen of Gloucester, New Bedford and Plymouth. New Englanders have always been premier shipbuilders and sailors, and today one of the greatest pleasures is to ride a Maine windjammer, an excursion boat or a tiny sailboat.

The ocean also tempers the weather, making summers cooler and winters less fierce. The seasons pull out all the stops here, parading four kinds of memorable variety every year. In warmer, more monotonous climes, the passing of time recedes to a blur.

New Englanders love and revere their covered bridges, their Revolutionary War–era, Federal and Greek Revival homes, and their chowder made with milk, not tomato juice, thank you. To a real New Englander, there's nothing quite like the first cider of the fall, real native maple syrup or a clambake on the beach.

To give them credit, many dour old Yankees have expanded their tastes to include the flowers, glass arcades and gourmet restaurants of Quincy Market and whimsical things like balloon festivals.

Still, there is little of glitz about this region. New England simply is what it is, without apology. It's not an invented attraction but a real place, one that stands on the legitimacy and integrity of its origins.

This book was designed to help you explore this wonderful area. Besides leading you to countless popular spots, it will also take you to many off-the-beaten-path locales, places usually known only by locals. The book will tell the story of the region's history, its flora and fauna. Each chapter will suggest places to eat, to stay, to sightsee, to shop and to enjoy the outdoors and nightlife, covering a range of tastes and budgets.

The book sets out in Connecticut, taking visitors in Chapter Two through the rural outlying areas and along its pretty coastline. Chapter Three outlines tiny little Rhode Island's greatly unspoiled topography and gorgeous beaches, as well as elite Newport and historic Providence. Because of its dense population and diversity, Massachusetts is presented in four chapters. Quintessential Boston is explored in Chapter Four, from its Revolutionary War–era sites to Beacon Hill and Back Bay. Chapter Five covers all of Cape Cod, as well as the islands of Martha's Vineyard and Nantucket. Chapter Six moves along the Massachusetts Coast, from the North Shore to Plymouth and New Bedford on the South Shore. In Chapter Seven, you'll discover the Pioneer Valley and the Berkshires of central and western Massachusetts.

Chapter Eight covers Vermont, with its Green Mountains and covered bridges. Chapter Nine is dedicated to New Hampshire, land of sparkling lakes, the White Mountains and majestic Mount Washington. Last but by no means least, you'll explore the stately pine forests and rugged coast of Maine in Chapter Ten.

Wherever you choose to go, whatever you choose to see and do, you're bound to find something to like in this infinite variety. Generations of travelers have enjoyed New England's coast and mountains, forests and lakes, in all kinds of weather.

▼▼▼▼▼▼▼▼▼▼▼▼▼▼▼▼▼▼▼▼

The Story of New England

Geology is destiny, you might say. Certainly this is true in the case of New England. Some of the region's most famed symbols,

GEOLOGY

from stone walls, mill towns and rivers, to Bunker Hill, Walden Pond, Cape Cod and the White Mountains, sprang from geologic events.

New England is one of the oldest continuously surviving land masses on earth. In Cambrian times, half a billion years ago, New England was covered by a vast inland sea. When the earth's crust buckled and rose, it pushed up mountainous masses—the ancestors of the Berkshires and the Green Mountains. During the same era, a mass of hot molten rock gave birth to the White Mountains from deep within the earth.

Even while the mountains were rising, running water began to wear away at the land, leveling it and washing sediments down from the uplands. Finally all New England was reduced almost to sea level,

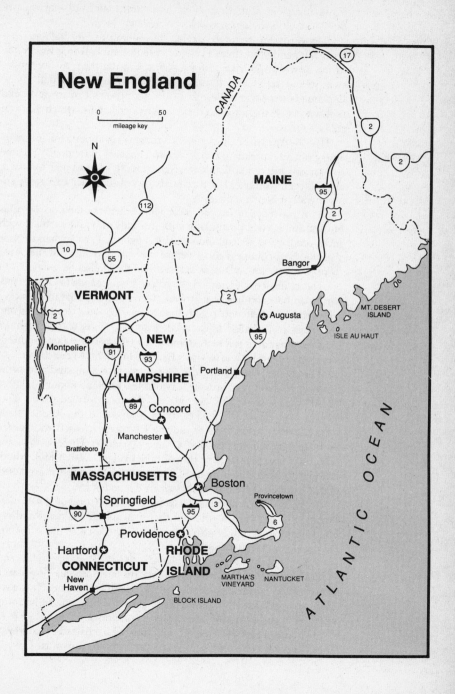

New England

0 — 50
mileage key

N

CANADA

MAINE

112

10

55

17

2

2

95

2

Bangor

2

VERMONT

2

Montpelier

91

NEW

93

HAMPSHIRE

Augusta

95

MT. DESERT
ISLAND

ISLE AU HAUT

Portland

89

Concord

Manchester

Brattleboro

MASSACHUSETTS

Springfield

90

Boston

Provincetown

3

6

95

Providence

Hartford

RHODE

CONNECTICUT

ISLAND

New
Haven

MARTHA'S
VINEYARD

NANTUCKET

BLOCK ISLAND

ATLANTIC OCEAN

like a flat plain. But some of the mountains survived, particularly those in the north, which was less completely leveled.

The earth's crust stirred again, 200 million to 300 million years later, but gently this time. The land rose just enough to give altitude to the slow-moving rivers of the plains, causing them to flow more swiftly, and set them off to carving out valleys. Eventually New Englanders would find these fast-flowing, powerful rivers and build mill wheels on them to run their factories and mills, which you can still see today.

The Ice Age seized the region in a frozen grip about a million years ago, gradually spreading and growing. The mass of ice finally became so vast and heavy that its own weight pushed it down and outward, and it began to move. For thousands of years, the ice cap grew, engulfing all of New England.

As it moved, the ice cap picked up boulders, some as large as houses, and carried them along with it. Fields of boulders, filled with rocks of all sizes, are common in New England. Farmers had to clear their fields of countless rocks before they could plant, and they used them to make stone walls, which still line the landscape today.

The ice moved in a southerly direction, from Canada to Long Island, paring off hills and ledges as it went. Some of the glacial till was clay, which sticks to itself more readily than to ice. Deposited clay formed into low-lying, oval-shaped hills called drumlins, many a mile or more long and a hundred feet high. Some of the region's most famous drumlins are Bunker Hill and World's End in Hingham, Massachusetts.

The glaciers came and went four times, retreating and advancing for over a million years, finally leaving New England about 10,000 to 12,000 years ago. The last glacial advance formed Cape Cod, Martha's Vineyard, Nantucket, Block Island and the Rhode Island shore. At the front of the advancing ice sheet, released rock debris built up a terminal moraine—a ridge of rubble. These islands and coasts are what remains of the morainal ridges. Watch Hill, Rhode Island, has been called by geologists "one of the finest examples of glacial dumping ground" in the eastern United States.

Large blocks of melting glacial ice formed kettle-hole lakes, deep bodies of water with a rounded shape, of which Walden Pond is a good example. It might also be said that kettle lakes make for fine ice-skating and ice-fishing.

HISTORY   New England is America's scrapbook, the memorabilia of a nation conceived on hardship and perseverance, faith and dreams. It is a riveting story of high adventure and the push for freedom, of ingenuity and despotism, of victory over adverse conditions.

The opening pages tell of Pilgrims who charted a course to Greenland but were blown far southward by violent winds. The year was 1000 A.D., and, according to Norse legend, Norseman Leif Ericsson landed in a strange place, probably along Maine's rocky coast. Discovering friendly Indians and fertile land where grapes and wheat grew wild, he dubbed his find Vinland the Good and returned to Norway with tales of a fascinating world.

More than 450 years would pass before European explorers would again call on the intriguing land. Navigator John Cabot, on assignment from England's King Henry VII and seeking a Northwest Passage to the East, explored the coasts of Maine and Massachusetts in 1497. He found no pass but claimed a considerable chunk of the New World—everything north of Florida and east of the Rockies—for the British crown.

Italian explorer Giovanni da Verrazano staked out the same coast some 27 years later, claiming the territory for his employer nation, France. Just prior to his visit, navigator Miguel Corte Real had been checking out the terrain for Portugal.

Dutch sailor Adriaen Block launched a coastal investigation in 1614, calling a Narragansett Bay island "Roodt Eyland," or Red Island, a likely precursor to Rhode Island. That same year, English captain John Smith mapped the Massachusetts coast and was taken by its beauty. A soldier of fortune, Smith wrote a glowing report of the intriguing land, describing its "sandy cliffes and cliffes of rock" planted with cornfields and gardens.

Though captivated by the new region, none of these adventurers did what seemed the most logical thing: settle the place. Of course, this white man's frontier had been inhabited at least five centuries by Algonquin tribes. A peaceful people who dwelled in wigwams, they were expert growers of corn, tobacco, pumpkins and other crops. They hunted forests plentiful with moose, deer, turkey and goose, and fished the streams and ocean for bass, salmon, lobster and clams, throwing the area's earliest clambakes.

The Algonquins were not populous. Small tribes, sometimes with as few as 200 Indians, were scattered among the forests and along the

A CORNUCOPIA OF HISTORY

It would be almost impossible to find another place in the United States so densely packed with history. You can barely take a step without stumbling over a colonial battlefield, a historic site or monument, or an 18th-century house. Before your eyes will come to life all that you learned in school about the birth of the United States. And every year or so, another New England town celebrates its 350th anniversary.

coast. The Pennacook tribe resided in what would become New Hampshire and Massachusetts; the Abenaki favored the New Hampshire area, too, as well as Maine. The Narrangansetts were natives of today's Rhode Island. All told, New England's Indians numbered about 25,000 when they welcomed the first permanent European settlers in 1620.

By the mid-1660s, Rhode Island received New England's first Jews and several hundred French Huguenots and Quakers.

Religious asylum, not adventure or fortune, is what those first real settlers were seeking. The Puritans, cut off from Anglican England because of their strict Protestant beliefs, read with interest John Smith's glowing report on the New World. Could it be their Utopia? They were anxious to find out.

In the spring of 1620, the Puritans struck a deal with the Plymouth Company to finance a settlement in the New World. By summer's end, 102 Puritans boarded the *Mayflower* for a rigorous, two-month journey to America. They first sighted land at Cape Cod, then cruised the coast for a month and landed at Plymouth Rock. On December 21, the Plymouth Colony was born.

That first winter proved brutal for the colonists as they fought scurvy, pneumonia and other diseases that killed nearly half their group. But springtime brought relief and the opportunity to plant crops, thanks to help from the Indians who were hospitable to their new neighbors. To celebrate the first anniversary of their friendship, the Pilgrims and Indians feasted together for three days that fall.

As word of the successful colony trickled back to England, more Puritans set out for the New World. In 1630, about 1000 Puritans on 11 ships landed at Salem during the "Great Migration." Drawn by a vast harbor filled with sea life, settlers moved southward and declared Boston their main colony. Fur-trading posts were established in Maine, and small villages sprang up in New Hampshire, Connecticut and Rhode Island.

By 1636, another 12,000 immigrants had arrived. Puritan ministers, sensing the need to train future leaders, founded Harvard College and set up a general court to govern the colonies. Local matters were dealt with by town leaders at regular meetings, the forerunners of today's town council sessions.

Ironically, those same Puritans who sought the New World for religious freedom would not tolerate other beliefs. In 1651, a visitor from the Rhode Island colony was publicly whipped for being a Baptist. Victims of English persecution, Quakers fleeing the Old World were arrested on ships in Boston Harbor before they ever set foot on the new land. And in 1659, two men and a woman were hanged in Massachusetts for espousing Quaker beliefs.

Religious dissidents fled to Rhode Island, which Puritans dubbed "the sewer of New England" and "Rogue's Island." But the tiny colony held fast to religious and social freedoms.

It was Puritan fanaticism that caused the untimely end of several other unfortunate New England souls. Witches, the Puritans said, were lurking about, possessed by demons and casting spells on innocent minds.

The accusations led to witch trials in Charlestown in 1648 and in Boston in 1655, but the most hideous ordeal occurred in Salem in 1692. After hundreds of people were imprisoned in a "Witch House," 19 were executed, including 80-year-old Giles Corey, who was pressed to death when he pled no-contest.

The Puritans were also a nightmare for the Indians. Determined to "save" them from their pagan ways, missionaries translated the Bible into Algonquin and set about converting new Christians. By the 1670s, nearly one-fourth of the Indian population had officially accepted the imposed faith. But it was not enough. The Puritans wanted not just mental converts but a race that would abandon its centuries-old customs, its very mode of existence.

As colonies expanded, the Indians got in the way. Several skirmishes ensued, but it was King Philip's War, from 1675 to 1676, that spelled the beginning of the end for the New England Indians. Pressured by colonists to abandon his land, chief Metacomet (King Philip) led a series of battles against his encroachers. He lost a decisive engagement, the "Great Swamp Fight" near Kingston, Rhode Island, when Massachusetts and Connecticut colonists burned wigwams, killing hundreds of women and children and disorganizing Indian forces.

Betrayed by a fellow Indian, King Philip was captured soon thereafter, his body beheaded and quartered. His head was displayed on a gibbet in Plymouth for 20 years as a reminder of white victory. Just four decades after the Indians had welcomed the first Puritans into their home, the Puritans had decimated them.

Eighteenth-century New England was a place of social, economic and political growth. Life centered around the ocean and rivers, as shipbuilding thrived in towns such as Portsmouth in New Hampshire, Groton in Connecticut, Kittery in Maine and, of course, Boston. Coopers, potters and furniture makers plied their trades along the waterfront, and coastal and international trade boomed.

Colleges and universities that today rank among the nation's best were established: Yale University, New Hampshire's Dartmouth College, and Rhode Island College, now Brown University. The influx of non-Puritans created a greater cultural and religious mix, and politics flourished as colonists demanded more autonomy from Mother England.

Determined to subdue its wayward child, England in 1764 imposed the Revenue Act, which levied duties on silk, sugar and some wines. Colonists rebelled and promptly boycotted the tariffs.

England didn't flinch. One year later, it slapped colonies with the Stamp Act, taxing commercial and legal papers such as newspapers and licenses. Outraged, colonists denounced the tax and refused to buy European goods. "No taxation without representation," they cried. Every colonial stamp agent resigned, and before the law could take effect November 1, Parliament repealed the act.

But England insisted on political and economic control. Several months later Parliament passed the Townshend Acts, imposing heavy taxes on paper, glass and tea. Colonists again rebelled, and England sent troops to squelch rioting in Boston.

By 1770, hoping to rid the city of "Redcoats"—the colonists' name for the British militia—Bostonians gathered at the Customs House and began taunting the sentry. Troops arrived, and after a series of violent skirmishes, they fired shots into the crowd. When the Boston Massacre was over, five colonials lay dead on King Street, present-day State Street.

England repealed most of the Townshend taxes, leaving duties on imported tea—then the most popular drink in America. New Englanders retaliated by buying smuggled tea. In 1773, when England's Tea Act flooded the market with cheap tea, agents would not accept deliveries—except for Governor Thomas Hutchinson in Boston.

When three tea-filled ships sailed into Boston Harbor, the Committees of Correspondence and Sons of Liberty—pre-revolutionary activists—blocked the piers. Governor Hutchinson refused to let the ships return to England, so protestors invited him to a little tea party.

Disguised as Indians, 60 Sons of Liberty boarded the ships on the night of December 16, 1773 and dumped 342 chests of tea into the harbor. It was a defiant move and an ominous portent of what lie ahead: revolution was in the air.

On April 19, 1775, a single musket discharge set off America's first full-scale war. "The shot heard 'round the world" was fired at the Battle of Lexington and Concord, an effort by the Redcoats to crush revolutionary uprisings around Boston.

Forewarned by Paul Revere that "the British are coming," 77 Minutemen crouched in early morning darkness, waiting for the Redcoat attack. The British advanced, killing eight rebels and wounding ten on the present-day Lexington Green before continuing to Concord. There they destroyed a cache of arms and were finally driven out.

The colonies rallied together. Vermont's Green Mountain Boys, led by Ethan Allen and Benedict Arnold, captured Fort Ticonderoga on Lake Champlain, blocking a British invasion from Canada. On June 17, 1775, New Englanders fought the war's first major engagement—known as the Battle of Bunker Hill although it was really fought on nearby Breed's Hill—on the Charlestown peninsula near Boston. After enduring two British attacks, the Americans ran short of ammunition and retreated.

Though a technical victory for England, Bunker Hill cost the crown more than 1000 troops—over twice the colonial losses. More important, it proved that the Minutemen volunteers were a match for the better-trained British army.

On July 4, 1776, the Declaration of Independence was adopted by the Continental Congress. The war raged on in surrounding states for six years, but New England was free.

Economic depression followed the war. Paper money was scarce, loans difficult to obtain and court foreclosures commonplace. When their new state government levied high taxes, Massachusetts farmers rose up in anger. Shays' Rebellion, which lasted from 1786 to 1787 but was unsuccessful at stopping the taxes, proved that democracy was still an elusive concept.

New England heralded the 19th-century with a burgeoning shipping industry, though the War of 1812 temporarily halted matters with stiff trade embargoes. With the advent of the cotton mill in Pawtucket, Rhode Island, weavers no longer had to work at home, though their 12-hour workdays and paltry wages led to the nation's first labor strike in 1800. Eli Whitney's cotton gin revolutionized the wool industry, and mills sprang up across New England. By the 1830s, Providence alone produced 20 percent of the country's wool.

As New England grew and the railroad headed west, settlers starting moving into the interior. Wilderness areas of northern Maine, Vermont and New Hampshire were slowly penetrated, and pioneers established small farms. But unforgiving soil and unpredictable weather squelched any hopes of real agriculture, and by 1860 farming as serious business ceased to exist in these states.

The Industrial Revolution sparked a mass immigration of Europeans, with hundreds arriving from England, Scotland, Italy and Portugal. Victims of the 1845 Great Potato Famine, thousands of Irish sailed to Massachusetts with dreams of a new life. By 1850, one of every ten New Englanders was foreign born. Only ten years later, 61 percent of Boston residents had been born abroad.

AMERICAN INGENUITY

Hundreds of inventions put New England at the forefront of the industrial age. Yale graduate Samuel Morse masterminded the telegraph and his own code, Elias Howe crafted the world's first sewing machine, and Charles Goodyear developed a type of commercial rubber, though he died $200,000 in the red. In Hartford, Samuel Colt opened a munitions factory and Francis Pratt and Amos Whitney manufactured machine tools and interchangeable parts.

Not all New Englanders welcomed so many immigrants with open arms. During the 1850s, several political monsters reared their ugly heads. The Know-Nothing Party blatantly opposed all immigrants, particularly the Irish. Together with virulent anti-Roman Catholic factions in Maine, the party burned several Catholic churches. The powerful Know-Nothings managed to control governorships in several states.

At the same time, the abolition movement gripped New England. Connecticut's Harriet Beecher Stowe raised public consciousness in 1852 with *Uncle Tom's Cabin*. A fervent opponent of slavery, William Lloyd Garrison published his *Liberator* newspaper for 34 years in Massachusetts, despite being dragged through streets by angry mobs and threatened constantly.

New England was also experiencing a cultural renaissance. The great "Flowering of New England" was centered in Boston. Now called the "Athens of America," the city saw the founding of such eminent institutions as the Museum of Fine Arts, the Boston Symphony Orchestra and the Boston Pops.

Great minds thrived across the region. Artists, thinkers and literary geniuses would set the dynamic tone in New England for centuries to come. People like Nathaniel Hawthorne and Oliver Wendell Holmes, Henry David Thoreau and Julia Ward Howe, Ralph Waldo Emerson and Robert Frost made New England an intellectual mecca.

By the turn of the century, an ethnic and political metamorphosis had taken place. The long-time bastion of Yankee Protestantism was now being run by Roman Catholics. In 1900, a majority of New England legislators were Catholic.

At the same time came a wave of corruption that would last for several decades. In Rhode Island, Republican "Boss" Charles R. Brayton built his regime by exchanging bought votes for "judgeships and other political jobs," charged journalist Lincoln Steffens. Brayton even paid "yellow dog" Democrats to be loyal to the machine. Iniquity reached its height in Boston's James Michael Curley, elected mayor four times between 1914 and 1950 and state governor from 1935 to 1937. The "Irish Mussolini" perfected ward politics, handing out jobs, favors and money to those who guaranteed his return to office.

The Depression crushed New England. Between 1929 and 1950, more than 149,000 textile workers lost their jobs as the manufacturing industry fell prostrate. Wages were slashed in half for those lucky enough to work, and hundreds of thousands lost their homes.

New England never fully rebounded from those difficult years. During the 1960s and early 1970s, foreign imports dealt a blow to most of the manufacturing left in the area. Void of natural resources such as oil and coal, the area was especially hard hit by the 1970s recession.

But today's New England has seen a rebirth of industry and technology. Modern enterprises have flourished, producing such far-reaching wonders as missile and space systems, jet aircraft engines, computers and computer equipment, and biomedical and photographic instruments. The new businesses circle Boston around Route 128 and spill over into Hartford, southern New Hampshire, Rhode Island and even Vermont's Burlington area.

Massachusetts and Connecticut boast one of the nation's largest pools of capital, with Boston claiming more than 50 insurance companies and about 35 percent of U.S. mutual fund holdings. The greater Boston metropolitan area is home to some 21 newspapers, 8 television stations, 31 radio stations and many libraries and museums of national stature.

Progressive New Englanders were among the first to push environmental issues to the national front, passing stringent air pollution and zoning laws. As early as the 1960s, rural Vermont banned billboards and nonreturnable bottles. Massachusetts passed the nation's earliest wetlands act.

Higher education is itself a leading "industry" of Massachusetts, the site of some 121 colleges and universities—47 in Boston alone. And New England's immense beauty and rich history make tourism the number two industry, second only to manufacturing.

Today, beyond the high-tech centers and tourist attractions resounds the inescapable presence of New England's colorful past: Revolutionary War monuments, 18th-century covered bridges and statehouses, steepled churches that held this country's first congregations.

One need only explore Paul Revere's House, the Bunker Hill Monument and the Granary Burial Ground in the Boston area to recognize the sites of this country's genesis. For New England's past is America's past. And the region remains a vital part of the nation's present and future.

The glorious flaming reds, oranges and yellows of a New England fall come from changes in its thick stands of hardwood trees, which cover more than three-quarters of the region. The most colorful displays are put on by sugar and red maples, beech, oak, birch, hickory and red oak (see "Fall Foliage: Nature's Kaleidoscope" in this chapter).

FLORA

Vast and stately pine forests blanket much of the north, creating its characteristic wild and rugged look. Among them are spruce, balsam fir and hemlock. Southern New England, too, has conifers throughout, the most common being white pine. Among the tallest of eastern trees, the sun-loving white pine may live 400 years or more.

New England grows some 2000 species of flowering plants and ferns. Wildflowers bloom in colorful profusion along the roadsides and in parks and forests. The leader of the wildflowers is the long-stemmed goldenrod, which occurs almost everywhere, as do black-eyed Susans, lupine, purple asters, daisies and Queen Anne's lace. Shady, moist habitats foster several species of orchids, with the pink lady's slipper being the showiest and most common.

Text continued on page 14.

Fall Foliage: Nature's Kaleidoscope

Like nature's last fling before a long slumber, the changing hues of New England's fall foliage precede winter with a fantastic display of color gone wild. Meadows are splashed with orange and purple, lakes appear ringed with fire and whole mountains turn from green to gold.

Better than any fireworks show, this phenomenon draws at least 2.8 million visitors to New England each year. Arriving by car, train, bus and bicycle, they pitch tents in forests, settle into cabins and resorts and pack the roadways everywhere. They come not just to marvel at the scenery but to be part of an all-encompassing experience.

The show starts up around mid-September with a few hints of scarlet and gold, as if the mountains were blushing. Then slowly, the blush becomes a sea of reds and orange and purples that melt together like rivers of shimmering watercolors. Each day brings new colors, new perspectives.

What makes it all happen? Prodded by cool nights and shorter autumn days, tree leaves abandon their green veneer to reveal hues ranging from crimson and sunburst to mahogany, violet and bronze.

Of course, each tree has its own brand of color. Maples flash a brilliant red leaf. Shagbark hickory leaves turn yellow and resemble hammered gold, while witch hazel's flaxen leaves camouflage small yellow flowers. The sumac sports purple saw-toothed leaves and fuzzy twigs resembling antlers. Thin and dainty, cherry leaves go from bright purple to bright yellow.

Then there's the clever speckled alder, a swamp dweller that doesn't change color at all. Its broad green leaves provide a nice contrast to all those reds and yellows and purples.

The farther north you are, the earlier the show starts. Northern areas of Maine, New Hampshire and Vermont set things off, sending waves of color southward as fall advances. The show usually winds down around mid-October, or after the first few frosts.

Though you can "see the leaves" change almost anywhere in New England, the best leaf-peeping exists in mountain areas. Reputed as one of the best fall-foliage spots in the world, New Hampshire's White Mountain National Forest offers 763,000 acres of uninterrupted timberland that explodes with continuous color.

Next door, Vermont's Green Mountain National Forest has miles of dense woods, gentle mountains and rushing streams that form a spectacular foliage backdrop. In Maine, head for the area around Machias known as **blueberry barrens**. A vast sweep of blueberry fields, the barrens turn flaming red in the fall and stretch as far as the eye can see. Maine's rock-lined coast also provides extraordinary foliage pageantry, with spiraling scarlet trees set against a sea of aquamarine.

Connecticut's foliage beauty lies in its diverse forests that provide the entire spectrum of colors. Travel from the pastel-colored oaks and birches along the coast to the deep red pepperidge trees in the southwest. Then cut up to the yellow and vermilion maple trees in the northwest corner.

Tiny Rhode Island is all ablaze with fall color, though it is most concentrated in the uplands. Located on the north and west corridors, the uplands are a picture of amber rolling hills, thick timbers and nearly 300 lakes and reservoirs rimmed with rainbow hues.

For a special foliage treat, head for Massachusetts' South Shore, where **cranberry bogs** stretch just south of Boston to Bristol. During October harvests, farmers flood the bogs, forcing the berries to the top of the marsh and creating a sea of bright crimson (see "Exploring Cranberry Country" in Chapter Six).

If you'd like to take home more than photographs, gather an assortment of your favorite leaves and branches. While they're still supple, press the leaves between layers of cardboard, then secure between heavy boards or books and tie tightly with rope. Store in a warm, dry place for ten days, making sure the rope is always snug.

Branches make beautiful bouquets once preserved. Simply split the stems at the base and cover with a solution of two parts water and one part glycerine. Store in a cool, well-ventilated area until leaves show a slight change in color. Remove and hang upside down until dry.

To get the scoop on leaf-peeping conditions, call the foliage hotlines (during fall months only) sponsored by each state: New Hampshire, 603-271-6870, 800-258-3608; Vermont, 802-828-3239; Maine, 800-533-9595; Connecticut, 860-258-4290; Rhode Island, 401-277-2601; Massachusetts, 617-727-3201. Some states supply foliage guides with tips on picture-taking and leaf identification.

A word of advice: fall-foliage season is the most popular vacation time in New England, so it's important to make travel arrangements far in advance—at least six months ahead of time.

Three of the most spectacular wildflower displays are given by the rhododendron, flowering dogwood and mountain laurel, the state flower of Connecticut, which occurs in southern New England. The mountain laurel's lustrous, dark green leaves and six-sided, pink-and-white blossoms form a dense, impenetrable thicket in the forest, sometimes up to 13 feet high.

At the shore grow miles and miles of shrubby wild beach roses with delicate scent and fragile petals of pink, white and fuchsia. Also along the shore grow beach peas, pitch pine, huckleberry, lowbush blueberry, sheep laurel and bayberry, from which the colonists made candles.

Wetlands are prevalent throughout New England, left by glacial action. Swamps, marshes and bogs all have their own little communities of plants, specially adapted to float on the water or emerge from it. Two very characteristic swamp plants are the purplish green skunk cabbage, with a strong odor like a skunk's, and Jack-in-the-Pulpit, which looks like a miniature preacher in a covered pulpit.

In the soft, dark muck and highly organic environs of marshes grow grasses, reeds and sedges such as cattails. Purple loosestrife now covers huge expanses of marsh and wet meadows. Other common marsh plants include duckweed, the smallest flowering plant known; blue flag, a kind of native iris; Joe-pye weed and yellow pond lily.

Sphagnum moss and sedges are partial to bogs, as are knee-high evergreen shrubs, bog laurel, bog rosemary and Labrador Tea, reputedly brewed as a substitute for tea in colonial times. In low-lying, sandy-floored bogs thrive cranberries, a mainstay of the Massachusetts economy.

FAUNA

No single animal is more ubiquitous in New England than the gray squirrel, which flirts its bushy tail as it races along telephone wires, up and down trees in city parks and through backyards. A close second is the dramatically colored eastern chipmunk. Though they are pests to the gardener and the householder, rabbits and woodchucks are numerous, too.

The black bear, New England's only bear, and the moose claim title to being the region's largest land mammals, favoring wilder woodland areas in the north. The homely moose, believe it or not, is a member of the deer family and lives in the deep cover of northern forests in Maine, New Hampshire and Vermont. Another large mammal favored by hunters is the white-tailed deer, which has a bushy white tail, big ears and long legs.

The fallow deer, a native of Asia Minor, was released on Nantucket and Martha's Vineyard. The deer became so numerous that they overran the islands and had to be thinned.

Smaller mammals include beaver, red foxes, raccoons, porcupines, skunks and possums. Pity the poor possum: he is poorly adapted to the cold, and many New England possums lose pieces of their paper-thin ears and bare tails to frostbite.

Off the rocky shores in northern coastal waters, harbor seals cavort, hauling out to sun themselves on islands and rocky shores. The coast is also home to the Atlantic white-sided dolphin and several species of whales, best seen up-close on whale-watching trips.

The clownlike Atlantic puffin can be seen on the rocky islets of Maine, the only place in the U.S. where you can spot this bird.

The arrival of spring in New England is announced vociferously by spring peepers, tiny frogs measuring little more than an inch long that climb trees to sing their lyrical nocturnal chorus.

Other native amphibians include the spotted salamander, green frog and bullfrog, a giant of native frogs, sometimes over eight inches long. Reptiles are represented by snapping turtles, painted turtles, box turtles, garter snakes and black racers. New England also has two poisonous snakes, the timber rattlesnake and the northern copperhead, although you will almost surely never see one, so rare and retiring are they.

Situated as it is right along the Atlantic Flyway, New England is a premier place for birding, especially during spring migration. More than 400 species have been sighted in New England, although more than half are transient migratories, shorebirds that rarely come ashore or accidentals carried in by storm winds. The single most characteristic bird is the gull, found everywhere along the coast.

Canada geese and cormorants have increased their range and numbers, as have ospreys, after being given special nesting platforms on Martha's Vineyard. The handsome loon rules the northern lakes. There are many species of ducks, in both fresh water and salt water.

Endangered species include the piping plover, roseate tern, peregrine falcon, upland sandpiper, short-eared owl and bald eagle, now nesting in the Quabbin Reservoir in central Massachusetts.

Where to Go

New England is no more all of a piece than is Europe. Deciding what to see and where to go is a tough choice. The good news is, you'll just have to keep coming back to get to know the real New England.

To help you with your decisions, we'll entice you with some brief descriptions of each state. To get the whole story, read the introductions to each chapter, then the more detailed material on the regions that appeal to you.

Connecticut packs several very different regions into its compact space. We first visit the southeastern part of the state, neighbor to New York. Failing in their effort to annex this corner, New Yorkers have nonetheless succeeded in remaking it in their own image: brimming with the fancy gourmet stores and chichi boutiques so vital to

Manhattanites. The state's northwest corner offers historic villages and picturesque lakes. The capital city is Hartford, also known as the insurance capital of the world. South along the coast stands the city of New Haven, an urban industrial center whose main claim to fame is Yale University. From New Haven to the Rhode Island border, coastal Connecticut strings together one pretty fishing and sailing village after another: Essex, Old Saybrook, Mystic and Stonington. Connecticut's rural northeastern corner is the least known and developed area.

With two feet in the ocean, **Rhode Island** boasts miles of sandy beaches with rolling surf rivaling those of the Cape. The coastal villages of South County have a quiet, antique charm, while Victorian Block Island is a little island lost in time. Newport's fabled elegance still shines today in the extravagant summer "cottages" built by Gilded Age multimillionaires. Providence, a revitalized urban center, stands tall with one of the nation's finest historic districts, showcasing restored 18th- and 19th-century period houses. Farther north, the Blackstone Valley, stretching from Pawtucket to Woonsocket and west, is known as the "birthplace of American manufacturing."

With its quaint, cobblestoned streets, old-fashioned neighborhoods and big-city charms, **Boston** delights all who visit. Here is where America's most iconographic history lives on, at such sites as Paul Revere's House and the Old North Church in the North End. Much of Boston sparkles with new polish, especially the waterfront. Perennial favorites include Quincy Market, the diminutive brick townhouses and sprightly gardens of Beacon Hill, the imposing brownstones of Back Bay and the soaring architecture of Copley Square. Across the Charles River sits Harvard Square, the thriving nexus of intellectual Cambridge. Rural Lexington and Concord are known for their colonial history.

Cape Cod and the Islands explores some of the most famous and popular areas of the state. Cape Cod is a favored spot for summer vacations. The North Cape is known for its quaint historical villages, the South Cape for Hyannis, home of the Kennedy clan, the Outer Cape for its beaches and sand dunes and Provincetown for its gay life. South of the Cape lie the islands of Martha's Vineyard and Nantucket, both prosperous whaling ports in their day and now drenched in the natural beauty of windswept moors, weathered cottages, pine woods and intimate beaches.

Wending its way hundreds of miles from Boston's North Shore to New Bedford in the southeast corner of the state, the **Massachusetts Coast** is studded its entire length with lovely resorts, fine sandy beaches and small fishing villages. Gloucester, Rockport and Salem are the highlights of the exclusive North Shore. The Plymouth area is rich in colonial history and lined with attractive fishing and farming villages with neat clapboarded 18th- and 19th-century sea captains' homes. New Bedford and Fall River have troves of whaling and textile history lore, respectively, as well as oodles of discount outlet stores.

Central and western Massachusetts includes a vast part of the state, from the old industrial city of Worcester west of Boston to the resort-oriented Berkshires on the western border. Rural hamlets, wildlife sanctuaries and state parks ring central Massachusetts, where Old Sturbridge Village re-creates the farming life of the 1840s. The Pioneer Valley stretches up the Connecticut River, through another large city with a rich industrial past, Springfield. A summer capital of music, dance and drama, the Berkshires are serene and sylvan settings of mountains, forests and lakes. Here Norman Rockwell made the streetscapes of Stockbridge famous. The Berkshires have produced a lovely commingling of luxurious resorts, charming inns, gourmet restaurants and ski havens.

No single New England state is more rural than **Vermont**, with its miles of open farmland, covered bridges, maple sugarhouses and small towns with classic village greens and general stores. Some of the best skiing in America is here, as is some of the best cheddar cheese you'll ever eat. Lying on Vermont's western border with New York is the magnificent Lake Champlain, named for explorer Samuel de Champlain and popular with boaters, swimmers and ice fishers. The most rugged region is the Northeast Kingdom, three northern counties bordering Canada that make up a realm of tiny townships, mountains, forests and isolated farms.

Though **New Hampshire**'s tiny seacoast measures a mere 18 miles, along it lies Portsmouth, a jewel of a town that is one of the most handsome refurbished antique settlements on the East Coast. Old textile mills and factories sprawl along the Merrimack River, while outlet stores and other commerce thrive in the state's prosperous, booming southern half. The northern half is a wilderness of lakes, mountains and evergreen forests. Large and beautiful bodies of water like Lake Sunapee and Lake Winnepesaukee, and the White Mountains offer sports enthusiasts numerous choices, as well as plentiful resorts. Weathered barns and country towns complete the scenery in the Monadnock Region.

Maine, the land of Downeast, has sent its most famous delicacy, Maine lobster, all over the world. In this state's wilderness and waterways live thick spruce forests, moose, black bear, loons and deer. More developed than the north, the southern coast presents low-key resort towns and outlet stores, as well as the city of Portland, a restored maritime Victorian jewel. North of Portland is the rugged, rockbound coast, the real Downeast, with its independent-minded towns of Damariscotta, Wiscasset, Camden and Castine. Out on

Mount Desert Island, the old-money resort of Bar Harbor reigns, alongside the splendid Acadia National Park. Maine is also Andrew Wyeth country, as seen in the turn-of-the-century world of Monhegan Island, just one of hundreds of islands in Casco Bay. To the north, the Maine woods offer an unparalleled wilderness experience, where visitors can travel for a hundred miles without spotting any sign of civilization. The lakes region provides scenic splendors and water sports galore.

When to Go

SEASONS

A constant battle wages here in New England between bristling battalions of cold, dry Canadian arctic air and laid-back, warm, humid air from the tropics. When these two mix it up, which is frequently, you have New England's legendary changeable weather. The morning may dawn fine and sunny, afternoon turn cold and foggy and nightfall bring a raging northeaster.

More than you might think, the weather varies from south to north. Weather in southeastern New England, tempered by ocean winds, is warmer. While mean temperatures for Connecticut range from 27 in January to 73 in July, in Vermont they go from 16 in January to 70 in July. And at the top of New Hampshire's Mount Washington, it may as well be Antarctica.

No matter how you slice it, winters are long and cold here, and the overall effect has been described as "nine months of winter and three of rough sledding." Winters are invariably colder in Vermont and Maine, where temperatures range from -10 to 10 and sometimes drop to -30. In southern New England, temperatures are more likely to hover in the 20s and 30s in winter.

In the north, snow arrives as early as Thanksgiving and stays on the ground into mid-April, but near the coast in the southeast, it's indecent of snow to put in an appearance until Christmas and subzero weather is almost unheard of. But don't be deterred by the long winter; that's what puts plenty of white stuff on the northern ski slopes.

And, inevitably, there comes the spring thaw, which in the northern country goes by the popular name of "mud season." When the frozen ground starts melting, the result is a muddy morass. Spring is a little less messy in the south, where by mid-March the songbirds are chirping away, followed by greening in another few weeks.

Summer sets in around about mid-June. Days are quite warm, with temperatures ranging from 70 to 90, turning to slightly cooler evenings, especially along the shore and in the mountains. Despite the tempering ocean breezes, summer can be humid, as well as foggy and rainy. The weather is hottest in central Massachusetts, in the dry valley of the Connecticut River.

Autumn may be the most wonderful season of all to visit, and certainly the most popular one. Fall colors are at their peak, and all the fall harvests of apples, cider, cranberries and pumpkins are in. Sunny days often warm up to "Indian summer" comfort, energized by cool, crisp nights. In the southeast, autumn lasts right into November.

Both autumn and winter are substantially drier than in other locales. Still, it manages to rain, snow or sleet about one day out of three, making for an annual precipitation of 42 inches and an annual snowfall in the mountains of 90 to 100 inches.

Hurricanes periodically strike the region with devastating intensity. This century's worst occurred in 1938 when entire coastal communities were swallowed by the sea. In the fall of 1991 another disastrous hurricane hit New England, damaging, among others, former President George Bush's family home in Kennebunkport, Maine.

Tourists flock to New England for fall-foliage season (mid-September through October), when it can be very difficult to get reservations. High summer (July through Labor Day) is also a busy time, especially along the coast. You might want to consider a visit to a seaside resort in the spring or fall, when rates are lower. Christmas, New Year's and ski season (late January through March) are popular times with tourists. During the low seasons of April, May and late October through late December, you'll have a much less crowded vacation and a much easier time getting reservations.

CALENDAR OF EVENTS

Each year, New England celebrates its colonial past by reenacting historic events that took place in all six states. Other annual observances celebrate the wonderful largesse of this region: apples, maple sugar, blueberries, scallops, clams. The list of merrymaking goes on, with art, music and dance festivals, and occasions honoring many New England traditions, such as shipbuilding, quiltmaking, sheep shearing and Shaker craftsmanship.

Boston   The **Chinese New Year** is celebrated in January or February, with three weeks of festivities.

JANUARY

Vermont   Sled dog races, parades and downhill and cross-country skiing events comprise the **Stowe Winter Carnival**.

Boston   The **New England Boat Show**, one of the largest on the East Coast, brings out the latest and fanciest in power and sail. Four of the city's biggest hockey-playing colleges (Harvard, Northeastern, Boston University and Boston College) face off in the **Beanpot Hockey Tournament**.

FEBRUARY

New Hampshire   The **Dartmouth College Winter Carnival** is an exuberant expression of fun during the winter doldrums.

Boston   The **New England Spring Flower Show** has been running for more than 100 years, giving a lift to winter-weary Bostonians. The **St.**

MARCH

Patrick's Day Parade thrown by the Irish of South Boston is one of the largest and most festive in America.

Maine   Appropriately, the **Sled Dog Races** take place in the frontier town of Rangeley. Maple sugarhouses statewide throw open their doors on **Maine Maple Sunday.**

APRIL

Boston   The nation's premier running event, the **Boston Marathon** is only one of several signal events on **Patriot's Day.** Other activities commemorating Revolutionary War events include a parade plus re-enactments of Paul Revere's famous ride and the Battle of Lexington and Concord.

Cape Cod and the Islands   During Nantucket's **Daffodil Festival,** hundreds of these sprightly blooms decorate shop windows.

Vermont   At the **Vermont Maple Festival** in St. Albans, sample maple products, watch contests and enjoy the entertainment.

MAY

Connecticut   Picnic-style lobster dinners, naturally, are the main event at the **Lobster Festival** at Mystic Seaport.

Rhode Island   **Gaspee Days** in Warwick, which run into June, commemorate the colonists' burning of Britain's H.M.S. *Gaspee* in 1772—one of the first acts of hostility leading to the Revolution—with historic re-enactments, a parade, arts and crafts, food and entertainment.

Boston   **Lilac Sunday** at the Arnold Arboretum finds 400 varieties of lilacs in bloom, and the Franklin Park Zoo hosts a colorful **Annual Kite Festival.**

Cape Cod and the Islands   Sandwich's **Heritage Plantation Rhododendron Festival** features blooms as far as the eye can see, plus lectures and plant sales.

Central and Western Massachusetts   The **Brimfield antique shows,** also held in July and September, draw more than 1000 dealers for week-long events in the small town of Brimfield.

Vermont   **Lilac Sunday** at the Shelburne Museum showcases this museum's stunning lilac collection.

JUNE

Connecticut   One-hundred-and-fifty species of rare, endangered or just plain lovely New England wildflowers are displayed at the **Wildflower Festival** at the University of Connecticut at Storrs.

Rhode Island   Providence's historic east side is on view during the **Festival of Historic Houses.**

Boston   The **Bunker Hill Day Reenactment and Parade** features contemporary patriots dressed in Revolutionary uniforms fighting the famous battle again.

Cape Cod and the Islands   At Hyannis' **Cape Cod Chowder Festival,** you can vote for the best chowder and enjoy live entertainment.

Massachusetts Coast   Anything made with fresh strawberries can be served at the **Annual Strawberry Festival** in Ipswich.

Central and Western Massachusetts Wine and cheese on the lawn while listening to the Boston Symphony Orchestra is the attraction of the **Tanglewood Music Festival**. One of the Northeast's best-known dance festivals, **Jacob's Pillow**, takes place in the Berkshires.

Vermont Hot-air balloons light up the scenery at the **Balloon Festival and Crafts Fair** in Quechee.

New Hampshire Local and national acts heat up the summer at the **Portsmouth Jazz Festival**.

Maine The **Old Port Festival** brings the historic part of Portland to life with a street fair of arts and crafts, music, jugglers, kids' events, song and ethnic foods. **Windjammer Days** in Boothbay Harbor show off these classic schooners under full sail in a dress parade.

Connecticut Soloists of national renown perform **Summer Music** at a scenic seaside setting at Waterford's Harkness Memorial Park.

JULY

Boston The **U.S. Pro Tennis Championship** draws thousands of tennis fans to the Longwood Cricket Club. Every weekend in July and August, **Italian street festivals** honor patron saints with colorful parades and festivities. The **Boston Harborfest** offers nearly a hundred activities celebrating the harbor at 30 sites, highlighted by a chowderfest and wingfest. Local restaurants serve up heaping samples of clam chowder as they battle for the tastiest bowl of "chowdah" as determined by popular vote at the **Chowderfest** on City Hall Plaza. The **Boston Pops Fourth of July Concert** on the Esplanade's Hatch Shell promises an evening of free music and glorious fireworks.

Cape Cod and the Islands In early July, the People of the First Light's **Mashpee Pow-Wow** is held at the Heritage Ballfield in Mashpee. The pow-wow attracts American Indians from all over the United States, as well as from Canada, Mexico and some Central and South American countries. In Sandwich, book lovers delight in the **Cape Cod Antiquarian Book Fair**, with more than 40 dealers, rare and out-of-print books, manuscripts and collectibles. The **Edgartown Regatta**, held on Martha's Vineyard, is one of New England's best and most serious yacht races. On Nantucket, the **Annual Billfish Tournament** is a big event where anglers compete for the biggest catch of each species.

Massachusetts Coast In Gloucester, the **Hammond Castle Annual Medieval Festival** has magic shows, music and merriment. **Race Week** in Marblehead includes sailboat races, parades and concerts.

Vermont The **Vermont Mozart Festival** presents more than two solid weeks of classical music and a "Mozart Odyssey" of dining and entertainment at the Trapp Family Lodge.

Maine The **Great Kennebec River Whatever Week and Race** is an apt name for a ten-day event that starts with vaudeville shows and street performers and climaxes with an eight-mile regatta of anything that floats.

AUGUST   **Connecticut**   The **Volvo International Tennis Tournament** show-cases top tennis stars in world-class play. A kinetic sculpture race kicks off the **SoNo Arts Celebration,** a weekend featuring live entertainment, art exhibits, a colorful puppet parade and dancing in the streets.

Rhode Island   Some of the world's best jazz musicians entertain the thousands sprawled out on the green lawns of Fort Adams State Park in Newport at the JVC **Jazz Festival.** B. B. King, Randy Newman and Leon Redbone have all performed at **Ben & Jerry's Newport Folk Festival.**

Cape Cod and the Islands   The **Falmouth Road Races** is the event of the year on the lower Cape, where the seven-mile race is run along the Shining Sea Path. On Nantucket, the **Annual Antique Show** offers quality antiques. Imaginations go wild at the **Sandcastle Contest** at Jetties Beach on Nantucket. In Oak Bluffs, on Martha's Vineyard, **Illumination Night** is pure magic, with hundreds of paper lanterns strung between the Gothic homes.

Massachusetts Coast   New Bedford's **Annual Feast of the Blessed Sacrament,** the largest Portuguese feast in America, features terrific ethnic food at budget prices.

New Hampshire   Some of the state's finest crafts are sold at the **Craftsmen's Fair of the League of New Hampshire Craftsmen Foundation** in Newbury. Thousands flock to Louden for the **New England 200,** an Indy car race at the New Hampshire International Speedway.

Maine   Hundreds of performers from around the world enliven Brunswick at the **Maine Festival of the Arts** with music, dance, crafts, demonstrations and food. An all-you-can-eat blueberry pancake breakfast starts off the week for the **Maine State Blueberry Festival** in Union.

SEPTEMBER   **Connecticut**   The South Norwalk **Oyster Festival** has something for everyone: oysters galore, seafood and ethnic foods, nationally known singers and bands, arts and crafts, tall ships and marine skills demonstrations.

Rhode Island   Cajun and bluegrass in New England? Yes, loads, not only music, but food and dance, at the **Cajun & Bluegrass Music & Dance Festival** in Escoheag at Stepping Stone Ranch.

Boston   The **Boston Film Festival** is held at the end of the month and includes feature-length movies by major studios as well as more unusual films from independent producers, students and foreign filmmakers.

Cape Cod and the Islands   The **Cape Cod Antique Market,** a large gathering of antique and collectible dealers, takes place at Barnstable County Fairgrounds in Falmouth. The **Harwich Cranberry Festival** includes ten days of parades, contests, fireworks and exhibits.

Wellfleet holds **Bygone Days,** a nostalgic weekend including a children's parade, a Cape Cod Shore dinner, fashion shows, church suppers, nature walks, quilt raffles and the Saturday Harvest Moon Dance. **Tivoli Day** is usually held on the second Saturday of the month in Oak Bluffs, on Martha's Vineyard, where there's a street fair and a 62-mile bike race.

Massachusetts Coast The **Essex Institute Harvest Festival** in Salem features demonstrations of 17th- and 18th-century domestic arts, folk dancing, music and food. At the **Gloucester Schooner Festival,** you can watch races, a boat parade and other maritime activities. **Plimouth Plantation Muster Day** includes antique militia weapons and defense displays, tactical moves, feasting and recreation.

Central and Western Massachusetts The **Big E,** or the **Eastern States Exposition,** in West Springfield is the East's largest annual fair, strong on agricultural and animal exhibits, horse shows and rides and food galore. King Kielbasa, "the world's biggest kielbasa," sets the tone for the **World Kielbasa Festival** in Chicopee.

New Hampshire The **Scottish Highlands Games** draws thousands of people to Lincoln, some who show up in kilts for highlander games and music.

Maine In Windsor, the **Common Ground County Fair** celebrates the rural Maine life with homegrown foods and locally produced crafts.

Boston More than 3000 oarsmen compete in the **Head of the Charles Regatta,** the largest one-day rowing event in the world.

Cape Cod and the Islands Island arts, crafts, workshops and exhibits take place during **Nantucket Heritage Days.**

Massachusetts Coast If ever a place looked haunted, it would be Hammond Castle in Gloucester, where on **Freaky Fridays** ghosts and ghouls spook and delight you as you tour this romantic castle. If you can make reservations well in advance and have a great Halloween costume, don't miss **Hammond Castle Halloween Ball** in the Great Hall, a costumed event right out of a horror novel. **Haunted Happenings,** Salem's citywide Halloween festival, includes haunted-house tours, costume parades, parties, magic shows, psychics and candlelight tours with, of course, witches.

Central and Western Massachusetts The **Topsfield Fair** is another vintage event, with sheep dog trials, ethnic foods and midway rides.

Maine More than 135 years old, the **Fryeburg Fair** sticks close to its agricultural roots during week-long festivities. **Lowell Celebrates Kerouac** stages poetry readings and organizes "beat" tours in honor of '50s literary giant Jack Kerouac who lived and worked in Lowell.

Massachusetts Coast **A Sea Captain Celebrates Thanksgiving,** an 18th-century banquet in Salem's House of Seven Gables, also includes discussions on meal preparation, dining customs and music of the

OCTOBER

NOVEMBER

time (reservations required). Have a traditional turkey dinner with all the trimmings in America's hometown, Plymouth, during its annual **Thanksgiving Dinner.**

Central and Western Massachusetts   Cascade mums, standard varieties and new hybrids are shown at the week-long **Chrysanthemum Show** at Smith College in Northampton.

DECEMBER   **Connecticut**   Lantern light tours and a **Carol Sing** mark Christmas at the Mystic Seaport Museum.

Boston   Staged by the Center of Afro-American Artists, Langston Hughes' **Black Nativity** is a holiday spiritual tradition. Hundreds of events mark **First Night**, an alcohol-free New Year's Eve celebration held throughout the city. There's a huge pageant, plus choral groups, ice sculptures, storytellers, acrobats, puppeteers and art and drama presentations. The **Boston Tea Party Re-enactment** finds patriots dressed as Indians throwing chests of tea into Boston Harbor one more time.

Massachusetts Coast   **Christmas as Imagined** in Newburyport includes Santa arriving by boat, a parade and tree lighting. It looks like something out of Dickens along the town's Main Street when the **Nantucket Christmas Stroll** takes place, with a weekend of carolers and other Yuletide festivities.

New Hampshire   The **Candlelight Stroll** at Strawbery Banke illuminates three centuries of houses.

▼▼▼▼▼▼▼▼▼▼▼▼
Before You Go

VISITORS CENTERS

As well as large cities, many small towns have chambers of commerce or visitor information centers that provide detailed information about the area you wish to visit; a number of these facilities are listed in *Hidden New England* under the appropriate state or region.

Travel information on Connecticut is available from the **Tourism Division.** ~ Department of Economic Development, 865 Brook Street, Rocky Hill, CT 06067; 860-258-4290, 800-282-6863.

For Rhode Island, contact the **Tourism Division.** ~ Department of Economic Development, 7 Jackson Walkway, Providence, RI 02903; 401-277-2601, 800-556-2484.

For Massachusetts information, contact the **Massachusetts Office of Travel and Tourism.** ~ 100 Cambridge Street, 13th floor, Boston, MA 02202; 617-727-3201, 800-227-6277.

For more detailed information on Boston, contact the **Greater Boston Convention and Visitors Bureau.** ~ Box 990468, Prudential Center Towers, Suite 400, Boston, MA 02199; 617-536-4100.

For information on vacationing in Vermont, write the **Vermont Department of Travel and Tourism.** ~ 134 State Street, Montpelier, VT 05602; 802-828-3237, 800-837-6668.

In New Hampshire, the contact the **Office of Travel and Tourism** for travel information. ~ Box 1856, Concord, NH 03302; 603-271-2666, 800-837-6668.

In Maine, write the **Maine Publicity Bureau.** ~ P.O. Box 2300, Hallowell, ME 04347; 207-623-0363, 800-782-6419.

Packing for a visit to New England is a little trickier than for other destinations. What you must take is dictated by the fickle Yankee weather, which might change at any minute. A warm, sunny day can turn cool and foggy without so much as a by your leave. The best bet is to bring layers of clothing that can be added or subtracted as needed. Even in the summer, bring some long-sleeved shirts, long pants and lightweight sweaters and jackets, along with your T-shirts, jeans and bathing suit.

Fall and spring call for a full round of warm clothing, from long pants and sweaters to jackets, hats and gloves. While fall days are often sunny and warm, fall nights can turn quite crisp and cool. Bring your heaviest, warmest clothes in winter: thick sweaters, knitted hats, down jackets and ski clothes.

Boston Brahmins notwithstanding, most of New England is a pretty casual place, especially in summer, when everyone has sand in his shoes. No one will look askance if you wear your deck shoes and L.L. Bean pants to dinner at most restaurants, particularly in coastal resort areas like Kennebunkport. New England is less casual, however, than a warm-weather resort, and you can't get into most restaurants or bars without a shirt or shoes, or if you're wearing a bathing suit.

Boston is the most conservatively dressed place you'll visit. Some downtown Boston restaurants have dress codes, requiring men to wear jackets and ties and women to be "appropriately attired."

New Englanders are used to rolling up their car windows every night in summer, knowing it may rain any night. Rain, though not usually heavy, is a big part of every season, so be sure to bring an umbrella and a raincoat, even in the summer.

Some of the streets are almost as old as New England itself. In many areas such as Boston, on these rough, cobblestone ways you need sturdy, comfortable shoes that can take this kind of beating and be kind to your feet. Women should never attempt to navigate cobblestone streets in high heels. Likewise, some New England shores can be rocky. A pair of rubber shoes or old sneakers for swimming is sometimes advisable.

Though New England is not the Caribbean, you can get just as impressive a sunburn here. Bring a good sunscreen, especially to the beach, where sand and water reflect the sun's rays more intensely. Bring insect repellant in the summertime as insurance against the greenhead flies at the shore and blackflies in the mountains.

For the northern woods of Maine and other out-of-the-way places, you'll have far fewer stores to rely on, so come prepared with whatever gear you'll be using. It's wise to consult a backpacking or camping supply store before you leave about what to bring for the weather conditions likely at the time of your travels.

When you come here, you'll need nothing but the best street and road maps. Many roads in New England are winding, poorly marked or not marked at all, following an age-old philosophy that if you live here, you know where you're going, and if you don't, you have no business being here anyway.

You may want to toss in an antique guide along with your other reading; the country's oldest antiques are for sale here. Last but not least, don't forget your camera for capturing quintessential New England vistas of lighthouses and white-steepled villages.

LODGING

Visiting New England is your opportunity to stay in some of the most historic lodgings this country has to offer. A number of them date to the 18th century, such as Longfellow's Wayside Inn in Sudbury, Massachusetts. Randall's Ordinary in North Stonington, Connecticut, dates to the 17th century.

New England is where the bed-and-breakfast movement gained ground in this country, and the region is thick with historic farmhouses and sea captains' homes turned into bed and breakfasts. These are often rambling, cozy affairs complete with fireplace, bookshelves and resident cat. But bed-and-breakfast booking agencies, especially in urban areas, also list host homes with a spare room, which isn't quite the same thing. Be sure to ask whether a bed and breakfast is a real inn or not.

In addition, accommodations include mom-and-pop motels, chain hotels and rustic seaside cottages where you'll awaken to the sounds of surf and crying gulls. Cities have the most deluxe highrise hotels, but outside urban areas, lodgings are generally casual and lowrise.

Whatever your preference and budget, you can probably find something to suit your taste with the help of the individual chapters in this book. Remember, rooms are scarce and prices rise in the high season, which is summer, fall-foliage time and Christmas throughout New England, and also includes ski season in northern areas.

There are lots of special weekend and holiday packages at the larger hotels, and off-season rates drop significantly, making a week- or month-long stay a real bargain.

Accommodations in this book are organized by state or region and classified according to price. These refer to high-season rates, so if you're looking for low-season bargains, be sure to inquire about them.

Budget lodgings generally cost less than $50 a night for two people and are satisfactory and clean but modest. *Moderate*-priced lodgings run from $50 to $90; what they offer in terms of luxury will depend on their location, but in general they provide larger rooms and more attractive surroundings. At *deluxe*-priced accommodations, you can expect to spend between $90 and $130 for a homey bed and breakfast or a double in a hotel or resort. In hotels of this price you'll typically find spacious rooms, a fashionable lobby, a restaurant or two and often some shops. *Ultra-deluxe* facilities, priced above $130, are a region's finest, offering all the amenities of a deluxe hotel plus plenty of luxurious extras, such as jacuzzis and exercise rooms, 24-hour room service and gourmet dining.

If you've got your heart set on a room with a water view, be sure to pin that down. Be forewarned that "oceanside" doesn't always mean right on the beach. If you want to save money, try lodgings a block or so away from the water. They almost always offer lower rates than rooms within sight of the surf, and the savings are often worth the short stroll to the beach.

> No spot in New England is more than a day's drive from any other.

Succulent native seafood stars at legions of New England restaurants, from lobster in the rough and tender bay scallops to codfish, mussels, steamers and milky clam chowder.

DINING

Besides seafood and traditional Yankee foods, New England restaurants also serve up ethnic cuisines of every stripe, plus gourmet foods and fast food. No matter what your taste or budget, there's a restaurant for you.

Within each chapter, restaurants are organized geographically. Each entry describes the cuisine and ambience and categorizes the restaurant in one of four price ranges. Dinner entrées at *budget* restaurants usually cost $8 or less. The ambience is informal, service speedy, the crowd often a local one. *Moderate*-priced eateries charge between $8 and $16 for dinner; surroundings are casual but pleasant, the menu offers more variety and the pace is usually slower. *Deluxe* restaurants tab their entrées above $16; cuisines may be simple or sophisticated, but the decor is plusher and the service more personalized. *Ultra-deluxe* establishments, where entrées begin at $24, are often the gourmet gathering places; here cooking is (hopefully) a fine art, and the service should be impeccable.

Some restaurants, particularly those that depend on the summer trade in coastal areas, close for the winter.

Breakfast and lunch menus vary less in price from one restaurant to another. Even deluxe establishments usually offer light breakfasts and luncheons, priced within a few dollars of their budget-minded competitors. These smaller meals can be a good time to test expensive restaurants.

New England is a wonderful place to bring children. Besides many child-oriented museums, the region also has hundreds of beaches and parks, and many nature sanctuaries sponsor children's activities year-round.

TRAVELING WITH CHILDREN

Quite a few New England bed and breakfasts don't accept children, so be sure of the policy when you make reservations. If you need a crib or cot, arrange for it ahead of time.

Travel agents can help with arrangements; they can reserve airline bulkhead seats where there is plenty of room and determine which flights are least crowded. If you are traveling by car, be sure to take along such necessities as water and juices, snacks and toys. Always allow extra time for getting places, especially on rural roads.

Hidden New England lists gay-friendly lodging, restaurants and nightclubs scattered throughout the six states. You can look in the index under "gay-friendly" travel to find these listings.

A first-aid kit is a must for any trip. Along with adhesive bandages, antiseptic cream and something to stop itching, include any medicines your pediatrician might recommend to treat allergies, colds, diarrhea or any chronic problems your child may have.

At the beach, take extra care with your children's skin the first few days, even though this is not the Caribbean. Children's tender young skin can suffer severe sunburn before you know it. Hats for the kids are a good idea, along with liberal applications of a good sunscreen. Never take your eyes off your children at the shore. If you are traveling in winter, never leave a child alone near a frozen lake.

All-night stores are scarce in rural areas, and stores in small towns often close early. You may go a long distance between stores that can supply you with essentials, so be sure to be well stocked with diapers, baby food and other needs when you are on the go. But all-night stores such as Store 24 and Christy's are plentiful in urban areas.

To find specific activities for children, consult local newspapers. The *Boston Globe Thursday Calendar* has especially comprehensive listings that cover a good part of New England.

The **Travelers Aid Society of Boston, Inc.** is a resource for any traveler in need and maintains booths at the major transportation terminals. Volunteers can arrange to meet young children who are traveling alone. ~ 17 East Street, off of Atlantic Avenue, Boston, MA 02111; 617-542-7286.

WOMEN TRAVELING ALONE

It is sad commentary on life in the United States, but women traveling alone must take precautions. It's entirely unwise to hitchhike and probably best to avoid inexpensive lodging on the outskirts of town; the money saved does not outweigh the risk. Youth hostels, college dorms and YWCAs are generally your safest bet for inexpensive lodging.

If you are hassled or threatened in some way, never be afraid to scream for assistance. It's a good idea to carry change for a phone call and to know the number to call in case of emergency. Most areas have 24-hour hotlines for victims of rape and violent crime. In the Boston area, call the **Boston Area Rape Crisis Center.** ~ 617-492-7273. In New Hampshire, contact **Sexual Assault Support Services.** ~ 603-436-4107. In Rhode Island, **Rape Crisis Unit** provides assistance. ~ 401-421-4100.

While New England is generally not known for its progressive attitudes, the people who live here tend to be very independent minded and not apt to stick their noses in other people's business. This allows gay or lesbian travelers to feel comfortable here. Whether you're interested in exploring the scenic rural backroads or sightseeing in the region's cities, New England has much to offer. The region also boasts several gay and lesbian hot spots to which this guidebook dedicates special "gay-specific" sections.

GAY & LESBIAN TRAVELERS

The first of these sections covers Boston's gay neighborhood in the city's South End. Both Boston and nearby Cambridge are home to large gay communities, with the South End area of Boston offering the greatest concentration of gay-friendly bars, nightclubs and restaurants (see "Gay Neighborhoods" in Chapter Four).

Located at the tip of Cape Cod and attracting gay and lesbian travelers from all over the world is the well-known resort mecca of Provincetown (see "Provincetown" in Chapter Five).

The bucolic Pioneer Valley in central Massachussetts, which includes the college towns of Amherst and Northampton, is more commonly known in the gay community as "The Happy Valley," and has one of the largest lesbian communities in the United States (see "The Happy Valley" in Chapter Seven).

Gay and lesbian publications providing entertainment listings and happenings are available in many of the region's towns. *The Metroline*, a free bi-monthly that you can find in cafés, covers Connecticut, Rhode Island and Massachusetts. ~ 860-570-0825. In Northampton, Massachusetts, pick up a copy of *The Lesbian Calendar* at area bookstores to get an update on local happenings. ~ 413-586-5514.

In Boston, you can get the weekly *Bay Windows* for entertainment listings. ~ 617-266-6670. The quarterly *Gay Community News* is available at bookstores for $3.50. ~ 617-262-6969. Boston also has the free *In Newsweekly*, available at cafés and bookstores. ~ 617-426-8246. In Maine and New Hampshire, the monthly *Community Pride Reporter* is available at bookstores and cafés. ~ 207-879-1342.

New England is a hospitable place for senior citizens to visit; countless museums, historic sights and even restaurants and hotels offer senior discounts that cut a substantial chunk off vacation costs. And many golden-agers from hotter climes flock to New England for its cool summers.

SENIOR TRAVELERS

The **American Association of Retired Persons** offers membership to anyone over 50. AARP benefits include travel discounts. ~ 3200 East Carson Street, Lakewood, CA 90712; 213-496-2277, 800-424-3410.

Elderhostel offers many, many educational courses in a variety of New England locations that are all-inclusive packages at colleges and universities. ~ 75 Federal Street, Boston, MA 02110; 617-426-7788.

Be extra careful about health matters. In New England's changeable and sometimes cold weather, seniors are more at risk of suffering hypothermia, especially during prolonged exposure to wind. Older travelers should be very careful when walking to beware of falls. Sidewalks may be poorly paved or buckled in places, and cobblestone streets are easy to lodge an ankle in.

Out-of-state prescriptions are not filled so try to bring extra of whatever medications you use. Or consider carrying a medical record with you, including your history and current medical status as well as your doctor's name, phone number and address. Make sure that your insurance covers you while you are away from home.

The **Travelers Aid Society of Boston, Inc.** can provide emergency financial assistance and medical and social service referrals, help find low-cost accommodations, give directions and information and assist with banking and check cashing, and train, plane and bus connections. Volunteers can arrange to meet travelers who have special needs. ~ 17 East Street, off Atlantic Avenue, Boston, MA 02111; 617-542-7286.

DISABLED TRAVELERS

New England has made real strides toward making its many attractions and services handicapped-accessible. Parking spaces for the handicapped are provided at most services and attractions, although few buses are handicapped-accessible.

Special escorted group tours are offered by **The Guided Tour.** ~ 7900 Old York Road, Suite 114-B, Elkins Park, PA 19027; 215-782-1370, 800-783-5841.

Access Tours specializes in travel arrangements for the handicapped with any disability. The helpful staff will generate travel reports that match your personal needs with detailed property access profiles. More than 175,000 companies are listed in their computer banks worldwide. ~ P.O. Box 356, Malverne, NY 11565; 516-568-2715.

There are many organizations offering general information. Among these are:

The **Society for the Advancement of Travel for the Handicapped.** ~ 347 Fifth Avenue, Suite 610, New York, NY 10016; 212-447-7284.

The **Travel Information Center.** ~ Philadelphia; 215-329-5715.

Mobility International USA. ~ P.O. Box 10767, Eugene, OR 90440; 503-343-1284.

Flying Wheels Travel. ~ P.O. Box 382, Owatonna, MN 55060; 800-535-6790.

Also providing information for travelers with disabilities is **Travelin' Talk**, a networking organization. ~ P.O. Box 3534, Clarksville, TN 37043; 615-552-6670.

The **Information Center for Individuals with Disabilities** provides information referral and problem-solving services for travelers with disabilities in Massachusetts. A list of hotels, restaurants and historic sites that are handicapped-accessible is also available. ~ 27-43 Wormwood Street, Boston, MA 02210; 617-727-5540, 800-462- 5015 in Massachusetts.

The **Spaulding Community Access Line** helps people find handicapped-accessible family activities, restaurants and cultural events in the greater Boston area. ~ 617-720-6659.

The **Travelers Aid Society of Boston, Inc.** can arrange for volunteers to meet handicapped travelers. ~ 17 East Street, off Atlantic Avenue, Boston, MA 02111; 617-542-7286.

FOREIGN TRAVELERS

Passports and Visas   Most foreign visitors are required to obtain a passport and tourist visa to enter the United States. Contact your nearest United States Embassy or Consulate well in advance to obtain a visa and to check on any other entry requirements.

Customs Requirements   Foreign travelers are allowed to carry in the following: 200 cigarettes (one carton), 50 cigars or two kilograms (4.4 pounds) of smoking tobacco; one liter of alcohol for personal use (you must be 21 years of age to bring in alcohol); and US$100 worth of duty-free gifts that can include an additional quantity of 100 cigars. You may bring in any amount of currency, but must fill out a form if you bring in over US$10,000. Carry any prescription drugs in clearly marked containers. (You may have to produce a written prescription or doctor's statement for the customs officer.) Meat or meat products, seeds, plants, fruits and narcotics are not allowed to be brought into the United States. Contact the **United States Customs Service** for further information. ~ 1301 Constitution Avenue Northwest, Washington, DC 20229; 202-927-6724.

Driving   If you plan to rent a car, an international driver's license should be obtained *before* arriving in New England. Some rental companies require both a foreign license and an international driver's license. Many car rental agencies require a lessee to be 25 years of age; all require a major credit card.

Currency   United States money is based on the dollar. Bills come in six denominations: $1, $5, $10, $20, $50 and $100. Every dollar is divided into 100 cents. Coins are the penny (1 cent), nickel (5 cents), dime (10 cents), quarter (25 cents). Half-dollars and dollar coins are rarely used. You may not use foreign currency to purchase goods and services in the United States. Consider buying traveler's checks in dollar amounts. You may also use credit cards affiliated with an American company such as Interbank, Visa, Barclay Card and American Express.

Electricity   Electric outlets use currents of 117 volts, 60 cycles. For appliances made for other electrical systems you need a transformer or other adapter.

Weights and Measurements   The United States uses the English system of weights and measures. American units and their metric equivalents are as follows: 1 inch = 2.5 centimeters; 1 foot = 0.3 meter; 1 yard = 0.9 meter; 1 mile = 1.6 kilometers; 1 ounce = 28 grams; 1 pound = 0.45 kilogram; 1 quart (liquid) = 0.9 liter.

▼▼▼▼▼▼▼▼▼▼▼▼▼▼

Outdoor Adventures

CAMPING

New England offers a rich spectrum of camping experiences, from sites in the deep wilderness of the White Mountains and the Green Mountains and quiet lakeside spots to protected forests and recreational vehicle parks.

For information on camping in the Green Mountain National Forest, contact the **U.S. Forest Service**. ~ RR#1, Box 1940, Manchester Center, VT 05255; 802-362-2307.

Brochures on camping in the White Mountains are available from the **White Mountain National Forest**. ~ 719 Main Street, Laconia, NH 03246; 603-528-8721.

In Connecticut, quite a few state parks and forests are open for camping. The **Bureau of Parks and Forests** has information on fees and regulations. ~ Department of Environmental Protection, 79 Elm Street, Hartford, CT 06106; 203-424-3015, 203-424-3200.

The beautiful Acadia National Park in Maine, as well as about half the state parks, permit camping. For information about Acadia, contact **Acadia National Park**. ~ P.O. Box 177, Bar Harbor, ME 04609; 207-288-3338. To find out about camping in state forests, contact the **Maine Forest Service**. ~ 22 State House Station, Augusta, ME 04333-0022; 207-287-2791. Or contact the **Bureau of Parks and Recreation**. ~ 22 State House Station, Augusta, ME 04333-0022; 207-287-3821. The **Maine Campground Owners Association** offers a free camping guide. ~ 655 Main Street, Lewiston, ME 04240; 207-782-5874. At privately owned campsites, facilities range from rustic basics in wilderness areas to fairly deluxe cabins and cottages. The **Maine Publicity Bureau** offers a current listing of trailer parks and campsites. ~ P.O. Box 2300, Hallowell, ME 04347; 207-582-9300.

For information on camping at Massachusetts state forest sites, contact the **State Division of Forests and Parks**. ~ 100 Cambridge Street, 19th Floor, Boston, MA 02202; 617-727-3180. A free guide, the *Massachusetts Campground Directory*, is published by the **Massachusetts Association of Campground Owners**. ~ P.O. Box 548, Scituate, MA 02066; 617-544-3475. This guide is also available from the **Massachusetts Office of Travel and Tourism**. ~ Department of Commerce, 100 Cambridge Street, 13th floor, Boston, MA 02202; 617-727-3201, 800-227-6277. Camping is also permitted on several of the Boston Harbor Islands (see the "Beaches & Parks" sections of Chapter Four).

New Hampshire Loves Campers, a free guide to New Hampshire campgrounds covering private, state and White Mountain National Forest campsites, is published by the **New Hampshire Campground Owners Association**. ~ P.O. Box 320, Twin Mountain, NH 03595; 603-846-5511, 800-822-6764.

In Rhode Island, the **Tourism Division** provides information on facilities and permits, and offers *The Rhode Island Camping Guide*, which lists state, municipal and private campgrounds. ~ Department of Economic Development, 7 Jackson Walkway, Providence, RI 02903; 401-277-2601 or 800-556-2484.

The **Vermont Department of Forests, Parks and Recreation** operates 35 campgrounds with 2200 campsites. ~ Agency of Natural Resources, 103 South Main Street, Waterbury, VT 05671; 802-241-3655. The state has about 90 private campgrounds. Write the **Vermont Association of Private Campground Owners and Operators** for a free brochure. ~ c/o Marguerite, 400 Woodstock Road, White River Junction, VT 05001; 802-296-6711.

WILDERNESS PERMITS Primitive campsites are provided in certain state parks and recreation areas. While wilderness camping away from designated areas is sometimes not allowed, in other cases it is allowable without a permit.

No permit is needed for wilderness camping in either the Green Mountain National Forest or the White Mountain National Forest. But Acadia National Park does not allow camping away from designated areas.

Connecticut allows backpack camping on state lands; a wilderness permit is needed. Contact the **Department of Environmental Protection**. ~ Eastern District Office, 209 Hebron Road, Marlborough, CT 06447; 860-295-9523. Or get in touch with the DEP's **Western District Office**. ~ 230 Plymouth Road, Harwinton, CT 06791; 860-485-0226.

In Maine and New Hampshire, no permit is required to camp in wilderness areas in state forests.

Rhode Island and Massachusetts do not allow camping outside designated camping areas in state forests.

Groups of more than ten people who wish to camp in wilderness areas in Vermont need a permit; contact the **Vermont Department of Forests, Parks and Recreation** for the location of the appropriate local district office. You can also contact the forestry department for a free brochure, the *Vermont Guide to Primitive Camping on State Lands*. ~ Agency of Natural Resources, 103 South Main Street, Waterbury, VT 05671; 802-241-3655.

BOATING

Boating is one of the most popular activities in New England. Sailboats, canoes, windjammers, power boats, cruise boats and ferries all ply the coastline and region's large lakes and rivers. You can bring your own boat and get your feet wet doing some New England cruising, or rent or charter a craft here. Each chapter in this book offers suggestions on how to go about finding the vessel of your choice.

Charts for boaters and divers are widely sold at marine shops and bookstores throughout New England.

Boating regulations vary slightly from state to state. In Connecticut, for a list of boating regulations and safety information, contact the **Department of Environmental Protection.** ~ Office of Parks and Recreation, Boating Safety Division, P.O. Box 280, Old Lyme, CT 06371; 860-434-8638.

For Rhode Island regulations, contact the **Department of Environmental Management.** ~ Office of Boat Registration and Licensing, 22 Hayes Street, Room 111, Providence, RI 02908; 401-277-6647.

Massachusetts boating information can be obtained from the **Division of Law Enforcement.** ~ 175 Portland Street, Boston, MA 02114-1701; 617-727-3905.

Vermont boating regulations can be obtained from the **Vermont State Police Headquarters.** ~ 103 South Main Street, Waterbury, VT 05671-2101; 802-244-8775.

In New Hampshire, contact the **New Hampshire Marine Patrol.** ~ 31 Dock Road, Gilford, NH 03246; 603-293-2037.

For Maine regulations, contact the **Department of Inland Fisheries and Wildlife.** ~ 284 State Street, Station 41, Augusta ME 04333; 207-287-2043.

Canoeing the region's many rivers is a rewarding experience. The **Connecticut River Watershed Council** can answer questions about canoeing the Connecticut, which winds through most of New England. ~ 1 Ferry Street, Easthampton, MA 01027; 413-529-9500.

Canoe trails in Connecticut are described in two free brochures from the **Bureau of Outdoor Recreation**—*Canoe Camping* and *Canoeing in Connecticut.* ~ Department of Environmental Protection, 79 Elm Street, Hartford, CT 06106-5127; 860-424-3015.

The **Vermont Department of Travel and Tourism** sends out travel guides with information about canoeing. ~ 134 State Street, Montpelier, VT 05602; 802-828-3237.

WATER SAFETY

Even in winter, you'll find diehard surfers and windsurfers riding the waves in their wetsuits. Swimming, waterskiing, jetboating and floating on inflatable rafts are popular activities in the summer.

People have drowned in New England waters, but drownings are avoided when you respect the power of the water, heed appropriate warnings and use good sense.

Wherever you swim, never do it alone. On the ocean or in large lakes like Lake Champlain or Lake Winnipesaukee, always face the incoming waves. They can bring unpleasant surprises even to the initiated. If you go surfing, learn the proper techniques and dangers from an expert before you start out. Respect signs warning of dangerous currents and undertows. If you get caught in a rip current or any tow that makes you feel out of control, don't try to swim against it. Head across it, paralleling the shore. Exercise caution in the use of floats, inner tubes or rafts; unexpected currents can quickly carry you out to sea.

There are some jellyfish that inflict a mild sting, but that is easily treated with an over-the-counter antiseptic. If you go scalloping or

Facts
and Foibles

Population—13.7 million
Square miles—66,608
Miles of coastline—6130
States with no coastline—1 (Vermont)
Square miles of lakes, rivers and streams—3660
Number of farms—28,500
Millionaires—23,900
Income per capita—$18,431
Number of Fortune 500 companies—49
Percentage of college graduates—18
Colleges and universities
    In New England—264
    In Massachusetts—121
    In Boston—47
U.S. presidents born here—7
Percentage of native New Englanders in population—67.8
Inventive inventions—laughing gas, frozen food, sandpaper, snow-
    making machines, basketball, Monopoly, chocolate chip cookies
Gallons of maple syrup produced annually in Vermont—half a million
Covered bridges in Vermont—109
Pounds of Maine lobster caught annually—23.5 million
Pounds of Maine blueberries picked annually—52.3 million
Bushels of New Hampshire apples picked annually—1.5 million
Miles of stone walls in Connecticut—50,000
Famous cookie named for a Boston suburb—Fig Newton, for Newton
Highest natural point—Mount Washington in New Hampshire (6288 feet)
Highest manmade point—John Hancock Tower in Boston (790 feet)
Nation's first
    Highway—Route 20, Old Boston Post Road, from Boston to New
    York City
    Synagogue—Touro Synagogue (1759) in Newport
    College—Harvard (1639) in Cambridge, Massachusetts
    Postage stamp—printed in Brattleboro, Vermont (1846)
    Recipient of Social Security—Ida Fuller of Ludlow, Vermont, in 1940
    received check #00-000-001 for $22.45
    Human Flying Stunt—John Childs (1757), using a half glider/half
    umbrella, jumped from the steeple of Boston's Old North Church

musseling, swim in or wade in murky waters where shellfish dwell, wear canvas or rubber shoes to protect your feet.

Remember, you are a guest in the sea. All rights belong to the creatures who dwell there, including sharks. Though they are rarely seen and seldom attack, they should be respected. A wise swimmer who spots a fin simply heads unobtrusively for shore.

Scuba divers should always put out a visible float or flag to warn approaching boats of their presence. On a boat or a canoe, always wear a life jacket; ocean and river currents can be very powerful.

If you're going canoeing or whitewater rafting, always scout the river from land before the first trip, and check the available literature. Rivers have danger areas such as falls, boulder fields, rapids and dams.

FISHING

Ever since the Puritans discovered salt cod, New Englanders have been fishing these waters. In the 19th century, men went down to the sea in ships after bigger fish—whales.

Today many people fish just for fun, casting a line into the surf off a rock jetty for flounder, striped bass or bluefish, or perhaps going out to sea for such deep-water game fish as bluefin tuna or shark.

For tamer activities, try harvesting mussels, scallops, littleneck clams or quahogs. And anyone can throw out a lobster pot or two and bring home a deluxe dinner.

Freshwater fishing in streams, lakes and ponds nets rainbow, brook and brown trout, as well as largemouth bass, northern pike, bullhead, perch, sunfish, catfish and pickerel. In cold northern lakes, you can catch lake trout, steelhead, landlocked salmon, smelt, sauger, walleye, largemouth and smallmouth bass, northern pike, muskellunge, yellow perch and channel catfish.

The most common saltwater fish are winter flounder and bluefish. Other saltwater species include striped bass, cod, tautog, mackerel, cod, haddock, pollock, weakfish and smelt.

While all six states require a license for freshwater fishing, no license is needed for saltwater fishing, with a few restrictions.

In Connecticut, freshwater fishing licenses can be bought from town clerks or sporting goods stores. For information on fishing regulations, contact the **Fisheries Division**. ~ Department of Environmental Protection, Room 255, 79 Elm Street, Hartford, CT 06106-5127; 203-424-3474.

In Rhode Island, freshwater fishing licenses can be bought at bait and tackle shops, all town clerks' offices, or from the **Department of Environmental Management**. ~ 22 Hayes Street, Providence, RI 02908; 401-277-3576.

For fishing in Massachusetts, contact the **State Division of Fisheries and Wildlife** and ask for the Abstracts of the Fish and Wildlife Laws. ~ 100 Cambridge Street, Room 1902, Boston, MA 02202; 617-727-

3151. A saltwater permit is required for tuna or lobster fishing; for this permit, contact the **State Division of Marine Fisheries**. ~ 100 Cambridge Street, Room 1901, Boston, MA 02202; 617-727-3193.

Fishing licenses in Vermont may be purchased from any town clerk or at many sporting goods stores, general stores, and state parks. The **Vermont Department of Fish and Wildlife** has details and maps in *The Digest of Fish and Wildlife Laws* and the *Vermont Guide to Fishing*. ~ Agency of Natural Resources, 103 South Main Street, Building 10 South, Waterbury, VT 05676; 802-241-3700.

For fishing fees and regulations in New Hampshire, contact the **New Hampshire Department of Fish & Game**. ~ 2 Hazen Drive, Concord, NH 03301; 603-271-3211.

TWO

Connecticut

Connecticut is the gateway to New England and it offers, despite its diminutive size, a sampling of everything that makes the region famous. Although it takes no more than two and a half hours to drive across the state, these 5000 square miles hold a surprising variety of riches: 250 miles of jagged shoreline; farms, woodlands, mountains and rolling hills; villages of white-clapboard houses huddled around classic greens; and cities rich in cultural offerings. Three hundred and fifty years of history are reflected in the varied architecture and in countless sites—vintage houses, museums, historical societies—that celebrate the forceful men and women who made Connecticut their home.

Shaped like a rectangle measuring about 90 miles from west to east and 55 miles north to south, Connecticut is bounded by New York State on its western border, Massachusetts to the north and Rhode Island to the east. The southern edge is traced by Long Island Sound, a sheltered arm of the Atlantic Ocean that was formerly a vital avenue of trade and transportation and is now a prime recreational asset. The state's other major waterway is its namesake: the Connecticut River, longest in New England, which roughly cuts the state in half and was the site of the earliest 17th-century settlements.

Indian names grace the rivers Housatonic, Quinnipiac and Naugatuck, as well as towns and villages like Cos Cob, Niantic, Saugatuck and Wequetequock. Most towns, however, bear names that have their roots in Great Britain—Windsor, Bristol, New Britain, Greenwich, Norwich—or in the Bible—Bethel, Goshen, Canaan, Bethlehem.

England, their land of birth, and the Puritan faith were crucial influences on the original settlers, who left the fledgling Massachusetts colony in 1633 to found the communities of Hartford, Windsor and Wethersfield on the Connecticut's fertile banks. A few years later, the three settlements joined together as the Hartford Colony—soon to become the Colony of Connecticut—and adopted the Fundamental Orders of 1639. This document, created as a framework for governing the colony, is regarded by many as the world's first written constitution. That's why the words "Constitution State" are heralded on automobile license plates.

Other, less glorious nicknames include "The Nutmeg State," a reference to the days of the itinerant Yankee peddler who went up and down the Atlantic seaboard door to door, selling anything the householder might need, including imported nutmeg, to add flavor to food. Legend has it that wily peddlers would leave the lady of the house holding a "wooden nutmeg"—a fake.

Be that as it may, few of those households could grow much of their own food, since the state's surface is largely glacial soil, too rocky for successful farming. From the beginning, many of the residents had to turn to other endeavors—commerce, shipping, insurance and, in time, manufacturing, which put the state on the map.

American Indians knew Connecticut as Quinnehtukqut, "long tidal river."

Towns and cities grew up around their factories—you'll see handsome brick or stone mills as you drive along the valleys of the Naugatuck, the Quinebaug and other rivers— and each locality became known by the product it manufactured. Waterbury was the brass city; New Britain was the hardware capital of the world; Danbury's fame was hats; Bristol boasted of its clocks.

As mills and factories grew, so did their need for workers. During the late 19th and early 20th centuries great waves of immigrants entered the state from Ireland, Italy, Germany, Poland—every country in Europe. The makeup of the population changed from a homogeneous nucleus of English Protestant descent to the mosaic of nationalities and ethnic groups that characterizes Connecticut's 3.9 million people today.

Industry continues to remain important to some extent: airplane parts are manufactured in East Hartford, helicopters in Stratford; in Groton, Electric Boat builds submarines. But changing patterns and needs across the nation have led to factory closings throughout the state, and to grave problems for older manufacturing cities. At the same time, a number of national corporations have moved their headquarters to Connecticut, creating new skylines and new work in cities like Greenwich, Danbury and Stamford. As a whole, the state continues to be one of the most prosperous in the country, although substantial segments of the population have been unable to share in the wealth.

Despite the importance of manufacturing, a large proportion of the land has remained rural, with vast acreage set aside for recreation and open space in more than 50 state parks and forests, as well as municipal parks and nature preserves. These peaceful oases are scattered throughout the state: along the shoreline, in the pastoral northern corners, even in the more populated valleys near the three largest cities— Bridgeport, Hartford and New Haven.

The landscape ranges from a level shoreline dotted with small beaches and coves through rolling country to the green-clad mountains of the northwest corner and gentle hills of the northeast. At the center is the Connecticut River Valley, once fertile farmland whose traditional crops, tobacco and corn, have largely given way to suburban growth in recent decades.

The central section of the state is home to several major universities: Yale in New Haven, Wesleyan in Middletown, Trinity College in Hartford. New London, on the southeastern coast, boasts Connecticut College and the Coast Guard Academy, while the University of Connecticut's main campus is in Storrs.

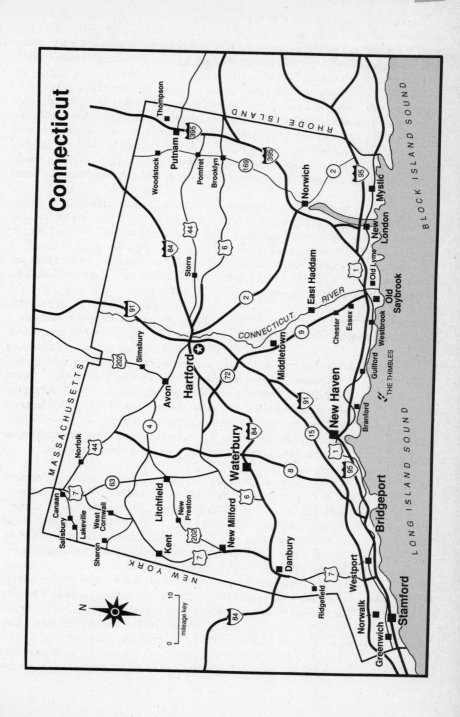

Though distances are short, the climate varies by several degrees from north to south, with snow and ice lasting longest in Litchfield County, the northwestern region. Winter temperatures can go below zero at times, though seldom for long; summer can be occasionally hot and humid. And yet each season brings its own rewards and calendar of attractions. Winter turns the hilly regions into scenes of skating and ice fishing on lakes and ponds, while downhill skiers rush to half a dozen well-equipped areas and cross-country buffs head for countless trails. In spring, the dogwood's snowy blossoms brighten the roadways, and mountain laurel, the state flower, paints hillsides the very palest pink. Summer is the favorite vacation season, a time of festivals and fairs, swimming, fishing and boating, and crowds of visitors at beaches and parks. Fall, some say, shows the state at its best, with maples, oaks, dogwoods, ferns, even the dreaded poison ivy turning the countryside into a symphony of orange, red and gold.

Connecticut can be explored from several points of entry, but chances are that visitors will be coming in from New York state. With this in mind, the chapter has been organized as one lengthy, S-shaped path, going from southwest to northwest; then to the Hartford area, more or less the state's center; south to New Haven; then east along the shore with a brief jog up the Lower Connecticut Valley; finishing up with the scenic, little-known northeast corner. It's a journey that could take a few days, a week or a lifetime spent discovering the treasures of this compact state.

Southwestern Connecticut

Guidebooks tend to dismiss southwestern Connecticut, which roughly corresponds to Fairfield County, as merely a bedroom community for New York City, not worthy of a visitor's time. In fact, it's far more complex—a mix of pretty residential towns with roots in the 17th and 18th centuries, once-thriving industrial cities struggling to find new roles for themselves and clusters of tall, sleek corporate headquarters that have transformed the county's way of life. What's more, although the area is far from rural, a surprising amount of open space has been preserved in state parks and nature preserves.

SIGHTS

A brief tour to sample this variety should start in **Greenwich**, the first town encountered on crossing into the state from the southwest. Famed as an exclusive residential enclave of affluent New York commuters, this community of 60,000 has acquired an additional role as a business center. A host of corporate office buildings draws some 20,000 workers from other towns, as well as hundreds of foreign executives. The old order changeth, even here!

HIDDEN ►

The beauty of the town remains, as does the atmosphere of quiet privilege. Visitors seeking a glimpse of the **great estates** that give Greenwich its special ambience should wander the "backcountry" roads north and immediately south of the Merritt Parkway, along Lake Avenue, North Street, Round Hill Road and smaller, bucolic lanes and drives—as long as they're not guarded by stone gateposts with "No Admittance" signs! It's a world of white churches and manicured country clubs, ancestral trees and lavishly landscaped grounds, with mansions, neo-Tudor or Colonial Revival, barely visible behind iron gates, stone walls and fences.

One former estate that, happily, is open to the public is the renovated **Bruce Museum,** housing American paintings, American Indian pottery and textiles, natural science and geologic displays and frequent exhibitions that reflect the eclectic nature of the holdings. Closed Monday. Admission. ~ 1 Museum Drive, Greenwich; 203-869-0376.

> Many of the "great estates" of Greenwich are owned by celebrities—Ivan Lendl, Leona Helmsley and Ivana Trump among them.

Another nearby attraction is the **Bush-Holley House,** devoted to the community's long and colorful history. Closed Saturday. Admission. ~ 39 Strickland Road, Cos Cob; 203-869-6899.

Putnam Cottage is a late-17th-century tavern and site of General Israel Putnam's 1779 daring escape against the redcoats—a favorite bit of local lore. Open Wednesday, Friday and Sunday. Admission. ~ 243 East Putnam Avenue, Greenwich; 203-869-9697.

Also worth checking out in Greenwich is the **Cavalier Galleries & Sculpture Garden,** which have a variety of contemporary paintings and more than 30 large-scale, modern figurative sculptures on display. ~ 405 Greenwich Avenue; 203-869-3664.

Driving east from Greenwich on Route 95, you'll spot **Stamford's** skyline, which appears as a forest of discordant office towers, huge corporate headquarters built since the 1960s that dwarf the few remaining older structures. An enlightened giant, the Champion International Corporation, houses a branch of New York's prestigious **Whitney Museum of American Art.** It's a handsome, sleek gallery space, with exhibits of 20th-century American art. Closed Sunday and Monday. ~ 1 Champion Plaza, at the corner of Atlantic Street and Treser Boulevard, Stamford; 203-358-7630.

Another interesting destination in Stamford is the **First Presbyterian Church,** a unique fish-shaped church that was designed by Wallace K. Harrison. ~ 1101 Bedford Street; 203-324-9522.

A few miles north of downtown you'll find the **Stamford Museum and Nature Center,** perhaps the most eclectic institution in the state. Set on more than 118 acres, the center offers, in nine widely scattered buildings, galleries devoted to art and American and natural history; an auditorium; a planetarium; an observatory; a small New England farm; and nature trails, picnic grounds and a small lake populated by all manner of geese, ducks and swans. This one's truly a treat for the whole family. Special seasonal programs are offered. Admission. ~ 39 Scofieldtown Road; 203-322-1646.

Just east of Stamford is **Darien,** one of Connecticut's most coveted addresses. Take time out to see the **Bates-Scofield Homestead,** a classic 1736 Connecticut saltbox house now used as a museum. All rooms, including the kitchen and the buttery, are fully restored with

18th-century furnishings and artwork. Open only on Thursday and Saturday. ~ 45 Old Kings Highway North; 203-655-9233.

Next stop along the shoreline is **Norwalk**, a city of 80,000 that was settled in 1645 and thrived on the coastal trade and manufacturing, then went into a slump. After years of neglect, the area closest to the harbor, **South Norwalk** (known as SoNo), has been restored, gentrified and listed in the National Register of Historic Places. Its major artery, **Washington Street**, is now a stroller's mecca offering dozens of shops and boutiques, art and craft galleries, restaurants and bars, all set in handsome 19th-century commercial buildings.

Around the corner, on five acres of riverfront, rises a more modern tourist draw, the **Maritime Center at Norwalk**. It includes an aquarium with 20 tanks that take you from salt marsh into open sea, sharks, harbor seals and all; a maritime museum displaying classic open boats; video games that teach marine skills such as designing the boat of your dreams; and, in a separate building, a high-tech, 337-seat IMAX theater with a six-story-tall screen that stretches 80 feet and provides three-dimensional laser light shows on weekends. Admission. ~ 10 North Water Street; 203-852-0700.

From an adjacent dock you can board **The Seaport Island Girl**, an open ferry that goes to the 1868 lighthouse on Sheffield Island, one of 20 that dot the nearby waters. Seasonal. Admission. ~ 132 Water Street; 203-838-9444, 800-220-9991.

Other vessels take longer jaunts around all the islands. Information about this and other attractions is available from the **Coastal Fairfield County Tourism Information Center**. ~ 297 West Avenue, Norwalk; 203-854-7825.

The center occupies the gate house to the **Lockwood–Mathews Mansion Museum**. This lavish residence, built in the 1860s in French Second Empire style, includes work by some of the finest cabinetmakers and craftsmen of the day. Saved from the bulldozer by local preservationists, it has been gradually restored room by room—frescoed ceilings, inlaid woodwork, glassed-in conservatory—and now serves as a museum of Victorian life. Admission. ~ 295 West Avenue, Norwalk; 203-838-1434.

Continue east and you'll soon come to **Westport**, a popular summer spot as well as a thriving community year-round. Its beaches are a magnet for visitors from inland and other parts of the coast. Take the second Westport exit northbound on Route 95 to reach **Sherwood Island**, a public beach with picnic tables, changing facilities and beachside refreshments.

A more beautiful beach—**Compo Beach**—is for Westport residents and anyone who doesn't mind paying $12 a day for parking ($25 on weekends and holidays). The price is ridiculously high, but that's what keeps the crowds from getting too big.

Westport is home to **The Nature Center for Environmental Activities,** a 62-acre wildlife sanctuary providing habitat for squirrels, birds, deer and other animals native to the region. The museum offers a variety of educational programs and live-animal touch tanks; the center also operates a rehabilitation program for injured animals. ~ 10 Woodside Lane; 203-227-7253.

From Westport, follow Greens Farms Road to Beachside Avenue, which will turn onto Pequot Avenue and take you right into **Southport,** one of Connecticut's most enchanting villages. Here you will find a stunning collection of houses, churches and public buildings crowding around the tiny Southport Harbor. Drive slowly down Pequot Avenue past the parade of homes in the Federal and Greek Revival style and later ones in all the variations we tend to lump together as Victorian.

◄ *HIDDEN*

After you pass a small cluster of stores and antique shops, take a right to the harbor, the original source of the wealth that created the handsome dwellings. The vessels that traded with Boston and New York from this small, sheltered port have given way to sailboats moored at the yacht club, but the homes built by the ship's owners and captains are still lived in and lovingly maintained. Park if you can, and walk up Harbor Road for a fine view of the watery landscape.

Bridgeport, the next city along Route 95, is the largest in the state and no one's dream of a tourist attraction, but **The Barnum Museum** will delight both children and adults. For Bridgeport, P. T. Barnum was more than the king of hoax and hokum, more than the creator of the legendary Barnum and Bailey Circus. He was a philanthropist and real estate developer, the city's mayor and its favorite son. The museum established in his will in 1891 is as flamboyant as he was, a gargoyled, towered and domed red building in the heart of the city, a reflection of his eclectic interests. Circus buffs will go straight to the third floor with its mementos of General Tom Thumb, the talented midget who achieved world fame; its big top memorabilia; and espe-

✔ CHECK THESE OUT—UNIQUE SIGHTS

- Step right up to a flamboyant exhibit of circus mementoes honoring Bridgeport's favorite son at The Barnum Museum. *page 45*
- Tread the same boards that George Washington did in 1781 on **Bull's Bridge,** one of two remaining covered bridges in the state. *page 55*
- Tour the homesteads of two of America's best loved authors, Mark Twain and Harriet Beecher Stowe, at Hartford's **Nook Farm.** *page 68*
- Stroll amid the Greek Revival architectural treasures constructed in the service of Academia at New Haven's **Yale University.** *page 74*

cially the 1000-square-foot scale model of "The Greatest Show on Earth," complete with over 3000 miniatures of acrobats, clowns, elephants, trains and tents, every tiny detail hand carved by a craftsman from a nearby town. Closed Monday from September through June. Admission. ~ 820 Main Street; 203-331-1104.

Bridgeport is also home to **The Discovery Museum**, an interactive art and science museum featuring hands-on exhibits in both disciplines. In the science section explore light, sound, computers, electronics and nuclear energy; in the arts section play with color, line and perspective. The Challenger Learning Center gives you the chance to go on a simulated space mission, and the planetarium offers daily shows on the stars and planets. The museum also has two art galleries with rotating exhibits. Children and adults alike will love this museum. Closed Monday. Admission. ~ 4450 Park Avenue; 203-372-3521.

In addition to the towns along the shores of Connecticut's southern coast, there are a few villages just inland that merit a visit. These include New Canaan and Ridgefield.

New Canaan is a quiet residential community that was settled in 1731. Throughout the town and along the winding roads that surround it are beautifully maintained New England homes and churches. One worthwhile stop is the **Silvermine Guild Arts Center**, an art school with galleries showcasing the works of member artists and artisans. ~ 1037 Silvermine Road; 203-966-5617.

Another spot to check out is the **New Canaan Nature Center**, a 40-acre preserve that encompasses a variety of habitats, including woodland, marshes and fields. Its Discovery Center offers interactive, educational exhibits on animal behavior that will intrigue youngsters. Closed Sunday and Monday. ~ 144 Oenoke Ridge Road, New Canaan; 203-966-9577.

Perhaps the most idyllic town in this busy part of the state is **Ridgefield**, a quintessential New England enclave of stately homes, ancient trees and mementos of battles long past. To reach Ridgefield, a bit farther inland than Bridgeport, take Route 123 through a corner of New York State to Route 35. Once a way station on the road from New York to Boston, the town provided inns for weary passengers. The tradition continues, with several old but up-to-date hostelries and one that now acts as a museum, the **Keeler Tavern**, whose most famous feature is a cannonball lodged into its wall during the Battle of Ridgefield, April 27, 1777. Benedict Arnold was a hero on that day! Closed January. Admission. ~ 132 Main Street; 203-438-5485.

Not far from the tavern, another 18th-century building has been transformed into the **Aldrich Museum of Contemporary Art**. Surrounding the historic main structure and its congenial addition is an outstanding sculpture garden representing the finest artists of the day. Closed Monday. Admission. ~ 258 Main Street; 203-438-4519.

LODGING

Surrounded by extensive, stately homes in an exclusive part of Greenwich known as Belle Haven, **The Homestead Inn** first saw life in 1799 as a farmhouse. It was converted to an inn 50 years later and eventually acquired a jaunty cupola, a Victorian wraparound porch and two outbuildings that also offer accommodations. A million-dollar renovation in 1984 supervised by designer John Saladino brought everything up-to-date, creating a graceful, sophisticated country inn with 23 guest rooms, ample public spaces and a three-star restaurant, all embellished with carefully chosen Victorian pieces. ~ 420 Field Point Road; 203-869-7500. ULTRA-DELUXE.

Set proudly among the tall new office towers of downtown Stamford, the **Stamford Marriott** boasts more than 500 elegant rooms and such amenities as an indoor-outdoor pool, racquetball courts, a rooftop jogging track and a revolving restaurant with views of Long Island Sound. It may not be everyone's ideal vacation hideaway, but its proximity to Route 95, the railroad station, cultural offerings and a major shopping mall makes it attractive. ~ 2 Stamford Forum; 203-357-9555, 800-228-9290, fax 203-324-6897. ULTRA-DELUXE.

Silvermine Tavern has a special charm that spells New England, even though it's just a hop from the New York state line. Well-known for its restaurant, this picturesque cluster of rambling, circa-1785 frame buildings offers ten comfortable bedrooms appropriately but not lavishly furnished with country antiques. Overlooking the mill pond and its waterfall, the complex is at the crossroads of a woodsy residential community. Continental breakfast. ~ 194 Perry Avenue, Norwalk; 203-847-4558, fax 203-847-9171. DELUXE.

A clutch of motels lines Route 1, the old Boston Post Road and now the area's crowded commercial strip. For one that's clean, quiet and operated by the same family for over 30 years—they live on the premises—try the **Garden Park Motel**. Their 21 units all have air conditioning, cable television, good bathrooms and firm mattresses; there's even a picnic table under a shady tree for the guests' use. Fancy, it's not, but it's cheap in an area that tends to be expensive. ~ 351 Westport Avenue, Norwalk; 203-847-7303. BUDGET.

The Inn at Longshore is an unusual place to stay: a ten-room inn with restaurant, lounge and banquet facilities in the midst of a town-owned golf course and park, with lawns that sweep down to Long Island Sound. The rooms (three of them are suites that can sleep four) are almost an afterthought, but they're tastefully done, with up-to-date bathrooms and views of white sails dancing on blue water. Guests may use town facilities, such as the golf course, swimming pool, and tennis court, on payment of a fee. Continental breakfast. ~ 260 Compo Road South, Westport; 203-226-3316. ULTRA-DELUXE.

The **Roger Sherman Inn** is located just outside the center of New Canaan. It's a small inn that dates back to around 1740. All seven

Victorian guest rooms are decorated with cherry-wood antiques, and several have sitting rooms. There is a restaurant on the premises. ~ 195 Oenoke Ridge, New Canaan; 203-966-4541. DELUXE.

In serene Ridgefield, set behind a wide lawn and ancient trees, sits **West Lane Inn**, a gracious dowager of a place built as a home in the early 1800s, embellished in the Victorian era and then converted to an inn in the late 1970s. There's a wide porch that wraps around two sides, with colorful hanging baskets and wicker furniture for lazy summer days. A great carved oak staircase leads up to 20 generous-sized rooms. All show restrained elegance, and each is individually designed with plush carpeting, fine upholstered pieces and period-style furniture. Continental breakfast. ~ 22 West Lane; 203-438-7323. ULTRA-DELUXE.

The Elms, operating as an inn since 1799, has been run by only four families in all these years. Today, the famed restaurant occupies most of the main building, with two bedrooms and two suites up a steep, cramped flight of stairs. The annex offers 16 accommodations—three of them suites—which are elegantly carpeted and appointed with attractive stenciled wallpapers and period furniture. Some of the rooms offer four-poster and canopied beds. The rooms over the restaurant are more casual, with rag rugs, hand-stenciled borders on the ceilings and bathrooms sporting a "country" look. Continental breakfast. ~ 500 Main Street, Ridgefield; 203-438-2541. DELUXE TO ULTRA-DELUXE.

DINING

For a glimpse of Connecticut dining at its classiest, start with **The Homestead Inn**. A 1799 farmhouse turned hostelry and exquisitely restored, the inn stands on a knoll in an exclusive residential area—a treat to the eye as well as the palate. In the restaurant, the ambience is classic French and subdued; the fare is French, sophisticated and up-to-date. Tables sparkle with Wedgwood and fine glass; service is proper. In the summer, you can enjoy the outdoor patio for lunch. ~ 420 Field Point Road, Greenwich; 203-869-7500. ULTRA-DELUXE.

Greenwich is also home to **Restaurant Jean-Louis**, a top-drawer French restaurant. Chef-owner Jean-Louis is well known in the culinary world for his masterful food preparation. The *prix-fixe* menu changes daily and may include such dishes as steamed lobster salad, scaloppine of salmon with parsley coulis, boneless quail stuffed with rice and truffles and venison with french lentils. Whatever the menu, everything is made from fresh, seasonal ingredients. The decor is high-tech, with mirrors and original French artwork on the walls. The restaurant is small, so reservations are *très* necessary. Closed Sunday. ~ 61 Lewis Street; 203-622-8450. ULTRA-DELUXE.

Among the myriad Italian restaurants in this part of the state, **Il Falco** is considered one of the best. Set in the heart of Stamford, this pleasant spot without glitz or pretension serves regional specialties that don't appear on every menu—gnocchi, *vitello tonnato*, fish in the style of various Italian cities—all cooked with imagination and care. Closed Sunday. ~ 59 Broad Street; 203-327-0002. MODERATE TO DELUXE.

A great diner to find your way to is **Bull's Head Diner**, which offers such favorites as sandwiches, stir-fry and roast chicken. The diner also serves up Greek specialties like spinach pie, moussaka and savory sampler plates. ~ 43 High Ridge Road, Stamford; 203-961-1400. BUDGET TO MODERATE.

Silvermine Tavern is a landmark: a country inn, popular for decades, with several antique-filled dining rooms and a romantic terrace for summer dining, overlooking a waterfall and pond. Offerings fit the colonial atmosphere: roast beef, seafood, poultry, pasta and the traditional old-time lobster pie. Closed on Tuesday from November through September. The Friday-evening Innkeeper's Dinner is a bargain, as are Sunday brunch and Thursday-night buffet. ~ 194 Perry Avenue, Norwalk; 203-847-4558. DELUXE.

If you're in the mood for Italian, choose **Maria's Trattoria**. This small and often noisy restaurant attracts a crowd of fanatical regulars who love both the food and the moderate prices. The menu offers all the old favorites—eggplant parmigiana, shrimp scampi, lasagna, scaloppine alla Sorrentina and fried calamari. Closed Sunday. ~ 172 Main Street, Norwalk; 203-847-5166. MODERATE.

South Norwalk, or SoNo, a restored 19th-century neighborhood, is a good place to window-shop for lunch or dinner. On rejuvenated Washington Street and the adjoining Main Street, you can read menus in restaurant windows and decide if you're in the mood for Italian, French, Mexican, Chinese, seafood or sandwiches, funky or chic. There's been some turnover among the tenants in this historic district, but **Jeremiah Donovan's** has been a lively meeting place for over a century, a wood-paneled Victorian saloon with unpretentious, inexpensive food—good burgers, salads, sandwiches, their special New England chowder and hearty bowls of chili—and a prodigious selection of beers. A collection of vintage prizefighter photos adorns the walls, legacy of a regional champ who owned the place many decades ago. ~ 138 Washington Street, South Norwalk; 203-838-3430. BUDGET.

Connecticut's largest city is Bridgeport, with 146,000 people, followed closely by Hartford and New Haven.

A newcomer in Westport that's getting very good press is the **Restaurant Zanghi,** located in the Inn at National Hall. The menu changes seasonally and features contemporary French and Italian cuisine. The open and airy dining room has high ceilings and large picture windows that look out onto the Saugatuck River and into the kitchen where you can watch the chef at work. Veal dusted with wild mushrooms and served with sun-dried tomato sauce and endive confit is an example of what you might find on the winter menu. ~ 2 Post Road West; 203-221-7572. DELUXE.

Nearby, in Westport's former library, is chef-owned **Café Christina**, an especially good choice for brunch. Menu offerings are largely country French and Italian—fresh pasta dishes and entrées like braised lamb shank with saffron mashed potatoes and roasted zucchini. For brunch try the poached eggs with fontina sauce, grilled pancetta and spinach on crispy polenta. For lunch you'll find salads, sandwiches and pizzas. ~ 1 Main Street; 203-221-7950. MODERATE TO DELUXE.

Over by Compo Beach is **Allen's Clam & Lobster House**. While it has the look of a tourist establishment, the food is unfailingly good. Choose from steak, chicken or lobster—their specialty—and a variety of other seafood. Located right on the water's edge, this restaurant has a resort feel to it during the summer months. Closed January. ~ 191 Hillspoint Road, Westport; 203-226-4411. MODERATE TO DELUXE.

Donuts don't often merit hymns of praise, but at the **Coffee An' Donut Shop** they are handmade by the owner, with lots of TLC, each morning before 7 a.m. The resulting confections—glazed, sugared, twirled with cinnamon, rolled in thick chocolate or filled with raspberry jelly—have made addicts for miles around and been dubbed best in the country by food critics of national renown. ~ 343 North Main Street, Westport; 203-227-3808. BUDGET.

Parc 1070 and the hotel that houses it are stepping-stones on the way to the long-awaited renaissance of downtown Bridgeport. The emphasis is on steaks, chops and prime rib roasts—back to the basics! The food is expertly prepared and served in bountiful portions—good reasons for dining in an area not previously known for its cuisine. ~ Bridgeport Holiday Inn, 1070 Main Street; 203-334-1234. MODERATE.

A Fairfield County grande dame, the **Roger Sherman Inn** stands in the heart of an attractive residential community. Once a classic country inn and restaurant known for American fare, the Roger Sherman was been totally—and tastefully—renovated in 1989 and

CONNECTICUT INVENTIONS

Among the products invented, or perfected, by Connecticut Yankees were hats, combs, pins, clocks, seeds, furniture, typewriters, axes, hardware of all kinds, vulcanized rubber, bicycles, textiles—both silk and cotton—silverware and firearms. Samuel Colt developed the Colt 45, "the gun that won the West," at his armory in Hartford. At his firearms factory near New Haven, Eli Whitney, who had previously invented the cotton gin, introduced the concept of interchangeable parts, which led to the flowering of the Industrial Revolution.

dedicated to French Mediterranean cuisine, with game and seafood high on the list of favorites. ~ 195 Oenoke Ridge, New Canaan; 203-966-4541. DELUXE TO ULTRA-DELUXE.

For a festive occasion, try **The Elms**, which has been greeting travelers since 1799. The handsome old white inn has changed a lot since then, needless to say. Its dining rooms are now gracious and serene, all flickering candles, flowered china and snow white linens, and they serve impeccably prepared continental fare. Veal is always a specialty, and seasonal game dishes such as pheasant and venison are widely praised. Closed Wednesday. ~ 500 Main Street, Ridgefield; 203-438-2541. DELUXE TO ULTRA-DELUXE.

For brunch in Ridgefield choose **Gail's Station House**. It's a funky little restaurant where the servings are huge, healthy *and* delicious—a rare combination. Cuisine is contemporary with foreign and regional American accents. For dinner try the rainforest stir-fry (roasted cashews and brown rice in a ginger sauce) or the salmon phyllo with mushroom duxelles and lemon mayonnaise with capers. The budget-priced brunch features corn-and-cheddar pancakes and skillet specials. ~ 378 Main Street; 203-438-9775. MODERATE.

Another good choice in Ridgefield is the **Hay Day Coffee Bar**, which is connected to the gourmet grocery store of the same name. There's a wonderful selection of salads, pastas and soups, as well as sandwiches such as grilled vegetables on Italian ciabotta bread and a California roll with jack cheese, alfalfa sprouts and avocado. ~ 21 Governor Street; 203-431-4400. BUDGET.

Run by an energetic local couple, busy **Ciao Café** is tucked in an unlikely spot behind Danbury's Main Street, not far from the train station. The decor in this small restaurant is simple with white linen tablecloths and black chairs and tables. The menu focuses on Italian dishes, with veal and inventive sauces playing major roles. Try to save room for the flourless chocolate cake. ~ 2-B Ives Street; 203-791-0404. MODERATE.

◄ HIDDEN

Owned and run by the same couple who began Ciao!, **Two Steps Downtown Grille** is just . . . two steps away, though quite different in decor and menu. This is more of a beer and finger-food kind of place. As you sip a draft beer and nibble on Buffalo wings, count the elaborately painted boots that hang from the ceiling; the owners, staff, and their friends decorated them. ~ 5 Ives Street, Danbury; 203-794-0032. MODERATE.

Greenwich Avenue, the main street of elite Greenwich, and the adjoining blocks on **Putnam Avenue** (Route 1) present a profusion of upscale apparel shops—skiwear to prom gowns, trendy to purest Ivy League. You'll also find fine jewelry, gourmet cookware, furniture and home accessories (check out the exquisite imported ceramics) at **Hoagland's of Greenwich**. ~ 175 Greenwich Avenue; 203-869-2127.

SHOPPING

Fairfield County is a shopper's dream come true. Most of the shoreline towns, as well as several major cities, offer such a variety of consumer experiences that people come from far and wide to browse and buy.

In Stamford, now a mini-metropolis, you can find stylish, established department stores such as **Lord and Taylor.** ~ 110 High Ridge Road; 203-327-6600.

Another choice is the Cadillac of downtown shopping malls, the seven-level **Stamford Town Center,** which is anchored by **Macy's** (203-964-1500), **Saks Fifth Avenue** (203-323-3100) and **Filene's** (203-357-7373). What more could one wish? Well, there are chic European shops like **Burberry's** (203-325-1450); prestigious American labels such as **Abercrombie and Fitch** (203-327-4840); **F.A.O. Schwarz** (203-324-1643) for the finest in toys; even a branch of **New York's Metropolitan Museum Shop** (203-978-0554)—all connected by high-tech escalators and glass-enclosed elevators and serviced by a mammoth parking garage. ~ 100 Greyrock Place.

Stamford is also home to a one-of-a-kind shopping experience: **United House Wrecking.** This huge store sells the salvaged remains of demolitions and estate sales—antiques, architectural items, and old lighting and plumbing fixtures. ~ 535 Hope Street; 203-348-5371.

Washington Street, the heart of South Norwalk's historic district, is great for browsing through a potpourri of small shops and boutiques devoted to home furnishings, both yesterday's and today's, quirky clothing, jewelry, high-tech lighting fixtures and French ceramics. If stringing beads is something you always wanted to try, **Beadworks** will show you how and sell you all the necessary materials. Beadwork classes are also offered. ~ 139 Washington Street, South Norwalk; 203-852-9194.

For an outlet mall experience, try **The Factory Outlets at Norwalk** located at 230 East Avenue, a former hat mill now devoted 26 stores bursting with designer clothes, shoes and accessories for men, women and children, as well as linens, luggage and gifts. Check out **The Company Store** for sportswear and leather goods. ~ 203-838-9921.

Other discount outlets are located up and down nearby West Avenue, including **Loehmann's,** the grandmother of all off-price designer clothing stores. ~ 467 West Avenue, Norwalk; 203-866-2548.

You can't leave Norwalk without a trip to **Stew Leonard's,** say its fans. "The World's Largest Dairy Store" is a near-supermarket with Disneyland overtones, where bigger-than-lifesize animated displays—cows, dogs, giant milk cartons—sing for your children's pleasure, if not yours. Its success is now legendary, largely because dairy products, meat, fish, fruit, veggies, baked goods and ready-cooked foods are super fresh and reasonably priced. ~ 100 Westport Avenue, Norwalk; 203-847-7213, 800-729-7839.

Back to more traditional shopping: a stroll downtown in Greenwich or in Westport provides a mall's worth of attractive shops and boutiques.

On Westport's short but lively Main Street you'll find predictable fashion names like **Laura Ashley**, **Ann Taylor**, **Barneys** and **Eddie Bauer**.

You'll also come across several uncommonly well-stocked bookstores, including **Klein's**, a sizable emporium that combines a vast choice of reading material with office supplies and equipment, cameras and stereos. ~ 44 Main Street; 203-226-4261.

Around the corner, **American Hand Craft Gallery** carries outstanding contemporary craft objects—glass, jewelry, ceramics, wood, fiber, metal—in a wide range of prices. ~ 125 Post Road East, Westport; 203-226-8883.

Westport is also home to **Save the Children**, where you can find all sorts of gifts—pottery, musical instruments, jewelry and neckties designed by kids around the world. ~ 54 Wilton Road; 203-221-4000.

Antique shops are ubiquitous in Fairfield County, as they are everywhere in the state. An extensive list of Connecticut's antique dealers is available from the Connecticut Department of Economic Development. ~ 865 Brook Street, Rocky Hill, CT 06067-3405; 860-258-4355.

One of the most attractive spots for viewing yesterday's treasures is **Cannon Crossing**, a pre–Civil War farm village. In the handful of small, picturesque buildings you'll also find dried floral arrangements, fine fireplace tools, quilts, pottery, glassware, antiques and a tiny restaurant in an old schoolhouse. ~ 30 Cannon Road, just off Route 7, Wilton; 203-762-3432.

Across the way is **St. Benedict Guild**, a cross-cultural shop selling clothing, jewelry and artifacts from around the world. ~ Cannondale Depot, 22 Cannon Road, Wilton; 203-762-3633.

There are also quite a few consignment stores in Fairfield County, especially on the Post Road, between Greenwich and Southport.

Another in the state's collection of oversized emporiums is **Danbury Fair Mall**. It's huge and glitzy, boasting **Macy's** (203-731-3500), **Filene's** (203-790-4000), a food court and a gaily painted carousel, in memory of the days when this vast site was the beloved Danbury Fairgrounds. ~ 7 Backus Avenue, Danbury.

NIGHTLIFE

The **Stamford Center for the Arts** Rich Forum, presents a dazzling potpourri: classical music, jazz, folk, musical theater, dance, all performed by nationally known artists on tour. ~ 307 Atlantic Street, Stamford; 203-325-4466.

In the same city, a cozy night spot called **Brennan's Restaurant** specializes in New Orleans–style jazz and blues. ~ 82 Iroquois Road; 203-323-1787.

There's dancing and then some at **Bopper's** in Stamford. On the main floor music from the '50s through the '90s is blasted while DJs lip-synch and dance along theatrically; downstairs in the **Underground** only '90s hip-hop is played. ~ 220 Atlantic Street; 203-357-0300.

For music and dancing, follow the crowds to **Shenanigan's**. There's live entertainment every night except Monday. This rustic brick and wood dance hall, located in a historic building, offers clas-sic rock-and-roll, R & B and occasional headliners like Bo Diddley and Bonnie Raitt. Cover. ~ 80 Washington Street, South Norwalk; 203-853-0142.

Downtown Cabaret Theater varies the formula by encouraging patrons to bring along their own picnic. ~ 263 Golden Hill Street, Bridgeport; 203-576-1636.

In tiny Georgetown, the **Georgetown Saloon** has country music on weekend nights, open mike on Wednesday, rock and blues on Thurs-day. Cover on Friday and Saturday. ~ 8 Main Street; 203-544-8003.

The **Charles Ives Center for the Arts** presents a dramatic outdoor classical music festival during the summer which caters to most pref-erences: classical, pops, jazz, country, music theater and dance. ~ West Side Campus, Western Connecticut State University, Danbury; 203-837-9226.

**BEACHES
& PARKS**

SHERWOOD ISLAND STATE PARK One and a half miles of wide, sandy beach front the calm waters of Long Island Sound, with the coast of Long Island visible on a clear day. Behind the beach are extensive open fields and groves of maples and oaks that shelter pic-nic tables. Two breakwaters offer fine saltwater fishing for bluefish, striped bass and blackfish in season. Pavilion with food concession stands, restrooms, bathhouses, lifeguards; day-use fee, minimum $5. ~ Exit 18 off Route 95 in Westport; 203-226-6983.

PUTNAM MEMORIAL HISTORIC PARK This 183-acre park was the site of the Continental Army's 1779 winter encampment, under the command of General Israel Putnam. Remains of the encampment can be viewed, as well as reconstructed log buildings. Hiking trails fan out into the woods; the pond is suitable for fishing and ice skating. Picnic area, historical site; day-use fee, minimum $5. ~ Three miles south of Bethel on Route 58; 203-938-2285.

▼▼▼▼▼▼▼▼▼▼▼▼▼
Northwest Corner

The northwestern corner of Connecticut is New Eng-land, just as you pictured it. There are big old white churches, Colonial houses, covered bridges, stone walls, winding roads and woods all around. To top it all off, there are quite a few fine restaurants, historic inns and an abundance of small shops and galleries. Litchfield County encompasses most of the area and is home to dozens of small villages, including one by the same name.

From southern points the Litchfield area—often referred to as the Litchfield Hills—can be reached by taking Route 684 to Route 84 east and then following Route 7 north (Exit 7) to New Milford, or by tak-ing Route 684 north to Route 22 and crossing over the state line on Route 55, heading into Gaylordsville.

Just north of New Milford, the road turns into a shunpiker's dream, a gentle rollercoaster with views of fields and streams and vintage houses. Just before Kent, stop at **Bull's Bridge**, one of two covered bridges in the state that cars can drive through—a most picturesque spot. Washington crossed it in March 1781, and it's said that one of his horses fell into the freezing Housatonic River and had to be pulled out.

The town of Kent boasts the **Sloane-Stanley Museum**, which contains Early American farm and woodworking tools collected by Eric Sloane, artist and writer, as well as some of his own oil paintings. The grounds include the ruins of Kent Iron Furnace, one of many used for smelting the iron ore that was the mainstay of the northwest corner from the mid-18th century until the close of the next. Closed Monday and Tuesday and November through mid-May. Admission. ~ Route 7; 860-927-3849.

A few miles later, on the right of the road, the 250-foot cascade of **Kent Falls** dominates an attractive state park (see the "Beaches & Parks" section below).

Then the road splits: Route 45 goes south to **Lake Waramaug**, a zigzagged, three-mile long body of water that has drawn visitors since the mid-1800s—by train back then. Drive all around it: the hilly, wooded shores shelter several inns, a state park and—surprise!—**Hopkins Vineyard**, with a winery housed in a restored 19th-century barn, where you can taste and buy both wines and various gourmet items. Since the late 1970s, even as dairy farms have gradually disappeared from the landscape, vineyards have sprung up, half a dozen at least and more to come. ~ 25 Hopkins Road, New Preston; 860-868-7954.

From Lake Waramaug it's a short drive to **Washington**, a pristine, white hilltop residential village built around a church. Less than two miles from there, on Route 199, is the **Institute for American Indian Studies**, with excellent exhibits, including a habitat trail, a simulated archeological site and an outdoor Indian village—a good way to learn about the region's earliest dwellers. Closed Monday and Tuesday from January through March. Admission. ~ 38 Curtis Road; 860-868-0518.

Litchfield is the most visited spot in the northwest corner, and its spare, graceful **Congregational Church**, built in 1828, rates among the finest in New England and the most photographed. ~ Junction of Routes 202 and 118.

There are two homes here that have been turned into museums. One is the **Tapping Reeve House and Law School**, America's first law school, which was founded in 1784. Open mid-May through mid-October. Admission. ~ 82 South Street, Route 63 South; 860-567-4501.

The other is the **Litchfield Historical Society Museum**, which owns a fine selection of 18th-century portraits, and houses items of the town's past and present. Closed Monday and mid-April through mid-November. Admission. ~ Corner of East and South streets; 860-567-4501.

For a walking tour map and information on events throughout the county, stop at the seasonal booth maintained on the green by the **Litchfield Hills Travel Council.** ~ 860-567-4506.

Despite its palpable concern for the past, Litchfield is very much alive and offers a variety of attractions, such as **Haight Vineyard and Winery**, with winery tours, tastings and vineyard walks. ~ 29 Chestnut Hill Road, off Route 118, one mile east of town; 860-567-4045.

Another worthwhile stop is **White Flower Farm**, a nationally known nursery with five acres of display gardens and 30 of growing fields. ~ Route 63, three miles south of town; 860-567-8789.

Or check out **White Memorial Foundation**, the state's largest nature center and wildlife sanctuary—an ideal place for lovers of the outdoors. ~ 80 White Hall Road; 860-567-0857.

In nearby Waterbury, the **Mattatuck Museum** exhibits artifacts such as clocks, novelty watches, art deco tableware and some of the buttons locally produced in this former "brass capital of the world." You can also visit a historic brass mill and a 19th-century boarding house highlighting immigrant memories, or peruse the galleries showcasing 18th-century furniture and American masters who have been associated with Connecticut. Closed Sunday in July and August and Monday year-round. ~ 144 West Main Street; 203-753-0381.

After enjoying the museum take the self-guided walking tour of the historic downtown district. Many buildings have been renovated thanks to the combined efforts of preservationists and developers. For further information, contact the **Waterbury Regional Convention and Tourism Bureau.** ~ 83 Bank Street, Waterbury; 203-597-9527.

There's no way to see all the picturesque little towns around these parts, but you should sample the northernmost ones, such as Norfolk, surrounded by mountains and state parks. Along the way, if you go by Route 7, you'll pass the much-photographed **covered bridge** at

LITCHFIELD'S LEGACY

Litchfield is as prosperous a town today as it was as an outpost and trading center; and, happily, it still centers on the handsome green that was laid out in the 1770s. The wide, maple-lined streets are edged with homes of unusual distinction, boasting past residents such as Aaron Burr, Ethan Allen and Harriet Beecher Stowe. Burr lived with his brother-in-law, Tapping Reeve; Allen was born on Old South Road, in a small privately owned house; the site on North Street where Mrs. Stowe was born bears a marker—the house itself was moved some years ago.

West Cornwall and the attractive cluster of homes and shops by its side. This section of the Housatonic River is much favored by devotees of kayaks and canoes, which can be rented both here and in **Falls Village**, a few miles to the north.

The **falls** in that town's name are channeled to provide electric power part of the year. In spring you have but to cross the bridge in the middle of town and you'll be rewarded by a dramatic rush of water to rival far more celebrated ones.

◄ HIDDEN

Alternatively, you could opt to drive north via the picturesque towns of Sharon, Lakeville and Salisbury, passing, along the way, some of the richest, most scenic farmland in the state. Either way, when you get to Canaan, just south of the Massachusetts line, stop by to see the unique **Union Station and Depot**, built in 1872 with two wings at right angles to each other, to service the two railroads that used to come this way. In our near-trainless times, the building houses office space and a restaurant. ~ Route 44, center of town.

Heading east along the swift Blackberry River, Route 44 takes you to tiny, serene **Norfolk**. Affluent families have maintained summer homes in this town since the 1880s, drawn by the cool mountain air and by the much-acclaimed **Chamber Music Festival**, held each year from June to August. ~ 860-542-3000

From here you can drive to several mountains with stunning views. You have to be on foot to appreciate Norfolk's exquisite green (Route 44), embellished by a fountain designed by Stanford White, eminent architect of the Gilded Age, and surrounded by graceful homes and the Congregational Church, built in 1813.

Each of the inns studded around serpentine Lake Waramaug has a distinct personality, and its own dedicated fans. Here's a selection:

LODGING

More cost-conscious travelers wishing to stay near the lake, yet who loathe roughing it at Lake Waramaug State Park, will find four bed-and-breakfast rooms about a mile up the hill at **Constitution Oak Farm**. It's a rambling 1830s farmhouse overlooking ten acres of corn, and its name comes from a majestic oak tree said to descend from the legendary one in which Connecticut's colonial charter was concealed. Two downstairs rooms have baths; those on the second floor share. Breakfast is in the guests' own living room. The owner collects many and sundry things—a boon to some, but irksome to those who dislike clutter. ~ 36 Beardsley Road, Kent; 860-354-6495. MODERATE.

Boulders Inn offers 17 rooms, six in the picturesque, turn-of-the-century main house, three in the carriage house and the rest in individual guest houses, all of which are set in the hill that rises immediately behind the inn. The rooms are decorated with flair: those in the stone-and-shingle main house have antique furniture and quilts; the carriage-house rooms have antiques and stone fireplaces, while the guest houses boast freestanding fireplaces. There's tennis on the premises, hiking on wooded trails and a small private beach with boats for the guests' use. Breakfast and dinner are included in the price of the room. ~ Route 45, New Preston; 860-868-0541, 800-552-6853, fax 860-868-1925. ULTRA-DELUXE.

The **Hopkins Inn** was named for the family who settled the northern shore of the lake in 1847, built a great rambling clapboard home and took in lodgers who came up from the city in the summer. Today, the graceful yellow home is best known for its restaurant, but it does rent 11 rooms and an apartment on the second and third floors. The rooms are bright, with Colonial-style wallpaper and country antiques—comfortable, not dramatic. Two share a bath, the others have their own, with old-fashioned tub or stall shower. Downstairs, a shaded terrace high over the lake affords spectacular views. The adjoining hillside is owned by Hopkins Vineyards, where visitors can taste and purchase locally produced wines. Closed from January through March. ~ 22 Hopkins Road, New Preston; 860-868-7295, fax 860-868-7464. MODERATE.

The **Inn on Lake Waramaug** boasts 23 guest rooms in three buildings: the main house, circa 1780, and two guest houses of later vintage. It's a little more formal than other lake hostelries, with rooms designed by professional decorators, an imposing dining room and amenities that include an indoor pool and a sauna. There's also tennis and a small sandy beach where refreshments are served, including lunchtime barbecues on summer weekends. Breakfast and dinner are included in the rates. ~ 107 North Shore Road, New Preston; 860-868-0563, 800-525-3466, fax 860-868-9173. ULTRA-DELUXE.

Atha House, a cozy Cape Cod–style home, is convenient to galleries and antique stores. This bed and breakfast has three rooms looking out on a big garden with evergreen, silver birch and dogwood trees as well as a Connecticut stone fence. There's a fireplace and piano in the living room. Pets welcome. ~ Wheaton Road, New Preston; 860-355-7387. MODERATE.

The small village of Washington is home to one of the state's most exquisite inns. Having recently reopened after a multimillion-dollar renovation, **The Mayflower Inn** has 25 lavishly decorated guest rooms filled with English and American antiques from the 18th and 19th centuries, most with four-poster, king-sized canopy beds. All rooms overlook the surrounding gardens and hills. ~ Route 47; 860-868-9466, fax 860-868-1497. ULTRA-DELUXE.

For visitors who prefer to stay in Litchfield, the area's most visited town, there's a choice of two inns, one old, one new but colonial in feeling. The **Litchfield Inn**, built circa 1980, works hard at being graciously New England even as it highlights facilities for conferences and banquets. Its 31 rooms are spacious and well appointed, with elegant bathrooms. Two units even have a dry bar. A continental breakfast is provided, and there's an elevator—a rare commodity among country inns. ~ Route 202; 860-567-4503, 800-499-3444, fax 860-567-5358. DELUXE.

Tollgate Hill Inn, built in 1745, is listed on the National Register of Historic Places as The Captain William Bull Tavern. As befits a tavern, you enter through the bar, and you can feel the pride of place in the fine way paneling and fireplaces have been restored. There's a top-rated restaurant. The 20 bedrooms are stylishly decorated with four-poster and canopied beds, authentic wallpapers and antique tables and chests. Continental breakfast. ~ Route 202, Litchfield; 860-567-4545, 800-445-3903, fax 860-567-8397. DELUXE TO ULTRA-DELUXE.

The **Blackberry River Inn**, built in 1763, is also listed on the National Register of Historic Places. Set on 17 acres of woodsy Berkshire foothills and complete with its own pool, tennis courts and cross-country ski trails, the inn offers 20 guest rooms, some in the handsome, light grey two-story main building, others in the adjoining carriage house, and a cottage. Most rooms have their own bath, with an occasional clawfoot tub; a few share. The public rooms have an informal, well-used atmosphere. Complimentary breakfast is served in the attractive dining rooms. ~ Route 44, Norfolk; 860-542-5100, fax 860-542-1763. MODERATE TO DELUXE.

A bed and breakfast furnished with antiques, **Greenwood's Gate** is a beautifully restored 1797 Colonial home. Each of the four deluxe suites has a luxury bathroom, bedroom and sitting room. Relax in the living room in front of the fireplace or lounge in the library with a book. ~ 105 Greenwoods Road East, Norfolk; 860-542-5439. ULTRA-DELUXE.

Manor House is a sumptuous bed and breakfast, an 1898 Tudor-inspired Victorian mansion with windows designed by Tiffany—he was a family friend. Up the handsome, carved cherry wood staircase, eight guest rooms—all with private bath, some with balcony and fire-place—have been done to a turn in period elegance. There's even vin-

---

✔ CHECK THESE OUT—UNIQUE LODGING

- *Budget:* Canoe or tube down the Farmington River—it's only moments away when you stay at the affordable family-owned **Hillside Motel**. *page 69*
- *Moderate:* Stay at **Constitution Oak Farm**, named for an oak tree in which Connecticut's original colonial charter was concealed. *page 57*
- *Deluxe:* Delight your children with the sheep, goats and Arabian show horses on the 33 acres at **Applewood Farms Inn**. *page 92*
- *Deluxe to ultra-deluxe:* Peer at, not through, the windows of the **Manor House**; these panes were designed by a family friend—Louis Comfort Tiffany. *page 59*

Budget: under $50 Moderate: $50–$90 Deluxe: $90–$120 Ultra-deluxe: over $120

tage clothing hung here and there, for decoration. A classy touch: breakfast—a very hearty one—can be served in the room, even in bed. ~ 69 Maple Avenue, Norfolk; 860-542-5690. DELUXE TO ULTRA-DELUXE.

In Salisbury, which is west of Falls Village and very close to the New York border, is **The White Hart Inn**. This carefully renovated three-story inn began operating in the early 19th century. Furnishings throughout include antiques and Chippendale reproductions. The 26 guest rooms are decorated in Early American style, some with four-poster beds. In winter guests can warm up in front of the fireplace in the Hunt Room, which features dark wood paneling and overstuffed leather chairs; in summer the large front porch with wicker furniture is inviting. ~ Village Green at Routes 41 and 44; 860-435-0030, fax 860-435-0040. MODERATE TO DELUXE.

Nearby you'll find **The Under Mountain Inn**, which is housed in an 18th-century farmhouse. A true inn, both breakfast and dinner are included in the tab. The seven guest rooms are named after famous sites in England, the owner's homeland. The Covent Garden room has a Shaker canopy bed and a cast-iron tub; Buckingham Gate is a large, sunny corner room with two canopy beds. The library is stocked with books on England, and the pub offers English ales. Breakfast alternates between English and American fare. Dinner features dishes such as steak-and-kidney pie and bread-and-butter pudding. ~ 482 Under Mountain Road, Salisbury; 860-435-0242, fax 860-435-2379. ULTRA-DELUXE.

DINING

Le Bon Coin serves French entrées such as dover sole Riviera, sweetbreads with various garnishes, châteaubriand, game and seasonal specialties. Located in a cottage reminiscent of the south of France, the two small dining rooms are decorated with impressionist paintings á la Toulouse-Lautrec. Closed Tuesday and Wednesday. ~ Route 202, New Preston; 860-868-7763. DELUXE.

Each of the several inns around Lake Waramaug has its followers, who proclaim it the best. The **Hopkins Inn**, a many-windowed, rambling mid-19th-century house, boasts a unique location, high on a hill overlooking sparkling blue water. On a warm day, sitting under the ancient trees on the terrace would be reason enough for deep content, but the eclectic continental menu casts its own spell. Austrian and Swiss traditions are emphasized; *wienerschnitzel* is a perennial favorite, as is trout, live from the inn's own tank, prepared *à la meunière* or *bleu*, the Swiss way. Closed Monday and January through March. ~ 22 Hopkins Road, New Preston; 860-868-7295. DELUXE.

The Mayflower Inn offers guests and passersby a highly respected restaurant. The cuisine is Continental with a Northeast accent. The salmon is hand smoked and the bacon is home cured. Dine in the garden room adorned with tapestries or in the clubroom done in brass, and feast on specialties like grilled veal with wild mushroom sauce. Although the decor and food are elegant, dress is informal. ~ Route 47, Washington; 860-868-9466 DELUXE TO ULTRA-DELUXE.

Several area places feature both lunch and take-out foods—a pleasant thought on days that call for a picnic. **The Pantry**, which doubles as a cookware shop and small restaurant, serves well-prepared entrées such as ham-and-leek quiche and shrimp-and-goat cheese pizza, as well as homemade soups, salads and desserts. Closed Sunday and Monday. ~ Titus Square, Washington Depot; 860-868-0258. MODERATE.

Spinell's leans more toward elaborate sandwiches such as sundried tomato, roasted red pepper and goat cheese on focaccia bread and homemade soups and salads. The baked goods are fresh every day, and there is a bright, pleasant room with tables and a counter for ordering lunch to go. ~ West Street, On-the-Green, Litchfield; 860-567-3113. BUDGET.

Tollgate Hill Inn is a 1745 tavern restored as an inn in admirably authentic fashion. Two intimate ground-floor dining rooms are most attractive, with dark, wide floor boards and paneling and just a few handsome antiques. Upstairs, the ballroom with its fieldstone fireplace and fiddlers' loft is used for Saturday dinner and Sunday brunch. Meals feature American cuisine with European touches, including many unusual seafood entrées. Closed Tuesday. ~ Route 202, Litchfield; 860-567-4545. DELUXE.

The **West Street Grill** is a good place to people-watch as well as feast on contemporary American dishes. Start with the specialty of the house—peasant bread with parmesan aïoli—then move on to the *nori*-wrapped salmon with marinated daikon radish and seaweed salad or roast leg of lamb with marinated eggplant, potato galette and tomato-and-olive compote. The decor is simple and sophisticated, with lots of black and white and low lighting. ~ 43 West Street, Litchfield; 860-567-3885. DELUXE.

Brookside Bistro stands in a cluster of picturesque old houses built next to the much-photographed covered bridge that spans the Housatonic River. On a summery day, one can dine on a deck overlooking a little stream with emerald banks. The interior is attractive as well, featuring butcher-block tables graced with flowers and lacy curtains. True to the name, the offerings feature traditional French bistro fare such as *coq au vin* and seafood au gratin. Seasonal produce and seafood are delivered several times a week. Closed Tuesday and Wednesday. ~ Route 128, West Cornwall; 860-672-6601. MODERATE.

Right on Main Street in the historic little town of Salisbury, you'll find the **Ragamont Inn**, where you can dine on a sheltered terrace or in one of two dining rooms. The Swiss-inspired cuisine features veal dishes, with *wienerschnitzel* gaining the most requests. Homemade pasta is another specialty: black pepper fettucine is one of the chef's creations, served with scallops or shrimp. Closed Monday and Tuesday and late October through early May. ~ 10 Main Street; 860-435-2372. DELUXE.

HIDDEN ▶

A welcome addition to good eating at the northernmost edge of the state is **The Cannery Café**, where canning jars, old and new and sporting many colors, are part of the attractive, unassuming decor. Here American country cooking is practiced with imagination, skill and a Cajun twist. For dinner try the jambalaya, fresh fish or grilled shrimp and pasta. Closed Tuesday. ~ 85 Main Street, Canaan; 860-824-7333. MODERATE.

SHOPPING

Every little town in this fashionable rural area hosts a variety of intriguing shops and boutiques, not to mention art galleries, craft studios and antiques of all kinds.

The Silo is an uncommon enterprise, a former barn with silo that combines a handsome art gallery with changing exhibitions, a cooking school and a store that stocks everything the home chef might ever need—all in a warren of quaint little rooms. ~ 44 Upland Road, New Milford; 860-355-0300.

Historic Litchfield is a paradise for lovers of antiques, who might strike gold right in the center of town, at **Thomas McBride Antiques**, for example. ~ 62 West Street, Litchfield; 860-567-5476.

Or head a few blocks west on Route 202 to reach **D. W. Linsley**, where English furniture is the specialty. ~ 499 Bantan Road, Litchfield; 860-567-4245.

For a complete list of antique stores in the area, contact the **Litchfield Hills Travel Council**. ~ P.O. Box 1776, Marble Dale, CT 06777; 860-567-4506.

You can window shop for elegant, country-style clothes or home accessories alongside the green, or half a mile west on Route 202 at Litchfield Common, an enclave of attractive shops. Flower lovers will want to visit **White Flower Farm**, a mail-order nursery known countrywide for its perennials, garden store and five acres of exquisite display grounds. ~ Route 63, Litchfield; 860-567-8789.

Alongside the picturesque covered bridge at West Cornwall, you can stroll into **Cornwall Bridge Pottery Store** and purchase attractive pots, lamps and tiles made by Todd Piker. ~ Route 7; 860-672-6545.

Should you wish to watch this fine craftsman at work, you're welcome to visit **Cornwall Bridge Pottery** on Route 7, one-half mile south of the junction with Route 4. ~ 860-672-6545.

Brass Bugle Antiques offers furniture, primitives, quilts, china and tools. One of the region's finest antique shops, it's located in an 18th-century barn. ~ Route 45, Cornwall Bridge; 860-672-6535.

If you like fruit and veggies really fresh, stop at **Ellsworth Hill Farm**. During June and July, you can pick as many strawberries as time and your aching back permit. The same applies for raspberries and apples in season. ~ Route 4, Sharon; 860-364-0249.

Salisbury's pretty Main Street is great for gazing at 19th-century homes and window shopping innumerable small, attractive shops that feature clothes, antiques, gifts and books. There are also unusual, exotic teas to buy or sip at tiny tables at **Chaiwalla**. ~ 1 Main Street; 860-435-9758.

In Riverton, traditional home of the celebrated Hitchcock chair, you can purchase recently made reproductions at the **Hitchcock Chair Factory Store**. ~Route 20; 860-379-4826.

NIGHTLIFE

Litchfield County attracts devotees of classical music to its two long-established summer festivals, both of which feature musicians of national and international renown. **Music Mountain** presents chamber music from June to September. ~ 225 Music Mountain Road, off Route 7, Falls Village; 860-824-7126. The **Norfolk Chamber Music Festival** lasts from June to August. ~ Battell Stoeckel Estate, Routes 44 and 272, Norfolk; 860-542-3000.

In stately Litchfield, the **Litchfield Inn** is the one place to go for a bit of music after dark. Thursday through Saturday, there's a variety of live bands and dancing. ~ Route 202; 860-567-4503.

The **Marbledale Pub** is located ten miles north of New Milford, and you'll find it lively every night, summer or winter. Locals, of the young and upscale kind, drop in before or after dinner to meet their friends, play a game of darts or pool and try their hand at one of the video games. ~ Route 202, Marblehead; 860-868-1496.

BEACHES & PARKS

MACEDONIA BROOK STATE PARK 🏃🛶 Numerous streams course through the forested 2300 acres of this park, and many trails traverse it. One trail reaches the crest of Cobble Mountain, almost 1400 feet, affording splendid views of the Taconic and Catskill Mountains in the adjoining states. Fish for brook, brown and rainbow trout. Picnic shelter and outhouses. ~ Four miles northwest of Kent off Route 34; 860-927-4100.

▲ There are 80 tent/RV sites (no hookups); $9 per night; no pets allowed.

KENT FALLS STATE PARK 🏃 The foaming waterfall that cascades 250 feet here is at its peak in springtime. It's popular in summer as well, when the welcome spray brings relief from the heat, and in the fall, when the surrounding 275 acres of woods turn red and gold. Then there are those who love the waterfall in winter, when frozen rivulets turn the mountainside to glistening abstract sculpture. You can admire it all from a grassy plain at road level, or you can view it from many different angles as you climb a wide, stepped pathway all the way to the head of the cascade. Picnic grounds, restrooms; day-use fee, minimum $5. ~ Four miles north of Kent on Route 7. Parking fee on the weekend; 860-927-4100.

LAKE WARAMAUG STATE PARK Ninety-five wooded acres front this scenic body of water. Visitors can swim or explore countless hidden coves in paddleboats and canoes that can be rented here. Fishing is good for bass, sunfish and perch. Bicycling along the quiet road around the lake is also popular, as is touring the nearby towns by car. Picnic shelter, restrooms, food concession stands, boat and canoe rentals; day-use fee, minimum $5. ~ On Lake Waramaug Road, off Route 45; 860-868-0220.

▲ There are 26 tent sites and 52 RV sites (no hookups); $10 per night. Some sites have lake views.

WHITE MEMORIAL FOUNDATION This 4000-acre nature sanctuary bordering scenic Bantam Lake is crisscrossed by 35 miles of wooded trails for hiking, birdwatching, horseback riding or cross-country skiing. The legacy of two visionary residents, this extraordinary preserve is dedicated to conservation education and research as well as recreation. A nature center and museum are open to the public as are the grounds. Picnic areas, restrooms, store, nature center. ~ On White Hall Road, off Route 202, Litchfield; 860-567-0857.

▲ There are 68 sites in several locations, including waterfront sites at popular Point Folly; $10.50 per night for tents and $12 per night for RVs. Tent-only sites are available at Windmall Hill; $7.50 per night.

HAYSTACK MOUNTAIN STATE PARK From the stone tower atop Haystack Mountain (1706 feet above sea level) visitors can see south as far as Long Island Sound and north to the Berkshires' peaks in Massachusetts. You can drive halfway up the mountain, then hike a steep half-mile to the top. Fall foliage is outstanding up there, as is June's show of mountain laurel in bloom. Picnic grounds, outhouses. ~ One mile north of Norfolk on Route 272; 860-482-1817.

▲ There is camping nearby at Taylor Brook Campground (Mountain Road off Route 8). The campground includes 40 tent/RV sites (no hookups); $10 per night.

HOUSATONIC MEADOWS STATE PARK Encompassing 451 acres, this park is set on a former flood plain and offers flyfishing for trout and bass in the Housatonic River. Visitors will find miles of hiking trails including Pine Knob Trail Loop, which gives hikers a view of the green valley. Camping is especially good and the fall foliage is fantastic. Picnic grounds, restrooms. ~ In Sharon on Route 7; 860-927-3238.

▲ There are 95 sites; $10 per night.

Practically smack dab in the middle of the state is Hartford, its capital. Many people know it only because it's where they send their insurance payments. Indeed, Hartford is home to dozens of insurance companies and, in fact, is the insurance capital of the world. But it's not all business in Hartford: the city—and its surrounding towns—offers a variety of historical and cultural attractions.

▼▼▼▼▼▼▼▼▼▼
Hartford Area

Route 44 heads southeast out of Norfolk, leading, some 35 miles later, to Hartford. It's a more scenic road to the state capital than the highways, one that offers the chance to stop at some attractive towns in the **Farmington Valley**. In fact, if you prefer small towns to city bustle, you could overnight there and take day trips into Hartford. For information about them, stop at the office of the **Greater Hartford Tourism District**. ~ 1 Civic Center Plaza, 3rd floor, Hartford; 860-520-4480, 800-793-4480.

SIGHTS

Take a brief detour south on Route 179 to the village of **Collinsville** for a glimpse of an intact 19th-century mill village—one of hundreds built across the state by the companies that gave them their names. The Collins Company was purveyor of axes and machetes to the world; the **Canton Historical Museum** features a wide array of Victorian collectibles and a charming railroad diorama circa 1900. Closed weekends from December through March; closed Monday and Tuesday the rest of the year. Admission. ~ 11 Front Street; 860-693-2793.

◄ HIDDEN

Continue on Route 179 into Route 4 as it follows the Farmington River into the residential town of **Farmington**, whose Main Street is a treasure trove of Colonial architecture. Just a few blocks away you'll find a little-known gem: the **Hill-Stead Museum**. Unique in many ways, Hill-Stead is a turn-of-the-century Colonial Revival country house built for an art-loving industrialist, Alfred A. Pope. It is furnished as if the Popes left yesterday, and on its walls hangs a breathtaking collection of impressionist paintings—works by Monet, Degas, Manet and their American contemporaries, Cassatt and Whistler. The residence was designed by the Popes' daughter, Theodate Pope Riddle, in collaboration with an architectural firm. The personality of this pioneering woman, who went on to become an architect at a time when that profession was unheard of for a female, comes through vividly on a guided tour of the house. And there's a fine, short videotape to enlighten one further. The grounds are noteworthy as well, with hiking trails in the woods and a sunken garden designed by landscape architect Beatrix Farrand. Admission. ~ 35 Mountain Road; 860-677-9064 or 860-677-4787.

If you're intrigued by this unusual woman and her work, head north of Farmington by way of Route 10 and take a left onto Old Farms Road. In a few moments you will come to the campus of

HIDDEN ▶ **Avon Old Farms School,** a boy's preparatory academy founded during the 1920s by Theodate Pope Riddle and designed by her in what is described as Tudor/Cotswold style—cottage-inspired buildings in reddish sandstone and dark timbers. It's private property, but nobody seemed to mind our driving through the picturesque campus. Old Farms Road winds its way north, emerging in the center of Avon, a busy suburban town that was once an agricultural community.

HIDDEN ▶ Not long ago, great **fields of shade tobacco** covered portions of this valley and that of the Connecticut River, a few miles to the west. Suburbanization, highways and, of course, the intense disfavor with which the evil weed is now regarded have cut sharply into this profitable business. Yet there are still some 1800 acres devoted to tobacco in the state. In summer, when the fields are covered by acres of netting, they create a unique, dramatic setting enhanced by the long, narrow red barns used for drying tobacco leaves. Go north on Route 10 through **Simsbury,** noting the many graceful 18th- and 19th-century buildings of this prosperous community. Two miles north of the town center take Hoskins Road, and you'll get a taste of this picturesque, surreal landscape.

From Route 10, as you look to the west, you'll see a ridge of hills topped by a stone tower, the centerpiece of **Talcott Mountain State Park,** which can be reached by Route 185. Hartford lies on the other side.

Truth is, **Hartford** suffers the same image problems that afflict other American cities, and there are many well-traveled residents of the state who've never been there. They're missing a lot. Its long and distinguished history—from newborn settlement in 1635 to shipping center throughout the 18th century, industrial leader in the 19th and capital of the insurance business to this day—is reflected in its varied architecture and active cultural life. For easier sightseeing, the city can be subdivided into three separate parts: downtown; the capitol area, on the opposite side of beautiful Bushnell Park; and Asylum Hill, where Mark Twain built his celebrated mansion.

Start at the dignified **Old State House,** designed in 1796 by Charles Bulfinch and used as the seat of the state's government until 1878, years during which Harford alternated as capital with New Haven. Part of the building is now used as a museum and part as a visitors center. ~ 800 Main Street; 860-522-6766.

Ask for the walking tour map of the city prepared by the **Greater Hartford Convention and Visitors Bureau.** It will guide you to two dozen landmarks, old and new. (As you've no doubt noticed, the former are being squeezed out by the latter). ~ 1 Civic Center Plaza, Hartford; 860-728-6789, 800-446-7811.

If the printed itinerary seems overwhelming, here's a shortened list: Walk by the **Richardson,** as it is known today, a massive, handsome brownstone building designed in 1876 by Henry Hobson

Richardson in his distinctive Romanesque style. It's just north of the Old State House, on Main Street. A few blocks south, and across the street, stands **Center Church**, built in 1807, whose white portico and ornate white spire contrast with the red brick of the facade. Next to it, the **Ancient Burying Ground** shelters gravestones that date back to 1640. ~ 675 Main Street.

Across the street is the **Wadsworth Atheneum**, America's longest continuously operating public art museum, opened in 1844 and later harmoniously enlarged. Walk up the steps of the towered, castlelike original building and turn around before entering. You'll be rewarded with an extensive view of Bushnell Park and the glimmering gold dome of the State Capitol across the park. Inside, you'll find a distinguished collection, strong in paintings of the Hudson River School, Colonial American furniture, African-American art and other works of this century. Yet the museum doesn't overwhelm you with size and arrogance; it feels friendly, somehow. Closed Monday. Admission. ~ 600 Main Street; 860-278-2670.

Nestled between the Atheneum and the fine **Municipal Building** of 1915 is **Burr Mall**, a small, endearing open space centered on Alexander Calder's giant sculpture *Stegosaurus*. The two classic buildings and the bright red steel abstract sculpture form a wonderful contrast.

◄ HIDDEN

On to the **State Capitol**, a monumental Victorian Gothic structure that can be toured, along with the new legislative office building, in

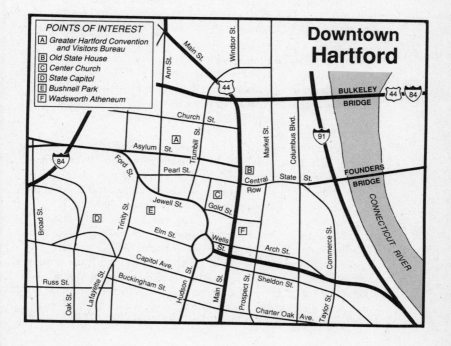

POINTS OF INTEREST
A Greater Hartford Convention and Visitors Bureau
B Old State House
C Center Church
D State Capitol
E Bushnell Park
F Wadsworth Atheneum

Downtown
Hartford

groups led by members of the League of Women Voters. The 1878 capitol is a sight to behold: gold-domed, turreted, mansarded, adorned with statues of Connecticut's greats (including Ella Grasso, the late governor and first woman to be elected to that post in her own right). It has undergone a superb, ten-year restoration, outside and in. The soaring, lavishly decorated interior is as exuberant as the facade; clearly Hartford was out to celebrate when it won the designation of sole capital over New Haven in 1875. ~ Tours: Capitol Information Desk and Tour Guide Service, 210 Capitol Avenue; 860-240-0222.

Hartford's venerable Old State House was almost bulldozed, until a vocal group of preservationists came to its aid.

The stately building across Capitol Avenue houses the State Library, the Supreme Court and the **Museum of Connecticut History,** which specializes in military, political and industrial history. Exhibits here include a collection of historic Colt firearms and a trove of documents such as the 1662 Royal Charter. Closed Saturday and Sunday. ~ 231 Capitol Avenue; 860-566-3056.

Asylum Hill is where Mark Twain built his Hartford residence, along with many eminent citizens of the 1870s who fled the downtown area for what was then considered the suburb. His mansion was part of **Nook Farm,** an enclave of writers and intellectuals that included Harriet Beecher Stowe. Admission. ~ 351 Farmington Avenue; 860-525-9317.

The **Mark Twain House** is a super-ornamented extravaganza where he wrote *Huckleberry Finn* and *Tom Sawyer.* It's closed on Tuesday during the winter. Admission. ~ 351 Farmington Road; 860-493-6411.

You can visit the **Harriet Beecher Stowe Home,** a discreet Victorian "cottage," on the same tour. Closed on Monday during the winter. Admission. ~ 73 Forest Street; 860-525-9317.

Located a few blocks away is the **Connecticut Historical Society Museum,** where a variety of lively exhibits will help you place the sights you've seen into historical context. Admission. ~ 1 Elizabeth Street; 860-236-5621.

Hartford's surroundings offer varied attractions that can be visited on day trips. Art buffs won't want to miss the **New Britain Museum of American Art,** which features a collection spanning 250 years and is strong on Hudson River School painters and artists of the 20th century. ~ 56 Lexington Street, New Britain; 860-229-0257.

North of the capital, the **New England Air Museum** exhibits 75 aircraft that trace the history of aviation. Admission. ~ Route 75, Bradley International Airport, Windsor Locks; 860-623-3305.

A mere three miles south of Hartford on Route 91, the town of **Wethersfield,** one of the original three settlements on the Connecticut River, is famed for its extensive historic district comprising 150 dwellings built before the mid-19th century. Several old Wethersfield homes are open to the public as house museums:

The **Webb-Deane-Stevens Museum** consists of three homes built, respectively, for a wealthy merchant, a diplomat and a craftsman, each representing a different style of 18th-century life. The Webb house was the setting for a conference between General George Washington and his French counterpart, Jean de Rochambeau, that led to the British defeat at Yorktown in 1781. Admission. ~ 211 Main Street; 860-529-0612.

Across the street, the **Hurlbut–Dunham House** is a stylish two-story brick Georgian-style building with Victorian porches and a belvedere. It features early 20th-century collections of the Dunham family, including paintings, glassware, china and ceramics. The house retains its original wallpaper. Closed Monday through Wednesday and the months of January and February. Admission. ~ 212 Main Street, 860-529-7656.

The **Buttolph-Williams House** is a late 17th-century "mansion house" with a collection of period furnishings. Its overhanging and small casement windows reflect the medieval character of the pilgrim century. Admission. ~ 249 Broad Street; 860-529-0460.

The **Old Academy** is a fine 1804 brick building in the federal style housing a library and several offices. ~ 150 Main Street.

Nearby is the **Wethersfield Museum** exhibiting the Wethersfield Historical Society's collection of local history. Admission. ~ Robert A. Keeney Memorial Cultural Center, 200 Main Street.

For information on the Old Academy or the Wethersfield Museum, contact the **Wethersfield Historical Society**. ~ 860-529-7656.

LODGING

For budget lodgings in the Farmington Valley, the place to go is the **Hillside Motel**, 17 miles west of Hartford. It's family owned and operated, and its 15 simple rooms—all with bath, four with cooking facilities—are clean, neat and air-conditioned, though there's nothing fancy. What's more, it's close to that great canoeing and tubing section of the Farmington River known as Satan's Kingdom. ~ 671 Route 44, Canton; 860-693-4951. BUDGET.

Avon Old Farms Hotel, once a small motel, has grown gradually into its present role as a major country hotel with 164 guest rooms. This multiwinged hostelry has a dining room, an outdoor pool, well-landscaped grounds and great views over woods and stream. You can choose from inexpensive lodging in the older motel—freshly painted and comfortable—to more expensive options in the three-story main wing, where the rooms are done in old New England elegance and the carpeted staircase in the lofty lobby just begs for Scarlett O'Hara to sweep down. ~ Junction of Routes 10 and 44, Avon; 860-677-1651, 800-836-4000, fax 860-677-0364. MODERATE TO DELUXE.

If a truly exquisite restoration makes your heart sing, then the **Simsbury 1820 House** is a must. Set on a knoll in the center of this historic small town, the three-story, four-chimney brick building was home to generations of distinguished Americans, including Gifford Pinchot, known as the father of the conservation movement. No pains were spared in transforming the graceful grey mansion and the nearby carriage house into a 32-room inn with a fine restaurant. Each room is carpeted and furnished with antiques, with imaginative use made of the nooks, crannies and arched windows. ~ 731 Hopmeadow Street, Route 10, Simsbury; 860-658-7658, 800-879-1820, fax 860-651-0724. DELUXE.

Behind the ornate 19th-century brick facade of the **Goodwin Hotel** in the heart of downtown, all is brand new. Once a distinguished apartment house, a local landmark, it was entirely rebuilt inside and appointed in a style that would have pleased the Hartford-born financier the hotel honors. Fine reproductions grace the 124 rooms and suites, service is personal and the ambience is gracious and subdued. Public spaces are adorned with works borrowed from the nearby Wadsworth Atheneum, one of the country's finest museums. Rates are expensive but lower on weekends and worth it if a touch of urban elegance fits in your plans. ~ 1 Haynes Street, Hartford; 860-246-7500, 800-922-5006, fax 860-247-4576. ULTRA-DELUXE.

A luxury downtown hotel that offers attractive weekend packages is the **Sheraton Hartford,** joined by a bridgeway to the Civic Center's many attractions. The Sheraton's rooms, almost 400 and generous in size, tend toward art deco furnishings. There's a health club, an indoor pool, a restaurant and, right next door, the award-winning Hartford Stage Company—food for both the body and the soul. ~ Trumbull Street at Civic Center Plaza; 860-728-5151, 800-325-3535, fax 860-240-7247. MODERATE.

Budget accommodations can be found on the outskirts of Hartford off Route 91 at Exit 27. Of several chain motels, the **Susse Chalet** seemed the most attractive, with an airy lobby, good size outdoor pool and standard motel rooms: clean and small but adequate. ~ 185 Brainard Road; 860-525-9306, 800-524-2538, fax 860-525-2990. BUDGET.

DINING

HIDDEN ►

"It's not fancy," said our informant, "but everyone likes it." And so it seemed, since **The Pie Plate** was crowded with a great variety of people. The Pie Plate offers tasty, homey fare in generous portions—New England–style pot pies, thick soups, a dozen dinner entrées and pies that really taste freshly baked. This Pie Plate, it turns out, has three siblings around the state, in Fairfield, Vernon and Waterbury, creations of two Connecticut men devoted to affordable quality food. What an idea! ~ 265 West Main Street, Route 44, Avon; 860-674-0087. BUDGET.

Apricots fronts a lively stretch of the Farmington River. You can sit on a riverbank terrace, drink or sandwich in hand, and almost feel the water as it leaps around shiny rocks. The ground floor of the old building, a former trolley stop, is devoted to a popular pub where the "happy hour" boasts a heaping tableful of complimentary food. Upstairs is the restaurant itself, an oasis of fine American cuisine where the deluxe to ultra-deluxe entrées most in demand are rack of lamb and swordfish. ~ 1593 Farmington Avenue, Farmington; 860-673-5405. BUDGET TO MODERATE.

The restaurant at **Simsbury 1820 House** is in what was once the cellar of the lovely old mansion. Room dividers give the illusion of intimate dining rooms, enhanced by several distinct styles of decor: exposed brick walls with arches in one area; patterned wallpaper for another; traditional prints of hunting scenes highlighting a third. The atmosphere is elegant and serene, the cuisine Continental. An additional pleasure is a drink on the spacious wicker-furnished veranda overlooking the gardens. ~ 731 Hopmeadow Street, Route 10, Simsbury; 860-658-7658. DELUXE.

A few blocks south of downtown Hartford, on and around Main Street, is an area that has sprouted some attractive new restaurants in recent years. **Max on Main**, one of the most popular with the upscale young crowd, serves eclectic American and Continental dishes in an uncluttered, sleek space, contemporary in feeling though the building itself is 19th century. The menu, which is written daily, might include grilled swordfish with roasted pepper sauce or leg of lamb with marinated portabella mushrooms. A house specialty always on the menu is the "stone pie" pizza, filled with a variety of exotic entries. Closed Sunday. ~ 205 Main Street; 860-522-2530. MODERATE TO DELUXE.

If a visit to the Wadsworth Atheneum is on your itinerary, consider staying for lunch at **The Museum Café**. It's an attractive, restful room off the rotunda on the main floor, enhanced by a changing selection of prints or paintings. Open only for lunch, it offers a dozen entrées that include stir-fried vegetables, fresh fish, chicken and sandwiches with a gourmet touch. There is also a Sunday brunch. Closed Monday. ~ 600 Main Street; 860-278-5989. BUDGET TO MODERATE.

When an inexpensive, quick meal is on the schedule, you might consider the food court at Civic Center or the handsomely restored Union Station, where various stands serve up Italian, Greek or Vietnamese food that you can take to a table at the glass-enclosed **Greenhouse Café**. BUDGET.

Another option is the Pavilion at State House Square, a stylish office-and-retail complex whose second floor boasts a dozen eateries. Try **The Natural**, which features healthy soups, salads and Mediterranean dishes like falafel, tabbouleh and hummus. ~ Food Court in the Pavilion at State House Square; 860-247-1627. BUDGET.

Canton abounds in antique shops, and there's action every Saturday night at 7:30 at **Canton Barn Auctions**. ~ 75 Old Canton Road, off Route 44; 860-693-0601.

SHOPPING

The **Farmington Valley Arts Center** comprises 20 artists' studios, a gallery with changing exhibitions and a shop that sells American contemporary crafts from all over the United States. It's an intriguing complex of handsome brownstone buildings scattered about a landscaped park. Closed Monday and Tuesday. ~ 25 and 27 Arts Center Lane, Avon Park North, Avon; 860-678-1867.

Riverdale Farms used to provide fresh milk to Hartford County. Today it houses 35 varied shops and services in 18 buildings, some old, some new but harmonious. There are fashions, gifts, jewelry, clothes, baked goods and special stores for people who like to knit and sew. ~ Simsbury Road, Avon; 860-677-6437.

In downtown Hartford you will find three shopping malls. First, there is the standard but extensive **Civic Center Mall**. ~ 1 Civic Center Plaza; 860-275-6100. The second is the historic **Richardson Mall**, housed in an 1863 landmark building. ~ 942 Main Street; 860-525-9711. The third is the dazzling newcomer, **The Pavilion at State House Square**. ~ 30 State House Square; 860-241-0100.

For unusual gifts, you might consider **The Museum Shop** at the Wadsworth Atheneum, which stocks a fine selection of art books, reproductions, prints, cards, elegant wrapping papers as well as games and books for enquiring young minds. ~ 600 Main Street, Hartford; 860-278-2670.

The shop at the **Old State House** leans more toward things historical, as befits this ancient, still lively institution. ~ 800 Main Street, Hartford; 860-522-6766.

NIGHTLIFE   **Bushnell Memorial Hall** has been a major performing arts center for half a century. The vast art deco auditorium is where audiences flock for concerts of the Hartford Symphony and other orchestras, the ballet and the opera, and touring dramas and musicals. ~ 166 Capitol Avenue, Hartford; 860-246-6807.

Hartford Civic Center schedules frequent, star-caliber entertainment. ~ 1 Civic Center Plaza; 860-727-8080.

Comics from major eastern cities take the mike at **Brown Thomson's Last Laugh Club**. Cover. ~ 942 Main Street, Hartford; 860-525-1600.

At **Bourbon Street North** it's rock, rhythm-and-blues and alternative music on Thursday and Saturday night; a deejay fires up on Friday. Cover. ~ 70 Union Place, Hartford; 860-525-1014.

Among lovers of jazz, one of the favorites is **The 880 Club**, where different groups perform Monday through Saturday. Closed Sunday. Cover. ~ 880 Maple Avenue, Hartford; 860-956-2428.

BEACHES & PARKS   **STRATTON BROOK STATE PARK** 🚶 🚴 🏊 ⛵ An unusual feature of this 148-acre park in the Farmington Valley is a shady bicycle trail built on a former railroad bed. It travels across woodlands and along several scenic brooks, then continues through a town forest. There are also hiking trails and a pleasant pond. Picnic shelter, restrooms, changing rooms. ~ Two miles west of Simsbury on Route 309; 860-658-1388.

TALCOTT MOUNTAIN STATE PARK 🏃 The views from this mountain, of the city of Hartford and the valleys of the Farmington and Connecticut rivers, have been favorites of painters for over 100 years. Atop the mountain stands handsome Heublein Tower, part of a residence deeded to the state by a prominent Hartford family. A one-and-a-half-mile hike leads from the parking lot to the tower, 165 feet high; the ground floor houses a museum of local history, open late April through October; closed Monday, Tuesday and Wednesday from April through Labor Day (860-677-0662 for information). Along the trail, you might see people hang-gliding: the mountain is considered a good jumping-off place for this sport. Picnic grounds, restrooms, museum, observation tower. ~ Three miles south of Simsbury, on Route 185.

▲ There is camping nearby at the American Region State Forest. The campground includes 30 tent/RV sites; $10 per night. ~ West River Road in Pleasant Valley; 860-379-0922.

DINOSAUR STATE PARK 🏃 This 70-acre park, set midway between Hartford and New Haven, boasts a geodesic dome exhibit center enclosing a celebrated exposure of rock. The ancient rock bears some 500 tracks made by dinosaurs of the Jurassic period—185 million years ago. Visitors may make plaster casts of some tracks from May through October, but materials are not provided. Call 860-529-5816 for information about casts. Extensive nature trails wind through the park. Picnic grounds, restrooms, exhibit center. ~ On West Street in the Rocky Hill area, one mile east of Exit 23 off of Route 91; 860-529-8423.

▾▾▾▾▾▾▾▾▾▾▾▾

New Haven Area

Located just about midway between the borders of New York and Rhode Island, New Haven is the last major hub you reach when heading north on Route 95. The city itself is a fascinating blend of old and new, urban center and university campus—a must on any tour of the state. Just to the east is a handful of towns—including Branford, Guilford and Clinton—that are home to historic homes and museums. Just offshore are the Thimble Islands, a galaxy of tiny islands.

New Haven was founded as an independent colony in 1638, but in 1784 it merged with Hartford to become co-capital of the state, which it remained until 1875. Although it shone as an industrial center in the 19th and early 20th centuries, the special flavor that sets it apart today is due in large part to the presence of Yale University, an institution that has shared the city's fortunes since 1718.

SIGHTS

New Haven was planned around a green at its founding, and happily the 17-acre square with its trio of churches in the center has been proudly maintained as open space and still acts as focus of the downtown area. Yale University forms the backdrop to the green's western edge, along College Street and fanning out across a dozen blocks west and north of it. Most of the cultural and architectural landmarks that define this uncommon city can be seen on a walk around the immediate area.

Yale University offers free guided tours of the campus. ~ Visitor Information Center, 149 Elm Street; 203-432-2300. The **Greater New Haven Convention and Visitors Bureau** provides maps and an outline for a walking tour of campus and civic landmarks. ~ 1 Long Wharf Drive; 203-777-8550, 800-332-7829.

Three hundred years of history and architecture can be traced on these rambles. For the earliest structures, start with the three graceful clapboard homes built by late-18th-century gentry at **149, 155** and **HIDDEN ►** **175 Elm Street**. The three facades, set among much grander, later buildings, give a glimpse of how the city looked 200 years ago. The only structures on the green itself are the churches—**Trinity, Center** and **United**—erected between 1812 and 1815 in Gothic, Georgian and Federal styles.

Yale's oldest remaining building, **Connecticut Hall,** is part of what is known as the old campus, which can be entered through **Phelps Gateway,** the school's massive front door at 344 College Street. It's a bulky, gambrel-roofed brick structure facing a statue of Nathan Hale, who lived there as a student.

Much of the architecture for which Yale is famous is 19th- and early-20th-century Gothic Revival. By crossing the Old Campus onto High Street, the visitor can wander past **Dwight Chapel** (1842), the first Gothic design; **Harkness Tower** (1917), whose turrets and pinnacles are a symbol of Yale itself; and **Sterling Memorial Library** (1927), a modern Gothic.

York Street, one block west of High, is also lined with Yale-related buildings, including the legendary **Mory's,** a private club celebrated in "The Whiffenpoof Song." ~ 306 York Street.

One of the finest contemporary complexes on campus rises just west of York Street: **Morse and Stiles Colleges,** designed in 1960 by Eero Saarinen, contrasting yet in harmony with the older buildings.

HIDDEN ► Don't miss Claes Oldenburg's powerful sculpture **Lipstick,** an anti-Vietnam War statement that dominates the courtyard of Morse College.

Another renowned 1960s structure is Gordon Bunshaft's **Beinecke Rare Book and Manuscript Library,** a granite and translucent marble landmark that seems to float above a sunken court featuring sculptures by Isamu Noguchi. Step inside to view a Gutenberg bible, original Audubon prints and other exhibits. Closed Sunday. ~ 121 Wall Street; 203-432-2977.

Down on Chapel Street, you come upon the **Yale University Art Gallery**, known for American, European, African, Asian and pre-Columbian works, as well as a special gallery devoted to the historical paintings of John Trumbull, the artist-patriot of the American Revolution. Designed by architect Louis I. Kahn, the gallery is exceptional for its use of interior space and light. One of its most appealing features is its idyllic **outdoor sculpture garden.** Closed Monday. ~ 1111 Chapel Street; 203-432-0600.   ◄ HIDDEN

Across the street you'll find the **Yale Center for British Art**, which was also designed by architect Louis I. Kahn and is also known for the quality of its collections. It boasts canvases by Turner, Gainsborough and Constable, among other renowned artists. Closed Monday. ~ 1080 Chapel Street; 203-432-2800.

New Haven has suffered its share of urban ills, and efforts to upgrade its image have sometimes been ill-advised. Two of the more successful projects are the recent creation of an entertainment district on College Street, centering on the renovated **Shubert** and **Palace** theaters (see "Theater in Connecticut" in this chapter).

Another area that has been successfully restored is **Wooster Square**,   ◄ HIDDEN
between Chapel and Greene streets, six blocks east of the green. This early 19th-century enclave of graceful homes, after years of neglect, is once again a fashionable in-town address.

Among the many cultural and recreational facilities in New Haven are the **Peabody Museum of Natural History**, with its famed dinosaur collection and a Pulitzer Prize–winning mural entitled *The Age of Reptiles*. Admission. ~ 170 Whitney Avenue; 203-432-5050.

Nearby, the **New Haven Colony Historical Society** contains furniture and decorative arts from early New Haven homes, an art gallery, a maritime collection and industrial displays. Closed Monday. Admission. ~ 114 Whitney Avenue; 203-562-4183.

Farther out Whitney Avenue you'll find the **Eli Whitney Museum**, dedicated to the New Haven industrialist who invented the cotton gin and then developed the concept of interchangeable parts, which led to modern mass-production methods. Displays trace 200 years of industrial growth on the site. Closed Monday and Tuesday. Admission. ~ 915 Whitney Avenue, Hamden; 203-777-1833.

On a day that calls for outdoor fun, consider a trip to **Lighthouse Point Park**, with facilities for picnicking and swimming and a classic old-time carousel. ~ 2 Lighthouse Road; 203-946-8005.

Or you may want to head for the **Shoreline Trolley Museum**, where you can ride classic, antique trolleys along a scenic three-mile route. Admission. ~ 17 River Street, East Haven; 203-467-6927.

East of New Haven, the shoreline is dotted with a string of attractive residential towns that started life as farming and fishing villages. Branford is about six miles east of town on Route 1. It's home to **Harrison House**, which was built in 1774 and is now a house museum filled with 18th- and 19th-century furnishings. Closed Sunday through Wednesday and October through May. ~ 124 Main Street; 203-488-4828.

Nearby is Bittersweet Farm, where the **Branford Craft Village** is located. The Branford Craft Village is both working farm and perennial crafts fair (see "Shopping" below) on 85 acres. There are more than two dozen shops and studios, a café and a play area for children. ~ 779 East Main Street; 203-488-4689.

HIDDEN ▶

Slightly south and just east of Branford is Stony Creek, from which cruises for the Thimble Islands sail. **The Thimbles**, some no larger than a rock that disappears at high tide, others topped by a single elaborate Victorian mansion or two, are an enchanting group of islands. They say Captain Kidd hid stolen treasures on one of these rocky outposts. You'll learn all about that, and other local legends, if you take one of the small **excursion boats** around this miniature archipelago. Seasonal. ~ *Volsunga III*, Town Dock; 203-481-3345; or *Sea Mist*, Thimble Islands Cruise, 34 Sachem Road; 203-481-4841.

Route 146 leads from Stony Creek to **Guilford,** a town that has preserved many pre-Revolutionary War houses, including the **Henry Whitfield State Museum**. This home of the town's first minister, built in 1639, is said to be both the oldest stone house in New England and the oldest building in Connecticut. The green is special, generous for a town of this size and evocative of an earlier time. The museum is closed Monday and Tuesday year-round; from mid-December through January, visits are by appointment only. Admission. ~ Old Whitfield Street; 203-453-2457.

A few miles farther east you might consider a swim at **Hammonasset Beach State Park**. It's Connecticut's largest public beach, over two miles long.

A worthwhile stop in **Clinton,** a picturesque, little seaside village made up of Colonial Cape Cod homes, is the **Stanton House,** built about 1790. Once a general store, it now exhibits items that would have been sold in that era, such as hardware, yard goods, spices and dishware. Closed Monday and from October through May. ~ 63 East Main Street; 860-669-2132.

LODGING   New Haven boasts a luxury urban inn, **The Inn at Chapel West,** housed in a restored 19th-century residence. The ten bedrooms, each with its own bath, are elegantly appointed with antique furnishings of different periods; the beds are four-posters, shiny brass or hand-turned wood, covered with colorful quilts or coverlets. Complimentary breakfast is served in the dining room; refreshments, in the late afternoon, are in the parlor. All this comfort and graciousness is just three blocks from Yale's campus and New Haven green. ~ 1201 Chapel Street; 203-777-1201, fax 203-776-7363. ULTRA-DELUXE.

The **Colony Inn** is a modern, five-story hotel with 86 attractive rooms done in French provincial style. Its convenient location makes it popular with Yale visitors as well as those sampling the city's theaters and museums. The Colony has its own indoor garage, a boon in the busy downtown area, as well as a restaurant and lounge with entertainment in the summer months. ~ 1157 Chapel Street; 203-776-1234, 800-458-8810, fax 203-772-3929. DELUXE.

The historic **Hotel Duncan**, a landmark since 1894, has probably seen better days, yet it must be the best buy in town. Behind its handsome Romanesque facade rise five floors of neatly furnished rooms with old-fashioned baths. No air-conditioning here, just fans to keep you cool on a hot day, and the pleasure of being part of a tradition. ~ 1151 Chapel Street; 203-787-1273. MODERATE.

East of New Haven, the shoreline towns are well stocked with budget- and moderate-price motels close to Route 95. **Holiday Inn Express**, a family-run facility only seven miles from New Haven, has 82 guest rooms, a pool and complimentary breakfast. It's also near Tweed–New Haven Airport and the popular Trolley Museum. ~ 30 Frontage Road, East Haven, at Exit 51; 203-469-5321, 800-465-4329, fax 203-469-2544. MODERATE.

DINING

The Chapel Street area is so rich in theaters, museums and scenic vistas of Yale that it's become a spawning ground for restaurants. **Bruxelles Brasserie**, in its black-and-white, stylish setting, specializes in roasted meat, fish and fowl, but you can also order pasta or pizza at almost any hour. ~ 220 College Street, New Haven; 203-777-7752. MODERATE TO DELUXE.

You'll find **Scoozzi's** down a flight of stone stairs, between the British Art Center and the Yale Repertory Theater. Location is everything, they say, but here the high-tech setting is attractive as well, and the trendy, Italian-inspired fare pleases the customers. ~ 1104 Chapel Street, New Haven; 203-776-8268. MODERATE.

Louis Lunch is one of New Haven's claims to fame—it seems Louis Lassen was the man who first put ground-up beef between two halves

---

✔ **CHECK THESE OUT—UNIQUE DINING**

- *Budget to moderate:* Indulge in a New Haven tradition—pizza—at two outstanding joints, the **Frank Pepe Pizzeria** and **Sally's Apizza**. *page 78*
- *Moderate:* Dine on down-home American cuisine at **The Cannery Café**, among dozens of colorful canning jars, old and new. *page 62*
- *Moderate to deluxe:* Join the crowd of seafood lovers and crack open the lobster shells with your bare hands at Noank's legendary **Abbott's Lobster in the Rough**. *page 93*
- *Ultra-deluxe:* Watch meals cooked Early American–style over massive fireplaces at the anything-but-ordinary **Randall's Ordinary**. *page 93*

Budget: under $8 Moderate: $8–$16 Deluxe: $16–$24 Ultra-deluxe: over $24

of a bun, back in 1903. The small brick building is considered a landmark; in fact, it was moved some years ago to save it from incoming bulldozers. It's old New Haven, where people talk to strangers, and the hamburger—a very fine one—is king. Closed Sunday and the month of August. ~ 261 Crown Street, New Haven; 203-562-5507. BUDGET.

The city's big Mexican restaurant is **Azteca**. In addition to customary Mexican favorites, like enchiladas and chicken mole poblano, there are quite a few American Southwest dishes on the menu. Try the blue-cornmeal crêpe with Southwest vegetables and manchego cheese or the catfish with pecan sauce and chorizo. The restaurant is decorated in southwestern pastels and local artwork. Closed Sunday and Monday during the summer and closed Sunday the rest of the year. ~ 14 Mechanic Street; 203-624-2454. MODERATE TO DELUXE.

Pizza on Wooster Street is a must in New Haven—you'll find no disagreement on that. But whether Pepe's is better than Sally's, or vice versa, is cause for arguments in this city that is considered the pizza capital of the state. There are numerous Italian restaurants lining the street, and all of them have lines that are long but friendly. Here are two favorites. Maybe you'll try them both, and then decide. One of the most popular is **Frank Pepe Pizzeria**. ~ 157 Wooster Street; 203-865-5762. BUDGET TO MODERATE. Another good spot to try is **Sally's Apizza** a few doors down. ~ 237 Wooster Street; 203-624-5271. BUDGET TO MODERATE.

As understated and attractive as the crafts complex that surrounds it, **Katherine's Bistro** is popular not just with those shopping for artwork here but also with residents who appreciate imaginative home cooking, varied daily. A wide array of hearty dishes are served here, and the popular country breakfast on Sunday includes homemade biscuits. Closed Monday. ~ Branford Craft Village at Bittersweet Farm, Branford; 203-488-9457. BUDGET TO MODERATE.

The **Stony Creek Market** has as many enthusiasts as do the enchanting islands it overlooks. Locals and visitors drop in and order their favorites—soups, unusual salads, breads, muffins and cookies still warm from the oven—then take their choices to a table inside or on the deck. Pizza and pasta are available at dinner Tuesday through Sunday. Food, views and friendly atmosphere vie for the raves. Closed Monday. ~ 178 Thimble Island Road, Stony Creek; 203-488-0145. BUDGET TO MODERATE.

SHOPPING   When in New Haven, do as the Yalies do—patronize the **Yale Coop**, two mammoth floors filled with everything needed by students—and other humans, too. Glance at the striking, geometric facade—a 1960s design by Eero Saarinen—before you succumb to temptation inside. Books are the main attraction here, a most extraordinary selection of titles, but you'll also find men's and women's dress and casual clothes, records and radios, computers and a travel agency. ~ 77 Broadway, New Haven; 203-772-2200.

Among the bountiful bookstores in this learned city is **Atticus Bookstore Café**, a great place to start reading that novel you just bought as you linger over a cappuccino or a sandwich. ~ 1082 Chapel Street; 203-776-4040.

The area around Chapel and College streets, home to theaters, museums and restaurants, is great for shopping, too. Some of the stores are multiples—Laura Ashley, The Gap—while others are New Haven originals. **Endleman Gallery** carries one-of-a-kind jewelry by over 100 American designers. ~ 1014-A Chapel Street; 203-776-2517.

The Endleman Gallery's offspring, **Endleman Two**, presents uncommon accessories and clothes. ~ 1044 Chapel Street; 203-782-2280.

Branford Craft Village at Bittersweet Farm is a delight—a cluster of some 20 workshops carved out of buildings that were part of a chicken farm. You can watch craftspeople at their work—woodworker, potter, glass blower, knitter, stained-glass artist—and order custom-made pieces or select from their ample stock. ~ 779 East Main Street, near Exit 56 on Route 95, Branford; 203-488-4689.

New Haven is blessed with an outstanding theater scene (see "Theater in Connecticut" in this chapter), frequent concerts by the New Haven Symphony and visiting artists and several late-night spots well worth a visit.

NIGHTLIFE

Toad's Place headlines local and national bands. Cover. ~ 300 York Street; 203-624-8623.

Boppers, like its older Hartford sibling, favors the songs of the 1950s and '60s and is housed in a re-created '50s diner. ~ 239 Crown Street; 203-562-1957.

HAMMONASSET BEACH STATE PARK

BEACHES & PARKS

Largest of Connecticut's shoreline parks, 919-acre Hammonasset offers a two-mile-long, wide sandy beach that's great for swimming, scuba diving and fishing. Patient anglers often reel in good-size bluefish, striped bass or blackfish. You can launch small sailboats at the boat ramp, hike along numerous hiking and biking trails and visit the nature center, which sponsors interpretive programs. Moreover, the park is ideally located for visiting the picturesque shoreline towns. Picnic grounds with shelter, restrooms, food concession stands, pavilion with changing rooms, nature center; day-use fee, minimum $5. ~ In Madison, one mile south of Exit 62 on Route 95; 203-245-2785.

▲ There are 550 tent/RV campsites (no hookups); most are located in open fields, a five-to-ten-minute walk from the beach; $12 per night.

Text continued on page 82.

Theater in Connecticut

Over the past two decades, this small state has been gaining a large reputation for excellent theater. Connecticut theater no longer means merely summer stock or road companies of successful Broadway shows. The state has seen a flowering of professional regional theaters, staging their own productions of classics and new plays and sending them forth into the national arena, where they have garnered many top awards.

New Haven, once known as a venue for New York producers testing out Broadway-bound plays, now boasts two prestigious producing companies of its own.

One is the 448-seat, thrust-style **Long Wharf Theater**. It's found in the heart of the city's wholesale market, adjacent to Route 95—a great location with no parking problems. Its season, from September through May, spans the spectrum of American and European drama and comedy, with an occasional musical or small-cast opera—outstanding productions that have gained recognition around the country. ~ 222 Sargent Drive; 203-787-4282.

The other one, the prestigious Yale Repertory Theater, is the professional adjunct of **Yale University School of Drama**, and its artistic director, Stan Wojewodski, Jr., doubles as dean of the drama school. Works such as Lee Blessing's *A Walk in the Woods*, Athol Fugard's *Master Harold ... and the Boys* and August Wilson's Pulitzer Prize–winning *Fences* made their debut in the attractive church-turned-theater and then went on to fame and fortune around the land. ~ 1120 Chapel Street; 203-432-1234.

The state capital is home to the **Hartford Stage Company**, winner of the 1989 Tony Award for Outstanding Achievement in Regional Theater. Housed in a contemporary, 489-seat theater downtown, the company is devoted to innovative, sometimes controversial interpretations of the classics, as well as new works by playwrights of today. The season is October through June. ~ 50 Church Street; 860-527-5151.

The **Goodspeed Opera House** is dedicated to the American musical—to reviving vintage ones and inspiring the new. The legendary *Annie* as well as *Man of La Mancha* were both seen for the first time in this Victorian jewel box on the Connecticut River, as were numerous song-and-dance gems from the past that went on to Broadway. The season is April to December. ~ Route 82, East Haddam; 860-873-8668. A second stage, the **Norma Terris Theater/Goodspeed-at-**

Chester, opened in 1984 to house workshops of new musicals-in-progress. ~ North Main Street, Chester; 860-873-8668.

The **National Theatre of the Deaf** makes its home in Connecticut, although it travels during most of the year. A professional ensemble of deaf and hearing actors, NTD combines the spoken word with sign language in unique performances that have touched the hearts of audiences in all 50 states and more than two dozen countries for 25 years. On summer Sundays, they offer free storytelling on the green in Chester. ~ 5 West Main Street, Chester; 860-526-4971, voice, or 860-526-4974, TDD.

The **Eugene O'Neill Theater Center** is a nationally known playwrights workshop created on a 90-acre estate overlooking Long Island Sound. Staged readings or run-throughs of works-in-progress are open to the public for a nominal fee during July and August. ~ 305 Great Neck Road, Waterford; 860-443-5378.

These are the big guns on the theater scene, the award winners whose names are recognized by stage buffs around the land. Each year also brings new professional theater groups, such as the **Music Theatre of Connecticut**. ~ 246 Post Road East, Westport; 203-454-3883. The **Music Theatre** performs at the Westport Country Playhouse, along with fine productions by talented campus and community groups. Moreover, there's original dinner theater and cabaret. (See the "Nightlife" sections in this chapter.) ~ 25 Powers Court.

Other showplaces present national tours of popular dramas and musicals. Foremost among them is New Haven's historic **Shubert Theater**, restored to its stylish 1914 sparkle and offering a varied fall, winter and spring season. ~ 247 College Street; 203-562-5666, 800-228-6622.

Connecticut's straw-hat circuit—how quaint that name seems nowadays—is comprised of numerous theaters, some old, some new, that present generally lightweight fare during the summer. Among them are **Gateway's Candlewood Playhouse**. ~ Junction of Routes 37 and 39, New Fairfield; 203-746-4441. In the Lower Connecticut River Valley, check out the **Ivoryton Playhouse**. ~ Main Street, Ivoryton; 860-767-8348. In the Northeast Corner is the **Connecticut Repertory Theater**. ~ Jorgensen Auditorium, University of Connecticut, Storrs; 860-486-3969. The **Oakdale Theater** is located north of the New Haven area. ~ 95 South Turnpike Road, Wallingford; 203-265-1501. In Southwestern Connecticut, the **Westport Country Playhouse** is one of the oldest summer theaters in the country. ~ 25 Powers Court, Westport; 203-227-4177.

Lower Connecticut River Valley

The Lower Valley of the Connecticut River—stretching north for some 30 miles from Old Saybrook, where the river empties into Long Island Sound, is a favorite destination for visitors from near and far. The area is studded with small scenic towns once known as shipbuilding and sea-going communities. Also blessed with numerous state parks, and sophisticated restaurants and lodgings, the Lower Valley provides a chance to get close to the longest waterway in New England, a river that was central to the development of the young nation.

SIGHTS

There's a highway information center on Route 95 (northbound) at Westbrook. You'd do well to begin this leg of the trip by stopping there, or contacting the **Connecticut River Valley and Shoreline Visitors Council** for information and detailed maps. ~ 393 Main Street, Middletown, CT 06457; 860-347-0028, 800-486-3346.

HIDDEN ►

In fact, Westbrook, on Long Island Sound, is a good place to begin your exploration of the valley. Take Route 1 east until it joins **Route 154**, then ramble with it past salt marshes, causeways and marinas through Old Saybrook, a town with shoreline along both Sound and river and many picturesque watery views.

Route 154 (natives call it the Shore Route) leads to **Essex** and points north, as does Route 9, which is speedier and beautiful in its own right, but the older road is best for antiquing and poking; it gives you more of a sense of place. Essex is one of the most visited towns in the state, and with good reason: it's a compact peninsula where the tree-lined streets end at the river and the white houses, set cheek-by-jowl, date back to 18th-century shipbuilding days. Beware of summer weekends, however: Essex's charms have been sung once too often.

At the foot of Main Street, with a river view to make you catch your breath, stands the **Connecticut River Museum**, housed in a restored 1878 warehouse where steamboats used to stop for freight and passengers on their way to Hartford or New York. Exhibits will help you place the river's role into perspective. Closed Monday. Admission. ~ Steam Boat Dock, 67 Main Street, Essex; 860-767-8269.

The **Valley Railroad** is a vintage steam train that winds its nostalgic way through the countryside for about a half hour to Deep River, the next town up the line. From there you may continue on by train or hop aboard a riverboat up the Connecticut River—and then climb back on the train to return to Essex. The combination train/riverboat trip takes about two-and-a-half hours. Admission. ~ 1 Railroad Avenue; 860-767-0103.

When you head north from Essex, go right at the turnaround at the head of Main Street and take River Road as far as Deep River—just keep bearing right when the road forks. It's a winding, narrow country road with views of quietly flowing waters and the forested banks across the way. Then back on Route 154 and on to **Chester**, a picture-postcard village with a short main street lined with charmingly eclectic buildings—a few shops, galleries and restaurants, all restored to a fare-thee-well. Should you be there in June, you'll want to know about the **Sunday afternoon storytellings** in words and pantomime held on the green, a present to the community by the award-winning **National Theatre of the Deaf**, a company that tours the world and makes its home in this town. ~ 5 West Main Street, Chester; 860-526-4971 or 860-526-4974 [TDD].

◄ *HIDDEN*

Since 1769, Chester has been the site of a ferry to the river's east bank. It's a few minutes' drive east of the town center, on Route 148. By all means, take it. The five-minute crossing operates continuously from 7 a.m. to 6:45 p.m. from April through November, at a minimal charge. Looming above you as you stand on deck you'll see what looks like a medieval fortress atop a steep wooded hill. It's **Gillette Castle**, Connecticut's own castle-on-the-Rhine, the creation of a turn-of-the-century actor/playwright who specialized in playing Sherlock Holmes. It took William Gillette five years to build his eccentric dream house, all to his own designs down to the ingenious locks for all 47 doors and the carved oak trim of the mammoth living room. At his death, it was purchased by the state, which made it the centerpiece of a popular state park with wonderful vistas, **Gillette Castle State Park**. Admission for castle only. ~ 67 River Road, East Haddam; 860-526-2336.

East Haddam, a few miles south on Route 82, holds what many consider the jewel of the valley: the **Goodspeed Opera House**. Built on the river in the elegant mansard-roofed style of 1876, this petite Victorian beauty was reopened in 1963 and dedicated to reviving American musicals of the past. Tours of the exquisitely restored interior can be taken on Mondays and Saturdays in July, August and September. (For performances, see the "Theater in Connecticut" feature in this chapter.) Admission. ~ Route 82, East Haddam; 860-873-8668.

The little town retains many well-kept buildings, reminders of the days when steamboats made regular stops, and sailing ships before them. High on a knoll is the little red schoolhouse where Nathan Hale taught in 1773–74, two years before he was hanged as a spy by the British.

A brief voyage on the Connecticut River gives new perspectives on the picturesque shores. **Camelot Cruises** offer lunch, dinner, Sunday brunch and murder mystery outings along the scenic Connecticut River. Also available are all-day trips across Long Island Sound. ~ 1 Marine Park, Haddam; 860-345-8591, 800-522-7463.

Old Lyme lies due south of East Haddam, at the eastern end of the highway bridge that spans the river as it flows to the sea. The town's wealth, reflected in extraordinarily handsome, spacious homes, was born in the days of clipper ships and the China trade, but at the start of this century Old Lyme became a magnet for artists drawn by its beauty and tranquil setting. They called themselves American impressionists: Childe Hassam, Willard Metcalf, Henry Ranger and others who stayed at "Miss Florence's" boardinghouse. Miss Florence Griswold was a ship captain's daughter and lover of art. Her home, built in 1817, is today the **Florence Griswold Museum**, with period furniture and changing exhibitions. Most interesting is the dining room, where the artists painted local scenes on wooden wall and door panels. A long, humorous vignette over the fireplace represents the congenial group at an imaginary fox hunt, each member in a characteristic pose. Closed Monday. Admission. ~ 96 Lyme Street; 860-434-5542.

When visiting the Connecticut River Museum, be sure to view the full-size replica of the ill-fated *American Turtle* (the world's first submarine), built just before the Revolutionary War.

The imposing **Congregational Church** that appears frequently in the impressionists' paintings stands at Lyme Street's south end. Admired though it is, it is a 1910 copy, faithful in all details, of the original 1816 structure, destroyed by fire. **The Lyme Academy of Fine Arts** continues the town's tradition with a variety of exhibits throughout the summer, as do several galleries on Lyme Street. Closed Monday. ~ 84 Lyme Street; 860-434-5232.

LODGING

Westbrook is blessed with that rarest of pearls, a bed-and-breakfast set right on the sea. At **Talcott House**—an 1890 dormered, shingled home—guests can cross the quiet street and go swimming, or they can sit in the spacious, informal living room and admire the view. The four guest rooms face the sea, have private baths and are all tastefully done with country antiques. Hearty full breakfast included. ~ 161 Seaside Avenue; 860-399-5020. DELUXE.

HIDDEN ►

For accommodations in the moderate range, it would be hard to beat the **Maples Motel**. Forty years of tender loving care by the same family have made it grow into a woodsy, attractive poolside complex of 18 units—some with cooking facilities—and seven "cottagettes" that can be rented by the week. Guests share a picnic area and may use a private sandy beach, minutes away. ~ 1935 Boston Post Road, Westbrook; 860-399-9345. MODERATE.

For many travelers, the words Connecticut Valley are interchangeable with the **Griswold Inn**. "The Gris" is a legend; a white, rambling landmark on the picture-postcard main street since 1776. Serving as a meeting place for the town, it's Olde New England to its very bones, with a taproom and restaurant, a gallery of vintage marine art and nightly musical jamborees. Twenty-six guest rooms and suites are housed in four period buildings. Some are remodeled; in others, the floors list to port or starboard, as if to remind you of the town's maritime past and its nautical present as well. Continental breakfast is included. ~ 36 Main Street, Essex; 860-767-1812, fax 203-767-0481. MODERATE TO DELUXE.

Copper Beech Inn is a classic: a sedate, gracious country inn with an award-winning French restaurant in what was once the home of a wealthy ivory merchant—the trade that put this little town on the map. Four of the 13 rooms are in the main house, meticulously appointed all, with charming old-fashioned baths and antique beds. Set back near the woods, the Carriage House has been remodeled with exquisite taste and a sense of romance, and its nine bedrooms all have jacuzzis and French doors leading out to a deck with sylvan vistas. Continental breakfast. ~ 46 Main Street, Ivoryton; 860-767-0330. DELUXE TO ULTRA-DELUXE.

Antique lovers won't know where to look first at **Riverwind Country Inn**. This bed and breakfast, in the center of one of the valley's quieter towns, is chockablock with country antiques and folk art—some from the owner's own family, others trophies of forays around the country. Rates for the eight attractively furnished, hand-stenciled rooms, all with bath, include a prodigious breakfast that reflects the innkeeper's southern background. ~ 209 Main Street, Deep River; 860-526-2014. DELUXE.

What could be more pleasant than to waltz across the street to **Bishopsgate Inn** after enjoying a nostalgic musical at Goodspeed Opera House? Or any time, in fact. The early 19th-century shipbuilder's house stands tall and handsome on a landscaped knoll, and the six guest rooms, all with theatrical names on the door, are done in good taste, with bathrooms carved out of the oddest places. Would you believe a former closet, for one? Breakfast is family-style, served in the spacious country kitchen. ~ Goodspeed Landing, East Haddam; 860-873-1677. MODERATE TO DELUXE.

The **Bee and Thistle Inn** is on every list of all-time favorites. A gambrel-roofed, mid-18th-century house, it's right next door to the Florence Griswold Museum on the town's major street, yet it's set back on extensive landscaped grounds that sweep down to the Lieutenant River, a branch of the Connecticut. Most of the ground floor is devoted to the popular restaurant. Eleven tasteful, uncluttered rooms occupy the second and third floors, each with its own decor, all with bath except for two that share. There's also a one-bedroom "Innkeepers Cottage" featuring a library with fireplace, kitchen and glass-enclosed sitting room. Rooms in the main house are moderate to deluxe; the cottage is ultra-deluxe. Closed for three weeks in January. ~ 100 Lyme Street, Old Lyme; 860-434-1667, 800-622-4946, fax 860-434-3402. MODERATE TO ULTRA-DELUXE.

The **Old Lyme Inn** is set in a farmhouse that dates back to the 1850s. The 13 rooms, five in the original farmhouse, are furnished with Victorian and Empire antiques. The honeymoon suites have four-poster beds, Victorian loveseats and marble-topped dressers. Guests can lounge in the library in front of the fireplace and choose from a variety of puzzles and games. A full country breakfast is served every morning. Four rooms on the first floor are wheelchair accessible. Gay-friendly. ~ 85 Lyme Street, Old Lyme; 860-434-2600, 800-434-5352, fax 860-434-5352. ULTRA-DELUXE.

DINING

Seafood lovers think of Westbrook as the home of **Bill's Seafood Restaurant.** Here at this informal spot, fried-clam aficionados gather inside or on the terrace overlooking the salt marsh. Fish, shrimp and lobster rolls have a place on the menu, as do hot dogs and burgers for the landlubber who gets dragged along, but it's the sweet, plump, lightly fried clams that are the attraction. ~ Boston Post Road at the Singing Bridge; 860-399-7224. BUDGET TO MODERATE.

The **Copper Beech Inn** is a landmark, a longtime favorite among followers of fine French cuisine. Set in a tree-shaded, 1890 home, it breathes Old World elegance and charm. Sterling silver, fresh flowers and fine china grace the tables in the three dining rooms; European antiques and Oriental carpets set the stage. Behind the inn is the greenhouse with wicker tables and chairs for the Saturday-evening cocktail hour; all in all, a most elegant place. Despite the high prices, you'll have to reserve well in advance, at least on weekends. Closed Monday April through December, Monday and Tuesday January through March and the first week of January. ~ 46 Main Street, Ivoryton; 860-767-0330. ULTRA-DELUXE.

Fiddlers is a pleasantly appointed, unpretentious place residents turn to when they want carefully prepared, really fresh seafood—chicken and meat, too. Fish entrées change according to the market and can be ordered to your taste—sautéed, poached, baked, broiled or mesquite-grilled. Closed Monday. ~ 4 Water Street, Chester; 860-526-3210. MODERATE TO DELUXE.

The **Wheat Market** creates gourmet sandwiches, as well as changing entrées, salads, soups and a famed deep-dish pizza to eat at tables or take along on a picnic. With Gillette Castle State Park just a five-minute ferry ride away, that might be just the ticket on a nice day. Closed Sunday. ~ 4 Water Street, Chester; 860-526-9347. BUDGET.

THE "GRIS"

Historic is a word used lightly around these parts, but surely it applies to the **Griswold Inn,** established in 1776. Go for lunch, dinner, the famous Sunday "Hunt Breakfast" or a drink, so you can view the warren of wood-paneled, evocative rooms that tumble one into the other. Partake of the New England specialties and other Americana on which the "Gris" has built its reputation, it's an experience one shouldn't miss. ~ 36 Main Street, Essex; 860-767-1812. MODERATE TO DELUXE.

For years, the **Bee and Thistle Inn** has been voted the most romantic restaurant in the state by readers of *Connecticut* magazine. It's true, the rambling rooms and porches exude an air of intimacy and warmth appealing to lovers, and other mortals as well. The offerings are elegantly served and very tasty: seafood, game, poultry, meats, each flavored with fresh herbs shipped in or picked from the sunken garden just outside the windows. Closed Tuesday and for three weeks in January. ~ 100 Lyme Street, Old Lyme; 860-434-1667. DELUXE TO ULTRA-DELUXE.

SHOPPING

Antiques are what most shoppers seek in this region, and every little town responds with its own array of specialized offerings. There's even the **Essex Saybrook Antiques Village**, where no fewer than 100 dealers hold forth in their own cluster of Colonial-looking buildings. ~ 345 Middlesex Turnpike, Old Saybrook; 860-388-0689.

The **Connecticut River Valley and Shoreline Visitors Council** has compiled a complete listing of antique shops in the area. ~ 393 Main Street, Middletown; 860-347-0028

Window shopping along Essex's lovely Main Street is a popular pastime—too popular, you might find, on summer weekends. Many of the stores' names will be familiar; some are originals, like **Swanton Jewelry**, experts in jewelry old and new. ~ 1 Griswold Square; 860-767-1271.

If herbs intrigue you, drive to the **Sundial Herb Garden** in tiny Higganum, where you can stroll through an 18th-century-style garden, then browse in the attractive barn-turned-herb-shop stocked with gourmet items, plants, books and a myriad of herbs for sale. Drop by for afternoon tea on Friday or make reservations for Sunday tea and a tour of the garden. Admission. ~ Route 81 to Brault Hill Road; 860-345-4290.

NIGHTLIFE

The elegant **Water's Edge Inn and Resort** offers live bands in the lounge on weekends and outdoor entertainment during the summer. ~ 1525 Boston Post Road, Westbrook; 860-399-5901, 800-222-5901

The **Griswold Inn** is a favorite meeting place after sundown. A landmark of this exquisite river town ever since 1776, "the Gris" boasts an old taproom as fine as any in the state. Nightly doings range from Dixieland to sea chanteys to traditional ballads or classic arias, all performed in a warm, friendly atmosphere. ~ 36 Main Street, Essex; 860-767-1812.

BEACHES & PARKS

SELDEN NECK STATE PARK This one is special, a 528-acre island in the Connecticut River accessible only by water—truly a place to get away from it all. You can hike along woodsy trails that lead to old rock quarries, explore the shore in your kayak or canoe or contemplate the wide, tranquil river. Outhouses, picnic tables, fireplaces. ~ The island is located two miles south of Gillette Castle State Park in East Haddam, which handles information and permits for both parks (call 860-526-2336). Canoes and kayaks can be launched at the ferry slip below the castle or anywhere along the Connecticut River; 860-526-2336.

▲ Four primitive tent sites are available for one-night stops by boaters only; $4 per person.

GILLETTE CASTLE STATE PARK ◡ One of the most popular destinations in Connecticut, this mountainside park is topped by the picturesque fieldstone structure built at the start of the century by William Gillette, a well-known actor (see the "Sights" section in this chapter). Views of the Connecticut River are spectacular, and you can hike on shady trails to the water's edge and watch the ferry plying its way between Chester and Hadlyme. Picnic grounds, restrooms, food concession stands, gift shop, horse-drawn carriage rides. ~ Four miles south of East Haddam, off Route 82. From the west bank of the river, take the ferry from Chester to Hadlyme and follow the signs up the mountain; 860-526-2336.

▲ A few primitive tent sites available for one-night stops for canoers and kayakers only; $4 per person.

Mystic Area

The easternmost stretch of the Connecticut coast is lined with towns and villages with deep maritime roots. These include New London, home to the U.S. Coast Guard Academy; Groton, the "submarine capital of the world;" Mystic, where the popular Mystic Seaport is located; and Stonington, where you'll find an impressive collection of 18th- and 19th-century buildings that were built for ship captains and other seafarers. Several of the east-coast towns were important whaling centers back in the early 1800s, which brought great prosperity to the area.

SIGHTS

The centerpiece of this chunk of the coast is the historic Mystic Seaport, which could keep you happily amused for hours, but you'll find quite a bit to see in the towns surrounding it.

It's best to stop at the information center on Route 95 at North Stonington (southbound) or contact the **Southeastern Connecticut Tourism District** to get the lay of the land—and of the water. ~ P.O. Box 89, 27 Masonic Street, New London, CT 06320; 800-863-6569.

New London, Groton, Mystic and Stonington grew prosperous as sea and river ports, and today, the recreational uses of this jagged coastline are central to the communities' appeal. Moreover, New London and Groton are home to water-related military facilities, some of which are open to the public. At the **United States Coast Guard Academy** visitors may tour the grounds, visitors center, museum, the chapel, some of the buildings and, when it's in port, the tall ship *Eagle*, used as a training vessel for the cadets. What a vision, when she sails down the Thames River and out to sea! ~ 15 Mohegan Avenue/Route 32, New London; 860-444-8270.

Another river scene great to behold is a submarine being towed by a tugboat to or from the United States Naval Submarine base on the Groton side of the Thames. In Groton, you can tour the **USS Nautilus**, the first nuclear-powered submarine, now a National Historic Landmark, permanently berthed and refitted to receive visitors. ~ Route 12; 860-449-3174.

Alongside is the striking, steel-and-glass **Submarine Force Library and Museum**, with hands-on, up-to-date exhibits that trace the history of the submarine from our friend Bushnell's *Turtle* to the sleek, high-tech models of today. ~ Route 12, Groton, 860-449-3174.

Boat tours of the Groton–New London area offer visitors a multitude of choices, including the two-and-one-half-hour educational cruise on the research vessel **Enviro-Lab**, where passengers learn about marine life firsthand. Open from mid-June through Labor Day. Admission. ~ Project Oceanology, 1084 Shennescossett Road, Avery Point, Groton; 860-445-9007, 800-364-8472.

Though the glories of whaling days are New London's main claim to fame—be sure to drive past the four magnificent 1832 temple-front mansions, known collectively as **Whale Oil Row** (105–119 Huntington Street)—the city has many strings to its bow: the lively town pier, with charter boats of all kinds; ferries that ply across the Sound to several island destinations; and some fine historic homes and museums.

◄ HIDDEN

Visitors of a literary bent will want to stop by the shorefront **Monte Cristo Cottage**, boyhood home of playwright Eugene O'Neill and the setting for his two autobiographical plays, *Ah! Wilderness* and *Long Day's Journey Into Night*. Closed in winter. Admission. ~ 325 Pequot Avenue, New London; 860-443-0051.

The Monte Cristo cottage is part of the **Eugene O'Neill Theater Center**, an organization devoted to developing new works for the stage. Some of the play readings, performances and rehearsals are open to the public. (See the "Theater in Connecticut" feature in this chapter.) ~ 305 Great Neck Road, Waterford; 860-443-5378.

Nearby is New London's **Ocean Beach Park**, with a broad expanse of fine sand, a boardwalk, amusement rides and vistas of passing ships, ferries and a handsome lighthouse. Admission. ~ Ocean Avenue; 860-447-3031, 800-510-7263.

Driving toward Mystic on Route 95, you'll arrive at a scenic overlook where **Mystic Seaport Museum** comes into view. Just for a moment—as you spot the masts of tall ships in the distance and the smaller craft that ply the Mystic River—you might really believe you're entering a 19th-century New England seaport. When you get there, you and thousands of others, a little of the magic wears off. Yet it's unique, this indoor/outdoor museum on 17 riverfront acres. Admission. ~ 75 Greenmanville Avenue; 860-572-0711.

Begun in 1929, Mystic Seaport has grown steadily, encompassing a coastal village—church, chapel, schoolhouse, pharmacy, bank, ship's chandlery—several buildings with indoor exhibits of figureheads, marine paintings and ship's models; a lively children's museum; a preservation shipyard where you can watch the craftsmen at work; and a collection of some 300 boats and ships headed by the *Charles W. Morgan* (1841), America's sole surviving wooden whaleship. Crowds or no crowds, you won't want to miss the opportunity to explore its decks, visit the cramped quarters where crews lived for years at a time and watch members of the staff set sails and climb the rigging as they sing traditional chanteys. An ideal time to go is on a drizzly, misty grey day, when visitors are fewer and the atmosphere even more evocative.

Having been transported into the reconstructed past, take time to roam the town of **Mystic** itself, where vessels of all kinds, including whalers, clipper ships and pleasure boats, have been built since the 17th century. You'll find streets, such as Gravel, Clift and High, edged with early- and mid-19th-century homes of ships' owners and captains. The small downtown bustles with visitors, all watching the parade of boats passing under the rare *bascule* bridge (that's French for seesaw) that opens hourly all summer long, while traffic stops dead. There are **windjammers** and all manner of craft available for cruises of an hour or a week. You can help sail, or not, according to the mood of the moment. For details, contact the Southeastern Connecticut Tourism District. ~ P.O. Box 89, 27 Masonic Street, New London, CT 06320; 800-863-6569.

Stonington, the easternmost coastline town in the state, is thought by many to be the most attractive. The densely settled, narrow tongue of land known as Stonington Borough, part of the larger town, is home port to Connecticut's one remaining commercial fishing fleet. Its compact streets are a treasury of architectural styles dating back to the 18th and 19th centuries, when generations of seamen sailed in locally built vessels to trade with China and as far as Antarctica in search of whales and seals. A pleasant walking tour of Main, Water and the short diagonal streets could begin at the **Old Lighthouse Museum**, where the 1823 granite lighthouse displays maritime exhibits and artifacts of early American coastal life. Be sure to climb the stone steps to the top of the tower where there is a wonderful view of three states and Long Island Sound. Closed from November through April. Admission. ~ 7 Water Street; 860-535-1440.

LODGING   Don't be lulled by the abundance of accommodations around New London and Mystic; in season, a good room can still be hard to get. There's a big cluster of motels at Exit 90 off Route 95, ranging in price from moderate to deluxe (less in winter and spring). Some other options, all within a few miles of the main attractions:

The **Lighthouse Inn** was the summer home of a steel magnate who decided, in 1902, to build a Spanish-style stucco "cottage" in the meadows overlooking the sea. The meadows have been rezoned residential, but the mansion makes an opulent 51-room inn, with a fine restaurant and individually designed, generous bedrooms with water views, antique furnishings and unusual details; a few even have ocean views. ~ 6 Guthrie Place, New London; 860-443-8411, fax 860-437-7027. DELUXE TO ULTRA-DELUXE.

The cozy **Shore Inne** is a seven-room bed and breakfast set among small homes right on the water—"like being in grandmother's cottage," the owner says. Grandma should consider new mattresses. Other than that, it's a great place to be: The views are splendid and you can walk to any of three private beaches nearby. ~ 54 East Shore Avenue, Groton Long Point; 860-536-1180. MODERATE.

◄ HIDDEN

The Inn at Mystic is a hilltop potpourri of accommodations: a fine motel and two historic buildings for a total of some 68 rooms. The exquisitely landscaped complex also includes an exemplary restaurant, tennis courts, a pool and a dock with rowboats and canoes. Rooms are individually designed and old-time in feeling, even in the motel. Not so the bathrooms, which are luxuriously up-to-date. Despite the feeling of elegant seclusion, you're only a mile away from Mystic Seaport. ~ Routes 1 and 27, Mystic; 860-536-9604, 800-237-2415, fax 800-572-1635. DELUXE TO ULTRA-DELUXE.

At the **Whaler's Inn** you'll find a variety of rooms housed in the inn itself and two motor courts. You couldn't be more "downtown": The famed bridge is within a few feet. There are two restaurants attached to the inn and a few rooms with fine views of the Mystic River

Mystic Area

and the Seaport, just a half-mile away. ~ 20 East Main Street, Mystic; 860-536-1506, 800-243-2588, fax 860-572-1250. MODERATE TO DELUXE.

HIDDEN ►

Two gems lie on the outskirts of Mystic. **Applewood Farms Inn**, an early 19th-century farmhouse complete with corn crib and barn, is a few miles north of Route 95 and the visiting crowds. Set on 33 acres and surrounded by farms, this is one bed and breakfast that actually welcomes children, who'll be enchanted by the horse, sheep and goats here and the 50 Arabian show horses next door. The house, a National Historic Register Landmark, is blessed with magnificent fireplaces, and the three common rooms and six guest rooms have distinct personalities, highlighted by an eclectic selection of period pieces. Breakfasts are uniformly bountiful, true country meals. ~ 528 Colonel Ledyard Highway, Ledyard; 860-536-2022, fax 860-536-4019. DELUXE.

The **Palmer Inn** is southern in inspiration, a columned, porticoed mansion built in this captivating little community in 1907. Here all is graciousness and Victorian elegance—carved mahogany paneling, stained glass, Oriental carpets on polished wood floors—in the main hall, the parlor and the sitting room as well as the six spacious bedrooms up the wide, curving stairs. ~ 25 Church Street, Noank; 860-572-9000. DELUXE TO ULTRA-DELUXE.

DINING

Lunching at the **Lighthouse Inn**, you'll glimpse an intriguing view of Long Island Sound between two rows of houses. These good-size 20th-century homes seem to be dollhouses, in contrast to the baronial grandeur of the inn's dining room—dark, heavy overhead beams and dark wainscoting, great fireplaces and heavy, almost grotesque chandeliers. Yet, though the dining rooms seat more than 200, business is brisk. And with good reason: the food is well prepared, heavy on seafood—a favorite around these parts. ~ 6 Guthrie Place, New London; 860-443-8411. MODERATE TO DELUXE.

For a meal or snacks at any time of day, the place to go, according to residents of the area, is **G. Williker's!**. It has a popular taproom and a friendly staff, the usual faux-Victorian decor and a variety of

UNDERWATER MYSTIC

You'll want to visit Connecticut's most popular attraction, **Mystic Marinelife Aquarium**. It boasts 48 fine indoor exhibits; outdoor habitats for sea lions, seals and penguins; a Marine Theater with hourly demonstrations starring trained whales and dolphins; and in summer, open classroom programs are available for children, requiring no reservations. Admission. ~ 55 Coogan Boulevard, Mystic; 860-536-3323.

excellent burgers and all-American favorites such as tacos and pizza. ~ 156 Kings Highway, Groton, Exit 86 on Route 95; 860-446-0660, 800-443-0611. BUDGET TO MODERATE.

Restaurant Bravo Bravo features cuisine with Italian and French accents. You may choose from entrées like veal medallions stuffed with garlic, spinach and cheese and topped with shiitake mushroom sauce, or garlic and tomato shrimp baked in a casserole. During the summer, enjoy the outdoor café where you can watch the best show in town: The old drawbridge that opens every hour to let boats go through. Closed Monday. ~ In the Whaler's Inn, 20 East Main Street, Mystic; 860-536-3228. BUDGET TO MODERATE.

If you're spending the day at Mystic Seaport, you'll want to know about **The Seamen's Inne,** located next to the Seaport entrance. It's a large, busy place, built to resemble the New England–style structures nearby, and it specializes in the appropriate fare—basically seafood. Portions are ample. ~ 65 Greenmanville Avenue; 860-536-9649. MODERATE TO DELUXE.

High on a knoll overlooking the harbor sits the **Flood Tide Restaurant**, a favorite with visitors to the town. Part of The Inn at Mystic but set apart on the unusually handsome grounds, this bright, airy dining room offers an ambitious continental menu with something for every taste. ~ Routes 1 and 27, Mystic; 860-536-8140. MODERATE TO DELUXE.

And then there's **Abbott's Lobster in the Rough**, a legend in is own time, a place where dining informally means sitting at waterfront picnic tables or in the simple dining room and truly using your hands for all they're worth. There's chowder, steamed clams, mussels and shrimp, but it's the lobster that has made Abbott's famous for 40 years—caught in local waters, steamed to just the right degree of tenderness. On a summer day, you can expect a wait, maybe a long one. But who minds waiting, when there's a harbor full of boats and a picturesque village to delight? Closed November through April. ~ 117 Pearl Street, Noank; 860-536-7719. MODERATE TO DELUXE.

In captivating Stonington, the **Harborview Restaurant** is considered one of the area's best. Classic French dishes rule the menu— bouillabaisse, mussels, veal in many guises. The ambience is elegant and subdued. ~ 60 Water Street; 860-535-2720. DELUXE TO ULTRA-DELUXE.

Right behind the Harborview, built on a pier, is **Skipper's Dock**, its sister restaurant. In this more casual spot, you can consume your fill of seafood on a terrace overhanging the water or in a glass-enclosed dining room decorated with buoys of all kinds. If you arrive by sea, you can tie up at no extra charge. Closed Monday and Tuesday. ~ 66 Water Street, Stonington; 860-535-2000. MODERATE TO DELUXE.

Randall's Ordinary is, in fact, unique. Everything on the menu at this inn-with-restaurant—that's what *ordinary* meant in days of yore—

is cooked over the fire in authentic Early-American fashion. Guests are invited to stand before the three massive fireplaces and watch dinner cooking; then it's brought to the table by servers in period costumes. The backdrop for this gastronomic journey into the past is a landmark 17th-century country home listed on the National Register of Historic Places. The price includes soup, an entrée of poultry, meat or fish, and dessert. ~ Route 2, North Stonington; 860-599-4540. ULTRA-DELUXE.

SHOPPING   Olde Mistick Village is an entire community of Colonial-style structures built in the early 1970s to house every kind of shop and boutique known to the traveler—60 businesses on 20 landscaped acres. A bit cutesy, but it's an attractive place for browsing, with winding lanes, a stream, benches, wonderful flowers, even an authentic-looking meeting house with slender steeple and bells that soothe the weary visitor with music. ~ Exit 90 off Route 95; 860-536-4941.

Within Mystic Seaport itself, the vast **Mystic Seaport Museum Stores** emphasize things nautical and traditionally New England: gifts, clothes, jewelry, foods, books, prints, reproductions from the museum's collection. A separate section houses the prestigious Mystic Maritime Gallery. ~ 860-572-0711.

> The river Thames is pronounced "Thaymes" hereabouts.

Stonington's Water Street offers a wealth of pristine buildings to admire, good antiquing and a clutch of interesting boutiques as well. At **Hungry Palette** you'll find exclusive, locally designed fabrics and clothes. ~ 105 Water Street; 860-535-2021.

Quimper Faïence imports its traditional, hand-painted dinnerware and accessories directly from France. ~ 141 Water Street, Stonington; 860-535-1712.

NIGHTLIFE   Ocean Beach Park presents nightly programs with top entertainment acts performing under a spacious tent close to the sea. ~ Ocean Avenue, New London; 860-447-3031, 800-510-7263.

Located on the Mashantucket Indian Reservation, **Foxwoods High Stakes Bingo and Casino** is New England's largest and the state's first gambling casino. It has over 200 gaming tables, several restaurants and other entertainment. It's open 24 hours a day, year-round. ~ Route 2, Ledyard; 860-885-3000, 800-752-9244.

After a heavy day of sightseeing in Mystic, try the bar at the **Captain Daniel Packer Inn**. The cozy, rustic room with its old fireplace is a favorite gathering place for residents of all ages. It features music Tuesday through Thursday and a relaxing atmosphere seven nights a week. ~ 32 Water Street; 860-536-3555.

BEACHES & PARKS   ROCKY NECK STATE PARK 🏃🏊⚓ The main attraction here is a one-mile sandy beach with excellent swimming and fishing, and a picturesque view of shorefront cottages across the bay. The 700-acre park also encompasses vast salt marshes sheltering a variety of bird life that can be viewed from trails and raised boardwalks. Picnic grounds, restrooms, bathhouses, food concession stands; day-use fee, minimum $5. ~ Three miles west of Niantic on Route 156; 860-739-5471.

▲ There are 169 campsites, 149 for tents and RVs, 20 for tents only (no hookups); $12 per night.

OCEAN BEACH PARK ⬥ This city-owned park has a one-mile-long, crescent-shaped beach of sparkling white sand, backed by an old-fashioned boardwalk for jogging or strolling. The beach has excellent swimming. Several of the amusement park rides it used to offer are now on hold, but the triple waterslide remains a big draw. There's also miniature golf, a gift shop, snack bars, an arcade and nightly entertainment under the stars. Olympic-sized pool, beach volleyball, picnic pavilion, restrooms and changing rooms; parking fee, minimum $2. ~ In New London; from Route 95, take Exit 82A northbound or Exit 83 southbound, then follow signs; 860-447-3031.

North of the bustling, sometimes crowded coastline lies the region that has dubbed itself "the quiet corner": Connecticut's little-known, unspoiled Northeast, rich in scenic and historic interest if not in per capita wealth. You'll find no corporate towers here, no hordes of tourists, but interesting small towns, some of them settled in the 18th century, and a wealth of green pastures, rolling hills, rivers and forests.

▼▼▼▼▼▼▼▼▼▼▼▼
Northeast Corner

The **Northeast Connecticut Visitors District** will supply brochures listing accommodations and points of interest. ~ P.O. Box 598, Putnam, CT 06260; 860-928-1228.

SIGHTS

To reach the quiet corner from the coast, the fastest route is 395, which branches off from Route 95 west of New London. If you're in Stonington, however, and don't wish to retrace your steps, a pleasant alternative would be Route 2, which winds its way through unspoiled rural areas to Norwich, a historic city at the head of the River Thames. At the junction of Routes 2 and 169, in Norwich, the old **Leffingwell Inn**, a former colonial "publique house" and now a museum, served as a meeting place for patriots in the Revolutionary War. Closed from mid-October to mid-May. Admission. ~ 348 Washington Street; 860-889-9440.

From there, Route 169 heads north and passes through the village of Taftville, past an immense, turreted brick construction handsome enough to serve as a king's castle. It's **Ponemah Mill**, a former cotton factory thought to have been the largest in the country and the most beautiful, many say. You won't find it on tourist itineraries—it's privately owned and now home to several companies—but it's an appropriate introduction to an area where the textile industry set the pattern of life from the mid-19th century until recent decades. When

◀ HIDDEN

the industry moved to the South, it left behind its footprints: imposing riverfront mills, each with its village where the workers lived. Many such complexes—some shuttered and depressed, others used for new purposes—hug the banks of the Quinebaug River, which flows close to Route 169.

The road also passes graceful colonial towns like **Canterbury**, with its neat village green, where the **Prudence Crandall Museum**, a National Historic Landmark, pays tribute to the resolute young teacher who dared to open a school for "young ladies of color" in 1833. The ensuing controversy led to imprisonment—happily, brief—and to the school's closing. Fifty years later, as a restitution of sorts, the state legislature granted Crandall an annuity of $400 per year. In 1995, Prudence Crandall became Connecticut's first official female state hero. Closed Monday and Tuesday and from mid-December through January. Admission. ~ Junction of Routes 14 and 169; 860-546-9916.

The courthouse where Crandall's trial took place is a few miles north, in **Brooklyn**, where it serves as the current town hall. Near it, on Brooklyn's green, is the first **Unitarian Church** in the state, a simple, elegant white structure built in 1771, with a Paul Revere bell in its lofty belfry.

HIDDEN ▶

The town is known for its agricultural fair in late August, but it also holds a hidden gem: **Old Trinity Church** (1771), bypassed by time and now open just once a year on All Saints' Day. From the town center, take Route 6 east for one mile, go left on Church Street and you'll find the serene white clapboard structure, with its arched windows and pedimented door, standing next to its ancient graveyard in a leafy grove, surrounded by cornfields.

Woodstock sits high on a hill overlooking a rich agricultural valley. Visitors come from far away to see **Roseland Cottage**, a bright pink Gothic-inspired mansion built in 1846 by Henry Bowen, a local boy who grew rich in business in New York, then turned his energies toward publishing an antislavery, staunchly Republican weekly called *The Independent*. The lavish house and gardens, which remained in the family for over 100 years, are intact, as is the tradition of festive Fourth of July parties on the grounds. Closed in the winter. Admission. ~ 556 Route 169, 860-928-4074.

Pomfret, site of an elite private school, has long been a magnet for affluent city families, who built substantial summer homes and landscaped gardens here.

Across the Quinebaug, and just a few miles from the Rhode Island and Massachusetts lines, the town of **Thompson** boasts a magnificent 19th-century mill fronting the river, as well as a classic residential area on a hilltop—one of the finest. Today, it's as composed and tranquil as any you'll find, with its traditional green—they call it a common here—fine meeting house and white or pale-yellow homes on shady streets. It was a busy crossroads in the past: two major turnpikes intersected there, Boston to Hartford and Providence to Springfield.

The two-story tavern built in 1814, the still-operating **Vernon Stiles Inn**, was a bustling meeting place for important, but weary stagecoach travelers from three states. It also did a brisk wedding business, as young lovers fled the stringent laws of the nearby states. The 19th-century innkeeper, Captain Stiles, administered the vows. Today's owners merely provide food and drink in an evocative, charming setting. Closed Tuesday. ~ Junction of Routes 193 and 200, Thompson; 860-923-9571.

After this spell of old-time tranquility, you'll be ready for the bustle and bounce of an up-to-date university campus. Route 44 will take you west to Storrs, part of the town of Mansfield, location of the main campus of the **University of Connecticut**. ~ Information Center on Storrs Road; 860-486-2000.

Now a prestigious university, "UConn" was founded in 1881 as an agricultural school. The sight of emerald pastures dotted with well-fed cows across the street from massive modern buildings makes an intriguing contrast. It also makes for great ice cream, which you can buy at the Dairy Bar, made every day. Refreshed, you'll want to stop at the **William Benton Museum of Art**, where wide-ranging exhibitions are displayed in an attractive, cathedral-ceilinged gallery. The Benton has the honor of being Connecticut's state art museum—a fitting way to finish up a tour. Closed Monday and between exhibits. ~ 245 Glenbrook Road, Storrs; 860-486-4520.

LODGING

The **King's Inn** makes a handy jumping-off place for exploring the "quiet corner" of the state. In decor, it tries to re-create old-time New England, but what it does best is supply 40 pleasant motel rooms, adding a pool and a restaurant for your convenience. ~ 5 Heritage Road, Putnam; 860-928-7961, 800-541-7304, fax 860-963-2463. MODERATE.

The 1825 **Inn at Woodstock Hill** is a Christopher Wren–style, three-story white building with black shutters. The 22 guest rooms are decorated in Waverly chintz with an assortment of antique cherry and maple furniture. Six of the rooms feature fireplaces and four-poster beds. Guests may linger at the piano in the living room or relax with a book in front of the fireplace in the library. ~ 94 Plaine Hill Road, South Woodstock; 860-928-0528, fax 860-928-3236. MODERATE TO ULTRA-DELUXE.

In recent years numerous new bed and breakfasts—small, for the most part—have sprouted in this little known area, where accommodations were once hard to find. The **Northeast Connecticut Visitors District** will help visitors find one that suits their needs. ~ P.O. Box 598, Putnam, CT 06260; 860-928-1228.

One bed and breakfast with a faithful following is **Altnaveigh Inn**, a 1734 farmhouse less than two miles from the University of Connecticut. The five well cared for rooms are located above a popular restaurant and are simply furnished. ~ Route 195, Storrs; 860-429-4490. MODERATE.

Several bed and breakfast reservation services will supply additional suggestions for accommodations throughout the state. Try the **Nutmeg Bed and Breakfast Agency.** ~ P.O. Box 1117, West Hartford, CT 06107; 860-236-6698, 800-727-7592. Another agency is the **Covered Bridge Bed and Breakfast Reservation Service.** ~ P.O. Box 447, Norfolk, CT 06058; 860-542-5944.

DINING

Some people plan a trip to this part of the state just to have a meal at the **Golden Lamb Buttery.** Located in a converted barn, it's country dining like you've never experienced. The menu generally includes classic American dishes and whatever's ready to be plucked from the garden. There's usually a wonderful soup to start, followed by a choice of entrées (duck, lamb, various seafood) prepared a different way every day. Throughout the meal a strolling guitarist lightly strums away. The restaurant is open May through New Year's Eve; closed Sunday and Monday. ~ Bush Hill Road, Brooklyn; 860-774-4423. ULTRA-DELUXE.

In Thompson, there's an institution called the **Vernon Stiles Inn**. Built as a stagecoach tavern in 1814, it has played many roles since then, the current one being that of restaurant. It's a rambling, two-story structure—several dining areas filled with country antiques, old tavern signs and other landmarks of its colorful past. The food is typically American with Continental overtones—steak, duckling, seafood and pasta. Closed Tuesday. ~ Junction of Routes 193 and 200; 860-923-9571. MODERATE TO DELUXE.

If you're tooling around the "Quiet Corner" and feel a sudden yen for a real, old-fashioned roadside diner, **Zip's Diner** is the answer to your prayers. It's a legacy from the 1950s with a jukebox at every booth; a true formica-and-stainless-steel classic that serves up pot roast, roast turkey, eggs any way you like, pie and ice cream and lots of hot, strong coffee. ~ Routes 12 and 101, Dayville; 860-774-6335. BUDGET.

A few miles from the University of Connecticut campus, and a favorite with the "UConn" crowd, is the **Mansfield Depot Restaurant.** The simple 1920s structure has been restored with restraint and good taste, in keeping with its origins as a small country station. The atmosphere is warm and comfortable and the food rates raves from faithful followers. It's regional American cuisine, with an emphasis on fresh fish, along with a choice of vegetarian entrées and specials. ~ 57 Middle Turnpike, Route 44, Mansfield; 860-429-3663. MODERATE TO DELUXE.

SHOPPING

The "quiet corner" offers its own array of antique shops on country roads or quiet main streets. Contact the **Northeast Connecticut Visitors District** for a complete list of the region's shops. ~ P.O. Box 598, Putnam, CT 06260; 860-928-1228.

Each town has its complement of boutiques and stores, but visitors seeking an unusual buying foray often head for one of the region's scenic vineyards: **Nutmeg Vineyard.** ~ 800 Bunker Hill Road, Coventry; 860-742-8402.

Another popular shopping destination is **Caprilands Herb Farm,** most famous of its ilk. On the extensive grounds stand a bookshop, a bouquet and basket shop, a restored 18th-century barn that carries herbs and spices, a greenhouse that sells seeds and plants, and an old farmhouse open for luncheon programs (daily, by reservation only), not to mention 31 different gardens featuring vegetables, herbs and herbal flowers. ~ 534 Silver Street, Coventry; 860-742-7244.

A welcome addition to the "quiet corner's" nightlife scene is **J. D. Cooper's Fine Food and Spirits** . This triple-threat establishment comprises a restaurant, a bar and the Cooper Stadium Sports Bar, where the whole family can enjoy darts, an oversized TV screen and several interactive video games. ~ 146 Park Road, Putnam; 860-928-0501.

NIGHTLIFE

The **Bidwell Tavern** dates from the 1800s, but the music that fills this rustic spot is up-to-date, contemporary acoustic. ~ 1260 Main Street, Coventry; 860-742-6978.

The **Jorgensen Auditorium** is the University of Connecticut's major performing center, presenting a year-round program of music, dance and theater performed by artists of international renown. ~ University of Connecticut, 2132 Hillside Road, Storrs; 860-486-4226.

MASHAMOQUET BROOK STATE PARK 🏃 🏊 ⛵ Two major hiking trails lead to the park's most famous feature: a wolf den where, in 1742, young Israel Putnam shot a wolf that had terrorized the population. Putnam became a local hero and later gained national fame as a Revolutionary War general. The park also boasts a small, clear pond for swimming and a brook for fishing. Located at the entrance is Brayton Grist Mill, last in the area, with its traditional machinery intact and a display of blacksmithing tools belonging to three generations of the same family. Picnic grounds, restrooms, concession stand, nature trail; day-use fee, minimum $5. ~ Five miles southwest of Putnam on Route 44; 860-928-6121.

BEACHES & PARKS

▲ There are 55 tent/RV sites for (no hookups); $9 per night.

Along the coast of Long Island Sound, fishing boats cast off daily with groups of passengers eager to try their luck. Among the party fishing boats that sail on specific schedules and can be boarded on first-come, first-served basis are the following:

▼▼▼▼▼▼▼▼▼▼▼▼▼
▼▼▼▼▼▼▼

Outdoor Adventures

SPORT-FISHING

MYSTIC AREA   In New London, at Thamesport Landing, you can try the **Wanderer.** ~ 800-882-1151. In Niantic, at Niantic Beach Marina, try the **Black Hawk II.** ~ 203-443-0663. At Mijoy Dock, check out the **Mijoy/Mijoy 747.** ~ 860-443-0663. At Captain John's Dock, there's the **Sunbeam Fleet**. ~ 860-443-7259. In Groton, at Hel-Cat Dock, try the **Hel-Cat II**. ~ 860-535-2066.

Charter fishing boats that can be booked by private groups are more numerous. A sampling follows:

LOWER CONNECTICUT RIVER VALLEY In Old Saybrook, at Saybrook Marine Service, there's the **Provider**. ~ 860-388-3614. At Saybrook Point Marina, try the **Sea Sprite**. ~ 860-669-9613.

MYSTIC AREA In New London, the **Lady Margaret** and the **Playing Hookey**, both at Thamesport Landing, and the **Wanderer in Noank**, at Noank Village Boatyard, can all be booked by calling 860-442-1151 or 800-882-1151. You can call the **Reelin'** in Noank. ~ 860-449-1980. Also in Noank is the **Trophy Hunter**. ~ 860-536-4460.

SAILING & WIND-SURFING

Sailing is a way of life along the Connecticut shoreline. Each harbor, big or small, shelters its own flotilla at the ready, and yet it's hard to find sailboats for rent. Here are a few suggestions:

SOUTHWESTERN CONNECTICUT In Westport, you'll find windsurfers and small sailboats at **John Kantor's Longshore Sailing School**. ~ 260 Compo Road South; 203-226-4646.

LOWER CONNECTICUT RIVER VALLEY **Colvin Yachts** offers a fleet of charter boats 22 to 36 feet in length; the smaller ones can be rented by the day, while the others are available only for a weekend or more. ~ 533 Boston Post Road, Westbrook; 860-399-6251, 800-850-7245.

MYSTIC AREA Mystic Seaport offers a different maritime experience, a sailing education program for young people aged 15 to 19 on the 61-foot schooner *Brilliant*. Youths act as crew for six-to-ten-day trips, under professional supervision. An adult version of the project involves four-day stints, from May to October. ~ 75 Greenmanville, Mystic; 860-572-0711.

CANOEING & KAYAKING

The Connecticut River lends itself to a variety of canoeing experiences, from guided overnight trips to rent-your-own. You can find out about canoe camping at three state parks by writing the **Department of Environmental Protection**. ~ Office of State Parks and Recreation, 165 Capitol Avenue, Hartford, CT 06106; 860-424-3015.

SOUTHWESTERN CONNECTICUT Canoeing and kayaking trips on rivers, lakes and Long Island Sound are arranged by the **Mountain Workshop**. Programs run anywhere from a day to two weeks. ~ P.O. Box 625, Ridgefield, CT 06880; 203-438-3640.

NORTHWEST CORNER For explorations of the Housatonic River by canoe or kayak, contact **Clarke Outdoors**. ~ Route 7, Box 163, West Cornwall, CT 06796; 860-672-6365. You can also try **Riverrunning Expeditions**. ~ Main Street, Falls Village, CT 06031; 860-824-5579.

HARTFORD AREA You can paddle the waters of the Farmington River by day or on moonlit nights through the services of the **Main**

Stream Canoe Corporation. ~ Route 44, P.O. Box 448, New Hartford, CT 06057; 860-693-6791.

MYSTIC AREA   You can rent your own canoe or kayak through **North American Canoe Tours, Inc.** ~ 65 Black Point Road, Niantic; 203-739-0791.

Golf courses dot the Connecticut landscape like dandelions on a lawn in spring. Here's a selection of those open to the public: **GOLF**

SOUTHWESTERN CONNECTICUT   In Stamford, try **E. Gaynor Brennan Golf Course.** ~ 451 Stillwater Road; 203-324-4185. Also in Fairfield County is **Ridgefield Golf Club.** ~ 545 Ridgebury Road, Ridgefield; 203-748-7008.

NORTHWEST CORNER   In Litchfield you'll find **Stonybrook Golf Club.** ~ 263 Milton Road; 860-567-9977. In New Milford, try the **Candlewood Valley Country Club.** ~ On Danbury Road off Route 7; 860-354-9359.

HARTFORD AREA   Of the many golf courses in the Hartford area you can try **Bel Campo Golf Club** in Avon. ~ 65 Nod Road; 860-678-1358. In Farmington, play the **Westwoods Golf Course.** ~ Route 177; 860-677-9192. In Hartford, check out the **Goodwin Park Golf Club.** ~ 1130 Maple Avenue; 860-956-360).

NEW HAVEN AREA   In New Haven, you can play 18 holes at the **Alling Memorial Golf Course.** ~ 35 Eastern Street; 203-946-8013.

LOWER CONNECTICUT RIVER VALLEY   At Old Saybrook, you can tee off near the sea at **Fenwick Golf Club.** ~ 580 Maple Avenue; 860-388-2516.

MYSTIC AREA   Stonington has the **Pequot Golf Club.** ~ Wheeler Road; 860-535-1898.

NORTHEAST CORNER   In scenic Woodstock, you'll want to try the **Harrisville Golf Course.** ~ Harrisville Road; 860-928-6098.

The state's ski areas improve on nature with snow-making machines.   **SKIING**

NORTHWEST CORNER   In Cornwall, hit the ski slopes at **Mohawk Mountain.** ~ Great Hollow Road, off Route 4; 860-672-6100.

HARTFORD AREA   In the Hartford area, you'll find good trails at **Ski Sundow.** ~ 126 Rathum Road, off Route 219, New Hartford; 860-379-9851.

LOWER CONNECTICUT RIVER VALLEY   Near Middlefield, try the runs at **Powder Ridge.** ~ 99 Powder Hill Road; 860-349-3454.

Ski Rentals   You can rent skis at **Action Sports.** ~ 1385 Boston Post Road, Old Saybrook; 860-388-1291.

There's no dearth of tennis courts in the state—schools, universities, clubs, hotels and municipalities are well supplied—but many are out   **TENNIS** of bounds to the visitor. Each local parks and recreation department has its own rules; try calling when you come to town or ask your innkeeper or hotel desk person to make arrangements for you if they don't have their own court.

HARTFORD AREA   Courts are open to the public at three of Hartford's parks: **Elizabeth Park West** (Prospect and Asylum streets), **Goodwin Park** (South Street and Maple Avenue) and **Keney Park** (Woodland and Greenfield streets). The city's Parks and Recreation Department can be reached at 860-722-6495.

Outside the city, you can play at **Sycamore Hills Park** and **Avon Middle School**. ~ West Avon Road, Avon; 860-677-2634. You can also check out the **Simsbury Farms Recreation Complex**. ~ 100 Old Farms Road, Simsbury; 860-658-3836.

NEW HAVEN AREA   In New Haven, you can play at **Edgewood Park** (Whalley Avenue), **East Shore Park** (Woodward Avenue) and **Cross High School** (Mitchell Drive). For information, call the Recreation Division at 203-946-8538.

LOWER CONNECTICUT RIVER VALLEY   In the Lower Connecticut River Valley, try **Old Saybrook Tennis and Swim Club**. ~ 299 Spring Brook Road, Old Saybrook; 860-388-5115. **Lyme Shores Racquet Club** also has courts available. ~ 22 Colton Road, East Lyme; 860-739-6281.

MYSTIC AREA   Farther east you can play at New London's **Toby May Field**. ~ Ocean Avenue; for information call the Recreation Department, 860-447-5230.

For tennis courts at **Mitchell College**, call 860-443-2811. In Groton, courts are available at **Farquhar Park** (Route 117), **Washington Park** (Mitchell Street) and **Fitch Senior High** (Groton Long Point Road).

NORTHEAST CORNER   As you head north, you can test your skills at **Roseland Park**. ~ Roseland Park Road, Woodstock; 860-963-7690. In Willmantic, check out the **Willimantic Recreation Park**. ~ Route 6 and Main Street, Willimantic; 860-456-3593, ext. 242. There are numerous courts on the campus of the **University of Connecticut**. ~ Storrs; 860-486-2837.

BICYCLING   Much of Connecticut is ideal for bicycle touring. The relatively gentle terrain and scenic back roads lend themselves to this unhurried form of exploration—except for the hillier northwest corner, which requires some strenuous pedaling. The **Connecticut Department of Transportation** publishes a free bicycle map that indicates touring routes, loop routes and the Connecticut section of the East Coast bicycle trail. It also lists bicycle and repair shops in the state. The suggested routes cover most of the state, avoiding city traffic and high-speed highways. ~ 2800 Berlin Turnpike, Newington, CT 06111; 860-594-2000.

HARTFORD AREA   In addition, two of the state parks provide special bicycle trails. At **Stratton Brook State Park** in Simsbury, not far from Hartford, the old railroad tracks have been replaced by an extensive bike trail traveling along a scenic brook.

MYSTIC AREA   At **Haley Farms State Park** in Groton, an eight-mile trail winds its way through the picturesque old shoreline farm.

Bike Rentals   A few inns and hotels keep a small fleet of bicycles for their guests. Other than that, there are no bikes for rent around Connecticut. Best bring your own, if pedaling is your pleasure.

HIKING

Although Connecticut is densely populated, a surprising amount of open space has been preserved and provided with trails suitable for hiking. The Connecticut Blue Trails System, established and maintained by the **Connecticut Forest and Park Association**, consists of more than 700 miles of cleared and well-marked woodland trails touching on every county. Contact them for a brochure describing the trails. ~ 16 Meriden Road, Rockfall, CT 06481; 860-346-2372.

In addition, a portion of the white-blazed Appalachian Trail crosses northwestern Connecticut, and many state parks and forests and nature preserves have created their own hiking routes. You may also call or write to the **Department of Environmental Protection, State Parks Division** for hiking maps and information. ~ 79 Elm Street, Hartford, CT 06106-5127; 860-424-3200.

SOUTHWESTERN CONNECTICUT   In **Devil's Den Preserve**, 20 miles of interconnecting trails cover a variety of terrain, from wetland, stream and pond through mature forest to rocky knolls with wide-open vistas. Take Exit 42 from the Merritt Parkway, go north on Route 57 for five miles, then east on Godfrey Road for one-half mile and turn left on Pent Road.

NORTHWEST CORNER   In Kent Falls State Park a steep trail (.25 mile) leads up the south side of the falls, across a bridge and down

---

✔ **CHECK THESE OUT—UNIQUE OUTDOOR ADVENTURES**

• Canoe the still, peaceful waters of the scenic **Farmington River** by day or, for a romantic touch, by moonlight. *page 100*

• Join the flotilla of water-lovers sailing and windsurfing in **Westport's** harbor. *page 100*

• Retrace a Revolutionary War path leading to caves that hid Loyalists on the eight-mile **Housatonic Range Trail**. *page 104*

• Don your cross-country skis and explore 35 miles of trails through Litchfield's countryside at the **White Memorial Foundation**. *page 64* more gradually on the north side, through dense woods and towering hemlock trees. The south side trail hugs the cascade itself, enabling hikers to view the falls from many angles. Call 860-927-3029 or 860-927-3238 for information.

The blue-blazed **Housatonic Range Trail** (8 miles) follows the general route of an old Indian trail along the hills above the Housatonic River. Along the way are several caves to explore—Tories' Cave is said to have sheltered Loyalists during the Revolutionary War—fine views of Candlewood Lake, the Housatonic and its verdant valley; occasional steep climbing and some areas of rough scrambling over boulders. The trail begins one-and-a-half miles north of New Milford on Route 7. Call 860-672-6139 or 860-927-3238 for information.

Macedonia Ridge Trail (6.7 miles) is a loop within Macedonia Brook State Park. The trail, which begins and ends near the parking area at the southern end of the park, crosses bridges and brooks, passes old charcoal mounds and climbs Pine Hill and Cobble Mountain, both with splendid views and demanding ascents. Call 860-927-3238 for information.

Bear Mountain Trail (5.6 miles) is a steep, rugged hike to the 2316-foot summit, which reveals a vast panorama of mountains, lakes and forests in three states, as well as of turkey vultures soaring along the edge of the plateau. This hike begins on Route 41, at a small parking lot three-and-two-tenths miles north of its junction with Route 44 in Salisbury.

HARTFORD AREA   **Heublein Tower Trail** (1.3 miles) is an easy walk along a section of the blue-blazed Metacomet Trail, which circles around a scenic reservoir and climbs steeply up to Heublein Tower in Talcott Mountain State Park. From the tower, you'll see the skyline of Hartford and, on the clearest of days, the distant mountains of Massachusetts and New Hampshire. Before setting out, check with a ranger for detailed directions. The park entrance is on Route 185 in Simsbury.

Windsor Locks Canal Trail (9 miles round-trip) provides a level hike along the towpath that follows a historic canal built in 1829 to bypass the Enfield rapids on the Connecticut River. The trail begins on Canal Road, off Route 159.

NEW HAVEN AREA   **Westwoods**, a 2000-acre open space in Guilford, is crisscrossed with hiking trails. By taking the white circle trail out and the orange one back, you'll have walked six mostly level miles along marsh boardwalks, stands of hemlock and laurel, rocks, ledges, an abandoned quarry and Lost Lake, a scenic halfway point for a picnic.

Sleeping Giant, two miles north of Hamden, is a series of mountaintops resembling an oversized reclining man. More than 32 miles of trails traverse the titan's anatomy—head, chin, chest—affording distant views of hills and cities. For a strenuous, up-and-down circuit of the major peaks (6 miles round-trip), follow the blue-blazed trail from near the parking lot all the way to the giant's right foot, then back on the white trail, with a detour to the stone tower for the loftiest vista.

LOWER CONNECTICUT RIVER VALLEY Devil's Hopyard Trail (4.5 miles) in East Haddam crisscrosses the state park of the same name, beneath ancient groves of hemlocks, across picturesque foot bridges and along Chapman Falls, which tumbles in a 60-foot cascade. It begins near the parking lot. Call 860-873-8566 for information.

MYSTIC AREA Bluff Point Trail (4.5 miles), in Bluff Point Coastal Reserve, leads from the parking area to the bluffs. Wander along the rocky, pristine beach, then wind your way back on a different trail through woods and salt marshes that cover this rare, undeveloped peninsula on Long Island Sound. Call 860-445-1729 for information.

NORTHEAST CORNER Wolf Den Trail (5 miles) lies within Mashamoquet Brook State Park and takes you, along up-and-down terrain, into Israel Putnam's celebrated cave. It also loops past a boulder known as Indian Chair and into diverse environments that include swampland and open fields, woods and streams and high ledges that offer fine vistas. The blue-blazed trail starts near the parking lot off Wolf Den Drive. Call 860-928-6121 for information.

Mansfield Hollow Trail (8 miles round-trip) is part of the much long, blue-blazed Nipmuck Trail. Starting in the parking lot of the Mansfield Hollow Dam Recreation Area, it winds along the Fenton River, then veers steeply up a hillside to emerge at a cliff known as 50 Foot, a fine lookout with views of eastern Connecticut. Call 860-455-9057 for information.

▼▼▼▼▼▼▼▼▼▼▼▼

Transportation

CAR

Four major highways thread their way through the state. Route 95, the Connecticut Turnpike, runs along the shoreline, all the way from the New York state line to Rhode Island. At New Haven, it connects with Route 91, which heads north through Hartford into Massachusetts. Route 84 enters the state at Danbury and runs northeast through Hartford to join with the Massachusetts Turnpike at Sturbridge. Route 15, the celebrated Merritt Parkway, winds its scenic way a few miles north of Route 95, then swings north at New Haven to join with Route 91. The major highways are all linked to each other by north–south roads set at convenient intervals.

Route 1, the old Boston Post Road, goes through the heart of all the coastline communities paralleling Route 95. Unfortunately, most of Route 1 has turned into a commercial strip, with just a few old buildings here and there to recall the historic roadway it once was.

AIR

The major airport in the state is Bradley International Airport in Windsor Locks, 12 miles north of Hartford. Airlines flying into Bradley include American Airlines, Business Express, Continental Airlines,

Delta Airlines, Northwest Airlines, Trans World Airlines, United Airlines and USAir.

Several bus and shuttle companies provide ground transportation from Bradley Airport. Call Bradley Airport Information for details. ~ 860-292-2000.

Taxi service is available 24 hours a day from the **Yellow Cab Company**. ~ 860-666-6666.

Three smaller airports offer limited service. **Groton–New London Airport**, on the southeastern coast, is serviced by USAir. At Bridgeport's **Igor Sikorsky Memorial Airport**, scheduled flights are offered by Business Express, Continental Express and USAir Express. **Tweed–New Haven Airport** is serviced by Continental Express, United Airlines and USAir Express.

Residents of the southwestern section of Connecticut tend to use New York City's two airports, **La Guardia** and **John F. Kennedy**. They are crowded and frantic, but all the airlines fly there; they are less than an hour's drive from the Connecticut line (more at peak traffic time) and connected by frequent limousine service. For information, call **Connecticut Limousine Service**. ~ 800-472-5466.

FERRY

Two auto ferry lines operate daily, year-round, from points on Long Island in New York state across Long Island Sound, to the Connecticut shore. On the **Bridgeport and Port Jefferson Ferry**, the trip from Port Jefferson, New York to Bridgeport, Connecticut takes approximately an hour and 20 minutes. You'll need a reservation if you want to bring your car along. ~ 203-367-3043.

The **Cross-Sound Ferry**, form Orient Point, New York to New London, Connecticut takes about the same amount of time. You'll need a reservation if you want to bring your car along. ~ 860-443-5281.

BUS

Greyhound (800-231-2222) and **Bonanza** (800-556-3815) bus lines provide scheduled interstate service for most points in Connecticut. Greyhound offers service from the following terminals: Bridgeport (203-335-1123), New Haven (203-772-2470), Hartford (860-522-9267) and New London (860-447-3841).

TRAIN

Metro North (New Haven Line) runs hourly trains (more frequent at commute time) from New York City's Grand Central Station to New Haven, with connecting service from Stamford to New Canaan, South Norwalk to Danbury and Bridgeport to Waterbury. ~ Reservations: 800-638-7646. At New Haven, Metro North connects with **Amtrak's** main line to Boston, with stops at Old Saybrook, New London and Mystic. Also at New Haven, Amtrak links with service to Hartford. Amtrak's service from Washington to Boston makes Connecticut stops at Stamford, Bridgeport and New Haven. ~ Reservations: 800-872-7245.

At Bradley International Airport, you'll find the following car rental agencies represented: **Avis Rent A Car** (800-331-1212), **Budget Rent A Car** (800-724-6203), **Dollar Rent A Car** (800-800-4000), **Hertz Rent A Car** (800-654-3131) and **National Interrent** (800-227-7368).

The **Norwalk Transit District** has city buses, some of which meet Metro North trains at the railroad station. ~ 203-853-3338.

Connecticut Transit Company operates frequent buses within the city of Hartford and offers service to outlying towns such as Windsor, New Britain, Middletown, Manchester and the Farmington Valley communities of Avon, Canton, Farmington and Simsbury.

Connecticut Transit Company also services the New Haven area with city buses as well as buses that go to East Haven, West Haven, Milford, Cheshire, Waterbury and Wallingford, and frequent commuter buses to the shoreline communities of Guilford, Madison and Clinton. ~ 860-525-9181 or 203-624-0151. **Dattco Bus Company** operates buses that go from downtown New Haven east along Route 1, making stops along the way to Old Saybrook. ~ 203-772-2072, 800-229-4879.

The **Southeast Area Transit District** runs buses that connect New London, Norwich, Groton, East Lyme, Jewett City, Montville and parts of Mystic. ~ 860-886-2631.

In Hartford, guided walking tours are offered on Sundays from June through October by the **Greater Hartford Architecture Conservancy**. ~ 278 Farmington Avenue; 860-525-0279.

In New Haven, visitors can tour the **Yale University campus** on guided walks that are conducted twice daily. ~ Visitor Information Office, 149 Elm Street; 203-432-2300.

Heritage Trails, offers daily scheduled tours of Hartford and vicinity, as well as less frequent visits to other parts of the state and dinner tours of historic Farmington sites. Reservations required. ~ P.O. Box 138, Farmington, CT 06034; 860-677-8867.

THREE

Rhode Island

Rhode Islanders don't think of their state as small; they see it as compact, easy to get around in. They point out with great pride that no place in the state is more than a 45-minute drive away from anywhere else. In fact, one of the quirky traits that set Rhode Islanders apart from the rest of us is their reluctance to drive "long" distances. (Any commute longer than ten minutes is considered grounds for changing either one's job or one's residence.)

It's not only the locals who benefit from all this cozy proximity. Rhode Island's easy-to-reach destinations make it an ideal state for visitors. In a single day, it's possible to swim in Narragansett Bay, lunch in Newport, tour a mansion or two and still be in Providence in time for dinner.

Rhode Island, as every schoolchild knows, is the smallest state in the union—a mere 1214 square miles to be exact. But crammed into this tiny package is an overload of good things. The state's statistics are impressive: 400 miles of coastline (and this in a state that measures only 48 miles from north to south) with over 100 public beaches, some 18,000 acres of parklands, 12 institutions of higher learning, as well as a statewide storehouse of historically significant spots.

Having mentioned some of the state's obvious attributes, let's peek at some of its hidden virtues. Perhaps the best-kept secret about Rhode Island is the immense diversity within its modest boundaries. Some of its sites are well known throughout the world. Surely everyone has heard of the glittering mansions of Newport, but how many tourists know it is also possible to hike through a natural "cathedral of forest" near the historic village of Hopkinton? And while probably every sailor on the East Coast has discovered the seaport haven of Block Island, how many have ventured north into Narragansett Bay to set sail for the solitary splendor of Prudence or Patience Islands?

Those travelers who seek an individual path could not have found a more appropriate state than this one founded on an individual search for religious freedom. Back in 1636 Roger Williams settled this territory after he could no longer tolerate the religious constraints of the early Boston Puritans. Migrating south with his wife and daughters, he stopped to settle with the friends he had made among the Narragansett Indian tribe. After years of setbacks and negotiations, in 1663 Williams succeeded in wresting a royal charter from England for his new territory, one that would also allow him to unite Providence with several other settlements nearby.

A truly enlightened clergyman, Williams' religious tolerance was universal; his new state embraced all faiths. Although Williams founded his own Baptist Church in 1639 (the building in Providence can still be toured), Quakers, Jews and any other group seeking religious freedom were wholeheartedly welcomed. (Touro Synagogue in Newport, built in 1763, stands today as the oldest Jewish house of worship in continental America.)

This sense of tolerance endured. Although Rhode Island did participate in the infamous "triangle trade" (slaves traded for molasses traded for rum), it was also the first colony to prohibit slavery. Rhode Island was also the first colony to declare independence from Great Britain. And at the end of the Revolutionary War, it was the last of the original 13 colonies to ratify the new Constitution, holding out until the Bill of Rights, guaranteeing individual liberties, was added.

America's industrial revolution began in Rhode Island in 1790, when Samuel Slater started operating the first water-powered cotton mill. That power was provided by the mighty Blackstone River, and the rest is American history. Other successful industrial endeavors in the state have included jewelry and silver manufacturing, both of which have drawn immigrants here from all over the world. The newcomers brought along ethnic riches that can still be found in the state's cuisine, architecture and even the spoken word.

During "La Belle Époque" right before the turn of the century, the seaside town of Newport became the darling of America's newly rich and famous, a status-conscious group who lavished their untaxable millions on opulent "summer cottages." Folks like the Vanderbilts, the Astors and the Belmonts vied to one-up each other architecturally in the designs of these palaces, as well as with the opulent furnishings within. It was truly a gilded age, the spoils of which we can all still marvel over.

But palaces of the past are only part of the splendor of today's Rhode Island, much of it to be found away from the cities. One glance at a map reveals why Rhode Island is nicknamed the "Ocean State": its flamboyant coastline can only be the handiwork of a creative sea. While its interior boundaries are the work of man (they are pure New England—ruler-straight and right-angled), it's a different story along the coast, where the relentless surf has carved out a wild, exotic profile, etching miles of extravagant bays and barrier beaches into the shores, capriciously sprinkling the expanse with an explosion of islands.

South County's coastal villages reflect this watery whimsy. From the westernmost reaches of Watch Hill up to Greenwich in the east, each small town harbors its unique bit of history and maintains its individual personality, yet each is linked to the others by common bonds—silken beaches that edge the coastline and a dependence on the sea.

Thirteen miles off this coast lies Block Island, offshore but very much a part of the makeup of South County. Aggressively underdeveloped (the resident islanders intend to keep it this way!), Block Island is a haven in the true sense of the word, with no traffic lights, no fast-food places and no neon. Peace, quiet and nature are the touristic lures here, combined with some world-class fishing and sailing.

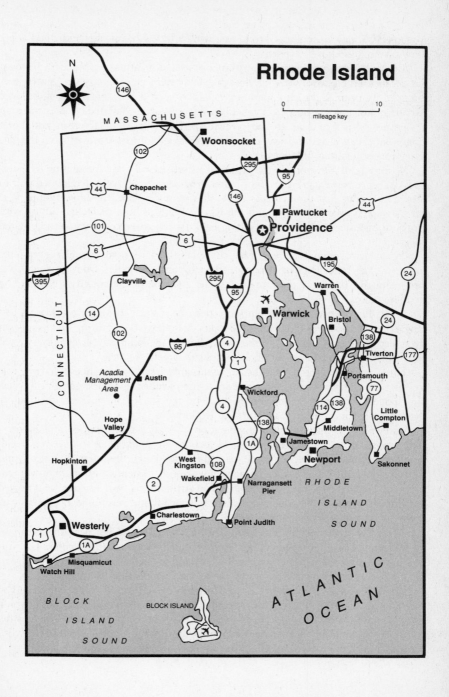

Rhode Island

MASSACHUSETTS

0 — mileage key — 10

Woonsocket

Chepachet

Pawtucket

Providence

Warren

Clayville

Warwick

Bristol

Tiverton

Little Compton

Portsmouth

Austin

Acadia Management Area

Wickford

Middletown

Hope Valley

Jamestown

Newport

Sakonnet

Hopkinton

West Kingston

Wakefield

Narragansett Pier

RHODE ISLAND SOUND

Charlestown

Westerly

Point Judith

Misquamicut

Watch Hill

BLOCK ISLAND SOUND

BLOCK ISLAND

ATLANTIC OCEAN

CONNECTICUT

Connected to South County by bridges across the broad expanse of Narragansett Bay is Newport County, occupying the islands the Indians named Conanicut and Aquidneck. Today visitors travel to Jamestown on little Conanicut Island, and the big draw on Aquidneck is Newport.

Although Newport is famous for its mansions and breathtaking beaches, the town has another, little-known side—its close proximity to relaxed country life. A mere ten-minute drive from all the glamour and the clamoring crowds of tourists along Bellevue Avenue stretch miles of bucolic farmlands, wilderness areas, deserted beaches and even a vineyard. A short drive to the postcard-perfect villages of Tiverton and Little Compton reveals a pastoral way of life that remains centuries removed from the glittering tourist passions of Newport.

Northwest of Newport, in the center of Rhode Island and representing its metaphysical heart as well, stretches the Greater Providence area. A get-acquainted visit to Providence helps first-time visitors establish a sense of place; the capitol building is here, as are Brown University and the Rhode Island School of Design, along with scores of historic buildings, some dating back two or three centuries to the original colony.

Providence combines the best of big-city/small-town; it's small enough for residents to know each other (Mayor Paolino personally answers letters from residents), yet large enough to support top-rate restaurants and one of the country's outstanding small museums.

Above Providence along the northern tier of the state, throughout the great rectangle of land known as the Blackstone Valley, folks have been gearing up to show off their special blend of treasures to the world. But for the moment, this densely forested river valley is yours to discover, its bounties still largely "hidden."

The Blackstone River itself is the key to this area. Its history includes a starring role in America's industrial revolution, and its future includes landmark status as a federally funded recreation heritage preserve. For the immediate present, the mighty Blackstone awaits your pleasure and your exploration.

Statewide, it is this appealing combination of big-city sophistication and country-style hospitality that makes Rhode Island such an intriguing place to discover. You'll note these qualities in the people you meet; they combine the best of both. Oh yes, and don't overlook their innate sense of independence—that legendary strength of will that surpasses even the rock-bound, generic version attributed to most Yankees. This rugged individuality—one of the principles on which Rhode Island was founded—comes naturally to the people of the Ocean State.

Weatherwise, temperate is the word. Much of the state lies near the ocean or Narragansett Bay, which plunges northward through Rhode Island's center. This watery influence results in light winter snowfalls and temperatures that reach the freezing mark only in January. In summers, the average temperature is around 72.

Rhode Island has another nickname, "America's First Resort." We're confident you will enjoy discovering this state for yourself. The only question is whether or not you'll want to share the tales of your adventures in this newfound playground. You may decide you want to keep all these treasures hidden just a while longer, before the word gets out and Rhode Island becomes everyone's favorite place in New England.

Officially, this southern tier of the state—extending from Connecticut along Block Island Sound and reaching into Narragansett Bay—is called Washington County. But you'll have trouble finding even one resident who calls it that. Rhode Islanders know this area as South County, and so should you if you want to be understood.

South County

South County truly *is* resort country; beach lovers from all over flock here every summer. Even many native Rhode Islanders maintain vacation homes in this coastal area, which provides great seaside escapes from urban pressures.

The sometimes unpronounceable names of many of South County's villages and waterways—Misquamicut, Cocumscussoc, Pettaquam-scutt—reflect the region's American Indian heritage. Roger Williams befriended the Indians when he settled Rhode Island and divided his time between Providence and North Kingstown (in South County), where he lived with his wife and two children from 1644 to 1650. The rolling farmlands and white-sand beaches of today's South County— a bucolic landscape mercifully lacking in high-rise condos and fast-food stores—make this history seem ancient indeed.

SIGHTS

Among the more high-profile residents of South County's villages are those who live in **Watch Hill**. (This select group strives for seclusion and anonymity, but their lavish dwellings continue to pique the imaginations of outsiders.) Although there's no formal "sightseeing route," many visitors love to drive through Watch Hill's quiet country lanes to ogle the tastefully lavish summer estates of these rich and reclusive folks. It seems that every turn in the road reveals a more lavish, more imposing "summer cottage." Although most were built decades ago, there are one or two new additions to the "Millionaires' Colony."

In town, at the foot of Bay Street, the country's oldest **merry-go-round** is still spinning its magic. Locals call it the "Flying Horse Carousel" because its gaily painted ponies are hung from chains that spin outward, so the horses "fly." Local custom decrees that as soon as a child's feet can touch the floor, he is too old to ride. Pint-sized riders still grab for the brass ring, squealing in triumph as they store less valuable rings on their horses' pointed ears for safekeeping.

In the nearby town of Westerly, **Wilcox Park**, an 18-acre haven right in the heart of town, has been an oasis for locals and visitors alike since 1898. Designed by a student of Frederick Law Olmsted, the park is listed in the National Register of Historic Places. In addition to biking and strolling by the beautiful flower beds, you can attend outdoor concerts here during the summer. ~ Tower Street; 401-596-8590.

Inland from South County's coastal areas, along Route 138, lies the century-old **Kenyon Grist Mill**. Run by the same family for years,

Text continued on page 116.

Rhode Island's Favorite Island

When describing Block Island, some liken it to Ireland. Many choose to rhapsodize over its bucolic charms, while others see it as a Victorian time warp. Block Island is all these ideals—and more. A modest triangle of land lying 13 miles off the coast of Rhode Island, it measures a scant three miles wide by seven miles long. Yet captured within its 11 square miles are vistas that do indeed recall Ireland at its best: verdant, rolling hills, neatly defined by rambling stone fences; grassy meadows strewn with wildflowers; ponds—over 365 of them (one for every day of the year); and always, the wild Atlantic crashing just off-shore.

As you approach Block Island by ferry, you'll first spot the chalky cliffs that rise 200 feet in a straight vertical from the thundering waves of the sound. It was from these cliffs that the resident Narragansett Indians once dispatched a band of off-islanders who attempted to conquer them; in a now famous battle, they pushed a band of invading Mohegans over the bluffs onto the rocks below.

Although the Mohegans are long gone, Block Island does seem lost in a former time. As the ferry slides into Old Harbor, passengers are greeted by an imposing phalanx of ornate Victorian buildings that stand shoulder-to-shoulder, facing out to sea. These grande dame structures are really most welcoming, offering bed and board to the island's multitudes of summer visitors—the same throngs who swarm the sidewalks of Old Harbor, slurping up mountains of homemade ice cream, purchasing enough "I ❤ Block Island" T-shirts to clothe the entire population of an emerging nation, and generally soaking up the festive salt-air island mood.

Do not misunderstand: Block Islanders are not about to let their idyllic spot fall prey to tourist trappings. There are no fast-food chains and not a glint of neon anywhere. No traffic lights wink on this island; in fact, there is no traffic to speak of. Visitors can get around in local taxis, or they can rent bikes or mopeds. (Mopeds, however, are discreetly discouraged.)

This is an island for travelers who truly want to commune with nature. Just minutes (even by bike) from the bustle of Water Street in Old Harbor, the island's only town, lies a three-mile swath of sand known as **Crescent Beach**. As the island's most popular bathing and sunning beach, Crescent may become too "crowded" for a loner's tastes. No problem: simply pick up your towel and mosey a few yards to the north where an isolated stretch of sand awaits.

Bikers are delighted to find the island's rolling hills offer just the right amount of challenge. The quiet roads wind past a handful of weathered-shingle cottages and a clapboard Victorian or two. But mostly, it is nature that's on view: brushy bayberry and scrub pines, grassy moors punctuated by ponds.

An astute naturalist will observe that there are very few trees standing on this island. Once there were many. That was back in the mid-1600s, when the first white settlers arrived. They felled the island's forests for lumber for their houses and barns, and for fuel. When that ran out, they burned peat from the marshes. Life has never been easy for islanders anywhere; but these early island dwellers had to cope not only with stern New England winters but also with the resident Indians who took a dim view of the new arrivals.

The white settlers, however, met no fate as harsh as the would-be Mohegan invaders, forced off the high cliffs at the southern end of the island. Today, these **Mohegan Bluffs** are still an awe-inspiring sight, attracting hordes of visitors who peer down at the crashing Atlantic 200 feet below, or who brave the climb down wooden stairs to walk the rock-strewn sands that border the wild ocean.

You might also want to visit the **Southeast Lighthouse** or **North Light-house**. The former has recently been relocated to escape rapidly eroding cliffsides and awaits reopening. The North Lighthouse has been renovated and now houses an interpretive exhibit on Block Island.

History teaches that several explorers "discovered" Block Island, among them Italian Giovanni Verrazano, who named it "Claudia," in honor of the mother of his patron, Francis I of France. But it was the Dutch navigator Adriaen Block who, in 1614, claimed this bit of land as his own, dubbing it "Adriaen's Eylant."

Today's Block Island is available to visitors on a limited basis. We mainlanders will never really belong; that privilege is only for the handful whose ancestors first settled here. But we are welcome to enjoy the bounties nature has bestowed: the wildlife that inhabits the marshy ponds; the quiet countryside; the pebbly beaches that ring the coastline and the migrating birds that swarm here each spring and fall.

At the entrance to Rodman's Hollow, an ancient glacial crevice that is now a wildlife refuge, locals have posted a hand-carved sign that admonishes all visitors: "This land has been dedicated for preservation in its natural state . . . please respect it so that all human, creature and plant life may share in its peace and beauty." A fitting sentiment that could easily be applied to all of Block Island.

The **Block Island Chamber of Commerce** can fill you in on anything else you want to know about the island. ~ Box D, Block Island, RI 02807; 401-466-2982.

Kenyon grinds the cornmeal that is the basic ingredient for proper Rhode Island johnnycakes. Tours of the facility—from the original stone grinding wheels to the Queens River behind the mill that once turned its wheels—can be arranged by appointment. Proprietors Paul Drumm Junior and Paul Drumm III love to talk about their mill and its history. Drop by for a chat, a look around or for some tips, recipes or cornmeal from the mill's country store. ~ Village of Usquepaugh, Glen Rock Road, West Kingston; 401-783-4054.

The history of American Indians in South County stretches some 12,000 years; this whole area is rich in artifacts and trails. A four-page drive tour through some of the best sightseeing territory—complete with drive guides, detailed maps and historical commentary—has been assembled by the **Museum of Primitive Art and Culture**. There are also self-guided walking tours of Mill Village. Open Tuesday, Wednesday and Thursday from Labor Day to Memorial Day; Wednesday only the rest of the year. ~ 1058 Kingstown Road, Peace Dale; 401-783-5711.

Back along the coast, you may want to stop in at the **South County Tourism Council**, where the folks can help with maps, brochures and information on the entire county. Closed Sunday. ~ 4808 Tower Hill Road, Wakefield; 401-789-4422.

From here the coast road starts winding north along Narragansett Bay. When you come to the village of Cocumscussoc north of Wickford, you'll find the building known as **Smith's Castle**. Although not a castle by traditional fairy tale standards, this 300-year-old woodframe house does harbor some impressive history, and 1.8 of its 23 acres are a National Historic Landmark. Roger Williams lived here and preached to the Indians in the mid-1630s, when the site was a trading post. Rebuilt in 1678 after a fire, it enjoyed celebrity as Updike Plantation and welcomed such famous guests as Benjamin Franklin and General Lafayette. Today, this grand era is memorialized by the 17th- and 18th-century household furnishings throughout the

✔ CHECK THESE OUT—UNIQUE SIGHTS

- Delight in the children's smiles as they ride the "flying horses" at Watch Hill's **merry-go-round**, the oldest in the country. *page 113*
- Fantasize about life as a Vanderbilt or Astor when you visit their lavish homes on the **Newport's mansions tour**. *page 124*
- Marvel at century-old trees and shrubs sculpted into a variety of whimsical shapes at Portsmouth's **Green Animals**. *page 127*
- Visit the small but impressive **Museum of Art—Rhode Island School of Design** housing treasures from Babylonian times to the present. *page 135*

house. Closed Tuesday and Wednesday. Admission. ~ 55 Richard Smith Drive; 401-294-3521.

On a newsworthy note: Experts at Brown University believe that America's oldest mass burial ground may lie beneath Smith's Castle property. In 1675, in the Great Swamp Fight with warring local Indian tribes, many colonists and Indians—including women and children—were killed. Archaeologists have conducted a dig at the site, where many of the colonists were buried.

Also near Wickford stands the **Gilbert Stuart Birthplace and Snuff Mill.** Sounds like an unlikely combination, but the famous "George Washington portraitist" was born here in this 1700 gambrel-roof house, next to where his dad owned and operated America's first snuff mill. Closed Tuesday and Wednesday. Admission. ~ Gilbert Stuart Road, Saunderstown; 401-294-3001.

Although Block Island is considered part of South County, this highly independent bit of territory 13 miles offshore marches to its own drummer. From its earliest days, when the native Narragansetts called it "Manisses," meaning "God's Little Island," this spirit has prevailed. (Dutch explorer Adriaen Block, in a 1614 visit, gave it his own name.) Many have compared Block Island's landscape to that of Ireland or Scotland. It's renowned for sightseeing of the natural kind; the island's remote location offers a unique closeness to nature. (See "Rhode Island's Favorite Island" in this chapter.)

LODGING

While visitors can always find one or two cookie-cutter chain hotels clustered near the larger towns, it is the rambling Victorians and out-of-the-way inns one remembers, and that tend to become a cherished part of the South County experience.

As with most New England resort areas, many lodgings here close for the winter. Rates, too, are seasonal; those indicated below reflect the heady rates of the peak summer season. Because of the crush of visitors, many places will also require two- or three-day minimum stays during high season and holiday weekends.

Personifying the genteel understatement of Watch Hill's old guard is the **Watch Hill Inn,** an 1890s white clapboard jutting out onto Little Narragansett Bay. The bay breezes cool the inn's 16 non-air-conditioned rooms. Decor is simple—wood four-poster beds with puffy quilts, a few period antiques. Some rooms feature modernized baths with stall showers replacing the vintage claw-footed tubs. Guests can rock on the wide porch that overlooks the water. ~ 38 Bay Street; 401-348-8912, 800-356-9314, fax 401-596-9410. DELUXE TO ULTRA-DELUXE.

Not to be confused with the Watch Hill Inn, the **Inn at Watch Hill** is a stretch of 16 modern motel-type suites atop the stores on the town's main drag. While the decor of each unit is utilitarian rather than posh, the views from each open-air deck is pure New England; from your vantage point you can check out everything going on in town, while just beyond the bay, vistas stretch on forever. Specify "Bay View" when reserving; several (designated "Village View") have obstructed views of the water. Each suite has a private bath and a kitchen area equipped with microwave, refrigerator and sink but without dishes or utensils. ~ 118 Bay Street; 401-596-0665, fax 401-348-0860. ULTRA-DELUXE.

Guests at **Pleasant View House** get the full ocean treatment. The wide swath of beach unfolds like a carpet just at the edge of the hotel's manicured lawns. The rambling, white wood exterior is accented with sail-blue canvas fronting each private deck. The atmosphere here is vintage seaside; dining rooms, both covered and outdoor, front the ocean, as do many of the guest rooms. Don't look for posh appointments; rooms are decorated in basic motel. But they're clean and comfortable, and the views from the private decks are well worth the price. ~ 65 Atlantic Avenue, Misquamicut; 401-348-8200, 800-782-3224, fax 401-348-8919. DELUXE TO ULTRA-DELUXE.

The **Shelter Harbor Inn** looks exactly the way a seaside country inn should look: a spanking white clapboard main building with contrasting window shutters, well-manicured and welcoming. This 1800s farmhouse, its landscaped grounds defined by rustic stone fences, is an inn as well as a popular restaurant. There are nine guest rooms in the main building, each with private bath and some with private sun deck, ten more in the converted barn nearby and four in the coach house. In each room antiques gleam with care, and bedsteads complement the period decor. The public rooms include a cozy library just off the sun porch bar. Breakfast included. ~ Route 1, 10 Wagner Road, Westerly; 401-322-8883, 800-468-8883, fax 401-322-7907. DELUXE.

Not all of South County's inns reflect a Yankee heritage. **The Villa**, with its Italianate decor and colorfully decorated swimming pool, is decidedly Mediterranean in ambience. Rooms are chock-full, if not

---

✔ CHECK THESE OUT—UNIQUE LODGING

- *Moderate:* Discover a true bargain at Warren's **Nathaniel Porter Inn**, a beautifully restored, red-clapboard Colonial hostelry. *page 140*
- *Moderate to deluxe:* Relax in a handmade Shaker-style four-poster bed at a Newport Colonial house, the **Admiral Farragut Inn**. *page 130*
- *Deluxe:* Cloister yourself at **Old Court Bed & Breakfast Inn**, a former Episcopal church rectory, now furnished with antique treasures. *page 139*
- *Ultra-deluxe:* Relish the seclusion of your own Victorian cottage set on a peninsula overlooking Narragansett Bay at **The Inn at Castle Hill**. *page 129*

Budget: under $50 Moderate: $50–$90 Deluxe: $90–$120 Ultra-deluxe: over $120

cluttered, with knickknacks. Enjoy a continental breakfast or the occasional afternoon snack around the pool. Gay-friendly. ~ 190 Shore Road, Westerly; 401-596-1054, fax 401-596-6268. DELUXE.

Nestled in a wooded inland setting and thoroughly steeped in old New England is the **General Thurston House**. A lovingly restored 1763 Colonial, this bed and breakfast wraps its guests in cozy country living. Each of the five guest rooms has a fireplace and Early American antiques, and several feature Victorian parlors. Every room comes with a decanter of sherry and freshly baked sweets. ~ Old Route 3, Hopkinton; 401-377-9049. MODERATE.

The Larchwood Inn sits on a hill above the country village of Wakefield, the quintessential manor house. Built in 1831, the three-story house shimmers with family history: one window in the dining room still bears the signature a daughter etched on the glass pane with her diamond engagement ring. Private baths can be requested, although some of the 12 guest rooms share facilities. There are also six additional units in the annex. Traditional dark wood headboards are brightened by country floral spreads and light streaming in through large windows. ~ 521 Main Street; 401-783-5454, 800-275-5450, fax 401-783-1800. MODERATE TO DELUXE.

Victorian is the word for most of the lodgings on Block Island. Imposing, gingerbread-trimmed structures dominate the island's ocean skyline. A word of caution: some "modernizations" may not please everyone. One such example might be the National Hotel's trendy front-porch scene. Although this place is well-known and located in the middle of the action, its amplified music and noisy camaraderie are not everyone's idea of an idyllic island vacation.

Presiding like a grande dame over all she surveys, the **Hotel Manisses** rules with Victorian splendor. Built in 1870 and restored by the Abrams family, innkeepers well known locally, the Manisses seems to personify Block Island's unique charm and individualism. In the wicker-appointed parlor leaded-glass windows rainbow the sunlight. There are a few surprises: several of the 17 guest rooms, like the Princess Augusta, feature jacuzzis; the Antoinette suite opens directly onto the front porch, providing handy access for anyone who dreads climbing stairs; the Pocahontas has its own private deck. ~ Spring Street; 401-466-2421. ULTRA-DELUXE.

The **1661 Inn and Guest House** combines Victorian charm with sweeping views of Old Harbor. Rooms with water views also sport private decks (the Ackurs room even has its own kitchenette). Guest quarters are antique-filled and sunny. The inn is known for its huge breakfast buffet, served overlooking the water. ~ Spring Street, Block Island; 401-466-2421, 800-626-4773, fax 401-466-2858. ULTRA-DELUXE.

Everyone in Watch Hill eats at the **Olympia Tea Room** at one time or another; just sit in the old mahogany booths and watch the local world go by. Owners Jack and Marcia Felber stress a modern

DINING

American cuisine with an emphasis on fresh seafood. It's a sort of back-to-the-future setting (waitresses wear formal black with white lacy collars and cuffs), but the menu is both homey and eclectic; the Olympia is as famous for its gutsy garlic-laced clam stew as for its dainty dessert pastries shaped like swans. Closed December through mid-May. ~ 74 Bay Street; 401-348-8211. MODERATE TO DELUXE.

The ideal country dining experience is alive and well at the **Shelter Harbor Inn**. Meals are served in several small rooms, each with its stone fireplace, burnished wooden chairs and wildflowers at every table. Selections reflect the local harvest, changing every season. Seafood, as you will have come to expect in this area, is fresh and excellent. Pasta dishes are well seasoned and imaginative. Try the local wine, "America's Cup," from nearby Sakonnet Vineyards. And for dessert, sample the Indian pudding, which arrives warm and fragrant. ~ Route 1, Westerly; 401-322-8883. MODERATE TO DELUXE.

At **Main Street Foods & Bakery** you can dine inside, seated at tables dressed with snowy napery, or take out treats for alfresco feasting. Chefs Christine and Michael Chapman serve breakfast (oven-baked German apple pancakes, french toast made from challah), lunch (fresh homemade pastas, pesto chicken sandwiches, special frittatas and quiches) and dinner (risotto of grilled chicken and Italian sausage, grilled duck breast with pecan marmalade). For dessert, try the lemon coconut layer cake. Closed Monday. ~ 333 Main Street, Wakefield; 401-789-0914. MODERATE TO DELUXE.

Yearn for some Italian food that's good and won't dent the budget? Head for **Term's**. Nothing fancy here, just lots of families, with kids running around. Lots of enjoyment, too, as everyone digs into heaping plates full of seafood marinara, special pastas and veal dishes. ~ 135 Boon Street, Narragansett; 401-782-4242. BUDGET TO MODERATE.

Haute cuisine served in rarified surroundings greets visitors to **Basil's**. With striped awnings outside and delicate floral wallpaper inside, Basil's is a tiny gem of European-style dining. The service is formal, and guests tend to dress up for the occasion (unusual in a seaside area). The menu includes many usual Continental favorites (*vol au vent*, beef Stroganoff, scallops Provençal), but owner and chef Vasilios Kourakis has an inspired hand with herbs and spices, so old favorites tend to become new favorites at first bite. Closed Monday. ~ 22 Kingston Road, Narragansett; 401-789-3743. DELUXE.

Eating at **George's of Galilee** has become a Rhode Island tradition. Diners at this casual, wood-paneled spot usually sit before huge windows that offer views of the fishing boat dock. Fare is a traditional mix of clam cakes, lobster, fish and pasta, plus beef and poultry items. Limited hours off-season. ~ 250 Sand Hill Cove Road, Narragansett; 401-783-2306. MODERATE.

Most visitors to Block Island feel they have stepped back in time, into a more gentle era. Among Block Island's bevy of Victorian mansions, the favored lodging is also the preferred dining spot. In summer the **Hotel Manisses** focuses its meal service on the flower-studded outdoor patio; and when chill winds blow in off the Atlantic, the focus shifts indoors, where crackling fires warm the spirits. Appetizers include a selection of fish smoked over aromatic woods right on the premises. Smoked bluefish is a perennial favorite. Seafood is featured, with some nice variations that include several low-calorie selections. ~ Spring Street; 401-466-2421. DELUXE.

Whether you fancy a sandy beach or a cliff-top ocean view, picnics will become an important part of your Block Island experience. Pick up your favorites at **Rebecca's Seafood.** Open mid-May through mid-October. ~ 435 Water Street, Old Harbor; 401-466-5411. BUDGET.

◄ HIDDEN

Or stop by the **Old Harbor Take Out,** then hop on your bike and head for your wilderness pleasure. Open mid-May through mid-October. ~ Water Street, Old Harbor; 401-466-2935. BUDGET.

Late-fall and early-spring daytrippers who come over to Block Island for a few hours of biking or hiking are often surprised to find the hotels and restaurants closed for the season. No problem. Just join the locals who head for the **Bethany's Airport Diner,** which serves basic breakfast- and lunch-counter meals all day, every day. Specialties are eggs Benedict and garden burgers. ~ State Airport; 401-466-3100. BUDGET.

◄ HIDDEN

The **Sun-Up Gallery** introduces the wonderful world of dazzling and upscale made-in-America crafts, jewelry and wearable-art fashions to this staid and conservative community. ~ 95 Watch Hill Road, Avondale; 401-596-3430.

SHOPPING

The **Hack and Livery General Store** is everything you ever dreamed a country store would be: more than 50 varieties of penny candy temptingly arrayed in glass canisters. Bet you can't walk out with only one of those tiny paper bags full of goodies. ~ 1006 Main Street, Hope Valley; 401-539-7033.

Antique lovers take heart; there are over 25 traditional antique dealers in South County, including **Frink's Collectibles**, with glassware, china, silver, lamps and toys from the 18th, 19th and 20th centuries. ~ Route 1, Dunn's Corners, Westerly; 401-596-2756.

Another antique dealer in the area is **The Artists Guild and Gallery**, which features 19th- and 20th-century art. ~ 5429 Post Road, Route 1, Charlestown; 401-322-0506.

For a brochure and map pinpointing every shop, contact the **South County Tourism Council**. ~ 4808 Tower Hill Road, Wakefield, RI 02879; 401-789-4422.

Near the waterfront, **Scarlett Begonia** is the place to go for quilts, pillows, jewelry, rugs and other handicrafts. ~ Dodge Street, Old Harbor, Block Island; 401-466-5024.

NIGHTLIFE   **The Windjammer** brings in big-city lights and stars for the under-30 set (or anyone else who thrives on megadecibel rock). Live bands perform every Friday and Saturday night in a room that holds about 800 people. ~ Atlantic Beach Park, 321 Atlantic Avenue, Misquamicut Beach; 401-322-9298.

Colonial Theatre offers drama, musicals and, in the summer, free Shakespeare performances in nearby Wilcox Park. ~ 3 Granite Street, Westerly; 401-596-0810.

What began as a two-story farmhouse in the seaside village of Matunuck back in 1891 is now the home of the famous **Theatre-By-The-Sea**. In 1931, Alice Tyler converted her farm's barn into a 500-seat theater, and the rest is show-biz history. Several stars, including Marlon Brando, got their start on these boards. Many vacationers plan their schedules according to the theater's productions: *George M!*, *La Cage aux Folles* and *Nunsense* were part of one bill. Theatre-By-The-Sea is part of both the state and the Federal Register of Historic Places. ~ 364 Card's Pond Road; 401-782-8587.

A handy addition to the farm-theater complex is the **SeaHorse Grill and Cabaret** which serves a popular (albeit incongruous) chicken cashew dish as well as seafood favorites before the show; after the show it offers entertainment and hors d'oeuvres to those who yearn to stay up a bit later. Cover for cabaret shows. ~ 364 Card's Pond Road; 401-789-3030.

BEACHES & PARKS   There are 19 government-managed preserves, state parks, beaches and forest areas in South County. The stretch of coastline from Watch Hill to Narragansett is made up almost entirely of sandy beaches.

HIDDEN ►   **NAPATREE POINT BARRIER BEACH** ⚓ This Watch Hill spit of land evokes a true wilderness feeling; cars are barred from this ecologically fragile, half-mile-long sandy fishhook, allowing the many species of shorebirds and human visitors to enjoy a peaceful coexistence. ~ At the westernmost end of Watch Hill.

MISQUAMICUT STATE BEACH ⚓ One of the largest and most popular beaches in New England, this is a good family beach, with surf that is usually mild and a gradual drop-off. The wide beach is equally good for lazing or walking, and the sand is of fine quality, although August can bring in an excess of seaweed. Picnic tables, snack bars, restrooms, bathhouse and changing rooms; day-use fee, minimum $4. Open from Memorial Day to Labor Day. ~ Along Atlantic Avenue in Misquamicut; 401-596-9097.

NINIGRET CONSERVATION AREA (EAST BEACH) ⚓ A four-mile-long swath of broad, sandy barrier beach between Ninigret Pond and Block Island Sound, this is considered by many to be the most beautiful in the state because of its undeveloped expanse of dunes and scrub pines. (The 1938 hurricane blew away all houses, and the state now forbids any development.) The beach is usually not crowded because the state strictly limits parking in the entire conservation area. (Get there early in the morning on weekends for a parking spot.) The beach has a rocky bottom with a steep drop-off about three feet out. There is a lifeguard in a designated area, but this beach can be dangerous for small children. Because of drop-off, waves tend to break hard close to shore. Portable toilets; day-use fee, minimum $4. Closed November through April. ~ At the foot of East Beach Road, off Route 1 in Charlestown; 401-322-0450.

▲ Permitted for four-wheel, camper vehicles only on barrier beach; $8 per night for residents, $12 for nonresidents.

ARCADIA MANAGEMENT AREA 🚶‍♂️ 🚴 🐎 🛶 🏊 🚤 🎣 Thousands of inland wilderness acres have been set aside in the northwest corner of South County and can be enjoyed by outdoor lovers at Rhode Island's largest recreation area. Because it lies along the Appalachian Trail, this park offers some excellent hiking opportunities. There's also boating and swimming from the sandy beaches of Browning Mill and Beach Pond during the summer months, and fishing in the freshwater pond and streams and rivers. Picnic areas, lifeguards. ~ The main entrance is off Route 165; 401-539-2356.

▲ The park has free hike-in tent camping and $15-a-night shelter camping. Camping requires a permit (free) available at park headquarters (260 Arcadia Road, Arcadia). If you don't find sufficient camping in the park, there's always **Oak Embers** (Escoheag Hill Road, West Greenwich; 401-397-4042), a private campground nearby. There are 50 seasonal RV sites with sewer hookups and 30 year-round RV hookup sites, both $18 per night, as well as tent sites ($16 per night).

EAST MATUNUCK STATE BEACH 🏊 Three-quarters of a mile of nice shoreline, sand dunes and, on a clear day, a nice view of Block Island, are yours at this popular family beach. A gradual drop-off makes East Matunuck a good place to take the kids. Picnic tables, bathhouse, restrooms, concessions, lifeguards; day-use fee, minimum $4. Open Memorial Day to Labor Day. ~ On Succotash Road off of Route 1 in South Kingston; 401-789-8585.

ROGER WHEELER STATE BEACH 🏊 Lying within the protective breakwater of Point Judith Harbor of Refuge, this wave-free spot known locally as Sand Hill Cove is an ideal swimming beach for families. The sand is fine and white, waters are calm and the drop-off is so gradual that it is often necessary to wade great distances just to reach waist-deep water. Picnic tables, restrooms, bathhouse, showers; day-use fee, minimum $4. Open May weekends and Memorial Day to Labor Day. ~ Off Sand Hill Cove Road in Narragansett, near Galilee; 401-789-3563.

NARRAGANSETT TOWN BEACH ⚲ 🏊 Voted the "best swimming beach in the state" by *Rhode Island Monthly* magazine, this swath is visible from every point in town and from every turn along the local stretch of scenic Route 1A. Just south of the elite Dunes Club, it's a quintessential New England beach with miles of fine white sand in a broad sweep from waterline to dune and rollers that can kick up enough to lure surfers in rough weather. The Northeast Surfing Championships are held here every fall. And for wanna-be surfers, free lessons are given by the pros every summer Wednesday at 12 noon. Bathhouse; lifeguards (seasonal); snacks available across the street. ~ On Route 1A, two miles east of Route 1; 401-783-6430.

Newport Area

You'll really understand just how much diversity Rhode Island crams within its tiny borders as you leave mellow South County and cross over Narragansett Bay to Newport, with its abundance of high-powered millionaires' yachts and extravagant mansions. These, of course, are the very elements that set Newport apart from other New England resort towns.

Modern-day Newport does retain its fair share of colonial history and landmarks, however. Founded in 1639 by settlers from Providence, the town became an important shipbuilding center and seaport, a landing site for the infamous "triangle trade" in molasses, rum and slaves. By the time of the Revolution, Newport was already prospering.

That prosperity would reach staggering heights during the next century, when wealthy families from New York and Philadelphia started building their summer mansions in this idyllic spot. It is really the lavish excesses of these "gilded age" palaces that everyone flocks here to see; we want an insider's glimpse into the lifestyles of the long-ago rich and famous.

SIGHTS

The **Preservation Society of Newport County** maintains eight historic house museums, five of them the most dazzling mansions along exclusive Bellevue Avenue. In each, the one-hour tours are well organized and quite thorough, given by guides who obviously love their work. You'll see examples of mind-boggling wealth and extravagance, holdovers from a pre-income-tax era when vast fortunes could be squandered on palatial "summer cottages" for families with Vanderbilt- and Astor-like reputations to uphold. The Preservation Society also offers combination tour tickets. All mansions are open daily from May through September with seasonal hours the rest of the year; call for more information. ~ 424 Bellevue Avenue; 401-847-1000.

Some of the mansions toured:

Château-Sur-Mer, built in 1852, remains one of the finest examples of lavish Victorian architecture in America. It was built for William Wetmore, who made his fortune in the China trade—hence, the Chinese "moongate" in the south wall. Admission. ~ Bellevue Avenue.

Cornelius Vanderbilt commissioned American architect Richard Morris Hunt to build **The Breakers** in 1895. It was designed to replicate the architecture of a massive, four-story Italian palace of the 16th century. After touring the 18th-century reception room, grand state dining room and the rest of the splendid interior, visitors can ramble through extensive grounds that overlook the ocean. If you only have time to tour one mansion, this is the one to see. Admission. ~ Ochre Point Avenue.

Rosecliff is architect Stanford White's own version of the Grand Trianon. It was built in 1902 for Mrs. Hermann Oelrichs and was the scene of many extravagant parties. Admission. ~ Bellevue Avenue.

Marble House is most often described as "sumptuous." It was built in 1892 for William K. Vanderbilt, and its interior boasts virtually no surface left ungilded, unmarbled or unembellished. Like The Breakers, it was designed by Richard Morris Hunt, who borrowed features from the Grand and Petit Trianons in Versailles. Out over the ocean end of the vast front lawn sits a charming and authentic Chinese teahouse. Closed October through December. Admission. ~ Bellevue Avenue.

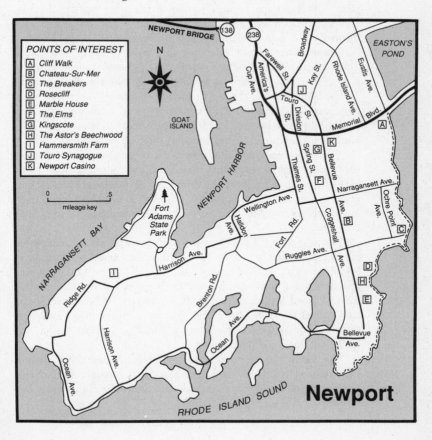

POINTS OF INTEREST

A Cliff Walk
B Chateau-Sur-Mer
C The Breakers
D Rosecliff
E Marble House
F The Elms
G Kingscote
H The Astor's Beechwood
I Hammersmith Farm
J Touro Synagogue
K Newport Casino

The Elms, as famous for its landscaped grounds as for its lavish, antique-filled interior, was built in 1901 for coal millionaire Edward Berwind to resemble the Château d'Asnières outside Paris. Closed October and November. Admission. ~ Bellevue Avenue.

Kingscote is less imposing than its neighboring "palaces." Built in 1839 in a cozy Victorian style, this red-roofed cottage is a charming hodgepodge of dormers, turrets and towers. It's also noted for its Tiffany glass windows and Oriental art. Closed October through March. Admission. ~ Bellevue Avenue.

Unlike the regular mansion tours (whose "gee-whiz" tones often teeter on the edge of sounding reverential), two are refreshing in their unorthodox approach: The Astor's Beechwood and Hammersmith Farm.

The Astor's Beechwood gives tours with an amusing twist: they are presented as living theater. Costumed actors appear as guides, gossipy servants, eccentric house guests and even as an Astor or two to lead "guests" through both upstairs and downstairs peeks into the life of the privileged in the 1800s. These tours are informative and fun for kids, a nice break from the formula format of the other mansions' tours. Closed mid-December through January. Open weekends only February through April. Admission. ~ 580 Bellevue Avenue; 401-846-3772.

Hammersmith Farm offers another kind of unique appeal: a down-to-earth peek into the contemporary old-money lifestyles of the Kennedy-Auchincloss dynasty. Hammersmith was a working farm in 1600s. More recently the farm's cottage and its 50 waterfront acres (landscaped by Frederick Law Olmsted) served as summer home to young Jacqueline Bouvier and as "Summer White House" to her husband, John F. Kennedy. Admission. ~ Ocean Drive; 401-846-0420.

The name **Newport Casino** refers not to gambling but to the elegant resort built in 1880 that now houses the International Tennis Hall of Fame and the Tennis Museum, as well as famed championship grass courts and court tennis (the "sport of kings"). Closed mid-November to mid-March. Admission. ~ 194 Bellevue Avenue; 401-849-3990.

Not *everything* in Newport has to do with gilded monuments to big bucks—the city is one of the oldest in the United States and has an intriguing history stretching back three centuries. One spot that has attracted a horde of historical theories yet remains a mystery is the **Old Stone Mill.** Some believe it was erected by Norsemen in the days of Leif Ericsson. Others date it to the 17th century or believe it to be the remains of a 17th-century windmill. ~ Bellevue Avenue and Mill Street in Touro Park.

The oldest library building in the United States, the **Redwood Library** was erected in 1748–1749 and today boasts an important collection of books and paintings, including several by Gilbert Stuart. ~ 50 Bellevue Avenue; 401-847-0292.

Nearby stands the **Friends Meeting House,** a Quaker worshipping place since it was built in 1699. The original large English Gothic structure has received two Colonial-style additions, in 1729 and 1807. The meeting house can be toured by appointment only. Admission. ~ Marlborough and Farewell streets; 401-846-0813.

A fine Colonial mansion dating to 1748, **Hunter House** was owned by Jonathan Nichols, the Deputy Governor of the time. Today it is a restored National Historic Landmark with an excellent collection of 18th-century Colonial furnishings, as well as paintings and other decorative objects. Open May through September and weekends only in April and October. Admission. ~ 54 Washington Street; 401-847-1000.

A good stress-buster is the **Newport Trolley Transportation,** which helps you beat Newport's summertime gridlock traffic. The trolley leaves from the Convention and Visitors Bureau and stops at all the mansions and major attractions. Fee.

Newport County Convention & Visitors Bureau is a bustling hub of traveler's information: helpful staff; brochures, maps and guides; multimedia video; and bus, trolley and tourist train terminal. ~ 23 America's Cup Avenue; 401-849-8048.

The towns of Middletown and Portsmouth share Aquidneck Island with Newport. In Middletown, the **Norman Bird Sanctuary** encompasses 450 acres of extraordinarily beautiful wilderness land. Wildlife (pheasant, nesting birds, rabbit and fox) inhabit the 30 acres of hay fields; there are woodlands, salt marshes and craggy ridges. An extremely active program includes guided trail walks, educational workshops, children's programs and themed hikes. Closed Monday from Labor Day to Memorial Day. Trail fee. ~ 583 Third Beach Road; 401-846-2577.

In Portsmouth, **Green Animals** is a whimsical garden of more than 80 century-old trees and shrubs sculpted in the European manner to resemble dogs, camels, goats, roosters, bears and even police officers

THE HOUSE THAT SURVIVED THE SONS OF LIBERTY

The oldest restored home in Newport, the **Wanton-Lyman-Hazard House** dates to 1675 and has seen a wealth of history all by itself. Several colonial governors called the place home, but its claim to fame was as the site of a riot following passage of England's infamous Stamp Act of 1765. It seems the stamp master lived in this house, which was nearly destroyed by a distraught Sons of Liberty mob. Today the house features period pieces and a colonial garden. Open June 15 through Labor Day (Thursday through Saturday in July and August, Friday and Saturday the rest of the summer). Admission. ~ 17 Broadway; 401-846-0813.

and sailboats. It's a treat for kids, a mecca for horticulture buffs. A Victorian toy collection is housed inside the country estate's 19th-century white clapboard house. Closed October through March. Admission. ~ 380 Cory's Lane; 401-847-1000.

Touro Synagogue at 85 Touro Street is the oldest Jewish house of worship in the continental U.S.—dedicated in 1763.

To increase the fun of the excursion out to Green Animals, hop aboard the historic **Old Colony & Newport Railway**. During the 21-mile, one-hour roundtrip you'll pass a number of the island's maritime sites. There's ample time for viewing the animals before the return train departs. Closed Monday, Tuesday and Friday during peak season; closed in the winter. Fee. ~ America's Cup Avenue and Bridge Street, Newport; 401-624-6951.

Across the Sakonnet River from Portsmouth lie the bucolic towns of Tiverton and Little Compton. Comparable to the fashionable bedroom communities found near any urban center, these towns have their fair share of power residents who share the country scene with the gentlemen farmers. Everything is peaceful here; strict zoning laws and sky-high real estate prices conspire to keep things that way.

HIDDEN ▶   **Sakonnet Vineyards** is the oldest of Rhode Island's three vineyards. Established in 1975, Sakonnet now produces a southeastern New England selection including their popular chardonnay and vidal blanc. There are guided tours and winetastings. ~ 162 West Main Road, Little Compton; 401-635-8486.

Sakonnet's vineyards and its scenic acres extend down to the banks of the river, an altogether idyllic picnic setting. Stop by the **Provender at Tiverton Four Corners**, a gourmet food emporium housed in an old mansard-roofed general store, to assemble your dream lunch, complete with fresh-baked bread. You can buy a bottle of wine at Sakonnet's tasting room and ask permission to picnic near the river. ~ 3883 Main Road, Tiverton; 401-624-8096.

LODGING   In addition to the usual chain hotels, Newport has an abundance of small bed-and-breakfast establishments. As one islander observed, "In this town, almost everyone has an extra room or two to rent." Don't be fooled by that gem of Yankee understatement; we have observed that, in this town where extravagant landmark mansions are almost the norm, the bed and breakfasts tend to follow suit.

The Wayside is a trim beige-brick Georgian mansion just across Bellevue Avenue from the famous Elms. Owners Dorothy and Al Posts have restored this sprawling 1896 home, creating a dozen guest rooms blessed with antique furnishings and majestic proportions—and each with its own private bath. There's even a heated pool in the back garden. ~ 406 Bellevue Avenue; 401-847-0302, 800-653-7678, fax 401-848-9374. DELUXE TO ULTRA-DELUXE.

The 1855 **Marshall Slocum Guest House** sits on a tree-lined, Norman Rockwell kind of street. An American flag flies overhead, and on the spacious front porch rocking chairs await your leisure. Inside, rooms are cheery and graced with antiques. Your gregarious innkeeper, Joan Wilson, who is creative both in the kitchen (fresh-baked quiches and muffins every breakfast) and in decorating, has chosen sunny yellows and marine blues to balance the house's original dark woods. Two of the five upstairs guest rooms have fireplaces and a private half-bath, while the others share three baths. Breakfast is served on the deck overlooking the sunny back garden in warm weather. ~ 29 Kay Street; 401-841-5120, 800-372-5120, fax 401-846-3787. MODERATE TO DELUXE.

The **Newport Marriott** is big, modern and close to the water. A number of the 317 rooms and seven suites command sweeping views of Newport Harbor. Glass-fronted elevators (often exasperatingly slow to arrive) seem to double as kinetic sculpture, providing space-age mobility to the lobby's plant-filled atrium design. Rooms feature a pastel decor and the usual complement of electronic equipment. Among the definite pluses: there's a health club and indoor pool in the hotel; the Gateway Center (Convention and Visitors Bureau) is next door; and shopping and waterfront browsing are within easy walking distance. ~ 25 America's Cup Avenue; 401-849-1000, 800-458-3066; fax 401-849-3422. ULTRA-DELUXE.

Viking Hotel is Newport's grande dame, a 1920s National Historic Landmark in red brick trimmed in white. The understatement of the tidy four-column entrance is deceptive; inside, the hotel is a sprawl of rooms and levels. There are 184 guest rooms, numerous dining rooms and a health club and pool. Rooms are a bit cramped, crammed with heavy antique reproduction four-posters and furniture. In summer, dining at the Garden Patio Café offers a charming alternative to the somewhat overpowering hotel atmosphere inside. ~ 1 Bellevue Avenue; 401-847-3300, 800-556-7126, fax 401-849-0749. DELUXE TO ULTRA-DELUXE.

The Inn at Castle Hill sits on 32 acres of secluded peninsula overlooking Narragansett Bay. Built in 1874 for international naturalist Alexander Agassiz, this weathered, shingled inn today retains most of its original Victorian charm. Its rambling structure yields ten guest rooms of unique shapes, bursting with antique decor. Bedrooms are furnished with mahogany four-posters, authentic washstands and upholstered slipper chairs, and are paired with large, modern baths. Six more guest rooms are found in cliffside harbor houses behind the main building, and beachfront cottages draw repeat visitors every year (weekly rates in the summer, nightly rates in the spring). The harbor house and beach cottages are closed in the winter. Guests like to gather before the unique inlaid-wood fireplace in the downstairs sitting room. ~ Ocean Drive; 401-849-3800. ULTRA-DELUXE.

Not everything in Newport is rarified and expensive. The **Newport Comfort Inn** offers visitors clean, comfortable and affordable lodgings. The 162 guest rooms are large and creatively decorated with

Colonial fabrics, contrasting carpeting and wooden spool head-boards. Amenities include no-smoking rooms, a lounge, heated in-door pool and Captain's Table Restaurant. ~ 936 West Main Road, Middleton; 401-846-7600, 800-556-6464, fax 401-849-6919. MOD-ERATE TO DELUXE.

The Admiral Inns, three historic houses within a couple of blocks of Newport Harbor, are well-kept secrets among regular Newport vis-itors. Each has a fascinating history and distinctive characteristics.

The graceful Italianate **Admiral Benbow Inn** was built in 1855 by Captain Augustus Littlefield. Its 15 rooms have brass beds, private baths, and the entire inn is air conditioned (which is welcome during Newport's steamy summers). ~ 93 Pelham Street; 401-848-8000, 800-343-2863, fax 401-846-8006. MODERATE TO ULTRA-DELUXE.

The **Admiral Fitzroy Inn**, the largest of the three inns, has 17 rooms, each with a private bath, an elevator, and a roof deck with a harbor view. Admiral Fitzroy commanded the *Beagle* during Charles Darwin's *Origin of the Species* voyage to the Galapagos Islands. ~ 398 Thames Street; 401-848-8000, 800-343-2863, fax 401-846-8006. MODERATE TO ULTRA-DELUXE.

During the Revolution, the **Admiral Farragut Inn**, built in 1702, housed two of the aides-de-camp of General Rochambeau, the French general who assisted George Washington throughout the war. The nine-room inn maintains its colonial air, with wide plank floors, twelve-over-twelve paned windows, and original cave mouldings. ~ 31 Clarke Street; 401-848-8000, 800-343-2863, fax 401-846-8006. MODERATE TO ULTRA-DELUXE.

The **Inntowne Inn** is located within easy walking distance of many Newport sights. All 26 rooms in this bed and breakfast are individu-ally decorated in Colonial style with lots of floral fabrics. Each room has a private bath and telephone; none have televisions. There are four floors but, unfortunately, no elevator. A continental breakfast and afternoon tea are included in the rate. All guests have free use of the nearby Marriott's health club and pool. ~ 6 Mary Street; 401-846-9200, 800-457-7803. DELUXE TO ULTRA-DELUXE.

The only bed and breakfast in the mansion district, the **Ivy Lodge** is a ten-room inn housed in a large Victorian. All rooms are individ-ually decorated in Victorian style. Eight have their own bathrooms, a rarity at most bed and breakfasts. Breakfast is always a treat here; you'll enjoy the homemade muffins and other baked goods. ~ 12 Clay Street, Newport; 401-849-6865. DELUXE.

DINING

As you might expect, the restaurant scene in this posh town can get quite fancy and expensive. For those who prefer a more laid-back ap-proach, there are many waterfront places that specialize in seafood, harbor views and relaxed enjoyment.

Non-guests are welcome to enjoy the legendary Sunday brunch at **The Inn at Castle Hill**. This three-story, weathered-shingle 1874

Victorian, with its peaked roof and turrets, overlooks the bay from its own peninsula. Inside, the chestnut paneling shines in the glow of Tiffany lamps. Oriental rugs accent hardwood floors. Brunch, served on the lawn or indoors in a gazebo-setting of green and white, combines just the right mix of formal and alfresco eating as you sit peacefully watching the sailboats on Narragansett Bay. The vast spread offers everything from breakfast items such as eggs Benedict to tempting entrées such as leg of lamb and whole poached salmon. Closed November through April. ~ Ocean Drive; 401-849-3800. ULTRA-DELUXE.

An atmosphere of elegance prevails at the **White Horse Tavern**, a restored 1673 colonial landmark. Although it's America's oldest tavern, don't expect a typical pub scene; this is one of Newport's finest restaurants. The White Horse's interior, too, remains true to its colonial heritage with huge fireplaces, exposed beams and lots of oil portraits of solemn-faced ancestors. While the menu varies with the season, you can count on always finding native seafood specialties like lobster White Horse Tavern or terra firma dishes such as beef tournedos and roast rack of lamb. Service is formal, lending additional panache to the elegant continental cuisine. ~ Farewell and Marlborough streets, Newport; 401-849-3600. DELUXE TO ULTRA-DELUXE.

While not strictly hidden, **Canfield House** is decidedly a find.   ◀ HIDDEN
Relying primarily on satisfied diners to spread its good word, Canfield's maintains a discreet elegance. An unpretentious Victorian building tucked away in a tiny alley off the main street, Canfield's began as a gambling casino, the joy and toy of Richard Canfield, a colorful figure in the gaming world of the early 1900s. Today's diners enjoy French and Continental classics in the main casino, under a vaulted ceiling of intricately carved cherry. Service is formal and attentive. Visitors and locals (many of whom come to celebrate special occasions) enjoy dressing up to complement the surroundings. Closed Monday. ~ 5 Memorial Boulevard, Newport; 401-847-0416. DELUXE.

- -

✔ CHECK THESE OUT—UNIQUE DINING

- *Budget:* Pick a table on the back deck of Cumberland's **The Granary** and dine on gourmet sandwiches while overlooking a waterfall. *page 146*
- *Moderate to deluxe:* Savor fresh country ingredients at Westerly's **Shelter Harbor Inn**, where the menu changes with the harvest. *page 120*
- *Deluxe to ultra-deluxe:* Surround yourself with elegance at America's oldest restaurant, the 1673 **White Horse Tavern**. *page 131*
- *Ultra-deluxe:* Climb aboard a refurbished railroad car and enjoy a sumptuous five-course meal on **The Newport Star Clipper Dinner Train**. *page 132*

Budget: under $8 Moderate: $8–$16 Deluxe: $16–$24 Ultra-deluxe: over $24

A Newport classic and the town's oldest waterfront restaurant, **Christie's** is where the young and restless rub elbows with blue bloods just off their yachts. Diners can choose the main dining room, the second-floor Victorian Topside room or one of the two more casual outdoor deck eating areas—all with sea views. There's also a dockside raw bar where people gather for cocktails and live entertainment. Fresh lobster, of course, is the specialty, along with a menu of seafood, steak and chicken dishes. ~ Christie's Landing, off Thames Street; 401-847-5400. DELUXE TO ULTRA-DELUXE.

La Petite Auberge is a chef-owned French restaurant in a Colonial building that dates back to 1714. The five intimate dining rooms feature lace tablecloths. During the summer months you can also eat outside on the patio. There are two menus: a deluxe-priced formal menu and a moderate-priced bistro menu. The bill of fare usually includes some chicken dishes, duck, trout, lobster and châteaubriand. ~ 19 Charles Street; 401-849-6669. MODERATE TO DELUXE.

If you've yearned to dine aboard the Orient Express, **The Newport Star Clipper Dinner Train** provides a handy American version. Two lavishly refurbished railroad cars roll sedately along tracks paralleling Narragansett Bay, making a three-hour journey to nowhere and back, allowing ample time for the five-course meal. Diners choose from entrées of beef, poultry or fish and have the option to take part in a murder-mystery show. The mood is festive, with many parties celebrating a special occassion. (The down side: Diners sometimes get very rowdy, and noise levels tend to magnify inside a space as small as a railroad car.) Reservations required; closed January and February. ~ Newport Depot, 19 America's Cup Avenue; 401-849-7550. ULTRA-DELUXE.

Andrew's at Eastgate is housed in space that was once a new car showroom. Bland and square on the outside, it's spacious and cozy with fireplaces and wood paneling inside. Chef and owner Andrew Gold has created a fresh, innovative menu that often sparks old favorites with a new twist. (One favorite: a cheddar burger with Cajun ketchup. Wonderful.) He also serves salads, grilled meat and sandwiches. ~ 909 East Main Road, Route 138, Middletown; 401-848-5153. MODERATE.

Sea Fare Inn dazzles with festive opulence: chandeliers glitter, and tables are decked in Sunday best, as are the patrons. The cuisine is American regional, of the unabashedly haute classical variety, the kind that requires (and receives) similarly haute service and attention to detail. Whether you're seated in the large, formal, pillared dining room or in what once was the sun porch of this Victorian mansion, you'll catch the festive spirit of the place. ~ 3352 East Main Road, Portsmouth; 401-683-0577. DELUXE TO ULTRA-DELUXE.

HIDDEN ►

The beachside line of people waiting to get into **Flo's Drive-in** is the first clue. A true "clam shack" and the best of the genre, this beachfront haven sells huge, puffy clamcakes, fried steamers and spicy "stuffies" (stuffed clams). Open Thursday through Sunday. ~ Park Avenue, Portsmouth. BUDGET.

In Newport even the shopping malls sport a nautical/historical air. **SHOPPING**
Bowen's Wharf is a mix of 18th-century wharf buildings and 19th-
century brick warehouses that make up today's complex of open-air
seafood restaurants, fashion boutiques and import shops. ~ Just off
America's Cup Avenue; 401-849-2120.

Brick Market Place is a three-and-a-half-acre complex of more
than 30 shops and restaurants along a—you guessed it—brick road.
The original site, a market and granary built in 1762, is now a
National Historic Landmark. ~ Between Thames Street and America's
Cup Avenue.

Antique lovers might want to slip into **The Nautical Nook**, where
the treasures include lots of those ships in full sail inside glass bottles.
Although the shop focuses on ship models, there are many other nau-
tically inspired items, such as prints, posters and navigational equipment. ~ 86 Spring Street; 401-846-6810.

Try **William Vareika Fine Arts** for 300 years worth of American
paintings, prints and drawings—many of Newport and Narragansett
Bay. It's a delight to shop in this museumlike setting. ~ 212 Bellevue
Avenue; 401-849-6149.

If lace is your first love, don't miss **Rue de France**, where imported
laces from France shape everything from window-hangings to dainty
camisoles. Some laces are sold by the yard as well. ~ 78 Thames Street;
401-846-2084.

Clustered in a 1750s landmark shingle-sided farm complex called
The Old Almy House are several charming country stores that have
everything from a "Gentlemen's Emporium" to a year-round Christmas store. ~ 1016 East Main Road, Portsmouth; 401-683-3737.

Tiverton Four Corners is a gathering of some very chic merchandise
presented in charming old-fashioned surroundings. On one corner,
the 1829 Josiah Wilcox House is home to **Peter's Attic**, specializing in
antiques, and an art gallery. ~ 3879 Main Road, Tiverton; 401-625-
5912. Nearby, **Provender at Tiverton Four Corners** purveys gourmet
imports as well as fresh-baked goods and fancy take-outs. ~ 3883
Main Road, Tiverton; 401-624-8096.

In summer, Newport's nightlife assumes world-class proportions with **NIGHTLIFE**
its famous festivals: the **August Jazz Festival** (401-847-3710), the
late-July **Folk Festival** (401-847-3710) and the mid-July **Newport
Musical Festival** (401-846-1133), which features classical concerts at
some of the most spectacular mansions of Bellevue Avenue.

Newport Playhouse & Cabaret Restaurant offers dinner theater
and cabaret on weekends. ~ 102–104 Connell Highway, near the foot
of the Newport Bridge; 401-848-7529.

Auld Mug Lounge features Saucy Sylvia on Thursday, Friday,
Saturday and Sunday. Saucy plays the piano and parodies favorites of
the '40s, '50s and '60s. ~ Newport Islander Doubletree Hotel, Goat
Island; 401-849-2600.

Red Parrot Restaurant and Bar has live jazz in the upstairs restaurant on Thursday, Friday and Sunday nights. ~ 348 Thames Street; 401-848-9920.

BEACHES & PARKS

Although not quite technically an island, Aquidneck Island has water along almost every inch of its four sides and an enviable selection of ocean, bay and river beaches facing in all directions.

FORT ADAMS STATE PARK Built in 1824 to protect the entrance to Newport Harbor, Fort Adams stands now as a National Historic Landmark, its stone fortress open for tours (fee), and its 21 acres of parklands offer a recreational haven for all. The park lies at the toe of Aquidneck Island's boot, facing Narragansett Bay. This vast grassy meadow—home to the Newport Jazz and Folk Festivals and other summer concerts—matches great sounds with spectacular sights such as views of the bay and its active boating scene. Picnic groves with grills, restrooms, lifeguards. ~ Located at the end of Fort Adams Road on Ocean Drive; 401-847-2400.

EASTON'S BEACH (FIRST BEACH) This swath has a real public beach atmosphere, the only one you're likely to find in the area. A mostly young crowd comes here. This stretch of beach curves, with rougher waves for surfers on the outer edges and a broad inner arc with calmer waters. The sand is fine and very soft, the beach wide. Restrooms, showers, lifeguards; restaurant, aquarium, boardwalk with amusements (miniature golf, bumper cars, carousel). ~ Located along Memorial Boulevard, from the northern end of the Cliff Walk southward to Middletown; 401-848-6491.

SACHUEST BEACH (SECOND BEACH) Its two miles of rolling dunes, fine sand and waves for surfing at one end make Sachuest the favorite local beach, and singles tend to congregate here. Beautiful views include St. George's School in the distance. There's surf fishing from the rocky coast. The beach abuts the 21 shoreline acres of the Norman Bird Sanctuary. Picnic tables, restrooms, showers, lifeguards, concession stand. ~ On Sachuest Point in Middletown; 401-849-2822.

▲ The campground (401-846-6273) offers 44 sites with full hookups and is open mid-May through September. Some sites are available on a first-come, first-serve basis; others must be reserved. Daily fees are $25 to $30 per site, with weekly and monthly discounted rates.

PEABODY BEACH (THIRD BEACH) This spot is ideal for families because it fronts the calm waters of the Sakonnet River. Its profile includes high dunes and a beach that's more soil than sand. It's also popular with windsurfers. The view across the river includes Little Compton's sweep of rolling hills. Restrooms, concession stand. ~ Off Third Beach Road in Middletown.

At a glance Rhode Island seems comprised of water first and land second. The reason for this is Narragansett Bay. Twisting southward from Providence and the Blackstone River, the bay permeates the state's rocky landscape, then spills into the Atlantic at Newport. If you follow this waterway you will see that it defines Rhode Island. The communities it touches thrive on fishing, shipbuilding and sailing. From the busy port of Providence to the Herreshoff Boatyard in Bristol (builders of the first torpedo boat in 1887) to the resorts and beaches of Warwick, the Narragansett is a saltwater net that holds the state together.

Providence Area

Within the city limits of Providence are enough historical treasures to satisfy even the most insatiable culture buffs—from the architectural beauties of Benefit Street to the marble dome of the State House, which gleams like a beacon above the skyline. The lofty College Hill area is home to Brown University and to a resulting Cambridge-like neighborhood of bookstores, boutiques and trendy restaurants. Revitalized sections—such as Corliss Landing—are springing up like mushrooms almost overnight, bringing new life and lifestyles into forgotten parts of town. There's a vitality, a zingy balance of part and future, to this place that *Newsweek* dubbed a "Hot City" in a late '80s poll of the country's "most livable cities."

This capital city of Rhode Island was also its first, established in 1636 by Roger Williams, founder of the Baptist Church, "in commemoration of God's Providence." Williams' religious bent extended even to the naming of local thoroughfares; visitors today walk along Benefit, Church, Benevolent, Hope and Friendship streets.

SIGHTS

Seven hills and the Providence River give the city its geographic complexity. Most fashionable addresses lie on the east side of town (not to be confused with the neighboring town of East Providence). College Hill is a steep incline dotted with many historic sites and crowned by the Brown University complex.

It is fitting to begin at the corner of Main and Waterman streets, site of Williams' **First Baptist Church**, built in 1775 (although his first congregation was founded in 1638). The 185-foot church steeple, visible from just about anywhere in town, was inspired by designs of Sir Christopher Wren. Actively used by its local congregation, the church opens its vast spaces every Memorial Day weekend for the commencement exercises of Brown University. ~ 75 North Main Street; 401-751-2266.

Nearby is the **Museum of Art—Rhode Island School of Design**, which is considered one of America's finest museums of its size. Housed within a deceptively unimposing 1877 six-story, Federal-style brick structure are three floors of artistic masterpieces with dates ranging from the ancient Egyptian period to the present. Throughout the exhibits, you'll encounter clutches of students studying and creating their own artworks; this museum is a treasured storehouse for RISD (pronounced Rizz-dee) students and faculty. Don't miss: the satiny Goddard-Townsend block and shell masterpiece (a 1760s mahogany desk and bookcase, one of only 12 still in existence, whose sibling piece fetched $12 million at a Christie's auction); the Babylonian lion bas-relief (605 B.C.); the impressionists (Manets and Monets); and the Rodin sculptures. Step into The Daphne Farago Wing for a look at the contemporary art collection, or wander through the museum's interior sculpture garden. Closed Monday. Admission. ~ 224 Benefit Street; 401-454-6500.

Benefit Street, which traces a path across College Hill's vertical pitch, boasts a "Mile of History," regarded by scholars as the highest concentration of historic buildings anywhere in America. Along this miracle mile are restored Colonial, Federal and 19th-century buildings, all carefully maintained. They are also homes and businesses, for this is a street of *living* history, as well. Every year, during the second weekend in June, a portion of Benefit Street—along with other historic areas—is open to the public for the "Festival of Historic Houses," a three-day celebration that includes tours, food events and sales. Contact the **Providence Preservation Society** for reservations or details. ~ 21 Meeting Street; 401-831-7440.

One of Benefit Street's historic beauties is the **Providence Athenaeum.** Founded in 1753 as one of this country's first libraries, it sits in Grecian splendor looking properly imposing and scholarly. The Greek Doric structure was completed in 1838. A wealth of rare and historic volumes is housed within, along with a bit of famous romantic history. It was here that Edgar Allen Poe met, loved and lost Sarah Helen Whitman, the inspiration for his "Annabelle Lee." ~ 251 Benefit Street; 401-421-6970.

A few blocks south stands the **John Brown House**, built in 1786 for one of the famous Brown brothers (whom locals refer to fondly as Nick, Joe, John and Moe). The name "Brown" is an integral part of Rhode Island history; the Browns were a merchant family who lived in Providence since the city's founding. This three-story brownstone and brick Georgian, which President John Quincy Adams once called "the most magnificent and elegant mansion I have seen on this continent," houses an extraordinary collection of 18th-century furniture—such as its nine-shell desk and bookcase, the latter considered to be the finest piece of American Colonial furniture in existence today. Closed Monday in March through December, and Monday through Friday in January and February. Admission. ~ 52 Power Street; 401-331-8575.

Brown University is indeed king of the hill, the nation's seventh oldest university, founded in 1764. ~ College Hill, end of College Street; 401-863-1000.

You'll feel the Ivy League influence throughout the sprawl of Gothic and Beaux-Arts structures and commons areas, dominated by the enormous **John D. Rockefeller, Jr., Library**, which houses Brown's general collections. ~ Prospect and College streets; 401-863-2167.

University Hall, a National Historic Landmark, served as a barracks and hospital for American troops during the Revolutionary War. ~ Prospect Street.

Before leaving College Hill, stop off at **Prospect Terrace**, the site of the Roger Williams Memorial, which overlooks downtown Providence. A tiny park is maintained here, making an ideal place for a picnic lunch. Enjoy the panoramic view while you digest all the history you've just seen and prepare to tour the city's other neighborhoods. ~ Congdon Street at Cushing Street.

Providence's downtown area is dominated by the **State House**, considered by some to be the most beautiful capitol building in America. The classic structure's white marble exterior dazzles in the sunlight. Its self-supported marble dome is the fourth largest in the world. A full-length portrait of George Washington, painted by Rhode Island's own Gilbert Stuart, hangs in the State Reception Room. Free tours of the capitol are given on weekdays. ~ Smith Street; 401-277-2000.

Several blocks south, you'll find **The Arcade**, an 1828 Greek Revival–style National Historic Landmark, now a three-story shopping mall. ~ 65 Weybosset Street; 401-598-1199.

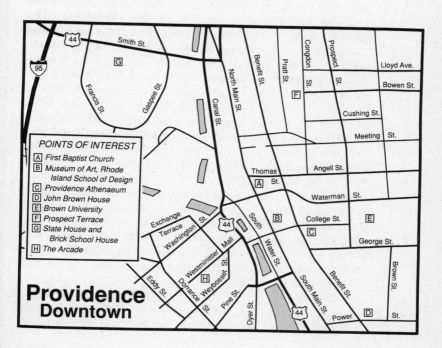

POINTS OF INTEREST
A First Baptist Church
B Museum of Art, Rhode Island School of Design
C Providence Athenaeum
D John Brown House
E Brown University
F Prospect Terrace
G State House and Brick School House
H The Arcade

Providence
Downtown

Many of these sites are covered in the "Walkie Talkies," 90-minute taped audio tours of the College Hill and downtown area with walk-along maps. They're available at the **Providence Preservation Society**. ~ 21 Meeting Street; 401-831-7440.

For further information on this area contact the **Greater Providence Convention & Visitors Bureau**. ~ 30 Exchange Terrace; 401-274-1636.

A short drive away is **Roger Williams Park**, Providence's favorite park since 1871, when Betsy Williams bequeathed her 102-acre farm to the city. Today this spacious parkland combines wilderness areas with such people pleasers as a zoo, complete with a community of penguins (admission), a lake and picturesque boathouse, a lakeside bandstand for concerts, a carousel, a nine-hole miniature golf course, kiddie bumper boats, pony rides, and a greenhouse of exotic plants and flowers. All this amid landscaped, wooded parklands in the heart of the city. ~ Elmwood Avenue; 401-785-9450.

Also in the park; the **Roger Williams Park Museum of Natural History** has a planetarium, cultural and wildlife exhibits and a model of Narragansett Bay. ~ 401-785-9457.

Across the Providence River, at the toe of the Bristol peninsula, nestles the serene haven of **Blithewold Mansion and Gardens**. Jutting spectacularly into Narragansett Bay, Blithewold dazzles with its verdant acres and landscape gardens that border the water. A 17th-century-style manor house, all stone and turrets, plays centerpiece to this bucolic setting. Here lived the Van Wickle family from 1894 until the last heir, Mrs. Marjorie Van Wickle-Lyon, died in 1976 and willed the estate to the Heritage Trust of Rhode Island. Visitors today can tour some of the Van Wickle's private rooms and wander around their gardens. New England's tallest giant sequoia stands here, 90 feet tall, 90 years old and thriving far from its West Coast homeland. Tour the 33 acres of rose gardens, rock gardens and bosquets on your own, or join one of the guided tours. Even winter is special here, with the mansion decked in bows and baubles, its Victorian tree stretching past the balcony to the second-floor ceiling. House closed on Monday, and months of November, January, February and March. Admission. ~ 101 Ferry Road, Bristol; 401-253-2707.

A short drive away, across the horseshoe cove of Bristol Harbor, is **Coggeshall Farm Museum**, a living history museum that represents a Rhode Island coastal farm in the 1790s. A costumed guide is often on hand to answer questions about the farm or the blacksmith shop on the premises. The monthly special programs—maple sugaring, 18th-century crafts demonstrations—are worth checking out. Admission. ~ Adjacent to the Colt State Park, Route 114, Bristol; 401-253-9062.

Across Narragansett Bay from Bristol lies Warwick, the second largest city in Rhode Island. Home to the state's only commercial airport, as well as to the largest concentrations of hotels and retail stores, it bills itself as "Rhode Island's Host City."

There's a bit of big city entertainment in Warwick at the **Rocky Point Amusement Park**, Rhode Island's largest. Rocky Point has 76 bayfront acres crammed with over 100 rides and games including the million-dollar Corkscrew Rollercoaster and the two-million-dollar, eight-story Free Fall. Closed after Labor Day until May. Admission. ~ 1 Rocky Point Avenue; 401-737-8000.

There are some large, urban hotels in the capital city, with several more under construction.

LODGING

The **Providence Biltmore** has traditionally been the area's biggest and best. The 217 guest rooms reflect a softer decor, with modern pastels in the carpeting and floral spreads. The lobby's grand staircase and glass-cage elevator continue to impress, as does the view from the Grand Ballroom. ~ Kennedy Plaza, Providence; 401-421-0700, 800-437-4824, fax 401-455-3050. ULTRA-DELUXE.

Judging from the number of briefcases and power suits, the **Providence Marriott** is a favorite site for local business meetings as well as a familiar setting for out-of-town visitors. The all-over design is classic Marriott, although the sprawling layout requires quite a hike to reach the guest room elevators. Rooms are standard issue, modern and clean, with no surprises either good or bad. The lobby bar tends to be very popular and noisy at night. The indoor/outdoor pool is also a gathering spot. ~ Charles and Orms streets, Providence; 401-272-2400, 800-228-9290, fax 401-421-8006. DELUXE.

The **Old Court Bed & Breakfast Inn** is an antique buff's delight. The building, which began as an Episcopal church rectory in 1863, was restored in 1985. Today each of its ten guest rooms is decorated in authentic treasures: four-poster beds, Victorian coverlets, period washstands. Reserve early; this inn is quite popular. ~ 144 Benefit Street, Providence; 401-351-0747, fax 401-272-6566. DELUXE.

FOURTH OF JULY EXTRAVAGANZA!

Nowhere in America is July 4th given such notice as in Bristol, where they've been celebrating since 1785, adding a bit more each year. Now, more than 250,000 visitors flood this tiny village in July (regular population: 21,625) to participate in its Independence Day celebration. The country's oldest parade marches along Route 114 (which features a red, white and blue stripe all year), and the festivities continue for days. For more information about this area, contact the Bristol County Chamber of Commerce. ~ 654 Metacom Avenue, Warren; 401-245-0750.

HIDDEN ►

The **Nathaniel Porter Inn** is a combination inn, restaurant and local success story. "Rescued" and painstakingly restored by the Lynch family, this red-clapboard Colonial house with its jaunty yellow trim now has three guest rooms, each with a private bath, and a shared sitting room on the second floor. Everything, from the stone fireplaces to the four-poster canopy beds, is authentic and charming. ~ 125 Water Street, Warren; 401-245-6622, fax 401-247-0244. MODERATE.

Radisson Airport Hotel is the practicum facility for Johnson & Wales University, a hotel, tourism and culinary institute. Opened in 1989, this state-of-the-art hotel offers such wide-ranging facilities and amenities as concierge services, whirlpool and free airport shuttle service. Even better, guests can be sure that the entire staff will be trying extra hard to please; they're students, and they're being graded on their performance. ~ 2081 Post Road, Warwick; 401-739-3000, 800-233-2066, fax 401-732-9309. DELUXE.

Master Hosts Inn, a 103-room economy motel, offers excellent value. Guests can look forward to complimentary continental breakfasts and airport shuttle service. ~ 2138 Post Road, Warwick; 401-737-7400, fax 401-739-6483. MODERATE.

DINING

In keeping with its role as state capital, university town and business center, Providence has developed into a sophisticated dining arena. The many local yuppie types demand it, and visitors can enjoy it. Happily, the focus on upscale eateries has not banished the plentitude of casual, ethnic restaurants.

Overlooking a small lake called Spectacle Pond, **Twin Oaks** serves seafood, steak and Italian dishes in their classic Rhode Island eatery south of Providence. The restaurant offers two contemporary indoor dining areas with lake views, plus outdoor seating. Closed Monday. ~ 100 Sabra Street, Cranston; 401-781-9693. MODERATE.

Fine Continental cuisine with a creative twist fills the menu at **Rue de l'Espoir**. Along with traditional items, the restaurant serves a host of original sauces. Specials change nightly and might include entrées like roasted filet of salmon with pistachio-basil crust and grilled chicken and pesto over three-cheese ravioli. Their "small plates," served with hot bread from the oven, are popular. The casual French-country decor features hardwoods and tables topped with red tile. Closed Monday. ~ 99 Hope Street, Providence; 401-751-8890. MODERATE TO DELUXE.

Al Forno was the inspiration of two local innovative foodies, George Germon and Johanne Killeen. Al Forno is renowned for its grilled pizzas (*al forno* means "from the oven"). The style is casual, but the food is serious, hearty and, most of all, good. Closed Sunday and Monday. ~ 577 South Main Street, Providence; 401-273-9760. MODERATE TO DELUXE.

Next door, the **Hot Club,** housed in what was once a factory boiler room, serves lighter fare like grilled chicken breast sandwiches, hamburgers and fried zucchini sticks. When the Hot Club moved here, it caused the waterfront area of Corliss Landing to become gentrified, elevating it to the status of "in" spot. ~ 575 South Water Street; 401-861-9007. BUDGET.

The Fish Company, which shares a common outdoor boardwalk along the river with the Hot Club, is a casual, trendy and romantic spot at sundown for appetizers and predinner drinks on the deck, where you can watch the boats pass. ~ 515 South Water Street; 401-421-5796. BUDGET.

Adesso bills itself as a "California Café" and specializes in mesquite grilling. Preferred seating is in the high, skylighted front room. Decor is minimalist, almost hard-edge. The wood-oven pizzas (topped with everything from barbecue chicken to smoked gouda) are popular favorites. Everything on the menu can be ordered to go. ~ 161 Cushing Street, Providence; 401-521-0770. MODERATE TO DELUXE.

In a building that resembles a huge Rubik's Cube, **Hemenway's** serves what some consider the area's best seafood. The room's simple black, white and rose tiled floor and high-ceilinged decor does not detract from the cuisine, although the spectacular views of the river do tend to vie strongly for one's attention. ~ 1 Old Stone Square, South Main Street, Providence; 401-351-8570. DELUXE.

Federal Hill, Providence's "Little Italy," is fairly bursting with wonderful ethnic restaurants; most are family-oriented with menus priced accordingly. A local favorite is **Angelo's Civita Sarnese Restaurant,** where the decor is strictly luncheonette (and includes a photo-collage of celebrity customers), the service is friendly and family-style and the cuisine is traditional, hearty and wholesome, with dishes like veal with roasted peppers and a variety of pasta specials. Closed Sunday from Memorial Day through Labor Day. ~ 141 Atwells Avenue; 401-621-8171. BUDGET.

A GREAT PLACE TO RETIRE

Rhode Island's reputation for championing personal freedoms is once again evidenced in today's newest minority: senior citizens. The state is second only to Florida in its over-65 population. It's especially curious that many of these seniors have moved here from other states, choosing to move to a place far from the Sunbelt's climate. Whatever the reasons for the influx (state statisticians are still puzzling over this one), it becomes fairly obvious that Rhode Island's winters cannot be regarded as a negative factor.

For a more upscale venue in the same neighborhood, you might sample the fine Italian cuisine at **Camille's Roman Garden**. Closed Sunday in June, July and August. ~ 71 Bradford Street; 401-751-4812. MODERATE TO DELUXE.

Across the Providence River in Bristol County is the **Nathaniel Porter Inn**. Dine indoors in the restored 1750 Colonial's front parlors with their authentic stenciled walls and brick fireplaces or in an enclosed courtyard. Winner of the 1989 Grand Master Chefs of America award, the inn's menu of seafood and game specialties changes seasonally, although two favorites always remain: their award-winning seafood chowder and the "Autumn Harvest" apple pie, voted "best in New England" by the readers of *Yankee* magazine. ~ 125 Water Street, Warren; 401-245-6622. MODERATE TO DELUXE.

HIDDEN ►

The tiny town of Warren is the "Clambake Capital of the United States." Local bakemasters take their titles very seriously around here; summer weekend **clambakes** are culinary poetry. All-you-can-eat for $15. Reservations are a must: call retired police chief Robert Perry. ~ 401-245-1977.

Once inside the cavernous barn of **Rocky Point Shore Dinner Hall**, you won't doubt their claim of being the world's largest. The quantities are award-winning, too, with heaps of their famous clam cakes, chowder, baked fish—anything from the sea. All with a view of Narragansett Bay. Closed from Labor Day to May. ~ 1 Rocky Point Avenue, Warwick; 401-737-8000. MODERATE TO DELUXE.

SHOPPING

Although there are a couple of vertical malls in downtown Providence, the best of the city's shopping is found in independent shops and boutiques all over town.

The Opulent Owl is typical of the innovative, trendy stores fronting South Main Street. Here, nifty gift items—unusual frames, fine china—share space with handsome housewares and accessories for the home. ~ 295 South Main Street; 401-521-6698.

The Arcade, which occupies three floors of an 1828 majestically columned marble National Historic Landmark building, bills itself as America's first shopping mall. It may be the oldest, but it's far from the nation's finest or most well-stocked. There are lots of small specialty shops to browse but nothing to lure the serious shopper. Closed Sunday. ~ 65 Weybosset Street; 401-598-1199.

The **Museum Gift Shop** harbors a wealth of reproductions, as well as jewelry, cards, textiles, sculptures, prints and books focusing on the art treasures exhibited throughout the museum. ~ Museum of Art—Rhode Island School of Design, 224 Benefit Street; 401-454-6500.

NIGHTLIFE

Two major theater experiences in town offer audiences both local repertory and touring company productions. **Trinity Repertory Company** is over 30 years old and going strong. This Tony award-winning repertory company supports a talented group of resident artists and also encourages audience participation. ~ 201 Washington Street; 401-351-4242.

Providence Performing Arts Center showcases national touring companies' road shows of Broadway and other hit productions. The PPAC is located in the landmark Loew's Theater, a 1920s beauty complete with vintage velvet seats and gilded ceiling. ~ 220 Weybosset Street; 401-421-2997.

An alternative gay and straight crowd frequents **Gerardo's**, a cavernous club with four bars, a dancefloor, pool tables and an outside garden area. Check out the Thursday night striptease show which features both sexes. Cover. ~ 1 Franklin Square; 401-274--5560.

Challenges Ultimate Sports Pub features wall-to-wall viewing: a theater-sized screen that dominates the room, plus individual sets at each booth and table. There are even videos of highlights and the best games to fill in the dreaded "off-game" times when no sporting event is being broadcast. ~ 52 Pine Street; 401-861-1385.

Cable Car Cinema and Café shows classics and foreign films in at-home comfort; half the regular theater seats have been replaced with overstuffed two-seater couches. There's a coffeehouse café serving sandwiches, calzones and pastries right in the theater building, with outdoor seating during good weather. ~ 204 South Main Street; 401-272-3970.

L'Elizabeth's looks like a cozy living room in a friend's home: intimate clusters of couches surround coffee tables topped with bowls of flowers. This intimate setting is popular for after-theater coffee and pastries, or for cocktails or drinks. ~ 285 South Main Street; 401-621-9113.

Providence Civic Center is the site of family shows, concerts and sporting events. ~ 1 La Salle Square; 401-331-6700.

Warwick Musical Theater is theater-in-the-round with a new twist; here, it's the stage that revolves. Open June through August. ~ 522 Quaker Lane, Warwick; 401-821-7300.

COLT STATE PARK Formerly the private estate of the Samuel Pomeroy Colt family, this Bristol park now provides a 443-acre outdoor haven to all families. A three-mile shore drive traces Narragansett Bay, and a network of bike paths (which links up with the "East Bay Bike Path") crisscrosses the wooded park. There's excellent saltwater fishing. In summer the Rhode Island Symphony gives occasional waterside concerts here. Picnic areas; restrooms; day-use fee, minimum $4. ~ Along Route 114 in Bristol; 401-253-7482.

GODDARD STATE PARK This beachfront park is beautifully maintained and provides outdoor recreation year-round. The old carousel building on the shore now serves

BEACHES & PARKS

as a performing arts center for band and jazz concerts during the summer. Spread throughout the 500 wooded acres are 18 miles of bridal trails (no horse rentals in the park), a nine-hole golf course and a picnic gazebo. Picnic areas, lifeguards, bathhouse, concession stands, boat ramp; day-use fee, minimum $4. ~ On Ives Road about one mile south of East Greenwich; 401-884-2010.

Blackstone Valley

To help pinpoint the Blackstone Valley area, visualize the state of Rhode Island as a layer cake: the Blackstone Valley forms the entire top layer. (And the icing, too, its fans would add.) The Blackstone River surges through the eastern portion of this layer with a force powerful enough to have altered the course of our country's history.

America's industrial revolution began in the Blackstone Valley. In 1793, Samuel Slater harnessed the potential of mighty Blackstone River (which subsequently became known as "the hardest working river in America"), creating the first factory in America able to produce cotton yarn by using water power.

Today this entire "top-layer" area is Rhode Island's undiscovered gem, a region dotted with historic industrial towns that lie within huge tracts of rural and forested wilderness areas. You'll drive along scenic country roads that meander past historic sites, charming villages, meticulously restored Colonial homes, antique stores and farm stands.

SIGHTS
The city of **Pawtucket,** located at the extreme southeastern edge of the region, is home to Mr. Slater's mill, the place where it all began. Fourth largest city in the state, Pawtucket (an Indian term meaning "falls of water") sits at the upper tidewaters of Narragansett Bay.

Slater Mill Historic Site was the site of the 1793 mill and cotton factory. Today, it is a National Historic Landmark. Visitors to this wooden building, resplendent in its original vivid yellow hue, can tour the museum, with its huge looms still intact. Next door is the original rubblestone Wilkinson building that houses the 16,000-pound waterwheel. The gallery upstairs features changing exhibits of textiles and other related topics. Closed Monday from June through Labor Day. Closed Monday through Friday from Labor Day through December and from March through May. Closed January and February. Admission. ~ 67 Roosevelt Avenue, Pawtucket; 401-725-8638.

Not far away is the **Children's Museum of Rhode Island**, a kiddie wonderland housed in the spectacular 1841 Queen Anne–style Pitcher-Goff House. The kids who swarm noisily all over the museum are oblivious to the house's proud history; they just love the hands-on (and often feet-on, too) exhibits. There's the room-sized floor map of Rhode Island to crawl over, complete with boats to push along Narragansett Bay and trains chugging along the Amtrak rails; all that funny old stuff in Great Grandmother's Kitchen; sitting in the comfy lap of Estrella, the giant chair; and the creative joys of making up and acting in one's own plays. Parents enjoy observing all this activity, too. But they can also explore the many design and architectural gems throughout the house. One such highlight is Colonel Goff's unique solution to a vexing ventilation problem: the ornate design of his library's ceiling conceals dozens of holes drilled to allow his dreaded cigar smoke to escape Mrs. Goff's detection. Closed Monday and the two weeks after Labor Day. Admission. ~ 58 Walcott Street, Pawtucket; 401-726-2591.

Nearby **Slater Memorial Park** is also fun for children and adults. The oldest "stander carousel" in the world is located here. This gem is a genuine Charles Looff creation and one of the few that remain of this master craftsman's handiwork. Built in 1895, it was installed in Slater Park in 1910 and has been thrilling children ever since. The park has ball fields and bike trails, a pond full of ducks and even a regulation lawn bowling green. ~ Newport Avenue, Pawtucket; 401-728-0500, ext. 251.

Also located within the park is the **Daggett House**, a 1685 farmhouse and the oldest home in Pawtucket. The Daggett House is open Saturday and Sunday from June through September as well as by appointment. Admission. ~ Newport Avenue, Pawtucket; 401-728-0500, ext. 251.

A few minutes drive north of Pawtucket is **Diamond Hill Vineyards**, which lies nestled in the beautiful Cumberland countryside. After a jostling drive over the private road that runs through fields of vines, you arrive at the trim, gray, 200-year-old home of the owners, the Berntson family, who welcome visitors and invite them to use the spacious porch and rolling front lawn for picnics. Inside there's a tasting room and gift shop. Closed Tuesday. ~ 3145 Diamond Hill Road, Cumberland; 401-333-2751.

Rhode Island is home to more than 20 percent of all Registered Historic Landmarks in the entire country.

One specialty of Diamond Hill: you can design your own customized labels (complete with photos, personal messages or whatever else) to paste on gift bottles of their fruit wines or nonalcoholic ciders.

While you're in the area, you might want to stop by the **Blackstone Valley Tourism Council** for maps, brochures and information about Blackstone Valley and its activities. ~ Blackstone Valley Electric Office Park, 640 Washington Highway, Lincoln; 401-334-7773.

A bit farther north lies Woonsocket, whose residential North End holds an unexpected treasure, the **B'nai Israel Synagogue**. This house of worship has a series of spectacular stained-glass windows designed by a disciple of Marc Chagall, as well as Milanese hand-blown glass chandeliers. It's listed in the *Encyclopedia Judaica* as one of America's premier synagogues. ~ 224 Prospect Street; 401-762-3651.

LODGING

Surprises await at the **Comfort Inn** in Pawtucket. There's an "Executive Section" where guest rooms are larger, more fashionably decorated and better appointed than in most chain hotels. The hotel also has a staff so courteous and helpful you'll be glad you stayed. ~ 2 George Street; 401-723-6700, 800-221-2222, fax 401-726-6380. MODERATE.

DINING

HIDDEN ►

In a restored 1911 grain shed, **The Granary** has been given new life as a gleaming 1990s-style food haven. Specialty foods such as nouvelle sandwiches and salads and gourmet cheeses can be taken out or eaten at small tables topped with pots of wildflowers. Best of all: munching your meal out on the Granary's back deck, which cantilevers out over Abbott Run, a postcard-perfect mill stream and waterfall. ~ Pole 157, Sneech Pond Road, Cumberland; 401-334-2036. BUDGET TO MODERATE.

Wright's Farm Restaurant is the undisputed king of the "chicken family-style" dinners that are unique to the Blackstone Valley. This meal must always include macaroni, roast chicken, salad, french fries and dessert—served and served until you can't eat another bite. Wright's Farm's dining room can accommodate 1500, so expect busloads of fellow diners, groaning boards and low prices. Closed Monday through Wednesday. ~ 84 Inman Road, Harrisville; 401-769-2856. BUDGET.

SHOPPING

This is *mill country*, birthplace of the mill-end and factory outlet concept. Among the many nearby, we especially like the **Slater Fabric Store**, where printed fabrics from well-known houses sell from $1.25 to $4 a yard. Store manager Nancy Lee remembers her goods and can locate a perfect match years after you've bought the original. ~ 727 School Street, Pawtucket; 401-725-1730.

Contact the **Blackstone Valley Tourism Council** for a brochure listing all of the factory outlets. ~ 640 Washington Highway, Lincoln; 401-334-7773.

HIDDEN ►

There are about a dozen antique stores in the tiny village of Chepachet in the town of Gloucester, but the undisputed star of the group is the **Brown & Hopkins Country Store**. As country stores go, this one is the genuine article; it's also one of the oldest continuously operated stores in America. Opened in 1809, Brown & Hopkins retains much of the old (the roll-top desk near the front door has been there since the Civil War era) while giving today's customers what they want (gourmet foods, hand-dipped candles, even penny candies). The antiques are displayed in room settings on the second and third floors. Owners Claudia and Joe Amaral also stock a popular 40-pound wheel of Vermont cheddar cheese. Closed Monday through Wednesday and the last two weeks of August. ~ 1179 Putnam Pike; 401-568-4830.

City Nights Dinner Theatre presents a series of dinner shows as well as matinee shows. A typical season includes mostly musicals and comedies as well as one drama. ~ 27 Exchange Street, Pawtucket; 401-723-6060.

Chan's is, in addition to being a popular Oriental restaurant, renowned throughout New England for its showcasing of international jazz artists. Host John Chan invites only the best to perform. ~ 267 Main Street, Woonsocket; 401-765-1900.

LINCOLN WOODS STATE PARK Over 600 acres of woodland make up this popular recreation area north of Providence. Visitors can swim in Olney Pond and hike or ride horses along the oak-bordered trails surrounding it. In the winter, people come here to skate, cross-country ski and snowmobile. Picnic areas, restrooms, bathhouse, playing fields, lifeguard, concession stand, horse rentals available right outside the park at Sunset Stables; day-use fee, minimum $4. ~ Entrances are located on Great Road, Route 123, and Twin River Road off Route 146 in Lincoln; 401-723-7892.

DIAMOND HILL PARK This woodsy hill is skirted by a mile-long ledge of quartz, thus the park's moniker. The 373-acre spot, crossed by hiking trails, is the site of summer festivals near the small pond. Picnic area, restrooms, ball field. ~ Off Route 114 on Diamond Hill Road in Cumberland; 401-728-2400, ext. 28.

PULASKI MEMORIAL STATE PARK Part of the 3500-acre George Washington Management Area, the park has 80 acres of red pine, white pine and oak woods that skirt Peck's Pond, whose beach is a main attraction for visitors here. Fishing is good for bass, perch and trout; swimming is excellent. You can also hike trails through the forest area or get a game going at the ball field. Picnic area, restrooms, changing room, ball field, lifeguard; day-use fee, minimum $4. ~ On Pulaski Road, off of Route 44 six miles west of Chepachet; 401-568-2013.

Known as the "Ocean State," Rhode Island is an angler's paradise. The New England Offshore Sportfish Tournament is held here every summer, with weigh-ins at the Ram Point Marina in Port Judith. Local waters teem with tuna, bluefin, albacore, marlin and shark. Charter boats abound, sailing from every port along the coast.

Outdoor Adventures

SOUTH COUNTY In South County, contact the Snug Harbor Marina Booking Service for charter fishing reservations. ~ 410 Gooseberry Road, Wakefield; 401-783-7766. On Block Island, contact G. Willy Makit Charters. ~ 401-466-5151.

NEWPORT AREA   **Fishin' Off**, a 36-foot Trojan sportfish sedan, offers everything including a videotaping of you landing that big one. No license is required for saltwater fishing. ~ Goat Island Causeway, Newport; 401-849-9642.

SAILING

While not every Sunday sailor gets to crew during Newport's famed America's Cup races, Rhode Island's bays, sounds and open ocean lure boating fans of all degrees of expertise. In fact, you don't even have to know how to sail at all; there are plenty of vessels that come complete with their own crews.

SOUTH COUNTY   In South County, you can choose from several power and sail charters at **Mill Cove Yachts**. ~ 1 Phillips Street, Wickford; 401-295-0504.

NEWPORT AREA   In Newport, **Newport Yacht Charters** has bareboat and crewed charters ranging from 35-foot schooners to a 120-foot sailboat, as well as power boats. ~ P.O. Box 1224, Newport, RI 02840; 401-423-2345. **Newport Sailing School and Cruises Ltd.** and **Newport Sailboat Harbor Tours** offer lessons as well as popular partial or full-day harbor cruises aboard 23-foot and 30-foot sloops. ~ 5 Beaver Road, Barrington; 401-683-2738, 401-246-1595.

WIND-SURFING

This sport, which requires both sailing and surfing skills to master, is also pretty to watch. All along Rhode Island's beaches the colorful sails of these water-skimming boards add to the beauty of the ocean views.

NEWPORT AREA   **Peabody Beach** in Newport is a popular windsurfing spot. If you'd like to give it a try, **Island Sports** gives group and private lessons and rents and sells boards and gear. ~ 86 Aquidneck Avenue, Middletown; 401-846-4421.

GOLF

Throughout the state many public courses welcome visitors.

SOUTH COUNTY   **Winnapaug Golf Course** is open to the public. ~ Shore Road, Westerly; 401-596-9164. Also in Westerly is the **Pond View Country Club**. ~ Shore Road, Westerly; 401-322-7870. In Hope Valley, try **Lindhbrook Country Club**. ~ Woodville-Alton Road, Hope Valley; 401-539-8700.

NEWPORT AREA   In the Newport area, try the semi-private **Green Valley Country Club**. ~ 371 Union Street, Portsmouth; 401-847-9543. You can also check out **Montaup Country Club**. ~ Anthony Road, Portsmouth; 401-683-9882.

PROVIDENCE AREA   In Providence, **Triggs Memorial Gold Course** is open to the public. ~ 1533 Chalkstone Avenue; 401-521-8460.

TENNIS

Tennis courts in Rhode Island range from the modest playground variety to the rarified splendor of the grass courts of Newport's venerable Casino. Regardless of their relative status, most require advance reservations.

SOUTH COUNTY   On Block Island, courts include **The Atlantic Inn** (401-466-5883), **The Block Island Club** (401-466-5939; fee) and **Champlin's Marine** (401-466-2641).

NEWPORT AREA   At the **International Tennis Hall of Fame,** you can play on the world-famous Newport grass courts. Lessons are available; reservations required to book one of the 13 courts. ~ 194 Bellevue Avenue; 401-849-3990.

PROVIDENCE AREA   In Providence, **Roger Williams Park** has ten beautiful clay courts. ~ Elmwood Avenue; 401-785-9450.

RIDING STABLES

Given Rhode Island's wealth of superb wilderness and parklands, one might expect to find a similar abundance of stables offering horseback rentals, but there are relatively few.

You can take a lesson and ride English style on 107 acres of back-country trails, seven days a week, at the **Richmond Equestrian Center.** ~ 124 Kenyon Hill Trail, Wyoming; 401-539-2979.

BLACKSTONE VALLEY   Guided rides are offered on the weekends at the **Stepping Stone Ranch.** ~ Escoheag Hill Road, West Greenwich; 401-397-3725. Lincoln's **Sunset Stables** also provides guided weekend rides through Lincoln Woods State Park. ~ Twin River Road, off Route 146, Lincoln; 401-722-3033.

BICYCLING

SOUTH COUNTY   For strong cyclists who can handle the hills, Block Island can be biking heaven, with its pristine byways and incredible views.

NEWPORT AREA   In Newport, you can cycle the lovely 15-mile Bellevue Avenue and Ocean Drive route that hugs the Atlantic. Across the Sakonnet River, there are 25 to 35 miles of quiet routes that meander through the peaceful villages of Tiverton and Little Compton.

✔ **CHECK THESE OUT—UNIQUE OUTDOOR ADVENTURES**

- Learn to surf from a pro at picture-perfect **Narragansett Town Beach,** site of the Northeast Surfing Championships. *page 124*
- Catch the breeze on a board in the calm waters of the Sakonnet River and windsurf **Peabody Beach.** *page 148*
- Blaze a path along oak-bordered woodland trails horseback riding through **Lincoln Woods State Park.** *page 147*
- Cycle along the water while taking in historic mansions on Newport's **Bellevue Avenue** and **Ocean Drive.** *page 149*

As you travel the state's multitude of country lanes, you'll understand why so many Rhode Islanders are avid cyclists.

PROVIDENCE AREA Rhode Island is a biker's paradise. There are bike lanes everywhere and even a special ten-foot-wide, 15-mile-long "East Bay Bicycle Path" that runs from East Providence to Riverside along scenic shoreline routes and through several state parks.

Bike Rentals Disappointingly few shops rent bikes in the state. In South County, a dependable choice is **Narragansett Bikes** ~ 1153 Boston Neck Road, Route 1A, Narragansett; 401-782-4444. On Block Island, visit **Esta's at Old Harbor.** ~ Water Street, Old Harbor, Block Island; 401-466-2651.

In Newport, **Ten Speed Spokes** rents mountain bikes and hybrids. ~ 18 Elm Street; 401-847-5609. You can also try **Adventure Water Sports.** ~ 2 Bowen's Landing; 401-849-4820.

The state's biking possibilities are superior enough to warrant bringing along your own cycle if you don't want to chance a rental.

HIKING The entire state of Rhode Island holds wonderful surprises both for serious hikers as well as those who simply enjoy meandering through the great outdoors. In the northern tier of the state, a unique two-state federal project, the Blackstone River Valley National Heritage Corridor, will develop miles of new trails along the banks of the river and the original tow paths along the canal. Even though not fully completed, this linear park offers endless opportunities to those who celebrate wilderness beauty.

SOUTH COUNTY The lowlands of South County are studded with great tracts of protected wilderness areas that are ideal for the hiking enthusiast.

Called "the most beautiful walk in Rhode Island," the **Long Pond–Ell Pond Trail** (4.5 miles) leads to three ponds through what locals call a "cathedral forest" of wild rhododendrons and hemlocks. Located in Hopkinton, this area is listed in the Registry of Natural Landmarks. Trailheads are located off North Road and off Cahouchet Road in Hopkinton.

Arcadia Park's **Yellow Dot Trail** (8 miles) can be followed via yellow spots painted on trees. It crosses much of the park's wooded wilderness. Call 401-539-2356 or 401-277-1157 for a list of hiking paths within the Yellow Dot Trail.

In the 29-acre Kimball Wildlife Refuge near Charlestown, the **Orange Trail** (1.5 miles) leads through postglacial forests of oaks and maples to Toupoyesett Pond. This trail is maintained by the Audubon Society (401-949-5454) for hiking, birding and photography.

At Rudman's Hollow on Block Island, venture upon **The Green Way Nature Trail** (3 miles), a silent wilderness where you'll encounter the "enchanted forest," rolling hills and open brush. Along the way you'll espy the foundation of an old mill and a cemetery—remnants of an old farm. The only sounds heard are bird calls; this glacial ravine provides sanctuary for over 200 species of migratory birds. The trail begins at Beacon Hill. For more information and trail maps, contact The Nature Conservancy (P.O. Box 1287, Block Island, RI 02807; 401-466-2129).

NEWPORT AREA The famous **Cliff Walk** (3.5 miles) in Newport must be counted as unique, if not the ultimate in hikes. Beginning at the Memorial Drive gate and winding its sometimes precarious way along and above the crashing waves, this scenic path provides "hidden" views of the front yards and facades of the town's great mansions, as well as sweeping views of Rhode Island Sound. Keep to the inside of the path because erosion has weakened the outer edges of some sections.

There are a dozen varied trails through the 450 acres of the Norman Bird Sanctuary in Middletown, ranging from the brief **Woodcock Trail** (.5 mile) that leads through level shrublands and a forest of black cherry and black locust, to the 300-million-year-old Paradise Rock formation known as **Hanging Rock Trail** (1 mile), along a 70-foot-high rocky ridge that overlooks the ocean, Gardiner's Pond and the marshlands.

BLACKSTONE VALLEY The **Blackstone River Valley National Heritage Corridor** encompasses both the canal tow paths as well as the river area itself. Covering over 45 miles in the region, the corridor will eventually contain miles of hiking trails. Although not yet a formal "hiking trail," a two-mile stretch of canal tow path in Lincoln provides a feel of what the finished park will offer. It's a flat walk bordered by flood plain meadows and dense forest; you will see great blue heron, woodchucks, rabbits and turtles along the way. ~ To get there, take Exit 10 off of Route 295 to Route 122 South (also called Mendon Road). Continue on for about one-and-one-half miles to Martin Street. Cross two bridges. Park in the pull-off at the second bridge. Skirt the orange guard rail and turn right. After one mile of hiking, you will see the old Captain Kelly house, the Ashton Mill and the dam. Turn back here.

◀ HIDDEN

Three marked trails crisscross the 77-acre Powder Mill Ledge Refuge in Smithfield. Owned by the Audubon Society of Rhode Island (401-949-5454), this refuge is home to many species of birds, spotted turtles, ducks and some snakes in forests of shagbark and pignut hickory, butternut and chestnut trees. The **Orange Trail** (1 mile) and the **Blue Trail** (1.5 miles) are graded as "easy," while the **Yellow Trail** (2 miles) is a bit more difficult. In winter, all three are groomed for cross-country skiing.

Transportation

▼▼▼▼▼▼▼▼▼▼

CAR

Route 95 traverses the state north and south, connecting Rhode Island to Connecticut and to the rest of New England. Along the coast, scenic 1A hugs the ocean shoreline, a slower but more beautiful drive.

AIR

T. F. Green Airport in Warwick is the state's only commercial airport. Regularly scheduled service is provided by America West, American Airlines, American Eagle, Business Express, Continental Express, Delta Airlines, Northwest Airlines, TWA Express, USAir Express and United Airlines.

New England Airlines operates daily five-minute commuter flights between Block Island and Westerly. ~ 401-596-2460.

Several limo and van companies link the airport to cities throughout the state: **Airport Taxi** runs to and from Warwick. ~ 401-737-2868. **Cozy Cab** runs daily shuttles to and from Newport. ~ 401-846-2500. **Cadillac Cab** goes to and from Providence. ~ 401-232-5731.

FERRY

Ferry service between Block Island and Galilee, Newport, New London and Providence is provided by **The Interstate Navigation Company**. Cars and passengers are transported on a year-round basis from Point Judith, although the schedule is abbreviated during off-season. Reservations for cars are essential year-round. ~ Galilee; 401-783-4613.

BUS

Scheduled and charter bus services connect all points within the state. **Bonanza Bus Lines** operates out of Providence. ~ One Bonanza Way, Providence; 401-751-8800. **Pawtuxet Valley Bus Lines** is based in West Warwick. ~ 76 Industrial Lane, West Warwick; 401-828-4100. **Rhode Island Public Transit Authority** (RIPTA) operates throughout the state. ~ 265 Melrose Street, Providence; 401-781-9400.

TRAIN

Amtrak's Northeast Corridor service connects Rhode Island with Boston and New York. There is frequent service to and from Providence at Union Station and less frequent service to Kingston Station. ~ Reservations: 800-872-7245. Union Station: 100 Gaspee Street; 401-727-7389. Kingston Station: Railroad Avenue, West Kingston; 401-783-2913.

CAR RENTALS

Major car rental agencies at the Warwick airport include **Avis Rent A Car** (800-331-1212), **Budget Rent A Car** (800-527-0700) and **Hertz Rent A Car** (800-654-3131).

Located across the street from the airport are **Dollar Rent A Car** (1989 Post Road; 800-800-4000), **National Interrent** (2053 Post Road; 800-328-4567) and **Thrifty Car Rental** (2329 Post Road; 800-367-2277).

Bus service throughout the state is provided by **Rhode Island Public Transportation Authority** (RIPTA). These buses can connect airport passengers with the Block Island ferry in Galilee, as well as direct service from Providence to Newport, Westerly and the South County beaches. ~ 401-781-9400.

PUBLIC TRANSIT

FOUR

Boston

A stately dominion of brick and brownstone, parks and trees, river and harbor, Boston has stood as the preeminent New England city for more than three and a half centuries. Holding fast to the tip of a tiny peninsula jutting into the Atlantic, the city grew and spread south and west through the centuries, but it's still compact and eminently walkable. Despite its tiny size, Boston has played a mighty role in history, a history etched in the minds of all Americans. For this is the birthplace of our nation, where Paul Revere made his dashing midnight ride, where "the shot heard 'round the world" was fired.

A city of fanatical Puritan roots, Boston has been mocked and scorned by more worldly others as dull, pious and provincial, no match for New York or Los Angeles in sophistication. Rich in artistic and intellectual life, Boston has still been notched down on the big-city scoresheet for its lackluster shopping, dining and hotel accommodations.

But Boston is changing its face. While still revering its history and roots, the city is searching for a new identity as a modern, stylish metropolis. In the 1980s, world-renowned chefs set up shop here, winning over Bostonians and food critics alike. The palatial shopping emporium Copley Place opened, anchored by flashy Dallas retailer Neiman Marcus, which would never have dared show its face here in the '50s. A building boom pushed up skyscraping, first-class hotels like the Westin, the Boston Harbor Hotel and the Four Seasons, as well as gleaming Financial District office towers. At the same time, old treasures like South Station and the Ritz-Carlton Hotel received much-needed face-lifts. Change continues in the 1990s. In 1995, the Boston Public Library completed a $50 million, three-part restoration project. In September 1995 the FleetCenter, a $160 million contemporary sports arena, opened to replace the antiquated Boston Garden.

The push for class continues with a grand project called the "Big Dig" begun in the late 1980s, which involves carving a giant tunnel to place the ugly, elevated Central Artery expressway underground, as well as building a third tunnel to the airport. The project's completion will bring light and spaciousness to the downtown area. And the city's main eyesore—the burlesque district known as the Combat Zone—has all but disappeared. Several restaurants, cafés and shops have sprung up in Boston's efforts to demolish the Combat Zone and expand the nearby theater district.

The city's Puritan roots were laid back in 1630, when a small band of English Puritans led by Governor John Winthrop arrived and settled on the peninsula. The colonists found Boston waters teeming with cod and, by the 1640s, were shipping dried cod to the West Indies and the Mediterranean. In exchange, they received sugar, gold and molasses. By the 1670s, Boston dominated the West Indian shipping business, and by 1700 it was the third busiest port in the British realm, after London and Bristol.

But Britain resented this young upstart colony and began to impose trade and tax restrictions. The growing city resisted, and soon colonial anger erupted into riots. The British responded by sending troops to occupy the city in 1768. Anti-crown tensions climaxed in the Boston Massacre in 1770, a clash between British soldiers and colonists in which five American men were killed.

More signal events on the road to independence followed in rapid succession. In the 1773 Boston Tea Party, 200 men dressed as Indians tossed three shiploads of tea into Boston Harbor as a protest against the English tea tax. King George closed the port and sent more troops to Boston.

The Revolution began in earnest in and around Boston. The first shots were fired at nearby Lexington and Concord in 1775. In the Battle of Bunker Hill, the British drove off the heavily outnumbered Americans, but only after sustaining severe losses. When George Washington fortified Dorchester Heights in a single night, the British were ousted forever. They evacuated the city on March 17, 1776, and fighting never again touched Boston.

With the ink dry on the Declaration of Independence, thoughts turned to commerce. But lost British markets pushed the city into a depression, and Boston began looking toward the Far East for trade, bringing in silks, spices and porcelain.

The city grew and thrived in the years after the Revolution. Fortunes were made by Boston's more prosperous merchants, a group of influential families who came to be known as the "codfish aristocracy." They dubbed themselves Boston Brahmins, smugly adopting the title of India's priestly caste. This small group counted among them the names of Cabot, Lowell and Hancock. They ruled the city with an unapproachable elitism, letting it be known that "the Lowells speak only to the Cabots, and the Cabots speak only to God."

The Brahmins built brick monuments to their prosperity on Beacon Hill, an elite residential district that defined the social character of Boston throughout the mid-19th century. Beacon Hill was home to such intellectuals as Francis Parkman, William James, Henry Wadsworth Longfellow, James Russell Lowell, Bronson Alcott, Julia Ward Howe and Horace Mann.

In the 1850s Boston become the premier builder of clipper ships, sending these graceful crafts around the world. To accommodate the growing trade, the city built many wharves along its waterfront. But the clipper era was cut short by the rise of steam-powered ships, which conservative Bostonians did not trust and would not build. Merchants shifted their capital to manufacturing, and the harbor went into a long decline.

The mid-19th century also saw the founding of some of Boston's most famed cultural institutions, among them the Boston Public Library, the Boston Symphony Orchestra, the Massachusetts Institute of Technology and Boston University, the first to admit women on an equal basis. The cultural richness produced a new nickname for the city: "The Athens of America."

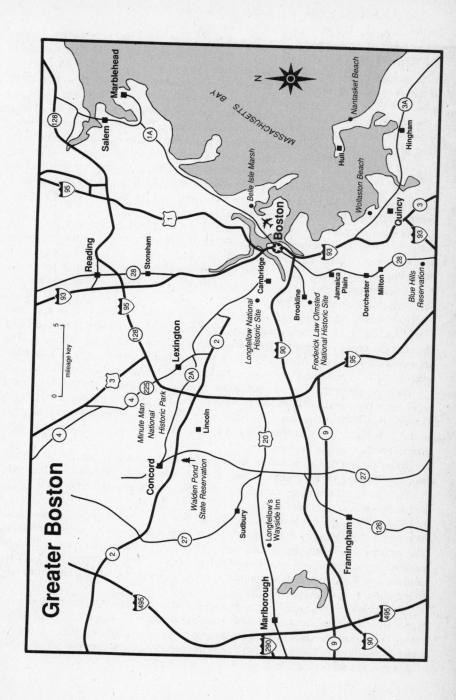

Greater Boston

Into this bustling urban area swarmed thousands of immigrants, led in the 1840s by the Irish, who had been forced from their homeland by the potato famine. The influx of Irish changed the character of this Yankee city forever. First blatantly discriminated against by old-line Bostonians ("No Irish need apply"), they grew in numbers great enough to win political power. The first Irish mayor was elected in 1885.

> The Boston Irish gave us such leaders as former Speakers of the House John W. McCormack and Tip O'Neill, James Michael Curley and the Kennedy clan.

Boston bloomed into an ethnic rainbow in the 1880s, when waves of Italians, Poles and Russians arrived, multiplying the population thirty-fold. At the same time, the city's area was itself multiplying. In the mid-19th century, Boston had begun filling in the bay between Beacon Hill and Brookline, a neighborhood now known as Back Bay. Other swampy land to the south was also filled and became the South End. By the turn of the century, Boston had tripled its size with landfill.

But soon after, Boston's economy suffered a tremendous decline that would last until the 1960s. The city lost its major port status to New York and Baltimore, and its textile, shoe and glass mills moved south in search of cheaper labor and operating costs. Population shrank in the 1940s and '50s, with Boston the only large city to decline in numbers during the postwar baby boom years. The city languished in the throes of this decline for decades.

Good times returned suddenly in the 1960s, as the Protestant elite and Irish Catholics finally cooperated in managing city affairs. Urban renewal projects created the new Government Center and the landmark Prudential and Hancock towers. The technological revolution of the 1970s and '80s enriched Boston's economy, with computer companies and think tanks springing up in Cambridge and Greater Boston.

With prosperity came urban problems. In the early 1970s, court-ordered busing among racially imbalanced schools sparked rioting and protests, particularly in South Boston and Charlestown. The crisis lasted several years. Racial strife eased somewhat in the 1980s and 1990s as blacks began to gain more power in local and state government and in private business.

Today Boston has a Democrat-controlled legislature and a reputation for liberalism, spearheaded by the reigning scion of the Kennedy clan, Senator Ted Kennedy. Breaking the Irish tradition, today's top city official—Thomas Menino—is the city's first Italian mayor.

Boston the city is home to a scant 650,000 souls. Many are under 30; thousands of students flood the city each September, injecting it with vitality and youthfulness. The weather is infinitely changeable, varying from warm, humid summers, when temperatures range from the 60s to the low 90s, to dry, crisp falls hovering in the high 40s (and the low 70s during Indian summer), to very cold winters, when temperatures dip to the 20s and 30s, occasionally falling below zero.

The nucleus of Boston proper is a pear-shaped peninsula. At its northernmost tip stands the North End, a small, Italian enclave clustered with shops, cafés and restaurants. The downtown area takes up most of the peninsula, winding between the waterfront and Boston Common from north to south and encompassing a Chinatown that is tiny yet rich in tradition.

High above Boston Common in regal splendor sits Beacon Hill, crowned by the State House and graced with bowfront brick homes, window boxes and hidden gardens. To the west of Beacon Hill lies its cousin, stately Back Bay, a place of wide boulevards and imposing brownstones. Back Bay also encompasses the architectural jewels of Copley Square: the Public Library, Trinity Church and the John Hancock Tower. Farther west is the Fenway, sprawling around its marshy gardens and home to baseball's famous Fenway Park.

A bit farther south lies the city's largest neighborhood, the South End, another 19th-century brick residential area in the process of gentrification. Cut off from eastern downtown by the Fort Point Channel, South Boston (not to be confused with the South End) is a primarily commercial area, home to the city's fish piers.

The residential neighborhoods, harking back to English architecture, have led to Boston's being characterized "America's most European city." But since Boston has added new space-age layers to the urban quiltwork of centuries, the city wears a more American and international face. Though the city took its time, it has come a long way from its Puritan roots and the days when books by male and female authors were separated on different shelves.

Somehow we know the Puritan roots will never die; the Sunday blue laws were rescinded only recently. And Boston will never be mistaken for wilder cities like New York or Los Angeles. It will always remain small, and never a province of punk hairdos. But nowadays, Boston has a lot less to apologize for on the big-city scoresheet and is becoming a first-class city in a class by itself.

▼▼▼▼▼▼▼▼▼▼
The North End

The North End is Boston's oldest, most colorful neighborhood. Today it's a tightly knit, homogeneous Italian community, established after a gradual takeover from pockets of Irish, Portuguese and Jewish residents starting in the late 19th century. The North End's mostly one-lane streets are crowded cheek-by-jowl with Italian restaurants and food stores. Many residents still greet each other in the language of the Old Country and hang their wash out between the alleys. All summer long, Italians celebrate their patron saints with picturesque weekend parades and street festivals.

On the roundish peninsula that is Boston, the North End juts north into Boston Harbor and is cut off from downtown by the elevated Southeast Expressway, which helps keep it a place unto itself. It's a spot where Boston history still lives.

SIGHTS

Probably no name evokes more romance in American history than Paul Revere. His famous ride warning of the British attack in 1775 has been chronicled the world over. The quiet little expanse of North Square, lined with cobblestones and black anchor chain, is where you come upon **The Paul Revere House**. This simple little three-story house with gray clapboards and leaded-glass, diamond-paned windows looks almost out of place in Boston today, and well it might. Built in 1680, it's the only example left in downtown Boston of 17th-century architecture. Revere lived here from 1770 until 1800, although not with all of his 16 children at the same time. Inside are period furnishings, some original Revere family items and works of silver. Admission. ~ 19 North Square; 617-523-1676.

Next door to Paul Revere's house and entered through the same courtyard is the **Pierce-Hichborn House**. Built about 1711 for glazier Moses Pierce, it's one of the earliest remaining Georgian structures in Boston. It later belonged to Paul Revere's cousin, boatbuilder Nathaniel Hichborn. Admission. ~ 29 North Square; 617-523-2338.

Also in North Square are the **Seamen's Bethel** (12 North Square) and the **Mariner's House** (11 North Square). An anchor over the door announces the Mariner's House, a place where, since 1838, a seaman has always been able to get a cheap meal and a bed for the night. Said the sailor-preacher of the Seamen's Bethel, "I set my bethel in North Square because I learned to set my net where the fish ran." Once a place where sailors worshipped, it's now a rectory office.

On a street noted for "gardens and governors" lived John F. "Honey Fitz" Fitzgerald, one of Boston's Irish "governors," a ward boss, congressman and mayor. His daughter Rose Kennedy was born in this plain brick building at **4 Garden Court Street**.

The **Old North Church** is the one from which the sexton hung two lanterns the night of Paul Revere's midnight ride ("one if by land, two if by sea"). This beautiful church has Palladian windows and a white pulpit inspired by London designs. The four trumpeting cherubim atop the choir loft pilasters were taken from a French pirate ship. Replicas of the steeple's lanterns may be viewed in the adjacent museum. ~ 193 Salem Street; 617-523-6676.

Directly behind Old North Church in the **Paul Revere Mall** stands a life-sized statue of Revere astride his horse—one of the city's most photographed scenes.

On the other side of the mall you'll come to **St. Stephen's Church**, a brick Federal-style church designed by the man who established that style, Charles Bulfinch, America's first native-born architect. The only Bulfinch-designed church still standing in Boston, St. Stephen's has a

✔ CHECK THESE OUT—UNIQUE SIGHTS

- Weigh your fruit, vegetables, meat and seafood on ancient metal scales at the 200-year-old **Haymarket**. *page 163*
- Explore Boston's early history at the **Old State House**, the seat of the British government before the revolution. *page 168*
- Walk on a footbridge through the echoing **Mapparium**, a 30-foot stained-glass globe of the world as it was in the 1930s. *page 203*
- Discover the 1937 **Gropius House** in Lincoln, designed by the founder of the German Bauhaus movement as his family home. *page 223*

bell and copper dome cast by Paul Revere. Inside are wedding-cake-white fluted pillars, balconies and Palladian windows, a pewter chandelier and an 1830s pipe organ. ~ Hanover and Clark streets.

Copp's Hill Burying Ground served as the cemetery for Old North Church in the 17th century. Set high on a little green knoll, it overlooks Boston Harbor and Charlestown, which was bombarded by British guns placed here during the Battle of Bunker Hill. Its simple gray headstones bear pockmarks from British target practice. Buried here are Increase and Cotton Mather, Puritan ministers who wielded considerable political clout. ~ Hull and Snowhill streets.

The widest street in all the North End is Hanover Street, a major center for shops and restaurants. Walking south on Hanover Street leads you straight to the **Haymarket–North End Underpass**, which leads under the Southeast Expressway to downtown. The underpass is lined with bright, primitive mosaics done by North End children, a kind of urban folk art. The walls of the underpass also sport the work of Sidewalk Sam, a well-known local sidewalk artist who paints brightly colored reproductions of works by the Italian masters.

◄ HIDDEN

Boston by Foot gives regular walking tours of the North End, as well as many other neighborhoods. Tours are available from May through October. Fee for tours. ~ 77 North Washington Street; 617-367-2345.

In the Italian North End, you can feast on pasta and regional dishes from one end to the other, stopping at little neighborhood "red-sauce" cafés, plush formal dining rooms or late-night espresso bars. Some of the best deals in Boston dining are here, with many restaurants offering moderate prices.

DINING

Neighborhood regulars favor **Pat's Pushcart Restaurant**, which specializes in northern Italian dishes and also serves up a lot of red sauce. In its casual, speakeasy ambience, the sole homage paid to decor is red tablecloths. But who cares when you can get such wonderful dishes as beef *braciolettini sorrento* and spaghetti marinara at these prices? Dinner only. Closed in July. ~ 61 Endicott Street; 617-523-9616. BUDGET TO MODERATE.

◄ HIDDEN

Mamma Maria's Ristorante is the queen of North End gourmet. Highly regarded, it's set in a ritzy townhouse bedecked with brass chandeliers, mirrors and peach-and-gray walls. An upstairs atrium overlooks Paul Revere's little house. Mamma Maria's menu is refreshingly free of red sauce, featuring the lighter, reduced-sauce dishes of Tuscany and Piedmont, which might include grilled swordfish on a bed of pesto garnished with lobster and baby vegetables. ~ 3 North Square; 617-523-0077. MODERATE TO DELUXE.

Café Paradiso is a favored haunt of local Italians. Downstairs is an espresso bar decorated with hanging plants, mirrors and colorful Italian cakeboxes. The spumoni is handmade, and the *gelato* and *granite* are freshly churned. Upstairs is a secluded, postage-stamp dining room set with white tablecloths, and a menu that offers Northern, Central and Southern Italian dishes. A house specialty is the Paradiso: veal, chicken or shrimp, baked with mushrooms, wine, butter, prosciutto and mozzarella. ~ 255 Hanover Street; 617-742-1768. MODERATE.

Café Vittoria is the most colorful of the espresso bistros. It might have been shipped here straight from Italy, so Old World is it. A massive and ancient espresso machine stands in the window, and latticework, marble floors and a mural of the Italian coast add to the feeling. Here's the place to indulge in a late-night espresso, cappuccino or Italian liqueur, accompanied by gelato or cannoli. ~ 296 Hanover Street; 617-227-7606. BUDGET.

If you can't visit the Sistine Chapel, you can still see its transcendent frescoes covering the ceiling at **Lucia's**. Art critics come to rave and art students to stare in awe. More magnificent ceiling frescoes show Marco Polo's visit to China, the 12 Apostles and the Last Supper. Lucia's chef hails from Abruzzi and prepares specialties from all over Italy, robust to light dishes, something for everyone. Try the *pollo all'Arrabbiata* or *maccheroni all'Arrabbiata* (angry chicken or angry macaroni). ~ 415 Hanover Street; 617-367-2353. MODERATE TO DELUXE.

Pizza is all that's served at **Pizzeria Regina,** and that's fine with the loyal clientele who jam the doorway at lunch and dinner waiting for one of the few tables inside. When you get in, you'll sit on high-backed benches at long, battered, heavy wooden tables, where you'll eat slice after slice of pizza served with pitchers of beer, soda or house wine. The service is fast, if sometimes curt, but that's the North End style. ~ 11½ Thatcher Street; 617-227-0765. BUDGET TO MODERATE.

The main attraction at **Michael's Waterfront** is its wine cellar; it has one of the best wine lists in town. The decor is part '90s-style fern bar and part library, and patrons are encouraged to page through or even borrow the books. Meals vary in quality; meat dishes are usually excellent, but the seafood is sometimes mediocre. ~ 85 Atlantic Avenue; 617-367-6425. MODERATE TO DELUXE.

At **La Famiglia**, the portions are so big and the prices so small, you can't believe it. Locals do believe, and they pack the uproarious place nightly to feast on gargantuan helpings of spaghetti and meatballs, lasagna, linguine with clam sauce and other *delicioso* pasta. As the name suggests, the small, bright low-decor eatery is family-owned. Enjoy the reasonable prices *and* leave with leftovers. ~ 112 Salem Street; 617-367-6711. MODERATE.

SHOPPING The North End is a food lover's shopping dream, chock full of wine and cheese shops and bakeries.

Since **Bova's Bakery**, at the corner of Salem and Prince streets, is open 'round the clock, it's a great place to satisfy late-night hunger pangs. It's also an ideal spot to hear local gossip. The well-connected

Bova family owns shops and apartments all over the North End, and the bakery serves as an apartment-hunters' clearinghouse for folks who are in the know. ~ 134 Salem Street; 617-523-5601.

For a pungent whiff of Old World ambience, head for **Polcari's Coffee Shop**, a tiny shop brimming with open bags of cornmeal and flour, wooden bins of nuts and jars of coffee beans. ~ 105 Salem Street; 617-227-0786.

At **A & J Distributors**, you can pick up almost any Italian cookware you want: pasta racks, painted pasta bowls, pizzaiole and waffle makers. ~ 226 Hanover Street; 617-523-8490.

Mike's Pastry is a popular spot for North End–residing yuppies to pick up a boxful of pastries for breakfast meetings downtown. A warning: The volume of goods available here far outweighs their consistent quality, so take your time to peruse the offerings. ~ 300 Hanover Street; 617-742-3050.

The downtown area comprises several distinct neighborhoods, sprawling around the peninsula and looping around Beacon Hill and the Boston Common. Although Boston's compactness makes it very easy to sightsee on foot, there is no convenient way to see these neighborhoods, and you'll find yourself doubling back more than once.

▼▼▼▼▼▼▼▼▼
Downtown

For visitors who would rather combine all their historic sightseeing into one trip, the **Freedom Trail** links 16 major historic sights from downtown to Beacon Hill, the North End and Charlestown. A walking trail map is available at the **Boston Common Visitor Information Kiosk**, which is conveniently located at the entrance to the Park Street T stop and is within a couple blocks of the stops for all four T lines. ~ 147 Tremont Street; 617-536-4100.

SIGHTS

You can also pick up maps at the **Prudential Visitors Center**. ~ 800 Boylston Street, Prudential Plaza; 617-536-4100, 800-374-7400.

But if you do nothing but walk the Freedom Trail, you will have missed many of Boston's riches. We have chosen to show you a route that covers many more sights than the Freedom Trail: It loops northward from the North End to the old West End, back down through Government Center and Quincy Market, and out to the Waterfront. Then it goes up State Street, down through the Financial District to Chinatown and the Theater District, and finally back up Washington Street to Boston Common. Since all these neighborhoods are so small, there's no need to treat them as separate geographic areas. But when a sight lies within the boundaries of a particular downtown neighborhood, we'll be sure to let you know.

When you come out the North End Underpass, you'll be crossing Blackstone Street, home to **Haymarket** (covering several blocks of Blackstone Street), the country's oldest market, in operation more than 200 years. On weekends, open-air vendors hawk fruits and vegetables, meats, fresh fish and crabs, crowding over several blocks. Ancient hanging metal scales are used to weigh purchases. Prices are good here, but don't try to touch anything without permission—the vendor will scream.

HIDDEN ▶ You'll find the **Boston Stone** easily enough by looking behind the Boston Stone Gift Shop. A round brown stone embedded in the rear corner of the house and dated 1737, it was brought from England and used as a millstone to grind pigment. A tavern keeper named it after the famous London Stone and used it as an advertisement. ~ Marshall and Hanover streets.

Behind Marshall Street is the **Blackstone Block**, tiny alleyways that are the last remnants of Boston's 17th-century byways, the oldest commercial district. Their names, Marsh Lane, Creek Square and Salt Lane, represent the early topography of Boston's landscape.

The **Union Oyster House**, built in the 18th century, became a restaurant in 1826, making it the oldest continuously working restaurant in America. Here Daniel Webster drank a tall tumbler of brandy and water with each half-dozen oysters, and he rarely had fewer than six plates. Before it was a restaurant, exiled French King Louis Phillipe taught French here to wealthy ladies. Upstairs in 1771, Isaiah Thomas published *The Massachusetts Spy*, one of the first newspapers in the United States. ~ 41 Union Street; 617-227-2750.

At the western edge of Boston's peninsula, stretching from the Southeast Expressway to Storrow Drive, is an area that used to be known as the West End. Once rich in many-quilted ethnic groups, it's now a mostly commercialized neighborhood. The area around North Station and the Boston Garden has begun to sprout new restaurants, while a few of the old-time sports bars have become trendy hangouts for a younger crowd.

Located next to the site of the hallowed Boston Garden, the state-of-the-art **FleetCenter** opened in September 1995. With 19,000-plus seats, luxury suites, spacious concourses and air-conditioning, the Center is a far cry from Boston's beloved, but outdated Garden. Home to the Boston Celtics and Bruins, the shiny new FleetCenter still sports the famous parquet floor and banners. ~ 1 FleetCenter, Boston; 617-624-1000.

Not on the peninsula at all, but out in the middle of the Charles River, is the **Museum of Science**, reached via the Charles River Dam. The star of the museum is the state-of-the-art Omni Theater, whose 76-foot domed screen and surrounding sound systems make you feel as though you're actually whizzing down Olympic slopes on skis, moving underwater through the Great Barrier Reef or breaking through the Antarctic's icy underwater depths. The museum also houses live animal exhibits, the Hayden Planetarium and changing

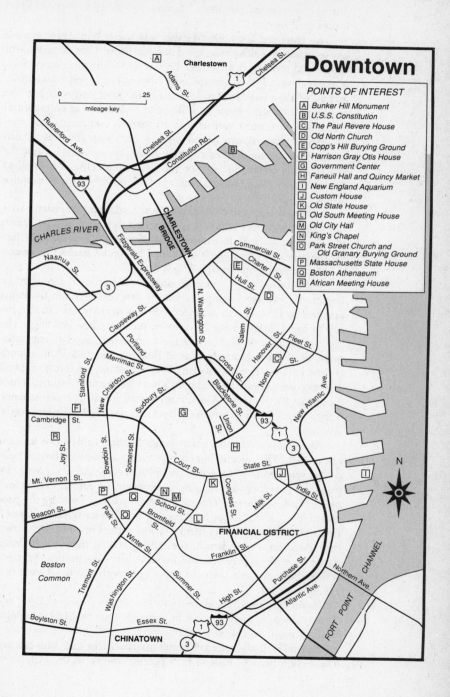

Downtown

POINTS OF INTEREST

- A Bunker Hill Monument
- B U.S.S. Constitution
- C The Paul Revere House
- D Old North Church
- E Copp's Hill Burying Ground
- F Harrison Gray Otis House
- G Government Center
- H Faneuil Hall and Quincy Market
- I New England Aquarium
- J Custom House
- K Old State House
- L Old South Meeting House
- M Old City Hall
- N King's Chapel
- O Park Street Church and
     Old Granary Burying Ground
- P Massachusetts State House
- Q Boston Athenaeum
- R African Meeting House

displays on foreign cultures. Admission. ~ Science Park, O'Brien Highway, Boston; 617-723-2500.

The Harrison Gray Otis House was the first of three Boston houses Charles Bulfinch designed for his friend Otis, a prominent lawyer and member of Congress. Built in 1796, the three-story brick house is classically symmetrical, with rows of evenly spaced windows and a Palladian window. Inside is one of the most gorgeous interiors in Boston, rich with imported wallpapers, opulent swag curtains and carpeting, gilt-framed mirrors, Adams mantels and neoclassical motifs framing every doorway and window. Surviving abuse as a bathhouse, Chinese laundry and rooming house, the building became the headquarters of the Society for the Preservation of New England Antiquities in 1916. Closed Sunday. Admission. ~ 141 Cambridge Street; 617-227-3956.

Right next door is the **Old West Church,** a handsome Federal-style brick building with a cupola and pillars on three stories. The British tore down its original steeple to prevent signaling across the river during the siege of 1776. Rebuilt in 1806, it houses a Charles Fisk organ. ~ 131 Cambridge Street; 617-227-5088.

A short walk up Cambridge Street brings you to Government Center, a sprawling brick plaza with multilevel stairs and fountains designed by I. M. Pei, an architect who was to change the face of the city in the 1960s, leaving his imprint on many key buildings. The plaza contains two of Boston's most important government structures, the **John F. Kennedy Federal Building** and **City Hall,** a modernistic-looking inverted pyramid. An abstract sculpture entitled *Thermopylae,* inspired by Kennedy's book *Profiles in Courage,* stands facing the JFK Building. A mass of twisting forms, it takes its name from a Greek battle in which the Spartans fought the Persians to the last man.

For a figure so flamboyant as **James Michael Curley,** one statue is not enough. The colorful but corrupt Curley dominated Boston politics for years, from 1914 to the late 1940s, serving as mayor, congressman and governor and figuring prominently in Edwin O'Connor's novel *The Last Hurrah.* This four-term mayor was loved by the poor and fond of calling Boston bankers the "State Street Wrecking Crew." Behind City Hall, two very lifelike bronze statues immortalize Curley, one sitting on a park bench, the other standing right on the brick pavement with no pedestal. Tourists have been seen patting the stomach of the standing Curley, so temptingly portly is it. ~ Union and Congress streets.

If you walk down the stairs at the rear of Government Center and across Congress Street, you'll be entering Quincy Market, one of Boston's most popular destinations.

Faneuil Hall was the city's central market in the mid-18th century. The second floor of Faneuil Hall became known as the "Cradle of

Liberty," as it resounded with the patriotic rhetoric of James Otis and Samuel Adams in the years leading to the Revolution. On the fourth floor is a museum and armory of the **Ancient and Honorable Artillery Company**, the nation's oldest military group, founded in 1638. Look up to see the four-foot-long gilded copper grasshopper weathervane, a familiar Boston landmark and symbol. ~ Off Congress Street; 617-338-2323.

Quincy Market is another historic marketplace, built in 1826 by Mayor Josiah Quincy to expand Faneuil Hall. In a move that has been imitated by almost every major city, Quincy Market, along with its twin flanking arcades, the North and South Markets, was renovated in the 1970s into shops and restaurants that have become a major tourist draw for the city. The cobblestoned mall is a street festival by day, a lively nightspot in the later hours. It's wonderfully decorated during the holidays. ~ Off Congress Street.

If you walk out the rear of Quincy Market and under the Southeast Expressway across busy Atlantic Avenue, you'll arrive at the waterfront.

When Atlantic Avenue was built in the 1860s, it sliced right through the center of many of the great old wharves, including **Long Wharf,** the oldest existing one in Boston. Built in 1710, Long Wharf was named for its length—formerly 1800 feet. The British marched up Long Wharf when they occupied the city in 1768, only to retreat back down it when they were evacuated in 1776. Long Wharf also saw the departure of the first missionaries to Hawaii in 1819 and played a role in the 1850s California gold rush, when thousands of New Englanders departed for San Francisco.

Buildings imitating Renaissance palazzos and Greek temples were built in the 19th century along Rowes, India, Central, Long, Commercial, Lewis, Sargent's and Union wharves. **Lewis Wharf,** formerly Clarke's Wharf, was once owned by John Hancock. Nathaniel Hawthorne served as a customs inspector at Long Wharf. By the mid-19th century, the wharves were a center of clipper trade with China, Europe, Australia and Hawaii.

ADVERTISING—EARLY AMERICAN STYLE

Some say the **Steaming Teakettle**, a huge copper kettle hung outside the doorway at 65 Court Street at the edge of Government Center, is America's oldest advertising sign. It once announced the operations of the Oriental Tea Company, Boston's largest tea company. Made by city coppersmiths, it holds 227 gallons, two quarts, one pint and three gills. It gives you a warm feeling to see the teakettle steaming away, especially on a cold day. Ironically, it's now advertising a coffee shop.

Some of the old wharf buildings, which once housed ships' chandlers and sail riggers, have been renovated into shops, offices and restaurants, including the **Pilot House**, **Mercantile Wharf** and **Chart House**, the only surviving late-18th-century building on the waterfront. ~ Off Atlantic Avenue.

Central Wharf is home to the **New England Aquarium**, signaled by a bright red, 45-foot wind sculpture. Bostonians like to congregate to watch the harbor seals in the outdoor pool. Inside, the Giant Ocean Tank is home to 95 species of exotic reef fish, sea turtles, sharks and moray eels. Sea lions perform next door on board the Discovery, a floating theater. Admission. ~ Central Wharf, off Atlantic Avenue; 617-973-5200.

Waterfront Park is a neatly landscaped pocket park with brick walkways and benches that offers a lovely harbor view along with respite. Dedicated to the late matriarch of the Kennedy clan, the Rose Fitzgerald Kennedy Garden is a lovely spot at any time of year, but especially when it is in full bloom early in the summer. It's not far from Mrs. Kennedy's birthplace in the North End. ~ North of Long Wharf on Atlantic Avenue.

From the wharves, you can take cruises of Boston Harbor, a great way to while away an afternoon or evening and see the city skyline. One boat line there is **Boston Harbor Cruises**. ~ 1 Long Wharf; 617-227-4320. Another servicing the harbor is **Massachusetts Bay Lines**. ~ 60 Rowes Wharf; 617-542-8000.

If you're into swashbuckling stories with a bit of history added on, try **Harboring Boston's Mysteries** for an aquatic tour of Boston with a cast of buccaneers and pirates. Closed Tuesday. ~ Long Wharf; 617-542-2525.

From Long Wharf, walk up State Street. In a couple of blocks, you'll come to the granite Greek Revival **Customs House**, built between 1837 and 1847, where inspectors once examined all cargoes arriving at the wharves. Incongruously, this building also became Boston's first skyscraper in 1915, when the great clock tower was added. The clock, broken for many years, was restored in the late 1980s, and its bright blue and gold face now glows handsomely at night, visible from great distances. ~ McKinley Square at State and India streets.

The **Cunard Building** was built in 1902 for the Cunard Steamship Line, owners of the ocean liner *Queen Elizabeth II*. Twin brass anchors flank its doors, festooned with dolphins and seashells. ~ 126 State Street.

The oldest surviving public building in Boston, the **Old State House** is a pretty little brick building dwarfed by the surrounding skyscrapers. The bronze lion and unicorn atop its gables stand as symbols of the English crown. Until the American Revolution, this was the seat of British government. A ring of cobblestones outside marks the site of the Boston Massacre, the signal event launching the Revolution. A museum since 1882, the Old State House features winding galleries of exhibits on the building's history and architecture, early Boston and maritime history, including memo-rabilia, ship's models, paintings and prints. Admission. ~ 206 Washington Street, corner of State Street; 617-720-3290.

Right next door, **National Park Service Visitor Information** has a good selection of maps, tour books and brochures and also sponsors ranger-guided tours to national park sites, including some Freedom Trail stops. ~ 15 State Street; 617-242-5642.

> Countless notables spoke at the Old South Meeting House, including Samuel Adams, John Hancock and, later, Oliver Wendell Holmes.

An outdoor flower market fronting the brick, Colonial-style **Old South Meeting House** adds to its charms. Built in 1729, Old South has high-arching Palladian windows, white pulpit and candlelight chandeliers. Many crucial meetings leading to the American Revolution took place here, including the debate that launched the Boston Tea Party. Though Old South was repeatedly ravaged—the British turned it into a riding school complete with jumping bar, and it was forced to serve as a temporary post office after a devastating fire in 1872—it has been restored to its 18th-century look. Taped presentations re-create the famous Tea Party debate and others. Structural renovations begun in the fall of 1995 are scheduled to be completed by winter of 1997. Admission. ~ 310 Washington Street, corner of Milk Street; 617-482-6439.

Milk Street leads into the heart of the Financial District, a warren of streets stretching south from State Street to High Street and east to Washington Street. Dominated by towering banks and office buildings, the Financial District was considerably built up in the 1980s with bold new buildings, provoking controversy over their design in tradition-minded Boston. One of these—the **Bank of Boston**—is laughingly called Pregnant Alice because of its billowing shape. ~ 100 Federal Street.

In its marching devastation, the Great Fire of 1872 leveled 60 acres of downtown Boston. The spot where the fire was arrested on its northeastward path is noted on a bronze plaque on the front of the U.S. Post Office at Post Office Square, the corner of Milk and Devonshire streets.

Two bonanzas await in the lobby of the **New England Telephone building**. One, a massive mural called *Telephone Men and Women at Work*, circles the rotunda 360 and depicts decades of telephone workers, from 1880s switchboard operators to later engineers, cable layers and information operators. The other reward is Alexander Graham Bell's Garret, a dark little corner filled with memorabilia surrounding the birth of the telephone in Boston in 1875. The garret looks much as it did when Bell worked in it at its original location at 109 Court Street. (A **bronze plaque** at Government Center in front of the John

◄ HIDDEN

F. Kennedy Federal Building marks that spot, where sound was first transmitted over wires in the fifth-floor garret.) ~ 185 Franklin Street.

At 100 Summer Street stands a mobile that looks like a giant yellow lollipop tree, an ebullient surprise in a city where there is not much outdoor public art. Bostonians call it "the lollipops," but its real name is **Helion,** one of a group of pieces called "windflowers" by sculptor Robert Amory.

HIDDEN ►

Walk south down Summer Street, until you come to **South Station.** South Station was a grand old station house in its day, in fact the largest in the world at the turn of the century. After a thorough restoration completed in 1989, this pink granite beauty stands tall and proud. Ionic columns, a balustrade and clock with eagle decorate the curved Beaux-Arts facade stretching for two blocks. South Station today serves as a transportation hub for subway, rail and bus connections. The interior, designed to resemble a European market square, sparkles with polished marble floors and brass railings and is filled with restaurants, shops and pushcart vendors. ~ Summer Street and Atlantic Avenue.

Across the street, you can tour the **Federal Reserve Bank,** which processes millions of dollars worth of currency every day. The Fed's unusual design—it looks like a giant white washboard, and there's a gap where the fifth floor should be—is intended to withstand down drafts and wind pressures. The Fed, which boasts a lobby full of sculpture and murals, also hosts jazz and classical concerts and changing art and crafts exhibits. Call 617-973-3454 for a performance schedule. The Fed is open to the public Monday through Friday; reservations are required for tours. ~ 600 Atlantic Avenue, corner of Summer Street; 617-973-3451.

HIDDEN ►

Winthrop Lane, a tiny brick-lined channel between Arch and Devonshire streets, contains one of the most interesting pieces of public art in Boston, entitled *Boston Bricks: A Celebration of Boston's Past and Present.* In 1985 artists Kate Burke and Gregg Lefevre created bronze reliefs of various Boston personages, scenes and stories and placed them along this red-brick shortcut that's used by folks who work in the financial district. Take the time to peruse the bricks here; you'll recognize some things—the Red Sox, the swan boats in the Public Garden lagoon—and wonder about others.

South Station is just a hop, skip and a jump from **Chinatown,** bounded by Essex and Washington streets and the Southeast Expressway. Compared to Chinatowns in other major cities, Boston's is geographically quite small, just a few blocks long. But this Chinatown was much larger decades earlier, before the Southeast Expressway was built, cutting a wide swath through the district. The Tufts New England Medical Center, too, took a great chunk of Chinatown land when it was built. Now hemmed in by the Expressway and the Combat Zone, Chinatown has little room to grow. But don't be fooled by its physical size: Boston' densely populated Chinatown makes it the third largest Chinese neighborhood in the country.

The Chinese were first brought to Boston to break a shoe industry strike in the 1870s, coming by train from the West Coast. They settled close to South Station because of the convenience of the railroad. First living in tents, the Chinese eventually built houses or moved into places previously inhabited by Syrians, Irish and Italians.

Despite its small size and recent influx of Thai and Vietnamese immigrants, Chinatown is intensely and authentically Chinese. Signs are in Chinese characters, and the area is densely packed with Chinese stores and restaurants. Even the phone booths are covered with Chinese pagodas.

The **Chinatown gates,** a bicentennial gift from Taiwan, stand at the intersection of Beach Street and Surface Road, marking the entrance to Chinatown. White stone with a massive green pagoda on top, they are guarded fore and aft by stone Chinese Foo dogs and sport gold Chinese characters on green marble. The classic characters are not readily translatable in modern Chinese, but they embody such moral principles as propriety, righteousness, modesty and honor.

At the corner of Harrison Avenue and Oak Street is the large **Unity/Community Chinatown Mural,** painted in 1986, which depicts the history of the Chinese in Boston. Among its pigtailed Chinese figures are construction workers, a launderer and women at sewing machines. Other scenes show the Chinese learning to read, protesting to save their housing and gaining access to professional careers.   ◀ HIDDEN

Although you may not want to take one home, you can see live chickens squawking in stacks of wire crates at **Eastern Live Poultry,** where locals line up to buy them "live or dressed." ~ 48 Beach Street; 617-426-5960.   ◀ HIDDEN

Few people know that **Edgar Allan Poe** had a long history in Boston, so in 1989 a memorial bronze plaque was erected to his memory at the corner of Boylston Street and Edgar Allan Poe Way. Born here, Poe was the son of actors at the Boston Theatre. He published his first book, lectured and enlisted in the army in Boston.

The **Grand Lodge of Masons** is decorated with blue and gold mosaics of masonic symbols, and its grand lobby houses a small exhibit of masonic memorabilia. ~ 186 Tremont Street, corner of Boylston Street; 617-426-6040.   ◀ HIDDEN

Walk over to Tremont Street, and head south. In short order you'll be in the Theater District, centered on Tremont Street, Warrenton Avenue and Charles Street South. Boston has a lively and prestigious theater scene, with many tryouts moving on to Broadway. Among the half dozen or so nationally known theaters is the **Colonial,** the oldest continuously operated theater in America, built in 1900. At that time the sumptuously decorated Colonial was considered one of the most elegant theaters in the country, with its 70-foot Italian-marble vestibule and foyer rich with ceiling paintings, cupids, plate mirrors, bronze staircases and carved wood. George M. Cohan, Noel Coward, Fred Astaire, Katharine Hepburn and the Marx Brothers have trod its boards. A 1995 restoration gave the theater a refreshing facelift and brought back the original writing table, located outside the ladies' lounge, that Rodgers & Hammerstein used when they wrote *Oklahoma!* ~ 106 Boylston Street; 617-426-9366.

Formerly the Metropolitan Theater, the splendid **Wang Center for the Performing Arts** was built in 1925 as a palace for first-run movies in the Roaring Twenties. Restored to its original grandeur, it is opulently decorated with gold leaf, crystal, mirrors and Italian marble, and was designed to be reminiscent of the Paris Opera and Versailles. This 3610-seat theater is one of the largest in the world, and has hosted a variety of artists including Yo-Yo Ma, Luciano Pavarotti, Benny Goodman and the Grateful Dead. The Center is listed on the National Register of Historic Places and opens its doors for public tours on selected weekdays. ~ 270 Tremont Street; 617-482-9393.

HIDDEN ►

The **Chinese Culture Institute** opened in 1980. It houses a gallery where rotating exhibits of Chinese paintings, sculpture, ceramics and folk art are shown. The institute also produces concerts, plays, dance recitals and lectures. ~ 276 Tremont Street; 617-542-4599.

At the corner of Tremont Street and Charles Street South, **Eliot Norton Park** stands where Chinatown and the Theater District meet Bay Village. The city completed a much-needed renovation of this urban oasis in August 1994; new lights and green lawns now brighten this once dark, dank and dangerous place. The park is appropriately dedicated to the dean of American drama critics.

Boston's famed **Combat Zone** on lower Washington Street should be added to the endangered species list. As the pace of development quickened in the late 1970s, its former horde of topless lounges, sleazy bars and adult bookstores and movies shrank to a pathetic few blocks that would be the scorn of any true big-city habitué.

Downtown Crossing is the heart of downtown shopping. Lunchtime shoppers crowd the brick pedestrian mall at the corner of Washington and Summer streets, fronting on Macy's and Filene's, one of Boston's oldest department stores. Downtown Crossing is street entertainment at its most diverse. Pushcart vendors and street musicians—one day a Peruvian folk band, the next a rock group—vie for space in the crowded mall. A one-man band is a permanent local fixture.

The **Old Corner Bookstore**, now called the Globe Corner Bookstore, was a literary hub in the mid-19th century (see "Boston Area Bookstores" in this chapter). Covered with billboards in the 1950s, it was once threatened by urban renewal but saved by preservationists. ~ 1 School Street, corner of Washington Street; 617-523-6658.

Old City Hall, a grand French Second Empire building, was renovated in the 1970s into offices and a French restaurant. As one of the first 19th-century Boston buildings to be recycled, it helped spark the preservationist movement. In front of Old City Hall stands the **Franklin Statue**, an eight-foot bronze tribute to Benjamin Franklin. Relief tablets at the base illustrate scenes from his career as printer, scientist and signer of the Declaration of Independence. ~ 45 School Street.

Bromfield Street, a short lane located between Washington and Tremont streets, is chock-full of tiny camera shops, jewelers and watchmakers, stamp traders, pawnshops and a couple of tiny cafés. There are some interesting historical buildings sprinkled along the street, including the home of Revolutionary War hero Thomas Cushing, who held meetings here with the Adamses, Thomas Paine and other cronies.

The **Omni Parker House** is the oldest continuously operating hotel in America, first opening in 1855. Soon after, it became a hangout of the Saturday Club, a literary group whose members included Nathaniel Hawthorne, Ralph Waldo Emerson, Henry Wadsworth Longfellow, James Russell Lowell, Oliver Wendell Holmes and John Greenleaf Whittier. This little group founded the *Atlantic Monthly*. ~ 60 School Street; 617-227-8600.

King's Chapel looks morosely like a mausoleum. Its steeple was never finished, so its Ionic columns flank a bare, squat granite building. The inside, however, is gorgeous, with carved Corinthian columns and pewter chandeliers. The first Anglican church in New England, King's Chapel eventually became the first Unitarian church in the United States. King's Chapel became famous for its music, since it was the first church in Boston to have an organ—the Puritans didn't believe in music at Sunday services. The chapel is open to the public Monday through Saturday from June through Labor Day. It is open Monday, Friday and Saturday the rest of the year. ~ Corner of Tremont and School streets; 617-523-1749.

Beside the church is **King's Chapel Burying Ground**, the oldest cemetery in Boston. It contains the graves of John Winthrop, the colony's first governor, and William Daws, the minuteman who helped Paul Revere warn the colonists the British were coming.

Park Street Church is one of Boston's most beautiful churches, with its white Christopher Wren spire and brick exterior. It was known as Brimstone Corner during the War of 1812 because gun powder was stored in its basement. Here William Lloyd Garrison made his first antislavery speech, and the song "America" was sung for the first time. ~ Park and Tremont streets; 617-523-3383.

Next door is the **Old Granary Burying Ground**, which took its name from a large grain storehouse the Park Street Church replaced. Buried here are Paul Revere, Boston's Mother Goose (Elizabeth Ver Goose, who became known for her nursery rhymes) and three signers of the Declaration of Independence, including John Hancock. You can't see exactly where each is buried, since the headstones were rearranged for the convenience of lawn mowing. Death's heads, skeletons and hourglasses were popular headstone motifs here.

Times have changed considerably at **Boston Common**, a large tract of forested green, America's oldest public park. In 1634, its acres served as pasture for cattle, training grounds for the militia and a public stage for hanging adulterers, Quakers, pirates and witches. A few steps from the visitor kiosk is **Brewer Fountain**, brought from Paris by Gardner Brewer in 1868 for his Beacon Hill home and later donated to the city. Notable among the statuary on the Common is the **Soldiers and Sailors Monument** high on a hill, whose figures represent history and peace.

Today, downtown office workers use the crisscrossing paths as shortcuts to work, and it's a popular spot for jogging, Frisbee-tossing, dog walking, concerts and community events. You might wander into **Park Street Station**, the first station built on the nation's oldest subway, which opened in 1897.

Boston Common is the first jewel in Boston's **Emerald Necklace**, a seven-mile tracery of green that loops through and around the city, all the way to Jamaica Plain, Brookline and Fenway. It was designed in the early 1900s by famed landscape architect Frederick Law Olmsted, who believed that parks could provide a psychological antidote to the noise, stress and artificiality of city life. The Emerald Necklace also includes the Public Garden, the Commonwealth Avenue Mall, the Back Bay Fens, Olmsted Park, Jamaica Pond, Franklin Park and the Arnold Arboretum. The Boston Parks and Recreation Department (617-635-7383) conducts periodic walking and bicycling tours of the entire Emerald Necklace. Other parts of the Necklace will be dealt with under their appropriate neighborhoods.

Leaving the edge of Boston Common, you can walk up Park Street, which brings you to Beacon Hill.

LODGING

A small luxury hotel with 152 rooms, the **Bostonian** stands right next to Faneuil Hall and Quincy Market. In its lobby are two exhibits on early Boston firefighting. Besides one of the city's top-rated restaurants, the Bostonian has a multiple-story terraced atrium. A typical room might have a rose carpet and contemporary furnishings like glass-topped tables and white love seats. The bathroom is spacious, with double sinks and a large oval tub. Six rooms even have hot tubs and fireplaces. Complimentary use of a nearby health club is offered. ~ North and Blackstone streets; 617-523-3600, 800-343-0922, fax 617-523-2454. ULTRA-DELUXE.

The **Boston Harbor Hotel** is simply the most visually stunning hotel to be built in Boston in many years. Set right on the harbor and designed in grand classical style, the brick structure is pierced with an 80-foot archway. The waterfront side is lined with Venetian-style piers and crowned with a copper-domed rotunda observatory. A cobblestone courtyard reaches toward the ornate marble-floored and crystal lobby. Many of the 230 guest rooms have magnificent water views and feature dark wood furniture in a green decor, marble-topped nightstands and paintings of birds. The hotel has a health club and spa, sauna and lap pool, and an award-winning restaurant and bar. ~ 70 Rowes Wharf; 617-439-7000, 800-752-7077, fax 617-345-6799. ULTRA-DELUXE.

One of New England's top-rated hotels, the 288-room **Four Seasons Hotel** overlooks the Public Garden. Interiors reflect the Victorian residential character of Beacon Hill, with a grand staircase leading up from the lobby and, in the rooms, leather-topped writing desks, fresh flowers in the bathroom and marble-topped vanities. Duvets are handed out in winter, and there's a spa, whirlpool, exercise room, masseur and lap pool with a view of Beacon Hill. ~ 200 Boylston Street; 617-338-4400, 800-332-3442, fax 617-426-7199. ULTRA-DELUXE.

The **Hotel Méridien** is one of the country's most highly acclaimed hotels. It opened in 1981 in the former Federal Reserve Bank, built in 1922, a Renaissance Revival granite and limestone structure modeled after a Roman palazzo. Many original interior architectural details remain, including elaborate repoussé bronze doors, gilded, coffered ceilings and sculpted bronze torchières. The Julien Lounge is dominated by two massive N. C. Wyeth murals depicting Abraham Lincoln and George Washington. The hotel has 326 rooms, two restaurants, two bars, an indoor lap pool and health club facilities with whirlpool and sauna. The generous-sized guest rooms are elegantly cozy, with varied color schemes. A matching two-toned silver embroidered sofa and club chair contrast a black lacquer writing desk, and you will find granite vanities and marble floors in the bathrooms. ~ 250 Franklin Street; 617-451-1900, 800-543-4300, fax 617-423-2844. ULTRA-DELUXE.

✔ **CHECK THESE OUT—UNIQUE LODGING**

- *Moderate:* Join budget-minded travelers at **Florence Frances'**, a 150-year-old internationally decorated brownstone in the Fenway. *page 200*
- *Deluxe:* Stay in the heart of Cambridge and enjoy the collegial ambience at the **Harvard Manor House**. *page 215*
- *Deluxe to ultra-deluxe:* Rest your weary bones at **Longfellow's Wayside Inn**, immortalized by America's most famous 19th-century poet. *page 223*
- *Ultra-deluxe:* Situate yourself just steps away from Quincy Market at downtown's legendary and classy **Omni Parker House**. *page 176*

Budget: under $50   Moderate: $50–$90   Deluxe: $90–$120   Ultra-deluxe: over $120

Owned by a Swiss company, the 500-room **Swissôtel Boston** is run with legendary Swiss efficiency and hospitality. Conveniently located to everything, the hotel has every luxury you could ask for: 24-hour room service, bathroom telephones, spa, Olympic-size pool with outdoor terrace, sauna, an exercise room, one restaurant and a lounge, where tea and pastries are served in the afternoon. The decor mixes Colonial and European styles, with impressive antique furniture and paintings, Waterford crystal chandeliers and imported marble. Rooms are smartly finished in green, mocha or rose. ~ 1 Avenue de Lafayette; 617-451-2600, 800-621-9020, fax 617-451-0054. ULTRA-DELUXE.

Omni Parker House is a fabled Boston institution. Many celebrities have stayed here, from Charles Dickens and John Wilkes Booth to Hopalong Cassidy. Its lobby is decorated in the grand old style, with carved wood paneling and gilt moldings, a carved wooden ceiling, bronze repoussé elevator doors and candlelight chandeliers. In the heart of downtown, it's just steps away from Quincy Market. Rooms have writing desks and wing chairs, beige carpeting, pink floral spreads and marble baths. ~ 60 School Street; 617-227-8600, 800-843-6664, fax 617-725-1638. ULTRA-DELUXE.

There are at least half a dozen bed-and-breakfast agencies in Boston, offering accommodations in host homes from downtown to Cambridge and the suburbs.

Bed & Breakfast Associates Bay Colony has rooms in 150 homes, most with continental breakfast and private bath, many offering Waterfront, Midtown, Back Bay or Beacon Hill locations. Accommodations range from a bow-windowed room with pine floors, antique brass bed and fireplace in a South End Victorian townhouse, to Beacon Hill and Back Bay homes close to the Public Garden. One of the best deals for the money. ~ P.O. Box 57166, Babson Park Branch, Boston, MA 02157; 617-449-5302, 800-342-5088, fax 617-449-5958. MODERATE TO DELUXE.

Breakfast is always included in rooms booked through **Greater Boston Hospitality**, which offers dozens of listings, with many in Back Bay, Beacon Hill and Cambridge. Host homes include a converted Georgian carriage house in Brookline and a classic 1890 Back Bay brownstone appointed with 18th-century mahogany furniture and floors and Oriental rugs. Gay-friendly. ~ P.O. Box 1142, Brookline, MA 02146; 617-277-5430, fax 617-277-5430. BUDGET TO DELUXE.

DINING

HIDDEN ▶

Downtown dining covers a wide spectrum, from traditional Yankee bastions to sprightly outdoor cafés and inexpensive ethnic eateries.

Haymarket Pizza fronts right on Haymarket, a weekend open-air food market, and the surrounding crowds make it hard to get in the door. But if you do, you'll find some of the best cheap pizza in Boston. ~ 106 Blackstone Street; 617-723-8585. BUDGET.

The **Commonwealth Brewing Co.** makes its own beer in the basement, serving nine styles of ale on tap. A vast hall lined with huge copper vats, beer kegs, copper-covered tables and a brass-railed bar, the dining room is popular with sports fans from nearby FleetCenter where the Boston Celtics play. You can watch the beer being made behind glass walls (weekend tours available). Chow down on hearty fare like three-alarm chili, steak and fish and chips. ~ 138 Portland Street; 617-523-8383. BUDGET TO MODERATE.

Most tourists walk right by **The Marshall House** on their way to the picturesque Union Oyster House, the famous hostelry just down the street. Locals prefer this less crowded and less expensive alternative in this pocket of cobblestoned streets and brick sidewalks. Large portions of chowder, fish and chips, burgers and icy cold beer, all excellent, are served by friendly staff with thick Bahston accents. ~ 15 Union Street; 617-523-9396. BUDGET TO MODERATE.

◄ HIDDEN

You can't beat the **Union Oyster House** for historic atmosphere. In 1742 it was a dry goods store and in 1775 became a center for fomenting revolutionary activity. The restaurant opened in 1826, and Daniel Webster was fond of slurping down oysters at its U-shaped oyster bar, still standing today. Little alcoves with wooden booths and bare wood tables wend around the several wood-paneled dining rooms, and there are ship's models, a mahogany bar and antique wooden pushcarts in this casual and roisterous eatery. The menu features chowders, seafood and New England shore dinners. ~ 41 Union Street; 617-227-2750. MODERATE TO DELUXE.

Noisy and chaotic, **Durgin Park** is legendary for its rude waitresses and community tables set with red-and-white-checked cloths. A Boston institution founded in 1827, it dispenses such solid and hefty Yankee fare as prime rib, corned beef and cabbage, franks and beans, corn bread and Indian pudding. ~ 30 North Market, Faneuil Hall; 617-227-2038. BUDGET TO DELUXE.

Far above the crowded bustle of Quincy Market, you can dine in removed splendor at **Seasons**, one of Boston's top-rated restaurants. Widely spaced tables, gold-rimmed china, mocha banquettes, crisp white napery and mirrored ceilings add to the mood. A creative New American menu is served, changing seasonally, which might include seared quail with polenta and sausage or roasted monkfish with lobster roe. ~ 9 Blackstone Street at North Street, Faneuil Hall, in the Bostonian Hotel; 617-523-4119. DELUXE TO ULTRA-DELUXE.

Featuring fantastic views of the water and the city, **Cornucopia** showcases innovative New American cuisine. Specialties change with the season, but you can always order a New England lobster dinner. An outdoor café serves lunch and dinner in season. ~ 100 Atlantic Avenue; 617-367-0300. MODERATE TO DELUXE

The **Boston Sail Loft** stretches back and back, out onto the harbor for some wonderful views. Some of the best potato skins in town are to be had here, along with burgers, sandwiches, pastas and fish plates, in a nautical atmosphere. ~ 80 Atlantic Avenue; 617-227-7280. MODERATE TO DELUXE.

The **Chart House** is one of Boston's most historic restaurants. Set on cobblestoned Long Wharf, it was built in 1760 and served as John Hancock's counting house. His black iron safe is embedded in the upstairs dining room wall. The Chart House carries a marine motif all the way, with gilt-framed black-and-white pictures of ships, as well as model ships. Famed for its dense mud pie, Chart House also dishes up hearty steaks and seafood. Dinner only. ~ 60 Long Wharf; 617-227-1576. MODERATE TO ULTRA-DELUXE.

So, you want it kosher? You can get it at the **Milk Street Café**, a cozy Financial District cafeteria that dishes up some of the best inexpensive homemade food in the city: soups, sandwiches, salads, muffins, bread and desserts such as homemade brownies and cookies. Breakfast and lunch. ~ 50 Milk Street; 617-542-3663. BUDGET.

With its tall oak doors lettered in gold, **Tatsukichi** looks like a foreign consulate. The food is just as impressive: almost 50 kinds of sushi and the famed house specialty, *kushiage*, skewers of battered and fried meats and seafood. Dine Japanese-style in a light wood and beige tatami room, or at a Western-style table. ~ 189 State Street; 617-720-2468. MODERATE TO DELUXE.

Julien manages to be both sprightly and elegant, with its impossibly high rose-colored ceilings and massive crystal chandeliers. Wing chairs and rose banquettes guard your privacy, and softly shaded table lamps cast a romantic glow. When the waiter removes the silver cover from your plate with a *"Voilà!"* you'll find a light but vibrant hand has seen to the sauces. The seasonally changing menu emphasizes regional foods, which might include Long Island duckling with yellow vegetable roots or roasted Maine lobster with a lemon, herb, butter and mushroom soufflé. Closed Sunday. ~ 250 Franklin Street, in the Hotel Méridien; 617-451-1900. ULTRA-DELUXE.

The sumptuous surroundings at **Essex Grill** hint at days when the building was an opulent hotel. Ornate columns add to the European-style elegance, while the dining room is a feast of contemporary design. The popular grill, now residing in an office complex, changes weekly and specializes in Mediterranean and seafood dishes such as sautéed scallops and blackened salmon. Closed Sunday. ~ 695 Atlantic Avenue; 617-439-3599. MODERATE TO DELUXE.

HIDDEN ► Five take-out restaurants with open kitchens surround a group of tables at the **Chinatown Eatery**, where the same type of chaos reigns as at a Hong Kong food market. Wall-mounted menus are hand-printed in Chinese and English, and Asians predominate among the diners. Taken together, the restaurants offer some 400 items, covering Szechuan, Hunan, Mandarin and Cantonese cuisines. Open from 11 a.m. til 2 a.m. ~ 44 Beach Street, second floor. BUDGET.

HIDDEN ► The best Chinese seafood restaurant in Boston's tiny Chinatown district is **Chau Chow**. The decor is cafeteria-minimalist, and the well-meaning staff is practically non-English speaking, but Bostonians of all ethnicities ignore the communication problem—they queue up in long lines for fabulous shrimp, crab, sea bass and other delectables. ~ 52 Beach Street; 617-426-6266. BUDGET.

A thoroughly Chinese lobby greets diners at the **Imperial Tea-house** in the heart of Chinatown, with Chinese lanterns and gold dragons. Known for its dim sum, the restaurant also serves Mandarin cuisine to lots of appreciative locals. ~ 70 Beach Street; 617-426-8543. BUDGET TO MODERATE.

Representative of the new Southeast Asian immigration to China-town is **Pho Bolsa**, an inexpensive Vietnamese restaurant that also serves Thai and Chinese cuisine. You can choose from noodle dishes, a variety of soups and excellent seafood entrées. ~ 1 Stuart Street; 617-695-1843. BUDGET TO MODERATE.

China Pearl specializes in Cantonese and Mandarin cuisine. Locals form long lines for their dim sum and seafood specialties. ~ 9 Tyler Street; 617-426-4338. MODERATE.

At **Ho Yuen Ting Seafood Restaurant**, no-frills service and decor don't diminish the excellent seafood specialties: dishes of shrimp, lobster, crab, clams, conch and snails. ~ 13-A Hudson Street, 617-426-2316. MODERATE.

The Blue Diner and the **Art Zone** co-exist to create one of the most unusual restaurants in Boston. The tables are glass-topped, square boxes that each contain the work of a local artist. Some of the funky contents include odd pinball machines, snippets of love letters and ceramic animals. The menu boasts southern barbecue specialties like pulled pork, catfish, fried okra and classic diner fare such as flapjacks, New York egg creams and "wets"—homemade french fries swimming in gravy. Open seven days a week, the diner serves food 'round the clock from Tuesday through Saturday. ~ 150 Kneeland Street; 617-695-0087. MODERATE.

✔ **CHECK THESE OUT—UNIQUE DINING**

- *Budget to moderate:* Overlook the lack of decor at South Boston's **No-Name Restaurant** and enjoy the fresh fish straight off the local fishing boats. *page 210*
- *Moderate to deluxe:* Take in the transcendent frescoes on the ceiling at **Lucia's**, an artful eatery serving tasty Italian cuisine. *page 162*
- *Moderate to deluxe:* Immerse yourself in history at what was once Daniel Webster's favorite oyster bar, the **Union Oyster House**. *page 177*
- *Deluxe to ultra-deluxe:* Play the role of diner at **Upstairs at the Pudding**, located in the infamous Hasty Pudding Club and Theatricals institution. *page 217*

Budget: under $8 Moderate: $8–$16 Deluxe: $16–$24 Ultra-deluxe: over $24

Be sure to ask for a table by the window at **Aujourd'hui** so you will have a view of the Public Garden below. Tables are set with one-of-a-kind antique service plates, complemented by antique paintings and a display of porcelain. The regional American menu features game, poultry and seafood dishes. There's also a low-cholesterol menu. In addition to the regular menu, you can try the "Nightly Tasting Menu," either traditional or vegetarian, which offers five courses of the chef's evening specialties. One block from the theater district, this is a great place for *après*-theater. Dinner only. ~ 200 Boylston Street, in the Four Seasons Hotel; 617-451-1392. DELUXE TO ULTRA-DELUXE.

A bright red railing leads upstairs to Boston's greatest culinary adventure at **Biba**, where chef Lydia Shire and sous-chef Susan Regis are unafraid to create from any palette: Chinese, French, Italian, Indian. Where else would you get lobster satay with green papaya and winter mint or beef short ribs with cumin seeds and cilantro? Her upstairs dining room feasts the eyes, too, with rich colors and primitive Mediterranean motifs set off by yellow walls. The menu is seasonal. ~ 272 Boylston Street; 617-426-7878. DELUXE TO ULTRA-DELUXE.

SHOPPING   Next to the FleetCenter—the last place you'd expect to find a shopping mecca—is **Boomerangs**, a fundraising venue for the AIDS Action Committee that's chock full of recycled housewares and clothing. Brand-name quality goods are also donated by such retailers as Filene's Basement and Urban Outfitters. ~ 60 Canal Street; 617-450-1500.

The biggest tourist shopping mecca in Boston continues to be **Quincy Market**, just a few steps from Faneuil Hall. A Boston marketplace since 1826, Quincy Market is the centerpiece of three shopping arcades filled with more than 150 shops and two dozen food stands and restaurants. Outside the market are a profusion of cheery flower and balloon stands, and under its glass-canopied sides are pushcart vendors selling novelty products. Flanking Quincy Market are two more arcades, the North Market and the South Market. Among the more intriguing shops is **Purple Pizazz** (617-742-6500), where everything is purple—T-shirts, stuffed animals and novelties. And, who could resist **Puzzle People** (617-248-9629), a "maze" of puzzle jewelry, books, jigsaw puzzles and other brain teasers? Also browse **Banana Republic** (617-439-0016), purveyors of travel and safari clothing. **The Nature Company** (617-227-5005) sells animal videos, telescopes, sundials and a wide selection of nature books.

For such a small area, Chinatown has more shops than you might imagine. If you've never experienced Chinese pastries, your mouth will water for them at **Hing Shing Pastry**, where you can see the bakers at work. ~ 67 Beach Street; 617-451-1162

HIDDEN ►

Professional-quality Chinese cooking equipment is sold at **Chin Enterprises, Inc.**, including traditional Chinese chopsticks and two-foot-diameter woks. ~ 33 Harrison Avenue; 617-423-1725.

If there is such a thing as a vintage joke shop, **Jack's Joke Shop** is it. Open since 1922 and still run by the original family, the shop is festooned with dozens of elaborate Halloween masks and wigs, inflatable skeletons and glasses with noses and mustaches. ~ 38 Boylston Street; 617-426-9640.

Downtown Crossing is the heart of downtown shopping. A brick pedestrian mall at the intersection of Washington and Summer streets, it fronts on **Macy's** (formerly Jordan Marsh), one of Boston's oldest department stores. ~ 450 Washington Street; 617-357-3000. Down the street, **Filene's** has been one of its rivals since the mid-19th century. ~ 426 Washington Street; 617-357-2100.

No shopping tour would be complete without a visit to **Filene's Basement**, the country's oldest bargain store, founded in 1908, which has made a legend out of off-price shopping. In the 1940s, 15,000 women once stormed the doors to get the last dresses to leave Paris before the German occupation. Detractors say merchandise slipped during the 1980s, when the Basement opened 22 stores in six states. But the Basement is always crowded with women, who used to try on clothes in the aisles until dressing rooms were installed in 1989, and who don't mind the flaking paint and exposed piping when they can pick up designer dresses for less than ten percent of retail price after three markdowns. Or, on occasion, an $80,000 sable coat for $5000. ~ 426 Washington Street; 617-542-2011.

NIGHTLIFE

Boston's arts scene has rich centuries of history behind it and is expanding all the time. The **Bostix Booth** at Faneuil Hall offers half-price tickets for many performance events on the day of the show, cash only, first-come, first-served. ~ 617-723-5181.

THE BEST BARS   There's a Boston bar for everyone: young singles, bricklayers and stevedores, the State House crowd, Financial District workers, Cambridge academics, sports fans, the Irish.

The **Bell in Hand Tavern** is Boston's oldest tavern, opened in 1795, and retains a cozy, colonial feeling. ~ 45 Union Street; 617-227-2098.

Irish brogues roll so thickly at the **Black Rose** that it sounds like Dublin. Irish beers, Irish folk music and a rollicking good time are house specialties. Cover on the weekends. ~ 160 State Street; 617-742-2286.

The **Last Hurrah**, features a piano player in the early evening with DJ music on the weekend. ~ 60 School Street, in the Omni Parker House; 617-227-8600.

HIDDEN

The **Littlest Bar** is just that—Boston's smallest tavern. There are five stools at the bar and four tiny tables behind them. The noise from the television is often deafening, but this is a fun place to have a quick drink before dinner; most locals haven't heard of it, either. ~ 47 Province Street; 617-523-9766.

NIGHTCLUBS AND CABARETS The **Roxy** is a beautiful and elegant art deco–style club where people like to really dress up. Friday is international night. Dress code. Cover. ~ 279 Tremont Street, in the Tremont House; 617-338-7699.

A view of the city from the 33rd floor is offered at the prosperous **Bay Tower Room**, where a four-piece orchestra plays. ~ 60 State Street; 617-723-1666.

A tropical paradise complete with 20-foot royal palms awaits guests of **Zanzibar**, which offers rock and Top-40 music. Cover. ~ 1 Boylston Place; 617-351-7000.

The **Orpheum Theater** hosts nationally known rock performers. ~ One Hamilton Place off Tremont Street; 617-482-0650.

THEATER AND DANCE Boston's theater district is tightly clustered on lower Tremont Street and several blocks west. Many of these host pre-Broadway tryouts and national touring companies. One such venue is the **Colonial Theatre**. ~ 106 Boylston Street; 617-426-9366. Another worth checking out is the **Shubert Theatre**. ~ 265 Tremont Street; 617-426-4520. Popular contemporary plays are offered by the **Wilbur Theatre**. ~ 246 Tremont Street; 617-423-4008.

The opulent **Wang Center for the Performing Arts**, formerly a Roaring Twenties movie palace, sponsors extravaganzas in dance, theater, music and film. ~ 270 Tremont Street; 617-482-9393.

The **Boston Ballet** performs classics like *The Nutcracker* and contemporary works at the Wang Center. ~ 19 Clarendon Street, Boston; 617-695-6950.

Musical comedies are the specialty at **The Charles Playhouse**. ~ 74–76 Warrenton Street; 617-426-6912. **Stage II** (downstairs) has been home to the country's longest-running nonmusical play, *Shear Madness*, a comedy whodunit. ~ 74–76 Warrenton Street; 617-426-5225.

▼▼▼▼▼▼▼▼▼▼▼
Beacon Hill

Beacon Hill got its name from a beacon that stood atop it in 1634 to warn colonial settlers of danger. "The Hill" used to be much taller; it was leveled by 60 feet to make way for residential building in the 19th century.

After a building boom, Beacon Hill fast became the most elite section of the city, home to doctors, lawyers, writers and intellectuals. Oliver Wendell Holmes called it "the sunny street that holds the sifted few." The first formal residents of the neighborhood were John Singleton Copley and John Hancock. Later residents included Daniel Webster, Louisa May Alcott, William Dean Howells, Henry James and Jenny Lind.

SIGHTS No single section of town is more elegant than Beacon Hill. This charming area still looks like a 19th-century neighborhood with its gas lamps, brick sidewalks and narrow, one-lane streets that wind up and down the hill. Its later brick rowhouses were designed in fine Federal style, with symmetrical windows, fanlight door windows, black shutters and lacy black iron grillwork. Beacon Hill residents love windowboxes and gardens, and many of the houses have beautiful hidden walled gardens. These are opened to the public during the **Hidden Gardens of Beacon Hill** walking tours in the spring, sponsored by the Beacon Hill Garden Club. ~ P.O. Box 302, Charles Street Station, Boston, MA 02114; 617-227-4392.

The crown of Beacon Hill, at its summit, is the **Massachusetts State House**, a grand replacement for the old State House downtown. After the American Revolution, state leaders wanted a more elegant home for the prosperous new government. Charles Bulfinch designed it for them in 1795 in federal style, with a gold dome, brick facade, Palladian windows and white Corinthian columns and trim. A free, weekday tour of the interior is well worthwhile, but be sure to make advance reservations. An impressive rotunda, floors made of 24 kinds of marble, unique "black lace" iron grillwork stair railings, stained-glass windows and decorated vaulted ceilings are all part of the appointments. Don't miss the Sacred Cod in the House of Representatives, a wooden fish hung there in 1784 to symbolize the importance of the fishing industry to Massachusetts. ~ Beacon and Park streets, 617-727-3676.

The **Old Court House**, now the Suffolk County Courthouse, has a grand rotunda with vaulted ceilings decorated with gilt rosettes and figures of cherubs, urns, scrolls and trumpet-blowing figures. Stone caryatids line the rotunda, representing Justice, Fortitude, Punishment, Guilt, Reward, Wisdom, Religion and Virtue. ~ Pemberton Square.

Many come to admire **Louisburg Square**—between Mt. Vernon and Pinckney streets—for its sheer beauty. The centerpiece of the square is a serene oval park with a tall black iron fence, ringed with brick bowfront houses. Louisburg Square looks so much like London that a British film company produced *Vanity Fair* here in the 1920s. Louisa May Alcott lived at number 20.

Although the **Rose Standish Nichols House Museum** was not fashionable for its time, it is a fine example of the late 19th-century row house. Standish Nichols was quite a personage in her day. A noted landscape architect and pacifist, she traveled around the world and was a friend of Woodrow Wilson. Designed by Charles Bulfinch, her home is filled with rare antiques such as Renaissance Flemish tapestries, statuary by noted American sculptor Augustus Saint-Gaudens and unusual imitation leather wallpaper gilded with gold. Tours run frequently from May through October; call for reservations during the winter months. Admission. ~ 55 Mt. Vernon Street; 617-227-6993.

The house at **85 Mt. Vernon Street** was Harrison Gray Otis's second Bulfinch-designed home, while **45 Beacon Street** was his third, an unheard-of extravagance.

A grander library than the **Boston Athenaeum** would be hard to find. The interior features high, vaulted ceilings, pillared archways, scores of marble busts, solid wood reading tables and red-leather, brass-studded armchairs. Founded in 1807 by a group including the Reverend William Emerson, father of Ralph Waldo Emerson, it's one of the country's oldest independent libraries. Its picture gallery and sculpture hall served as Boston's first art museum, and the library still maintains an impressive collection of art today, including works by Gilbert Stuart, John Singer Sargent and Chester Harding. The library is also noted for its collections of 19th-century American prints, Confederate state imprints and books from the libraries of George Washington, General Henry Knox and Jean Louis Cardinal Cheverus. Public tours are given by appointment on Monday through Saturday. ~ 10½ Beacon Street; 617-227-0270.

The **Appleton-Parker Houses**, twin Greek Revival houses alike in every detail, were built for two wealthy merchants. At number 39, Fanny Appleton married Henry Wadsworth Longfellow in 1843. Number 40 is now the home of the Women's City Club. ~ 39–40 Beacon Street.

At 63–64 Beacon Street you can see a few panes of the famous **Beacon Hill purple glass**, with hues caused by a reaction of sunlight. It acquired cachet, along with everything else traditional on "the Hill."

It is intriguing that while most people think of Beacon Hill as a Brahmin bastion, in the 19th century its north slope was the heart of Boston's emerging free black community. Blacks arrived in Boston as slaves in 1638. By 1705, there were more than 400 slaves, and a few free blacks, who settled in the North End. In the 19th century, most blacks lived in the West End, and on Beacon Hill, between Joy and Charles streets. The free blacks worked hard to provide decent housing and education for their own, and to help end slavery.

HIDDEN ►

A number of their houses and public buildings still stand, and you can see them on the 14-stop **Black Heritage Trail**.

Walking tour maps of the trail are available at the Boston Common Visitor Information kiosk and at the **Museum of Afro-American History**, a stop on the trail. The museum is closed on weekends. ~ 46 Joy Street; 617-742-1854.

Among the public buildings on the Black Heritage Trail are the **African Meeting House**, the oldest standing black church in America. Built in 1806, it was known in the abolitionist era as the Black Faneuil Hall. It was here, in 1832, that the New England Anti-Slavery Society was founded, with black leader Frederick Douglass and abolitionists William Lloyd Garrison and Charles Sumner speaking from the platform. ~ 8 Smith Court.

A stirring tribute to the first black regiment recruited for the Civil War stands at the corner of Beacon and Park streets, and marks the start of the Black Heritage Trail. A bas-relief sculpture by Augustus Saint-Gaudens, the **Robert Gould Shaw and 54th Regiment Memorial**

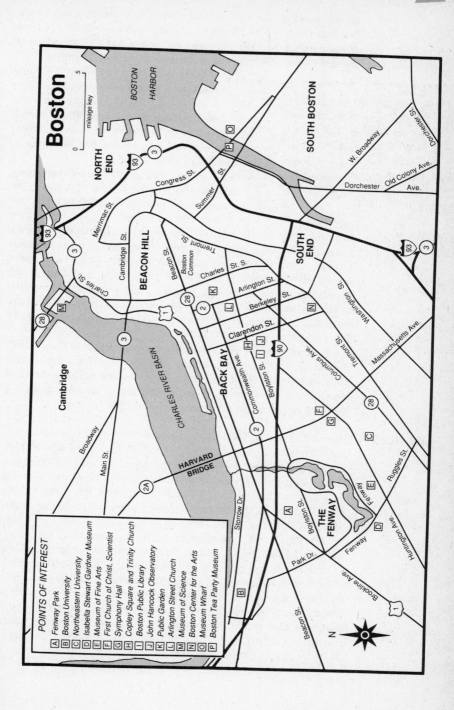

Boston

mileage key
0 ———— 5

BOSTON HARBOR

NORTH END

Congress St.
Summer St.
Merrimac St.
Cambridge St.

BEACON HILL

Beacon St.
Tremont St.
Boston Common

Charles St. S.

Arlington St.
Berkeley St.
Clarendon St.
Boylston St.

BACK BAY

Commonwealth Ave.

Charles St.

CHARLES RIVER BASIN

Cambridge

Broadway
Main St.

HARVARD BRIDGE

Storrow Dr.

SOUTH BOSTON

W. Broadway
Dorchester St.
Dorchester Old Colony Ave.
Ave.

SOUTH END

Washington St.
Massachusetts Ave.
Tremont St.
Columbus Ave.

Ruggles St.

THE FENWAY

Fenway
Park Dr.
Fenway
Huntington Ave.
Brookline Ave.
Beacon St.

Boylston St.

N

POINTS OF INTEREST

- A Fenway Park
- B Boston University
- C Northeastern University
- D Isabella Stewart Gardner Museum
- E Museum of Fine Arts
- F First Church of Christ, Scientist
- G Symphony Hall
- H Copley Square and Trinity Church
- I Boston Public Library
- J John Hancock Observatory
- K Public Garden
- L Arlington Street Church
- M Museum of Science
- N Boston Center for the Arts
- O Museum Wharf
- P Boston Tea Party Museum

shows the regiment on the march with their young white leader, Bostonian Robert Gould Shaw, and an angel flying overhead. The black military role in the Civil War won new recognition with the release of the film *Glory*, which chronicles the story of the 54th Regiment.

The trail also takes you to one of the first schools for black children and to homes built by free blacks, among them the **Lewis and Harriet Hayden House**, which served as an Underground Railway station and was visited by Harriet Beecher Stowe. ~ 66 Phillips Street.

Tiny one-lane **Acorn Street**—just south of Louisburg Square between Cedar and Willow streets—is one of the few old cobblestone streets left on Beacon Hill, and a very picturesque one it is. Coachmen and servants for nearby mansions used to live here.

On an entirely different note, television history is also alive and well in Beacon Hill. Like homing pigeons, all tourists head for "Cheers," so we may as well get it out of the way. The setting for the television show was the **Bull and Finch Pub**, not to be confused with the impostor, Three Cheers, at 390 Congress Street. Even though the Bull and Finch has made such a big business out of all this—selling "Cheers" T-shirts, mugs and hats in the Hampshire House lobby upstairs—it's a bar with real atmosphere. Originally an English pub, it was dismantled and shipped here, complete with old leather and walnut paneling. ~ Downstairs at 84 Beacon Street; 617-227-9605.

Yet another point of television trivia can be found in Beacon Hill. Private eye Spenser of "Spenser for Hire" lived above a Boston firehouse, which he entered through a bright red door. The firehouse is right next to the Charles Street Meeting House on Mount Vernon Street, at the corner of River Street.

LODGING

Beacon Hill Bed & Breakfast, a pretty six-story brick rowhouse, is in a quiet residential neighborhood on the lower slope of Beacon Hill, just two blocks west of Charles Street. Each of the three high-ceilinged guest rooms has a fireplace and a private bath. Most rooms have a view of the Charles River; some look out over the lovely Gothic Revival Church of the Advent, across the street. ~ 27 Brimmer Street; 617-523-7376. DELUXE TO ULTRA-DELUXE.

The **Eliot and Pickett Houses** is a bed-and-breakfast inn in two wonderful 1830s brick townhouses, with a total of 20 bedrooms (nine in Eliot House and eleven in Pickett House). Wall-to-wall carpeting, central air conditioning and rather generic Federal-style reproduction furniture make for a comfortable though not overly quaint inn. Guests may prepare their own meals in the houses' kitchens, and a complimentary breakfast is available daily. Handicapped-accessible rooms are available. ~ 6 Mt. Vernon Place; 617-248-8707, fax 617-367-3237. MODERATE TO DELUXE.

A real find, far less pricey than downtown hotels, is the **John Jeffries House**. It offers 46 spacious studio apartments and suites, most with kitchenettes, in a renovated turn-of-the-century house overlooking Charles Street. Guest quarters are furnished in tasteful pastels, with dark reproduction furniture, large windows and contemporary bathrooms. There is also a large and comfortable lobby. ~ 14 Embankment Road; 617-367-1866. MODERATE TO ULTRA-DELUXE.

Two steps from the State House, **The Black Goose** specializes in provincial Italian cuisine. Take care not to load up on the home-baked *focaccia* bread. Likewise the *caprese* salad, a mound of plum tomatoes, mozzarella and basil. Save room for the tasty entrées—among the menu of pastas and grilled meats and fish are linguine *basilico*, grilled marinated pork loin and Caribbean seafood-chicken stew. Contemporary dash has been added to the dining room, originally part of a historic hotel. ~ 21 Beacon Street; 617-720-4500. MODERATE TO DELUXE.

Along with its chic boutiques, Charles Street is lined with restaurants representing many ethnic cuisines.

Beacon Hill is the last place you'd expect to find supreme cuisine with reasonable prices. But **Rebecca's Restaurant** is such a place, a terrific neighborhood eatery with inventive New American dishes. Its little wood tables and booths are always crowded with locals who come for delights such as grilled salmon with mustard dill vinaigrette and roasted vegetables or veal scallopine with fresh artichoke, mushrooms, lemon and capers in a white vermouth sauce. Go casual or dressy: The mood here is super-relaxed. ~ 21 Charles Street; 617-742-9747. MODERATE TO DELUXE.

Café Bella Vista is a great coffeehouse where you can linger over an espresso or cappuccino and feel welcome in a European way. Its café chairs are always crowded with young students munching on hearty Italian sandwiches. Specialties are fresh *gelato* and desserts such as espresso-bean cake, chocolate-bean cake and *tiramisu*. ~ 30 Charles Street; 617-720-4505. BUDGET.

Good and spicy Thai food stars over the decor at **The King and I**. Start off your meal with *satay* and Thai rolls, then move on to dancing squids, seafood *panang* or any number of chicken, duck, beef, tofu and noodle dishes. ~ 145 Charles Street; 617-227-3320. BUDGET TO MODERATE.

Step into a Tuscan village at **Ristorante Toscano**, whose dining room has exposed brick walls hung with paintings of the Italian countryside and antique Italian cookingware and pottery. Feast on Florentine cuisine including homemade pastas and game dishes. The *tiramisu* is a dessert standout. ~ 47 Charles Street; 617-723-4090. DELUXE TO ULTRA-DELUXE.

SHOPPING   At the foot of Beacon Hill, little Charles Street is thickly lined with antique shops, art galleries and specialty stores.

Quirky bargains lie in store at the **Beacon Hill Thrift Shop**, where Beacon Hill matrons bring their best silver along with bric-a-brac. ~ 15 Charles Street; 617-742-2323.

If you stop by **Rouvalis Flowers** you can take home an exotic plant or flower. The shop has a wonderful selection of topiary trees and orchids as well as unusual ginger and heliconia. Shipping is available. ~ 40 West Cedar Street; 617-720-2266.

Fanciful handcrafted wood items abound at **In the Woods**, from yo-yos and birdhouses to breadboards and garden benches. ~ 102 Charles Street; 617-523-0797.

An amazing selection of beautifully colored and embroidered western-style leather boots awaits at **Helen's Leather**, along with leather coats, briefcases and belts. ~ 110 Charles Street; 617-742-2077.

One of Charles Street's oldest and most respected antique shops is **George Gravert Antiques**, which carries fine antiques. Open Monday through Friday during the summer; call for hours the rest of the year. ~ 122 Charles Street; 617-227-1593.

You ought to be able to find the perfect brass drawer pull at **Period Furniture Hardware**, which carries a full line of reproduction hardware. ~ 123 Charles Street; 617-227-0758.

NIGHTLIFE   Despite its fame as the "Cheers" bar, **Bull and Finch Pub** is a watering hole with character. The venerable English pub features big brews, burgers and an uproarious crowd. ~ Downstairs at 84 Beacon Street; 617-227-9605.

The **Sevens Ale House** is a better Boston neighborhood bar than the nearby Bull and Finch Pub. Decorated in dark, mellowed wood, and with photos of patrons finishing the Boston Marathon and other local events, The Sevens is small and lively, lacks tourists, and is blessed with some of the friendliest staff we've ever met. ~ 77 Charles Street; 617-523-9074.

▼▼▼▼▼▼▼▼▼▼
The Back Bay

Although it started life as a mud flat, Back Bay fast became a fashionable neighborhood. As the city grew, it started running out of room in its original peninsula surrounding Boston Common, so it began filling in the tidal flats of the Back Bay in 1858, the largest land reclamation project of its time. Some 450 acres of marshland were turned into usable land over 20 years.

Given all this room to plan, Back Bay is the only place in town laid out with any perceivable logic. Streets follow an orderly grid, with cross streets named alphabetically for palatial ducal mansions: Arlington, Berkeley, Clarendon, Dartmouth, Exeter, Fairfield, Gloucester and Hereford.

The centerpiece of this grand reclamation project is **Commonwealth Avenue**. Patterned after the Champs Élysées, it's a wide boulevard with a grass strip mall that runs right through the heart of the Back Bay. "Comm Ave," as it's called by natives, is lined with stately brownstones and many historic buildings. Newbury, Beacon and Marlborough streets parallel Comm Ave. Fashionable Newbury Street is lined with chic boutiques, expensive jewelry, fur and clothing stores, art galleries, antique stores and loads of restaurants. Back Bay crosses Massachusetts Avenue, which natives shorten to "Mass Ave," and ends at Kenmore Square.

To the north, the Back Bay ends at the Charles River, where the wide, grassy Esplanade is a popular sunning spot in warm weather. Also on the Esplanade is the **Hatch Memorial Shell**, where the Boston Pops Symphony Orchestra performs summer concerts.

If Boston Common is Boston's Central Park, then the **Public Garden** is its Tuileries, the first botanical garden in the country. Lavishly landscaped with flowers and trees, it's home to the **Swan Boats**, which circle the weeping willow–draped lagoon in season. The famous Swan Boats were launched in 1877 by Robert Paget, who was inspired by the swan-boat scene in Wagner's opera *Lohengrin*. The same family continues to operate them. Also in the Public Garden is some notable statuary: **George Washington** on horseback and abolitionist Wendall Phillips. ~ Bordered by Beacon, Charles, Arlington and Boylston streets.

If you walk straight through the Public Garden gates at the corner of Beacon and Charles streets, you'll come upon **Mrs. Mallard and her brood of eight ducklings** stretched out in a row behind her, all heading for the pond. Placed here in 1987, the bronze, larger-than-life statues represent the ducks made famous in Robert McCloskey's children's story *Make Way for Ducklings*. Every Mother's Day, the ducklings are feted on Duckling Day with a parade and festival sponsored by the Historic Neighborhoods Foundation. ~ 2 Bedford Street; 617-426-1885.

◄ HIDDEN

Ever since opening in 1927, the **Ritz-Carlton** has catered to a select clientele. The 17-story brick building overlooking the Public Garden, while not particularly striking on the outside, is the epitome of old elegance inside, where the lobby is graced with a large curving staircase and antique touches such as an exquisite brass railing. The original owner would never permit a reservation without researching the client's reputation in the Social Register or business directories. Many notable people have lived at the Ritz, including Charles Lindbergh and Winston Churchill. Many more have stayed here, among them Rodgers & Hammerstein, Albert Einstein, the Duke and Duchess of Windsor, Tennessee Williams and John F. Kennedy, even Lassie and Rin Tin Tin. ~ 15 Arlington Street; 617-536-5700.

Down the street, the Georgian-style **Arlington Street Church** features a tall and graceful steeple fashioned in the style of Christopher Wren. ~ Arlington and Boylston streets.

The Beaux-Arts **Berkeley Building** looks like a wedding cake, so curlicued and beribboned is its frothy white bas-relief terra cotta molding. Tiers of windows are trimmed in sea green, and a black marble entrance sign is flanked with dolphins and sea serpents. Built in 1905, it formerly housed Boston's design center and was beautifully restored in 1989. ~ 420 Boylston Street.

There's no better way to view Boston than from the 60-story **John Hancock Observatory**, the tallest building in New England. From 740 feet up, you can see the State House, the White Mountains of New Hampshire and the South Shore. Besides the great view, there are exhibits, a film, photographs and a sound and light show on Boston history. Down on the ground, the Hancock's shimmering glass sides serve as a fantastic mirror, reflecting the surrounding buildings as clearly as a photograph. Admission. ~ 200 Clarendon Street, Copley Square; 617-572-6429.

The **New Old South Church** is where the congregation of the Old South Meeting House moved in 1875, after they decided their Washington Street neighborhood had become too noisy to hear the sermon. The Gothic facade is dominated by a tower and carved stone rosettes. Inside are Venetian mosaics and 15th-century stained-glass windows depicting the Prophets, the Evangelists, the miracles and the parables. ~ Corner of Boylston and Dartmouth streets.

The heart of this area is gorgeous **Copley Square** named for artist John Singleton Copley. Boston's religious and intellectual center at the end of the 19th century, the square is dominated by two architecturally imposing structures, Henry Hobson Richardson's Trinity Church and Charles McKim's Boston Public Library. ~ Boylston Street, located between Clarendon and Dartmouth streets.

The French-Romanesque, medieval-style **Trinity Church**, built in 1877, is visually stunning inside and out. One of Richardson's most brilliant creations, Trinity Church has an enormous tower reminiscent of the domes of Venice and Constantinople. Inside, rich colors and exquisite Moorish details cover the vaulted ceiling, rotunda and walls, and there are John LaFarge frescoes and stained-glass windows. Tours to the public run throughout the summer. Call for arrangements from October through April. ~ 206 Clarendon Street; 617-536-0944.

Much more than a library, the **Boston Public Library** houses art and architectural treasures. A wide marble staircase, Corinthian columns and frescoes grace its grand entrance hall (at the side door). Inside are murals by John Singer Sargent, paintings by John Singleton Copley, sculptures by Augustus and Louis Saint-Gaudens and bronze doors by Daniel Chester French. Inspired by Italian Renaissance palaces, it was opened in 1895. Take time to sit in the lovely central courtyard, where you'll find a fountain and benches. ~ 666 Boylston Street; 617-536-5400.

The grande dame of Boston's vintage hotels is the **Copley Plaza Hotel**, built in 1912 in high Victorian style. It boasts a wide stone facade, whose curving center echoes the bowfront homes of Back Bay and Beacon Hill. Inside, marble and crystal appointments set off an elegant lobby topped with a trompe l'oeil painting of the sky. The internationally known Copley Plaza has served as a resting place for a dozen presidents and European royalty. ~ 138 St. James Avenue; 617-267-5300.

Like the Hancock, the **Skywalk Observatory** at the Prudential Tower gives you a bird's-eye view of downtown, this time a 360 one. Commonly called "the Pru," the Prudential Center was built in the early '60s as another piece of urban renewal. It houses shops and offices, and in front of it is a cast bronze statue called *Quest Eternal*, representing man reaching for the heavens. The tower is accessible for daylight or starlight viewing, from 10 a.m. to 10 p.m. Admission. ~ 800 Boylston Street, Prudential Center; 617-236-3318.

The building at **314 Commonwealth Avenue** was created in the 1920s in an 1899 mansion modeled after a Loire Valley château. Its medieval-looking exterior has sculptured stone cherubs and gargoyles looking down from its battlements. Inside the building are spectacular bas-relief mahogany walls, gold-leaf carved ceilings, stained-glass windows and an ornately carved marble staircase.

Nowhere is the opulence of the Back Bay Victorians more amply evidenced than at the **Gibson House**, now a museum and location of the Victorian Society in America, New England chapter. Built for the prominent Gibson family in 1859, the Italian Renaissance Revival home is richly furnished with gold-embossed wallpaper and black walnut paneling, imported carpets and most of the Gibson family china and porcelain. Tours are available Wednesday through Sunday. Admission. ~ 137 Beacon Street; 617-267-6338.

The **Institute of Contemporary Art** has won an international reputation for its wide-ranging artistic events, held here for more than half a century. Housed in an old Boston firehouse, the ICA often shows experimental or controversial works, among them art exhibits, films, videos, music events, lectures and literary readings. Open Wednesday

THE SKY IS FALLING

When the John Hancock Observatory was built in the late 1960s, architects argued bitterly that the rhomboidal building designed by I. M. Pei would ruin the character of Copley Square. The blue glass windows of this landmark have become collectors' items, ever since they fell out onto the sidewalk in the early 1970s. They were replaced at a cost of more than $8 million.

through Sunday, with special guided tours on Saturday and Sunday. Admission. ~ 955 Boylston Street; 617-266-5152.

A major convention hall, the **John B. Hynes Veterans Memorial Convention Center** was extensively renovated and rebuilt in the late 1980s. Call for a schedule of the numerous conventions and expositions, including a college-fest weekend, bridal expo, and a lumberjack convention! ~ 900 Boylston Street; 617-954-2000.

LODGING

The vintage 1927 **Ritz-Carlton** sparkles after an extensive restoration. A standard room is spacious and airy, with a high ceiling, brown floral drapes and spread and French provincial furnishings. On the walls are prints of antique engravings of Boston and Bunker Hill. The bathroom has polished white marble floors and antique fixtures. Besides an in-house health and fitness facility with sauna and massage, the 278-room Ritz offers complimentary use of a full-service health club nearby. The hotel has two restaurants, an afternoon tea lounge and a bar. ~ 15 Arlington Street; 617-536-5700, 800-241-3333, fax 617-536-1335. ULTRA-DELUXE.

The grande dame of Boston hotels is the **Copley Plaza,** built in 1912. The hotel was famed for throwing such sumptuous affairs as an "Evening in Venice," with gondolas floating on the parquet floor, converted to the Grand Canal. Every president since Taft has stayed here, as well as royalty from eight countries. JFK was a regular visitor. The Copley Plaza's elegant lobby is appointed with coffered gold ceilings decorated with a trompe l'oeil painting of the sky, marble columns and floors, crystal chandeliers and French provincial furniture. The hotel has two restaurants and a lively bar. The 373 bedrooms are decorated with dark period furniture and warm floral patterns, while bathrooms feature vintage marble and chrome fixtures. ~ 138 St. James Avenue; 617-267-5300, 800-822-4200. ULTRA-DELUXE.

Built in 1891, the vintage stone **Copley Square Hotel,** completely renovated, draws lots of families and Europeans to its cozy, friendly 143 rooms. Though the rooms are on the smallish side, they're comfortably appointed with modern furniture and fabrics in blues, greens and mauves. ~ 47 Huntington Avenue; 617-536-9000, 800-225-7062, fax 617-236-0351. ULTRA-DELUXE.

Real working fireplaces add to the considerable vintage charms of the **Lenox Hotel.** Opening at the turn of the century, the 214-room Lenox was popular with such entertainers as Enrico Caruso, who pulled his private streetcar up to the door. The lobby wears its original Gilded Age elegance of soaring white columns, gold-leaf moldings, marble fireplace and handsome royal-blue-and-white decor. A standard room has a Colonial-style chandelier, a rocking chair, high ceilings and a Colonial ambience. ~ 710 Boylston Street; 617-536-5300, 800-225-7676, fax 617-236-0351. ULTRA-DELUXE.

Beacon Inn Guest Houses has 25 less-than-lovely rooms with twin beds; in the summer 30 units are available. Still, these are reasonably priced rooms in the heart of Back Bay, with kitchenettes, air conditioning and private baths. Gay-friendly. ~ 248 Newbury Street; 617-262-1771. MODERATE.

A pretty streetside patio and stately brownstone facade greet guests of the **Newbury Guest House**. Besides its superb location on fashionable Newbury Street, the restored 1882 inn offers 32 guest rooms with pine plank floors, high ceilings and reproduction Victorian furnishings. Some have bay windows, and all have private baths, televisions and telephones—rarities in a small inn. Continental breakfast included. Gay-friendly. ~ 261 Newbury Street; 617-437-7666, fax 617-262-4243. DELUXE.

Popular with gays, **463 Beacon Street Guest House** also draws a mixed clientele. Twenty rooms, all with stove or microwave and refrigerator, make this turn-of-the-century brownstone an excellent value. The five-story walk-up also offers short-term lodging in Back Bay, business services and a laundry. ~ 463 Beacon Street; 617-536-1302, fax 617-247-8876. MODERATE TO DELUXE.

One of the city's smallest, most charming hotels, the **Eliot Suite Hotel** was built in 1925 by the family of Charles Eliot, a Harvard president. The renovated hotel has a warm, welcoming feeling. Its soft green-colored lobby is set with Queen Anne chairs, sofas and crystal wall sconces. Rooms are furnished with antique-style furniture and chintz fabric. Some have kitchenettes. ~ 370 Commonwealth Avenue; 617-267-1607, 800-443-5468, fax 617-536-9114. ULTRA-DELUXE.

◄ HIDDEN

The first independent luxury hotel built in Boston in 40 years, the **Colonnade**, opened in 1971, sparked the citywide hotel building boom a decade later. Recognized for its contemporary European atmosphere, the Colonnade has renovated its 288 rooms with classy mahogany and oak furnishings with copper or rose accents. The hotel has a restaurant as well as Boston's only rooftop pool. ~ 120 Huntington Avenue; 617-424-7000, 800-962-3030, fax 617-424-1717. ULTRA-DELUXE.

For less expensive lodging in Boston, rent a furnished room from **Comma Realty, Inc.**. Units with kitchens, rented weekly, are plain but clean with twin beds and funky bathroom fixtures. ~ 371 Commonwealth Avenue; 617-437-9200.

The circa 1860 **Oasis** caters to a gay crowd but draws a mixed clientele. Sixteen rooms feature antiques and queen-sized beds. Located on a quiet street, the inn serves continental breakfast in the living room. ~ 22 Edgerly Road; 617-267-2262, fax 617-267-1920. MODERATE.

The **Ritz-Carlton Dining Room** offers one of the most serene and traditional dining spots in Boston. Overlooking the Public Garden, this sparkling, elegant place features cobalt blue Dutch crystal chandeliers, French provincial-style furniture, blue-and-gold fringed drapes and swan-shaped table vases in honor of the Swan Boats. The Continental menu changes daily but might include such wonderful entrées as lob-

DINING

ster in bourbon sauce, venison, pheasant or whole dover sole sautéed with pine nuts and lemon butter. There are almost 20 desserts, ranging from *bavorois à l'orange* to *crêpes Suzettes flambées*. The **Roof Garden**, open from May through September, offers open-air continental dining and dancing. ~ 15 Arlington Street; 617-536-5700. DELUXE TO ULTRA-DELUXE.

Though it emulates a Parisian bistro about as successfully as a McDonald's, the **Café de Paris** offers better fare than McD's: croissants, omelettes, crêpes and the best chicken sandwich in Boston, with cafeteria-style service. ~ 19 Arlington Street; 617-247-7121. BUDGET.

High-end Chinese cuisine in a unique setting is what you'll get at **Bernard's at Copley**. Cantonese and Szechuan dishes debut in a tiny formal dining room that looks a bit like a dancefloor with its light-bedecked black ceiling. ~ 545 Boylston Street; 617-236-4040. DELUXE.

Graced with a cathedral ceiling painted with a blue sky and birds, the **Small Planet Bar and Grill** exudes a stylish informality. Here, paella, pastas, stirfries, and innovative sandwiches—grilled portabello mushroom burger with pesto, or a tasty vegetable burger—are among the menu's offerings. Conveniently, the café chairs and tables move outdoors in summer. ~ 565 Boylston Street; 617-536-4477. MODERATE TO DELUXE.

Skipjack's Seafood Emporium boasts one of the biggest and most varied seafood menus in Boston—over two dozen kinds of fresh fish daily, ranging from tuna, trout and salmon to lesser-known moonfish, parrot fish and opakapaka. The decor is far from traditional: glass block and glitzy red and blue neon, and changing exhibits of local artists. ~ 199 Clarendon Street; 617-536-3500. MODERATE TO DELUXE.

Boston's only Hungarian restaurant, the **Café Budapest** has a romantic Old World ambience complete with pianist and violinist, crystal chandeliers, leaded-glass windows and a coat of arms over the fireplace. Try the iced cherry soup or wild mushrooms in paprika sauce for appetizers, followed by any of 38 entrées, including *wienerschnitzel à la Holstein*, sauerbraten, beef *gulyas* or beef stroganoff, and apple and cherry strudel desserts. ~ 90 Exeter Street, in the Copley Square Hotel; 617-734-3388. DELUXE TO ULTRA-DELUXE.

The **Café Promenade** has a light and airy feel to its wide-windowed dining room, with caneback chairs, green, rose and white decor and banks of fresh flowers. A continental cuisine of steaks, seafood and sandwiches is offered. The restaurant serves breakfast, lunch, dinner and Sunday brunch. ~ 120 Huntington Avenue, in the Colonnade Hotel; 617-424-7000. MODERATE TO DELUXE.

Beautiful people dine at **Davio's**, a stylish Italian restaurant with primo service and real panache. Brick walls, white linens and soft lighting create an intimate milieu for superb creations such as crispy duck with gingered noodles and spicy green beans in a blackberry sauce, and Tuscan marinated chicken breast with pepperoncini, kalamata olives, tomatoes and potatoes. ~ 269 Newbury Street; 617-262-4810. DELUXE.

A cozy little basement restaurant, the **Kebab n' Kurry** smells of the spices of India. The tables are set with pink cloths and silk scarves embroidered with lion hunts and elephants, set under glass. Authentic curries from North India, Bombay and South India include chicken, lamb, fish and shrimp and a wide variety of vegetarian dishes. ~ 30 Massachusetts Avenue; 617-536-9835. MODERATE.

If your experience with Asian food begins and ends with chicken fried rice, **Wild Ginger Bistro** is a fun place to try out some unusual tastes. Thai, Korean, Chinese and Japanese foods mix surprisingly well in this small, somewhat stylish (but not at all trendy) café-type restaurant. ~ 95 Massachusetts Avenue; 617-267-2868. MODERATE.

SHOPPING

Back Bay is another of the city's densest shopping districts, concentrated on fashionable Newbury Street, lined from end to end with chic boutiques.

Shreve, Crump & Lowe, a Boston jeweler since 1800, has always been the place to go for fine gold and silver jewelry. ~ 330 Boylston Street; 617-267-9100.

A gold swan sculpture over the door signals the **Women's Educational and Industrial Union,** founded in 1877 by a group of socially concerned women, the same year the Swan Boats set sail. Its shop sells Italian pottery, jewelry, women's accessories, stationery, cards, children's clothing, even antiques. ~ 356 Boylston Street; 617-536-5651.

Shoes with a cluster of plastic bananas à la Carmen Miranda? You'll find them at **Alan Bilzerian,** a chic shop filled with avant-garde clothing for men and women. ~ 34 Newbury Street; 617-536-1001.

Lou Lou's sells old and new tableware from planes, ships, hotels and restaurants. It's fun to browse through this funky store. ~ 121 Newbury Street; 617-859-8593.

London Lace specializes in reproduction Victorian lace patterns made on the only Victorian machinery left in Scotland. Items include lace curtain panels, table runners, tablecloths and antique linens. ~ 167 Newbury Street; 617-267-3506.

The shopping jewel of this area is brass- and marble-bedecked **Copley Place** on upper Huntington Avenue, resplendent with indoor waterfalls and trees. The Copley Place complex also includes the Westin and Marriott hotels, and the shopping mall is in between the two, connected to both hotel lobbies. A glass pedestrian bridge carries shoppers over Huntington Avenue to the Prudential Center.

Opened in the mid-1980s, Copley Place holds 100 upscale stores, anchored by classy Dallas import **Neiman Marcus** (617-536-3660). Copley Place also houses outlets of **Polo–Ralph Lauren** (617-266-

4121), **Gucci** (617-247-3000), **Enrico Celli** (617-247-4881), **Bally of Switzerland** (617-437-1910) and **Louis Vuitton** (617-437-6519).

Who would mind buying used men's and women's clothing when it's as fashionable and "gently worn" as that at **The Closet**? Only the latest clothes in the finest condition are accepted. ~ 175 Newbury Street, downstairs; 617-536-1919.

The **Society of Arts and Crafts** is the oldest nonprofit craft organization in the United States, founded in 1897. At its two galleries you can buy whimsical animal sculptures, papier-mâché masks and furniture with real personality, as well as pottery and jewelry. ~ 175 Newbury Street, 617-266-1810; and 101 Arch Street, 617-345-0033.

With its outrageous cards and T-shirts, screaming toy axes and pounding pop music, **In Touch** puts you in touch with strange gifts. ~ 192 Newbury Street; 617-262-7676.

HIDDEN ▶ Step into **Selletto** for handmade products, always enhanced by piñon and cedar incense, where wares come from a worldwide network of artists. There are wreaths, dried flower arrangements and even hand-carved marble peaches from Tuscany. ~ 244 Newbury Street; 617-424-0656.

Copley Place's much older cousin is the **Prudential Center**, anchored by **Saks Fifth Avenue** (617-262-8500) and **Lord & Taylor** (617-262-6000). The Pru's new look includes a network of glass-roofed pedestrian streets lined with shops.

The best place in town to find cards, prints and posters is **Art to Go-Go** If a poster's not in stock, don't despair—they'll special-order anything for you from their many catalogs. An in-house frame shop with a friendly resident framer is an added plus. ~ 259 Newbury Street; 617-536-3560.

The **Tower Record Building** is a bold, winged stone creation by revolutionary architect Frank O. Gehry. The largest Tower store in the United States, it holds three floors of all the music anyone could want: classical, country, folk, rock, soul, reggae and gospel. ~ 360 Newbury Street; 617-247-5900.

NIGHTLIFE For a special evening drink, head for the dark-paneled **Ritz Bar**, where tradition and Brahmin propriety rule. ~ Ritz-Carlton, 15 Arlington Street; 617-536-5700.

The **Boston Camerata**, formed in 1954, offers medieval, Renaissance and early baroque concerts, both vocal and instrumental. ~ 140 Clarendon Street; 617-262-2092.

The **Lyric Stage Company of Boston**, Boston's oldest resident professional theater company, performs revivals and premieres, and Dylan Thomas' *A Child's Christmas in Wales* every Christmas. ~ 140 Clarendon Street, Copley Square; 617-437-7172.

The ornate **Plaza Bar**, was built in 1912; you can still sidle up to its original brass and wooden bar. There is cabaret from fall to spring, and jazz during the summer months. ~ 138 St. James Avenue, in the Copley Plaza Hotel; 617-267-5300.

Theater-goers and other performing-arts fans may purchase half-price, day-of-show tickets at **Bostix**. Shaped like an enormous webbed wooden mushroom, the booth also serves as a full-service box office and Ticketmaster outlet for performing arts events in and around Boston. ~ On the northwest corner of Copley Square.

For deejay-generated disco music, gays head to **Chaps**. Women are also welcome at this high-energy club which includes a separate lounge off the throbbing dancefloor. Cover. ~ 27 Huntington Avenue; 617-266-7778.

Boston nightlife doesn't get more local than the **Pour House**, where an uproarious underground bar features blues and psychedelic music. ~ 909 Boylston Street; 617-236-1767.

Middle-class disco pleases the middle-class crowds at **Club Nicole** in the Back Bay Hilton's basement. ~ 40 Dalton Street; 617-267-2582.

Housed in a renovated police station, **Division 16** features recorded big band and swing music amidst pink neon, pink walls and art deco wall sconces. ~ 955 Boylston Street; 617-353-0870.

During the Boston Marathon, you can't get in the doors of the **Eliot Lounge**, which is decorated with sports memorabilia and photos and the flags of marathon winners' countries. ~ 370 Commonwealth Avenue, in the Eliot Hotel; 617-262-1078.

The western side of Massachusetts Avenue edges over to the Fenway, the area surrounding the **Back Bay Fens**, another piece of the Emerald Necklace. Fens, from an Old English word meaning low wetlands or marshes, describes the area aptly. Along its sprawling length are several creeks and ponds, a rose garden and private garden plots, remnants of Boston's wartime "Victory Gardens."

▾▾▾▾▾▾▾▾▾▾
The Fenway

No one thinks of the Fenway without **Fenway Park**, the home of the Boston Red Sox and the Green Monster, the famous left-field wall. Fenway Park remains one of the homiest and most old-fashioned ballparks in the country. Built in 1912, it is one of the few baseball parks with a playing surface of real grass. The Green Monster is there to protect the ballfield from the Massachusetts Turnpike, and vice versa. ~ 4 Yawkey Way; 617-267-1700.

SIGHTS

The campuses of two well-known Boston colleges are also in the Fenway—**Boston University**, along Commonwealth Avenue, and **Northeastern University**, south of Huntington Avenue.

Visible from Kenmore Square is the brightly lit, red-white-and-blue **Citgo Sign**, a gasoline advertisement and relic of the 1950s. It is the last of six similar signs in the United States.

Housed in a 15th-century-style Venetian palazzo, the **Isabella Stewart Gardner Museum** is a little jewel of a museum. It contains the

Text continued on page 200.

Boston Area Bookstores

Boston is a book lover's delight, brimming with bookstores full of quirky personality, charm and the imprint of history. These shops display a colorful, individual stamp, with secondhand shelving, hand-lettered signs and perhaps a beat-up leather chair or two or a resident dog.

Boston's most famous literary emporium is the **Globe Corner Bookstore**. In the mid-19th century, it was called the Old Corner Bookstore and was a literary haunt of Hawthorne, Longfellow, Lowell, Emerson and Holmes, as well as Dickens and Thackeray when they were in the United States. Today the store's two floors burst with books about world travel and New England. ~ 1 School Street; 617-523-6658.

The **Brattle Book Shop** claims the title of being the successor to America's oldest continuous antiquarian bookshop, dating from the 18th century. Used books sit on battered gray steel shelving and range from fiction, humor and poetry to history, genealogy and heraldry. Old *Life* magazines dating to 1936 march up the stairway and through history, covered with the faces of Tallulah Bankhead, Betty Grable and Hedy Lamar. ~ 9 West Street; 617-542-0210.

The intimate **Glad Day Bookshop** houses a comprehensive collection of gay and lesbian literature, magazines, newspapers, travel guides and music. The bookstore also hosts monthly readings by authors. ~ 673 Boylston Street; 617-267-3010.

Good food and good books go hand in hand, and never more so than at **Trident Booksellers & Café**. Trident claims the prize for being funky: the province of young hippies dressed in black, a plethora of Third World, gay and alternative publications, and a menu of homemade soups and sandwiches tailored to a struggling writer's budget. It also sells bonsai trees, incense and myrrh, self-improvement videos and campy black-and-white postcards. ~ 338 Newbury Street; 617-267-8688.

An astonishing 25 bookshops surround Harvard Square. Established in 1856, **Schoenhof's Foreign Books, Inc.** is America's oldest comprehensive foreign-language bookstore. It carries reference books in over 240 languages, among them Swahili, Urdu, Tibetan, Navajo and classical Greek and Latin, whatever you need to complete a master's or Ph.D. Still, the shop is not too pedantic to sell children's favorites like *Le Petit Prince* and *Babar*. ~ 76-A Mt. Auburn Street, Cambridge; 617-547-8855.

Where else but Cambridge could a poetry-only bookshop exist? The **Grolier Poetry Book Shop Inc.**, founded in 1927, is America's oldest continuously operating poetry bookshop, carrying over 14,000 titles from all periods and cultures. Supported by friends of Conrad Aiken, who lived next door in 1929, the shop grew into a meeting place for such poets as Ezra Pound, Marianne Moore and T. S. Eliot. The shop sponsors an annual international poetry prize and a reading each semester. ~ 6 Plympton Street; 617-547-4648.

Many Harvard Square bookshops specialize in rare and out-of-print books. Among them is **James & Devon Gray Booksellers** featuring rare books—in any language or on any subject—published before 1700. Among the obscure and hard-to-find volumes are a first edition of Edmund Spenser's *The Faerie Queene* and manuscripts by John Dryden. ~ 12 Arrow Street; 617-868-0752.

For new and used titles on history, philosophy and medieval times, visit **Starr Bookshop, Inc.** You'll also find a concentration of academic books from university presses. ~ 29 Plympton Street; 617-547-6864.

Seven Stars breathes New Age culture. Besides such titles as *Everyday Zen*, *Spiritual Emergency* and *The Dynamics of the Unconscious*, the shop sells Tarot cards, incense and gorgeous chunks of amethyst and other crystals, which some believe have healing powers. The shop sponsors lectures and workshops in yoga, channeling and the meaning of myths and dreams. ~ 58 John F. Kennedy Street, Cambridge; 617-547-1317.

A couple of miles out from Harvard Square, **Kate's Mystery Books** is a mecca for mystery lovers and writers. Opening on Friday the 13th in 1983, the store has a black cat logo and walls lined with several hundred black cat figurines. About 10,000 new and used titles range from Dashiell Hammett and Agatha Christie to Tony Hillerman and Robert Parker. A special section focuses on mysteries set in New England. Mystery Writers of America, New England Chapter, meets here, as does the Spenser Fan Club. Kate's hosts author readings and signings at least once a week. ~ 2211 Massachusetts Avenue, Cambridge; 617-491-2660.

This is just a sampling of Boston's bookstores, large and small. In this area of scholars and writers, there's a bookstore for everyone, with almost 300 listed in the Yellow Pages. That's one for every 2500 inhabitants.

personal collection of Mrs. Isabella Stewart Gardner, amassed over a lifetime of travel to Europe. "Mrs. Jack," as she came to be called, was considered somewhat eccentric and outrageous by proper Bostonians, and she collected what she liked. Her booty includes Italian Renaissance, 17th-century Dutch and 19th-century American paintings, as well as sculpture, textiles, furniture, ceramics, prints and drawings. Admission. ~ 280 The Fenway; 617-566-1401.

Not far from the Gardner Museum is the **Museum of Fine Arts**, world famous for its exceptional collections of Asian, Greek, Roman, European, Egyptian and American art. The MFA also holds impressionist paintings and works by such American masters as John Singer Sargent, John Singleton Copley and Winslow Homer. The MFA regularly attracts mega-exhibitions, such as traveling shows of Renoir and Monet works. Don't miss the Japanese gardens, and the little first-floor café. Admission. ~ 465 Huntington Avenue; 617-267-9300.

LODGING

The Buckminster, a friendly lodging house with 100 rooms, is an inexpensive alternative to the higher-priced inns and hotels in nearby Back Bay. The hotel is on three floors of a nice old building in the heart of the vibrant Kenmore Square area. Rooms and suites tend to be large; all are furnished with reproduction furniture. The Buckminster's prime attraction is its thoughtful convenience to travelers who are staying for more than one night—each floor has a kitchen and full laundry facilities. If only there were hotels like this in every city! ~ 645 Beacon Street; 617-236-7050, 800-727-2825, fax 617-262-0068. MODERATE TO DELUXE.

HIDDEN ►

The best deal for budget-minded travelers in Boston just has to be **Florence Frances'** 150-year-old brownstone with four guest rooms that share baths and priced on the low side of moderate. Florence has traveled around the world and decorated each room individually with an international flair. The Spanish Room, done in red, black and white, has a display of Spanish fans on the wall. The living and sitting rooms are beautifully furnished with antiques and a collection of Royal Doulton figurines. There is also a community kitchen. ~ 458 Park Drive; 617-267-2458. MODERATE.

The **Boston International American Youth Hostel** represents the rock bottom of Boston accommodations, both in terms of price and amenities. Dormitory-style rooms hold six beds, with males and females kept separate. You must provide your own sheets (or rent them), and no alcoholic beverages are allowed. Non-AYH members can stay here by paying a small extra charge for an introductory membership. The hostel can accommodate 190 people. There are laundry and kitchen facilities and a lounge with piano and juice machine. ~ 12 Hemenway Street; 617-536-1027. BUDGET.

The **YMCA** welcomes both male and female guests. Generously appointed, the YMCA has a comfortable wood-paneled lobby, an indoor pool, laundry facilities and cafeteria. But rooms are cell-like and furnished with Salvation Army–style furniture. ~ 316 Huntington Avenue; 617-536-7800. BUDGET.

You'll halfway expect the girl from Ipanema to stroll into **Buteco**, so Brazilian and laid-back is it. Framed photos of Brazil line its white walls, Brazilian music plays softly and tables are simply set with oilcloth covers and fresh yellow primroses. A standout is the *feijoada*—the Brazilian national dish, a stew of black beans with pork, sausage and dried beef, served with rice (available on weekends only). There is also a wide variety of chicken and vegetarian dishes. Also try the homemade soups and desserts, among them caramel custard and guava paste. ~ 130 Jersey Street; 617-247-9508. BUDGET TO MODERATE.

The walls of **Bangkok Cuisine** look like a museum, lavishly covered with elaborate framed pictures of Thai motifs in gold leaf: a peacock, villagers with elephants, Buddhist figures. Warm orange lights and crystal-and-brass chandeliers add to the exotic flair. Entrées include deep-fried whole fish, hot and sour dishes, curry dishes and rice and noodles. ~ 177-A Massachusetts Avenue; 617-262-5377. BUDGET TO MODERATE.

The music of psychedelic '60s groups, '50s jazzmen and other performers of yesteryear rules at **Looney Tunes**, where you can buy used records on the cheap. ~ 1106 Boylston Street; 617-247-2238.

The **Rathskellar**, fondly called the Rat, first showcased The Police and the Talking Heads and is still a loud hole-in-the-wall offering alternative rock bands. Cover for basement shows. ~ 528 Commonwealth Avenue; 617-536-2750.

The **Avalon Ballroom**, one of the city's largest dance clubs, plays progressive and Top-40 sounds for avid dancers, and hosts top names like Eric Clapton and the artist formerly known as Prince. Cover. ~ 15 Lansdowne Street; 617-262-2424

Next door, one of the trendiest dance clubs is **Axis**, which features progressive music. Sunday is gay night, though a real mixed crowd turns out. Cover. ~ 13 Lansdowne Street; 617-262-2437.

The very upscale **Karma** features live jazz on Thursday, international music on Friday and plain old dance music on Saturday. If you want to sidestep the stringent dress code (jackets for men, semi-formal for women) go on Wednesday night, which is gay night. However, you'll still have to be at least 23 years old to get in. Cover. ~ 7 Lansdowne Street; 617-421-9595.

The leather and Levis crowd likes to cruise down to **The Boston Ramrod** There's a special two-stepping night at this gay-only bar which also offers pool. ~ 1254 Boylston Street; 617-266-2986.

A high-energy crowd dances at **Quest** to deejay music on four floors that represent earth, wind, fire and water. Saturday and Monday are gay nights. ~ 1270 Boylston Street; 617-424-7747.

A little farther out of the neighborhood are a couple more clubs. **The Paradise** draws SRO crowds for its national headliners in live rock music and dance. Closed Sunday. ~ 967 Commonwealth Avenue; 617-562-8804.

The Tam O'Shanter always gets the audience dancing with live jazz, blues and rhythm-and-blues in an unpretentious, down-home setting. Cover. ~ 1648 Beacon Street, Brookline; 617-277-0982.

Built around a beautiful flowered courtyard, the Isabella Stewart Gardner Museum offers weekly chamber music concerts from September through May.

CLASSICAL MUSIC & THEATER   Under the direction of Seiji Ozawa, the prestigious **Boston Symphony Orchestra** presents more than 250 concerts annually. ~ 301 Massachusetts Avenue; 617-266-1492.

Its **Boston Pops**, with the youthful Keith Lockhart as conductor, performs lighter favorites in spring and free outdoor summer concerts at the Hatch Shell on the Esplanade.

The Handel and Haydn Society is the country's oldest continuously active performing arts group, started in 1815. They perform instrumental and choral music, and Handel's *Messiah* at Christmas. ~ 300 Massachusetts Avenue; 617-266-3605.

The Huntington Theatre Company, Boston University's resident company, specializes in classics, comedies and musicals. No summer performances. ~ 264 Huntington Avenue; 617-266-3913.

The South End

Boston's largest neighborhood is also the least known. Like the Back Bay, it was built on filled land, preceding Back Bay by more than a decade. Victorian brick row houses rose apace as residences for the middle class and well to do. Today, the South End is listed on the National Register of Historic Places as the largest concentration of such houses in the United States.

After the panic of 1873, banks foreclosed on the area, and those who could afford to moved to Back Bay. The area was carved up into rooming houses and factories and became an immigrant ghetto of more than forty nationalities, notably black, Syrian, Hispanic and Lebanese.

The South End languished for decades, but when Boston's economy rebounded in the 1960s, so did this neighborhood. Since 1965, a new influx of middle-class professionals has renovated old row houses and partly gentrified the area. Not all of the South End has risen again, however, and there are still blighted, unsafe areas. But today the neighborhood is a vital center of artistic activity, and many artists live here. Fashionable shops, restaurants and nightclubs line the main thoroughfares of Columbus Avenue and Tremont Street. The area along Columbus and Shawmut avenues between Massachusetts Avenue and Arlington Street is a largely gay neighborhood with many restaurants and nightclubs. For more information on this area, see "Gay Neighborhoods" below.

The South End stretches hundreds of blocks, bounded roughly by the Southeast Expressway, Herald Street, the tracks of the MBTA's Orange Line and Huntington Avenue. Although the South End is a massive area to explore on foot, annual house tours are given in the fall by the **South End Historical Society**. Admission. ~ 532 Massachusetts Avenue; 617-536-4445.

At the corner of Huntington Avenue and Massachusetts Avenue is the famous **Symphony Hall**. Designed in 1900, it's so acoustically perfect it's known worldwide as a "Stradivarius among halls." The Boston Symphony Orchestra celebrated its 100th anniversary here in 1981. ~ 301 Massachusetts Avenue; 617-266-1492, 800-274-8499.

Across the street is another handsome brick building. **Horticultural Hall** is the third home of the Massachusetts Horticultural Society, the oldest active incorporated society of its kind in America, founded in 1829. The society maintains the largest and finest horticultural library in the world. This 1901 Beaux-Arts building features limestone and terra cotta cornices and moldings ornately carved with fruits and garlands. Closed Sunday. ~ 300 Massachusetts Avenue; 617-536-9280.

The **First Church of Christ, Scientist** is the world headquarters of Christian Science, founded in 1879 by Mary Baker Eddy. The mother church is topped by an imposing dome and set in a brick pedestrian plaza with a reflecting pool designed by I. M. Pei. Take a walk through the echoing **Mapparium** in the Christian Science Monitor building, a unique 30-foot stained-glass globe with a footbridge through it, for a peek at how the world looked in 1935. Tours are available throughout the week and weekend; church services are also open to the public. ~ 175 Huntington Avenue; 617-450-2000.

Once second in size only to the U.S. Capitol, the building that formerly housed the **Chickering Piano Factory**, now a craft guild, has been a Boston landmark since 1853. The pianos made here until 1929 were played not only in Victorian drawing rooms but in the concert halls of Europe and South America. Founder Jonas Chickering was said to be just like his pianos: "upright, grand and square." The building now serves as living, work and exhibition space for artists and musicians. ~ 791 Tremont Street.

◄ *HIDDEN*

Although it has only one guest room, the **Terrace Townehouse** is a hidden jewel. This 1870 townhouse has been richly redecorated; its glowing salmon-painted hallway is hung with 17th- and 18th-century French and English engravings. The French Dining Room (formerly the house dining room, now a guest bedroom) is done entirely in French antiques, including an armoire, crystal chandelier and canopied bed. Breakfast is served in bed on antique china, or on the rooftop garden in the summertime, and tea is served in the library in the afternoon. ~ 60 Chandler Street; 617-350-6520, fax 617-482-8474. DELUXE TO ULTRA-DELUXE.

◄ *HIDDEN*

The **Berkeley Residence/YWCA** offers the most basic budget accommodations for women in the city. No men are allowed outside the public areas. Rooms have twin beds with chenille spreads and battered blond furniture, and bathrooms are down the hall. There are laundry facilities and a cafeteria. ~ 40 Berkeley Street; 617-482-8850. BUDGET.

DINING

Ever since yuppies began moving into the South End in the 1970s and 1980s, restaurants have been springing up left and right, from small inexpensive cafés to upscale eateries.

HIDDEN ►

Don't look for any silverware at **Addis Red Sea Ethiopian Restaurant**, the nation's first authentic Ethiopian restaurant. A very African decor features authentic basketweave straw tables in a bright geometric pattern, low, carved wooden chairs, and paintings of African villagers. Platters of food cover the entire table surface. Ethiopian *injera* bread is served with chicken, lamb, beef and vegetarian dishes. The chef uses all-natural herbs and spices. ~ 544 Tremont Street; 617-426-8727. BUDGET TO MODERATE.

One of the South End's favorite breakfast and lunch hangouts is **Charlie's Sandwich Shoppe**. It's open early in the morning, and it's a great place for home-baked muffins, pancakes, sandwiches, burgers and conviviality, since you'll be sharing a table. Breakfast and lunch only. Closed Sunday. ~ 429 Columbus Avenue; 617-536-7669. BUDGET TO MODERATE.

Anchovies is a tiny Italian restaurant with large wooden booths, murals on the walls and a bar that's very popular with the locals. The menu offers huge plates of pasta and homemade pizzas. ~ 433 Columbus Street; 617-266-5088. BUDGET.

SHOPPING

Some of the city's most fanciful and free-spirited boutiques lie on Tremont Street and Columbus Avenue.

Jesse Jackson's **Sticks and Stems** features delightful warm-weather greenery such as bromeliads and birds of paradise. Jackson grows the beauties on his Palm Beach, Florida property, and personally updates his shop selections every two weeks. Call ahead for hours. ~ 585 Columbus Avenue; 617-247-2274.

NIGHTLIFE

The glitz of L.A. has come to Boston with the **Hard Rock Café**, a temple to rock history filled with such memorabilia as Elvis' white boots and Jimi Hendrix's jacket, and gold and platinum records from many groups. Elvis, Chuck Berry and Jerry Lee Lewis stare down from stained glass. ~ 131 Clarendon Street; 617-424-7625.

Wally's Café is everything that an old-time jazz club should be—small, smoky, dark and host to lots of talented musicians, including plenty of students from the Berklee School of Music, which is just a few blocks away. ~ 427 Massachusetts Avenue; 617-424-1408.

Boston's gay community is continually growing, and its collection of gay spots is always expanding. While gay activities and nightlife are found throughout Boston and Cambridge, the highest concentration is found in several blocks of South End, one of the city's most diverse neighborhoods. Bounded by Columbus and Shawmut avenues, and Arlington Street and Massachusetts Avenue, this area is home to an array of gay restaurants, cafés, bars and nightclubs.

Gay Neighborhoods

If this part of South End reminds you of Beacon Hill, it's no wonder. The same hidden gardens and black iron grillwork decorate many facades. The oval-shaped **Union Park** resembles Beacon Hill's Louisburg Square. **West Rutland Square**, too, is a lovely little landscaped patch.

SIGHTS

If you're interested in learning more about Boston's gay history, pick up a copy of LOCATION: A Historical Map of Lesbian and Gay Boston. It chronicles three centuries of Boston's landmarks and gay leaders, writers and personalities. You can find it at **Glad Day Bookshop**. ~ 673 Boylston Street; 617-267-3010. Or you can order it in the mail by sending $2 to BGLAD (Boston Gay/Lesbian Architects and Designers). ~ 168 West Brookline Street, Boston, MA 02118; 617-859-3055.

The **Boston Center for the Arts**, also known as the Cyclorama, is the center of South End arts activity. Built in 1884 to exhibit a huge circular painting, The Battle of Gettysburg, now in Pennsylvania, it's also where Albert Champion developed the spark plug. Its large rotunda hosts art exhibits, plays, festivals and an annual antique show. ~ 539 Tremont Street; 617-426-5000.

Right next door to the Boston Center for the Arts is the **Mills Gallery**, which specializes in exhibits by South End artists. These might include crafts, sculpture, oil paintings and gouache, and are always intriguing. Closed Monday and Tuesday. ~ 549 Tremont Street; 617-426-7700.

At the very northeast corner of the South End lies **Bay Village**, which used to be known as South Cove, bordered by Arlington, Tremont and Stuart streets and Charles Street South. This cluster of narrow little streets displays the most charmingly antique character in the area. Gaslights stand on the sidewalks outside these Victorian row houses decorated with black shutters and windowboxes, black iron grilled doorways and hidden, sunken gardens in backyards.

Although not everything matches, the tub may be chipped and hallways are narrow and dark, the **Chandler Inn** offers 56 rooms. Rooms are clean and appointed decently enough, in blues and greens and new oak furniture, with all the basic amenities. The bar is a popular gay hangout. Gay-friendly. ~ 26 Chandler Street; 617-482-3450, 800-842-3450, fax 617-542-3428. MODERATE.

LODGING

DINING

Kick back in one of the booths at **Mario's**, a gay restaurant featuring inexpensive Italian food. In addition to pasta, you'll find steak and seafood specials. ~ 69 Church Street; 617-423-6969. BUDGET TO MODERATE.

Decorated in Christmas kitsch, Elvis busts and retro paraphernalia, the **Delux Café and Lounge** features a cheap, eclectic and tasty assortment of pub grub until 11:30 every night. Try the grilled chicken sandwich with homemade chutney, the shepherd's pie or the hot chili. ~ 100 Chandler Street; 617-338-5258. BUDGET.

Geoffrey's Café & Bar is a Parisian-style bistro with crimson walls, oversized French paintings and large picture windows overlooking the street below. Breakfast is served daily until 3 p.m., and there's a wide selection of gourmet salads, sandwiches and tapas. The wine bar is open until midnight. ~ 578 Tremont Street; 617-266-1122. BUDGET TO MODERATE.

A local favorite for fresh, tasty food is the always-crowded **Jae's Café and Grill**. The health-conscious menu travels the Far East with selections from Korea, Japan and Thailand. Try the *karbi* (marinated barbecued beef spareribs), crispy *pad thai* noodles or a sampling of tidbits from the downstairs sushi bar. Indoor or outdoor seating is available. ~ 520 Columbus Avenue; 617-421-9405. BUDGET TO MODERATE.

The charming **Claremont Cafe** is a cozy neighborhood establishment featuring outstanding fare blending South American and Mediterranean cuisine. Entrées include grilled marinated lambchop with Tunisian coriander eggplant puree and braised cod with kalamata olives. The Claremont is also famous for its Sunday brunches. Closed Sunday evening and Monday. ~ 535 Columbus Avenue; 617-247-9001. MODERATE TO DELUXE.

NIGHTLIFE

A gay video bar catering to men and women, the **Luxor** specializes in comedy, classic Hollywood and alternative films. The bar is split into different rooms that you can choose from depending on what you like: dancing, talking or making out. Downstairs, the casual **Jock's Sports Bar** is also frequented by a gay crowd. ~ 69 Church Street; 617-423-6969.

Inside the **Napoleon Club** the gay crowd enjoys show tunes at the downstairs piano bar. Upstairs there's a cover charge for the dance music. ~ 52 Piedmont Street, Bay Village; 617-338-7547.

Jacques' has something for everyone, as long as you enjoy female impersonators mixed with your live rock, jazz and salsa. The clientele is diverse—there are gay, straight and lesbian couples and groups of gawkers. Cover. ~ 79 Broadway, Bay Village; 617-426-8902.

Club Café, an avant-garde club, sponsors nationally known jazz musicians, attracting a gay and straight crowd. Cover for live shows. ~ 209 Columbus Avenue; 617-536-0972.

Fritz, located in the Chandler Inn, is a casual gay bar that's usually crowded with regulars. ~ 26 Chandler Street; 617-482-4428.

At the **Delux Café and Lounge** the cool crowd consists of rockers and artists, both gay and straight. The decor is funky, the drinks are cheap and the music ranges from Frank Sinatra to older punk. ~ 100 Chandler Street; 617-338-5258.

Not to be confused with the South End, South Boston lies directly east of it. Despite its name, South Boston juts farther east into the Atlantic than any other point in the city, cut off from Boston by the Southeast Expressway and the Fort Point Channel. Everyone here calls it "Southie," especially the Irish who call it home.

▼▼▼▼▼▼▼▼▼
South Boston

The Irish poured into South Boston in the early 19th century, attracted by the work opportunities of the glass, iron and shipping industries. They stayed, and today this is the most predominantly Irish community in Boston, evidenced by the riotous St. Patrick's Day parade. The Irish are fiercely proud of their L Street Brownies, a local swim club that has won national publicity for swimming every day, even in January.

Ideally positioned for shipping, the peninsula is lined with commercial fishing and shipping piers. The **Fish Piers**, near the World Trade Center and Jimmy's Harborside on Northern Avenue, are a lively scene at dawn, when the fishing boats return to port to unload their catch. The fresh catch is sold at a lively auction right off the boats to retailers.

SIGHTS

Three bridges link South Boston with downtown: the Summer Street Bridge, the Northern Avenue Bridge and the Congress Street Bridge, with its Chinese lantern–style, wrought-iron lamps.

When you cross the Congress Street Bridge, you may not quite believe your eyes, but the first thing you'll see is a giant milk bottle. The 30-foot **Hood Milk Bottle** was a vintage lunch stand from the 1930s and sells snacks again today.

The Hood Milk Bottle signals the beginning of Museum Wharf, a mini-park of several museums. The Children's Museum and the Computer Museum are both housed in the same brick building, a former wool warehouse whose large windows and wool bays lend themselves nicely to exhibit spaces.

You don't have to be a kid to enjoy the **Children's Museum**, a gigantic toy box filled with four floors of hands-on fun where you can make giant bubbles or play instruments in a rock band. The exhibit on multiculturalism was the first of its kind. Closed Monday during winter. Admission. ~ 300 Congress Street; 617-426-6500.

As the world's only museum devoted solely to computers, the **Computer Museum** aptly dramatizes the swift pace of technology. Forty years of computing history are on display, starting with parts of an early Air Force vacuum-tube computer that occupied a four-story building. There are robots, animated films and a host of microcomputers to play with. To see how computers work, take a stroll through the giant Walk-Through Computer with its 25-foot keyboard and bumper car–sized mouse. Closed Tuesday during winter. Admission. ~ 300 Congress Street; 617-426-2800.

The last member of Museum Wharf is the **Boston Tea Party Ship & Museum,** a floating museum where you can board a two-masted brig and throw your own chest of tea into the harbor (it'll be retrieved by an attached rope for another visitor to heave). Displays here are lively and informative, explaining the events surrounding the 1773 dumping of 342 chests of tea overboard, a tax protest that was one of many spurs to the American Revolution. Open from March through December. Admission. ~ Congress Street Bridge; 617-338-1773.

A spanking white building with a flag-lined boulevard, the **World Trade Center** replaced the drab old Commonwealth Exhibition Hall in the 1980s. It hosts many of Boston's biggest trade shows, including the Boston Boat Show. ~ 164 Northern Avenue; 617-439-5000.

Four kinds of granite decorate the exterior of the **Boston Design Center,** New England's major design center. Architects and designers come here from miles away to search out the latest and chicest in interior designs. Outside the building stands an imposing cast of Auguste Rodin's sculpture *Cybèle*. Closed Saturday and Sunday. ~ 1 Design Center Place; 617-338-5062.

The work of painters, photographers, sculptors and others is on view at the **Fort Point Artists' Community Gallery.** You can also visit individual artists' studios by appointment. Look for them along the 200 to 300 blocks on A Street. Many gallery showings are free and open to the public. Call for showings and times. Closed Monday through Wednesday. ~ 300 Summer Street; 617-423-4299.

Dorchester Heights Monument is where George Washington set up his guns and forced the British to evacuate Boston in 1776, never to return. The British were astounded to see these guns, which had been dragged 300 miles by oxen from Fort Ticonderoga. A 215-foot marble tower marks the spot. ~ 456 West 4th Street; 617-242-5642.

Out at the very tip of South Boston, **Castle Island** is a windswept place of green lawns and high granite ramparts, a fine spot for picnicking and exploring. A series of eight forts has stood here since 1634, making it the oldest continuously fortified site in North America. The island was held by the British during the Revolution until Washington forced them out, from his vantage point at Dorchester Heights. The current fort, the star-shaped **Fort Independence**, was built in 1851. ~ End of Day Boulevard.

On a peninsula just south of South Boston lies Dorchester, once the home of the country's oldest chocolate manufacturer, the Walter Baker Chocolate Factory, founded in 1780. Today Dorchester is a quiet, residential area known for its characteristic three-story houses called triple deckers.

Don't miss the **John F. Kennedy Library and Museum**, a stirring place to visit both inside and out. In a parklike setting by the ocean that JFK loved so well, the striking, glass-walled building was designed by I. M. Pei. The museum houses JFK's papers, photographs, letters and speeches, and personal memorabilia such as his desk and rocking chair. Also housed here are Ernest Hemingway's papers, which may be viewed by appointment. Admission. ~ Columbia Point, Dorchester; 617-929-4523.

> More artists live in the old high-ceilinged, industrial buildings of the Fort Point Channel area than anywhere else in the city.

The **Franklin Park Zoo**, once rated one of the country's ten worst zoos by *Parade* magazine, has made some dramatic improvements. The most impressive is an African Tropical Forest that opened in 1989. Inside the 75-foot-high bubble live tropical birds, antelopes, a pygmy hippo and gorillas, among other tropical denizens. Admission. ~ 1 Franklin Park Road, Roxbury; 617-442-4896.

As you walk east on Northern Avenue, it becomes the Fish Pier, a crowded place of fish processing plants and wharves. Not surprisingly, the Fish Pier is home to a spate of seafood restaurants, some of them among the city's finest.

DINING

Located right here on the Fish Pier, two of Boston's most famous restaurants, Jimmy's Harborside and Anthony's Pier 4, have waged a decades-long battle for supremacy in harborside seafood dining. Both eateries offer a long list of fresh fish, from Boston scrod to steamed, boiled or baked lobster, as well as floor-to-ceiling windows with smashing views of Boston Harbor.

Albanian immigrant Anthony Athanas started life in Boston as a shoeshine boy and built the reputation of his **Anthony's Pier 4** with backbreaking work. The smiling Anthony has posed with Liz Taylor, Red Skelton, Gregory Peck and Richard Nixon, whose photos gaze down from the walls. Despite its fame, Anthony's has its detractors, who say the seafood doesn't live up to its reputation, the expansive dining halls process guests like a factory and the wait for a table is too long. Still, Anthony's has the largest wine list in Boston, and there is outdoor seaside dining on yellow-awninged terraces. ~ 140 Northern Avenue; 617-482-6262. MODERATE TO ULTRA-DELUXE.

We much prefer **Jimmy's Harborside**, founded in 1924 by Greek immigrant Jimmy Doulos, the "Chowder King," whose first customers were fishermen at a nine-stool cafeteria. Since then, President John F. Kennedy, his brother Bobby Kennedy, Tip O'Neill and Bob Hope have dined here, leaving their autographed photos on the wall. The seafood here is served in a nautical decor where the bar is a boat and waiters wear gold-braided blue jackets. ~ 242 Northern Avenue; 617-423-1000. MODERATE TO DELUXE.

The **Daily Catch** helped pioneer the open kitchen. Its Sicilian menu offers more than a dozen fresh New England fishes and shellfish, as well as black pastas made with squid ink. Bare wood tables and paper placemats suit the Fish Pier's working-class ambience. The restaurant also has locations in the North End and Brookline. ~ 261 Northern Avenue; 617-338-3093. MODERATE TO DELUXE.

HIDDEN ►

Largely undiscovered, the **International Food Pavilion** upstairs at the World Trade Center is one of the least expensive places to eat with a view in Boston. It serves cafeteria-style Chinese, Italian and American food at white tables overlooking the harbor. Breakfast and lunch. ~ 164 Northern Avenue; 617-439-5000. BUDGET.

The **No-Name Restaurant** not only has no name, it has no decor either. Famed for the freshness of its fish bought right off the boats, the No-Name always has long lines. ~ 15½ Fish Pier; 617-338-7539. BUDGET TO MODERATE.

▼▼▼▼▼▼▼▼▼▼▼▼
Charlestown

Across the river but still considered part of Boston, Charlestown is an area that has become increasingly popular among the yuppie set. This is the oldest part of town. It was founded in 1630 by a small band of Puritans who later abandoned it, moving across the river to Boston. Much of Charlestown was destroyed by the British in the Battle of Bunker Hill, so few 18th-century houses stand today.

SIGHTS

A walk over the river on the Charlestown Bridge brings you to the Charlestown Navy Yard, the berth of the **U.S.S. Constitution**, the oldest commissioned vessel in the world. It won its nickname of Old Ironsides when British cannon fire bounced off its sturdy oak hull in the War of 1812. A handsome black-and-white frigate, the *Constitution* once required 400 sailors to hoist its sails. While you can tour the decks and down below, lines are always long; try at lunchtime. Admission. ~ 617-242-5670.

Across the yard from Old Ironsides is the **Constitution Museum**, which houses exhibits on Old Ironsides' many voyages and victories, memorabilia and paintings. Admission. ~ Charlestown Navy Yard, Building 22; 617-426-1812.

Nearby is the **Commandant's House**, a handsome brick Federal-style mansion where Navy officers lived. ~ Charlestown Navy Yard.

The **Bunker Hill Monument** actually stands atop Breed's Hill, where the Battle of Bunker Hill was in fact fought. This encounter became legend with the words of Colonel William Prescott to his ammunition-short troops: "Don't fire until you see the whites of their eyes." The cornerstone of the 220-foot Egyptian Revival granite obelisk was laid in 1825 by General Lafayette, with Daniel Webster orating. There are 294 steps to the observatory, which affords a magnificent view of the city and the harbor. ~ 43 Monument Square; 617-242-5641.

Companion exhibits at the **Bunker Hill Pavilion** include a multi-media slide show with 14 screens re-enacting the battle. Admission. ~ 55 Constitution Road; 617-241-7575.

Mention Charlestown to a Bostonian and chances are you'll find yourself at **Olive's**. The food is New England with northern Italian and Mediterranean twists. Reservations are not taken for groups of fewer than six, so expect to wait for a table. Open for dinner only, Tuesday through Saturday. ~ 10 City Square; 617-242-1999. DELUXE TO ULTRA-DELUXE.

DINING

The **Warren Tavern** dates to 1780, and the small, clapboarded house with gaslights was patronized by Paul Revere and George Washington. The inside appears dark and Colonial, with heavy beamed ceiling, wood planked floors, candelabra wall sconces and punched-tin lights, thick lace tablecloths and a roaring fire. The solid fare includes steaks, seafood and a tavern burger with peddler fries. The tavern also makes its own brand of fried bread for dessert. ~ 2 Pleasant Street; 617-241-8142. MODERATE TO DELUXE.

Everyone thinks of Cambridge and Boston together, as if they were two sides of the same coin. While Cambridge is actually a separate city, it lies directly across the Charles River from Boston, and the lives of the two cities are very much entwined, linked by a series of foot and vehicular bridges.

Cambridge

Cambridge was founded in 1630, originally named New Towne, and was the colony's first capital. In 1638, two years after the founding of **Harvard**, the nation's oldest university, the city was renamed after the English university town where many Boston settlers had been educated.

Today Cambridge is still very much an intellectual center, home to Nobel Prize winners, ground-breaking scientists and famous writers, among them John Kenneth Galbraith, David Mamet and Anne Bernays. Cambridge became the heart of what came to be nicknamed "Silicon Valley East" when high-tech companies blossomed here during the 1960s and 1970s, as well as in outlying towns scattered along the Route 128 beltway. These think tanks and computer companies fueled a boom in the Massachusetts economy and its population.

Not all of Cambridge is serious or intellectual. It's given life and vitality by throngs of young students, ragtag protesters handing out leaflets, cult followers and street musicians.

The heartbeat of Cambridge is **Harvard Square**, where life revolves around the many bookstores, coffeeshops, boutiques and newsstands. In the very center stands the **Out of Town Newspapers** kiosk, a Harvard Square landmark for many years, famous for its thousands of national and foreign periodicals. ~ 617-354-7777.

SIGHTS

Right next to it you'll find the **Cambridge Discovery Information Booth**, which dispenses tourist information and walking maps. ~ 617-497-1630.

No one would come to Cambridge without taking a walk through **Harvard Yard**. A stroll of the yard's winding paths, stately trees, grassy quadrangles and handsome brick buildings is a walk through a long history of higher education. Six U.S. presidents have graduated from Harvard.

Enter the main gate by crossing Massachusetts Avenue. On the right, you'll see **Massachusetts Hall**, built in 1718, the college's oldest remaining hall. In the quadrangle of the historic Old Yard, on the left, tucked between Hollis and Stoughton Halls, is a little jewel of a chapel. **Holden Chapel**, built in 1742, has blue gables decorated with scrolled white baroque cornices, ahead of its time in its ornateness.

Along the diagonal path that cuts across Old Yard is the **Statue of John Harvard** by Daniel Chester French, called the statue of the "three lies." Besides giving the wrong date for Harvard's founding, the statue is actually not of John Harvard at all, but of a student model instead; and John Harvard is not the college's founder but its first great benefactor.

Harvard's famed **Widener Library** stands in the New Yard, a massive building with a wide staircase and a pillared portico. With nearly three million books, Widener ranks as the third largest library in the United States, second only to the Library of Congress and the New York Public Library.

Straight across from it is the **Memorial Chapel**, built in 1931 with a Bulfinch-style steeple in memory of the young men of Harvard who died in World War I. Their names are listed in brass on the walls.

Harvard is also home to a spate of museums known the world over for their esoteric collections, including three art museums:

The **Busch-Reisinger Museum** is noted for central and northern European works of art from the late 19th and 20th centuries. Admission. ~ 32 Quincy Street; 617-495-9400.

The **Fogg Art Museum** holds European and American art, with a notable impressionist collection. Admission. ~ 32 Quincy Street; 617-495-9400.

Ancient, Asian and Islamic art are the specialties at the **Sackler Museum**. Admission. ~ 485 Broadway at Quincy; 617-495-9400.

The University Museum consists of four natural history museums. **The Botanical Museum** holds the internationally famed handmade Glass Flowers, showcasing more than 700 species. At the **Museum of Comparative Zoology**, the development of animal life is traced from fossils to modern man. **The Mineralogical and Geological Museum** has a collection of rocks and minerals, including a 3040-carat topaz. **The Peabody Museum of Archaeology** displays artifacts from the world over, including Mayan and American Indian relics. Admission. ~ 26 Oxford Street; 617-495-3045.

Under the spreading chestnut tree/ The village smithy stands;/ The smith a mighty man is he/ With large and sinewy hands. These words from Longfellow's famous poem "The Village Blacksmith" were written about a real blacksmith, who lived in a house in Boston built in 1811. It's now the **Blacksmith House Bakery** with an outdoor café in warm weather and upstairs seating in cooler weather. Old World pastries and cakes are made here the same way they have been for decades. Breakfast, lunch and afternoon tea are served. ~ 56 Brattle Street; 617-354-3036.

Harvard Lampoon Castle, a funny-looking building with a round brick turret and a door painted bright red, yellow and purple, befits

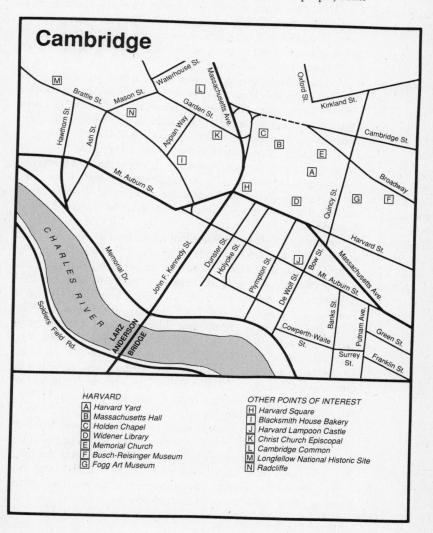

Cambridge

HARVARD
A Harvard Yard
B Massachusetts Hall
C Holden Chapel
D Widener Library
E Memorial Church
F Busch-Reisinger Museum
G Fogg Art Museum

OTHER POINTS OF INTEREST
H Harvard Square
I Blacksmith House Bakery
J Harvard Lampoon Castle
K Christ Church Episcopal
L Cambridge Common
M Longfellow National Historic Site
N Radcliffe

its occupants: the publishers of Harvard's longstanding satirical magazine, the Harvard Lampoon. ~ 57 Mt. Auburn Street at Bow Street.

Christ Church Episcopal, a simple gray-and-white structure with a squat steeple, is Cambridge's oldest church. George and Martha Washington worshipped here on New Year's Eve 1775. ~ Zero Garden Street; 617-876-0200.

The **Longfellow National Historic Site** is where poet Henry Wadsworth Longfellow lived for 45 years and wrote most of his famous works. Painted a cheery yellow and accented with black shutters, the house was built in 1759 for a well-to-do Tory and years later was used by Washington as his headquarters during the siege of Boston. The house has many fine Victorian furnishings, among them Longfellow's desk, quill pen and inkstand. The house also contains Longfellow's personal 10,000-book library and his 600,000-piece collection of family papers. Closed November through April. Admission. ~ 105 Brattle Street; 617-876-4491.

A handsome, slate-blue Georgian house with black shutters, the **Hooper-Lee-Nichols House** was built by a physician named Richard Hooper. Later it was the home of Joseph Lee, a founder of Christ Church, and then the home of George Nichols. Open Tuesday and Thursday. Admission. ~ 159 Brattle Street; 617-547-4252.

The western end of Brattle Street is called **Tory Row** because of the lovely homes built there by wealthy Tories in the 18th century. A fine example is at Number 175, the **Ruggles Fayerweather House**, first the home of Tory George Ruggles, later of patriot Thomas Fayerweather. The house served as an American hospital after the Battle of Bunker Hill.

Just down the street sits **Radcliffe College**, once a women's branch of Harvard but now fully integrated into the university. The gates to **Radcliffe Yard** are entered off Brattle Street, between James Street and Appian Way. As you walk the path, the four graceful brick main buildings of the campus will be in a semicircle to your right. First is **Fay House**, a mansion built in 1807, the administrative center. Next you'll find **Hemenway Gymnasium**, which houses a research center that studies women in society. Third is **Agassiz House**, fronted by white classical pillars, which holds a theater, ballroom and arts office. Last is the college's renowned **Schlesinger Library**, which contains an outstanding collection of books and manuscripts on the history of women in America, including papers of Susan B. Anthony, Julia Ward Howe and Elizabeth Cady Stanton.

Who says taking the subway has to be grim? The newest Red Line stations, opened in the 1980s, showcase major works of art in the country's first and largest program of its kind, **Arts on the Line**. Artworks range from stained-glass walls and bronze sculptures to a bright red windmill sculpture, a shimmering mobile and a whimsical mural of black-and-white cows. A favored piece is *Lost Gloves*, immortalized in bronze along an escalator railing. People inevitably reach out to touch these gloves as they ride.

A few miles east of Harvard Square lies Cambridge's other famous college, the **Massachusetts Institute of Technology** (M.I.T.). Offering a premier education in engineering and technology since 1865, M.I.T. draws students from all over the world, including China, Japan and Vietnam. In distinct contrast to the hallowed ways of Harvard, M.I.T. students are famed for their witty irreverence and contests they to outdo each other in intellectual pranks. One of their episodes involved placing a car on top of a campus building. Fittingly, the campus looks modern and high tech, with geometrical buildings designed by Eero Saarinen.

LODGING

Set in an office tower and shopping complex, the 296-room **Charles Hotel** is just steps away from Harvard Square. Rooms are styled in grays and blues, with a Shaker-style bed, upholstered loveseat and armchair, and new oak armoire. The gray-tiled bath has a second phone and TV and pink-and-gray marble counters. There are two restaurants and one of the city's best jazz bars, as well as a health spa with steam room, sauna and whirlpool. ~ 1 Bennett Street at Eliot Street; 617-864-1200, 800-637-7200, fax 617-864-9715. ULTRA-DELUXE.

A relatively inexpensive but still convenient place to stay in Cambridge is the **Harvard Manor House**. Although some rooms are on the smallish side, this 72-room private hotel has nicely appointed digs with contemporary furniture and floral spreads. ~ 110 Mt. Auburn Street; 617-864-5200, 800-458-5886, fax 617-864-2409. DELUXE.

The **Inn at Harvard** is the new kid on the block. It's wonderfully situated, a couple blocks from Harvard Square. The label "inn" seems a little inappropriate, however, since it's more of a standard hotel (in fact, it's a Doubletree property). Even so, it has its charms; there's a wonderful atrium lobby area that's four stories high, open to balconies and guest rooms, very much like a Renaissance palazzo. The 113 rooms are well appointed with cherry furnishings and original artwork from the Harvard Fogg Museum. ~ 1201 Massachusetts Avenue; 617-491-2222, 800-222-8733, fax 617-491-6520. ULTRA-DELUXE.

Some of the least expensive, albeit plainest, accommodations are to be had at the **Irving House** near Harvard Square. This woodframe

WASHINGTON'S COMMAND

Under an elm tree on the grassy **Cambridge Common**, General Washington took command of the Continental Army in 1775. A plaque and monument to Washington mark this spot. Nearby are three old black cannons, abandoned by the British at Fort Independence when they evacuated in 1776. ~ Massachusetts Avenue and Garden Street.

walk-up offers 58 plain but clean rooms. Your best bets are the top floor units featuring skylights, private baths and wall-to-wall carpets. ~ 24 Irving Street; 617-354-8249, 800-854-8249, fax 617-576-2814. MODERATE.

Look for some 20 artworks from the Arts on the Line Project at the Harvard, Porter, Davis and Alewife T stations.

The stepped, pyramidal walls of the **Hyatt Regency Cambridge** sit right on the banks of the Charles River, offering splendid views of the Boston skyline from many rooms. A 14-story atrium lobby has a semitropical feeling, from the Australian finches in a glass cage to a large fountain and towering potted plants and trees. Lighted glass elevators whoosh you up through the atrium, past a trompe l'oeil mural of an Italian villa and a 100-foot-high glass wall. The 469-room hotel has two restaurants, a lap pool and a health club with sauna, whirlpool and steam bath. The fair-sized rooms have natural woods, contemporary furnishings and carpeting, plus marble vanities in the bathroom. ~ 575 Memorial Drive; 617-492-1234, 800-233-1234. ULTRA-DELUXE.

HIDDEN ►

A 20-minute walk from Harvard Square, **A Cambridge House** is a special place to stay. A private home built in 1892 with a wide pillared porch, it's listed on the National Historic Register. Beautifully restored and richly furnished with floral print fabrics, patterned wallpapers, period antiques and Oriental rugs, the living room, den and dining room offer guests luxurious spaces. Each of the 16 rooms is individually decorated with antiques. The room we saw had a canopied bed with a white lace duvet and a working fireplace. A full breakfast is complimentary. ~ 2218 Massachusetts Avenue; 617-491-6300, 800-232-9989, fax 617-868-2848. DELUXE TO ULTRA-DELUXE.

DINING

A retrofit, '50s-style decor of diner stools, neon and a black-and-white-tiled floor enlivens the **East Coast Grill**. The southern grilled ribs, pork and chicken are served with coleslaw, baked beans, corn bread and watermelon, and hot drinks to match: blue, green and gold margaritas. Appetizers are equally muscular, notably the "sausage from hell." Leave room for chocolate mayonnaise cake. Dinner only. ~ 1271 Cambridge Street; 617-491-6568. MODERATE.

Next door, East Coast Grill operates a take-out stand, **Jake & Earl's Dixie Barbecue**, serving the same menu at budget prices. *People* magazine hailed it as one of America's ten best barbecue joints, and who are we to argue? Presided over by a plastic bust of Elvis, Jake and Earl's hews to such "barbecue rules to live by" as, "If it ain't got smoke, it's a joke!" ~ 1273 Cambridge Street; 617-491-7427. BUDGET.

It would be hard to find a friendlier place than the **Casa Portugal**, one of only a handful of Boston Portuguese restaurants. Imbibe the Latin mood set by black iron lanterns, red-vested waiters and folk art murals of bullfights and musicians. *Chourico* arrives in a small, flaming grill, followed by spicy dinners of marinated pork cubes with potatoes or mussels, linguica and onions, and squid stew, all served with thickly cut Portuguese french fries. There's a good selection of Portuguese wines and beers, and espresso and cappuccino to top it all off. ~ 1200 Cambridge Street; 617-491-8880. MODERATE.

Just over the Cambridge-Somerville line, in a somewhat scruffy neighborhood, **Dalí** has the best Spanish food in the metropolitan area. Make a meal of several different *tapas* and a bottle of hearty Iberian wine. Dinner only. ~ 415 Washington Street, Somerville; 617-661-3254. MODERATE TO DELUXE.

◄ HIDDEN

The family-owned **La Groceria** looks like an Italian trattoria, with its striped awning, lattice ceiling and exposed brick wall. Famed for its hot antipasti and homemade pasta, La Groceria does old-style Northern Italian dishes such as lasagna, eggplant parmigiana and a seafood marinara that must be eaten to be believed. Its splendid dessert case offers cannoli, *tartufo* and *zuppa inglese*. Ask for the Godfather Family room, a beaded alcove, if it's available. ~ 853 Main Street; 617-876-4162. MODERATE TO DELUXE.

African folk art hangs on the walls of the green, black and white dining room of **Asmara,** one of the many Ethiopian eateries in Greater Boston. Chicken, lamb, beef, fish and vegetarian entrées are to be eaten without silverware, in the Ethiopian manner. ~ 739 Massachusetts Avenue; 617-864-7447. BUDGET.

The owners of **The Harvest** researched European cafés to come up with their decor mixing brightly patterned upholstered banquettes with wooden shutters and tables and a Parisian bar. There is also a fenced-in terrace for dining during the summer. The clientele is ultra-Cambridge—you'll sit next to architects and psychiatrists. The more formal dining room is quieter than the café, and changes color schemes with the season. The menu features American game and seafood. It changes daily at the moderate-priced café, weekly at the deluxe-to-ultra-deluxe-priced dining room. ~ 44 Brattle Street; 617-492-1115. MODERATE TO ULTRA-DELUXE.

Upstairs at the Pudding is located at the home of a Harvard institution, the Hasty Pudding Club and Theatricals. The stairway and dining room walls are a gallery of old theatrical posters from Pudding productions dating to the 1800s. Despite its emerald green walls and pink tablecloths, the dining room has the casual feel of a historic college dining room. Upstairs at the Pudding offers one of the top dining experiences in Greater Boston, mixing Northern Italian cuisine with seasonal ingredients from seven continents. Menu selections include fresh local seafood, rack of lamb and venison. While the fixed-price menu is tabbed ultra-deluxe, an à la carte menu is available for mere deluxe prices. ~ 10 Holyoke Street; 617-864-1933. DELUXE TO ULTRA-DELUXE.

The **Coffee Connection** serves the best coffee in Greater Boston, and the most varieties of it. There are also teas, cocoas and European pastries. Small and intimate, the Coffee Connection is permeated with the thick aroma of fresh-roasted beans. There's almost always a wait at this popular coffeehouse. ~ In The Garage, 36 John F. Kennedy Street; 617-492-4881. BUDGET.

HIDDEN ►   Run by a group of transplanted Londoners, **Shay's** is a fairly authentic English-style pub right in the heart of Crimson territory, with a good selection of U.S. and U.K. draught beers and pub grub. ~ 58 John F. Kennedy Street; 617-864-9161. BUDGET TO MODERATE.

The **Algiers Coffeehouse** is one of Cambridge's most Bohemian eateries. With its 50-foot domed ceiling, white stucco walls and copper embellishments, it feels like a cross between a Moroccan palace and a mosque. The menu has a Middle Eastern flavor, with lentil falafel and *baba ganoosh*. An immense lunch buffet is available Monday through Friday. There are 16 kinds of coffees and hot drinks, teas, iced drinks and Arabic pastries. ~ 40 Brattle Street; 617-492-1557. BUDGET.

HIDDEN ►   Tucked a few blocks away from busy Harvard Square, **Café Pamplona** is a tiny basement-level café that serves Spanish dishes, pastries and strong coffee. During the summer, there are a few tables outside on a brick patio. ~ 25 Arrow Street; no phone. BUDGET TO MODERATE.

HIDDEN ►   **Troyka** is a real Russian restaurant. Even if its interior has the unfortunate look of a gulag dining hall, its hearty peasant fare includes borscht, piroshki, meat-potato pie and Russian dumplings. Russian cakes and meringues appear on the dessert list. ~ 1154 Massachusetts Avenue; 617-864-7476. BUDGET TO MODERATE.

Shades of the Southwest pervade the **Cottonwood Café**, decorated in green-and-purple neon and spiky cactus plants. A southwestern-style menu includes desert pizza, made with chicken, cheese, olives and jalapeños served on a deep-fried tortilla; enchiladas; rocky mountain lamb; grilled chicken or shrimp in barbecue sauce; and Hill Country mixed grill. ~ 1815 Massachusetts Avenue; 617-661-7440. MODERATE TO DELUXE.

SHOPPING   Harvard Square offers a wealth of shopping, from eclectic boutiques to upscale chain stores. Most notable in this intellectual bastion are the many bookshops surrounding the square. (See "Boston Area Bookstores" in this chapter.)

Yet another Harvard institution is the **Harvard Coop**, formed in 1882 by several Harvard students as a cost-saving measure. The Coop holds three floors of men's and women's clothing, calculators, games and toys, and an astonishing selection of records, art prints, posters and books. ~ 1400 Massachusetts Avenue; 617-499-2000.

Colonial Drug is like a European perfume shop, with more than 500 kinds of fragrances. ~ 49 Brattle Street; 617-864-2222.

HIDDEN ►   The creativity of Cambridge-area artists is for sale at the **Cambridge Artists Cooperative**, a treasure trove of whimsical and beautiful things: handmade paper face masks, fiber animals, Raku bowls, handmade quilts and hand-painted silk scarves. ~ 59-A Church Street; 617-868-4434.

Jasmine/Sola/Sola Men is the best source for up-to-the-minute clothing and shoes that are wearable as well as fashionable. The accessories selection is extensive, too, particularly the wall stocked full of women's hosiery. ~ 37-A Brattle Street; 617-354-6043.

Urban Outfitters features two floors of ultra-cool home furnishings, clothing and jewelry. Downstairs, there's a great bargain basement. ~ 11 John F. Kennedy Street; 617-864-0070.

Little Russia sells authentic Russian lacquered boxes and nesting dolls, jewelry, illustrated Russian fairy tales and pins of Lenin, Stalin and Trotsky. ~ 99 Mt. Auburn Street; 617-661-4928.

◄ HIDDEN

Grendel's Den is a comfy pub in the basement of Grendel's Restaurant, with brick walls, plank floors, and a bar you can really lean on. ~ 89 Winthrop Street; 617-491-1160.

NIGHTLIFE

One of the best jazz showcases in Greater Boston, the **Regattabar** offers an intimate jazz experience in a sophisticated club environment. The Regattabar regularly features such headliners as Wynton Marsalis, Ahmad Jamal and Stephane Grapelli. Cover. ~ 1 Bennett Street, in the Charles Hotel; 617-864-1200.

Ever since 1969, **Café et Club Passim** has been going strong as a showcase for acoustic folk performers, including Tracy Chapman, Jimmy Buffett and David Bromberg, in a clean-cut, no-alcohol basement coffeehouse. No Sunday performances; reservations for performances are suggested. Cover. ~ 47 Palmer Street; 617-492-7679.

Harvard's professional theater company, **American Repertory Theatre** produces world premieres and classical works, often taking a nontraditional approach. Their **New Stages** initiative mounts innovative productions in more intimate venues throughout Cambridge and Boston. ~ 64 Brattle Street; 617-547-8300.

Scullers is in an unlikely place—on the second floor of the Doubletree Guest Suite Hotel in one of the uglier buildings along the Charles. Don't let the location or the architecture dissuade you—this classy jazz club (with a terrific view of the Charles, by the way) has big-name acts Tuesday through Saturday evenings. Cover. ~ 400 Soldiers Field Road, Brighton; 617-562-4111.

The **Plough and Stars** is that rare thing, an uncorrupted working-class bar where habitués are logo-capped, burly types who belly up for live, boisterous entertainment. Black-and-white caricatures of

EXTRA! EXTRA!

The **Out of Town Newspapers** kiosk has been declared a National Historic Landmark. Set right in the middle of Harvard Square and surrounded by traffic, the kiosk carries more than 3000 newspapers and magazines from all over the world. ~ Zero Harvard Square; 617-354-7777.

neighborhood regulars line a whole wall. ~ 912 Massachusetts Avenue; 617-492-9653.

You never know what you'll hear on open mike nights at the **Cantab Lounge**, but the rest of the time it's soulful rhythm-and-blues bands in a let-it-all-hang-out playpen. Cover. ~ 738 Massachusetts Avenue; 617-354-2685.

For the last several years, the coolest area in metro Boston has been in Cambridge—Harvard Square's scruffy cousin, Central Square, which is about two-thirds of the way down Massachusetts Avenue from Harvard to M.I.T. *The* nightspot in this haven of coolness is the **Middle East**, which has three venues for live music: Upstairs, Downstairs and the Bakery. There's a mix of music and clientele here—from Michelle Shocked to Morphine, for example, as far as national acts go—and you're as likely to see underage high school (and college) kids as graying rock fans. Cover charge on most nights. ~ 472 Massachusetts Avenue; 617-497-0576.

An industrial dance club with a flair for art, **Man Ray** serves up progressive and alternative music. Gay nights are Thursday (men) and Sunday (women). Creative attire is encouraged. Cover. ~ 21 Brookline Street, in Central Square; 617-864-0400.

Named for the carved wooden amphibians overlooking the bar, **Toad** teems with music lovers of all ages enjoying live bands seven nights a week. Aimee Mann has even been spotted in this tiny no-cover hotspot. ~ 1912 Massachusetts Avenue; 617-497-4950.

Native son Pat Metheny occasionally stops in to jam at **Ryle's**, which features nightly jazz, R & B, Latin music and swing in a casual atmosphere. Cover. ~ 212 Hampshire Street; 617-876-9330.

▼▼▼▼▼▼▼▼▼▼
Outlying Areas

Although many tourists never leave the bounds of Boston and Cambridge, there is much of interest in the surrounding towns, many of which serve as bedroom communities for Boston workers and have rich colonial histories, too.

SIGHTS

Due east of the city and bordering the Fenway, Brookline is one of the more prestigious and wealthy residential surrounding towns. The architect of Boston's Emerald Necklace lived and worked in a little house in a quiet Brookline neighborhood, where he often took his work outside to a landscaped hollow.

HIDDEN ►

At the **Frederick Law Olmsted National Historic Site**, you can tour the house and grounds and see many of his landscape plans, memorabilia and photographs. Open Friday through Sunday. ~ 99 Warren Street; 617-566-1689.

President John F. Kennedy was born in Brookline in 1917, in a little house now restored to its period appearance as the **John F. Kennedy National Historic Site**. The house holds much JFK memorabilia, including his crib and some of his toys. Closed Monday and

Tuesday, and from late October through early May. Admission. ~ 83 Beals Street; 617-566-7937.

South of Brookline lies Jamaica Plain, which is technically part of Boston. The star of Jamaica Plain is the **Arnold Arboretum of Harvard University**, one of the more remarkable green strands in Boston's Emerald Necklace. The 265-acre preserve was established in 1872, and growing here are more than 5000 kinds of trees and plants from around the world. The arboretum has one of the oldest and largest lilac collections in North America, 200-year-old bonsai trees and rare specimens from China. A two-mile walk along a nature trail takes visitors through meadows and over valleys and hills, offering serene and secluded vistas of these special collections. ~ 125 Arborway; 617-524-1718.

To the southeast, the working-class city of Quincy may look uninteresting, but it happens to be the "City of the Presidents"—birthplace of John Adams and his son John Quincy Adams, the second and sixth U.S. presidents. There are several sights surrounding the Adams family history.

At the **Adams National Historic Site** stands an elegant gray Colonial house built in 1731, home to four generations of Adamses. The house is set on several acres strikingly set off with formal gardens that create a beautiful profusion of color in spring and summer. Inside the house are many original furnishings, including portraits of George and Martha Washington, Waterford candelabra and Louis XV furniture. There is also a cathedral-ceilinged library with 14,000 original volumes. As the Adams family prospered, John and his wife, Abigail, who moved into the house in 1787, enlarged it from 7 to 20 rooms. The National Park Service gives excellent tours. Closed mid-November through mid-April. Admission. ~ 135 Adams Street; 617-773-1177.

Nearby and part of the same site are the **John Adams** and **John Quincy Adams Birthplaces**, a pair of simple saltbox houses where the two presidents were born, built in 1663 and 1681. Admission. ~ 133 and 141 Franklin Street; 617-773-1177.

East of the Adams National Historic Site lies the **Quincy Homestead**, home to four generations of Edmund Quincys, the family of Dorothy Hancock. The fourth Edmund Quincy's daughter Dorothy married John Hancock, who was born in Quincy. A Colonial-style herb garden and authentic period furnishings embellish the 1686 house, and one of Hancock's coaches is displayed. Closed late May through April. Admission. ~ 1010 Hancock Street; 617-472-5117.

The 1872 Gothic Revival **Adams Academy** was founded by John Adams and is home to the **Quincy Historical Society**. Exhibits show the city's industrial history. ~ 8 Adams Street; 617-773-1144.

Dominating downtown Quincy Square is a beautiful granite church, **United First Parish Church**, designed by Alexander Parris and built in 1828. The church crypt holds the remains of John Adams, John Quincy Adams and their wives. ~ 1306 Hancock Street.

Across the street is **City Hall**, designed in 1844 in Greek Revival style by Bunker Hill architect Solomon Willard. And near City Hall is the **Hancock Cemetery**, dating to about 1640, where John Hancock's father is buried, as are Quincy and Adams ancestors.

The Old Ordinary counted Daniel Webster among its patrons.

A few miles south of Quincy lies one of the South Shore's most attractive coastal communities, **Hingham**, settled in 1635. Sailing yachts bob in its picturesque harbor, and the downtown retains the characteristics of a small village, with mom-and-pop shops, restaurants and a vintage movie theater surrounding Hingham Square. A drive along the long and wide **Main Street** rewards you with views of stately 18th- and 19th-century homes sporting neat black shutters. A number of them are on the National Register of Historic Places. These houses are private, but many are open to the public during the **Hingham Historical Society's** annual house tour in June, reputed to be the oldest historical house tour in the country, held since 1924. ~ Old Derby Academy, 617-749-7721.

There are two private houses worth a drive by. One is the **Hersey House**, a handsome gray mansion in Italianate style, with a flat-roofed, pillared porch, which dates to the 1850s and was once home to John Andrew, the Civil War governor of Massachusetts. ~ 104 Summer Street. The other is the **Joshua Wilder House**, a beautifully restored house that probably dates to 1760. ~ 605 Main Street.

The Old Ordinary, a house dating to 1680, numbered among its many owners tavern keepers who provided an "ordinary" meal of the day at fixed prices. Halfway on the day-long stagecoach ride from Plymouth to Boston, the Old Ordinary did a brisk business. Additions were made to the house in the mid-18th century. Now a museum of Hingham history, the house has an 18th-century taproom, complete with wooden grill, pewter plates and rum kegs. There's also an 18th-century kitchen outfitted with large hearth and butter churn, and a library, dining room and front parlor. Upstairs are four bedrooms furnished in period style. There are some rare objects among the collection, including "mourning" samplers, made to honor the dead; chinoiserie; a 17th-century Bible box; an 18th-century Queen Anne mirror; and paintings of Hingham ships that sailed to China. Closed mid-September through mid-June. Admission. ~ 21 Lincoln Street; 617-749-0013.

The Puritan congregation of the **Old Ship Church** gathered in 1635. Built in 1681, it is the oldest building in continuous ecclesiastical service in the United States. Unlike later New England churches with white spires and sides, Old Ship was probably built of somber gray, wooden clapboards in Elizabethan Gothic style. The original color is under dispute due to some recently analyzed paint samples. Crafted by ships' carpenters, the church has curved oak roof frames like the knees of a ship, and the unusual roof structure resembles an inverted ship's hull. ~ 90 Main Street; 617-749-1679.

Surrounding the Route 128 beltway are several more towns of interest to the traveler. A large and urbanized town about 20 miles west of Boston, Framingham offers a lovely respite within the **Garden in the Woods**, the largest collection of native plants in the Northeast. You can meander 45 acres of woodland trails, planted with some 1500 varieties of flora. Specially designed garden habitats include woodland groves, a lily pond, bog, limestone garden, pine barrens and meadows. Closed from November through mid-April. Admission. ~ Hemenway Road; 508-877-7630.

◄ HIDDEN

A few miles north of Framingham lie the endearing green colonial towns of Sudbury and Lincoln, still quite rural in character. Just off the historic Old Post Road, **Longfellow's Wayside Inn** is a wonderful place to visit, or stay. Built about 1700, the inn was made famous by Longfellow's cycle of poems, *Tales of a Wayside Inn*, which includes "Paul Revere's Ride." Historic structures include an 18th-century grist mill and a little red schoolhouse. Restored in 1923, it's a fully functioning inn and restaurant. ~ 63 Wayside Inn Road, Sudbury; 508-443-8846.

Walter Gropius, founder of the Bauhaus school of art and architecture in Germany, had his family home in the rolling green hills of Lincoln. The first house he designed upon his arrival in the United States in 1937, **Gropius House** embodies those principles of function and simplicity that are hallmarks of the Bauhaus style. The house has works of art and Bauhaus furnishings. Open only the first weekend of the month from November through May. Admission. ~ 68 Baker Bridge Road, Lincoln; 617-259-8843.

Set in a wooded green 30-acre park, the **DeCordova and Dana Museum Sculpture Park** has a collection of 20th-century American art, including paintings, sculpture, graphics and photography. Outdoor summer jazz concerts are given on the grassy lawn at the amphitheater. Admission. ~ Sandy Pond Road, Lincoln; 617-259-8355.

There's a great deal of historic ambience to **Longfellow's Wayside Inn**, which the poet made famous in his *Tales of a Wayside Inn*. The innkeepers have kept a number of the original rooms furnished with period items, including the bed chamber where Longfellow stayed in 1862. You are welcome to tour all these rooms, as well as several historic buildings on the grounds, including a grist mill and the little red schoolhouse of "Mary Had a Little Lamb" fame. Of the inn's ten rooms, only two are in the older part of the inn. Eight are in a modern addition and feature Colonial reproduction furniture, traditional colors of cranberry and green, and new oak floors. The two rooms in the original inn have wide-planked floors and hand-hewn ceiling beams. But they have tiny bathrooms with cramped showers. The inn has a wonderful restaurant that serves traditional country fare. Full breakfast included. ~ 63 Wayside Inn Road, Sudbury; 508-443-1776. DELUXE TO ULTRA-DELUXE.

LODGING

DINING

Don't be deterred by the strip-mall surroundings of **La Paloma,** complete with laundromat, sub shop and package store. La Paloma has won several awards from *Boston* magazine including six "Best Mexican Restaurant" awards. People line up outside the doors on weekends for the first-rate Mexican food, including beef and chicken fajitas, Mexican paella and *gorditos* (fried tortillas topped with homemade sausage and sour cream). The dining room feels as warm and festive as a Mexican village, with peachy-colored walls, dim lantern light, airy latticework, tiled floors and Mexican paintings and folk art. Closed Monday. ~ 195 Newport Avenue, Quincy; 617-773-0512. BUDGET TO MODERATE.

HIDDEN ►

The British Relief is a welcoming spot indeed, housed in a red brick storefront and modeled on a British soup kitchen. Vintage signboards and photographs following the soup kitchen theme hang on the walls. The homey furnishings include a massive carved oak table that seats at least ten, and ancient wooden booths. Cafeteria-style service dishes up hearty homemade soups, salads and sandwiches. The restaurant also operates a deli counter with gourmet take-out. Breakfast and lunch only, except for Thursday-night dinner. Closed Sunday. ~ 152 North Street, Hingham Square, Hingham; 617-749-7713. BUDGET.

Visions of Longfellow will come to mind immediately when you enter **Longfellow's Wayside Inn.** Before lunch or dinner, you can tour the period rooms of the original inn and several historic buildings on the grounds. Ask for a table in the small and intimate Tap Room, which has a truly Colonial ambience. Small and intimate, the Tap Room has two fireplaces, ladderback chairs and brown-and-white-checked tablecloths. The menu features hearty game and seafood dishes such as an 18th-century wayfarer might have dined on: prime rib, rack of lamb, roast duckling, goose, and sole. For dessert, there are deep-dish apple pie and baked Indian pudding. ~ 63 Wayside Inn Road, Sudbury; 508-443-1776. MODERATE TO DELUXE.

NIGHTLIFE

Ballroom dancers from 18 to 80 love **Moseley's on the Charles** for its large ballroom and 1940s ambience complete with sparkling ceiling globe. Cover. ~ 50 Bridge Street, Dedham; 617-326-3075.

BEACHES & PARKS

BOSTON HARBOR ISLANDS 🏃 🚣 🚤 🛥 Some 30 islands lie in Boston Harbor, scattered along the coast from Boston south to Quincy, Hingham and Hull, with eight of them comprising a state

HIDDEN ►

park. The Puritans used these islands for pastureland and firewood, and there are tales of buried pirate treasure and ghosts haunting old Civil War forts. Each island has a unique flavor and character.

Peddocks Island, a 113-acre preserve of woodlands, salt marsh, rocky beaches and open fields, has a turn-of-the-century fort, a wildlife sanctuary and an old cottage community, as well as a visitors center with displays detailing the island's history.

Peaceful and primitive **Lovells Island** is characterized by long beaches and diverse wildlife, rocky tidepools and sand dunes. This is the only island where swimmimg is allowed.

The smaller **Georges Island**, the most developed in the park, is dominated by Fort Warren, a National Historic Landmark built between 1833 and 1869. Construction was overseen by Sylvanus Thayer, the "Father of West Point."

Other islands in the park system include **Gallop's, Grape, Bumpkin** and **Great Brewster**. Swimming is permitted on Lovells Island only. Fishing is good from the rocky shores and public piers on all the islands except Peddocks; you'll find lots of flounder, cod, haddock, pollack and striped bass. Picnic areas, restrooms, park rangers, nature trails, fort tours, historical programs, boat docks, concession stand on Georges Island. Open from Memorial Day through Labor Day. Information: Peddocks, Lovells and Georges islands are administered by the regional Metropolitan District Commission; contact the MDC's Harbor Region Office. ~ 98 Taylor Street; Dorchester; 617-727-5359. Grape, Bumpkin, Brewster and the other islands are state-owned; contact the Boston Harbor Islands State Park. ~ 349 Lincoln Street, Hingham; 617-740-1605. Georges Island serves as the entrance to the park and provides free inter-island water taxis from Memorial Day to Labor Day; for information, call the Department of Environmental Management. ~ 617-740-1605. The islands are also accessible through Bay State Cruise Company. ~ 66 Long Wharf and Commonwealth Pier; 617-723-7800. The Friends of the Boston Harbor Islands sponsors special boat trips and tours. ~ 617-740-4290.

A There are free primitive sites on Peddocks and Lovells islands (free MDC permit required), and on Grape and Bumpkins islands. No water or electricity; outhouses available.

BELLE ISLE MARSH 🏃 This preserve holds 241 acres of one of the largest remaining salt marshes in Boston. Typical of the wetlands that once lined the shores of the Massachusetts Bay Colony, Belle Isle Marsh is a special place where you can see lots of wildlife and salt marsh plants, a rare experience in an urban area. Nature trails, observation tower. ~ At Bennington Street in East Boston; 617-727-5350.

◄ *HIDDEN*

NANTASKET BEACH 🏄 🏊 Once a classy mid-19th-century resort with grand hotels rivaling those in Newport, the Nantasket Beach area later declined into a tacky strip of bars, fast-food stands and Skeeball arcades. Still, this three-and-a-half-mile barrier beach is one of the nicest in the area, with clean white sand and a wide open vista of the Atlantic Ocean. The water is always good for swimming, and after a storm there's enough surf to go bodysurfing or windsurfing. Picnic areas, restrooms, lifeguards, shade pavilions, boardwalk, restaurants and snack stands. ~ On Nantasket Avenue, at the terminus of Route 228 in Hull; 617-925-4905.

WOLLASTON BEACH 〰 Come high tide, the beach virtually disappears, so narrow is this two-mile stretch of sand. The beach is backed by a wide seawall and a parking strip along its entire length. Here people like to sunbathe in lawn chairs or draped across the hoods of their cars, and to walk their dogs, giving this beach a distinctly urban feel. The sand here is gravelly and often crowded, but the beach does have a splendid view of the Boston skyline. ~ Picnic areas, restrooms, bathhouses, playground; snack bars and restaurants across the street with great fried clams. ~ On Quincy Shore Drive, south on Route 3A from Neponset Circle, Quincy; 617-727-5293.

BLUE HILLS RESERVATION 🚶🚴🏇🚣🛶🏊〰 This 7000-acre park is the largest open space within 35 miles of Boston. Great Blue Hill, the highest point on the Massachusetts coast south of Maine, is the site of the oldest weather station in North America. The reservation comprises dozens of hills, forested land and several lakes and wetlands, as well as 150 miles of hiking, ski touring and bridle trails. There's the **Trailside Museum,** a natural history museum with live animals and exhibits, and 16 historic sites, including the 1795 Redman Farmhouse. ~ 1904 Canton Avenue, Route 138, Milton; 617-333-0690.

Houghton's Pond, with its calm waters and sandy bottom, offers particularly good swimming for children. Ponds are stocked with trout, bass, bullhead, perch and sunfish. Picnic areas, restrooms, lifeguards, snack bar, tennis courts, golf course, small downhill ski run with ski rentals, ballfields, nature programs. ~ Reservation headquarters are on Hillside Street next to the police station in Milton, where maps are available; 617-698-1802.

▲ The Appalachian Mountain Club operates 20 cabins in the reservation on Ponkapoag Pond (5 Joy Street, Boston; 617-523-0636); camping rates range from $16 to $22 per night. Reserve these well ahead of time. Outhouses; no water or electricity. The MDC may restrict camping beginning in the 1996 summer season, so call ahead.

MIDDLESEX FELLS RESERVATION 🚶🚴🏇🏊〰 "Fells" is a Scottish word meaning wild, hilly country, which aptly describes the 2000-plus-acre terrain of this reservation. These rugged highlands were first explored in 1632 by Governor Winthrop, first governor of the Massachusetts Bay Colony. They were acquired as public parkland in 1893, and a 19th-century trolley line brought in droves of picnickers. The region has been used for logging, granite quarrying, ice harvesting and water power for mills that manufactured the first vulcanized rubber products. Fifty miles of hiking trails and old woods roads run through the Fells. For anglers, Fellsmere, Doleful, Dark Hollow and Quarter Mile ponds hold sunfish, catfish, perch, pickerel and bass. Horses are allowed, though there are no stables. Picnic areas, skating rink, swimming pool. ~ Six miles north of Boston, off Exits 32, 33 and 34 from Route 93; 617-662-5214.

Just outside of Cambridge, the two towns of
Lexington and Concord are forever linked by the
historical events of April 19, 1775, when the first
battle of the Revolutionary War took place. The British planned to
advance on Concord from Boston to seize the colonials' military supplies. Warned by Paul Revere the night before, farmer/soldier Minutemen had mustered early before dawn on the Lexington Green.

Lexington & Concord

About 77 men at Lexington Green, and hundreds more at Concord, fought off 700 highly trained British regulars. With heavy casu-
alties, the British retreated back to Boston. "The shot heard 'round the
world" had been fired, launching the American Revolution.

Between the two towns you can spend a couple of days visiting battle sites and monuments. When you arrive in Lexington, a few miles
north of Lincoln off Route 128, stop first at the **Lexington Visitors
Center** for maps and brochures, and to see a diorama of the battle. ~
Lexington Green, 1875 Massachusetts Avenue; 617-862-1450.

SIGHTS

Across from Lexington Green, in the center of town, stands the
Minuteman Statue, a simple bareheaded farmer holding a musket.
The statue's rough, fieldstone base was made of stone taken from the
walls the American militia stood behind as they shot at the British.
This statue has become symbolic of Lexington history. ~ Battle Green,
intersection of Massachusetts Avenue and Bedford Street.

On the green next to the Visitors Center is the yellow, woodframe
Buckman Tavern, built in 1709. This is where the Minutemen gathered to await the British after Revere's warning. Smiling elderly ladies
wearing mobcaps and long skirts guide you through the house, with
its wide-planked floors and 18th-century furniture and musket displays. Admission. ~ Lexington Green, 1 Bedford Street; 617-862-5598.

About a quarter mile north of the green is the **Hancock-Clarke
House**, where Samuel Adams and John Hancock were staying that
fateful night. Revere stopped here to warn them. John Hancock's father built this pretty little woodframe house with 12-over-16 windows
around 1700. Admission. ~ 36 Hancock Street; 617-861-0928.

The little red **Munroe Tavern,** built in 1695, served as British
headquarters, and housed wounded British soldiers after the battle.
The tavern has been maintained as it was, and there are mementos of
a 1789 visit by George Washington. Admission. ~ 1332 Massachusetts Avenue; 617-862-1703.

The **Jonathan Harrington House**, now a private residence, was the
home of Minuteman fifer Jonathan Harrington, who died in his wife's
arms after being fatally wounded in the battle. ~ Harrington Road.

The **Museum of Our National Heritage** has changing exhibits on
American history in four galleries. Past programs have included ret-
rospectives on Ben Franklin, Paul Revere and the USS *Constitution*,
plus exhibits of clocks, furniture and swords from different periods.

There are also permanent exhibits on the American Revolution and Masonic lodges. ~ 33 Marrett Road; 617-861-6560.

Within the 750-acre **Minute Man National Historic Park** are several more sites involved in the Battle of Lexington and Concord. In this peaceful, sylvan spot, it's hard to picture the bloody carnage of the historic battle. A wide, pine-scented path leads to the site of the **Old North Bridge** spanning the Concord River, a 1956 replica of the bridge where Concord Minutemen held off the British. Another **Minute Man Statue** stands across the river, made of melted 1776 cannon, designed by Daniel Chester French. This one shows a farmer with gun and plow in hand. ~ Route 2A, Concord; 508-369-6993.

At the **Visitors Center** are a film and exhibits. ~ 174 Liberty Street.

Concord is also famed as the home of four great literary figures of the 19th century: Nathaniel Hawthorne, Ralph Waldo Emerson, Henry David Thoreau and Louisa May Alcott.

The **Old Manse** was home not only to Emerson but also to Hawthorne, who lived there with his wife for two years, while writing *Mosses from an Old Manse*. The restored house is filled with Emerson and Hawthorne memorabilia. Closed Tuesday and from late October through mid-April. Admission. ~ Monument Street near North Bridge; 508-369-3909.

The Alcott family lived at **Orchard House** for almost 20 years. Here Louisa May Alcott wrote her most famous novels, *Little Women* and *Little Men*. Closed first two weeks in January. Admission. ~ 399 Lexington Road; 508-369-4118.

Ralph Waldo Emerson House is where Emerson lived for almost 50 years, with Thoreau, Hawthorne and the Alcotts as his frequent guests. Almost all furnishings are original. Closed Monday through Wednesday and from late October through mid-April. Admission. ~ 28 Cambridge Turnpike; 508-369-2236.

The **Concord Museum** contains Revolutionary War artifacts, literary relics and other historic items associated with Concord. Emerson's study was reconstructed and moved here, and the Thoreau Room holds the simple furniture Thoreau made for his cabin at Walden Pond. Admission. ~ 200 Lexington Road; 508-369-9609.

At the **Thoreau Lyceum** is a replica of the cabin Thoreau built on Walden Pond. Headquarters of the Thoreau Society, the lyceum has a research library and sponsors lectures about the writer. Admission. ~ 156 Belknap Street; 617-259-9411.

Few places have been more indelibly stamped by the presence of one individual than **Walden Pond State Reservation**. "I went to the woods because I wished to live deliberately, to front the essential facts of life, and see if I could not learn what it had to teach, and not, when I came to die, discover that I had not lived," wrote Thoreau in his famous account of his two years spent in a little cabin in these woods, beginning in 1845. Thoreau occupied himself studying nature, fishing and hoeing his bean crop. Today, Walden Pond offers less solitude—it's almost al-

Lexington and Concord

LEXINGTON

LEXINGTON
- A Lexington Green
- B Visitors Center
- C Minuteman Statue
- D Buckman Tavern

LEXINGTON TO CONCORD
- E Hancock-Clarke House
- F Munroe Tavern
- G Museum of Our National Heritage
- H Walden Pond State Reservation

Bedford St. *Hancock St.* *Harrington Rd.* A C D B *Meriam St.* *Massachusetts Ave.* *Clarke St.*

LEXINGTON TO CONCORD

Bedford St. *Minute Man National Historic Park* 4 128 *Lowell St.* *Hancock St.* *Adams St.* *Massachusetts Ave.* E *Woburn St.* Concord 2 2 *Lexington Rd.* **Lexington** *Bedford St.* *Great Rd.* 2A *Marrett Rd.* F G 2A H *Walden St.* 225 Lincoln **East Lexington**

CONCORD

I *Monument St.* J *Lowell Rd.* 62 *Bedford St.* *Main St.* 2A *Lexington Rd.* K L M N *Walden St.* *Cambridge Turnpike* *Hawthorne Ln.*

CONCORD
- I Minute Man Statue
- J Old Manse
- K Orchard House
- L The Wayside
- M Ralph Waldo Emerson House
- N Concord Museum

ways crowded. But you can swim or fish in the pond, or perhaps try a little boating. Nature trails wind around the pond, and there are picnic tables. You can also visit the little cairn of stones that marks the cabin site. Admission. ~ Route 126 off Route 2; 508-369-3254.

Concord is also known for **Concord grapes**, developed and cultivated here by Ephraim Wales Bull.

LODGING

If you're looking for an inexpensive place to stay right in the middle of Lexington, you might stop at the **Battle Green Motor Inn**. The 96 rooms in this L-shaped motel surround two courtyards graced with tropical plants and a heated swimming pool. Inside, guest rooms sport blond furniture and a colonial decor. ~ 1720 Massachusetts Avenue; 617-862-6100, 800-343-0235, fax 617-861-9485. MODERATE.

Concord is greener and more rural than Lexington, making it a more restful place to stay. You can't stay there without stumbling over history.

The **Hawthorne Inn**, built around 1870, is situated on land that once belonged to Emerson, the Alcotts and Hawthorne, and stands right across the street from the Hawthorne and Alcott houses. The homey inn has seven rooms, three furnished with canopied, antique four-poster beds covered with handmade quilts, as well as Colonial-patterned wallpapers and Oriental rugs. The private baths are large and nicely redone. Rates drop significantly during the off-season. ~ 462 Lexington Road, Concord; 508-369-5610. ULTRA-DELUXE.

Right on the town green, the **Colonial Inn** dates to 1716. The original part of the house was owned by Thoreau's grandfather. Although the inn has 49 rooms, few are in the historic old inn. Thirty-two rooms are in a newer wing added in 1961 and are comfortable but bland. The 15 rooms in the original part of the house are larger and have a more historic ambience, with wide-planked floors, hand-hewn beams and four-poster beds. The inn has a restaurant with two taverns. ~ 48 Monument Square, Concord; 508-369-9200, 800-370-9200, fax 508-369-2170. ULTRA-DELUXE.

DINING

For a quick bite and a break from sightseeing, stop for an excellent coffee and pastry at **One Meriam Street**, a cozy and casual café-style eatery. They also serve pancakes, omelettes, sandwiches, burgers and

WAYSIDE WRITERS

The Alcotts and Nathaniel Hawthorne lived at **The Wayside**. The Alcotts lived there for several years while Louisa was a girl. Hawthorne bought the house in 1852 and wrote his biography of Franklin Pierce here. Closed Wednesday and from late October through mid-April. Admission. ~ 455 Lexington Road; 508-369-6975.

salads. Breakfast and lunch seven days a week. ~ 1 Meriam Street, Lexington; 617-862-3006. BUDGET.

Yangtze River Restaurant specializes in Polynesian cuisine, as well as Szechuan and Cantonese favorites. The dining room is noisy and casual, with a jungle of greenery and exposed brick walls. ~ 21–25 Depot Square, Lexington; 617-861-6030. BUDGET TO DELUXE.

Not everyone will appreciate **The Willow Pond Kitchen,** but we do. Its ma-and-pa, down-home atmosphere hasn't changed since the 1930s, with decor that features moth-eaten stuffed fish, wildcats and opossum, plus tacky formica tables and battered wooden booths. Paradoxically, good food is served, including cheeseburgers, lobster rolls and lobster pie, steamed clams and a fine roster of beer and ale. ~ 745 Lexington Road, Concord; 508-369-6529. BUDGET TO MODERATE.

For some traditional Yankee fare in a historic setting, try the **Colonial Inn.** Built in 1716, the original part of the house was owned by Thoreau's grandfather. There are five dining rooms, each with its own Colonial-inspired decor. The menu includes prime rib, steak, scrod and lobster. ~ 48 Monument Square, Concord; 508-369-9200. MODERATE TO DELUXE.

▼▼▼▼▼▼▼▼▼▼▼▼▼▼

Outdoor Adventures

SAILING

Sailing the blue waters of the Charles on a breezy day with views of both the Boston and Cambridge skylines is a moment to be savored. **Community Boating** rents boats to visitors who pass a test and buy a two-day membership. ~ 21 Embankment Road, Boston; 617-523-1038. You can rent boats, with a captain, at the **Boston Sailing Center.** ~ 54 Lewis Wharf; 617-227-4198. You can also try the **Boston Harbor Sailing Club.** ~ 72 East India Row; 617-523-2619.

WHALE WATCHING

Boston is within easy reach of Stellwagen Bank, a major feeding ground for whales. You can go whalewatching from April through October with the **New England Aquarium** ~ Central Wharf; 617-973-5277. Or you can try **Bay State Cruise Company** ~ 66 Long Wharf; 617-723-7800. **A. C. Cruise Line** also has whale-watching charters. ~ 290 Northern Avenue; 617-261-6633.

JOGGING

Jogging is very big in Boston, where half the population seems to be in training for the Boston Marathon. The most popular running paths are along both sides of the green strips paralleling the Charles River, which run more than 17 miles. For information call the **USA Track and Field.** ~ 2001 Beacon Street, Brookline; 617-566-7600. Another safe place to jog is the two- and three-mile trails in the **Breakheart Reservation.** ~ 177 Forest Street, Saugus; 617-233-0834.

ICE SKATING

Skaters have been rounding the curves of the lagoon in the Public Garden and the Boston Common Frog Pond for more than a hundred years. The Charles River is almost never frozen enough for skating, but the MDC maintains 21 public indoor rinks, some with rentals available. ~ 20 Somerset Street; 617-727-9547.

The **Skating Club of Boston** also has public skating and has rentals. Admission. ~ 1240 Soldier's Field Road, Brighton; 617-782-5900.

SKIING

Cross-country skiers have a number of options. The **Weston Ski Track** has gently sloping trails that run over a golf course; lessons and rentals are available. ~ 200 Park Road, Weston; 617-891-6575. The **Lincoln Guide Service** also offers lessons and rentals. ~ Conservation Trail, Lincoln; 617-259-9204. The **Middlesex Fells Reservation** has a free six-mile trail, suiting a variety of skill levels, but you have to pay for the trail maps. ~ 1 Woodland Road, Stoneham; 617-662-5214. **Wompatuck State Park** has relatively easy trails, with free trail maps at the park headquarters. ~ Union Street, Hingham; 617-749-7160.

GOLF

You can tee up at numerous public golf courses. In Hyde Park, visit **George Wright Golf Course**. ~ 420 West Street; 617-361-8313. In Quincy there's the **Presidents Golf Course**. ~ 357 West Squantum Street; 617-328-3444. **Braintree Municipal Golf Course** is an option in Braintree. ~ 101 Jefferson Street; 617-843-9781. In Newton, try the **Newton Commonwealth Golf Course**. ~ 212 Kenrick Street; 617-630-1971. Another choice is **Stow Acres Country Club**. ~ 58 Randall Road, Stow; 508-568-8690. Lastly, there's the **Colonial Country Club** in Lynnfield. ~ 1 Audubon Road; 617-245-9300.

TENNIS

The **Metropolitan District Commission** (MDC) maintains 45 courts in the city and greater Boston. ~ 20 Somerset Street; 617-727-9547. Cambridge, too, has public courts. ~ Information: 617-349-6231.

There are numerous private clubs; one open to the public is the **Sportsmen's Tennis Club**. ~ Franklin Field Tennis Center, 950 Blue Hill Avenue, Dorchester; 617-288-9092.

BICYCLING

Biking is popular around Boston's scenic waterways, including the Charles River, although we wouldn't recommend it in the narrow, congested downtown streets. The Charles River Esplanade on the Boston side of the Charles River has a well-marked 18-mile route named the **Dr. Paul Dudley White Bike Path**, which goes from Science Park, through Boston, Cambridge and Newton, ending in Watertown. The **Stony Brook Reservation Bike Path** runs four miles through forests in West Roxbury/Hyde Park. ~ Turtle Pond Parkway, West Roxbury, Hyde Park; 617-698-1802. The **Mystic River Reservation** also has a nice bike path, 3.5 miles long, that runs from the Wellington Bridge in Somerville along the Mystic River to beyond the Wellington Bridge in Everett. Some of the best and least crowded biking in the area is at **Wompatuck State Park**, where there are 12 miles of trails through old forest groves. ~ Union Street, Hingham; 617-749-7160.

If you're up for a really challenging route, try the 135-mile **Claire Saltonstall Bikeway**, the first segment of which runs from Boston to Bourne at the entrance to Cape Cod. Continuing segments follow the Cape Cod Rail Trail all the way to Provincetown at the tip of the Cape.

For information on area biking, contact the **Bicycle Coalition of Massachusetts**. ~ 214-A Broadway, Cambridge; 617-491-7433. You can also try the **Charles River Wheelmen**. ~ 1 Belnap Road, Hyde Park; 617-325-2453.

Bike Rentals   To rent a bike in the Boston area, contact the **Community Bike Shop**. ~ 496 Tremont Street; 617-542-8623. Or you can call **Earth Bikes**. ~ Huntington Avenue; 617-267-4733.

HIKING

Scant miles outside the urban clatter of downtown Boston, Massachusetts turns to rolling green hills, river valleys and pine and hardwood forests. A surprising number of parks and wildlife sanctuaries are to be found in these rural country towns, where you can hike scenic trails, short or long.

OUTLYING AREAS   The **Quincy Quarries Footpath** (2.5 miles) leads past steep quarry walls, the first commercial railway in America and an 1898 turning mill, used to cut and polish the Quincy granite columns and slabs that went into many famous buildings in America.

The main path at **World's End** (4.5 miles) winds uphill and down ◄ HIDDEN
over a little peninsula extending north from Hingham into Massachusetts Bay. Its beautifully landscaped, gently curving roads were laid out by landscape architect Frederick Law Olmsted for a housing development that was never built. The wide, grassy path meanders through meadows and marshland, past rocky, glacial drumlins, through avenues of English oaks, pine and red cedars, and up a steep knoll with a knockout view of the Boston skyline, one of the best on the South Shore.

The **Ponkapoag Trail** (3.5 miles) in the Blue Hills Reservation circles Ponkapoag Pond, passing through wetlands and a golf course. From it, the Ponkapoag Log Boardwalk crosses a floating bog, filled with highbush blueberries, blue flag iris and Atlantic white cedar.

✔ **CHECK THESE OUT—UNIQUE OUTDOOR ADVENTURES**
- Climb aboard a **whale-watching charter** to Stellwagen Bank, a major feeding ground for whales. *page 231*
- Grab your skates and join a hundred-year-old tradition: ice skating on the **Boston Common Frog Pond**. *page 231*
- Ascend a rugged trail through volcanic rock and carpets of Canada mayflower on Middlesex Fells Reservation's **Skyline Trail**. *page 234*
- Sail the blue waters or cycle the 18-mile shoreline of the scenic **Charles River**. *pages 231, 233*

Little-known and little-used, Stony Brook Reservation allows you to walk in solitude among peaceful woods along the **Bearberry Hill Path** (3 miles). The trail leads into the woods toward Turtle Pond, then returns via the east boundary asphalt bicycle path leading past a swampy thicket and a golf course.

The **Skyline Trail** (6.8 miles) in the Middlesex Fells Reservation is a rugged trail that climbs many rocky knobs running between two observation towers. Scenery varies considerably along the way, from a pond with water lilies and frogs, to volcanic-rock-covered hills, wild hardwood forests, an old soapbox derby track, carpets of Canada mayflower and swampy areas.

Although you will do so with crowds of others, you can walk the shores Thoreau walked at **Walden Pond** in Concord. A 1.7-mile circuit trail winds through woods along the crystal clear waters of the pond. At the cabin site where Thoreau lived for two years, travelers from all corners of the globe have piled up stones in memoriam.

▼▼▼▼▼▼▼▼▼▼▼ Transportation

CAR

If you arrive in Boston by car, you'll have to watch closely for road markings; routes change numbers and names frequently. Also, roads will be tied up well into the mid-1990s by a major project designed to construct a third harbor tunnel and to depress the Central Artery underground. No one in his right mind would want to bring a car to downtown Boston, where narrow, confusing streets are ruled by legendarily homicidal drivers. Save the car for touring the suburbs of Greater Boston or outlying areas.

From the north, **Route 95** follows a curving, southwesterly path to Boston, changing to **Route 128** as it forms a beltway around the city. **Route 93** runs directly north-south through Boston; its downtown portion is called the Central Artery, and it's known as the John Fitzgerald Expressway and the Southeast Expressway between Boston and Route 128 in Braintree. **Route 90**, the Massachusetts Turnpike, heads into and through Boston from the west. From the south, you can reach Boston by Route 95, **Route 24** or **Route 3**.

AIR

Logan International Airport, the busy and crowded main airport serving Boston, is two miles north of the city in East Boston. Numerous domestic and international carriers fly in and out of Logan, including Aer Lingus, Air Atlantic/Canadian Air, Air Canada, Air France, Alitalia Airlines, American Airlines, British Airways, Continental, Delta Airlines, El Al Israel Airlines, Lufthansa Airlines, Northwest Airlines, Sabena Belgian World Airlines, Swissair, TAP Air Portugal, Trans World Airlines, United Airlines, USAir and Virgin Atlantic Airways.

Limousines and buses take visitors to numerous downtown locations, including **Carey Limousine** (617-623-8700), **Commonwealth Limousine Service** (617-787-5575) and **Peter Pan Bus Lines** (617-426-7838, 800-237-8747).

You can also take the subway from the airport, by taking a free Massport bus to the Blue Line stop. The slickest way to get downtown is to hop the **Airport Water Shuttle**, bypassing traffic altogether for a scenic seven-minute ride across Boston Harbor. ~ 617-330-8680.

Greyhound Bus Lines has bus service to Boston from all over the country. The main downtown terminal is at South Station. ~ 720 Atlantic Avenue; 800-231-2222. **Bonanza Bus Lines** serves Boston from Cape Cod. ~ 145 Dartmouth Street at Back Bay Station; 617-720-4110, 800-556-3815. **Peter Pan Bus Lines** runs between Boston and New York, New Hampshire and Cape Cod. ~ 700 Atlantic Avenue; 617-426-7838, 800-237-8747. **Concord Trailways** runs from points in New Hampshire only. ~ 700 Atlantic Avenue; 617-426-8080, 800-639-3317.

BUS

Amtrak services many destinations from Boston including San Francisco, Chicago and New York. ~ South Station, Summer Street at Atlantic Avenue; 617-482-3660, 800-872-7245.

TRAIN

Parking grows scarcer and ever more expensive, and you can easily see Boston on foot, but if you must rent a car, you can do so in the airport terminal at **Alamo Rent A Car** (800-327-9633), **Avis Rent A Car** (800-331-1212), **Budget Rent A Car** (800-527-0700), **Dollar Rent A Car** (800-800-4000), **Hertz Rent A Car** (800-654-3131), **National Interrent** (800-227-7368) and **Thrifty Car Rental** (800-367-2277). **American International Rent A Car** (617-237-6500) offers free airport pickup service.

Used-car rentals in the area include **U-Save and Choice Auto Rental** (617-254-1900) and **Adventure Rent A Car** (617-783-3825).

CAR RENTALS

Boston's subway system is operated by the **Massachusetts Bay Transportation Authority**, MBTA, popularly called the "T." In the 1980s, the MBTA spent $2.5 billion to improve and expand the system, and there are sparkling new stations on both the Red and Orange Lines. The T has four lines, the Red, Blue, Green and Orange, which will get you almost anywhere you want to go quite handily. The basic fare is 85 cents. Special multiple-day discount passes can be bought at many T stations and the visitor booths throughout the city.

The MBTA also operates a fleet of buses providing extensive coverage of Boston and Cambridge. Exact change is required for the 60-cent fare. ~ 617-722-3200.

PUBLIC TRANSIT

Several cab companies serve Logan Airport, including **Boston Cab** (617-536-5010), **Cambridge Taxi Company** (617-876-5000), **Checker Cab** (617-497-1500), **Red and White Cab** (617-242-5000) and **Town Taxi** (617-536-5000).

TAXIS

FIVE

Cape Cod and the Islands

Every year starting in June, close to 3.5 million people invade this foot-shaped peninsula, grappling with horrendous traffic and crowded beaches just to be on their beloved Cape Cod. It's easy to understand why.

The Cape has it all: silver gray saltbox cottages, historic villages, sports, seafood, art, first-rate theater and more. But those attributes aren't the real reason people come here. It's the land itself. With its ethereal light, comforting woodlands and 300 miles of majestic, untamed shoreline, Cape Cod reaches deep into the soul. Formed 12,000 years ago from an enormous glacier that left in its wake a unique and magical landscape of sand dunes, moors, salt marsh and ocean vistas, the Cape has a staggering number of utterly beautiful beaches and natural parks.

Linked to the Cape in the minds of many travelers (although definitely *not* in the minds of residents) are the nearby islands of Martha's Vineyard and Nantucket, wealthy enclaves where celebrities find retreat and make their homes along quiet or dramatic seascapes, beside purple heath or in museum-perfect villages dotted with historic buildings. Following in the footsteps of Lillian Hellman and Dashiell Hammett, folks like William Styron and Walter Cronkite have moved to Martha's Vineyard. Smaller Nantucket has one lovely town filled with museums, galleries and history, plus great wild beaches and backroads. Everyone calls Nantucket and Martha's Vineyard "the Islands"—except the people who live there. Don't even *suggest* that the "islanders" are connected to the Cape unless you want to start a row.

The Cape's first visitors were the Pilgrims, who landed near Provincetown just long enough to write the Mayflower Compact before heading off to Plymouth. As Massachusetts thrived after the Revolution, Nantucket and Martha's Vineyard joined other coastal areas as major whaling ports.

In the 1800s, artists and writers such as Henry David Thoreau discovered the Cape. Tourists were soon to follow, and these once-isolated fishing communities were never the same again.

Tourism has taken its toll. The Cape has a commercial side, complete with tired-looking shopping malls, pizza parlors, video arcades, tract houses and ugly motels. But it's easy to avoid all that if you know where to go.

The 70-mile-long Cape projects out into the ocean in an east-west direction for about 35 miles, then becomes narrower and turns northward. Practically everything worth seeing here lies along the shore, so an ideal way to explore is to follow the northern coast along Cape Cod Bay to the tip in Provincetown, then go back down along Nantucket Sound to Falmouth and Woods Hole. This is the route we will take.

We have labeled the first segment the North Cape, which follows scenic Route 6A along the north shore past some of the Cape's most charming historic villages. Route 6A eventually joins with busy Route 6 and soon arrives at Eastham. Here begins the Outer Cape area, the region known for sand dunes, rolling moors, impressive beaches and the bohemian and tourist enclave of Provincetown. Route 28 runs back along South Cape past a couple of attractive villages and some of the region's less-scenic commercial areas (including Hyannis, home to the Kennedy clan). This section ends at the scientific community of Woods Hole, noted for its oceanographic institute. We then journey to those two pearls off the Cape's southern coast, Martha's Vineyard and Nantucket.

Touring this area, perhaps you'll understand what inspired Thoreau to write *Cape Cod*. There's something here, though, that can't be put into words, a special chemistry and charisma that draw people back year after year, generation after generation.

▼▼▼▼▼▼▼▼▼▼▼▼ The North Cape

Hugging Cape Cod Bay along Route 6A are the beautiful historic villages of Sandwich, Barnstable, Yarmouth, Dennis and Brewster. Once known as Olde Kings Highway, Route 6A is a tree-lined road that dips and turns past lovely old homes, sweeping lawns, stone walls, duck ponds, museums, elegant restaurants and antique stores.

SIGHTS

Sandwich, the first town we reach, is very green, woodsy and English looking. It dates back to 1639 and has a 17th-century grist mill. Sandwich has more sights than any town on the Cape except Brewster. Maps are available at the **Cape Cod Canal Region Chamber of Commerce**. Open in summer only. ~ 70 Main Street, Bourne; 508-759-3122.

Near the heart of the village stands **The Hoxie House**, one of the oldest houses in Sandwich. Built around 1675, this modest saltbox structure has furnishings that are impressive in their simplicity and ingenuity. A 1701 Connecticut blanket chest with inlay is spectacular; chairs turn into tables and benches into beds. Closed after Columbus Day through early June. Admission. ~ Water Street, Route 130; 508-888-1173.

A few doors down is the **Thornton W. Burgess Museum** dedicated to the author of *Old Mother West Wind* and other children's tales.

This homey little cottage overlooking an idyllic, willow-lined duck pond contains a large collection of books by Burgess, beautiful old book illustrations and a gift shop with children's books. Closed Sunday and Monday from January through March. Admission. ~ 4 Water Street, 508-888-4668.

Heritage Plantation has a 1912 carousel, an antique car collection (including a stunning Dusenburg once owned by Gary Cooper), a military museum and an art museum. If cars, folk art or military history interest you, you'll be impressed. The military museum has 2000 hand-painted miniatures and all sorts of replica flags and firearms. The art museum includes an impressive collection of antique weathervanes, early American primitive and western art including many Currier and Ives lithographs, and cigar-store carved figures. The plantation's 76 acres of gardens are so perfectly manicured they look artificial. Closed November through Mother's Day. Admission. ~ Pine and Grove streets, 508-888-3300.

In the heart of Sandwich village is the **Sandwich Glass Museum**. In 1825 Deming Jarves, a Bostonian, built a glass factory in Sandwich because of its convenient water access to Boston and abundant wood

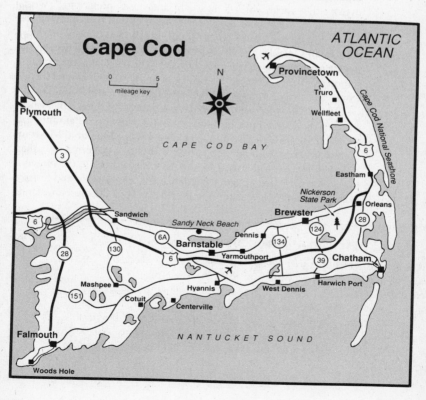

supply for the furnaces, and also because he thought his employees wouldn't squander their money on city temptations, as they had in Boston. His formula worked, and in no time Sandwich became renowned for its glass.

The museum's collection includes everything from jars, nursing bottles and tableware to saucers, vases and candlesticks. A lot of the glass is displayed on shelves in front of large picture windows. Sun illuminates the glass, and it lights up the museum in a kaleidoscope of sparkling colors. Closed Monday and Tuesday from November through March; closed in January. Admission. ~ 129 Main Street, Town Hall Square; 508-888-0251.

A few steps away from the Glass Museum you'll find **Yesteryears Doll Museum**, two floors packed with every antique doll and accessory imaginable—princesses, nurses, Indians, doll furniture, houses, paper dolls, baby buggies, parasols and much more. Closed Sunday and closed November through Memorial Day. Admission. ~ Main and River streets; 508-888-1711.

The Green Briar Jam Kitchen and the **Old Briar Patch Conservation Area** are east of the center of town. "'Tis a wonderful thing to sweeten the world which is in a jam and needs preserving," wrote Thornton W. Burgess to Ida Putnam. As a boy Burgess roamed the woods around Ida's jam kitchen. Today, the Burgess Society produces natural jams, pickles and jellies from Ida's recipes. Nestled deep in the woods next to a pond, the old-fashioned kitchen looks like an illustration from one of Burgess' books. Peter Rabbit and his animal friends would have loved it here. ~ Discovery Hill Road; 508-888-6870.

East of Sandwich lies the popular resort town of **Barnstable**, where some of the Cape's most beautiful inns and tempting restaurants and shops are located. You'll find the **Donald Trayser Memorial Museum**, a brick structure built in 1856, which was once a custom house, then a post office. Named after a local patriot and historian, the museum includes a potpourri of artifacts related to Cape Cod life and history, such as Indian tools and ships in bottles. Next to the museum stands

✔ CHECK THESE OUT—UNIQUE SIGHTS

- Enter Peter Rabbit's world and sample the tasty jams concocted in the old-fashioned kitchen at **Green Briar Jam Kitchen**. *page 240*
- Imagine yourself in Cornwall, England as you stroll among the rolling moors surrounded by the sea in Cape Cod's **Truro**. *page 249*
- Marvel at the only architecture native to Martha's Vineyard—brightly painted whimsical little cottages—at Oak Bluffs's **Cottage City**. *page 269*
- Stroll through the weathered fishing village of **Dutcher's Dock** on Martha's Vineyard, where simple, gray shingled houses front the harbor. *page 272*

the oldest wooden jail in the United States (circa 1690), whose walls are covered with graffiti written by seamen. Closed Monday, and from mid-October through mid-June. ~ Route 6A; 508-362-2092.

Farther along Route 6A, Yarmouthport is the site of two historic homes with impressive antiques. A white Greek Revival home with black shutters, **Captain Bangs Hallet House** is furnished with elegant settees, tables and chairs, and many classic old toys such as a rocking horse with real animal hide and hair. Open Thursday, Friday and Sunday in July and August; open Sunday in June and September; closed October through May. ~ 11 Strawberry Lane; 508-362-3021.   ◄ HIDDEN

The 1780 **Winslow Crocker House**, a shingled Georgian with handsome wood paneling and an impressive walk-in fireplace, has a rare 17th-century wooden cradle and blanket chest, a Windsor writing chair and many more valuable antiques. Admission. ~ Route 6A, Yarmouthport; 508-362-4385.

Brewster has a couple of sights for children and history buffs. The **New England Fire and History Museum** displays hand- and horse-drawn fire equipment that makes you wonder how they ever put out fires, and a full-scale model of Ben Franklin's first Philadelphia firehouse. Kids like all the bells and fire alarms that are constantly sounding off here. Closed after Columbus Day through Memorial Day. Admission. ~ 1439 Main Street, Route 6A; 508-896-5711.

The **Cape Cod Museum of Natural History** has a working beehive and occasional guided walks through the salt marsh behind the museum. Admission. ~ Main Street, Route 6A; 508-896-3867.

The Cape has some of the most beautiful inns in the country, plus hundreds of other accommodations in every price range, location and style imaginable. If you plan to stay for at least a week, think about renting a house, apartment or condo; it's usually less expensive than a hotel. Contact the **Cape Cod Chamber of Commerce** for names of realtors handling rentals in a particular area. ~ Junction of Routes 6 and 132, Hyannis, MA 02601; 508-362-3225.   **LODGING**

Located in the heart of Sandwich village, **The Village Inn** is a renovated 1830s Federal-style house. Without sacrificing historic details, the owners have made everything look fresh and new. The eight soothing, uncluttered guest rooms, decorated in shades of raspberry and moss, have lace swag curtains, Colonial armoires and pickled four-poster beds. All of the wood furniture is custom made. A wraparound front porch is a good spot for people watching. Closed December through March. ~ 4 Jarves Street; 508-833-0363, 800-922-9989. MODERATE TO DELUXE.   ◄ HIDDEN

The Daniel Webster Inn is one of the few full-service hotels on historic Route 6A. The Federal-style 47-room hotel is so much bigger than the other buildings in Sandwich, it looks a little out of whack. But the inside is very warm and cozy. Guest rooms are done in shades like gold and raspberry or smoke and rose, and are decorated with reproduction Colonial furniture and wing-back chairs; some beds have canopies. Brick paths lead through graceful flower gardens to a gazebo and pool area. The hotel has a restaurant and three dining rooms. Rates available with or without breakfast and dinner. ~ 149 Main Street, Sandwich; 508-888-3622, 800-444-3566, fax 508-888-3566. DELUXE TO ULTRA-DELUXE.

The **Seth Pope House 1699** is a tiny, three-room bed and breakfast thoughtfully run by owners Beverly and John Dobel, two midwestern transplants. Unlike many bed and breakfasts there's a sense of privacy here since all three guest rooms have their own private baths. Each room is individually decorated with beautiful antiques, including a pencil-post bed in the Colonial Room—sneak a peek at it if you can. Comfort is important here; the beds are big with an abundance of pillows. A full breakfast is served by candlelight in the morning. Closed late October through March. ~ 110 Tupper Road, Sandwich; 508-888-5916, 800-699-7384. MODERATE.

The **Beechwood** is one of the prettiest inns on Route 6A. An ancient weeping beech tree shades a good portion of this buttery yellow, gabled Queen Anne Victorian and its lovely wraparound porch. The entire house is furnished with fine antiques. In the Cottage room you'll find a rare 1860 hand-painted bedroom set, in the Marble room a graceful marble fireplace and 19th-century brass bed. The Garret room on the third floor has steeply angled walls and a half-moon window overlooking Cape Cod Bay, while the popular Rose room features a fainting couch at the foot of an antique four-poster bed and a working fireplace. It doesn't matter where you stay—all six guest rooms are wonderful. A full breakfast is served in the wood-paneled dining room and tea on the porch. ~ 2839 Main Street, Barnstable Village; 508-362-6618, 800-609-6618, fax 508-362-0298. DELUXE TO ULTRA-DELUXE.

Built in 1812, the **Wedgewood Inn** sits on a little hill overlooking historic Route 6A. Surrounded by stately elm trees and stone walls,

---

✔ CHECK THESE OUT—UNIQUE LODGING

- *Moderate:* Save your pennies at Brewster's **The Poore House**, an affordable old inn set amid a profusion of flowers and greenery. *page 243*
- *Moderate to deluxe:* Luxuriate at Martha's Vineyard's **Duck Inn**, a health-oriented B & B offering massages and an outdoor hot tub. *page 276*
- *Deluxe:* Marvel at the 35-foot hall at the historic **Mostly Hall**—a Greek Revival mansion designed in the New Orleans garden-district style. *page 262*
- *Ultra-deluxe:* Breathe in the scent of flowers in one of the quaint, rose-covered cottages at Nantucket's **The Summer House**. *page 285*

Budget: under $50   Moderate: $50–$90   Deluxe: $90–$120   Ultra-deluxe: over $120

the Colonial inn makes a lasting impression. Guest rooms sport hand-crafted cherry wood pencil-post beds, antique quilts and wideboard floors and fireplaces. The decor is an elegant interpretation of Early American styles. A full breakfast is included in the rate. ~ 83 Main Street, Route 6A, Yarmouthport; 508-362-5157, fax 508-362-9178. DELUXE TO ULTRA-DELUXE.

A rambling white 1875 Victorian close to the beach, the **Four Chimneys Inn** is the kind of place where you can plop down on the living room couch in front of the fire and settle in for a good read selected from the study. Homey and low-key, the eight guest rooms (three with fireplaces) are large, white and airy with high ceilings and chenille comforters. A large yard with a garden surrounds the house, which sits well back from the road. ~ 946 Main Street, Dennis; 508-385-6317, 800-874-5502, fax 508-385-6285. MODERATE TO DELUXE.

The **Isaiah Clark House**, an 18th-century sea captain's home, is surrounded by five acres of gardens, fruit trees and wild berry patches. Impeccably appointed with Shaker and Colonial antiques, many of the guest rooms have stenciled walls, canopy beds, sloping pine floors and fireplaces. Breakfast is served in an appealing room with an enormous fireplace—guests linger here all morning long. Pre-dinner get-togethers and a full breakfast are included. ~ 1187 Main Street, Brewster; 508-896-2223, 800-822-4001, fax 508-896-7054. DELUXE.

A large turn-of-century gray-and-white house, the **Old Sea Pines Inn** used to be a girls' school. The spacious public and 21 guest rooms are comfortably furnished with antique brown wicker, slip-covered chairs and sofas. A wraparound porch with rockers, perfect for reading or snoozing, overlooks a yard shaded by pine and oak trees. A full breakfast is served in a bright renovated dining area with many skylights. Closed January through March. ~ 2553 Main Street, Brewster; 508-896-6114, 508-896-8322. DELUXE.

You get a lot for your money at **The Poore House**, one of the few bargains on Route 6A. A charming old inn with dark green shutters, the place offers bright and cheery guest rooms with painted floors and some antique furnishings. A full breakfast is served in a cozy living room or patio. Behind the inn stands an attractive garden shop and nursery. Potted flowers and plants arranged along the stone driveway create a profusion of color. (Since you're saving so much money here, consider dining at Chillingsworth (see "Dining" below), one of the Cape's most elegant and expensive restaurants. It's within walking distance.) ~ 2311 Main Street, Brewster; 508-896-2094. MODERATE.

The **Daniel Webster Inn** is so Colonial looking, you expect it to serve traditional New England fare, but the menu is rather diversified. While the menu changes yearly, specials change every four to six weeks and cover a wide range of tastes. The award-winning restaurant boasts an extensive wine cellar. Meals are served in the very formal Webster Room with peach walls, mahogany chairs and brass

DINING

chandeliers; the Heritage Dining Room, featuring antiques, walk-in fireplace and grand piano; or in the greenhouse conservatory overlooking a garden. Breakfast is also available. ~ 149 Main Street, Sandwich; 508-888-3622. MODERATE TO DELUXE.

The place to go for breakfast in Sandwich is **Marshland**. A diner-cum-bakery, it's locally famed for its reasonably priced, hearty and reliably good food. It has all the customary breakfast dishes plus lots of daily specials like pancakes, omelettes and hash. Be sure to order a home-baked muffin; they're celestial. ~ 109 Route 6A; 508-888-9824. BUDGET.

Barnstable Tavern and Grill serves traditional lunch and dinner fare such as steak *au poivre*, mussels marinara, shrimp scampi and pasta. Located in a small complex of shops, the restaurant creates a pleasant Early American feeling with Windsor chairs, folk art, brass light fixtures and blond wood floors. The friendly bar is a good place for a drink, and different varieties of wine are served by the glass. ~ 3176 Main Street, Route 6A, Barnstable; 508-362-2355. MODERATE TO DELUXE.

Abbicci serves contemporary Italian cuisine in an 18th-century Cape Cod cottage on one of the prettiest stretches of historic Route 6A. A good spot for a special lunch or dinner, the restaurant has an imaginative, occasionally changing menu. Dishes have included grilled veal chop with a porcini madeira sauce, *osso bucca alla Milanese*, and pan-seared halibut with lemon caper anchovy sauce. Cozy yet sophisticated, it has a number of small dining rooms with low ceilings, Windsor chairs and white tablecloths. ~ 43 Main Street, Route 6A, Yarmouthport; 508-362-3501. MODERATE TO DELUXE.

HIDDEN ►

Cozy little **Margarite's Restaurant** is a perfect spot for sinfully good desserts and a cappuccino, as well as breakfast, lunch and dinner. Located in a small, Colonial-style shopping complex, it resembles a country tea room with ruffled curtains, cranberry tablecloths and an antique wood-burning stove. The traditional menu features quiche,

---

✔ **CHECK THESE OUT—UNIQUE DINING**

- *Budget to moderate:* End your day at the beach with a basket of fried clams on the deck at **Kadee's Lobster and Clam Bar** in Orleans. *page 263*
- *Moderate to deluxe:* Experience legendary **Ciro & Sal's**, an atmospheric Provincetown institution serving fine Italian food. *page 256*
- *Deluxe:* Overlook sand dunes, rolling green pastures and idyllic Menemsha harbor from the deck of Chilmark's seafood haven, **Home Port**. *page 278*
- *Deluxe to ultra-deluxe:* Make time for romance at the flower-covered **Le Chanticleer**, where you'll dine on traditional French cuisine. *page 287*

Budget: under $8 Moderate: $8–$16 Deluxe: $16–$24 Ultra-deluxe: over $24

french toast and eggs for breakfast; sandwiches, salads and chowder for lunch; prime rib, stuffed shrimp, veal marsala and pasta for dinner. Desserts change daily. One popular offering is the Hot Fudge Pie. A cross between chocolate fudge and cake, it's very thick, gooey and good. ~ 800 Main Street, Route 6A, Dennis; 508-385-3279. MODERATE TO DELUXE.

Gina's By The Sea, a sweet little white-shingled restaurant within walking distance of Chapin Beach, is far more sophisticated than it looks. The predominately Italian menu changes daily and includes entrées like shrimp scampi, mussels marinara and red snapper with champagne sauce. Ruffled curtains, white tablecloths and plain wooden chairs create a casual elegance. ~ 134 Taunton Avenue, Dennis; 508-385-3213. MODERATE TO DELUXE.

◄ HIDDEN

You might find yourself sitting near a well-known actor at the **Green Room,** located on the grounds of the Cape Playhouse. Banks of windows on three sides of the attractive white and green restaurant with ivy-accented valences overlook sweeping lawns and flower gardens. The Continental menu includes a host of fish, chicken and steak dishes. Closed November through April. ~ Off Route 6A, Dennis; 508-385-8000. MODERATE TO DELUXE.

The food's hearty and predictable, the service fast and friendly at **Marshside Restaurant,** a glorified coffee shop popular with locals. Omelettes, bagels, pancakes and french toast are some of the breakfast offerings. Lunch items include lobster salad, quesadillas and fried clams. At dinner it's fried clams, stuffed shrimp, steak, chicken picatta and daily specials. The decor is kitchen-cute with fake Tiffany lamps, bentwood chairs and ruffled curtains. The back room has a spectacular view of a salt marsh meadow. ~ 28 Bridge Street, East Dennis; 508-385-4010. BUDGET TO MODERATE.

◄ HIDDEN

The **Bramble Inn** is one of those restaurants people always rave about. Housed in a Greek Revival farmhouse on scenic Route 6A, the place offers a *prix-fixe* menu that changes daily. Dinner is served in four small dining rooms complete with Queen Anne chairs, fresh flowers, antiques and china blue walls. Innovative dishes have included grilled seafood in curry sauce, smoked bluefish pâté, and rack of lamb with garlic and rosemary. Closed January through March. ~ 2019 Main Street, Route 6A, Brewster; 508-896-7644. ULTRA-DELUXE.

The blond wood floors, floral drapes, ceiling fans and cloth napkins of the **Brewster Fish House Restaurant** creates a quaint and casual atmosphere. Its small, imaginative menu features dishes such as calamari with tomato-red aïoli and grilled Atlantic salmon with pancetta and a mild Dijon mustard sauce. ~ 2208 Main Street, Route 6A, Brewster; 508-896-7867. MODERATE.

◄ HIDDEN

Elegant and expensive, **Chillingsworth** has been repeatedly praised by the *New York Times* and *Esquire*. The menu changes daily, utilizing seasonal and fresh ingredients. The food is French American, with dishes such as loin of veal with sun-dried tomatoes, risotto and sage, and free-range chicken with greens, chili brown sauce and sweet potato chips. Located in a 300-year-old, tree-shaded Colonial house, the restaurant has dining areas combining modern and traditional decorative touches such as contemporary artwork, antique mirrors and white tablecloths. Lunch, brunch and bistro dinners are served in the greenhouse and garden. After lunch, browse in the restaurant's antique and pastry shop. The seven-course dinner is served at two seatings. The main dining room, closed on Monday, is ultra-deluxe. Bistro dining in the garden is moderate to deluxe. Closed Thanksgiving through Memorial Day. ~ 2449 Main Street, Route 6A, Brewster; 508-896-3640. MODERATE TO ULTRA-DELUXE.

SHOPPING   Some of the Cape's best shopping is along Route 6A, which is lined with antique stores and artists studios selling pottery, weavings, handcrafted furniture and more.

With its sloping wood floors and wainscotting, **The Brown Jug** looks like an old general store. But it sells fine quality, hand-blown antique glass. Many of the pieces were made in Sandwich in the 19th century. ~ 155 Main Street, Route 6A, Sandwich; 508-833-1088.

The Blacks Handweaving Shop has beautiful handwoven coverlets, throws, place mats, hats, gloves and wallhangings in lush colors—rich navy and cream, dusty lavender and grey, russet and forest green. The store is in a large barnlike room where you can watch owners/designers Bob and Gabrielle Black working at one of the many looms. ~ 597 Main Street, Route 6A, West Barnstable; 508-362-3955.

Even if you don't intend to shop to buy a weathervane, stop by **Salt and Chestnut**. It's like a weathervane museum. The Salt and Chestnut sells new and antique hand-hammered copper weathervanes in a myriad of styles—a witch on a broom, mermaid, lobster, sailboats, dogs, elephants, deer and more. ~ 651 Main Street, Route 6A, West Barnstable; 508-362-6085.

Design Works specializes in antique Scandinavian pine armoires, mirrors, chairs, settees and white linen and lace napkins, tablecloths and bed accessories. ~ 159 Main Street, Route 6A, Yarmouthport; 508-362-9698.

Originally a general store that also housed a church on the second floor, the **Parnassus Book Store** has a wealth of marine and Cape Cod book titles. ~ 220 Old King's Highway, Route 6A, Yarmouthport; 508-362-6420.

One of the nicest sights on Route 6A is the vibrant display of fresh produce and flowers at **Tobey Farm Country Store**. Stop here in the summer for fresh native corn, peaches and plums, and in the fall for pumpkins and apples. The white clapboard farm also sells reasonably priced dried wreaths made from German statice, rose hips, lavender, yarrow, dried pink rosebuds, baby's-breath, purple statice and eucalyptus. ~ 352 Main Street, Route 6A, Dennis; 508-385-2930.

Even if you can't afford anything at **Kingsland Manor**, stop and browse through its labyrinth of beautiful rooms and gardens filled with exquisite American and European antiques. ~ 440 Main Street, Route 6A, West Brewster; 508-385-9741.

Heritage Plantation Concerts offers a diverse program including jazz, ethnic and folk music, banjo music, Scottish pipe bands, chorale groups and big bands. Closed late October through Mother's Day. ~ Pine and Grove streets, Sandwich; 508-888-3300.

NIGHTLIFE

Established in 1926 and America's oldest summer theater, **The Cape Playhouse** presents well-known plays and musicals such as *The Sound of Music*, *Ain't Misbehavin'* and *Noises Off*, performed by Hollywood and Broadway stars. Lana Turner, Gregory Peck and Henry Fonda have been on stage here. Nostalgic and romantic-looking, the Playhouse is in an 1838 meetinghouse surrounded by graceful lawns, gardens and a Victorian Gothic ticket booth. Closed mid-September through late June. ~ Route 6A, Dennis; 508-385-3911.

The Cape Museum of Fine Arts' **Cinema Club**, on the grounds of the Cape Playhouse, shows quality films, both new and old, such as *Henry V* with Laurence Olivier, *Ginger and Fred* and *House of Games*. Films are shown only in fall and winter months. ~ Route 6A, Dennis; 508-385-4477.

Barnstable Comedy Club Community Theater, founded in 1922, is the oldest amateur theater group on the Cape. Throughout the year it gives major productions and workshops. Kurt Vonnegut, an alumni of the Club, acted in many of its earlier productions. ~ Route 6A, Barnstable Village; 508-362-6333.

North Cape beaches are on protected Cape Cod Bay. They tend to be quiet and calm, with gentle surf and scenic vistas of soft sand dunes and salt marsh.

BEACHES & PARKS

SANDY NECK BEACH & THE GREAT MARSHES 🏃 🏊 This area has all the ecological treasures for which the Cape is known. Very straight and long, beautiful Sandy Neck Beach offers a 360 view of the ocean and rippling sand dunes bordered by the Great Marshes, 3000 acres of protected land harboring many species of marine life and birds. The sand is ideal for beach-combing, and trails meander through the dunes and marsh. Restrooms, snack bar; groceries a short drive away in Sandwich; parking fee, $8. ~ Take Sandy Neck Road off Route 6A in Sandwich to the beach in Barnstable.

GREY'S BEACH 🏊 This small, quiet beach is perfect for children. But the main reason people come here is to stroll along the long, elevated walkway stretching across the marsh that skirts the beach. The walkway permits a close-up view of marsh flora and fauna, and from a distance it appears to be floating in grassy water. There's not much to do here, but this area is quite beautiful, especially at sunset. Picnic tables, playground, restrooms, lifeguards; groceries nearby in Yarmouth; information, call the Yarmouth Chamber of Commerce, 508-778-1008. ~ Off Route 6A on Centre Street in Yarmouth.

CHAPIN BEACH The sand-strewn road leading to Chapin Beach passes gentle sand dunes and small, unpretentious, summer cottages. A pleasant spot for walks along the shore, the thin, slightly curved, dune-backed beach has soft, white sand ideal for clean, comfortable sunbathing. Restrooms; groceries nearby in Dennis. ~ Off Route 6A on Chapin Beach Road in Dennis.

HIDDEN ► **PAINE'S CREEK BEACH** There are better beaches nearby for sunning and swimming, but Paine's Creek is ideal for quiet walks through timeless scenery bathed in golden light. Weatherbeaten skiffs are moored along the shore, and Paine's Creek, a gentle slip of a stream, winds through a salt marsh meadow down to a narrow strip of soft beach surrounded by tiny coves and inlets. Groceries nearby in West Brewster, parking fee, minimum $5; information, call the West Brewster Chamber of Commerce, 508-255-7045. ~ Off Route 6A on Paine's Creek Road in West Brewster.

NICKERSON STATE PARK This 2000-acre park looks more like the Berkshires than Cape Cod. Dense pine groves, meadows and jewel-like freshwater ponds with beaches are home to abundant wildlife including red foxes and white-tailed deer. There is so much to do here—hiking, biking, motor boating, canoeing—it gets very crowded in the summer. Quiet beaches and hiking trails can be found around Little Cliff and Flax ponds. In winter there's cross-country skiing and ice-skating on the ponds. Fishing is excellent at Higgins Pond, which is stocked annually with trout; you can swim in freshwater ponds. Picnic areas, restrooms, showers, ranger station, interpretive programs; groceries a short drive away in Brewster. ~ Off Route 6A in Brewster; 508-896-3491.

▲ There are 418 tent/RV sites (no hookups) on a first come, first served basis (reservations accepted April through October); $12 per night. Winter camping is allowed for self-contained RVs; $5 per night.

▼▼▼▼▼▼▼▼▼▼▼▼
The Outer Cape

Route 6A ends at Orleans, where it intersects with Route 6 and leads to Eastham. At this point the character of the landscape changes dramatically. The woods disappear and the sky opens up to reveal towering sand dunes, miles of silver marsh grass and windswept moors. At the very tip is Provincetown, one of the Cape's largest communities.

About 50 percent of the Outer Cape is under the jurisdiction of the Cape Cod National Seashore, a natural playground with miles of bicycle paths, hikes and the Cape's most dramatic beaches (see the "Beaches & Parks" and "Hiking" sections in this chapter).

Fort Hill in Eastham offers a mesmerizing view overlooking Nauset Marsh that's so beautiful it doesn't seem real. Once productive farmland, the marsh today is laced with wavy ribbons of water that wind through downy, soft green-gold marsh grass past old farmhouses, stone walls and ponds complete with adorable ducks. Trails meander through this area, which is a special resting place for blue herons. ~ Off Route 6.

Near the Fort Hill parking lot is the **Edward Penniman House**, a fairy-tale-like, red-and-yellow French Empire house with an enormous archway of whale jaw bones at its gate. Built by an eccentric whaler in the 19th century, the whimsical structure contrasts dramatically with the Cape's simple saltbox homes. ~ Off Route 6, Eastham.

After Eastham is **Wellfleet**, an unpretentious, wiggle-your-toes-in-the-sand kind of place with a surprising number of good art galleries and gourmet restaurants. On Saturday nights in the summer, many galleries have openings that feel like neighborhood block parties. Wellfleet has many year-round residents, and they all seem to know each other.

Before heading into town, stop at the **Wellfleet Chamber of Commerce** for a gallery guide. ~ Route 6; 508-349-2510.

On the way to Wellfleet is **Uncle Tim's Bridge**, a low wooden boardwalk that goes over a field of silvery marsh grass to a small wooded hill. A dreamy sort of place shrouded in delicate mist in the morning and soft mellow light in the afternoon, it's perfect for a picnic or quiet walk.

North of Wellfleet lies magnificent **Truro**, a vast treeless plain of rolling moors surrounded by water and some of the state's most impressive sand dunes. Named after an area of Cornwall, England that's similar in appearance, Truro is a wonderful area for picture taking.

To capture the essence of Wellfleet, stay at the **Holden Inn**, a long, white farmhouse-style building. There's nothing fancy about the place, but like Wellfleet, it has an easy, casual feeling. Located on a shady country lane five minutes from the wharf, the inn offers 27 well-kept rooms (some with shared bath) with ruffled white curtains and floral wallpaper or wood paneling. Closed mid-October through mid-April. ~ 140 Commercial Street, Wellfleet Bay; 508-349-3450. MODERATE.

Restaurants on the Cape fall into three categories: expensive French/nouvelle cuisine, surf and turf and coffee-shop fare. If you crave variety, head for the Outer Cape. Wellfleet has a surprising number of excellent, imaginative restaurants.

The **Bayside Lobster Hutt**, a noisy, friendly place, is perfect after a day at the beach. Located on a country road leading to Wellfleet's galleries and harbor, it looks like an old white schoolhouse. On the

SIGHTS

◄ *HIDDEN*

◄ *HIDDEN*

◄ *HIDDEN*

LODGING

◄ *HIDDEN*

DINING

Text continued on page 252.

The Land of Lighthouses

Massachusetts' prominence as a shipping and fishing center made lighthouses essential early in its history. The first lighthouse in America was built in Boston Harbor on Little Brewster Island in 1716. During the years to follow, 60 more were built all along the coast.

The majority of lighthouses have been well preserved, and many are still in use, although the lighthouse keeper has gone the way of time.

Today lighthouses are automated and unmanned. Lighted buoys, radio communications, radar and high-tech navigational equipment, electronic fog signals and the Coast Guard offer additional protection to seafaring vessels. Shipwrecks are practically unheard of these days.

A few beacons are privately owned, but most are maintained by the Coast Guard or local historic organizations. What follows is a guide to some of the most beautiful and historically significant lighthouses.

Built in 1797, **Highland Lighthouse Station** in Truro, Cape Cod, is better known as Cape Cod Light. It stands on clay bluffs overlooking an area once known as "the graveyard of ships" because hundreds of vessels went aground here before the lighthouse was built. Visible 20 miles out to sea, this classic white-and-black lighthouse is surrounded by scenic Cape Cod National Seashore and commands a magnificent view.

Located within the Cape Cod National Seashore, **Race Point Lighthouse**, built in 1816, guards the entrance to Provincetown Harbor. Surrounded by wild, windswept dunes, it is accessible only by four-wheel-drive vehicle or by foot. Even after the lighthouse was built, from 1816 to 1946 more than 100 shipwrecks occurred in this treacherous area.

Plymouth Lighthouse, established in 1768, is located on a beautiful bluff at the end of a peninsula that stretches from Duxbury to Plymouth Harbor. During the Revolutionary War, a British ship fired a cannonball at the lighthouse, but it barely made a dent. Destroyed by fire in 1801, it was rebuilt in 1843 and is one of Massachusetts' most scenic lighthouses.

Scituate Lighthouse, built in 1811 on Cedar Point at the entrance to Scituate Harbor, is maintained by the Scituate Historical Society. It's no longer in use, but an event that took place here during the War of 1812 gave this lighthouse historic distinction. In September 1814, Rebecca and Abigail Bates, the lighthouse keeper's young daughters, were alone in the lighthouse, when they spotted British war ships heading for the harbor. Frantic to do something, they started playing military songs on a drum and fife. The music made the British think the American Army was amassing, and they hightailed it back to the high seas. The girls became local heroes.

Minot's Lighthouse, which dates to 1850, is built on a ledge one mile offshore from Cohasset. The ledge can only be seen at low tide. Most of the time the lighthouse looks as if it's floating in water. Since it was built in a highly dangerous area, men working on the lighthouse were washed out to sea by strong waves and currents. In 1851 a ferocious storm destroyed the lighthouses and two keepers died. Because of these tragedies the lighthouse was thought to be haunted by the ghosts of those who perished at sea. A museum in Cohasset contains many artifacts and historical information on the lighthouse.

Annisquam Harbor Lighthouse is on Wigwam Point at the mouth of Annisquam River on the North Shore. Built in 1801, this lighthouse doesn't have historic significance, but it is one of the most scenic in all of Massachusetts. It's located off the beaten path: to get there, take Route 127 to Annisquam and turn right at the village church, then right into Norwood Heights and follow the road to the water.

roof, a fisherman statue hauls an enormous red lobster into a boat. Everyone sits at long picnic tables. Buoys and fish nets decorate the walls. The menu features lobster, flounder, steamed clams, scallops and shrimp. There's a raw bar and salad bar, as well as a take-out window where you can order clambake picnics. Closed September through Memorial Day. ~ 91 Commercial Street, Wellfleet; 508-349-6333. MODERATE TO DELUXE.

The Lighthouse is a Wellfleet institution. If you want to mingle with the locals, come here in the morning for breakfast. The ambience is strictly coffee shop, as is the food, which includes french toast, bacon and eggs, fried seafood, sandwiches, hamburgers and the like. Located in the center of town, it has a kitschy miniature lighthouse on its roof that is impossible to miss. ~ Main Street; 508-349-3681. MODERATE TO DELUXE.

Sweet Seasons is an exceptionally pretty restaurant overlooking an idyllic duck pond surrounded by rushes, flagstone paths, locust trees and woods. The pale gray and apricot restaurant serves dishes such as grilled swordfish, shrimp with feta cheese, tomatoes and ouzo, sliced island pork and potted crab and shrimp. Closed September through May. ~ The Inn at Ducke Creeke, Main Street, Wellfleet; 508-349-6535. MODERATE TO DELUXE.

Painters is a great place to go for a eclectic American fusion cuisine. Located in a 1750 Cape house, the restaurant serves mouthwatering dishes such as roasted pork with spicy peanut sauce, and sautéed scallops with oyster mushrooms and asparagus served with a ginger cream sauce. Closed Tuesday, and January through April. ~ 50 East Main Street, Wellfleet; 508-349-2134. MODERATE TO DELUXE.

BEACHES & PARKS

FIRST ENCOUNTER BEACH ≋ This is where the Pilgrims first encountered the Wampanoag Indians, who were not exactly happy to see them. Six years earlier an English slave dealer had kidnapped some of them to sell in Spain. When the Pilgrims arrived a mild skirmish broke out, but no one was hurt and the Pilgrims made a hasty retreat. Sandy paths lead through dense green grass to this striking beach bordered by a vast marsh meadow and brilliant sky. The long, wide beach attracts a relatively quiet crowd in the summer. Restrooms, groceries are a short drive away in Eastham; day-use fee, $5. ~ Take Samoset Road off Route 6 in Eastham.

THE CAPE COD NATIONAL SEASHORE 🚶 🚴 ≋ This 27,000-acre ecological wonderland includes endless stretches of unbelievably beautiful beaches, 60-foot sand dunes, steep cliffs, wind-bitten moors, salt marsh, freshwater ponds and woodlands. Undisturbed and undeveloped, the area runs from Chatham to Provincetown and is laced with some of the Cape's finest hiking and bicycle trails (see the "Bicycling" and "Hiking" sections at the end of this chapter).

What follows are some of the National Seashore's most renowned beaches and ponds. For more information visit the **Salt Pond Visitors Center.** ~ Route 6, Eastham; 508-255-3421. The **Cape Cod National Seashore Headquarters** is also helpful. ~ Route 6, South Wellfleet; 508-349-3785.

COAST GUARD BEACH 🏖 🏊 "On its solitary dune my house faced the four walls of the world," wrote Henry Beston of the place he built in 1927 on this extraordinary beach. In 1978 the house washed away in a storm, but Beston's experiences are chronicled in a wonderful book, *The Outermost House*, available at most Cape Cod bookstores. Rugged and wild Coast Guard Beach goes on for as far as the eye can see. Bordered by cliffs, marsh grass and tributaries, a red-and-white coast guard station sits on a bluff overlooking the beach. The beach is ideal for long walks, sunbathing, swimming (although the sea can be rough at times) and surfing. Restrooms, showers, lifeguards; groceries are nearby in Eastham; day-use fee, $5. ~ Take Doane Road off Route 6 near Eastham.

NAUSET LIGHT BEACH & MARCONI BEACH 🏖 These impressive beaches—bordered by towering, shrub-covered cliffs—are right next to each other. Long, steep wooden stairways descend to the clean, white sand beaches. The imposing cliffs and expansive vistas make you feel very small and in awe of it all. Walk north along the shore for a quiet spot in the summer, when the beaches get crowded. Swimming is excellent, but watch undertow. On the road to Nauset Beach is Nauset Light, a classic red-and-white lighthouse, one of the most photographed sights on Cape Cod. Restrooms, showers, lifeguards; groceries in Eastham or Wellfleet; day-use fee, $5. ~ Nauset Light is off Route 6 at the end of Cable Road and along Nauset Light Beach Road in Eastham. Marconi is off Route 6 on Marconi Beach Road in Wellfleet.

GREAT POND & LONG POND 🏖 Wellfleet has some of the most idyllic freshwater ponds on the Cape. Less than a mile from wild-looking shoreline, these two offer a completely different nature experience. Densely wooded and pine-scented, they look like mountain ponds. The sparkling water is fresh and invigorating. Long Pond has a lovely shaded grassy area with picnic tables, a small sand beach and a float in the water. Great Pond is approached via wooden steps leading down from the parking lot overlooking the pond. It has a pretty sandy beach. Half-hidden houses lie along some of the shore. You must live or be staying in Wellfleet to go to either pond, and nonresidents must purchase a permit. Picnic tables; groceries are found nearby in Wellfleet; information, call the Beach Sticker House, 508-349-9818. ~ To reach Great Pond, take Calhoon Hollow Road off Route 6 in Wellfleet; for Long Pond, take Long Pond Road off East Main Street in Wellfleet.

◄ HIDDEN

Provincetown

▼▼▼▼▼▼▼▼▼ Provincetown, at the Cape's outer tip, is nestled on a hill overlooking the bay. Everything good and bad about Cape Cod can be found here: elegant sea captains' mansions, a honky-tonk wharf, dazzling beaches, first-rate museums, schlocky galleries, hamburger joints and gourmet restaurants.

The people are equally diverse. Provincetown has a large gay population, as well as artists and writers, Portuguese fishermen, aristocrats, beer-guzzling rabble-rousers and plenty of tourists. Similarly, Provincetown's many attractions draw all types of visitors, but the town is particularly popular among gay travelers. The gay scene is everywhere, ranging from the beaches to the boulevards to the bars. Every hotel and restaurant in the area welcomes gays and lesbians and in many cases caters primarily to them, as is noted in the reviews below.

Of all the towns on the Cape, Provincetown has the most interesting history. The Pilgrims landed here in 1620 before going to Plymouth, and in the 18th and 19th centuries it was a prominent whaling and fishing port, attracting many Portuguese settlers who still fish the waters today.

Around the turn of the century, artists and writers, such as Eugene O'Neill, started moving to Provincetown, and it became one of America's most renowned artists colonies. A renaissance period flourished until about 1945, when tourism evolved and many artists scattered for quieter parts of the world.

SIGHTS
To immerse yourself in Provincetown's artistic past, get a copy of *Walking Tours No. 2 and 3* from the Provincetown Heritage Museum, or contact the **Provincetown Chamber of Commerce**. These pamphlets list the name and address of every famous writer and artist who ever lived here. Their former homes aren't open to the public, but it's fun to walk by 577 Commercial Street and imagine what it was like when O'Neill rented a room there. ~ 307 Commercial Street, MacMillan Wharf; 508-487-3424.

Provincetown Heritage Museum provides an overview of the town's historic and artistic past. The *Rose Dorothea*, the world's largest indoor model of a fishing schooner, fills up the entire second floor of the museum. Other exhibits include hand-painted Peter Hunt furniture featuring seascapes, photographs of artists at the turn of the century and many paintings. Closed from Columbus Day through Memorial Day. Admission. ~ 356 Commercial Street; 508-487-7098.

Walk east on Commercial Street, the main drag, to the **Provincetown Art Association and Museum** for the best art on the Cape. The museum exhibits work by noted Provincetown artists. In the winter, the museum is open on weekends only. Admission. ~ 460 Commercial Street; 508-487-1750.

For a picture-postcard view of Provincetown and the surrounding seashore and sand dunes, visit the **Pilgrim Monument and Provincetown Museum**. The 252-foot granite tower, with 30-foot arches and turrets, was copied from the Torre del Mangia tower in Siena, Italy. The museum houses an eclectic collection that includes everything from a model of a Thai temple, antique dolls, Wedgwood china, primitive portraits and scrimshaw to figureheads, a captain's cabin from a whaling ship and Provincetown's oldest fire engine. Closed December through March. Admission. ~ High Pole Hill; 508-487-1310.

Open mid-May to mid-October, **The Outermost Hostel** offers accommodations in five cottages. Amenities are standard hostel: shared baths, common kitchen and lounge. One unique feature is the hostel's key system, which allows entry to your room during the day. Gay-friendly. ~ 28 Winslow Street; 508-487-4378. BUDGET.

A short walk through the artsy East End brings you to and from **Windamar House**, a peaceful white clapboard guesthouse that caters mainly to women. The six rooms and two efficiency apartments vary from attractive to elegant, but the inn's prettiest areas are its spectacular gardens. Continental breakfast is provided in the common room, where guests are also welcome to watch television and videos or use the microwave to prepare snacks. Closed January through mid-February. ~ 568 Commercial Street; 508-487-0599. MODERATE TO DELUXE.

LODGING

The **Brass Key Guesthouse**, one of the only small inns in P-town with a private pool, is also one of the area's best gay-friendly inns. The owner's background in the high end of the hotel trade shows in his attention to the details that count—elegant, yet comfortable furniture, sparkling clean bathrooms, meticulous landscaping and friendly staff. Some rooms have private whirlpool baths and working fireplaces. ~ 9 Court Street; 508-487-9005, 800-842-9858, fax 508-487-9020. ULTRA-DELUXE.

For a free directory of gay- or lesbian-owned hotels, restaurants, bars, shops and services, stop by the **Provincetown Business Guild.** ~ 115 Bradford Street; 508-487-2313, 800-637-8696.

When you see the carefully restored 18th-century sea captain's home that is the **Fairbanks Inn**, you might well expect high prices; however, you would be wrong. Despite the charming building and fairly extensive amenities (working fireplaces and air conditioning in most of the rooms, for example), the 15 guest rooms are quite reasonably priced, all year-round. Wide plank floors and wainscoting, large, airy rooms and four-poster beds complete the picture. Gay-friendly. ~ 90 Bradford Street; 508-487-0386, 800-324-7265. MODERATE TO ULTRA-DELUXE.

The centrally located **Heritage House** offers great people watching and ocean views from the large upper veranda. This Cape Cod–style home, which dates from 1856, has 13 guest rooms furnished with an eclectic assortment of antiques. Guests are welcome to show their stuff on the baby-grand piano downstairs. Closed mid-November through March, but the owner is willing to accommodate special requests. Gay-friendly. ~ 7 Center Street; 508-487-3692. MODERATE.

HIDDEN ►

With its dark wood shingles, sky-blue shutters and nursery-rhyme garden, the **Bradford Gardens Inn** looks like an illustration from a Mother Goose book. One of the most inviting cottages in Provincetown, the Bradford has 18 guest rooms and apartments, most with working fireplaces. An apartment on the side of the house with its own entrance has a sitting room, brick fireplace and garden view. A full gourmet breakfast is served by the cozy fireplace. Gay-friendly. ~ 178 Bradford Street; 508-487-1616, 800-432-2334. DELUXE TO ULTRA-DELUXE.

The **Asheton House** makes an elegant first impression. A beautiful, curved two-sided stairway leads to the front door of this pristine white 1840 house surrounded by brick paths and an English boxwood garden. The three guest rooms are decorated differently. The handsome Captains room (shared bath) has a four-poster bed, neutral color scheme and antiques. The suite comes with a working fireplace, a harbor view and oversized bathtub. Safari room is spacious, although its grass cloth wallpaper seems more 1966 than 1840. Gay-friendly. ~ 3 Cook Street; 508-487-9966. MODERATE TO DELUXE.

Built in 1820, the **Watership Inn** is popular with gay men and women. Located on a quiet street yet close to everything, the inn features guest rooms with arched beamed ceilings and antiques. Some have private decks. Breakfast is served on an outdoor deck or in an attractive living room with vaulted ceilings and a bank of french doors leading out to a yard where volleyball is played in the summer. The inn offers terrific off-season bargains. ~ 7 Winthrop Street; 508-487-0094, 800-330-9413. MODERATE TO DELUXE.

If you're in the mood for a splurge during your visit to the Outer Cape, the beautiful Federal-style **Red Inn** is your best choice. Carefully renovated in 1992, the four rooms and efficiency apartments are carefully furnished with lovely antique furniture and original artwork, and each room has a spectacular view of Provincetown Harbor and Cape Cod Bay. The inn's fabulous restaurant is a treat, too. ~ 15 Commercial Street; 508-487-0050. ULTRA-DELUXE.

DINING

Provincetown restaurants serve everything from Italian, French, vegetarian and Continental to nouvelle, meat-and-potatoes and bistro-style fare.

Ciro & Sal's is one of Provincetown's most legendary restaurants. Established in 1951 as a coffeehouse for artists, it grew into a full-fledged restaurant serving classic Italian food. In 1959 Sal left and opened his own restaurant (described below). Dripping with atmosphere, the basement dining room resembles an Italian wine cellar with a low ceiling, slate floor and candle-lit tables. An upstairs dining room overlooks a garden. Popular dishes include linguine with seafood in a plum tomato sauce, poached bass with clams and veal tenderloin with mozzarella and prosciutto. Tasty Italian bread is baked on the premises. ~ 4 Kiley Court; 508-487-0049. MODERATE TO DELUXE.

Sal's Place is cozy and intimate. In this seaside cottage with Italian ambience, Chianti bottles hang from the low-beamed ceiling, bay windows are draped with lace curtains and a Modigliani poster adorns a wall. The menu includes 12 kinds of pasta, veal dishes and inventive seafood entrées such as flounder stuffed with shellfish and broiled salmon with balsamic vinegar and capers. Closed November through April. ~ 99 Commercial Street; 508-487-1279. MODERATE TO DELUXE.

With its teal and gray cloths, cream walls and casablanca ceiling fans, **Gallerani's Café** attracts locals and out-of-towners alike. The prices are a bargain, the food is down to earth and so is the crowd. The room is bright and airy, and the long bar in back is a pleasant place for a drink. Open for dinner only, Gallerani's serves dishes such as baked stuffed lobster, filet mignon and a variety of pastas. Closed Monday and Tuesday from Labor Day through May. ~ 133 Commercial Street; 508-487-4433. MODERATE TO DELUXE.

Café Heaven is located on a part of Commercial Street away from the touristy hoopla. Housed in an old storefront with large picture windows, the restaurant is bright and uncluttered, with white wooden tables and light brown carpeting. A colorful mural by nationally known artist John Grillo adorns one wall. The food is hearty and all American—bacon and eggs, Portuguese french toast, omelettes, tasty scones, lusty sandwiches, gourmet burgers and salads such as chicken tarragon. This popular hangout for gays and lesbians is open for breakfast, lunch and dinner. Closed November through mid-April. ~ 199 Commercial Street; 508-487-9639. BUDGET TO MODERATE.

SHOPPING

Remembrances of Things Past is fun to explore even if you aren't in the mood to buy. It's full of nostalgic memorabilia from the '20s to the '50s—phones, jewelry, sports memorabilia and vintage photographs of Elvis, Marilyn and Lucy. ~ 376 Commercial Street; 508-487-9443.

Marine Specialties sounds like a straightforward place, but it's not. Housed in a barnlike room, this eclectic shop is jammed with all sorts of reasonably priced oddball nautical and military items such as antique brass buttons, old fashioned oars, bells, baskets, antique diving gear, fog horns, vintage shoe carts, Army and Navy clothing, flags, bicycle lights, shells and fishing nets. Even people who hate to shop love this place. ~ 235 Commercial Street; 508-487-1730.

NIGHTLIFE

Provincetown has first-rate gay and lesbian entertainment—everything from afternoon tea dances, cabaret and ministage productions to piano bars, discos, you name it. Here are some of the most popular hot spots, a few of which draw straights and gays alike

The Post Office Café Cabaret is the spot for lesbians in the summer, when it presents noted female performers such as Teresa Trull. The café is a good place to hang out. Closed from Labor Day through Memorial Day; the cafe does open for Women's Week during the second week of October. ~ 303 Commercial Street; 508-487-6400.

A popular spot for quality entertainment is the **Town House Restaurant**. During the summer it offers a variety of acts—piano music, drag shows and comedians. Cover for most shows. ~ 291 Commercial Street; 508-487-0292.

Female impersonators bring to life such legends as Judy Garland and Pearl Bailey at the **Crown and Anchor**, housed in a historic waterfront building. This place attracts gays, lesbians and straights. Cover. ~ 247 Commercial Street; 508-487-1430.

The hottest gay bar and disco in town is the **Atlantic House**. ~ 4-6 Masonic Place; 508-487-3821.

The **Pied Piper** was cited by *Time* magazine as "the best women's bar" in the country. Locals say the best time to go is after ten for the dancing, but they also offer afternoon tea dances. Closed from October through March. ~ 193-A Commercial Street; 508-487-1527.

During the summer a popular activity for gays is the afternoon tea dance at **The Boatslip Beach Club**, a full-service resort on the beach. Closed from November through mid-April. ~ 161 Commercial Street; 508-487-1669.

BEACHES & PARKS

RACE POINT BEACH & HERRING COVE BEACH 🏃🚴🏊 "Here a man may stand, and put all America behind him," wrote Thoreau in his book *Cape Cod*. Located at the end of the Cape, both beaches have magnificent 360° views of brilliant sky, ocean, dunes and a silver sea of beach grass. On cloudy days, the winds shift, the colors change and a minimalist environment unfolds. When the sun shines, everything shimmers. Both beaches offer long stretches of clean white sand surrounded by acres of untouched land. Bicycle paths and hiking trails are everywhere. Restrooms, showers, lifeguards, snack bar (Herring Cove only); groceries nearby in Provincetown; day-use fee, $3; parking fee, $5. ~ To reach Race Point, take Race Point Road off Route 6; for Herring Cove, take Province Land Road.

▼▼▼▼▼▼▼▼▼▼▼

The South Cape

This part of the Cape is a hodgepodge of scenic villages, inexpensive motels, mini-malls and gas stations. To explore it from Provincetown, head back on Route 6 to Route 28 in Orleans, a pleasant yet unassuming residential area. At Chatham, Route 28 swings around to the west and runs along the south shore of the Cape along Nantucket Sound.

SIGHTS

Chatham, one of the most stylish towns on the Cape, has exquisite inns, good restaurants and beautiful shops. It's a very Ralph Lauren kind of place where everyone looks as though they play tennis.

Chatham's **Information Booth** is in the middle of town. ~ 533 Main Street; 508-945-5199.

At the end of Main Street, you run into **Shore Road**, lined with graceful oceanfront homes and a classic lighthouse across from the Coast Guard station.

Located nearby is the **Old Atwood House Museums and Murals Barn,** an unassuming-looking 1752 brown-shingle house exhibiting antiques, seashells and Sandwich glass. Right next to the house, a barn displays compelling murals by realist painter Alice Stallknecht. The murals depict Chatham townspeople of the 1930s in religious settings, such as Christ preaching from a dory below the Chatham lighthouse. Open Tuesday through Friday from mid-June through late September. ~ 347 Stage Harbor Road; 508-945-2493.

◄ *HIDDEN*

Monomoy National Wildlife Refuge, a sandy, nine-mile-long island immediately off the coast of Chatham, is home to over 300 species of birds, many on the endangered species list. The island is accessible by private boat or by car via the dike, and parts of it are off limits to the public.

West of Chatham is Harwich Port, a lovely residential area, followed by Dennis Port, West Dennis, West Yarmouth and Hyannis, considerably less attractive spots. This stretch of Route 28 is mostly gas stations, coffee shops and cheap motels. But if you've had it up to here with history and quaint villages, this area is great for slumming. There are 11 miniature golf courses in the region, and one of the best is **Pirates Cove.** The Trump Tower of miniature golf, it has an elaborate pirate ship in a fake pond surrounded by terraced rock cliffs and gushing waterfalls. Closed early November through mid-April. ~ 728 Main Street, South Yarmouth; 508-394-6200.

Because the Kennedys live in **Hyannis,** people usually expect it to be glamorous and beautiful, but most of the town is very commercial. The Kennedys live in the one nice area. People come to Hyannis for three reasons: the airport, ferries to the Islands, and spying on the Kennedys.

At the western end of the South Cape is **Falmouth,** a large and bustling town with a beautiful village green surrounded by some of the Cape's loveliest historic homes. One of these, which houses the **Falmouth Historical Society,** is a creamy yellow, hip-roofed 1790 Colonial building with a widow's walk. ~ Village Green, Palmer Street.

Six miles north of town, **Ashumet Holly Wildlife Sanctuary** offers tours as well as nature trail walks. Admission. ~ Off Route 151 and Currier Road; 508-563-6390.

The rest of downtown Falmouth isn't as scenic, but it does have a number of beautiful, high-quality clothing and home furnishing stores. The **Falmouth Chamber of Commerce** is located right off Main Street. ~ 20 Academy Lane; 508-548-8500, 800-526-8532.

Immediately south of Falmouth is Woods Hole, a small, deeply wooded, hilly village that's home to the **Woods Hole Oceanographic Institute.** The Institute isn't open to the public; it's strictly a research facility ranked in stature alongside Scripps Institute of Oceanography in California.

However, the nearby **National Marine Fisheries Service Aquarium** is open to the public in the summer. Its sole function is to preserve regional species, hence everything in its 16 major display tanks is native to the area: cod, lobster, flounder. The aquarium also has a seal tank. From mid-September through mid-June the aquarium is open on weekends only. ~ Water Street; 508-548-7684.

LODGING   A romantic, dark brown 1807 farmhouse, the **Nauset House Inn** is within walking distance of beautiful beaches. One of the inn's most memorable features is a magnificent 1907 conservatory with white wicker furniture, exotic plants and grapevines. Each of the 14 guest rooms is individually decorated, and may feature tiny floral-print wallpaper, stenciling and antiques such as a hand-painted Victorian cottage bed. Most of the guest rooms in the main house and carriage house have private baths. ~ 143 Beach Road, East Orleans; 508-255-2195, fax 508-896-2524. MOD-ERATE TO DELUXE.

Even though the Kennedy compound (near Ocean Street) is surrounded by tall hedges, all day long tour buses prowl this area, hoping to catch a glimpse of one of the clan. Their efforts are almost always in vain.

Chatham Bars Inn, one of Cape Cod's most luxurious grand resorts, looks like the kind of place where everyone should be wearing white linen and playing croquet. Built in 1914 as a hunting lodge, the horseshoe-shaped gray-shingled inn sits high on a gentle hill overlooking Pleasant Bay. An expansive brick veranda runs the length of the inn. The inviting lobby, luxurious rooms and comfortable cottages reflect the original beauty of this historic building with antique reproductions and period pieces like Vanderbilt Casablanca fans, authentic Victorian mantels and Hitchcock chairs. The 20-acre resort has a private beach, heated swimming pool, tennis courts, fishing, sailing, windsurfing, golf, magnificent theme gardens and two restaurants. Breakfast and dinner included. ~ 297 Shore Road, Chatham; 508-945-0096, 800-527-4884, 508-945-5491. ULTRA-DELUXE.

HIDDEN ►   **Inn Among Friends** is located three blocks away from the historic Chatham Lighthouse. The small, attractive inn stands in an exclusive residential neighborhood of winding streets and impeccably restored oceanfront homes. Chatham village is about a ten-minute walk. The inn's rooms are decorated with Early American touches such as wall stenciling and antique furnishings. The Break-Away Café is located in front of the inn. Closed January through March. ~ 207 Main Street, Chatham; 508-945-0792, 800-750-0792. MODERATE TO DELUXE.

Most of Chatham's hotels are expensive, but not the **Bow Roof House**, a real bargain. Located in the heart of the high-rent district, five minutes from the beach, this cozy 200-year-old sea captain's house feels comfortable and casual. A patio overlooking a scenic, winding road makes an ideal spot for tea or cocktails in the afternoon. Guest rooms are appointed with Colonial bedspreads and nondescript furniture, but they're far apart and private. ~ 59 Queen Anne Road; 508-945-1346. MODERATE.

Motels aren't known for beautiful landscaping, but **Pleasant Bay Village Motel** is a welcome surprise. Located across from salt marsh, ponds and ocean, Pleasant Bay boasts impeccably maintained rock and flower gardens that are so lush you hardly notice the 58 nondescript guest rooms and apartments. Closed November through April. ~ 1191 Orleans Road, Route 28, Chatham Port; 508-945-1133, 800-547-1011, fax 508-945-9701. ULTRA-DELUXE.

Accommodations in Harwich Port are limited and expensive, but **Harbor Walk** is an exception. The white 1880 bed and breakfast with gingerbread trim is within walking distance of the town's exclusive beaches. Six guest rooms (two with shared bath) are decorated with a mix of new and antique furnishings. A porch runs the length of this house overlooking the yard. A full breakfast is included. ~ 6 Freeman Street; 508-432-1675. MODERATE.

◄ HIDDEN

Augustus Snow House is one of the most beautiful inns in New England. Every inch of this magnificent Queen Anne Victorian is flawless. It's known for its fabulous wallpapers—some have ceiling borders of antique roses or clusters of fall flowers that look hand painted. Then there are the unbelievable bathrooms—one has an antique Victorian mahogany sink, another a black-and-white diamond tile floor and claw-footed tub. The dazzling public rooms are appointed with thick oak and mahogany paneling, moreen drapes, etched-glass french doors and period antiques. Located in a quiet, affluent town, the inn has five guest rooms and serves a full breakfast. ~ 528 Main Street, Harwich Port; 508-430-0528. ULTRA-DELUXE.

Route 28 from Dennis Port to Hyannis is dotted with one indistinguishable motel after another. However, if you head south toward the beach you'll find some nice alternatives, like **The Lighthouse Inn**. This sprawling, 61-room, Old World resort is remarkably affordable for Cape Cod. Located on the ocean, the inn is formed around a lighthouse that stood at nearby Bass River during the 19th century. The ambience is friendly and unpretentious. Activities include shuffleboard, horseshoes, miniature golf, tennis, hiking in nearby woods, swimming in the pool or ocean and nightly entertainment. A children's director provides daily family activities, as well as day and evening babysitting. Guest rooms in the main inn are simply furnished, and separate cottages are also available. ~ 1 Lighthouse Inn Road, West Dennis; 508-398-2244. ULTRA-DELUXE.

◄ HIDDEN

Located in elegant Hyannis Port, the **Simmons Homestead Inn** was once a country estate. Built in 1820, this gracious inn is furnished with quality antiques, canopy beds, white wicker and brass. Sweeping porches overlook gardens leading down to Simmons Pond. Unlike those in most old inns, the ten guest rooms here are fairly large. ~ 288

Scudder Avenue; 508-778-4999, 800-637-1649, fax 508-790-1342. DELUXE TO ULTRA-DELUXE.

HIDDEN ►   Tucked away on a tree-lined street in elegant Centerville is **The Inn at Fernbrook,** a large, graceful Victorian with wraparound porches, gables and turrets. The understated decor doesn't compete with the dramatic house. The six guest rooms and garden cottage are beautiful and unusual. The Spellman Room, named after Cardinal Francis Spellman, a former owner of the house, has a pyramid-shaped ceiling, stained-glass windows, tiled fireplace and enormous Georgian canopy bed. Not surprisingly, it resembles a church. For all its grandeur, there's something serene and unaffected about Fernbrook. It's a good place for collecting one's thoughts. ~ 481 Main Street; 508-775-4334, fax 508-778-4455. DELUXE TO ULTRA-DELUXE.

HIDDEN ►   **Horizons Inn** is in a magical little neighborhood of turn-of-the-century, dairy-barn-shaped houses with turrets, gables and gingerbread. Hidden from tourists, the inn sits on a bluff overlooking the ocean. Its craftsman-style public rooms have dark oak paneling and bookshelves. Four comfortable guest rooms are simply furnished. Closed from Columbus Day through Memorial Day. ~ 2 Wyoming Avenue, Falmouth Heights; 508-548-3619. MODERATE TO DELUXE.

The **Village Green Inn,** a white clapboard house with green shutters and a picket fence, is typical of many of the homes in Falmouth's historic district. Guest rooms are decorated with antiques; two of the five rooms have working fireplaces. One room has impressive wood inlay floors; all rooms have a TV. Full breakfast included. ~ 40 West Main Street, Falmouth; 508-548-5621. DELUXE TO ULTRA-DELUXE.

In 1849 Captain Albert Nye built **Mostly Hall** for his southern bride, who refused to live in a traditional Cape Cod house. Typical of houses in New Orleans' garden district, this striking, raised Greek Revival mansion has ten-foot windows, louvered shutters, a wraparound veranda, wrought-iron fence and a 35-foot center hall—which is why it's called Mostly Hall. Only steps away from Falmouth's historic village green, this elegant inn is set well back from the road and hidden from view by trees and bushes. The six guest rooms are spacious and airy, furnished with antiques, including canopied, four-poster beds. Full breakfast included. Closed January. ~ 27 Main Street; 508-548-3786, 800-682-0565. DELUXE.

DINING   The Mad Hatter might have enjoyed **The Arbor.** Fanciful and eclectic, it has a front yard filled with goofy junk—a bear riding a bicycle, a big wagon wheel. The inside is a hodgepodge of antique clutter— old bottles, vintage photos, tinware, colored pitchers. Tables are set with mismatched china. Somehow it all comes together in a magical way. The menu is as varied as the decor. Many dishes are elaborate and rich—saltimbocca, veal marsala, sweetbread with ham and mushroom caps. Behind the restaurant, the Binnacle Tavern is a cozy spot for a drink and light entrées. The Arbor is open Friday through Sunday from Columbus Day through December and from Valentine's Day through Memorial Day; it is closed during January until Valentine's Day. The Binnacle Tavern is open Thursday through Sunday from Labor Day to Memorial Day. ~ Route 28, Orleans; 508-255-4847 (restaurant), 508-255-7901 (tavern). MODERATE TO DELUXE.

Woods Hole is primarily a scientific community, and it looks and feels like a small university town, with a good bookstore, craft galleries and cafés. This is also where you can catch a ferry for the islands—Martha's Vineyard and Nantucket.

Kadee's Lobster and Clam Bar is a colorful, inexpensive sea shanty draped with lobster traps and buoys. The menu includes steamers, lobster, corn-on-the-cob, kale soup and chowder. An outdoor patio shaded by umbrellas is the perfect spot for beer and fried clams after a day at the beach. Closed from Labor Day through Memorial Day. ~ 212 Main Street, Orleans; 508-255-6184. BUDGET TO MODERATE.

A popular local hangout, especially on Saturday nights, **Land Ho** is a fish and chips place. The new white clapboard restaurant has red-and-white checked tablecloths, dark wood walls and nautical decorative touches. The menu offers classic Cape Cod fare—fried and broiled seafood, hearty salads, fries and burgers. The bar is a friendly watering hole. ~ Route 6A and Cove Road, Orleans; 508-255-5165. BUDGET TO MODERATE.

On their days off, chefs from the Cape's most noted restaurants often dine at **Nauset Beach Club**, on the road to beautiful Nauset Beach. The small grey-shingled restaurant offers consistently good, reasonably priced Northern Italian fare such as saltimbocca, caesar salad, a wide range of seafood dishes such as grilled shrimp scampi and a host of creative pasta dishes. Closed Sunday and Monday after Columbus Day until Memorial Day. ~ 222 Main Street, East Orleans; 508-255-8547. MODERATE.

◄ HIDDEN

The **Impudent Oyster** is the place to go for traditional or exotic seafood in an informal setting next to a park. The lunch and dinner menus change seasonally. Many of the dishes have Chinese or Mexican ingredients, such as Szechuan beef and shrimp satay or mussels. There are also excellent non-seafood items, such as the chicken enchiladas *rojas* and steak *au poivre*. The cheerful restaurant has skylights, a cathedral ceiling and stained-glass panels. Prices are considerably lower during the winter. ~ 15 Chatham Bars Avenue, Chatham; 508-945-3545. MODERATE TO DELUXE.

In historic Chatham village, **Christian's** draws an attractive tennis and yachting crowd. The bar does as much business as the two restaurants combined. A formal dining room on the ground floor, appointed with Oriental rugs, dark wood floors and lace tablecloths, serves dishes such as codfish with champagne hollandaise sauce, seafood sauté, veal chops and boneless split duck. An informal, wood-paneled restaurant and bar on the second floor serve pasta, quiche, hamburgers and sandwiches. ~ 443 Main Street; 508-945-3362. MODERATE TO DELUXE.

The **Chatham Bars Inn**, one of the Cape's most luxurious resorts, also has an excellent restaurant. The food, service and location are superb, the crowd elegant old money. The large dining room overlooking the water is decorated in soothing shades of beige, rose and navy. In the summer the restaurant offers a menu of healthful, low-calorie dishes such as steamed halibut, and raspberry torte, plus a regular dinner menu—grilled swordfish and tournedos of beef. Reservations are mandatory if you aren't a guest at the inn. Available for private events only from mid-November through December; breakfast only from January through mid-May. ~ 297 Shore Road, Chatham; 508-945-0096. ULTRA-DELUXE.

It looks like something out of a Popeye cartoon. Half of **The Lobster Boat** is a gray-shingled Cape Cod cottage with cheerful red window boxes, and the other half is an enormous red, white and blue lobster boat that seems to have grown out of the restaurant's side. The dining room overlooks a small harbor, and the decor is very yo-ho-ho with captains chairs, dark wood and rope. The atmosphere is free and easy, and the menu features lobster, as well as a variety of fried, sautéed and broiled seafood. Closed from late October through early April. ~ 681 Main Street, West Yarmouth; 508-775-0486. MODERATE TO DELUXE.

HIDDEN ▶   At **Mildred's Chowder House** you'll find a crowd of fanatical regulars. All the favorites are available: thick chowders, steamers and scrumptious lobster rolls. The restaurant looks like a coffee shop, but that's not the point. ~ 290 Iyanough Road, Hyannis; 508-775-1045. MODERATE.

Penguins Sea Grill serves classic New England–style dishes, such as baked stuffed lobster and grilled salmon, as well as Italian favorites, sushi and New York sirloin. Brick walls, mahogany chairs, natural-finish oak tables, linen napkins and waiters outfitted in long, white, bistro-style aprons contribute to the upscale ambience. Closed Monday during winter and closed in January. ~ 331 Main Street, Hyannis; 508-775-2023. MODERATE TO DELUXE.

An attractive, reasonably priced nouvelle Italian restaurant, **Gone Tomatoes** is in Mashpee Commons, an upscale outdoor mall that resembles an old-fashioned Cape Cod village. The clapboard restaurant has lofty ceilings, cream-colored walls, honey-warm wood and terra cotta floors. Fare includes thin-crusted focaccia pizza, pasta, grilled swordfish with basil butter, and veal chop with marsala and rosemary.

A take-out counter sells desserts, pasta, salads, sandwiches and espresso. ~ 11-A Steeple Street, Mashpee; 508-477-8100. MODERATE.

The Regatta of Cotuit is considered one of the top restaurants on the Cape. Housed in a Federal-style mansion that dates back to 1790, it specializes in New American cuisine with French and Asian touches. Selections include a wild mushroom strudel with a sauce of five mushrooms, a sautéed sesame swordfish steak and a house-smoked broiled salmon filet with a roasted pepper vinaigrette. They also do wonderful things with striped bass, lobster and shrimp. A dessert not to miss is the Chocolate Seduction Cake with sauce *framboise* and *crème anglais*. There are eight little dining rooms, all warmed by fireplaces on cool nights. ~ Route 28, Cotuit; 508-428-5715. DELUXE TO ULTRA-DELUXE.

Set in an 18th-century, red-and-white inn on the edge of a duck pond, the **Coonamesset Inn** serves seafood Newburg, oysters on the half shell, quahog chowder, Indian pudding and other classic New England dishes. The Cahoon Room, one of three dining rooms serving breakfast, lunch and dinner, features primitive paintings by artist Ralph Cahoon depicting life on Cape Cod. The inn and restaurant are tastefully decorated with Shaker and Colonial furnishings. Closed Monday in December; open on weekends only from January through late April. ~ Jones Road and Gifford Street, Falmouth; 508-548-2300. MODERATE TO DELUXE.

Located on a winding country road, **Peach Tree Circle** is the perfect place for lunch on a lazy summer day. A combination restaurant, farm stand, gourmet health food store and bakery, it is shaded by large graceful trees. Fresh flowers and vegetables are sold in front of the small grey building with nasturtiums climbing its walls. Lunch offerings include big, healthy sandwiches, quiche, chowder, garden salad, fruit and cheese. ~ 881 Old Palmer Avenue, Falmouth; 508-548-2354. BUDGET.   ◄ HIDDEN

The **Regatta of Falmouth By-the-Sea** is the mother restaurant to the Regatta of Cotuit. Set at the water's edge, it offers stunning views from two large dining rooms. The cuisine is French with an emphasis on seafood. Lighter fare is offered on a special café menu. Open May through September. ~ 217 Clinton Avenue, Falmouth; 508-548-5400. DELUXE TO ULTRA-DELUXE.

Locals come to **Fishmonger's Café** because it isn't as touristy as some of the other Woods Hole restaurants. The café serves California food—avocado tostada, tabouli, garden vegetable salad—and Cape Cod classics like fried clams, grilled fish and chowder. The atmosphere is casual, the decor salty dog. Paned windows overlook the harbor, and there's a counter where you can have lunch or a beer while you're waiting for the ferry. Closed on Tuesday from Labor Day through Memorial Day. ~ 56 Water Street; 508-548-9148. BUDGET TO MODERATE.

The place to go for a rawbar in Woods Hole is **Shuckers**. It's a bustling little spot, on the water, with table service provided by college students. In addition to rawbar offerings, you can choose from a tempting selection of seafood dishes and lobster rolls that just hit the spot. Shuckers serves its own home-brewed beer, Nobska Light. ~ 91 A Water Street; 508-540-3850. MODERATE.

SHOPPING   Aptly named **Bird Watcher's General Store** sells anything having to do with birds—field guides, binoculars, 25 kinds of birdbaths, bath heaters, birdfeeders and carving kits. It's also got coffee mugs, T-shirts, stamps, floor mats and pot holders adorned with birds. ~ 36 Route 6A, Orleans; 508-255-6974.

For beautiful hand-painted dishes from all over the world and European kitchen utensils, visit **Chatham Cookware**, a blue-and-white cottage-style store. Fresh and sweet, it also sells excellent bakery goods, deli items and coffee. ~ 524 Main Street, Chatham; 508-945-1550.

There are countless stores on Cape Cod selling nautical decorative items, but few are as classy as **The Regatta Shop**. Here you find silver dolphin bracelets, sleek hand-carved house signs, colorful fish-shaped magnets and a wide collection of museum-quality maritime posters. ~ 582 Main Street, Chatham; 508-945-4999.

The Spyglass is a wonderful salty dog store filled to its dark brown rafters with antique telescopes, microscopes, opera glasses, barometers, nautical antiques, paintings and tools. ~ 618 Main Street, Chatham; 508-945-9686.

NIGHTLIFE   Musical acts, comedies and plays are presented at the **Academy Playhouse**, in a former town hall built in 1837. ~ 120 Main Street, Orleans; 508-255-1963.

Asa Bears, a lounge and restaurant in a Victorian mansion, offers a little bit of everything—jazz, classical guitar and dance music. Entertainment takes place in the attractive library lounge. ~ 415 Main Street, Hyannis; 508-771-4444.

Duval Street Station draws a gay and lesbian crowd for dancing to deejay music Thursday through Sunday nights. During the summer you can gather around the baby-grand and sing along to your favorite showtunes. Cover charge on weekends. ~ 477 Yarmouth Road, Hyannis; 508-771-7511.

Cape Cod Melody Tent, an enormous theater-in-the-round, hosts big names such as Willie Nelson, Tony Bennett, Kenny Rogers, Bob Newhart and Ray Charles. Closed after Labor Day through Memorial Day. ~ 21 West Main Street Rotary, Hyannis; 508-775-9100.

South Cape beaches are usually big and wide with huge parking lots and ample facilities. Located in residential neighborhoods, they're popular with college students and families. Because this is the ocean side of the Cape, the water tends to be rougher than on the North Cape.

BEACHES & PARKS

HARDINGS BEACH 🏊 Big, straight and long, this popular beach attracts a gregarious crowd of kids. Expensive houses on a hill overlook Hardings, a spot good for swimming, sunning and hanging out with the neighbors. Modest little sand dunes with paths running through them lead down to the beach. Restrooms, showers, lifeguards, snack bar; groceries nearby in Chatham. ~ Take Barn Hill Road off Route 28 to Hardings Beach Road in Chatham; 508-945-5158.

WEST DENNIS BEACH 🏊 🏄 The view at the end of this sprawling beach, where the Bass River empties into the Atlantic, is of old summer houses with green lawns spilling down toward docks dotted with boats. There's even a windmill. West Dennis Beach attracts big summer crowds; its parking lot can accommodate 1600 cars. Popular with surfers, families and teens, the beach is bordered by flat salt marsh laced with tributaries from the river. Restrooms, showers, lifeguards, swings, snack bar; groceries nearby in Dennis; day-use fee, $8. ~ Take School Street off Route 28 to Lighthouse Road in West Dennis; 508-398-3568.

ASHUMET HOLLY WILDLIFE SANCTUARY 🚶 A treat for birdwatchers and botany enthusiasts, this 45-acre reserve abounds with many varieties of holly grown by the late Wilfred Wheeler, who donated the land to the Audubon Society. You're definitely out in the wilds here, and nothing looks manicured or fussed over. An easy-to-maneuver trail goes past a pond, forest, dogwoods, rhododendrons and a grove of Franklinia, an unusual, fall flowering shrub discovered in Georgia in 1790. Wildlife includes catbirds, so named because they make a meowing sound, belted kingfishers and pond critters such as ribbon snakes, catfish and turtles with bright yellow heads and dark shells. Since 1935, a barn on the property has been a nesting site for swallows. Every spring up to 44 pairs arrive to nest, then depart in late summer. Groceries are found nearby in Mashpee; day-use fee, $3. ~ 286 Ashumet Road in East Falmouth; 508-563-6390.

◄ HIDDEN

OLD SILVER BEACH 🏊 This spot, popular with a college-aged crowd and locals, doesn't look like a typical Cape Cod beach. A large, modern resort is situated on the north end, and most of the beach houses in the immediate area are fairly new. A lovely cove to the south is protected by wooded cliffs jutting down to the shore. The beach itself is somewhat rocky. Swimming is calm; lessons are available. Restrooms, showers, lifeguards, snack bar; groceries are nearby in Falmouth; parking is $10 per day. ~ Off Route 28A on Quaker Road in Falmouth; 508-548-8500.

Martha's Vineyard

▼▼▼▼▼▼▼▼▼▼▼ With its museum-perfect villages, Gothic Victorians and scenery that mimics the coast of Ireland, it isn't any wonder this enchanting island swells from around 12,000 year-round residents to more than 80,000 in the summer.

Discovered in 1602 by the English explorer Bartholomew Gosnold, it was named by him for its proliferation of wild grapes. Who Martha was is anybody's guess, but legend has it she may have been Gosnold's daughter or his mother.

An active whaling port in the 19th century, "the Vineyard," as it's often called, became a popular summer resort in the 20th century. Today it is a summer home to an impressive number of celebrities fiercely protected from ogling tourists by proud locals. Vacationing notables such as President Bill Clinton and Princess Diana have also spent time on the Vineyard.

One way not to impress the natives is to rent a moped. In the summer these noisy (but fun to drive) motorized bicycles sound like swarms of angry bees. They're considered a menace on the road, and bumperstickers that read "Outlaw Mopeds" are everywhere.

Only 20 miles long and 10 miles wide, the Vineyard can easily be toured in a day. Ferries dock at Oak Bluffs or Vineyard Haven, or you can fly in (see the "Transportation" section at the end of this chapter). The Vineyard's three major towns—Vineyard Haven, Oak Bluffs and Edgartown—are on the northeast side of the Island. The western end, known as "up-island," is comprised of bucolic farmland, moors and magnificent beaches.

SIGHTS In the '30s, Lillian Hellman and Dashiell Hammett spent their summers in **Vineyard Haven**, and ever since writers have been coming to this friendly, unpretentious town. Vineyard Haven has never attracted tourists like Edgartown, the island's main resort town, and therein lies its charm. It has the best bookstore (Bunch of Grapes), attractive shops, restaurants and a handful of wonderful inns. It's also home to the **Martha's Vineyard Chamber of Commerce**. ~ Beach Road; 508-693-0085.

One historical sight of note here is the **Seaman's Bethel Museum and Chapel**, established in 1893 to provide spiritual guidance to seamen and a refuge to shipwreck victims. Today it is part of a larger organization that still offers social services and ministry to seafarers. The bethel is open to the public, and the small museum houses a collection of seafaring artifacts. ~ 15 Beach Street; 508-693-9317.

Nearby stand the **Old Schoolhouse and Liberty Pole Museum**. The schoolhouse, a sweet-looking, one-room, white-clapboard building with artifacts related to early island life, is right in the heart of town. The museum takes its name from an American Revolutionary War incident: British sailors tried to steal the Liberty Pole to replace a broken mast on their ship, but three young girls blew up the pole before the sailors could get their hands on it. ~ 110 Main Street, 508-693-3860.

Oak Bluffs is only a couple of miles away. A must-see here is the **Martha's Vineyard Camp Meeting Association**, also known as **Cottage City**, right off the main drag through town. In 1835, Methodist church groups started holding annual summer meetings in Oak Bluffs, with hundreds of families living in tents for the occasion. Over time the tents were replaced by tiny whimsical cottages with Gothic windows, turrets, gables and eaves dripping with gingerbread and painted in a riot of colors—pink, green and white; peach, yellow and blue. Called "campground Gothic Revival," this is the only architecture native to the Vineyard. In mid-August, on Illumination Night, a custom dating back to 1870, hundreds of colorful glowing Oriental lanterns are strung up all over the cottages, creating a dazzling display of light. ~ Off Circuit Avenue.

With the exception of Cottage City and Ocean Park—a genteel neighborhood of Queen Anne Victorians overlooking the water on the road to Edgartown—most of Oak Bluffs is hamburger restaurants and T-shirt and souvenir shops. It has a funky, saltwater-taffy kind of charm. In the center of town is the **Flying Horses Carousel**, an antique, hand-carved wooden carousel still in operation. In the glass eye of each horse is a replica of a small animal. The carousel opens on Easter Sunday and closes mid-October. ~ Circuit and Lake streets; 508-693-9481.

Not far from Oak Bluffs is elegant **Edgartown**. With its narrow streets, brick sidewalks, graceful yachts and pristine Greek Revival and

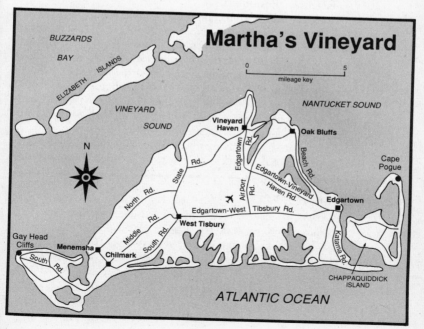

Federal-style architecture, it looks like a living museum. Prim, proper and perfect, Edgartown can sometimes appear a bit too perfect.

Edgartown has always been a town of considerable wealth and power. Prosperous whaling captains retired here, building magnificent homes along **North Water Street** that can still be seen today. Today's residents include many Boston Brahmin families. Life revolves around the formidable yacht club, where expert sailor Walter Cronkite reigns supreme.

The main thing to do in Edgartown is walk along its tree-lined streets window shopping and admiring the homes. The **Dukes County Historical Society**, tucked away on a beautiful side street, maintains a museum exhibiting scrimshaw, ship models, period costumes and whaling gear such as harpoons. Admission. ~ Cooke and School streets; 508-627-4441.

With exquisitely preserved details that include an enclosed cupola, roof and porch balustrades, shallow hipped roof, large window panes and a portico, the 1840 **Dr. Daniel Fisher House** is the Vineyard's best example of Federal-period architecture. Dr. Fisher was Martha's Vineyard's 19th-century Renaissance man—he was a doctor, whaling magnate, banker, merchant and miller. The house is now the headquarters of the Martha's Vineyard Preservation Trust, which saves, restores, and makes self-sufficient any important island buildings that might otherwise be sold for commercial purposes or radically remodeled. Unfortunately, the house is not open to the public for tours. ~ 99 Main Street, Edgartown.

The **Vineyard Museum** comprises several buildings, including the 1765 Thomas Cooke House, a fine example of pre-Revolutionary architecture that once served as a customs house. The house, which has undergone little renovation since the mid–19th century, contains relics of the Vineyard's whaling days, including scrimshaw and other artifacts. The original lens from the Gay Head Lighthouse is housed here; it's illuminated for a few hours each night. From Labor Day through June, the museum is open only Wednesday through Saturday. Admission. ~ 8 Cooke Street, Edgartown; 508-627-4441.

Right off the coast of Edgartown is **Chappaquiddick Island**. Called "Chappy" by locals, it is accessible by ferry (see the "Transportation"

WINERIES IN MASSACHUSETTS?

From Menemsha head back to Vineyard Haven via North Road and State Road, which goes by **Chicama Vineyards**. Massachusetts' first winery, it offers guided tours and winetastings in an appealing shop that sells wine, homemade jam, mustard and herb vinegar. ~ Stoney Hill Road, West Tisbury; 508-693-0309.

section at the end of this chapter). There's not much to do here except go to the beach and take long walks. The island, of course, is noted for the tragic auto accident involving Senator Edward Kennedy that resulted in the death of a young woman. Chappaquiddick Road ends at Dyke Bridge, site of the mishap, which has now fallen apart and is off limits to cars and people. The island's only other road, Wasque Road, leads to Wasque Point, a beautiful natural area.

The up-island section of the Vineyard includes West Tisbury, Chilamark and Gay Head, bucolic rural areas with lush green farms, meadows and scenic harbors. To explore this area from Edgartown, take the Edgartown–West Tisbury Road. It cuts through the middle of the island.

About the only thing in West Tisbury is **Alley's General Store**, where locals sit on the front porch drinking coffee and glaring at tourists. ~ State Road; 508-693-0088.   ◀ *HIDDEN*

On Saturday mornings, the big social event is the outdoor produce market at **Agricultural Hall**, down the road from Alley's. Don't be fooled by the casual way the locals are dressed. Look closely and you'll see Rolex watches, $600 cowboy boots and maybe, if you're lucky, James Taylor. This area of the island is where many accomplished writers, musicians and artists make their homes.   ◀ *HIDDEN*

From West Tisbury, follow the road to **Chilmark**. At the center of Chilmark, **Beetlebung Corner** is an intersection of the main up-island roads: Middle Road, South Road, State Road and Menemsha Cross Road. The intersection was named for a grove of beetlebung trees, the New England name for tupelo trees, which are unusual in the northeastern U.S. A very tough wood, tupelo proved to be excellent for making wooden mallets, or beetles, and plugs, or bungs, that stopped up the holes of the wooden barrels used to store whale oil.

At Beetlebung Corner, bear left onto South Road, heading toward Gay Head. After a mile, you'll pass over a bridge. Nashaquitsa Pond, or Quitsa, depending on who's talking, will be on your right, and Stonewall Pond on your left. About one-tenth of a mile farther, the road heads up a hill. Halfway up the hill, pull over to the wide spot on the side of the road. This is called the **Quitsa Overlook**. Get out   ◀ *HIDDEN*
of the car to look out over Quitsa and Menemsha ponds. Past the ponds is the tiny village of Menemsha, then Vineyard Sound, the Elizabeth Islands and Woods Hole and Falmouth on the mainland.

About half a mile farther along on the road to Gay Head, there's another wide spot in the road with room on both sides for two or three cars to pull over safely. This is where the locals park their cars and bikes, then walk over to drink from a fresh, sweet **aquifer**. This   ◀ *HIDDEN*
water is considered an antidote for various afflictions, from stress to the common cold to the occasional hangover.

The road ends at **Gay Head Cliffs**, towering ocean cliffs formed by glaciers over 10,000 years ago. Laced with multicolored bands of rust, lavender, wheat and charcoal, constant erosion over the millenniums has washed away most of the vibrant hues. This popular tourist attraction is approached by a path lined with chowder and gift shops owned by the native Wampanoag people.

Leave the Gay Head Cliffs area via Lighthouse Road, then turn left onto State Road. When you get to Beetlebung Corner, turn right onto Menemsha Cross Road, which takes you to **Menemsha Creek** and **Dutcher's Dock**, a lovely fishing village of simple, weathered gray shingled houses and short, sturdy docks. The channel seems to be impossibly narrow to be a working harbor, yet it's nearly constantly used by hardworking fishing folks.

LODGING   Upon entering the **Captain Dexter House**, you are greeted by the inviting aroma of cinnamon, cloves and warm bread. This meticulously restored 1843 white clapboard inn has sloping wood floors, Oriental rugs, fireplaces and antiques. It's luxurious but not pretentious. The eight rooms are appointed with contemporary furnishings, Colonial antiques and period reproduction wallpaper; some have fireplaces and four-poster beds with lace canopies. A very warm and friendly place. Closed late November through March. Gay-friendly. ~ 100 Main Street, Vineyard Haven; 508-693-6564. DELUXE TO ULTRA-DELUXE.

Crocker House Inn is tucked away on a quiet side street within walking distance of Vineyard Haven and the harbor. The eight guest rooms in this shingled Victorian are masterfully decorated. The octagonally shaped Lace Room romances you with a working fireplace, antique furnishings and an abundance of lace amidst a violet and white room. For serious getaways, try the Loft, a private room with harbor views and a balcony. Closed mid-November through mid-March. ~ 4 Crocker Avenue, Vineyard Haven; 508-693-1151, 800-772-0206. MODERATE TO ULTRA-DELUXE.

HIDDEN ►   A classic 1918 craftsman-style bungalow and a Cape Cod–style shingled carriage house make up the **Thorncroft Inn** which rests on a quiet, tree-lined residential street. There's nothing very craftsman-like about the decor, which leans toward country Victorian. Catering to couples on romantic getaways, nine of the 13 guest rooms have working fireplaces and four-poster lace-canopy beds, and some have jacuzzis. One of the best things about Thorncroft is its enormous breakfast of buttermilk pancakes, bacon, french toast, quiche, Belgian waffles, stuffed croissant sandwiches and more. ~ 278 Main Street, Vineyard Haven; 508-693-3333, 800-332-1236. ULTRA-DELUXE.

The front lawn of the **Lothrop Merry House** stretches down to a small beach that overlooks busy Vineyard Haven harbor. Guests enjoy their continental breakfast on a terrace overlooking this pretty vista. The seven pleasant guest rooms vary in their amenities—some have private baths, some have working fireplaces and some have fine views of the harbor. ~ Owen Park, Vineyard Haven; 508-693-1646. DELUXE TO ULTRA-DELUXE.

Just up the road from the center of Oak Bluffs is the **Admiral Benbow Inn**. What makes it stand apart from many inns is that it has all the New England touches, but not a don't-put-your-drink-on-this-table attitude. The 1870s house is a beauty. All seven rooms are attractively furnished with some antique pieces, big comfortable beds and private baths. ~ 520 New York Avenue; 508-693-6825, 800-331-1787. DELUXE TO ULTRA-DELUXE.

Right across the street from busy, picturesque Oak Bluffs Harbor, the **Wesley Hotel** is the last of the seven large oceanfront hotels that graced Oak Bluffs during the turn of the century. The Carpenter Gothic–style building, a traditional Gothic design elaborately constructed with wood, is wrapped with a wide, welcoming veranda. The hotel's 82 fairly large bedrooms are comfortably furnished. Closed October through Memorial Day. ~ 1 Lake Avenue; 508-693-6611, 800-638-9027, fax 508-693-5389. DELUXE.

At the top of Circuit Avenue, you can't miss the **Oak Bluffs Inn**— it's the pink building on the left with an enormous cupola atop the third story. Guests are encouraged to climb up to the cupola to take in the view of Oak Bluffs' rooftops and the ocean beyond. The inn's guest rooms and common areas are filled with fine examples of cottage-style furniture, prints and wall coverings. All nine rooms (some convertible to suites) have private baths, bright bathrooms and views of charming Oak Bluffs. Closed November through April. ~ Corner of Circuit and Pequot avenues, Oak Bluffs; 508-693-7171, 800-955-6235. DELUXE TO ULTRA-DELUXE.

The shingled, gingerbreaded 1872 **Oak House** is appropriately named—there's oak, oak everywhere, from the walls to the ceilings to the fine examples of antique oak furniture. The large wraparound veranda has wonderful rocking chairs and swings where many guests spend a lot of time relaxing and looking out across Seaview Avenue to the ocean. Many rooms have private balconies. All eight guest rooms and both suites have private baths, and all but two have water views. Closed mid-October through mid-May. ~ Corner of Seaview and Pequot avenues, Oak Bluffs; 508-693-4187, fax 508-696-7385 DELUXE TO ULTRA-DELUXE.

Carly Simon, James Taylor, John Kennedy, Jr., Caroline Kennedy Schlossberg, Diana Ross, Beverly Sills, Walter Cronkite, Mike Wallace, William Styron and Art Buchwald all have homes on "the Vineyard."

The **Arbor** is a quintessential New England cottage, fresh and white with a winsome vine-clad arbor, brick path and English garden. Located a couple of blocks from Edgartown's shopping district, the inn offers guest rooms simply but attractively appointed with antiques and fresh cut flowers. Continental breakfast is served in the old-fashioned formal parlor or in the garden. ~ 222 Upper Main Street, Edgartown; 508-627-8137. DELUXE TO ULTRA-DELUXE.

Built in 1840 by Edgartown's leading physician, Dr. Clement Frances Shiverick, the **Shiverick Inn** is a fantastic example of the high

Greek Revival style. Inside, the common areas and ten guest rooms are furnished with fine antiques and pieces of art of the same period. All guest rooms have fireplaces and private baths; most have air conditioning and queen beds. The library on the second floor has a terrace that looks out over the Old Whaling Church. In the backyard, there's a small flagstone terrace and flower garden. An expanded continental breakfast is served in the airy Garden Room. ~ 5 Pease's Point Way, Edgartown; 508-627-3797, 800-723-4292, fax 508-627-8441. ULTRA-DELUXE.

Edgartown Commons has 35 comfortably furnished efficiencies, from studios to one- and two-bedroom apartments. Outside, there are grills and picnic tables, a play area for the kids and an outdoor swimming pool. Closed late October through early May. ~ Pease's Point Way, 508-627-4671, 800-439-4671. MODERATE.

The **Harbor View Hotel** is Edgartown's only waterfront resort with conference facilities. Its 124 rooms, suites and cottages all have private bath, telephone and cable television. Rooms are generously proportioned, and decorated with wicker chairs, glass-topped tables, armoires, antique prints and watercolor landscapes by local artists. The hotel's gazebo is one of the most- photographed structures on the Edgartown waterfront. True to its name, the Harbor View does indeed have some of the best views of Edgartown's harbor. ~ 131 North Water Street; 508-627-7000, 800-225-6005, fax 617-261-7304. ULTRA-DELUXE.

The **Tuscany Inn at the Captain Fisher House** reflects the innkeepers' flair for balancing color, space and magnificent furniture. The result is an inn with an elegant, airy feeling. The eight bedrooms are all doubles with private bath (one detached), and many have whirlpool baths. Full breakfast is served in the tile-floored dining room or, in warm weather, on the flagstone terrace, with a fountain, iron benches and a hammock nearby. Closed January through mid-March. ~ 22 North Water Street, Edgartown; 508-627-5999, fax 508-627-6605. ULTRA-DELUXE.

For an inn with such a prestigious address, the **Shiretown Inn** has pretty good prices. Some rooms are furnished with antiques and have private entrances; others, especially those in the carriage houses in the back of the inn, are quite plain, rather than quaint. All have private bathrooms. ~ North Water Street, Edgartown; 508-627-3353, 800-541-0090. MODERATE TO ULTRA-DELUXE.

HIDDEN ►   With its elaborate windows and dormers, **The Victorian Inn** looks formal from the outside, but it's an easygoing place located one block from Edgartown harbor. Guests enjoy the cool, private garden in the summer. The 14 guest rooms are sweet and tidy with canopy beds, floral wallpaper, antiques and some antique reproductions; a few rooms have private balconies. ~ 24 South Water Street, Edgartown; 508-627-4784. DELUXE TO ULTRA-DELUXE.

The **Charlotte Inn** is one of the most elegant and luxurious inns in America. A sparkling white 1860 sea captain's house, it is nestled amid a profusion of flowers, lawns, wisteria and latticework. Guests check in at a gleaming English barrister's desk. Twenty-five meticulous guest rooms are appointed with fine English antiques, hand-painted china and equestrian prints. Suites, located in separate buildings, are quite extravagant—one has its own English cottage garden, another a bedroom balcony and palladium window. A continental breakfast is served in the inn's restaurant, L'êtoile, one of the finest dining establishments in New England. ~ 27 South Summer Street, Edgartown; 508-627-4751, fax 508-627-4652. ULTRA-DELUXE.

The homey, unpretentious **Summer House** is a place for vacationers who enjoy staying in a B & B that really is someone's home. There's a big, beautiful, very private front yard with a wonderful ivy-covered wall as a backdrop. The two large bedrooms have king-size beds. Closed mid-September through May. ~ 96 South Summer Street, Edgartown; 508-627-4857. DELUXE.

◄ HIDDEN

Hostelling International—Martha's Vineyard is an ideal place to stay on the Vineyard if you want to spend a lot of time biking. It's on the edge of the Correlus State Forest, which is crisscrossed with bike paths. The hostel was the first purpose-built youth hostel in the U.S. when it was built and opened in 1955. Sleeping areas are dormitory-style bunk beds and are separated by sex. Bring your own linens or rent them; blankets and pillows are furnished. Bathrooms are large, as they are shared by all (also segregated by sex). There's also a fully equipped kitchen. Hostels aren't for everyone, but if you know what to expect, this is a good one. Closed mid-November to mid-March. ~ Edgartown–West Tisbury Road, West Tisbury; 508-693-2665. BUDGET.

Talk about off the beaten path. **Lambert's Cove Country Inn** is down a long country road deep in the woods. Surrounded by vine-covered stone walls, expansive lawns and apple orchards, the white clapboard inn is appointed with Shaker and Colonial-style antiques. Some of the 15 guest rooms have private decks, and one has a greenhouse sitting room. Guests have access to Lambert's Cove Beach, one of the Vineyard's most beautiful private beaches. ~ Lambert's Cove Road, West Tisbury; 508-693-2298. ULTRA-DELUXE.

◄ HIDDEN

One look at the **Captain R. Flander's House** and you understand why it was featured in Martha Stewart's *Wedding Book*. The rambling, 18th-century farmhouse sits on a grassy knoll overlooking ancient stone walls, rolling meadows, grazing horses, a sparkling pond, ducks and woodlands. Chilmark is so peaceful and bucolic, it's no wonder the rich and famous have chosen to live here. The inn is simply furnished, but with scenery like this who needs decoration? Guest accommodations (some with shared bath) are comfortable and sparsely appointed with antiques and country-style furnishings. ~ North Road, Chilmark; 508-645-3123. DELUXE TO ULTRA-DELUXE.

HIDDEN ►

Breakfast at Tiasquam lies on a slight hill overlooking rolling farmland, ponds and woods. This beautiful bed and breakfast is a tribute to fine 20th-century craftsmanship. Bathroom sinks are hand-thrown by local potter Robert Parrot, the exquisite cabinets are custom-made, doors are solid cherry, skylights are everywhere and some of the furnishings are by Thomas Moser, known for fine-crafted Shaker furniture. At breakfast, guests are served cinnamon french toast, corn-blueberry pancakes, freshly caught fish and more. ~ Off Middle Road, Chilmark; 508-645-3685. DELUXE TO ULTRA-DELUXE.

The emphasis is on the luxury of spare decorations and peaceful surroundings at **Menemsha Inn and Cottages,** which is situated on ten and a half acres of tranquil forest in beautiful Menemsha. There are six luxurious suites in the Carriage House, nine smaller, bright and lovely rooms in the inn's main building, and 12 fairly spartan house-keeping cottages. All rooms and cottages have private bath, and each cottage has a screened-in porch, fully equipped kitchen, outdoor shower, barbecue and wood-burning fireplace. There's a tennis court on the grounds, too. Closed late October through late April. ~ North Road between Menemsha Cross Road and Menemsha Harbor; 508-645-2521. DELUXE TO ULTRA-DELUXE.

The nice folks at **Up-Island Real Estate** manage and rent properties for homeowners all over Gay Head, Menemsha, Chilmark and West Tisbury. They have houses and prices to suit nearly everyone. ~ State Road, Chilmark; 508-645-2632. BUDGET TO ULTRA-DELUXE.

HIDDEN ►

Duck Inn is a health-oriented bed and breakfast that offers a variety of luxuries, including massages, post-massage relaxation in the inn's outdoor hot tub, all-natural fibers on the comfortable beds, and delicious breakfasts that accommodate vegetarians, vegans and flesh-eaters alike. Some of the island's most spectacular beaches are but a few minutes' walk through the waving beach grass. The five guest rooms are furnished eclectically with a duck motif, oriental prints and funky old calendars and posters. The suite in the basement has a large fireplace and a private bath; the other four rooms share two bathrooms. In residence: the inn's mascot, Oralee, a black Vietnamese pot-

IT'S CHEAPER IN THE GREAT OUTDOORS

Webb's Camping Area has 150 large campsites on 90 acres of pine groves. Backpackers and cyclists have their own area separate from cars and trailers. There's a small store with groceries and campers' essentials, a dumping station, hot and cold showers in impressively clean bathrooms, laundry facilities and a playground. Closed the Sunday after Labor Day through mid-May. ~ Barnes Road, Oak Bluffs; 508-693-0233. BUDGET.

belly pig. Gay-friendly. ~ Off State Road, Gay Head; 508-645-9018. MODERATE TO DELUXE.

The Outermost Inn is on a 20-acre piece of land that has the island's second-most spectacular ocean view. (For the best, walk a few hundred yards up the hill to the Gay Head lighthouse.) The inn has six rooms and one suite, all with private bath and one with a private whirlpool. Teal-blue carpets in the halls, unpainted furniture, subdued colors and natural fabrics suit the inn's location perfectly; nothing detracts from the location or the views. This is one of the most romantic inns in coastal New England; it's worth the splurge. Closed November through mid-April. ~ Lighthouse Road, Gay Head; 508-645-3511, fax 508-645-3514. ULTRA-DELUXE.

Only Edgartown and Oak Bluffs serve liquor, but you can bring your own when you dine in other towns.

DINING

A grey-shingled saltbox overlooking the harbor, rustic **Black Dog Tavern** is a Vineyard institution popular with the yachting crowd. The best place to sit in the summer is an enclosed porch with beautiful ocean views. The fare is traditional—clams casino, codfish, roast duckling—with an emphasis on fresh seafood. ~ Beach Street Extension, Vineyard Haven; 508-693-9223. DELUXE TO ULTRA-DELUXE.

Café at the Tisbury Inn, a trendy establishment with deco light fixtures, grey industrial carpeting, and a Lambert's Cove beach-scene mural, attracts a young, stylish crowd. The menu includes grilled meat, poultry and seafood with different sauces such as Mediterranean or marinara. Other dishes include grilled lemon-pepper chicken, pasta pesto, seafood enchiladas and pastas. An awning-covered outdoor patio in front is a good spot for people watching in the summer. ~ Main Street, Vineyard Haven; 508-693-3416. DELUXE.

Papa's Pizza isn't your average pizza parlor. This place has class. Located in a bright red, white and green storefront, it has an enormous dining room with a tin ceiling and walls, antique brass light fixtures and long wooden tables. The counter in back is solid granite—an elegant touch. Papa's serves lasagna, pizza, pasta and subs. The portions are healthy and hearty. ~ 158 Circuit Avenue, Oak Bluffs; 508-693-1400. BUDGET TO MODERATE.

A high-profile watering hole and restaurant that resembles a French bistro, **The Oyster Bar** attracts a chic, festive crowd. The green-and-yellow facade has rows of french doors that open to a cavernous dining room with tin ceilings, marbleized columns and an impressive 35-foot mahogany bar. People come here for oysters and champagne or a full meal. The menu includes dishes such as seafood pizza, wild smoked Scottish salmon appetizer and many grilled, sautéed and baked seafood and non-seafood dishes such as veal loin. Closed October through April. ~ 162 Circuit Avenue, Oak Bluffs; 508-693-3300. ULTRA-DELUXE.

David Ryan's Restaurant is the kind of place where you stop for a drink and end up staying for hours. It's a restaurant/bar where you can order anything from a burger to a pita pizza to a big bowl of pasta topped with tasty sauce. Downstairs is informal with high stools situated around tall tables; upstairs has a selection of booths and tables. ~ 11 North Water Street, Edgartown; 508-627-4100. MODERATE TO DELUXE.

Small, white and bright, **Savoir Fare** is a perfect spot for dinner. The cooking is done behind a counter piled high with delicious cakes and cookies baked on the premises. Dishes include oyster brie soup, caesar salad with grilled chicken, ceviche, goat cheese tart with sun-dried tomatoes, and roasted garlic. Closed January through March. ~ Post Office Square, Edgartown; 508-627-9864. DELUXE TO ULTRA-DELUXE.

L'étoile, in the Charlotte Inn, is perfect for a special occasion. An incredibly beautiful restaurant, it's in a 19th-century conservatory with skylights, bowed windows, a flagstone floor and lush plants. In this romantic, fantasylike environment, contemporary French cuisine is served. The *prix-fixe* menu offers fresh game and seafood entrées. Sauces are light and aromatic, flavored with fresh herbs, exotic fruit, shiitake mushrooms and shallots. Dinner only. ~ 27 South Summer Street, Edgartown; 508-627-5187. ULTRA-DELUXE.

On the way to Gay Head is the **Feast of Chilmark** where you can indulge in American-style food such as roasted rack of lamb with a cognac glaze. The bi-level restaurant serves dinner only. An art gallery is on the mezzanine. Closed on Monday and Tuesday from Labor Day through Memorial Day; open on weekends only during winter; closed in January. ~ Beetlebung Corner, Chilmark; 508-645-3553. MODER-ATE TO ULTRA-DELUXE.

Even if you're not knocked out the by the surf-and-turf menu (steak, salad, lobster, etc.) at **Home Port,** come here for the mesmer-izing view. The rustic, brown-shingled restaurant overlooks sand dunes, rolling green pastures and idyllic Menemsha harbor. An out-door patio is available for summer dining. Closed mid-October through March. ~ Basin Road, Chilmark; 508-645-2679. DELUXE.

Small, exclusive **Beach Plum Inn** is easy to miss. A tiny sign points the way down a dirt road to a building without a sign that looks like a private home with a terraced rock and flower garden. Once you've figured out where to go, you'll be glad you came. The intimate din-ing room has large picture windows overlooking Menemsha Harbor, a white grand piano and subtle mauve and green decorative touches. Diners have a choice of five *prix-fixe* dinner entrées that must be or-dered in advance when making reservations. The cuisine features items such as steamed lobster, duck with honey-curry sauce and rack of lamb. Closed Columbus Day through Memorial Day. ~ North Road, Menemsha; 508-645-9454. ULTRA-DELUXE.

Bunch of Grapes Bookstore is a writers' hangout. The best bookstore on the island, it has shelves well-stocked with quality fiction and poetry. The store regularly hosts autograph parties. ~ 68 Main Street, Vineyard Haven; 508-693-2291.

Linen, antique English pine furniture, knubby hand-knit sweaters and hand-painted coffee mugs can be found at **Bramhall & Dunn**. ~ Main Street, Vineyard Haven; 508-693-6437.

Take It Easy Baby is a very hip used clothing store selling leather bomber jackets, vintage Hawaiian shirts, designer women's wear and incredibly chic Canadian foul weather gear such as flannel-lined sou'westers. This is a fun store for the terminally cool. ~ 142 Circuit Avenue, Oak Bluffs; 508-693-2864.

In the Woods, a cavernous red brick room, sells handsome hand-crafted wooden spoons, plates, bread platters, bowls, cutting boards, Christmas ornaments, tables and benches. Prices are reasonable, and the craftsmanship is superb. ~ 55 Main Street, Edgartown; 508-627-9853.

SHOPPING

Throughout the year at the **Vineyard Playhouse**, the Island's only professional theater, local and equity actors star in Broadway plays such as *Noises Off* and *Falsettos*. ~ Church Street, Vineyard Haven; 508-693-6450,

Island Theatre Workshop is the Vineyard's oldest theater. Year-round it presents a wide range of plays and musicals performed by Vineyard actors. With no permanent home, it stages productions at different locations throughout the island. ~ P.O. Box 1893, Vineyard Haven; 508-693-4060.

Atlantic Connection, a hopping dance and music club, has live bands and entertainment. Cover. ~ Circuit Avenue, Oak Bluffs; 508-693-7129.

Old Whaling Church Performing Arts Center offers cultural lectures, classic films, concerts and plays throughout the year. Located in an 1843 Greek Revival church, the center has featured stars such as Patricia Neal, Andre Previn and Victor Borge. ~ Old Whaling Church, 89 Main Street, Edgartown; 508-627-4440 or 508-627-8017.

NIGHTLIFE

Beaches in rural West Tisbury, Chilmark and Gay Head are dramatic, untamed and less crowded than beaches near the Vineyard's three towns. But the parking lots are for residents only, and in the summer guards check to see if cars have resident stickers. Nonresidents ride bikes to these beaches. Shore fishing is excellent from all south shore beaches.

BEACHES & PARKS

FELIX NECK WILDLIFE SANCTUARY 🏃 A 350-acre haven for wild animals, birds, flora and fauna, the sanctuary has six miles of easy walking trails through salt marshes, thick forests and open meadows of wildflowers. The area is managed by the Felix Neck Wildlife Trust. It is also affiliated with the Massachusetts Audubon Society. There are year-round activities for children and adults, including guided nature walks and bird-watching trips geared toward novices and experts alike. Restrooms, interpretive exhibit center, gift shop, library; admission (free for Audubon Society members). ~ Three miles from the center of Edgartown on the Edgartown–Vineyard Haven Road, off State Road, between Oak Bluffs and Edgartown; 508-627-4850.

NANTUCKET SOUND BEACHES Strung together along protected Nantucket Sound are Oak Bluffs Town Beach, Joseph A. Sylvia State Beach, Bend-in-the-Road Beach and Lighthouse Beach. This is where the movie *Jaws* was filmed, but don't panic, this isn't shark country. The narrow, gently curved shoreline has clean sand and calm water. Swimming lessons are offered at some of the beaches, and bicycle paths run alongside the shore, which is bordered by ponds, salt marsh and summer homes. A stately lighthouse overlooks Lighthouse Beach. Lifeguards; groceries in Oak Bluffs or Edgartown. ~ Along Beach Road between Oak Bluffs and Edgartown.

SOUTH BEACH Also called Katama Beach, this popular, three-mile-long, Atlantic-facing beach runs into Cape Pogue and the Nantucket Sound Beaches. Wide, expansive and flat, it is surrounded by heath dotted with 20th-century homes—a rare sight in Martha's Vineyard. In the summer the air is soft and warm from southeasterly winds. The beach is ideal for swimming and body surfing (watch undertow), and fishing is excellent. Lifeguards; groceries two miles away in Edgartown. ~ Off Katama Road, south of Edgartown. You may take a shuttle bus from the center of town.

FULLER STREET BEACH A favorite among the many young folks who spend the summer in Edgartown, it's a quick bike ride away and a great place to take a break from Edgartown's other, more crowded beaches. There are no facilities or lifeguards. ~ At the end of Fuller Street near Lighthouse Beach.

HIDDEN ► **CAPE POGUE WILDLIFE REFUGE & WASQUE RESERVATION** If you want to get away from it all, take the two-minute car and passenger ferry from Edgartown to these wilderness areas on Chappaquiddick Island, an undeveloped peninsula of vast, empty beaches and moors. The refuge and reservation are adjacent to each other and form the northeastern tip of the Vineyard. Both offer an assortment of low dunes, ponds, tidal flats and cedar thickets. Wildlife abounds, including noisy least terns, piping plovers, common terns and American oystercatchers. East Beach, part of the Cape Pogue Wildlife Refuge, is the best spot for swimming (although it is sometimes rough), and is a great spot to catch blue fish. The closest groceries are in Edgartown; day-use fee, $3. Closed late October through Memorial Day. ~ Cape Pogue is at the end of Chappaquiddick Road on the other side of Dyke Bridge. The bridge is closed now and access to Cape Pogue is limited to four-wheel-drive vehicles with permits. Wasque Point is at the end of Wasque Road; 508-693-7662.

MANUEL CORRELEUS STATE FOREST 🏃🚲 Right in the center of the Vineyard lie 3900 acres of towering evergreens, scrubland, ponds and streams. Laced with bicycle paths, as well as hiking trails carpeted with soft, thick pine needles, the cool, hushed forest offers a peaceful respite from the Vineyard's wind-bitten moors and wide-open beaches. Groceries in Edgartown or West Tisbury. ~ Off Airport Road between West Tisbury and Edgartown.

LONG POINT WILDLIFE REFUGE 🏊🎣 A never-ending, loosen-your-teeth dirt road is the only way to get to this mystical, magical wildlife refuge. The road forks here and there; just stay on the widest part and eventually you come to a small parking lot (seasonal parking with a fee). Shortly beyond lies an endless grass and huckle-berry-covered heath that looks like a prairie with two enormous ponds. Tisbury Great Pond and Long Cove are home to black ducks, bluebills, ospreys, canvasbacks and swans. Beyond the ponds you'll discover a sea of silver beach grass and a white sand beach. Swimming and fishing are good, although the waters can get rough. Groceries 15 minutes away in West Tisbury. ~ This place is very difficult to find. It's one mile west of Martha's Vineyard Airport off Edgartown–West Tisbury Road on Deep Bottom Road, a deeply rutted dirt road without a sign. It's best to ask locals for directions.

GAY HEAD BEACH 🏊🎣 Adjacent to the multi-colored Gay Head Clay Cliffs, a national landmark off-limits to the public, this 7.4-acre, flat, sandy beach is extremely popular in the summer. Gay Head is great for sunning, fishing, swimming and beachcombing, but be cautious of the surf. Although it is illegal, nude swimming is popular here. It costs $10 to park at the lot behind the dunes. You may be better off taking the Up Island Shuttle Bus that runs in the summer. Restrooms, snack bars; parking fee, $10. ~ At the western tip of the Vineyard at the end of State Road, which is also called South Road in Gay Head.

CEDAR TREE NECK SANCTUARY 🏃 The raucous chirping of king fish-ers, song sparrows and Carolina wrens is the first thing to greet you ◄ *HIDDEN* at this 300-acre preserve. This is their kingdom, and what a spectac-ular place it is. Follow one of two well-marked paths through hilly woods of beech, sassafras, red maple, hickory oak and beetlebung. Soon the sky opens up, and, out of nowhere, extraordinary vistas appear of deep ponds, rolling sand dunes and the ocean beyond. Paths lined with ferns, moss and mushrooms lead down through the woods to an elevated catwalk and the shore. Unfortunately, picnicking is not allowed, and swimming is prohibited in the sanctuary. Groceries in West Tisbury. ~ From State Road in West Tisbury, take Indian Hill Road to a dirt road with a Cedar Tree Neck sign. The road goes down a hill to the parking lot.

▼▼▼▼▼▼▼▼▼▼

Nantucket

Located 30 miles out to sea from Cape Cod, this magical, fog-shrouded island is a study in contrasts. With its historic homes and cobblestone streets, it looks like storybook land, circa 1800. Yet it has sophisticated New York City/San Francisco–style restaurants and Madison Avenue shops. Outside of town, Nantucket is a bittersweet world of rolling moors, wild roses and windswept saltbox cottages that appear to have sprouted from the earth itself.

Nantucket was first sighted in 1602 by Captain Bartholomew Gosnold on his way to Martha's Vineyard. English settlers and Quakers farmed the land until the 1830s, when it was one of the busiest whaling ports in the world, a fact noted by Herman Melville in *Moby Dick*. In the 1870s, when kerosene started to replace whale oil as a fuel source and whales were becoming scarce, the industry started to decline and Nantucket lost 60 percent of its population. A depression followed, but around the turn of the century tourism blossomed and the island prospered once again.

Nantucket is so small and flat you can zip across it on a bicycle in about two hours or by car in 30 minutes. There are almost as many bicycle paths as roads, and bicycle rental shops abound on the wharf where the ferries dock. Like Martha's Vineyard, the only way to get here is by ferry or plane (see the "Transportation" section at the end of this chapter).

SIGHTS

There is only one town, Nantucket, but it can occupy you for hours or days if you enjoy historic homes, museums, fine restaurants, shopping and gallery hopping.

At the foot of Main Street and the wharf is the **Nantucket Island Chamber of Commerce**, where you can pick up a 300-page color guidebook, *Official Guidebook to Nantucket*, a comprehensive resource guide. Benches are everywhere, so you can sit down and map out an itinerary or just people watch. During summer months the town is packed with tanned college kids, prosperous-looking couples, and families on vacation and some wide-eyed day-trippers from the Cape and nearby Martha's Vineyard. Tail-wagging Labradors wander about, and the local gentry stand on corners sipping coffee and chatting. ~ 48 Main Street; 508-228-1700.

The **Whaling Museum** is a couple of blocks north of the Chamber of Commerce. A former candleworks with enormous cross beams, this rustic old building is as fascinating as its exhibits, which include a whale skeleton, a lighthouse lens and a whaleboat. Closed October through April. Admission. ~ 5 Broad Street; 508-228-1736.

The **Jethro Coffin House** is Nantucket's oldest house. Built in 1686, this classic saltbox is characteristic of late-17th-century Massachusetts Bay Colony homes. ~ Sunset Hill and West Chester streets.

If you walk up Main Street past the shops, you'll find many elegant mansions built during the heyday of whaling.

Nearby stands the **Maria Mitchell Science Center**. Mitchell, a Nantucket native, was the first person to discover a comet with a telescope, and the first female member of the American Academy of Arts and Sciences. The center, named in her honor, includes a natural science museum with an impressive insect collection, a library, aquarium, observatory and the house in which Mitchell was born. The center conducts summer field trips. Closed September through mid-June. Admission. ~ Vestal and Milk streets; 508-228-9198.

For a heady dose of Nantucket country life, visit **Siasconset**, a doll-sized hamlet of 17th-century pitched-roofed cod fisher shanties transformed into beguiling summer homes. In spring and early summer this endearing village looks as though it's been attacked by roses. Everywhere you look wild pink roses are climbing over fences, up sides of houses and over roofs, creating a dusty pink, grey and sage landscape.

Called "Sconset" by nearly everyone, the village lies seven and a half miles from Nantucket town on Milestone Road, which is bordered by a smooth, flat bicycle path. There isn't much to do here except enjoy the scenery and go to the beach. Sconset has a couple of restaurants, including renowned Chanticleer, and Summer House, one of Nantucket's prettiest inns.

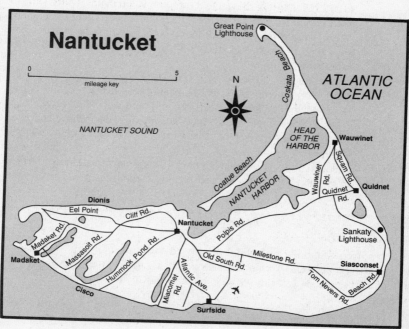

On the way back to town, take scenic Polpis Road. It goes past **Sankaty Lighthouse** and **The Moors**, magnificent, wind-bitten low-lying land that resembles a Persian carpet in the fall.

HIDDEN ►

The road also passes the **windswept cranberry bogs**, where you can watch cranberries being harvested in the fall (also see "Exploring Cranberry Country" in Chapter Six for information about cranberry growing on the South Shore).

The rest of Nantucket is all huckleberry covered-heath dotted with houses surrounded by spectacular beaches (see "Beaches & Parks" below).

LODGING

Nantucket has an astonishing number of inns and bed and breakfasts, but perhaps the most well-known is the **Jared Coffin House**. Built in 1845 by wealthy shipowner Jared Coffin, it features guest and public rooms appointed with antiques, Oriental rugs, crystal chandeliers, period wallpaper, marble fireplaces and canopy beds. A busy, festive establishment, it feels like a big city hotel of the 19th century. Sixty guest rooms span four different buildings. ~ 29 Broad Street; 508-228-2400, 800-248-2405, fax 508-228-8549. ULTRA-DELUXE.

Right down the street from the Jared Coffin House is one of the island's few bargain spots, **The Nesbitt Inn**. The white Victorian was built in 1872 as an inn and has been operated by the Nesbitt family since 1914. Most of the original furniture still remains. One room has a wood-rimmed bath tub that accommodates two. There are 13 guest rooms, each with a sink and shared bath. The inn's front porch is a great place for people watching. ~ 21 Broad Street; 508-228-0156. MODERATE.

Anchor Inn, a narrow grey clapboard house with green shutters and window boxes, is typical of Nantucket's many bed and breakfasts. Old and quaint, with narrow halls and sloping wood floors, it offers 11 cozy guest rooms, some hidden under dormers and eaves in small irregular spaces. Once the home of the Gilbreth family of Frank Gilbreth's *Cheaper by the Dozen*, the Anchor is furnished with Colonial and Shaker-style antiques. A continental breakfast is served in a cheerful blue-and-white breakfast room, and a brick patio.

CLASSIC OLD NANTUCKET

On Prospect Street stands the **Old Mill**, a classic red-and-grey shingled windmill that's one of Nantucket's most photographed sights. In the summer when the mill is operating you can see the intricate wooden gears that used to grind corn.

Closed January through mid-March. ~ 66 Centre Street; 508-228-0072. MODERATE TO DELUXE.

The **Woodbox Inn** is one of Nantucket's oldest and most delightful inns. Built in 1709, it exudes New England charm, with low-beamed ceilings, wood-paneled walls and walk-in fireplaces. The three guest rooms and six suites are furnished entirely in period antiques. Located in a quiet part of town away from all the hoopla, it has an excellent restaurant that can get a little noisy on weekends. Closed January through May. ~ 29 Fair Street; 508-228-0587. DELUXE TO ULTRA-DELUXE.

The **Wauwinet**, a lavish resort outside of town, is decorated to the hilt with country pine antiques, green wicker, primitive folk art, Victorian carpet runners, white wainscotting and pickled floors. The 35 guest rooms sport gentle sea breeze colors like pale smoke, sage and cream. Guests receive complimentary Crabtree and Evelyn toiletries. White wrought-iron furniture sits prim and proper on a vast lawn overlooking Nantucket Bay, and cushioned wicker furniture lines a bayside porch. Guests are transported to and from town in a shuttle bus. The Wauwinet is one of the most expensive inns on the island, attracting a well-heeled young crowd. There's a restaurant on the premises. Closed mid-October through mid-May. ~ 120 Wauwinet Road; 508-228-0145, 800-426-8718, fax 508-228-6712. ULTRA-DELUXE.

The **Summer House**, a rose-covered structure overlooking the ocean, is quintessential Nantucket, the kind of place you dream about but rarely find. Not surprisingly, it once graced the cover of *New York* magazine. Quaint little low-slung, vine-clad cottages surrounding the main house look as though they were designed by and for elves. But they're much bigger and lighter than they seem, and the decor blends just the right mix of rustic country charm. Rooms have features such as a fireplace, jacuzzi, rough-hewn beams, painted wood floor and rosebud wallpaper. There's a lively restaurant. Closed late October through late April. ~ 17 Ocean Avenue, Siasconset; 508-257-4577, fax 508-257-4590. ULTRA-DELUXE.

If you haven't stayed in a youth hostel since you gave up your backpack, you might want to try it again when you see Nantucket's **Star of the Sea Youth Hostel**. Located across from Surfside Beach, this historic wooden A-frame building looks like a cross between a Swiss chalet and a church. Originally a life-saving station, it today attracts a lot of young people, Europeans, senior citizens and cycling groups. Volleyball is played in a large yard in back bordered by sand dunes. The rows of twin beds inside remind most people of camp. As with most youth hostels, Star of the Sea is closed to guests during the day. ~ For reservations, write or call American Youth Hostels, 1020 Commonwealth Avenue, Boston, MA 02215; 617-731-6692. BUDGET.

◄ HIDDEN

DINING

Among Nantucket's astonishing number of sophisticated restaurants, one of the best is **Le Languedoc**. Elegant and hushed, it has taupe walls, contemporary art and dark carpeting that are strictly big-city, yet its navy-and-white checked tablecloths and Windsor chairs add a touch of French country. The menu includes pan-roasted lobster with garlic-thyme potatoes; soft-shell crab; Black Angus tenderloin of beef; and rack of lamb. A lot of care goes into the presentation. Ultra-deluxe in the upstairs dining room; moderate in the bistro downstairs. Closed mid-December through mid-May. ~ 24 Broad Street; 508-228-2552. MODERATE TO ULTRA-DELUXE

American Seasons serves American country specialties such as pan-fried sweetbreads with ragout of wild mushrooms, grilled tuna with a spicy vegetable sauce and sautéed rabbit with sundried tomatoes. The restaurant is in a white cottage with window boxes spilling lush pink impatiens. The green-and-white interior is romantically lit with hurricane lamps, and New Age music plays softly in the background. The crowd is young, happy and casual. Closed November through early April. ~ 80 Centre Street; 508-228-0397. ULTRA-DELUXE.

People stand in line for **The Brotherhood** because it serves reasonably priced basics—burgers, sandwiches and fried fish—in an 1840 whaling bar with a low ceiling, brick walls and weathered wooden tables. The Brotherhood is one of the few restaurants that serve until 12:30 a.m. Closed in February. ~ 23 Broad Street. BUDGET TO MODERATE.

The Atlantic Café is on a street that should be called Hamburger Row. Every restaurant on this block serves the same thing—burgers, beer and rock-and-roll. You can smell the fried food before you get here. The restaurant attracts families with small children. The Atlantic is a clean-looking establishment with white walls, wood beams and a bar in the middle surrounded by wooden chairs and tables. Closed late December through early January; closed Monday and Tuesday early January through April. ~ 15 South Water Street; 508-228-0570. MODERATE TO DELUXE.

Espresso Café is good for a cappuccino and a designer brownie, picnic fixings or a casual lunch or dinner. There are paddle fans, a black-and-white tile floor, a tin ceiling and a tree-shaded brick patio out in back. The food is trendy and hearty—cassoulet, soup, chili, pasta, thick pizza piled high with "yuppie" ingredients such as sun-dried tomatoes and goat cheese. ~ 40 Main Street; 508-228-6930. BUDGET.

One of Nantucket's most beautiful and versatile restaurants, the **Boarding House** has a shady brick patio that's perfect for people watching and a lovely bar and café with floor-to-ceiling windows. (A woman could come to the bar alone and feel totally at ease.) A formal dinner is served in the cellar, a grottolike, candle-lit room with cream-colored arched walls. Dishes change frequently. Popular offerings, many served in both the café and dining room, include seared tuna with wasabi aioli and soy ginger glaze, and twin lobster tails grilled with buerre blanc and mashed potatoes. ~ 12 Federal Street; 508-228-9622. DELUXE TO ULTRA-DELUXE.

Le Chanticleer is one of New England's most romantic restaurants. In spring, the many-windowed, gray-shingled house is covered with climbing roses, and the garden is a riot of pink, white and lavender flowers. The menu features traditional French cuisine—foie gras, lobster soufflé, fresh figs in sweet white wine and herbs, trout with salmon mousse and lobster ginger sauce. Many locals prefer the restaurant for lunch; the *prix-fixe* dinner is a major production. Closed November through mid-June. ~ 9 New Street, Siasconset; 508-257-6231. DELUXE TO ULTRA-DELUXE.

SHOPPING

Hoorn Ashby Gallery, one of Nantucket's most beautiful galleries, sells American and European contemporary paintings, antique hand-painted blanket chests, French-country porcelain and more in a sun-filled room with wood-paneled walls, tall columns, wainscoting and high ceilings. ~ 10 Federal Street; 508-228-9314.

Many shops in Nantucket sell handwoven goods, but Nantucket Looms blankets, throws and shawls are a cut above the rest. Popular designs include a voluminous, fluffy white blanket with thin navy stripes, and a pale pink shawl laced with foggy grey threads. ~ 16 Main Street; 508-228-1908.

Four Winds Craft Guild specializes in the island's two oldest crafts: antique and new lightship baskets and scrimshaw. The former are tightly woven, bowl-shaped baskets used as purses or decorative items; scrimshaw are items decoratively carved from whale bone and teeth. Both crafts were created in the 18th century by lighthouse keepers and sailors with idle time on their hands. Lightship purses are a status symbol among the island's conservative ladies. The older the basket, the better. ~ 6 Straight Wharf; 508-228-9623.

Brimming with hidden delights, Vis-A-Vis offers an eclectic mix of goods ranging from hand-knit sweaters, bathing suits and antique hooked rugs, to quilts and jewelry. Women and children can find something to wear to the beach, a wedding or an evening on the town. ~ 34 Main Street; 508-228-5527.

NIGHTLIFE

The Nantucket Arts Council presents classical music concerts in the old Coffin School and local churches from September to June. ~ Box 554; 508-228-1216.

In summer, Nantucket Musical Arts Society gives classical concerts in the First Congregational Church located at 62 Centre Street. ~ Box 897; 508-228-1287.

Throughout the year, **The Theatre Workshop of Nantucket** stages plays such as *Arsenic and Old Lace*, *Pantomime* and *Don't Dress for Dinner*. ~ Bennett Hall, 62 Centre Street; 508-228-4305.

Actors Theatre of Nantucket has something for everyone: serious drama, light comedy (like Neil Simon's *Lost in Yonkers*), musicals, modern dance, comedians and more. A children's matinee series features musicals, magicians and plays. Open Memorial Day to Columbus Day. ~ 2 Centre Street; 508-228-6325.

For evening cocktails and live entertainment in a comfortable old tavern, try the **Tap Room at Jared Coffin House**. ~ 29 Broad Street; 508-228-2400.

Fun, funky and informal, **The Chicken Box**, a bar with live entertainment, presents a variety of bands—rock-and-roll, reggae, rhythm-and-blues and others. Open year-round. Cover for bands. ~ 16 Daves Street; 508-228-9717.

BEACHES & PARKS

Bike paths go to Madaket, Dionis, Surfside and Siasconset Beaches, and fishing is great from those on the south shore. Nantucket doesn't have parks, per se, but the **Nantucket Conservation Foundation** owns and manages more than 8200 acres of undeveloped land open to the public to explore. Foundation land is identified by roadside maroon posts topped with a wave and seagull logo. If you want to know more, stop in and talk to the foundation folks, a friendly group of people who are happy to discuss the island's flora and fauna. ~ Larsen-Sanford Center, 118 Cliff Road; 508-228-2884.

DIONIS BEACH If it weren't for a white rock on which the word Dionis is painted, you'd never find this beach, which is ideal for swimming, picnics and cookouts (fire permits available from the Nantucket fire station). Beyond the large dirt parking lot, a path leads through tall sand dunes to the beach. These are dunes protected from natural erosion and people by a fence. The beach has some rocks and seaweed. During low tide, a sand bar stretches out into the water quite a distance. Lifeguards; groceries are found in downtown Nantucket. ~ Three miles west of town off Eel Point Road in Dionis.

MADAKET BEACH One of Nantucket's most beautiful bicycle paths ends at this spectacular western-facing beach. Everything about this long, wide beach is just right. The sand is white and clean, the surf fantastic, the sunsets the best on the island. It's also one of the best spots on Nantucket to fish. Lifeguards, restaurant; groceries nearby in downtown Nantucket. ~ At the end of Madaket Road in Madaket.

HIDDEN ► **CISCO BEACH** The road to this out-of-the-way beach goes past scenic Hummock Pond and rolling heathlands. The wide-open beach is a free and easy place where you can walk for miles on white sand. It's popular with seasoned beach rats and young surfer types. Lifeguards; groceries are in downtown Nantucket. ~ At the end of Hummock Pond Road in Cisco, four miles southwest of town.

SURFSIDE 🚴 ⛱ 🏊 🧺 ⚓ Narrow sand paths lace the moors leading to this massive beach. Because Surfside is only three miles from town, it gets very crowded in the summer. But it's a great beach—big, long and wide with small rolling dunes to explore and the best surf on the island. Surfside attracts families and college students. To get away from the crowds, walk east along the shore toward Siasconset and soon you'll discover long stretches of blissfully empty beach. Restrooms, showers, lifeguards, snack bar, bike path. ~ At the end of Surfside Road, three miles south of town.

SIASCONSET BEACH 🚴 ⛱ This lovely eastern-facing beach six miles from town is in the village of Siasconset. People make a day out of bicycling or driving here to explore the beach and the village. Part of the beach is surrounded by grassy cliffs and dunes, then the land dips and becomes flat. To the left of the beach is Sankaty Lighthouse and the summer community of Quidnet. Walk south along the beach for an empty spot. Because of the wind, seaweed can be a problem. Lifeguards; groceries and restaurants a short walk away. ~ Seven miles east of town at the end of Milestone Road in Siasconset.

GREAT POINT, COSKATA & COATUE BEACHES ⛱ ⚓ If you really want to leave civilization, consider exploring this narrow stretch of uninhabited land that wraps around Nantucket Harbor. It's like one giant sand dune surrounded by water. Driving through this desertlike landscape is an adventure, and those who make the trek can swim in calm waters lapping a deserted white sand beach and view a nesting ground for eagles, clam and oyster ponds, the remains of a shipwreck and the Great Point Lighthouse. There's Fantastic shore fishing at Great Point, the northernmost point of land; swimming is calm on Nantucket Sound but not recommended on the Atlantic side, where the current and undertow are rough. Driving in this area requires an expensive ($65) permit and a four-wheel-drive vehicle equipped with everything you need to dig yourself out of a deep sand rut. Permits are available at the Wauwinet Gate House on Wauwinet Road (508-228-0006). Great Point Natural History Tours (508-228-6799) offers a three-hour guided tour over ten miles of beaches; other tours and fishing excursions are advertised in the local paper. ~ At the northeast end of the island at the end of Wauwinet Road off Polpis Road.

◄ *HIDDEN*

SANFORD FARM 🚶 ⛱ Owned by the Nantucket Conservation Foundation, this former dairy farm consists of 767 acres of classic Nantucket countryside. A magical place for quiet walks and private picnics, it has 15 miles of trails meandering through rare maritime

◄ *HIDDEN*

heathlands that look like Scotland. Follow the trail past long and winding Hummock Pond down to the empty beach, which offers good swimming (but beware the undertow). In spring and summer Sanford Farm is lush with wildflowers, but its most beautiful time is fall, when the land is a tapestry of burgundy, sage, rose, gold and ivory. Deer can be spotted early in the morning and at dusk. Rare short-eared owls nest on the ground in the grass, and turtles live in the pond. Groceries are located 15 minutes away in downtown Nantucket. ~ West of town off Madaket Road near the intersection of Cliff Road and Madaket.

Outdoor Adventures

Cape Cod, Martha's Vineyard and Nantucket offer a staggering number of opportunities for fishing, boating and other water sports, as well as cycling, golf, tennis and more.

FISHING

Blue fish, striped bass, tuna, cod and flounder are abundant. No license is required to fish, and tackle shops are everywhere. For detailed information on what to catch when, where and how, call the Massachusetts Division of Marine Fisheries. ~ 100 Cambridge Street, Room 1901, Boston, MA 02202; 617-727-5074.

NORTH CAPE Among the hundreds of charter and party boat outfits on Cape Cod, one of the most reputable is **The Albatross**. ~ Sesuit Harbor, East Dennis; 508-385-3244. The **Naviator** also comes highly recommended. ~ Wellfleet town pier; 508-349-6003. **Teacher's Pet** also has a good reputation. ~ Hyannis Harbor; 508-362-4925.

MARTHA'S VINEYARD Martha's Vineyard has **Larry's Tackle Shop**. ~ 141 Main Street, Edgartown; 508-627-5088. In Nantucket there's **Albacore**. ~ Straight Wharf; 508-228-5074.

WATER SPORTS

Cape Cod abounds with marinas and harbors where you can rent sailboats, windsurfing equipment, canoes and more. Try these establishments:

NORTH CAPE In West Dennis, there's **Cape Cod Boat Rentals**. ~ Route 28; 508-394-9268.

OUTER CAPE In Wellfleet, check out **Jack's Boat Rental**. ~ Route 6; 508-349-9808; Gull Pond, Wellfleet, 508-349-7553; and Nickerson State Park, Brewster, 508-896-8556.

PROVINCETOWN In Provincetown, there's **Flyer's Boat Rental**. ~ 131-A Commercial Street; 508-487-0898.

SOUTH CAPE In Harwich Port, try **Cape Water Sports**. ~ Route 28; 508-432-7079.

MARTHA'S VINEYARD For sailboat charters, rentals or lessons on Martha's Vineyard, there's **Wind's Up**. ~ 95 Beach Road, Vineyard Haven, 508-693-4252. You can also try **Laissez Faire**. ~ 8 Owen Park,

Vineyard Haven; 508-693-1646. **Ayuthia Charters** offers half-day and evening harbor sunset sails on beautiful wooden yachts. ~ Coastwise Wharf, Vineyard Haven; 508-693-7245.

NANTUCKET In Nantucket, **Force Five Jetties** rents windsurfing gear, kayaks and sailboats. ~ North Beach Street; 508-228-5358.

SOUTH CAPE Among the many excursions departing from Cape Cod, try **Hyannis Whale Watcher Cruises.** ~ Millway Marina, Barnstable Harbor, Hyannis; 508-362-6088. In Provincetown there's **Dolphin Fleet Whale Watch.** ~ MacMillan Pier; 508-255-3857.

WHALE WATCHING

SOUTH CAPE In Cape Cod rentals and instructions are available at **Cape Cod Diver's.** ~ 815 Main Street, Harwich Port; 508-432-9035. You can also try **East Coast Divers.** ~ 237 Falmouth Street, Hyannis; 508-775-1185.

SCUBA DIVING

Cape Cod has many scenic public courses.

GOLF

NORTH CAPE To tee off in this area, try **Ocean Edge.** ~ 832 Village Drive, Brewster; 508-896-5911.

OUTER CAPE **Highland Golf Club** is located right near the Cape Cod National Seashore. ~ Lighthouse Road, Truro; 508-487-9201.

SOUTH CAPE In this area, you'll want to try **Harwich Port Golf Club.** ~ South Street, Harwich Port; 508-432-0250. **Fairgrounds Golf Course** is an 18-hole course with a driving range, motor and pull carts, rentals and pro shop and a restaurant and lounge. A large sign at the driving range warns players to "Stop driving when planes approach." If you wait around for a while, you'll see why; the course is close to an airport that launches gliders. Sometimes the planes fly so low you can wave to the passengers. ~ 1460 Route 149, Marstons Mills; 508-420-1142.

MARTHA'S VINEYARD On Martha's Vineyard you'll want to try **Mink Meadows Golf Course.** ~ Franklin Street, Vineyard Haven; 508-693-0600. In Oak Bluffs, **Farm Neck Golf Course** offers beautiful scenery. ~ County Road; 508-693-2504.

NANTUCKET You can tee off at **Miacomet Golf Club.** ~ West Miacomet Road; 508-228-9764. Or play your 18 holes at **Siasconset Golf Club.** ~ Milestone Road, Siasconset; 508-257-6596.

Most Cape Cod towns have a number of municipal courts. For names and addresses in specific towns, call the **Cape Cod Chamber of Commerce.** ~ Junction of Routes 132 and 6, Hyannis; 508-362-3225.

TENNIS

NORTH CAPE A privately owned court in the area is **Mid-Cape Racquet Club.** ~ 193 White's Path, South Yarmouth; 508-394-3511.

PROVINCETOWN **Bissell Tennis Courts** is a privately owned court. ~ 21 Bradford Street; 508-487-9512.

MARTHA'S VINEYARD   Tennis is very popular on Martha's Vineyard. Municipal courts are at Church Street in Vineyard Haven, Niantic Park in Oak Bluffs, Robinson Road in Edgartown, Old Country Road in West Tisbury and the Chilmark Community Center on South Road.

NANTUCKET   **Brant Point Racquet Club** has nine clay courts. ~ 48 North Beach Street; 508-228-3700. **Jetties Beach Public Tennis Courts** is right near town. ~ Bathing Beach Road; 508-325-5334.

RIDING STABLES

Liability insurance has gotten so high, most stables won't rent horses, but a few still do.

SOUTH CAPE   On the Cape there's the **Deer Meadow Riding Stable**. ~ Route 137, East Harwich; 508-432-6580.

MARTHA'S VINEYARD   **Southshore Stables** has trails with views of the beach and through the forest. ~ West Tisbury–Edgartown Road, Martha's Vineyard; 508-693-3770.

BICYCLING

Cape Cod, Martha's Vineyard and Nantucket are a cyclist's paradise. The flat landscape is laced with miles of smooth, paved bicycle paths that meander past sand dunes, salt marsh, woods and pastures. What follows is a modest sampling of some of the best rides. Local chambers of commerce can provide more comprehensive information.

Short Bike Rides, by Edwin Mullen and Jane Griffith (Globe Pequot Press) is a handy little book that describes 31 bike rides on Cape Cod, Nantucket and Martha's Vineyard.

NORTH CAPE   The **Cape Cod Rail Trail**, an eight-foot-wide bicycle path, runs along the old Penn Central Railroad tracks from Route 134 in South Dennis to Locust Road in Eastham past classic Cape Cod scenery—ponds, forest, saltwater and freshwater marsh, cranberry bogs and harbors.

OUTER CAPE   **Head of the Meadow**, a moderately hilly bicycle path in the Cape Cod National Seashore in Truro, traverses some of the

✔ **CHECK THESE OUT—UNIQUE OUTDOOR ADVENTURES**

- Follow a path through woods of sassafras and hickory oak beneath skies filled with kingfishers at **Cedar Tree Neck Sanctuary.** *page 281*
- Cycle through the vast expanses of grassy knolls known as The Highlands on the Outer Cape's **Head of the Meadow trail.** *page 292*
- Grab your board and hang-ten or windsurf the waves at Nantucket's **Cisco and Surfside beaches.** *pages 288, 289*
- Fish, canoe, bicycle or cross-country ski at the North Cape's 2000-acre **Nickerson State Park**, where wildlife is abundant. *page 248*

Cape's most dramatic scenery including The Highlands—vast expanses of grassy knolls. The 3.3-mile path starts at Head of the Meadow Road off Route 6 and ends at High Head Road.

PROVINCETOWN Talk about dramatic scenery. The **Province Lands Trail** dips and turns past towering sand dunes, silvery mounds of wavy beach grass, two magnificent beaches and the Province Lands Visitors Center. The path starts at Herring Cove Beach parking lot at the end of Route 6 and includes many places where you can stop and picnic.

SOUTH CAPE The **Shining Sea** bicycle path between Falmouth and Woods Hole is popular with experienced cyclists because it's hilly in some areas and very scenic. The 3.3-mile path runs along Palmer Avenue in Falmouth, then down a hill past deep woods and historic homes, and it ends at Woods Hole harbor.

MARTHA'S VINEYARD The **Oak Bluffs–Edgartown–Katama Beach** bike path on Martha's Vineyard is smooth and easy, even though it's ten miles long. Departing from Oak Bluffs, the flat path runs along the shore past lovely old homes, beaches, ponds and salt marsh to historic Edgartown, then through heathland dotted with occasional houses to magnificent Katama Beach.

From Vineyard Haven, the hale and hearty bicycle to **Menemsha** and **Gay Head** via State Road to West Tisbury, then Middle Road to the end. The ride is hilly in parts, but the scenery is breathtaking. The beaches in this area have residents-only parking lots, so bicycling is the only way a nonresident can enjoy them.

NANTUCKET Bicycling on Nantucket is a snap. Smooth, flat bike paths parallel the island's two main roads. The five-mile **Madaket** bicycle path is the most scenic, dipping and winding past moors and ending at Madaket Beach, the western tip of the island. The sevenmile **Siasconset** path is a straight, flat line that goes past barren scrub pine and sandy scenery, ending at the village of Siasconset on the eastern end of the island.

Bike Rentals Practically every town on Cape Cod has a couple of bike rental shops. In South Yarmouth, try **The Outdoor Shop**. ~ 50 Long Pond Drive; 508-394-3819. In Eastham there's **The Little Capistrano Bike Shop**. ~ Salt Pond Road, Route 6; 508-255-6515. In Provincetown, you can check out **Arnold's**. ~ 329 Commercial Street; 508-487-0844. Falmouth Heights offers **Holiday Cycles**. ~ 465 Grand Avenue; 508-540-3549. Martha's Vineyard has **Anderson's Bike Rentals** in Oak Bluffs. ~ 14 Saco Avenue; 508-693-9346. In Edgartown there's **R. W. Cutler Bike**. ~ 1 Main Street; 508-627-4052. Nantucket's wharf has many bicycle rental shops; one of the biggest outfits is **Young's Bicycle Shop**. ~ 6 Broad Street, Steamboat Wharf; 508-228-1151.

HIKING   Otherworldly sand dunes, heaths that recall those across the Atlantic, sheltering forests and salt marshes are just a few of the environments available to hikers on Cape Cod and the Islands. You can trek through wilderness areas or stick to spots close to town. For more information on hikes throughout the state, contact the **Massachusetts Department of Environmental Management Trails Program**. ~ 100 Cambridge Street, Boston; 617-727-3160.

NORTH CAPE   **Talbot's Point Salt Marsh Trail** (1.5 miles), off Old Country Road in Sandwich, offers excellent views of the Great Marsh. The trail winds through red pine forest, along the fern-filled marsh and past cranberry bogs and the state game farm, where thousands of quail and pheasant are raised.

OUTER CAPE   **Nauset Marsh Trail** (1 mile) offers some of the Cape's lushest scenery. The trail starts at the Salt Pond Visitors Center in North Eastham and goes past the shoreline of Salt Pond and Nauset Marsh, then rises through pastoral farmland filled with beach plums, bayberries and cedars.

A mesmerizing view of salt marsh and the ocean beyond greets you at **Goose Ponds Trail** (1.5 miles) in the Wellfleet Bay Wildlife Sanctuary. The path leads through forest down a slight grade past Spring Brook to marshlands covered with wild lupine. A wooden boardwalk leads to a secluded beach. Among the many species of bird life are white-bottomed tree swallows nesting in bird houses located throughout the sanctuary.

Great Island Trail (8.4 miles), a wind-bitten wilderness, is best in the morning when the sun isn't too intense. Located at the end of Chequesset Neck Road in Wellfleet, the trail borders tidal flats, grassy dunes, pitch pine forest, the ocean and meadows where purple marsh peas and fiddler crabs flourish. Great for solitary beachcombing, the trail offers a number of spectacular views.

PROVINCETOWN   You'll find hikers and bikers on the **Beech Forest Trail** (1 mile), which winds to the Cape's most monumental sand dunes. Most of the trail wanders through cool beech forests and past freshwater ponds, and at one point it opens up to reveal the desert-like sand dunes. It starts on Race Point Road in Provincetown. Call 508-487-3424 for more information.

MARTHA'S VINEYARD   **Felix Neck Wildlife Sanctuary Trail** (1.5 miles), off the Edgartown–West Tisbury Road, offers many opportunities to view ducks, swans, otters, muskrats, egrets, harrier hawks and other wildlife. The trail winds past waterfowl ponds, salt marsh, the end of a peninsula, wetland vegetation and oak forest. It ends at the sanctuary's exhibit building, which has aquariums, wildlife displays, a library and a naturalist gift shop. ~ Information: 508-627-4850.

NANTUCKET   Nantucket's only marked hiking trail is the **Sanford Farm–Ram Pasture Walking Trail**, offering 15 miles of wilderness to explore. In addition, the Nantucket Conservation Foundation also owns parcels of wilderness the public can explore. For more on this, see the "Beaches & Parks" sections in this chapter. Following are two of the most scenic areas in which to hike:

Tupancy Links, off Cliff Road immediately west of town, is laced with paths that overlook Nantucket Sound. A former golf course, today it is a big open grassy field offering dramatic views.

Alter Rock off Polpis Road in the central moors is crisscrossed with unmarked paths and rutted dirt roads. Dotted with kettle hole ponds, rocks and scrub oak thicket, the scenery is classic heathland. A four-wheel-drive is recommended.

For more information on hiking trails on Nantucket, call 508-228-1700.

Transportation

Special note: For up-to-the-minute information on every conceivable way to get to Martha's Vineyard, Nantucket and Cape Cod short of walking on water, call the **Massachusetts Office of Travel and Tourism.** ~ 100 Cambridge Street, Boston; 617-727-3201.

CAR

Route 6 cuts through the middle of Cape Cod, ending at Provincetown. **Route 6A** runs along the north side of the Cape, and **Route 28** runs along Nantucket Sound. Both routes connect with Route 6 in Orleans.

AIR

Five airports serve Cape Cod and the Islands: **Logan International Airport** in Boston, Barnstable Airport and Provincetown Municipal Airport on Cape Cod, Martha's Vineyard Airport and Nantucket Memorial Airport.

Barnstable Airport in Hyannis is served by Cape Air, Delta, Island Air, Nantucket Airlines, Northwest Air Link and USAir Express.

Cape Air services **Provincetown Municipal Airport.**

Flying into **Martha's Vineyard Airport** are Cape Air, Continental Express, Northwest Air Link and USAir Express.

Nantucket Memorial Airport is serviced by Cape Air, Continental Express, Delta, Nantucket Airlines, Northwest Express and USAir Express.

For ground transportation from Barnstable Airport to Logan Airport and areas throughout southern Massachusetts, contact ABC **Airport Coach** (508-747-6622) or **Nauset Taxi** (508-255-6965).

Taxis and car rentals listed below provide ground transportation to all other airports except Logan.

FERRY & BOAT

Ferries and boats between Boston, Cape Cod, Martha's Vineyard and Nantucket require reservations during the summer. Throughout the year, the **Steamship Authority** transports cars and passengers from

Route 28 to Woods Hole to Oak Bluffs and Vineyard Haven, as well as from Hyannis to Nantucket. ~ 509 Falmouth Road, Mashpee; 508-477-8600.

The following ferries and boats operate seasonally and do not transport cars: **Hy-Line** takes passengers to and from Hyannis, Nantucket and Oak Bluffs on Martha's Vineyard. ~ Ocean Street Dock, Hyannis; 508-775-7185. **Martha's Vineyard Ferry** operates between New Bedford and Vineyard Haven on Martha's Vineyard. ~ 1494 East Rodney French Boulevard, Billy Woods Wharf, New Bedford; 508-997-1688. **The Island Queen** goes between Falmouth and Oak Bluffs on Martha's Vineyard. ~ 75 Falmouth Heights Road, Pier 45, Falmouth; 508-548-4800. The **Chappaquiddick Ferry**, universally known as the "Chappy ferry," travels between Edgartown and Chappaquiddick Island year-round. ~ Dock and Daggett streets, Edgartown, Martha's Vineyard; 508-627-9427.

BUS

Greyhound Bus Lines offers frequent service to Newburyport and Boston. ~ 2 South Station, Boston; 617-526-1801, 800-231-2222.

Bonanza runs buses to and from Logan Airport, Hyannis, Woods Hole, Falmouth, Bourne, New Bedford, Fall River, Connecticut, Rhode Island and New York. ~ 59 Depot Avenue, Falmouth; 508-548-7588, 800-556-3815.

Plymouth and Brockton Street Railway Company has year-round express service to and from Boston's Logan Airport and local service along Route 6 on Cape Cod from Sagamore to Provincetown. ~ 8 Industrial Park, Plymouth; 508-746-0378.

Peter Pan Bus Lines offers service to Hyannis from Mount Holyoke, Springfield, Newton, Worcester and Albany, New York. ~ 555 Atlantic Avenue, Boston; 800-343-9999.

TRAIN

Amtrak runs between Boston and Hyannis with summer bus connections to towns throughout Cape Cod. The Amtrak "Cape Codder" runs between New York and Hyannis from May to September. ~ South Station, Summer Street at Atlantic Avenue, Boston; 800-872-7245.

CAR RENTALS

Car-rental agencies at Barnstable Airport include **Avis Rent A Car** (800-331-1212), **Hertz Rent A Car** (800-654-3131) and **National Interrent** (800-227-7368).

Thrifty Car Rental (800-367-2277) serves the airport in Provincetown.

Martha's Vineyard Airport has **Thrifty Adventure Car and Moped Rentals** (for cars, 508-693-1959; for mopeds, 800-367-2277), **All-Island Rent A Car** (508-693-6868), **Budget Rent A Car** (800-527-0700) and **Hertz Rent A Car** (800-654-3131).

Nantucket Memorial Airport agencies include **Budget Rent A Car** (800-527-0700), **Hertz Rent A Car** (800-654-3131) and **Nantucket Windmill Auto Rental** (800-228-1227).

Cape Cod Regional Transit Authority B-Bus Service offers door-to-door minibus service (reservations required) and makes six daily roundtrips between Barnstable and Woods Hole. ~ Old Chatham Road, South Dennis; 508-385-8326, 800-352-7155.

On Martha's Vineyard, from late May to mid-October, **Island Transport** runs shuttle buses between Vineyard Haven, Oak Bluffs and Edgartown. Less frequent service is available up-island; call the above number for schedules. Nantucket doesn't have public transportation. Most people get around with rental cars or bicycles. ~ 508-693-1589.

PUBLIC TRANSIT

Taxis serving airports on the coast are as follows: Barnstable Airport, **All Points Taxi** (508-778-1400), **Hyannis Taxi** (508-775-0400), **Town Taxi of Cape Cod** (508-771-5555) and **Yarmouth Taxi** (508-394-1500); Provincetown Airport, **Mercedes Cab** (508-487-3333); Martha's Vineyard Airport, **Adam Cab** (508-627-4462); Nantucket Memorial Airport, **All Points Taxi** (508-228-5779).

TAXIS

SIX

Massachusetts Coast

Immortalized in the past by Herman Melville in *Moby Dick*, the Massachusetts coast today remains fertile territory for the imagination. This magnificent stretch of windswept coast abounds with historic seaside villages, vintage lighthouses, glorious beaches and history that reads like an adventure story complete with witches and pirates, authors and artists, Pilgrims and American natives, sea captains and Moby Dick.

An ethnic melting pot of Portuguese fishermen, Yankee blue bloods, old salts and the Irish (who seem to be everywhere), coast residents are very proud of where they live. North Shore loyalists wouldn't think of moving to the South Shore, and vice versa. What unifies everyone is the sea. Rich and poor alike have miniweather stations on their roofs to determine wind direction, and everyone reads tide charts. Kids learn how to fish, sail and dig for clams when they're five years old.

That all-encompassing sea is, of course, what lured Europeans to these shores in the first place. One hundred years before the Pilgrims stepped foot on Plymouth Rock, English adventurers fished the waters around the Massachusetts coast. Between 1600 and 1610, explorers Samuel de Champlain and Bartholomew Gosnold sailed to Gloucester.

Aboard the *Mayflower*, 102 Pilgrims landed in Plymouth in 1620, establishing the first permanent settlement in New England. By 1640, about 2500 of the new settlers lived in eight communities. Although they came to America to seek religious freedom, the Pilgrims persecuted Quakers and anyone else who didn't adhere to their strict Puritan religion. Their intolerant thinking helped fuel one of the most infamous pieces of American colonial history—the Salem witch trials of 1692. Salem had been founded six years after Plymouth. Here the Puritans tried to impose their religious laws on rowdy fishermen who lived in nearby Marblehead, but adultery and drunkenness won out. The Puritans were more successful in their witch hunt—20 people, most of them women, were executed for practicing "witchcraft" in a single year.

The gruesome trials took place during a time when witchcraft was thought to be the cause for any unexplained event. Similar trials and executions occurred throughout New England and Europe, but Salem had the dubious distinction of executing the most women in the shortest amount of time.

Fortunately by the 1700s the focus was more on commerce than religion. Salem sailing vessels had opened routes to the Orient, thus establishing the famous China trade and Salem's reputation as a major port. When the Revolutionary War broke out in 1775, America didn't have a Navy, so Salem sea captains armed their merchant vessels and fought the British.

For the next 150 years, shipbuilding, the China trade and commercial fishing flourished along the Massachusetts coast, particularly in the towns north of Boston. Concurrently, New Bedford, near Rhode Island, became a leading whaling port.

All this maritime activity brought great prosperity to the coast. Fortune and adventure lay in wait for any man willing to risk his life on a whale boat or ship bound for the Orient to obtain ivory, spice, silver and gold. It was an exciting, swashbuckling time, filled with tall tales and tragedy. The widows' walks on many historic homes in towns such as Newburyport are a sad reminder of the men who never returned from the sea.

Evidence of the wealth gleaned during these years is apparent in the amazing number of 18th- and 19th-century mansions built by sea captains that dot the coast. Impeccably restored by a people in love with the past, these coast homes make up an architectural feast bulging with Greek Revival, Federal, Queen Anne, Victorian Gothic, Colonial and classic saltbox structures. Historic villages and buildings throughout the area enable visitors to see the evolution of America's unique architectural style.

By the mid-1800s everything along the Massachusetts coast started to change. Salem's prominence as a seaport was over. Its harbor was too shallow for the new, faster clipper ships, and railroads provided cheaper and more rapid shipping service. The whaling industry also started to decline as petroleum replaced whale oil and whales became scare. Eventually the entire industry vanished, plummeting New Bedford and other whaling ports into serious depressions.

The Industrial Revolution came along in the nick of time, and manufacturing businesses started to sprout along the Massachusetts coast and throughout New England. In the late 1800s, New Bedford and Fall River became leading textile manufacturers, but this prosperity was short lived. Prior to the Depression, union problems and cheaper labor in the South wiped out the textile industry.

While the coast economy was transforming itself in the mid-1800s, two other developments were evolving that would change the flavor of the coast forever. Tourism began to bloom on Cape Cod, and artists and writers discovered the inspirational charms of the coast.

Rudyard Kipling and Winslow Homer lived north of Boston in Rocky Neck, one of the country's oldest artist colonies. Nathaniel Hawthorne wrote about Salem, which he called home, in the *House of the Seven Gables*. Melville immortilized whaling in New Bedford. To this day, creative people are drawn to the Massachusetts coast, now supported by light industry, fishing and a tourist industry that just keeps growing.

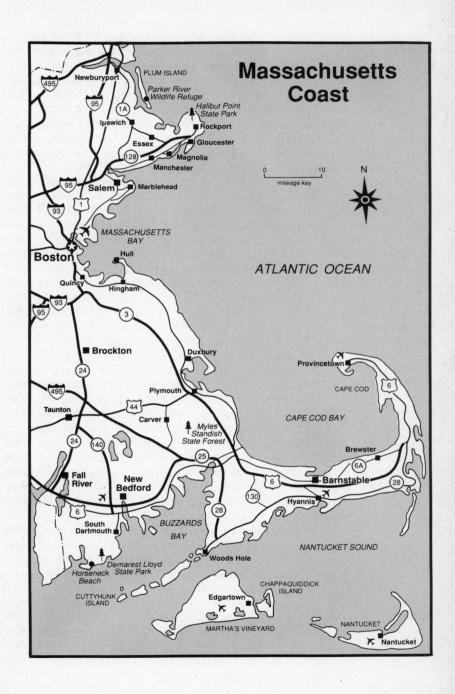

Massachusetts Coast

PLUM ISLAND

Newburyport

Parker River
Wildlife Refuge

Halibut Point
State Park

Ipswich

Rockport

Essex

Gloucester

Magnolia

Manchester

Salem

Marblehead

MASSACHUSETTS
BAY

Boston

Hull

ATLANTIC OCEAN

Quincy

Hingham

Brockton

Duxbury

Provincetown

CAPE COD

Plymouth

Taunton

Carver

Myles
Standish
State Forest

CAPE COD BAY

Brewster

Fall
River

New
Bedford

Barnstable

Hyannis

South
Dartmouth

BUZZARDS
BAY

NANTUCKET SOUND

Horseneck
Beach

Demarest Lloyd
State Park

Woods Hole

CUTTYHUNK
ISLAND

CHAPPAQUIDDICK
ISLAND

Edgartown

NANTUCKET

Nantucket

MARTHA'S VINEYARD

0   10
mileage key

N

We have divided the coast into two geographic areas. The North Shore (everything above Boston to the New Hampshire border) and the South Shore (Plymouth and the area from Cape Cod to the Rhode Island border). Cape Cod and the Islands have always attracted the lion's share of tourists, but the North Shore and South Shore offer more opportunities to discover hidden villages, inns, restaurants, beaches and more.

The North Shore wears many faces. Immediately north of Boston are the affluent commuter towns of Magnolia, Manchester and Marblehead, where prep schools, yachts and turn-of-the-century seaside mansions are a way of life.

Beyond these towns are Salem, known for architecture, witches and maritime museums; Gloucester, a major fishing port; Rockport, an artist-colony-turned-resort; Essex and Ipswich, pastoral areas with antiques and seafood; and Newburyport, a scenic 19th-century town on the New Hampshire border.

The South Shore is a patchwork of wealthy commuter towns, Portuguese neighborhoods, blue-collar communities and cranberry farms. Its three main towns include Plymouth, "America's Home Town," New Bedford and Fall River. You'll find Pilgrim lore, factory outlets, whaling museums, scenic ports, winding rivers and coastal pastures.

The coast has milder weather than the rest of the state. Summer temperatures range from the 60s to the 80s. Humidity can be a problem, especially along the North Shore, although ocean breezes keep things from getting too unbearable. In the fall temperatures range from the around 45 to 65. Rain is unpredictable and can happen any time of year.

Traditionally the Massachusetts coast has been a summer destination, but more people are starting to visit in the fall, when prices decline along with the crowds. But no matter when you visit you're bound to be impressed. The scenery is unparalleled, the architecture magnificent, the history fascinating, the seafood plentiful.

▼▼▼▼▼▼▼▼▼▼▼▼▼▼
The North Shore

The North Shore is a real sleeper. Unspoiled and relatively uncommercial, it's a place where you can still discover hidden inns, restaurants, beaches and parks. An explorer's destination, it's perfect for people who like to go it on their own.

From Marblehead immediately north of Boston to Newburyport on the New Hampshire border, this craggy stretch of coast offers tremendous diversity. Marblehead has magnificent yachts; Salem means witches and maritime history; gritty Gloucester is filled with old salts; Rockport has art and beautiful inns; Essex offers antiques; Ipswich has the best seafood; and Newburyport displays 19th-century elegance.

The North Shore is a vacation area and bedroom community to Boston populated by investment bankers, Yankee blue bloods, fishermen, artists and history buffs. In the 18th and 19th centuries, the country's most magnificent ships were built in North Shore towns, bringing great wealth to the area.

SIGHTS

To explore this area from Boston, take the Callahan tunnel to Routes 1A and 129 north to **Marblehead,** a small village of clapboard houses, hollyhocks and cobblestone streets. Marblehead is sailboat country. All summer long the harbor is alive with some of the most sophisticated racing vessels in America.

A good place to picnic and enjoy the harbor view is at **Crocker Park** at the western end of Front Street, high on a hill. Marblehead's **Old Town**, which surrounds the harbor, dates back to before the Revolution and is a very pleasant place to stroll. It has many interesting shops and casual restaurants.

The **Marblehead Chamber of Commerce** maintains a visitor information booth at the corner of Pleasant and Spring streets. ~ 62 Pleasant Street; 617-631-2868.

Historic sights in Old Town include **Abbot Hall**, the Victorian town hall that houses the famous historic painting *The Spirit of '76* by Archibald Willard. Visitors are free to wander in and view this dramatic work of art. ~ Washington Street; 617-631-0528.

◄ HIDDEN

Right down the street is the **Jeremiah Lee Mansion**, a Georgian home built in 1768 for Colonel Lee, a Revolutionary War patriot. The guided tour is packed with entertaining anecdotes: We learn, for example, that the extrawide stairway in the entrance hall was designed by Mrs. Lee so women could swoop down the stairs in their enormous hoop skirts without knocking over their escorts. Closed from mid-October through late May. Admission. ~ 161 Washington Street; 617-631-1069.

Salem, the largest North Shore town, is only ten minutes away from Marblehead on Route 114. People come here for architecture, maritime museums, Nathaniel Hawthorne and, of course, witches. This beautiful historic town is so civilized and proper looking, it's hard to believe the 1692 witchcraft trials ever took place here.

This macabre piece of American history began in a very innocent way. A group of teenage girls, who had learned black magic from a West Indian woman named Tituba, were diagnosed as bewitched. All hell broke loose, and everyone started accusing everyone else of being a witch. In the nine months to follow, 20 women were hanged and 150 imprisoned. The hysteria came to an end when the wives of prominent men were accused of being witches.

Salem's three witch exhibits are somewhat commercial, but kids love them. Every day in the summer, children wearing pointed black hats and capes purchased at nearby witch boutiques stand in long lines waiting to get in. The saving grace of the exhibits is that they are in historic buildings—not re-creations of haunted houses.

Salem Witch Museum is an audio-visual sound-and-light show. Life-size dioramas are spotlighted during the show to illustrate the events of the 1692 witch trials. Admission. ~ 19½ Washington Square North; 508-744-1692.

Witch House is the restored 1642 home of witch trial judge Jonathan Corwin. A narrated tour describes the style of life during this era and examines the process of the witch trials. Admission. ~ 310½ Essex Street; 508-744-0180.

Witch Dungeon Museum re-enacts the witch trials. Admission. ~ 16 Lynde Street; 508-744-9812.

Tourist information is available at the **National Visitors Center.** ~ New Liberty Street; 508-740-1650. Or contact the **Chamber of Commerce.** ~ Old Town Hall, 32 Derby Square; 508-744-0004. An easy way to see historic sights is to follow **Salem's Heritage Trail,** a self-guided walking tour indicated by a red line painted on the street.

To understand the real story of Salem, which was a major port in the 18th and 19th centuries, visit the **Peabody Essex Museum.** The Liberty Street site houses a treasure trove of objects acquired during Salem's active China trade days, such as an elaborate, moon-shaped, hand-carved wooden Chinese bed. A geneology research library and original witch trial documents are some of the highlights. The Essex Street site consists of a history and decorative arts museum and four impeccably restored homes and gardens dating from 1684 to 1818. The houses are fascinating, especially if toured in chronological order, and the architecture and craftsmanship are superb. Anyone who has ever renovated an old house will appreciate a special exhibit about the painstaking efforts that go into museum restoration work. Since bright colors were a sign of wealth in the 19th century, the 1804 Gardner-Pingree House, a fine neoclassical building, holds a few surprises. The kitchen is deep salmon and green; one bedroom wears a vivid peacock blue hue, while another sports canary yellow. Admission. ~ East India Square; 508-745-9500, 800-745-4054.

Chestnut Street is one of the most architecturally significant avenues in America. Many of its mansions were designed by Salem's famed Federal-period architect and woodcarver, Samuel McIntire. These brick and wood houses are simple in their design, yet the overall effect is graceful and elegant.

Pickering Wharf, a short walk from Chestnut Street, is a new but made-to-look-old commercial development of tourist shops and chain restaurants. About a block east stands **Derby Wharf**—a good area for strolling along the harbor.

Even though it's often crowded with tourists, there's something romantic and compelling about the **House of Seven Gables,** located

---

✔ CHECK THESE OUT—UNIQUE SIGHTS

- Delve into literary history at the 1668 **House of Seven Gables,** memorialized by Nathaniel Hawthorne in his famous novel. *page 304*
- Don't be fooled by what looks to be a normal cottage—Rockport's **Paper House** is constructed entirely out of newspaper. *page 306*
- Experience 17th-century life at the authentic **Plimoth Plantation,** where villagers in period costumes speak to you in Old English. *page 320*
- Climb aboard a half-scale model of a fully rigged 19th-century whaling ship at the **New Bedford Whaling Museum.** *page 322*

down the street from Derby Wharf. Built in 1668, the dark, almost black house is framed by ocean and sky. The tall, imposing gables look a bit like witch hats (although this thought probably wouldn't come to mind in another town). Inside, a labyrinth of cozy rooms with low ceilings, narrow passageways and secret stairs add to the ancient feeling of the place. The guided tour includes a good short film about how the house inspired Nathaniel Hawthorne to write his famous novel. Admission. ~ 54 Turner Street; 508-744-0991.

Northeast of Salem on scenic Route 127, which hugs the coast, are the residential towns of Manchester and Magnolia, known for their old money, private schools and magnificent mansions.

Right off Route 127 is **Hammond Castle Museum**, a popular spot ◀ HIDDEN
for weddings. Perched on the edge of a steep, windswept cliff, this seaside castle looks like something out of a Gothic novel. Built by John Hays Hammond, Jr., creator of the radio remote control, the house features an eccentric collection of medieval artifacts. Closed Monday through Wednesday from Labor Day through the end of September; closed in October; open weekends only from November through Memorial Day. ~ 80 Hesperus Avenue, Gloucester; 508-283-2080.

Three miles from Hammond Castle on Route 127 is **Gloucester**, the oldest seaport in the United States. Home port to approximately 200 fishermen, it has a salty dog ambience that brings you back to the real world after Hammond Castle. Overlooking the harbor stands the town's famed **Gloucester Fisherman** statue, *Man at the Wheel*, commemorating "They that go down to the sea in ships."

There's not much to see and do in Gloucester, but the **Cape Ann Chamber of Commerce** in the center of town deserves a visit. ~ 33 Commercial Street; 508-283-1601. The largest tourist information center on the North Shore, it has a hotel hotline for last-minute accommodations. ~ 800-321-0133.

A short hop from Gloucester, off Route 127, is **Rocky Neck Art Colony**, one of the country's oldest artist colonies, dating back to the 18th century. Winslow Homer and Rudyard Kipling lived here. Today it is a quainter than quaint seaside village with tiny houses, restaurants and galleries.

Down the road from Rocky Neck is **Beauport Museum**, a sprawl- ◀ HIDDEN
ing oceanfront English manor formerly owned by noted decorator Henry Davis Sleeper. From 1907 to 1934 Sleeper spent a fortune decorating all 40 rooms with a vast collection of American and European antiques, tapestries, wood paneling from abandoned old homes and much more. An informal pale green dining room has a worn brick floor and two long wooden tables set with a beautiful collection of colored glassware that reflects the light coming in from a bank of ocean-facing windows. Surprisingly, the overall effect is of an intimate English cottage. Closed mid-October through mid-May. Admission. ~ 75 Eastern Point Boulevard, East Gloucester; 508-283-0800.

Ten minutes from Gloucester on Route 127 is **Rockport**, the quintessential New England seaside village and the North Shore's only resort town. Until the mid-19th century, Rockport was a quiet fishing village. Then artists discovered its scenic charm, and the proverbial seascape was born. Today tourists flock to Rockport in the summer. The town is rather commercial, but the beautiful harbor and windswept rocky coast that originally attracted artists are still here to enjoy.

Bearskin Neck, a narrow peninsula jutting out into the ocean, is one of Rockport's main tourist attractions. It's lined with Lilliputian-sized wooden fishermen's cottages transformed into restaurants and galleries selling everything from T-shirts and seascapes in every style imaginable to model ships made of cut-up beer cans. Overlooking the harbor, off Bearskin Neck, is Motif #1, a red lobster shack, so named because it has been painted by so many artists.

About two miles south of downtown Rockport is the **Rockport Chamber of Commerce**. ~ 3 Main Street; 508-546-6575. The folks here can point out local sights such as the eccentric **Paper House**. At first it looks like a normal cottage, but it's made entirely out of newspaper. Even the furniture and fireplace are rolled paper. Elis F. Stedman, its creator, started the house in 1920; it took 20 years to complete. Closed from Labor Day through Memorial Day. Admission. ~ 52 Pigeon Hill Street; 508-546-2629.

The rural villages of **Essex** and **Ipswich** are about 30 minutes north of Rockport. Essex is famous for its antique stores (see the "Shopping" section below), Ipswich for its clams. A pleasant day can be spent antiquing and enjoying fresh, affordable seafood at one of the many roadside eateries in this area.

This route takes you right past **John Whipple House**, a steeply pitched-roofed house built circa 1655 and occupied by the Whipple family for over 200 years. As did many colonists, the Whipples built their home in the post-Elizabethan style popular in England at the time. It has a lovely Colonial-style garden and is located in a semirural area close to other historic buildings. Closed Monday and Tuesday and from mid-October through late April. Admission. ~ 53 South Main Street, Ipswich; 508-356-2811.

Just before the New Hampshire border, about 30 minutes north of Ipswich, lies the handsome 19th-century town of **Newburyport**. When the fog rolls in and the smell of brine and fish fills the air, you can walk along narrow streets bearing names like Neptune and imagine what it was like 100 years ago when this was a major shipbuilding center.

In the late 1970s the downtown area overlooking the harbor was renovated from top to bottom. Today, Newburyport's 19th-century brick buildings are so spit-and-polish clean, the town literally sparkles. As in many European towns, there's a central plaza overlooking the harbor where you can sit and watch the world go by. The shops and restaurants are quite tasteful; T-shirt and souvenir shops are the exception. **Greater Newburyport Chamber of Commerce** is in the heart of downtown. ~ 29 State Street; 508-462-6680.

For a healthy dose of the good life circa 1850, walk along **High Street** (Route 1A), which is lined with immaculate 19th-century Federal-style mansions built by sea captains. For a peek inside, visit **Cushing House**, home of the Historical Society of Old Newbury. It has 19th-century antiques, plus a genealogical library, French garden and carriage house. Closed Sunday and Monday and from November through April. Admission. ~ 98 High Street; 508-462-2681.

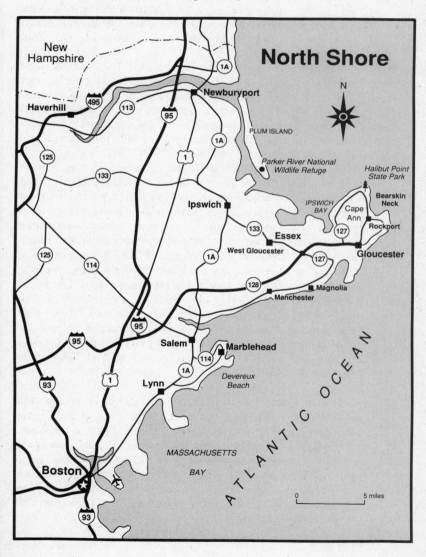

LODGING

Many of the North Shore's accommodations are in the resort town of Rockport. A sprinkling of motels can be found along Route 127, but they're short on charm and expensive.

Pleasant Manor Inn, an 1872 Victorian, is located on a historic street surrounded by other impressive homes. A grand staircase leads to 12 good-sized guest rooms. Some furnishings are a bit drab, but the inn's wide hallways, tall ceilings and many fireplaces are impressive. The inn has a homey, laid-back feeling, which is perhaps why it attracts the serious sailors from around the world who come to Marblehead, a yachting center. A tennis court is located behind the house; each room has a coffeemaker, and a hearty continental breakfast is served. ~ 264 Pleasant Street, Marblehead; 617-631-5843. MODERATE.

HIDDEN ►

A modest-looking green clapboard house, **The Nautilus Guest House** doesn't have a sign outside. "People just know about it," says the owner. Four plain and simple guest rooms with contemporary furnishings occupy the second floor (no private baths). The house stands on a narrow street across from the busy harbor and the Driftwood, a colorful, sea-shanty-style restaurant popular with fishermen and locals. ~ 68 Front Street, Marblehead; 617-631-1703. MODERATE.

The **Stephen Daniels House** is like a trip back in time. Built in 1667 by a sea captain, it is one of the few bed and breakfasts around here furnished entirely with museum-quality antiques. The five guest rooms have enormous walk-in fireplaces, low beamed ceilings and age-worn pine floors. It's located on a quiet, historic street within walking distance of everything, although the sign outside is small and easy to miss. ~ 1 Daniels Street, Salem; 508-744-5709. DELUXE.

If you can't live without a telephone, color television, air-conditioning and room service, stay at **The Hawthorne Hotel.** One of the few real hotels on the North Shore, this impeccably restored Federal-style building is located across from Salem Common. Eighty-nine guest rooms are tastefully decorated with reproduction Colonial antiques. Elegant public rooms have wood paneling, brass chandeliers and wing-back chairs. ~ 18 Washington Square West, Salem; 508-744-4080, 800-729-7829, fax 508-745-9842. DELUXE TO ULTRA-DELUXE.

The **Old Corner Inn** is a small, unpretentious and very casual inn in a building that dates back to 1865. It's within easy reach of Singing Beach and the village of Manchester. The nine rooms (six with private baths) are simply but comfortably furnished with some antiques. A couple of rooms have four-poster beds and working fireplaces; the bathroom of room number one has a ball-and-claw bathtub. Advance reservations are a must in the summer months since it's the only inn in Manchester. ~ 2 Harbor Street; Manchester by the Sea; 508-526-4996. MODERATE TO DELUXE.

There's something incredibly lovable about the **White House**, a cross between an inn and a motel. Surrounded by a well-coifed lawn steps away from the heart of little Magnolia, it has a total of 16 rooms, six fitting beautifully into the charming-inn category (antique furnishings, all sorts of little Victorian touches), and another ten rooms that are traditional motel accommodations. The latter are actually quite comfortable, each with two big double beds, a television, a private entrance and a parking spot—a welcome change from the inns that sometimes compromise on privacy. A continental breakfast is included. ~ 18 Norman Avenue, Magnolia; 508-525-3642. MODERATE.

Beach lovers enjoy the **Blue Shutters Inn**, a lovely old house across the street from Good Harbor Beach, one of the North Shore's most beautiful strips of sand. The inn sits on the outskirts of a secluded, affluent residential area overlooking the ocean and a vast expanse of scenic salt marsh. Blue and white throughout, the inn offers ten rooms and three individual apartments (weekly rental only), all with ocean views and sporting furnishings that are homey, simple and sparkling clean. Breakfast included. ~ 1 Nautilus Road, Gloucester; 508-281-2706. MODERATE TO DELUXE.

Only a ten-minute walk from Gloucester's famed fisherman statue, **Spruce Manor Motel and Guest House** has economical accommodations to satisfy all tastes. The main guest house, a lovely Victorian built in 1900, has 11 bed-and-breakfast-style guest rooms, some with turret-shaped ceilings and oversized beds. Next to the guest house are one-story motel units overlooking Annisquam River, plus a salt marsh and estuaries. The decor is plain and unobtrusive. Closed November through March. ~ 141 Essex Avenue; 508-283-0614, fax 508-283-0614. MODERATE.

A 1791 Colonial bed and breakfast, **The Inn on Cove Hill** is a five-minute walk from Bearskin Neck, Rockport's main tourist at-

✔ **CHECK THESE OUT—UNIQUE LODGING**
- *Budget:* Overlook a scenic three-block-long seaside village from your balcony at the white-clapboard **Mattapoisett Inn**. *page 325*
- *Moderate:* Join sailors from around the world who dock for the night at Marblehead's 19th-century Victorian **Pleasant Manor Inn**. *page 308*
- *Moderate to deluxe:* Shake the sand from your shoes at **Blue Shutters Inn**, across from exquisite Good Harbor Beach. *page 309*
- *Deluxe to ultra-deluxe:* Check in for the night at **Yankee Clipper Inn**, where JFK and Jackie once spent the night. *page 310*

Budget: under $50 Moderate: $50–$90 Deluxe: $90–$120 Ultra-deluxe: over $120

traction. Eleven guest rooms have wide pine plank floors, beautiful restored moldings, antiques, queen-size canopy beds, country quilts and Laura Ashley–style wallpaper. In summer a continental breakfast is served in the garden; in spring and fall it's served in bed. Shared bath, budget; private bath, moderate to deluxe. Closed from late October through mid-April. ~ 37 Mount Pleasant Street, Rockport; 508-546-2701. BUDGET TO DELUXE.

HIDDEN ►

The **Old Farm Inn** looks like the original Sunny Brook Farm. Built in 1779, the barn-red inn is shaded by glorious weeping willow trees. Only ten minutes from downtown and within walking distance of Halibut Point State Park, it's a good place for getting away from it all without going to extremes. Four guest rooms in the main house (some featuring sitting rooms) have gun stock beams, wide pine plank floors, fireplaces and antique quilts. Four large guest rooms in a newer building (some with kitchenettes) are decorated with country-style prints, but they lack the charm of the other rooms. Closed December through March. ~ 291 Granite Street, Rockport; 508-546-3237, 800-233-6828. MODERATE TO DELUXE.

JFK and Jackie once slept at the **Yankee Clipper Inn**, one of Rockport's finest hostelries. The main inn, a stately white oceanfront mansion, has magnificent wood-paneled public rooms appointed with model ships, Oriental rugs, paintings and elegant yet comfortable furniture. The Quarterdeck, a separate building built in 1960, has panoramic ocean views and a traditional look. The Bulfinch House, an 1840 Greek Revival building across the street, has fine period details but limited ocean views. Most of the 26 guest rooms are nondescript, but what they lack in decor is made up for by location. The inn has a good restaurant, saltwater swimming pool, gazebo and nature paths. Breakfast included. Closed from late October through mid-March. ~ 96 Granite Street, Rockport; 508-546-3407, 800-549-3699, fax 508-946-9730. DELUXE TO ULTRA-DELUXE.

The **Peg Leg Inn**, a white clapboard Colonial, is only steps away from the beach. One of the inn's five buildings is on the ocean and commands the highest rates, but it has spectacular views, a large, sweeping lawn and a granite gazebo. The 33 guest rooms are furnished with chenille bedspreads, braided rugs and reproduction Colonial furnishings and wallpaper. Closed from late October through mid-April. ~ 2 King Street, Rockport; 508-546-2352, 800-346-2352. MODERATE TO DELUXE.

Rockport's **Seaward Inn**, a rambling brown-shingle building, sits on a beautiful bluff overlooking the ocean. Surrounded by flower gardens, lawns and stone walls, it has a spring-fed swimming pond and bird sanctuary laced with nature paths. Cottages with kitchenettes and fireplaces, located behind the main inn, are ideal for families. Thirty-eight guest rooms, some with ocean views and fireplaces, are simply appointed with homey-looking Colonial-style furnishings. The Adirondack-style chairs on a grassy knoll overlooking the windswept shore are perfect for relaxing and reading. Rates include a full breakfast. ~ 62 Marmion Way; 508-546-3471, 800-648-7733. DELUXE TO ULTRA-DELUXE.

A reasonably priced bed and breakfast in the heart of Rockport is hard to come by, but **Lantana House** fits the bill. The three-story cedar shake-shingled inn has seven charming guest rooms, each with distinctive decor. The third floor boasts a suite with a kitchenette. There are two decks where guests can enjoy breakfast or a quiet afternoon. Common areas are decorated with the innkeeper's artwork and book collections. All rooms have private baths, and continental breakfast is included. ~ 22 Broadway; 508-546-3535, 800-291-3535. DELUXE TO ULTRA-DELUXE.

Guests at the **George Fuller House** will get the full Essex treatment. The house was built in 1830 by shipwrights who built many of the fishing schooners that plied Cape Ann's waters during the whaling era. Many of the original Federal-style details have been preserved, including the interior folding shutters, paneling and carved fireplace mantels. The seven rooms are furnished with antiques and reproductions; all have private baths and canopy beds and three have working fireplaces. The innkeepers serve a full breakfast every morning in the dining room, and tea is available on the porch or in the living room in the late afternoon. ~ 148 Main Street, Route 133, Essex; 508-768-7766, 800-477-0148, fax 508-768-6178. MODERATE TO DELUXE.

The **Clark Currier Inn** is a beautiful 1803 Federal home in the square style of the period. The woodwork and other details throughout the house are splendid, and the antiques and reproductions are, for the most part, true to the Federal period. The eight rooms are individually named for former owners or well-known visitors. Most rooms have canopy beds, and some have twin beds or are convertible to suites for parents who would rather have their children sleeping in an adjoining room. All rooms have private baths. The backyard boasts a lovely garden and a gazebo. ~ 45 Green Street, Newburyport; 508-465-8363, 800-360-6582. DELUXE.

Morrill Place, a three-story, 1806 Federal-style mansion, stands on historic High Street, where wealthy shipbuilders lived in the 19th century. The inn's 12 spacious guest rooms are beautifully decorated. The Henry W. Kinsman room (named for a former owner) is a rich hunter green with an enormous white canopy bed, while the Daniel Webster room has a four-poster antique bed and sleigh dresser. Rooms on the third floor are less formal but charming in their own way, with Colonial-style antiques. Some rooms share baths; pets are allowed. Breakfast is included. ~ 209 High Street, Newburyport; 508-462-2808, fax 508-462-9966. MODERATE.

◄ *HIDDEN*

DINING

Rockport has the majority of restaurants on the North Shore, but few are outstanding. Restaurants with a steady local clientele in nearby towns are generally better.

Rockport is a dry town, thanks to Hannah Jumper, a temperance supporter. In 1856 after a raucous Fourth of July celebration, Hannah convinced town fathers to outlaw liquor. Even today you can't buy it in a store or order it in a restaurant. But you can buy liquor in Gloucester, which is only ten minutes away, and bring it to any Rockport restaurant.

HIDDEN ►

King's Rook, a romantic café and wine bar, serves many varieties of hot chocolate, coffee, tea, imported beer and ale, wine, sherry, apéritifs and champagne. Also available are light entrées such as pesto turkey sandwiches, thin-crust gourmet pizza, pâté, cheese, sausage, soup and salad. The restaurant's low-beamed ceiling, soft peach walls, lace café curtains, candlelight and classical music create an intimate atmosphere favored by couples. ~ 12 State Street, Marblehead; 617-631-9838. BUDGET.

The **Driftwood Restaurant** is something of an institution. Homey, friendly and colorful, it attracts fishermen in the wee hours (it opens at 5:30 a.m.) and young professionals late on weekend mornings. The fare is traditional and plentiful: ham and eggs, pancakes, fried dough, clam chowder, burgers, fried seafood. The interior of this modest little establishment is plain and simple with red-and-white checked tablecloths. Tables are jammed close together, and there's a counter. Breakfast and lunch only. ~ 63 Front Street, Marblehead; 617-631-1145. BUDGET.

If the diner urge strikes, head for **Red's Sandwich**. Its booths and two horseshoe-shaped bars are always crowded with regulars who all seem to know one another. The menu includes all the diner favorites, from pancakes at breakfast to burgers for dinner. Outside there's a little courtyard area for warm-weather meals. ~ 15 Central Street, Salem; 508-745-3527. BUDGET.

✔ CHECK THESE OUT—UNIQUE DINING

- *Budget:* Immerse yourself in "New England's largest breakfast menu" at Kingston's ramshackle **Persy's Place**. *page 328*
- *Budget to moderate:* Travel back in time to **Woodman's**, a roadside institution where nothing but the prices has changed since 1914. *page 314*
- *Moderate to deluxe:* Join the Republicans or Democrats at **Tammany Hall**, a local restaurant serving such entrées as the Henry Cabot Scrod. *page 313*
- *Deluxe:* Feast in a former iron foundry at **Crane Brook Restaurant and Tea Room**, the perfect stop after touring cranberry country. *page 328*

Budget: under $8 Moderate: $8–$16 Deluxe: $16–$24 Ultra-deluxe: over $24

A good spot for a casual lunch or dinner, **Tammany Hall** is fa-   ◀ *HIDDEN*
vored by locals and not as touristy as the restaurants at nearby Pickering Wharf. Complementing the restaurant's political theme, two
benches sit in front of the building—one for Republicans and one for
Democrats. The cozy wood and brass restaurant serves hamburgers,
ribs, sandwiches and entrées with names like Henry Cabot Scrod. ~
208 Derby Street, Salem; 508-745-8755. MODERATE.

The **Bistro at 2 Main Street,** *the* place to eat lobster in a town that
literally lives on seafood, is an unpretentious little restaurant with a
pleasant clientele and enormous portions. Dinner only. ~ 2 Main
Street, Gloucester; 508-281-8055. MODERATE TO DELUXE.

The North Shore has two first-rate gourmet delis perfect for un-
forgettable picnics. **Grange Gourmet** and **Bruni's** offer items such as   ◀ *HIDDEN*
breakfast pastries, leek soup, cucumber soup, homemade salsa and
chips, tortellini primavera salad, chicken salad with green grapes and
almonds, breakfast pastries, healthy sandwiches, gourmet desserts
and baked goods. You can also pick up different types of coffee and
tea, natural sodas and more. ~ Grange Gourmet: 457 Washington
Street, Gloucester; 508-283-2639. Bruni's: 36 Essex Road, Route 133,
Ipswich; 508-356-4877. BUDGET.

The Greenery, located near the entrance to Bearskin Neck, has
sandwiches, a salad bar, bakery goods and desserts to go. The back
dining room facing the harbor serves all these dishes plus entrées such
as pesto pizza, lobster, crab quiche and seafood casserole. The restaurant is appointed with blond wood, brass light fixtures and touches
of green throughout. Closed from November through March. ~ 15
Dock Square, Rockport; 508-546-9593. MODERATE TO DELUXE.

Portside Chowder House is a good place for a cup of chowder on
a cold, blustery day. Cozy and tiny, the dark wood restaurant has
low-beamed ceilings, a fireplace and Windsor chairs. Specialties include New England and corn chowder, grilled sausage, crab and
chicken. Lunch served year-round, dinner in summer only. ~ 1 Doyle's
Cove Road, Rockport; 508-546-7045. BUDGET TO MODERATE.

Like many Rockport restaurants, the **Cutty's Harbour Café** serves
classic entrées—Cajun-style shrimp, lobster linguine, fried calamari—
but it prepares the food with more care than most of the competition.
Sit at the upper-level dining room overlooking the harbor. A roaring
fire adds to the romantic atmosphere of this eatery. Closed November
through February. ~ 14 Bearskin Neck; 508-546-2180. MODERATE.

Follow Bearskin Neck as far as it goes (resisting the urge to stop
for a lobster roll or bowl of chowder along the way) and you reach
My Place By-the-Sea. Here the view of the ocean competes with the
food for your attention. If the weather's nice, grab a table outside: this
is Cape Ann's prettiest dining spot. For both lunch and dinner you'll
find lots of seafood specialties, including lobster prepared several different ways. The lunch menu also includes an array of salads and

sandwiches. Closed November through March. ~ 68 Bearskin Neck, Rockport; 508-546-9667. MODERATE TO DELUXE.

Downhome and fun, **Woodman's** (124 Main Street, Route 133, Essex; 508-768-6451) hasn't changed anything except the prices since it opened in 1914. This roadside institution claims to have created the fried clam. The menu includes steamers, lobster, clam cakes, scallops and corn on the cob. Sit inside at old wooden booths or outside at picnic tables in back. There's a raw bar upstairs and a full liquor bar downstairs. Locals like to come here after a day at nearby Crane's Beach. ~ 124 Main Street, Route 133, Essex; 508-768-6451. BUDGET TO MODERATE.

Tom Shea's is a fine quality seafood restaurant with large picture windows overlooking Essex River—a perfect spot for watching the sunset. The wooden interior gives the restaurant an understated, nautical look. The fare is traditional—baked stuffed lobster, fried clams, stuffed sole, grilled teriyaki shrimp, pasta, Cajun dishes plus some beef and chicken dishes. ~ 122 Main Street, Route 133, Essex; 508-768-6931. MODERATE TO DELUXE.

HIDDEN ►

Chipper's River Café is great for casual fare in an idyllic setting overlooking Ipswich River. Tucked behind the Choate River Bar, the restaurant has a sign that's small and easy to miss. Chipper's imaginative, health-conscious menu, tile floors, natural wood, art prints and jukebox make it look and feel like a California restaurant. In the summer you can sit outside overlooking the river and quaint bridge. Dishes include chargrilled mustard lemon chicken, and changing pasta dishes. Next to the restaurant is Chipper's Bakery, a good source for picnic fare. ~ 1–3 Market Street, Ipswich; 508-356-7956. BUDGET TO MODERATE.

Classical music, candlelight, gold gilt mirrors and mismatched antiques give **Scandia** a romantic look. The menu changes with the seasons and the chef's whims. Entrées might include veal and lobster sauté with sweet butter or scallop chowder. The homemade salad

MEALS, MUSIC AND MEMORABILIA

The Rudder, an eclectic waterfront restaurant, is so popular Bostonians drive here just for dinner. The decor features a crazy mix of memorabilia collected by owner Evie Parsons, including hundreds of menus from around the world tacked to the low-beamed ceiling. Eyeglasses left here by Judy Garland are displayed in a glass jewelry box. And the food is good too, offering a little bit of everything—pasta, fried clams, steak, escargot. At night the place gets jumping to live piano music and after-dinner sing-alongs. Lunch is served only on weekends. ~ 73 Rocky Neck Avenue, Gloucester; 508-283-7967. MODERATE TO DELUXE.

dressings are excellent—fennel herb, maple curry, tomato cheddar and more. Reservations are a must. ~ 25 State Street, Newburyport; 508-462-6271. MODERATE TO DELUXE.

Fowle's Coffeehouse is a nostalgic, 1930s-style soda fountain and tobacco stand with authentic art deco decor. It features fresh pastries and freshly roasted coffee, as well as soups served in bread bowls, and sandwiches. The adjacent newsstand offers over 3000 magazine titles. ~ 17 State Street, Newburyport; 508-463-8755. BUDGET.

Grog is a large, dark, woody college bar–type place in a noncollege town. The burgers and Caesar salads are particularly good, and the cheerful staff may entice you into hanging out for longer than you'd planned. ~ 13 Middle Street, Newburyport; 508-465-8700. BUDGET TO MODERATE.

Located in a former tavern, **Antique Wear** offers beautiful earrings, stick pins, broaches, pendants and tie pins made out of antique buttons, some dating back to the 18th century. ~ 82–84 Front Street, Marblehead; 617-639-0070.

SHOPPING
◄ *HIDDEN*

In Salem, the **Peabody Museum Gift Shop** offers a wonderful assortment of prints, shipbuilding kits and maritime souvenirs, as well as posters and regional history books. You'll also find children's books, Indian jewelry and ceramic plates from China. ~ 161 Essex Street; 508-745-1876.

Across from the House of Seven Gables is **Ye Old Pepper Candy Companie**. Established in 1806, it claims to be the oldest candy store in America. Specialties include gibralters, black jacks and other old-fashioned candies made on the premises. ~ 122 Derby Street, Salem; 508-745-2744.

Nearby you'll find the **Pickering Wharf Antique Gallery**, which at first glance looks like your garden-variety antique shop. Upon closer examination—walk to the back and turn left—you'll find an astounding arena for dozens of antique dealers. This monster building used to be a theater-in-the-round. ~ Pickering Wharf; 508-741-3113.

◄ *HIDDEN*

One of Salem's biggest attractions is a witch shop owned by Jody Cabot, the city's most illustrious witch. **Crows Haven Corner** is filled with gargoyles, unicorns, crystal balls, magic wands and the full assortment of herbs, powders and seeds necessary for attracting good spirits or scaring off bad ones. ~ 125 Essex Street; 508-745-8763.

Don't leave Salem without stopping off at **Harbor Sweets**. Here you'll find sloop-shaped chocolates (a combination of white and dark chocolate with almond butter crunch) that are frighteningly delicious. You can take a tour of the factory if you call ahead for an appointment. Fortunately, Harbor Sweets does mail-order, so before leaving fill out an address card to receive mailings. At Valentine's Day you can order a dozen tiny red boxes of sloops for all the loves in your life. ~ 85 Leavitt Street; 508-745-7648.

Hanna Wingate House sells American pine antiques, French country furniture and accessories. Closed January and February. ~ 11 Main Street, Rockport; 508-546-1008.

New England Goods specializes in wooden toys, salt-glazed pottery, Maine wind bells and other quality crafts made in New England. ~ 65 Main Street, Rockport; 508-546-9677.

Rockport has almost as many galleries as bed and breakfasts. The majority sell seascapes—some good, many bad. For an excellent selection of Rockport art, visit the **Rockport Art Association**. All the work on view is for sale. ~ 12 Main Street; 508-546-6604.

HIDDEN ►   **Walker Creek**, a real find, offers reasonably priced, finely crafted wood tables, hutches, four-poster beds, one-of-a-kind pieces and custom work loosely based on Shaker or Colonial designs. ~ 57 Eastern Avenue, Route 133, Essex; 508-768-7622.

Essex's 25 antique dealers run the price-range gamut. Always ask a dealer if you can do better on a price—you're expected to bargain. Don't hope for major savings, however. The **White Elephant** is bargain basement heaven. ~ 32 Main Street; 508-768-6901. At the high end of the spectrum is **A. P. H. Waller & Son** which carries quality European antiques from the 18th and 19th centuries. ~ 140 Main Street; 508-768-6269. **The Scrapbook** specializes in antique and decorative prints, as well as maps from the 16th to 19th centuries. ~ 34 Main Street; 508-768-7404. **Main Street Antiques** has antique wicker. ~ 44 Main Street; 508-768-7039. **North Hill Antiques** has 18th and 19th-century furniture. ~ 155 Main Street; 508-768-7365.

If you've ever spent a lengthy period of time in the British Isles, and you miss such examples of British cuisine as Bovril, Ir'nbru or Smarties, you'll have a ball at **Best of British**, which imports a variety of English, Scottish and Welsh goods for Anglophiles who just can't do without 'em. ~ 22 State Street, Newburyport; 508-465-6976.

NIGHTLIFE   Every Sunday afternoon Le Grand David and his Spectacular Magic Company perform a highly skilled magic show at the **Cabot Street**

HIDDEN ►   **Cinema Theatre**, featuring levitations, vanishing acts, comedy and song-and-dance routines, complete with outrageous costumes and sets. The rest of the week the theater shows first-rate foreign and domestic films. ~ 286 Cabot Street, Beverly; 508-927-3677.

Symphony by the Sea concerts take place in the Peabody Museum's spectacular East Indian Marine Hall and the Peabody City Hall Wiggen Auditorium on Lowell Street. Formal winter and informal summer concerts are concluded by a reception with the musicians. ~ 161 Essex Street, Salem; 508-745-4955.

The **Gloucester Stage Company**, under the direction of playwright Israel Horovitz, stages first-rate plays in an old fish warehouse from March through December. ~ 267 East Main Street, Gloucester; 508-281-4099.

The **Rockport Chamber Music Festival** performs in the Hibbard Gallery of the Rockport Art Association during the month of June. ~ 12 Main Street; 508-546-7391.

Castle Hill Festival presents a wide range of summer musical concerts (jazz, reggae, classical) in Castle Hill mansion or on the manicured grounds. ~ P.O. Box 563, Ipswich; 508-356-4351.

The Grog is an attractive restaurant and cabaret with live entertainment ranging from reggae, rock and rhythm-and-blues to oldies and dance bands. Cover. ~ 13 Middle Street, Newburyport; 508-465-8008.

BEACHES & PARKS

DEVEREUX BEACH 🏊 🛶 On the causeway leading to scenic Marblehead Neck, Devereux is a small, clean beach. There's a lot to see here. The affluent town lies immediately behind the beach on a hill, while across the street lies a windsurfing cove and busy Marblehead harbor. Devereux is popular with families and teens, yet, unlike most North Shore beaches, it isn't always packed on summer weekends. Swimming and fishing are good here. Picnic areas, restrooms, playground, lifeguard, bike rack, restaurant, groceries five minutes away in Marblehead; out-of-town parking fee, $3. ~ On Ocean Avenue, to the south of Marblehead harbor.

◄ HIDDEN

SALEM WILLOWS 🏊 🚣 🛶 Don't be thrown off by the tawdry-looking Chinese take-out joints and arcade you see when you enter the parking lot. Salem Willows holds some pleasant surprises, including a nostalgic old amusement park overlooking Salem Sound that is shaded with graceful willow trees planted in 1801 to provide a protected area for smallpox victims. Next to the park is a small beach. People come here to stroll in the park, admire the view, rent rowboats and fish from the shore or a short pier. The waters are a little rough, and may not be ideal for swimming. Locals swear by the popcorn and chop suey sandwiches sold in the parking lot. Picnic areas, restrooms, lifeguards, snack bar, rowboat rentals; groceries are located ten minutes away in downtown Salem. ~ Located at the end of Derby Street in Salem.

SINGING BEACH 🏊 🛶 This jewel of a beach, only a quarter mile long, has pristine sand that literally squeaks underfoot. Hidden away in a lovely affluent neighborhood, the beach is surrounded by steep cliffs and spectacular mansions. The crowd matches the conservative neighborhood—blond and preppy. The changing rooms and parking lot are for residents only, and parking in the immediate area is impossible. But that doesn't keep out-of-towners away. Bostonians like this beach so much, they take the commuter train to Manchester, then walk one long, sweaty half mile to the shore. Restrooms, lifeguard, snack bar; groceries a mile away in town; day-use fee, $1. ~ At the end of Beach Street in Manchester.

GOOD HARBOR BEACH 🏊 ⛵ Located in a spectacular natural setting outside of Gloucester proper, this sweeping, half-mile beach is all ocean, sand dunes, marsh grass and big sky. A small shrub-covered island, positioned between two rocky headlands and accessible at low tide, is fun to explore. The beach is raked clean every day in the summer. Closed early September through Memorial Day. Restrooms, showers, lifeguard, snack bar; groceries are ten minutes away in Gloucester; parking fee, minimum $10. ~ On Thatcher Road in East Gloucester; 508-281-9790.

HIDDEN ▶ **WINGAERSHEEK BEACH** 🏊 This gentle, sloping, fine sand beach on Ipswich Bay is surrounded by rocks, tall marsh grass and homey summer cottages hidden in the woods. There are also tidepools to explore. The beach is quite close to downtown Gloucester and Rockport, but it feels as though it's far out in the country. Families with young children frequent this beach because it has good climbing rocks that aren't too slippery. Restrooms, showers, lifeguards, snack bar; groceries are 15 miles away in Gloucester. Closed early September through Memorial Day. ~ On Atlantic Street in West Gloucester; 508-281-9790.

ROCKPORT BEACHES 🏊 Rockport has two small beaches right in the heart of town. **Front Beach**, a favorite with small children, has a parallel sidewalk that gives everyone in town a perfect view of the beach. **Back Beach** is on the other side of a small bluff and is much more private. Restrooms, lifeguards are stationed on Front Beach, snack bar. ~ Both beaches are on Beach Street in Rockport.

HIDDEN ▶ **HALIBUT POINT STATE PARK** 🏃 🏊 ⛵ This wild and rugged 54-acre oceanfront park, formerly the site of a granite quarry, has one of the most spectacular views on the North Shore. A walking path goes past the old quarry down a gentle incline to a vast, treeless plain of scrub thicket and wildflowers overlooking the ocean. The stark, rugged shoreline has tidepools and smooth granite rocks large enough for a group of people to picnic on. Swimming is permitted, but not recommended since the shore is covered with big, slippery rocks. Restrooms, walking trails, guided tours; groceries are in Rockport; parking fee, $2. ~ Three miles north of Rockport off Route 127; 508-546-2997.

HIDDEN ▶ **THE COX RESERVATION** 🏃 Formerly the home of famed muralist Allyn Cox, this 31-acre salt marsh farmland is now headquarters for the Essex County Greenbelt Association. Peaceful and pastoral, it has paths leading through gardens of perennials and roses, salt marsh, woods, orchards and open farmland down to winding Essex River. Artists come here in the late afternoon when the river and graceful marsh grass are bathed in a soft golden light, creating a dreamlike environment. It's easy to see why a muralist lived in this romantic and private place. Groceries nearby in Essex. ~ Off Route 133 in Essex; 508-768-7241.

CRANE'S BEACH MEMORIAL RESERVATION This massive, four-mile, dune-backed beach is surrounded by over 1000 acres of salt marsh, shrub thicket and woods. In the off-season, the wide beach seems to go on forever. In the summer it's wall-to-wall people. Nature and beachgoers coexist peacefully, however. At certain times of the year, sections of the beach are fenced off to protect nesting birds. A boardwalk leading to the beach protects sand dunes and marsh grass. Restrooms, showers, lifeguards, snack bar; groceries are nearby in Ipswich; day-use fee, minimum $5. ~ Located on Argilla Road in Ipswich; 508-356-4354.

PARKER RIVER NATIONAL WILDLIFE REFUGE This magnificent oceanfront wildlife refuge on Plum Island is only about ten minutes from downtown Newburyport, but it feels very far away from civilization. One-third of Plum Island is covered with ramshackle summer beach houses; the rest is the refuge—4662 acres of bogs, tidal marshes, sand dunes and beach. It's a good beach for surf fishing, although a strong undertow discourages swimming. A boardwalk leads to the beach, and a trail meanders throughout the refuge. The abundant wildlife includes seals, geese, ducks, deer, rabbits and over 300 species of birds. Parker River is dearly loved by Newburyport residents. From April through August, most of the beach is closed to accommodate nesting piper plovers. Restrooms. ~ On Plum Island in Newburyport; 508-465-5753.

The South Shore

The South Shore is a mix of cranberries and Pilgrims, historic whaling ports, Portuguese bakeries, factory outlets, blue-collar workers and blue bloods. It is comprised of small scenic villages, pastoral farmland and three main towns— Plymouth, about 50 minutes south of Boston, and New Bedford and Fall River, next to each other and close to the Rhode Island border.

Each town has a different personality and history. Plymouth, of course, is where the Pilgrims landed. New Bedford, an active fishing port, was once the whaling capital of the world. Fall River, a factory outlet mecca, was a leading textile manufacturer at the turn of the century.

Sights, accommodations and restaurants are limited in Fall River and New Bedford. People usually visit these towns on their way to and from Cape Cod or Boston. Plymouth is much larger and draws over one million tourists annually. It has enough historic sights to occupy an entire weekend, although most people can't take more than a day of Pilgrim lore.

SIGHTS

To reach Plymouth from Boston, go south on Route 3 or take scenic Route 3A. It winds along the coast past beautiful, affluent commuter villages with lovely coves and harbors, old lighthouses, stately mansions and winding streets.

HIDDEN ►

Right before Plymouth is wealthy **Duxbury**, an aristocratic residential area of elegant homes. Stop by **The King Caesar House**, one of the state's most beautiful historic homes, located off Route 3A on a winding coastal road. A fresh yellow-and-white, Federal-era mansion with green shutters, a sweeping lawn and climbing roses, the house stands across from a massive stone wharf where ships were once rigged. The house has finely crafted wood cornices, moldings, fanlights and balustrades, plus original hand-painted French wallpaper and fine antiques. Admission. ~ King Caesar Road.

From Duxbury head south for **Plymouth**. "America's Home Town" can't seem to make up its mind whether to be a tourist trap or a scenic, historic village. The town is a jarring mix of historic homes, cobblestone streets, '50s-style motels, souvenir shops, a tacky waterfront and tour buses everywhere you look. It's not particularly scenic in parts, yet the town is rich with historic sights.

Plymouth is small, and without trying you bump into everything there is to see here. The **Plymouth Area Chamber of Commerce** has walking-tour maps. ~ Water Street; 508-830-1620. So does **Destination Plymouth**. ~ 508-747-7525.

The first thing everyone heads for is **Plymouth Rock** on Water Street on the harbor. Believed to be the landing place of the Pilgrims, it is housed inside a Greek canopy with stately columns. Don't expect to see a big impressive rock; it's only large enough to hold two very small Pilgrims.

Right next to the rock is the **Mayflower II**, a brightly painted reproduction of the real *Mayflower* that looks like the pirate ship at Disneyland. The self-guided tour, which features characters in period costume, is worthwhile, even though there's occasionally a line to get in. The *Mayflower* is shockingly small. It's hard to imagine how 102 people ever survived 66 days at sea in such cramped quarters. Admission. ~ State Pier; 508-746-1622.

For more Pilgrim lore, head for **Pilgrim Hall Museum**, on the main drag. Continuously operating since 1824, the museum houses the nation's largest collection of Pilgrim possessions, including richly styled Jacobean furniture and the relic of a ship that brought colonists to America. Its hull is made out of naturally curved tree trunks and branches, a crude but effective design. Closed in January. Admission. ~ 75 Court Street; 508-746-1620.

Three miles south of Plymouth is **Plimouth Plantation**, a "living museum" where men and women in period costumes portray the residents of a 1627 Pilgrim village. This sounds contrived, but it's authentic and well-done. The re-created village, on a dusty, straw-strewn road overlooking the ocean, is comprised of many wooden dwellings with deeply thatched roofs. There's not a modern detail in sight—just the village, the ocean and settlers going about the daily tasks of the time, tending the vegetable garden or building a house with 17th-century

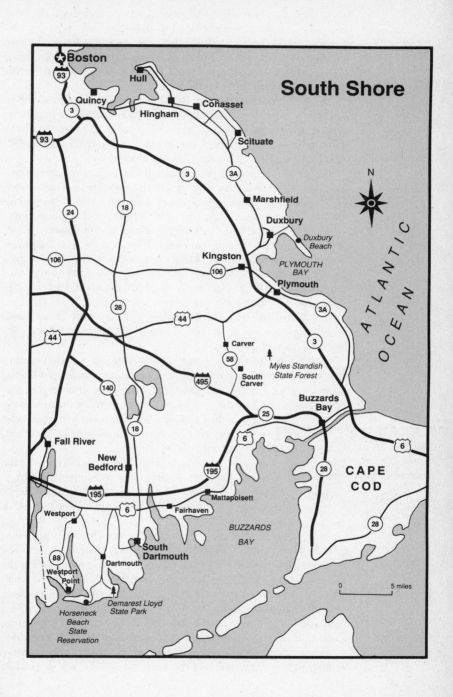

South Shore

Boston

93

Hull

Quincy

3

Hingham

Cohasset

93

Scituate

3

3A

24

18

Marshfield

106

Duxbury

Duxbury Beach

Kingston

PLYMOUTH BAY

106

28

Plymouth

44

3A

44

Carver

3

58

South Carver

Myles Standish State Forest

140

495

Buzzards Bay

25

18

6

Fall River

6

New Bedford

28

195

CAPE COD

195

6

Mattapoisett

Westport

6

Fairhaven

BUZZARDS BAY

88

South Dartmouth

28

Westport Point

Dartmouth

Demarest Lloyd State Park

Horseneck Beach State Reservation

N

ATLANTIC OCEAN

0   5 miles

tools. The villagers speak in Old English, and you can ask them questions about anything—including the politics of the 17th century. There's also a Wampanoag Indian site that re-creates a typical native encampment with woven and bark dome-shaped dwellings. Closed from late November through March. Admission. ~ Route 3A, Warren Avenue, Plymouth; 508-746-1622.

HIDDEN ▶

From Plymouth go west on Route 44, then south on Route 58 to rural **Carver**, cranberry capital of the world. In the fall the harvesting process, a breathtaking sight, can be witnessed from the road. There's also an antique train visitors can ride and a cranberry winery. (See "Exploring Cranberry Country" in this chapter.)

About a half-hour's drive southeast of Carver lies the former whaling town of **New Bedford**, which gained immortality in Herman Melville's *Moby Dick*. It still looks and feels a lot like a 19th-century whaling city, with a bustling waterfront and large Portuguese population.

Until the early 1980s the waterfront area was in disarray. Then, to attract tourists, the town restored more than 100 buildings. Fortunately New Bedford didn't go overboard with cute, contrived tourist attractions. Today it has a number of fine museums, restaurants, antique shops and galleries alongside the harbor. There's something genuine and tasteful about this miniature city.

The New Bedford Visitors Center occupies a restored brick building, sharing space with a French bakery and chowder shop. ~ 47 North 2nd Street; 508-991-6200.

Rotch-Jones-Duff House and Garden Museum is a 19th-century Greek Revival with a picturesque rose garden that becomes a Christmas showplace during the holidays and is the site of summer concerts. Named for three families who owned the property, it features many of their fine antiques. This 28-room mansion is one of the region's best. Admission. ~ 396 County Street, New Bedford; 508-997-1401.

The coast is dotted with majestic sea captains' homes, many of them now inns.

For three sights that shouldn't be missed, begin with the Whaling Museum. Continue on to Seaman's Bethel, a church across from the whaling museum, and County Street, where wealthy sea captains built homes in the 19th century.

Start with the **The New Bedford Whaling Museum**, then enter Seamen's Bethel, and New Bedford won't look the same again. The museum depicts whaling's profound impact on this town, telling the story beautifully with large, dramatic paintings of life aboard whaling ships and an enormous mural created in 1848. You can climb aboard a half-scale model of a fully rigged whaling ship housed in a large room with harpoons and figureheads. The museum is spacious, airy and absorbing. Admission. ~ 18 Johnny Cake Hill; 508-997-0046.

Across the street is **Seamen's Bethel**, where whalers prayed before setting out to sea. The pulpit of this plain, sturdy church is shaped like

a ship's bluff bows. Its walls are covered with memorial tablets to men
who died at sea. A visit to this church is a sobering experience.

"Nowhere in America will you find more patrician-like houses,"
wrote Herman Melville of **County Street**, located a few of blocks up
a slight hill from the whaling museum. The impeccably restored
Federal-style mansions and elaborate Victorians along this street illustrate how grand life was in 19th-century New Bedford.

◀ *HIDDEN*

For a unique change of pace, consider visiting **Cuttyhunk**, an island 14 miles offshore from New Bedford accessible by ferry (see the
"Transportation" section at the end of this chapter). It's part of the
Elizabeth Islands, a chain of 16 tiny islands, 14 of them owned by the
Boston Brahmin Forbes family. The island is practically all sand and
scrub bushes with a rocky beach. It does have a general store, two
restaurants and about 100 homes. Cuttyhunk is the opposite of busy,
crowded Cape Cod—there's nothing to do but walk and fish—and
therein lies its charm.

◀ *HIDDEN*

Immediately southwest of New Bedford off Route 6 are the affluent rural communities of **Dartmouth** and **Westport**, where you'll find
some of the most exquisite coastal farmland in all of Massachusetts.
Like Kentucky bluegrass country, this area has miles of ancient stone
walls, lovely old houses, shingled dairy barns, rolling pastures and elegant horse farms.

Off Slocums Road in South Dartmouth sits **Padanaram**, a fashionable yachting resort on Apponagansett Bay. It's home to the famous
boatyard Concordia, where beautiful old wooden yachts are restored.
The village is only two blocks long, but it has a number of fine restaurants and shops.

Not far from Padanaram is **The Lloyd Center for Environmental
Studies**, a nonprofit organization that studies coastal and estuarine environments. Open to the public are an aquarium, resource library and
changing exhibits featuring such work as naturalist photography. The
best thing here is the dazzling view from the observation deck, which
overlooks winding Slocums River and miles of wetlands. The center offers weekly walks, canoe trips and educational programs. Closed
Monday. ~ 430 Potomska Road, South Dartmouth; 508-990-0505.

◀ *HIDDEN*

Heading back to New Bedford, you can take Route 195 west to
Fall River 15 minutes away. Factory outlets (see the "Shopping" section below) and Battleship Cove are this town's claims to fame.

At the turn of the century Fall River had more than 100 textile
mills, but in 1927 the industry sagged and the town went through serious hard times. Today its large granite mills are occupied by electronic and metals firms and factory outlets, but the effects of the depression still linger.

Fall River's downtown has been spruced up, but there are so many
"for lease" signs tacked to its grand 19th-century buildings that the
town looks a little lost.

HIDDEN ►   **Columbia Street,** the Portuguese section of downtown, is a colorful place to stroll, sample treats from the many good bakeries and discover the beautiful mosaic sidewalks. For travel information, call the **Bristol County Convention and Visitors Bureau.** ~ 70 North 2nd Street; 508-997-1250, 800-288-6263.

There's also an information center at **Battleship Cove,** a harbor and park area right in town off Route 195 at exit 5. Docked in the water at Battleship Cove are a World War II battleship, destroyer, attack submarine and PT boat that you can tour. Not surprisingly, these vessels, which are in excellent condition, are filled with children playing war. Hundreds of scout troops make pilgrimages to this John Wayne playground. Admission for boat tours. ~ 508-678-1100.

Next to the boats is the **Fall River Heritage State Park Visitors Center.** It has an attractive waterfront park and a building with a number of exhibits about the town's former textile industry. A moving slide show documents the appalling working conditions, accidents and deaths suffered by children and adult immigrants who worked in the mills. ~ 200 Davol Street; 508-675-5759.

LODGING   Plymouth has an abundance of very ordinary motels that attract families and tour groups. Accommodations are limited throughout the rest of the South Shore, but there is a sprinkling of hidden bed and breakfasts that are quite special.

HIDDEN ►   For a romantic getaway try the **Windsor House Inn,** 15 minutes north of Plymouth. This graceful old inn stands on a street lined with houses listed on the National Register of Historic Places, and it's next to a classic white-steepled church. Down the street are a few elegant little shops, a French bakery and small wharf. Windsor House has two tastefully decorated guest rooms and a beautiful suite with pale blue wood-paneled walls and blue-and-white stenciling. All rooms are furnished with Shaker and Colonial-style antiques. A dark, cozy restaurant on the ground floor looks like an old seafaring tavern. ~ 390 Washington Street, Duxbury; 617-934-0991, 800-934-0993. MODERATE TO DELUXE.

Route 3A in Plymouth is lined with indistinguishable motels, but the **Cold Spring Motel** is one of the most attractive. The 40-year-old, reasonably priced motel is in pristine condition and beautifully landscaped. In the summer thick yellow marigolds border brick paths leading to the 33 guest rooms. These are spacious and simply appointed with standard-issue motel furniture. Closed from December through March. ~ 188 Court Street; phone/fax 508-746-2222, 800-678-8667. MODERATE.

The **John Carver Inn,** a large, imposing, Colonial-style hotel, attracts tour groups and gets very crowded in the summer. But it's in the most scenic part of Plymouth, across the street from a row of 17th-century historic homes and a beautiful grist mill. Seventy-nine guest rooms are decorated in soft shades of beige and Colonial-style reproduction antiques. A full-service hotel, it has a restaurant, lounge, gift shop and pool. ~ 25 Summer Street, Plymouth; 508-746-7100, 800-274-1620, fax 508-746-8299. MODERATE TO DELUXE.

In the small town of Carver, the heart of cranberry country, **On Cranberry Pond** is a great place to stay if you want to get away from the crowds in Plymouth (which is just 25 minutes away). The house is surrounded by ponds, horse pastures, and cranberry bogs. The three high-ceilinged bedrooms are furnished with contemporary pieces. The enormous back porch is a great place to while away a morning or an afternoon. ~ 43 Fuller Street, Middleboro; 508-946-0768. MODERATE TO DELUXE

Off-the-beaten-path **Mattapoisett Inn** is in a scenic little seaside village of doll-sized clapboard houses with white picket fences and window boxes. The inn stands right across the street from the harbor. The village, which is only three blocks long, consists of a small dock, an art gallery, a coffee shop and the inn. The white-clapboard inn with black shutters has a restaurant and pub on the ground floor. Three spacious guest rooms upstairs all have balconies overlooking the ocean. The rooms aren't "decorated," but they're neat, clean, bright and comfortable. ~ 13 Water Street, Mattapoisett; 508-758-4922. BUDGET.   ◄ *HIDDEN*

A 1760 brown-shingle bed and breakfast, **The Edgewater** is so close to the water you'd swear you were on a boat when you look out the window. The inn seems miles away from civilization, yet it's only a five-minute drive from New Bedford's historic wharf district. A perfect spot for romance, the handsome house has soft taupe walls and crisp white arched moldings. The blue-and-white Captain's Suite, the best room in the house, has a sitting room, fireplace and spectacular views. The other four guest rooms are attractive and comfortable. All are appointed with contemporary and antique furnishings. ~ 2 Oxford Street, Fairhaven; 508-997-5512. MODERATE.   ◄ *HIDDEN*

Salt Marsh Farm, a 200-plus-year-old farmhouse, is in the heart of pastoral South Dartmouth. A perfect retreat for nature buffs, the house is on a 90-acre preserve with trails leading through hay fields, woods and wetlands. Bikes are available to guests eager to explore the grounds. Salt Marsh Farm feels like another world and time. The floors are uneven, the doorways low and the rooms small, but it has comfortable, home-spun charm. Afternoon tea is served by the fireside in the common sitting room. Sunny guest rooms are furnished with antiques, and a full breakfast is served in an attractive dining room with a beautiful old fireplace. ~ 322 Smith Neck Road; 508-992-0980. MODERATE.

One of the best things about **The Little Red House** is the beautiful backyard overlooking a stone-walled horse farm. Guests can relax in the gazebo and throw apples to the horses. The barn-shaped red   ◄ *HIDDEN*

Text continued on page 328.

Exploring Cranberry Country

Hidden away in Carver, a scenic rura area ten minutes east of Plymouth, you'll find one of Massachusetts' most spectacular and least-known autumn attractions—**cranberry harvesting**. If you think fall foliage is a beautiful sight, wait until you see this dazzling display of color.

Cranberries are the state's number one agricultural product, valued at $100 million annually. Around 458 growers work more than 12,000 acres of cranberry bogs. Little Carver alone produces half the nation's crop, while Cape Cod and Nantucket also have cranberry farms.

One of the few fruits native to North America, cranberries were known to Indians as sassamenesh. They ate the tart red berries raw and mixed them with venison and fat to make small cakes called pemmicans. The cranberry's slender, cone-shaped flower reminded early European settlers of the beak of a crane—hence the present name.

Harvest time starts September 15 and continues until the first week of November. During this time, restaurants and bakeries in southern Massachusetts use the berry in a number of creative dishes, ranging from cranberry horseradish and salsa to cranberry soup, bread, muffins, sorbet and tarts.

To explore the cranberry bogs, from Plymouth take Route 44 east to Route 58 south. Bogs line both routes, and the harvest process is very easy to see from the road. Many farmers don't mind if you observe from the elevated dirt paths bordering the bogs, just as long as you stay well out of their way.

The short, scruffy, dark green cranberry vines are grown in shallow bogs surrounded by deep woods. When the cranberries are ripe, they are picked by either dry or wet harvesting. Dry-picked berries are often sold fresh, while wet-picked fruit usually becomes canned or frozen cranberry sauce.

Dry-harvested berries are combed off the vine with a machine. But it's wet harvesting that's the real treat to watch. First the bogs are flooded with about 18 inches of water. Then farmers in bright yellow slickers cut the fruit off the vine with large water reels that look like giant eggbeaters stirring up a waterfall of crimson berries. The buoyant berries float to the water's surface, creating a scarlet sea surrounded by a fiery ring of woods ablaze with fall colors.

The wind blows the floating berries to one end of the pond, where they are corralled with wooden booms. Giant vacuum cleaners then suck the berries into dechaffing machines. Helicopters and trucks transport the berries to packing houses, where they are graded according to size, color and quality.

It's easy enough to explore the bogs on your own, but if you want more information and an official tour, there are a number of options. Right in Plymouth is the **Cranberry World Visitors Center**. Operated by Ocean Spray, it has exhibits of harvesting equipment, historic and current photographs, two demonstrations of cranberry bogs and free cranberry juice. Guided tours are available. It's educational, but nothing compared to seeing the real thing. Closed from December through April. ~ 225 Water Street; 508-747-2350.

Plymouth Colony Winery, off Route 44, is in a former berry-screening house in the middle of a ten-acre cranberry bog. It offers free tastings, plus a tour of the winery and bogs. Open weekends only in the winter, closed in January. ~ 56 Pinewood Road, Plymouth; 508-747-3334.

bed and breakfast is new but has an antique appearance. It's located in a pleasant residential neighborhood of mostly 20th-century homes. Padanaram village is close by. The house is spotless and the decor country-cute with pineapple stencil wallpaper, wooden hearts, ruffles, canopy beds and more. ~ 631 Elm Street, South Dartmouth; 508-996-4554. MODERATE.

DINING

The Inn for All Seasons is a Victorian mansion set in a forested hilltop setting. Choose from one of four carpeted dining rooms brought up-to-date with contemporary furniture, or dine outside on the brick patio overlooking a garden. Entrées include veal Oscar, fruits de la mer and chicken parmigiana. You may also want to sample the popular scallops wrapped in bacon or oysters Rockefeller. Chocoholics will definitely want to try the mousse cake. Closed Monday. ~ 97 Warren Avenue, Plymouth; 508-746-8823. MODERATE.

Though a magnet for tourists, **The Lobster Hut** should not be avoided. Here you can feast on clam chowder, fried clams and lobster at outdoor picnic tables overlooking the harbor, or you can eat inside, though the atmosphere may be a bit too fast-food for your liking. Closed January. ~ On the Town Wharf, Plymouth; 508-746-2270. BUDGET TO MODERATE.

HIDDEN ►

A ramshackle brown-shingle restaurant a few miles north of Plymouth, **Persy's Place** claims to have "New England's largest breakfast menu," and that's no joke. The menu takes about an hour to read, but some of its offerings include fish cakes, buttermilk pancakes, chipped beef on toast, catfish and eggs, hickory-smoked bacon, finnan haddie, no-cholesterol eggs, waffles and much, much more. The restaurant looks like a cross between a coffee shop and a country general store. Breakfast and lunch only. ~ 117 Main Street, Route 3A, Kingston; 617-585-5464. BUDGET.

HIDDEN ►

Hidden and lovely **Crane Brook Restaurant and Tea Room** is a must if you're touring cranberry country. Located in a former iron foundry, the cozy, antiques-filled restaurant overlooks a pretty pond and is surrounded by woods, pastures and cranberry bogs. The restaurant started out serving only tea and pastries, but now it also

DINE PORTUGUESE

There are many Portuguese restaurants in New Bedford, but one of the best is **Café Portugal**. A large, festive restaurant popular with Portuguese families, it features house specialties such as an enormous platter of succulent shrimp and marinated steak served with eggs on top. With its acoustical tile ceiling and plastic flower arrangements, Café Portugal looks a little bit like a banquet hall. Closed Monday and Tuesday. ~ 1280 Acushnet Avenue; 508-992-8216. MODERATE.

offers lunch and dinner. A perfect place for a long, leisurely lunch, the Crane Brook has a changing menu of dishes such as grilled duck breast sandwich and imaginative salads for lunch; rack of lamb and spicy pork loin roast for dinner. Closed Monday and Tuesday. ~ 229 Tremont Street, South Carver; 508-866-3235. DELUXE.

Candleworks is housed in an 1810 granite candle factory half a block from New Bedford's major sights. A pink, atriumlike room in front is appointed with wooden tables and Windsor chairs. The main dining room has a low-beamed ceiling and rich wood. The menu features Italian cuisine and a wide variety of American food including veal medallions sautéed with lobster and asparagus; breast of chicken stuffed with prosciutto, provolone and roasted peppers and served with a pesto cream sauce; and grilled swordfish with lemon butter. ~ 72 North Water Street; 508-997-1294. MODERATE.

Bridge Street Café in the heart of Padanaram, attracts a young, well-dressed crowd. Clean and crisp, with slate floors, the café has an outdoor deck overlooking the town and harbor. Daily specials range from Creole-grilled swordfish, scallops and pesto pasta, to tuna and shrimp brochette and grilled sirloin. Favorite appetizers include smoked brook trout and smoked eastern salmon served with capers and mustard sauce. The house specialty is the grilled barbecue lamb. And you can't leave without trying one of Sally's outrageous desserts! Call for seasonal schedule. ~ 10-A Bridge Street, South Dartmouth; 508-994-7200. DELUXE.

It may look like a coffee shop, but **Bayside** serves classic clam-bar fare as well as such specials as chicken burritos and eggplant parmigiana. More "in" than it seems, the restaurant has a clientele ranging from construction workers, senior citizens and families to yuppies and arty types dressed entirely in black. Bayside overlooks rolling pastures, salt marsh, stone walls and the ocean. ~ 1253 Horseneck Road, Westport; 508-636-5882. BUDGET TO MODERATE.

◄ HIDDEN

The South Shore is outlet country. Fall River has over 100 outlets, and New Bedford and Plymouth have quite a few, too. Until the 1980s these were novel, but today there are so many discount shopping places across the country that they don't seem unique. Choices are somewhat limited because the same brands are sold everywhere: Bass, Farberware, American Tourister, Jonathan Logan, Van Heusen and Vanity Fair to name a few.

SHOPPING

Cordage Park, housed in a former brick cordage rope factory, is an attractive marketplace with specialty shops and a weekend flea market. The lovely old building is surrounded by ponds, fountains, gazebos, rolling lawns and flower gardens. ~ Route 3A, North Plymouth; 508-746-7707.

Howland Place is the Rodeo Drive of factory outlets. Located in a restored brick building that could pass for a fancy mall, it has retailers including Calvin Klein, Andrew Marc, Kemar and Anne Klein, to name a few. Discounts range from 20 to 70 percent. ~ 651 Orchard Street, New Bedford; 508-999-4100.

Salt Marsh Pottery specializes in hand-painted pottery and tiles designed with wildflower motifs. ~ 1167 Russells Mills Road, South Dartmouth; 508-636-4813.

Fall River Outlets: Driving the expressway in Fall River, you can't help but notice the mammoth, six-story granite textile mills transformed into factory outlets. To visit them from Route 195, which runs through town, take Route 24 south to the Brayton exit and follow the signs. All the outlets are close together, and each building has between 50 and 100 retailers selling clothes, dishes, sheets, towels, jewelry, handbags and more. Prices are rock bottom, and the merchandise is pretty low-end. Natural fiber clothing is difficult to find.

NIGHTLIFE   Free concerts at the **Village Landing Gazebo** range from swing bands to Irish balladeers to children's shows. ~ 182 Water Street, Plymouth.

Bands can be heard free on weekends at the **Sheraton Plymouth Pub.** ~ Village Landing, 180 Water Street, Plymouth; 508-747-4900.

Zeiterion Theatre presents a wide range of musical and dramatic performances—everything from Emmylou Harris, *Dreamgirls* and the Mantovani Orchestra to *Man of La Mancha* and the stars of the "Lawrence Welk Show." Located in historic downtown New Bedford, the Zeiterion is a masterfully restored 1923 vaudeville theater with gilded Grecian friezes, elaborate crystal light fixtures and a glamorous atmosphere. ~ 684 Purchase Street, New Bedford; 508-994-2900.

BEACHES & PARKS   **DUXBURY BEACH** ✎. This five-mile stretch of clean white sand is one of the finest barrier beaches on the Massachusetts coast. The beach juts out into Cape Cod Bay and is bordered by a little harbor on one side and the Atlantic on the other. Stretches are dotted with salt marsh, and parts are accessible only by four-wheel-drive vehicles. Located in an affluent residential neighborhood, it attracts a well-heeled crowd. Restrooms, showers, changing room, lifeguards, snack bar, restaurant; groceries in Duxbury. ~ Off Route 3 on Route 139 in Duxbury, north of Plymouth; 617-837-3112.

MYLES STANDISH STATE FOREST 🚶 🐎 🚲 ✎ 🏕 🚌 ⛵ Locals joke that once you're in this 14,635-acre park, you'll never find your way out again. The park is enormous, and the roads winding through the forest and meadows seem to go on forever. Because of its size, it feels remote and peaceful even in the summer. Beautiful and clean, the park has 15 ponds with two beaches. You can fish most of the ponds and swim at College and Fearings beaches. Motorcycle, bicycle, bridle and hiking paths wind through the forest. Non-motorized boats are allowed. Picnic areas, restrooms, interpretive programs; groceries and restaurants in Plymouth and Carver; day-use fee, $2. ~ Off Route 3 on Long Pond Road in Plymouth; 508-866-2526.

▲ There are 450 tent/RV sites (no hookups) with restrooms, hot showers, fireplaces and picnic tables; $5 to $6 per night.

PLYMOUTH BEACH ⚓ 🏊 ☂ ⛵ Located in a half rural, half residential area, this straight, three-mile beach dotted with beach grass and clear stretches of sand serves as a nesting ground for migratory shore birds such as terns, plovers and sandpipers. The nesting area is fenced off for protection, but the birds are easily observed. In summer this busy beach attracts families and local kids. Restrooms, lifeguards, snack bar. ~ Off Route 3A, three miles south of Plymouth; 508-830-4095.

HORSENECK BEACH STATE RESERVATION 🚶 🚴 🏇 🏕 ⚓ 🏊 ⛵
This vast, breezy beach is one of the state's most spectacular and least known. Bordered by fragile dunes that create a barrier between the huge parking lot and the beach, it has crunchy white sand and fine waves. From Labor Day to April, horseback riding is allowed. **Gooseberry Neck** is a narrow, mile-long stretch of land jutting out into the ocean and laced with paths. There's an abandoned World War II lookout tower at the end. Right before Gooseberry Neck is a clam bar, a small parking lot and a tiny beach popular with windsurfers. Restrooms, showers, lifeguards, snack bar; groceries in Westport; day-use fee, $2. ~ At the end of Route 88 in Westport Point; 508-636-8816.   ◀ *HIDDEN*

▲ Permitted in 100 RV sites (no hookups) on a first-come, first-served basis; $6 to $7 per night.

DEMAREST LLOYD STATE PARK ⚓ This little-known state park has everything: natural grassy areas for picnics, rambling hills of beach grass, winding rivers, abundant wildlife—deer, hawks, egrets—and a fairly isolated beach. At low tide a long sand bar juts out into the calm, warm waters. Located in the bucolic Dartmouth area, Demarest is a real find. Closed from Labor Day through Memorial Day. Picnic areas, restrooms, showers, lifeguards; day-use fee, $2; groceries nearby in South Dartmouth. ~ At the end of Route 88, east of Horseneck Beach in South Dartmouth; 508-636-3298.   ◀ *HIDDEN*

▼▼▼▼▼▼▼▼▼▼▼▼▼

Outdoor Adventures

FISHING

Blue fish, striped bass, tuna, cod and flounder are abundant on the Massachusetts coast. No license is required to fish, and tackle shops are everywhere. For detailed information on what to catch when, where and how, call the Massachusetts Division of Marine Fisheries. ~ 100 Cambridge Street, Room 1901, Boston, MA 02202; 617-727-3193.

NORTH SHORE   Gloucester has **Captain Bill's Deep Sea Fishing**. ~ 33 Harbor Loop; 508-283-6995. In Newburyport there's **Hilton's Fishing Dock**. ~54-R Merrimac Street; 508-465-9885.

SOUTH SHORE   On the South Shore, try **Captain John Boats** for fishing and whale watching. ~ Town Wharf, Plymouth; 508-746-2643. **Captain Leroy Inc.** offers charter and party boat excursions. ~ Route 6, on the Fairhaven Bridge, New Bedford; 508-992-8907.

SAILING

NORTH SHORE Marblehead on the North Shore is sailboat country. **Coastal Sailing School,** the only rental outfit, has 24- to 30-foot boats and gives lessons. ~ P.O. Box 1001, Marblehead; 617-639-0553.

WHALE WATCHING

The Massachusetts coast offers an enormous number of whale-watch excursions, some conducted by naturalists.

NORTH SHORE Gloucester is the North Shore's gateway to whale watching. **Yankee Fleet** is the oldest and largest whale-watch outfit, plus it offers charter and fishing party excursions. ~ 75 Essex Avenue; 508-283-0313. Also try **Cape Ann Whale Watch.** ~ 415 Main Street; 508-283-5110. In Newburyport, there's **Newburyport Whale Watch.** ~ Hilton's Dock, 54 Merrimac Street; 508-465-7165. At the same location is **Hilton's Fishing Dock.** ~ 54 Merrimac Street; 508-465-9885.

SOUTH SHORE **Captain John Boats** departs from Plymouth Harbor. ~ Town Wharf; 508-746-2643. **Cape Cod Cruises** departs from Plymouth Harbor and also goes to Provincetown. ~ Town Wharf; 508-747-2400.

CANOEING & SEA KAYAKING

NORTH SHORE One of the most beautiful canoe trips in New England is along the North Shore's Ipswich River through the 3000-acre **Ipswich River Wildlife Sanctuary** where you can spot deer, beaver and fox among other animals. ~ Perkins Row, Topsfield; 508-887-9264. For canoe rentals contact **Foote Brothers Canoes.** ~ 230 Topsfield Road, Ipswich; 508-356-9771.

SOUTH SHORE South of New Bedford in Dartmouth are many rivers ideal for canoeing. The **Lloyd Center for Environmental Studies** organizes day-long canoe trips along beautiful nearby rivers. ~ 430 Potomska Road, South Dartmouth; 508-990-0505. **Palmer River Canoe** rents canoes. ~ 206 Wheeler Street, Rehoboth; 508-336-2274.

SCUBA-DIVING

NORTH SHORE In Danvers, the brave and the bold bare the chilly waters with **Northeast Scuba,** an outfit that teaches scuba diving, rents equipment and runs trips off the coast. ~ 125 Liberty Street; 508-777-3483.

ICE SKATING

SOUTH SHORE Ice sailing is a tradition on Watuppa Pond in Fall River. This graceful sport takes tremendous skill and specially designed sailboats. Rentals aren't available, but it's fun to watch these lighter-than-air boats glide along the icy pond.

GOLF

NORTH SHORE Public golf courses are rare on the North Shore, but there is one beautiful municipal course surrounded by deep woods, the **Beverly Golf and Tennis Club.** ~ 134 McKay Street, Beverly; 508-927-5200. **Harwich Port Golf** is a nine-hole public course. ~ Forest and South streets, Harwich Port; 508-432-0250.

SOUTH SHORE Golfing opportunities on the South Shore are limited. There aren't any public golf courses close to Plymouth, but about 30 minutes out of town is **Pembroke Country Club.** ~ West Elm Street, Pembroke; 617-826-0260. **Bay Point Country Club** is nearby. ~ Bay Point Drive, off Onset Avenue, Onset; 508-759-8802. Hilly **New Bedford Municipal Golf Course** offers golfers a challenging course. ~ 581 Hathaway Road, New Bedford; 508-996-9393.

NORTH SHORE The best spot for tennis in the North Shore is the **Beverly Golf and Tennis Club.** It has ten clay courts open to the public. A limited number of municipal courts are available throughout the North Shore towns. ~ 134 McKay Street, Beverly; 508-927-5200.

TENNIS

SOUTH SHORE On the South Shore, municipal courts can be found in New Bedford's woodsy **Buttonwood Park.** ~ Rockdale and Hawthorne avenues. You can also try **Hazelwood Park,** a city park with playgrounds. ~ Brock Avenue; 508-991-6175.

SOUTH SHORE **Chipaway Stables,** a mile north of New Bedford, has guided trail rides and hayrides through local woodlands. ~ 600 Quanapoag Road, North Dartmouth; 508-763-5158.

RIDING STABLES

The North Shore and South Shore have limited bike riding areas, but a few choice spots are described below.

BICYCLING

NORTH SHORE Cyclists in the North Shore area recommend riding along scenic **Route 127** between Beverly, Manchester and Magnolia. The tree-lined road dips and turns past seaside mansions and historic homes. It's cool and peaceful in the summertime.

SOUTH SHORE The **Westport** and **Dartmouth** area on the South Shore doesn't have many cars, and the flat country roads wind past elegant horse farms, pastures and ocean. From Route 195, take Exit 12 and head south to Chase or Tucker Road. At this point it doesn't matter which road you take; they're all lovely, and as long as you head south you'll wind up at the beach.

✔ **CHECK THESE OUT—UNIQUE OUTDOOR ADVENTURES**

- Windsurf one of the state's most spectacular and little-known beaches, breezy **Horseneck Beach State Reservation.** *page 331*
- Paddle through the 3000-acre **Ipswich River Wildlife Sanctuary**—one of New England's most beautiful canoe trips. *page 332*
- Witness the migratory patterns of giant sea mammals when you take a **whale-watching** charter in Gloucester. *page 332*
- Ascend rugged, rocky **Whale's Jaw Trail** through birch groves and cattail marsh to a huge granite boulder resembling a whale's jaw. *page 334*

Bike Rentals On the North Shore you can rent bikes at **Seaside Cycle**. ~ 23 Elm Street, Manchester; 508-526-1200.

HIKING The Massachusetts Coast offers excellent opportunities to hike through salt marsh, forest, sand dunes and moors bordering freshwater ponds and the ocean. Many of the hikes are short and easy. The rest of the coast has a limited number of marked trails. For more information on hikes throughout the state, contact the Massachusetts Department of Environmental Management Trails Program. ~ 100 Cambridge Street, Boston; 617-727-3160.

NORTH SHORE **Art's Trail** (1 mile), in Dogtown Common, a 3000-acre park in Gloucester, winds through red oak forest past a highland of scrub oak, grey birch, blueberries and huckleberries. Several low areas flood in late winter and spring, forming frog-breeding ponds. Of moderate difficulty, the trail is rocky in parts and requires careful walking.

Also in Dogtown Common, **Whale's Jaw Trail** (4.5 miles) is a rugged, rocky, hilly hike starting at Blackburn Industrial Park off Route 128. The trail meanders through former grazing land and past Babson Reservoir, birch groves and cattail marsh. It ends at the top of a hill, where you'll see an enormous split granite boulder that looks like a whale's jaw.

SOUTH SHORE **East Head Reservoir Trail** (3 miles roundtrip) starts behind the Myles Standish State Forest headquarters building in Plymouth. The best thing about this hike is that it covers the full spectrum of habitats in the 14,635-acre park. The relatively flat trail winds past deep forest, marsh, hard and soft wood groves and a pristine pond. A pamphlet available at the start of the hike explains the flora and fauna of each environment. A couple of benches are located along the way.

The **Turner Brook Trail** (2.5 miles) in Massasoit State Park in East Taunton meanders through white pine forest and hardwoods and past swamps and brooks. It edges Lake Rico and arrives at a large, secluded sandy beach. Along the way, you'll spot wildlife such as deer, fox, turkey and owls. Spur trails (8–9 miles) extend through campgrounds and other parts of the park. To get a map, call 508-824-0687 (summer only) or 508-822-7405.

▼▼▼▼▼▼▼▼▼▼

Transportation

CAR

On the North Shore, **Route 128** is the main artery connecting Salem, Manchester, Magnolia, Gloucester and Rockport. **Route 95** is the major north–south artery to Essex, Ipswich and Newburyport.

Route 3 links Boston to Plymouth and ends at the Sagamore Bridge to Cape Cod. **Route 195** is the main east–west artery connecting Fall River and New Bedford.

Many people visiting this area come into **Logan International Airport** in Boston (see Chapter Four). Also serving the southern coastal area is the New Bedford Airport.

Cape Air flies into **New Bedford Airport.**

Ferries and boats between Boston, Plymouth, New Bedford, Cape Cod, Martha's Vineyard and Nantucket require reservations during the summer.

The following ferries and boats operate seasonally and do not transport cars:

A. C. Cruise Lines goes between Boston and Gloucester from Memorial Day through Labor Day. ~ 28 Northern Avenue, Boston; 617-261-6633. **Cape Cod Cruises** goes between Plymouth and Provincetown. ~ State Pier, Plymouth; 508-747-2400. **Martha's Vineyard Ferry** operates between New Bedford and Vineyard Haven on Martha's Vineyard. ~ 1494 East Rodney French Boulevard, Billy Woods Wharf, New Bedford; 508-997-1688. The **Cuttyhunk Boat Line** connects New Bedford and Cuttyhunk Island. ~ Fisherman's Wharf, Pier 3, New Bedford; 508-992-1432.

Greyhound Bus Lines offers frequent service to Newburyport and Boston. ~ 617-526-1801, 800-231-2222. **Bonanza** runs buses to and from Logan Airport, Hyannis, Woods Hole, Falmouth, Bourne, New Bedford, Fall River, Connecticut, Rhode Island and New York. ~ 145 Dartmouth Street, Boston; 617-720-4110; 59 Depot Road, Falmouth, 508-556-3815.

Many Boston commuters live on the North Shore; hence **Massachusetts Bay Transit Authority** (617-722-5000) runs numerous buses from Boston's Haymarket Square and trains from North Station to Salem, Beverly, Gloucester and Rockport. **Cape Ann Transit Authority** (508-283-7916) provides bus service from Gloucester and Rockport.

Plymouth does not have public transportation. **Southern Eastern Regional Transit Authority** (508-997-6767) provides bus service throughout Fall River and New Bedford.

The New Bedford Airport is serviced by **Standard Taxi** (508-997-9404) and **Yellow Cab** (508-999-5213).

SEVEN

Central & Western Massachusetts

Take a good long breath once you arrive in this region, and prepare for a relaxing mix of the rural and the urbane: rolling hills and acres of cornfields, winding country roads that meander along rivers and streams, small museums, old houses, historic villages and college towns with maple-lined streets.

Don't bother to bring your high heels or tuxedo to central and western Massachusetts, unless you're spending a weekend in a fancy Berkshire resort. The mood here—and the dress code—is casual.

Culturally, economically and socially, this area has always been strongly defined by its landscape. The forests, fields and vistas of the Berkshire hills attracted poets and authors of a naturalist bent in the 19th century, and they in turn attracted the rich and famous, who built the elaborate estates of the so-called "Gilded Age." The majestic Connecticut River provided a transportation route as well as water power to generate the mills and factories in the last century. Those factories, along with the fertile soil along the Connecticut's shores, attracted immigrant mill workers and farmers, who helped make the area the breadbasket of New England for decades.

Europeans who first arrived here found primeval forestland as well as large, treeless stretches that had been settled by the Mohegan Indians, hunters who had journeyed from the Hudson River area, and by the Mohawks farther north.

Development first came to central and western Massachusetts in the early 17th century, as small forts like Deerfield were built and trading posts like Springfield sprang up along the Connecticut River. These settlements were significant to our nation's history, as they marked the first movement of the colonists into the interior of the Northeast and served as models for further exploration west.

In the 1800s, canals and mills were built in the southern end of the Pioneer Valley at South Hadley Falls. Within 30 years of its founding in 1850, the city of Holyoke, the first planned city in the country, would become the "Queen of Industrial Cities" and soon after "Paper City of the World."

Thousands of immigrants from Canada and Europe came to central and western Massachusetts in the late 19th century to work in the mills and factories, and to the east, Worcester was experiencing its historical pinnacle as a city where industrial innovation and forward thinking flourished.

As New England's manufacturing economy ebbed in the 20th century, so did the fortunes of the flourishing cities of Holyoke and Worcester, as well as the smaller rural mill towns. Other areas of the state found new economic life in high-technology industries, but for central and western Massachusetts, it's been a struggle. The area continues to rely largely on smaller manufacturing, education, agriculture and the service industries. As a result, there is a different standard of living in this region than in wealthier areas near Boston.

Today, though the three areas in this chapter are not so far apart geographically, each has its own identity. Central Massachusetts, with Worcester and Sturbridge as its hubs, is made up of small rural and mill towns. The Pioneer Valley, stretching up the Connecticut River, is shifting from an agricultural area into a bedroom community for Springfield and Hartford. The Berkshire area takes its influences more from New York City than from Boston, and it, too, is seeing changes as the manufacturing jobs that once served as the mainstay of the local economy have disappeared.

Many residents of eastern Massachusetts are unaware of just how rural this area is, and "westerners" often quip that the state ends at Interstate 495, which makes a large semicircle around Boston. Every once in a while a local politician brings up the idea of secession for central and western Massachusetts, partly because of the claim that the smaller cities and towns of the region don't get their fair share of state funds.

But it's also because people in this part of the state have a different way of thinking. There's a streak of high-mindedness and independence here that was already evident back in 1787 when Daniel Shays, a farmer from Hatfield, started the nation's first tax insurrection. It continues up to this day, with nearly a hundred citizens in the region who refuse to pay their taxes in protest of U.S. military policy.

Over the centuries, the region has drawn many writers: from Nathaniel Hawthorne (a Salem man who didn't like the Berkshires) and Herman Melville (a Pittsfield man who did). Comedian Bill Cosby has a home in the hills surrounding the Pioneer Valley, and Poet Laureate Richard Wilbur resides in Cummington, carrying on the tradition of poets William Cullen Bryant, who lived in the same town, and Emily Dickinson, who wrote in her home in the center of Amherst in the 19th century.

What all these people have found is a place that's close enough to city amenities and resources—New York is less than four hours away, Boston two—but far enough from the urban smog, crime and high cost of living.

Many current residents in this area first came here as students. In the 1960s, western Massachusetts was a haven for the "back to the landers," who found cheap land and stimulating political activities on the University of Massachusetts campus in Amherst. Like everyplace else, the area has mellowed, but for many, political activism remains an important part of life. Most municipal decisions, except in the cities, are made at traditional New England town meetings. The region is also rich with craftspeople and artists, drawn here for the area's natural beauty and solitude, and their works fill galleries and studios in even the smallest towns.

Education is big business in these parts: Worcester is home to Holy Cross, Clark University and Assumption College, while the Pioneer Valley boasts the so-called "Five Colleges"—the University of Massachusetts, Smith, Mount Holyoke, Hampshire and Amherst—as well as a number of prestigious private schools like Deerfield Academy and Northfield Mount Hermon. Williams College is in the Berkshire village of Williamstown.

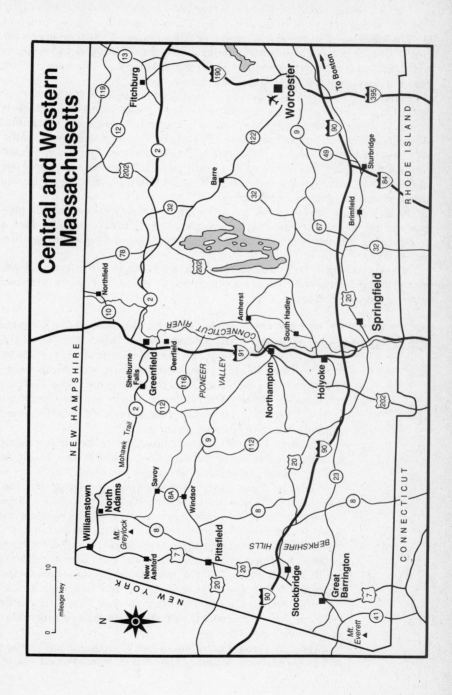

Central and Western Massachusetts

This is a special place, taken best at a slow pace. Don't try to do too much here; take the time to loll in a sidewalk café in Northampton or to lose yourself in any of the fine museums of Springfield, Worcester or Williamstown. Though summer is the closest thing to paradise in this region, other seasons have their special pleasures as well. Spend an autumn day climbing a mountain to see the foliage colors, or a winter weekend cross-country skiing at a cozy inn in the Berkshires.

Mark Twain's adage "If you don't like New England weather, wait a minute" applies here, and the weather can vary in locations only 20 miles apart in the Berkshires. Expect anything in winter, from brilliant, 50° days after a snowstorm, to stretches when the thermometer doesn't get above 20°. Early spring—maple sugaring season—will bring warmer days and freezing nights, while summer generally offers 70° to 80° days and, oftentimes, thunderstorms in the early evening. Indian summer is truly one of the most beautiful times in this area, with crystal blue skies, stunning foliage and temperatures that range in the 50s and 60s.

A visit to this region can put you in touch with life's simple pleasures. Like the pleasure of being outdoors and listening to the silence. The exhilaration of a hike down a forested trail. The fun of getting onto a backcountry road and not knowing where you'll end up.

If you're looking for an area that combines the serene pleasures of country life with abundant recreational and cultural opportunities, you will want to return again and again to this scenic refuge.

▼▼▼▼▼▼▼▼▼▼▼▼▼▼▼▼
Central Massachusetts

All too often travelers whiz through Central Massachusetts on the Mass Pike (Route 90) completely missing the attractions of the area. What a shame. This part of the state is home to several truly worthwhile attractions, including several museums in the city of Worcester (pronounced WUS-ter); Old Sturbridge Village, a living-history museum in Sturbridge; and the tiny town of Brimfield, which has been called the "flea-market capital of the world."

Thanks to Route 90, Central Massachusetts is a breeze to reach. In fact, Worcester is only an hour's drive west of Boston. People are often surprised to learn that Worcester's the second-largest city in New England. Perhaps even more surprising are its impressive contributions to education and commerce. It's home to a dozen colleges and was the birthplace of the ingenious machines that were the first to weave carpets and fold envelopes. The Valentine card was invented here, so was the cotton gin and the birth control pill. Abbie Hoffman, father of the Yippies, was born here; so was Clara Barton, mother of the Red Cross. Isaiah Thomas, publisher of the *Massachusetts Spy*, the country's first newspaper, gave the premiere New England reading of the Declaration of Independence here in Worcester, and the American Antiquarian Society he founded was the first national historical society in the country.

Worcester's proximity to Boston hasn't helped its cultural image, and its recent economic history has not been quite as grand. Like its neighbor Springfield to the west, the city's fortunes faded with the manufacturing economy, and it is still struggling to redefine itself. There's not much doing here, but the downtown area is in the process of restoration and revitalization, and there are some interesting museums and sights spread throughout the city.

The **Worcester Historical Museum** is housed in a Georgian Revival-style building and features a collection that details the settlement of the Worcester area. The library here has materials and books on local history for use by researchers. Closed Monday. Admission. ~ 30 Elm Street; 508-753-8278.

SIGHTS

Founded in 1812 by Isaiah Thomas, the **American Antiquarian Society** was this country's first national historical society. Its remarkable collection of printed material includes books, manuscripts, newspapers and ephemera produced in the United States before 1877. It also houses Thomas' printing press. Access to the library is limited, but tours of the collection and its conservation lab are offered on Wednesdays. Closed Saturday and Sunday. ~ 185 Salisbury Street; 508-755-5221.

The **Worcester Art Museum** has a fine reputation as one of the best art museums in New England and features a fine collection of European, Middle Eastern, Asian and early American works. Closed Monday and Tuesday. Admission. ~ 55 Salisbury Street; 508-799-4406.

On the outside, the **Higgins Armory Museum** is a steel-and-glass art deco building, but inside it's a castle filled with dozens of sets of armor collected over the years by John Woodman Higgins, who was a local steel magnate. The museum details the history of armor from the year 2000 B.C. to the present and even features a set of armor made for "Hell-Mutt" the hunting dog. There's a children's room where kids can try on helmets and medieval costumes. Closed Monday. Admission. ~ 100 Barber Avenue; 508-853-6015.

To the north of Worcester, the landscape opens up into the broad Nashoba Valley. It's worth the drive 20 miles north to visit the **Fruitlands Museums**. Fruitlands is an overlooked gem, with four small museums spread out on a hillside offering an expansive view of the valley. It was once the home of Bronson Alcott, father of Louisa May and founder of the transcendental movement of the 1840s, which espoused individualism and self-reliance, among other things, and included in its disciples Ralph Waldo Emerson and Henry David Thoreau. The **Fruitlands Farmhouse** has exhibits detailing the movement, while the **Shaker House** provides a look at Shaker life during the 19th century. The **Picture Gallery**, built by the museums' founder, Boston Brahmin Clara Endicott Sears, houses her collection of landscapes by several Hudson River School painters. The **American Indian Museum** has dioramas and artifacts relating to New England's

◄ *HIDDEN*

Indians, including Thoreau's collection of arrowheads. The grounds here are quite spectacular, so bring a picnic lunch and spend the day if you can. Closed Monday and mid-October through mid-May. Admission. ~ 102 Prospect Hill Road, Harvard; 508-456-3924.

West of Worcester, the land becomes less developed. You've now arrived in the real country. A good introduction to the history of this area comes in **Old Sturbridge Village**. Imagine a small New England village where time just stopped somewhere in the 1830s, and you'd probably conjure up a place like Old Sturbridge Village. It is a fascinating living history museum that re-creates New England life of that period, from the shoes on the feet of the costumed interpretive guides to the rooftops of the 40-odd restored buildings. Admission. ~ 1 Old Sturbridge Village Road; 508-347-3362, 800-733-1830.

Traveling the paths that wind through some 200 acres of the small village, gardens, farms and fields, you can learn how 19th-century potters, blacksmiths, basketmakers and other craftspeople created their wares. Every activity here is designed to bring the visitor back 150 years. They host a variety of special events, some of which are based on the seasons and include cider making, vegetable harvesting, preparation and eating of special Thanksgiving dinners, and craft and antique conferences. A good place for families, this is a must stop on any tour of the region. Closed Monday from November through April.

Driving west from Sturbridge on Route 20, you're on the open highway, traveling past forests and ponds to the small town of Brimfield, home of the famous **Brimfield Outdoor Antique Show**, a weeklong flea market extravaganza held three times a year, in May, July and September. Spread out along a mile-long stretch in the center of town, over 4000 dealers come here to sell their wares, from old postcards to fine European antiques. *The Brimfielder* is a guide to the different exhibitors, available at any local coffee shop or newsstand. For a schedule and detailed listing of exhibitors, send $5 to Quaboag Valley Chamber of Commerce. ~ P.O. Box 269, Palmer, MA 01069; 413-283-6149.

✔ CHECK THESE OUT—UNIQUE SIGHTS

- Imagine a small New England town where time stopped in the 1830s—you'll find it at **Old Sturbridge Village**, a living-history museum. *page 342*
- Witness the largest footprints in the world from the Triassic period, about 200 million years ago, at funky **Nash Dinosaur Land**. *page 348*
- Marvel at the natural marble bridge—the only one of its kind in North America—formed by melting glaciers in **Natural Bridge State Park**. *page 360*
- Visit "Mr. Barn," the man responsible for restoring some of New England's 300-year-old farm buildings at the **Babcock Barn Home**. *page 363*

For more information about the Worcester and Sturbridge area, contact the **Worcester County Convention and Visitors Bureau.** ~ 33 Waldo Street, Worcester, MA 01608; 508-753-2920.

Worcester has its share of chain motels, but Sturbridge, 18 miles southwest, offers a better variety of accommodations.

LODGING

Located near the busy University of Massachusetts Medical Center, the **Beechwood Hotel** is one of the town's newer hotels. The large round building has a lobby decorated with flagstone floors and light oak and lavender trim. The Beechwood offers 58 spacious guest rooms, including some fireplace suites, each decorated in pastels and wall-to-wall carpeting. The restaurant here has earned high praises from local food critics for its classic American cuisine. ~ 363 Plantation Street, Worcester; 508-754-5789, 800-344-2589, fax 508-752-2060. ULTRA-DELUXE.

The **Old Sturbridge Village Lodges and Oliver Wight House,** located at the entrance to Old Sturbridge Village, offers a variety of lodging that includes the 200-year-old Oliver Wight House, the Dennison Cottage suites and Village units. The Oliver Wight House, built in 1789, once served as a tavern providing food and lodging for farmers and travelers. The refurbished inn features ten large rooms nicely decorated with Federal-style pieces, including big four-poster beds. The Dennison Cottage offers two luxury suites in a 19th-century country decor with stenciled walls. The Village units are decorated in an Early American motif, with Colonial reproductions. Though the service is friendly here, the atmosphere is motel-like, without the personal interaction you get at a country inn. ~ Route 20 West, Sturbridge; 508-347-3327, 800-733-1830, fax 508-347-3018. MODERATE TO DELUXE.

A local institution, the **Publick House on the Common** was originally founded in 1771 by Colonel Ebenezer Crafts. The original building, which is listed on the National Register of Historic Places, has 16 rooms plus several restaurants and shops. It's surrounded by other accommodations, including the next-door Chamberlain House (a four-suite building) and a 100-room motor lodge. ~ Route 131 on the Common, Sturbridge; 508-347-3313, 800-782-5425, fax 508-347-1246. DELUXE TO ULTRA-DELUXE.

About a mile away is the **Colonel Ebenezer Crafts Inn** which is in a farmhouse dating back to 1786. The rooms here—the most charming of all the Publick House accommodations—have canopy or four-poster beds, some antique furnishings and an all-around peaceful feeling. ~ Fiske Hill Road, Sturbridge; 508-347-3313, 800-782-5425. DELUXE TO ULTRA-DELUXE.

Offering basic modern motel rooms, the **Sturbridge Coach Motor Lodge** has nicely kept grounds and a swimming pool and is convenient to Sturbridge, Worcester and Brimfield. ~ 408 Main Street, Route 20, Sturbridge; 508-347-7327, fax 508-347-2954. MODERATE.

Set on two acres and adjacent to a 100-acre park, **Wildwood Inn** is a century-old Victorian. Nine rooms feature twin, queen and four-poster beds (seven of them have private baths). Down comforters and handmade quilts are supplemented by electric blankets for those cold New England nights. In the warm months you'll gravitate to the wicker furniture on the wraparound porch. The country-casual parlor features antiques such as a spinning wheel and bed warmer as well as a fine library. Full breakfast and afternoon tea are delightful. ~ 121 Church Street, Ware; 413-967-7798. MODERATE.

Berkshire and Greater Springfield Bed and Breakfast is a reservation service that matches travelers with a number of private homes and small country inns in the Sturbridge area. ~ P.O. Box 211, Williamsburg, MA 01096; 413-268-7244.

DINING

Thai Orchid has received good reviews from locals. The Thai cuisine includes pineapple fried rice, chicken or shrimp and vegetables in peanut sauce, crisp fried tofu and other dishes, all served in the restaurant's quiet atmosphere. The decor here is spare and uncluttered, with white furnishings and wood paneling, creating an understated elegance. ~ 144 Commercial Street, Worcester; 508-792-9701. BUDGET TO MODERATE.

The Sunburst features natural foods for breakfast and lunch in a coffee-shop atmosphere. The muffins are excellent, as is the quiche and granola. Other items include fresh fruit bowls, sandwiches and "nogs," seasonal fruit mixed with milk and eggs. ~ 484 Main Street, Sturbridge; 508-347-3097. BUDGET.

A local dining institution, the **Salem Cross Inn** is a restored 1705 New England farmhouse filled with collections of antiques and photographs. The Salem family specializes in some unique eating events that include drinks in the old tavern downstairs, hayrides and sleighrides through their 600-acre farm. In the summer, their Drover's Roasts serve up a large side of beef, slowly cooked as it was in the 1700s, over a fieldstone open pit. In winter, the Hearthside Dinners on the weekends feature prime rib cooked on a 1700s roasting jack in the fieldstone fireplace and apple pie baked in the inn's 1699 brick beehive oven. These meals are worth rearranging your schedule for, and reservations are required. Closed Monday. ~ Route 9, West Brookfield; 508-867-2345. MODERATE TO DELUXE.

SHOPPING

Spag's is a Worcester institution, with three large buildings and an assortment of tents filled with, well, stuff, of all kinds: from small appliances to clothing to groceries. It's a warehouse-type operation where customers actually line up to get in the place. If you plan to do any heavy shopping, bring a tote or knapsack—vendors don't give out shopping bags. ~ Route 9.

Museum Gift Shop and **New England Bookstore at Old Sturbridge Village** are two outstanding shops that feature crafts made at

Sturbridge Village, as well as reproductions of early American items for the home. The bookstore features a wide selection of books about New England history, life and lore, including gardening and the home arts. ~ 1 Old Sturbridge Village Road, Sturbridge; 508-347-3362.

For a selection of reproductions of Shaker furniture, baskets, boxes and hand-cut stencils, visit the **Shaker Shop**. You can also buy authentic Shaker milk paint (yes, made with milk combined with lime and pigment). This old-fashioned product will not peel like modern paint mixtures. ~ 454 Main Street, Sturbridge; 508-347-7564.

Side Door Shop features home furnishings, reproductions of Early American furniture and decorative accessories. ~ Route 20, Sturbridge; 508-347-9500.

The Centrum is a 13,500-seat arena, offering rock and pop music concerts, as well as hockey and basketball games and conference events. ~ 50 Foster Street, Worcester; 508-798-8888.

NIGHTLIFE

Mechanics Hall, one of the finest pre–Civil War concert halls in the country, is especially noted for its fine acoustics. The hall draws folk, jazz and classical performers and has even been used for the recording of compact discs and records. ~ 321 Main Street, Worcester; 508-752-5608.

Algiers is open every night with live acoustic music on Thursday, Top-40 deejay music on Friday and Saturday and a jukebox other nights. Weekend cover. ~ 21 Foster Street, Worcester; 508-754-7742.

Sh'boom's is a club with a '50s style, with disc jockeys and dancing Wednesday through Saturday. Also here is **Polyester**, a "classic dance" (read: disco) club accessible through Sh'boom's. Cover Thursday through Saturday. ~ 215 Main Street, Worcester; 508-752-4214.

The **Spencer Country Inn** draws locals in their 20s and 30s for its live Top-40 bands on the weekends. The place has a pub-type atmosphere, with cozy booths and lots of antiques, including a horse-drawn carriage, and there's a large dancefloor and a big-screen TV for sports fans. Cover for bands. ~ 500 Main Street, Spencer; 508-885-9036.

Legends All-American Sports Bar has live Top-40 music and dancing Friday and Saturday nights. ~ Sturbridge Host Hotel, Route 20, Sturbridge; 508-347-7393.

Those in search of more low-key nightlife should try the popular **Ugly Duckling Loft**, the loft of the Whistling Swan. The place has a warm and relaxed atmosphere amid a brass and wood decor, with piano music Tuesday, Wednesday, Saturday and Sunday and a singing acoustic guitarist Thursday and Friday. ~ 502 Main Street, Sturbridge; 508-347-2321.

PURGATORY CHASM STATE RESERVATION 🏃 This park offers 960 acres of forestland, including the dramatic and unusual Purgatory Chasm. The chasm itself is a half-mile-long granite fissure, a sharp valley filled with huge boulders that have detached from the walls.

BEACHES & PARKS

Geologists can't seem to agree on exactly how the chasm was formed, and its mystery adds to the allure of the place. There are hiking trails, including a difficult one through the chasm. Picnic areas, restrooms. ~ On Purgatory Road, off Route 146, Sutton; 508-234-3733.

QUINSIGAMOND STATE PARK ⌇⌇ This 58-acre preserve is an urban park, offering a grassy, midday break for visitors to the Worcester area. There are several beaches, including Regatta Point and Lake Park. Crew teams from the area's colleges can often be found at Regatta Point, while Lake Park offers tennis courts and a track. Picnic areas, restrooms. ~ On Lake Avenue off Plantation Street exit from Route 290; 508-755-6880.

▲ Nearby, at the Sutton Falls Camping Area (90 Manchang Road, West Sutton; 508-865-3898), there are 60 sites for tents and 35 for RVs (hookups available); $15 to $18 per night.

▼▼▼▼▼▼▼▼▼▼▼
Pioneer Valley

The Pioneer Valley, actually a section of the Connecticut River Valley, stretches from the city of Springfield in the south to Brattleboro, Vermont, and beyond. Here you'll find an eclectic mix of old mill cities, semi-chic college towns and country villages, with tobacco, hay and cornfields in between. The farther north you travel from Springfield, the more country you'll find. Northampton and Amherst offer good restaurants and shops, while the towns in the surrounding hills are much more rural and relaxed, some with town commons and white-steepled churches, others with old iron bridges and brick factories along the rivers, remnants of the days when cutlery factories and paper mills fueled the region's economy.

Today, housing developments are starting to encroach on farmland, but the area is still remarkably rural in some parts. This area is known for its unique mix of Yankee stubbornness, ethnic influences and a '60s political outlook that remains even today.

SIGHTS

THE LOWER VALLEY Founded by fur trader William Pynchon in 1636, **Springfield** is the oldest settlement and the largest city in western Massachusetts, as well as the commercial hub of the region. Though it is a city that tries hard, Springfield's glory days seem to lie in the past. It does have a good collection of museums, however, that make it worth spending a rainy day here.

Overlooking the Connecticut River is the **Naismith Memorial Basketball Hall of Fame.** Basketball was invented here in Springfield in 1891, and this place is enjoyable even if you're not a sports fan. There are videos and plenty of interactive displays, including the Spalding Shoot Out, where visitors can shoot at baskets of varying heights while standing on a moving sidewalk. Admission. ~ 1150 West Columbus Avenue; 413-781-6500.

Court Square is a pleasant green space in the heart of Springfield bordered by the **Hampden County Courthouse**, the **Old First Church** and **Symphony Hall**. ~ Main Street, between Court and Elm streets.

From here it's a short hike up the hill to **The Quadrangle**, which features four museums (one admission charge admits you to all four) and the Springfield Library. ~ Springfield Library and Museums Association, 220 State Street; 413-739-3871.

The **George Walter Vincent Smith Museum** houses a collection of Oriental art, as well as 19th-century European and American paintings. Closed Monday and Tuesday. ~ On the Quadrangle; 413-733-4214.

Across the Quadrangle is the **Museum of Fine Arts**, which features a diverse collection of Chinese art and works from the early Renaissance to the 18th and 19th centuries. One gallery is devoted to impressionist, expressionist and early modern European works. Of special interest are the works of local 19th-century portrait artist Erastus Salisbury Field, whose gigantic *Historical Monument of the American Republic* is a mind-boggler. Closed Monday and Tuesday. ~ 413-732-6092.

The **Springfield Science Museum** offers exhibits in the natural and physical sciences, including a hands-on Exploration Center for children and the Seymour Planetarium. Closed Monday and Tuesday. ~ On the Quadrangle, State and Chestnut streets; 413-263-6800.

The **Connecticut Valley Historical Museum** offers a glimpse of the social and economic history of the Connecticut River Valley. Closed Monday and Tuesday. ~ On the Quadrangle; 413-263-6800.

Up the hill from the Quadrangle, on the campus of Springfield Technical Community College, is the **Springfield Armory National Historic Site**, established at a spot chosen by George Washington in 1794. The Springfield Armory produced the first U.S. military small arms—the Springfield rifle—bringing skilled workers to the area and setting the scene for the valley's industrial growth. Closed Monday between Labor Day and Memorial Day. ~ 1 Armory Square; 413-734-8551.

More information about Springfield is available from the **Greater Springfield Convention and Visitors Bureau**. ~ 34 Boland Way, Springfield, MA 01103; 413-787-1548.

Just north of Springfield are two great amusement parks. **Mt. Tom** is a ski area that serves double duty in the summertime with a water park and two hair-raising, 4000-foot drop alpine slides. The park offers activities for children of all ages, including an 8500-square-foot wave pool and two water slides. Admission. ~ Route 5, Holyoke; 413-536-0416.

Riverside Park is the largest amusement park in New England, an old-time place that features the Cyclone, one of the largest roller coasters in the country. Open daily in the summer, weekends only in

September, October, April and May. Closed November through March. Admission. ~ 1623 Main Street, Route 159, Agawam; 413-786-9300.

Traveling north from Holyoke, you start to get into farm-and-college country. Gradually, the mills and tenements fade away and the land becomes more open. The small town of South Hadley is the home of **Mount Holyoke College**. Established by Mary Lyon in 1837, Mount Holyoke is one of the oldest women's colleges in the country. The campus was designed by Frederick Law Olmstead, designer of Central Park, who used a variety of rare trees to provide form, beauty and consistency. A maple-lined road leads the traveler through the 800-acre campus, between two campus ponds and up to the wooded Prospect Hill, which has bridle paths and a lawn for picnics. ~ 50 College Street; 413-538-2000.

HIDDEN ►

On the Granby town line on Route 116 farther north is the funky and fascinating **Nash Dinosaur Land**, where 200-million-year-old dinosaur tracks were discovered in 1933. Geologist Carleton Nash and his son Cornell have built up a business over the past 50 years, excavating the tracks and building a small museum and shop to display the prints, some as tiny as chicken feet. The Nashes boast the largest footprint quarry in the world, as well as the largest footprints from the Triassic period; many pieces are for sale. Kids will love this place. Closed Monday, Tuesday and Wednesday from Labor Day to Memorial Day. Admission. ~ Route 116, South Hadley; 413-467-9566.

THE UPPER VALLEY **Northampton** counts among its past residents Calvinist minister Jonathan Edwards and President Calvin Coolidge, who also served as mayor. Sylvester Graham invented the graham cracker here, and in the early 1800s the place was a thriving industrial center for wool, buttons, paper, and later, cutlery.

Today, it is perhaps the most cosmopolitan town in western Massachusetts (some locals say too much so), with its mix of restored old buildings, galleries, restaurants and trendy Main Street boutiques. The home of Smith College, the town is a pleasant and lively place year-round but especially nice in summer, when the students have gone home.

Pioneer Valley is noted for its craftspeople who continue traditions started in the 17th century.

Smith College is located just outside of the town's center. One of the so-called "Seven Sisters" (as is Mount Holyoke), Smith's campus is quintessentially old-money New England, with old Gothic buildings and beautifully tended gardens. Among its attractions is the **Lyman Plant House**, a rambling, old-fashioned greenhouse filled with hundreds of different flowers, plants and trees and open to the public. The annual bulb show in early spring is a favorite visitor destination. Another idyllic spot is **Paradise Pond**, framed by weeping willows and elm trees and ideal for an afternoon picnic.

The **Smith College Museum of Art** houses works by Picasso, Degas, Monet and Winslow Homer, as well as local sculptor Leonard

Baskin and 19th-century local portrait artist Romanzo Elmer. Closed Monday. ~ 76 Elm Street at Bedford Terrace; 413-584-2700.

Calvin Coolidge, the nation's 30th president, attended Amherst College and settled in Northampton, where he practiced law and began his political career. Coolidge lived with his wife at **21 Massasoit Street**, and after his presidency the couple retired to The Beeches, a stately home located on Hampton Terrace. Both homes are private.

One fine old Gothic building is **The Forbes Library**, which houses many of Coolidge's papers. ~ 20 West Street; 413-586-0489.

For another example of Gothic architecture, visit **The Academy of Music**, a former opera house built in 1891 that now serves as a movie theater with occasional live performances. ~ 274 Main Street; 413-584-8435.

Historic Northampton operates three homes that highlight local history and daily life in Northampton over the past three centuries. The **Isaac Damon House** was built circa 1813 by Damon, a prominent New England architect of the day. The house includes an 1820 parlor display, changing exhibitions and a museum gift shop. ~ 46 Bridge Street; 413-584-6011.

The **Shepherd House** is furnished with the Shepherd family collection, including travel souvenirs from around the world. ~ 66 Bridge Street; 413-584-6011.

Built in the early 1700s, the **Parsons House** features an architectural tour; look inside the walls to see the various layers of wallpaper and paint from the 19th century. Guided afternoon tours are offered Wednesday through Sunday, March through December. ~ 58 Bridge Street; 413-584-6011.

For more information on the Northampton area, contact the **Greater Northampton Chamber of Commerce**. ~ 62 State Street, Northampton; 413-584-1900.

Follow Route 9 east across the Coolidge Bridge and you will reach Hadley, a farming town once noted for its asparagus and tobacco but now fast becoming a suburb. The **Hadley Farm Museum** is housed in a 200-year-old barn moved to the spot in 1929. The museum features a wonderful collection of farm tools, an 18th-century stagecoach, wagons and home utensils used during the 18th and 19th centuries. Closed Monday and from October through April. Admission. ~ Route 9.

Amherst is a pretty college town with shops and restaurants spread out along a maple-lined town common. Though it has been influenced by the gentrifier's wrecking ball, there's still a spark of politics in its downtown area, with tie-dye clad students petitioning against U.S. military policy or in favor of animal rights.

Founded in 1821, **Amherst College** gracefully borders the southern side of the Amherst common. With about 1600 students, Amherst is one of the smaller Ivy League colleges, and its campus architecture includes a rich mix of old ivy-covered halls and newer buildings. ~ 413-542-2000.

One of the newer buildings houses the **Robert Frost Library**, named for one of the college's better-known faculty members. Open daily when school is in session. ~ 413-542-2373.

The **Pratt Museum** houses a collection of local geological specimens, as well as the world's largest mastodon skeleton. Open daily when school is in session. ~ 413-542-2165.

The **Mead Art Museum** displays an outstanding collection of American art, with an emphasis on 19th- and early-20th-century works. In the summer, the museums are open on the weekends only; the library is open Monday through Friday. Open daily when school is in session. ~ 413-542-2335.

The **University of Massachusetts** is located at the other end of Amherst, and, with an enrollment of 23,000 students, is one of the largest universities in New England. ~ 413-545-0111.

"UMass" has come a long way from its beginnings as an agricultural land-grant college in 1863, and its campus buildings reflect that stretch, from the classic-style **Old Chapel** to the 26-story **W. E. B. Du Bois Library** that stands beside it. The library, as well as the **Top of the Campus** restaurant at the **Murray D. Lincoln Campus Center**, offer fine views of the Holyoke range.

The Campus Pond is the center of fair-weather activities, and the **Fine Arts Center** presents varied performances and includes an art gallery. ~ 413-545-2511.

For more information on the Amherst area, contact the **Amherst Area Chamber of Commerce**. ~ 11 Spring Street, Amherst; 413-253-0700.

Travel north on Route 116, and you'll leave the college towns behind. Here the landscape is punctuated by the long, faded red tobacco barns and cornfields whose crop will feed the area's dairy cows. Just off Routes 5 and 10 is **Historic Deerfield**. ~ Deerfield; 413-774-5581.

It's almost jarring to turn off the busy highway and onto the tree-lined main street of Deerfield, because you have, in a sense, left

THE "BELLE OF AMHERST'S" FAMILY HOME

The **Emily Dickinson Homestead** was the family home of "The Belle of Amherst," reclusive poet Emily Dickinson. The large brick house built by Emily's grandfather in 1813 is now owned by Amherst College, and it has become a mecca for poetry lovers. Part of the home is open to the public. Open Wednesday through Saturday from April through October and Wednesday and Saturday from November 1 through December 15. Closed the rest of the year. Admission. ~ 280 Main Street; 413-542-8161.

the modern world behind. The mile-long main street of this 300-year-old village (it's just called "The Street") is flanked by a dozen restored Colonial and Federal-style houses, all painted in the muted reds, blues and greys of bygone days. Here you can get a sense of the emerging Connecticut Valley architecture, which was different from the styles in England as well as the coastal New England towns. And the interiors at Historic Deerfield are just as faithful to the past as the exteriors; the village's collection of decorative arts and architecture has been compared to that of historic Williamsburg and the Winterthur Museum in Delaware.

Surrounded by farmland and meadows, Deerfield began in the 17th century as a tiny frontier outpost. The town was massacred by French and Indian attackers in 1675 in the Bloody Brook Massacre and virtually destroyed by a later attack in 1704. Testimony to that fateful day still stands: there's a door with a hatchet hole in it at the **Memorial Hall Museum**, one of the oldest local historical museums in the country. Admission. ~ Memorial Street; 413-774-7476.

The town recovered, and Deerfield went on to prosper as a center for commerce and agriculture, as well as an exchange post for travelers between Boston and points west. In 1952, Mr. and Mrs. Henry Flynt established Historic Deerfield, Inc. to carry out the restoration of the town, one of the first such undertakings in the country.

The **Sheldon-Hawks House** is the best-preserved Deerfield building from the 18th century, and the dark-stained, clapboard structure is one of the oldest houses in town, dating back to 1740. The woodwork is intact, and some of the furnishings are original Deerfield pieces. The Sheldon-Hawks displays New England furniture, European brass and English ceramics, while the **Wells-Thorn House** features a series of period rooms that illustrate the influence of the local economy and changing styles in home life in Deerfield from 1725 to 1850. There is no admission fee to Historic Deerfield, but one admission fee is charged to tour all the individual houses.

The Connecticut River is the backbone of this region, and from June to mid-October, the **Quinnetukut II Riverboat** cruises a 12-mile section of the river, giving you a look at the geology, history and natural beauty of the area. Closed Monday and Tuesday. Admission. ~ Northfield Mountain Recreation and Environmental Center, Route 63, Northfield; 413-659-3714.

If you're lucky enough to be in the area in the late summer or early fall, check out one of the region's many agricultural fairs. The **Eastern States Exposition** represents all six New England states and features music, food, agricultural contests, animal shows and much more. The exposition is held the third week of September in West Springfield. The **Cummington Fair** is another small-town beauty, held in the last week of August. This fair's highlights are its old engine display, square dancing and fireworks. The **Northampton Fair** is held during the first week in September at the Tri-County Fairground on Bridge Street in Northampton. The **Greenfield Fair** is the second week in September, at the Franklin County Fairgrounds on Wisdom Way in Greenfield.

For a complete listing of agricultural fairs around the state, write to the **Massachusetts Department of Food and Agriculture.** ~ 100 Cambridge Street, Boston, MA 02202; 617-727-3018.

> In the '80s, Jimmy Carter's daughter, Amy, '60s radical Abbie Hoffman, and a group of students from the University of Massachusetts put the CIA on trial—and won.

Route 5 north is a busy two-lane highway that will bring you to Greenfield and the beginning of a section of Route 2 known as **The Mohawk Trail**. The Trail is one of New England's oldest and finest touring roads, winding for some 60 miles past farm towns, forests and some of the best scenic views in western New England. The Trail is dotted with remnants of the 1950s heyday of automobile touring: cabins and old Indian souvenir shops, and several spots with lookouts boasting multistate views.

The Mohawk Trail is particularly popular in fall, when its hills offer spectacular foliage viewing. If you're traveling in early spring, however, **Gould's Sugar House** is a tasty stop. You're likely to find **HIDDEN ►** Edgar Gould out in the back boiling sap to make maple syrup, while his wife and grandchildren are in the restaurant serving it on waffles and pancakes. (Dill pickles are served on the side to cut the sweetness of the syrup!) Closed November through February. ~ Mohawk Trail, Shelburne; 413-625-6170.

There are many opportunities for picnicking along the Deerfield River, and you may want to stop in Shelburne Falls for supplies. **McCusker's Market** has a good deli and a supply of health foods, as well as Bart's ice cream, a local favorite. ~ State Street; 413-625-9411.

Take some time here to explore the lovely **Bridge of Flowers**, a former trolley bridge across the Deerfield River that has been converted into an incredible flower garden in bloom three seasons out of the year.

HIDDEN ► Across the bridge and down a side street, you'll find the **Glacial Potholes**, formed millions of years ago by "plunge pools" of waterfalls. For more information on local geology, pick up a copy of *Exploring Franklin County, A Geology Guide* at a local bookstore.

As you travel farther on the Mohawk Trail, the curves deepen in the road, and the mountains get steeper. At the crest of the hills, you'll reach Florida and **Whitcomb Summit**. The lookout tower here once appeared as an illustration on the cover of the *New Yorker*. Once one of the hottest tourist spots on the Mohawk Trail, the summit area has become a little honky-tonky, but the view remains spectacular. You can gaze back at the mountains you've just crossed. To the east you can see the huge reservoir that serves the Bear Swamp Hydroelectric Station in Rowe, and to the west, that's Mount Greylock—the tallest mountain in the state—rising up above the Berkshires.

For more information, contact **The Mohawk Trail Association**. ~ P.O. Box 722, Charlemont, MA 01339.

The Springfield area offers a large selection of chain motels and luxury hotels, while accommodations in the upper Pioneer Valley include more motels, country inns and bed and breakfasts. Advance reservations are strongly recommended in June, when college graduations and the American Council Crafts Fair are held, and in September, when the Eastern States Exposition and fall foliage bring a flurry of visitors.

The **Country Bed and Breakfast Association** offers information on 13 small bed and breakfasts located in the farm and hill towns of the Pioneer Valley. ~ P.O. Box 5, Buckland, MA 01338; 413-498-2692. BUDGET TO DELUXE.

The most elegant hostelry in the Pioneer Valley, the **Sheraton Springfield Monarch Place** has a plush lobby highlighted by marble, a 12-story atrium and amenities like an indoor pool with a sun deck. The 304 spacious guest rooms are decorated in soft pastels. There are also two restaurants, a lounge and a health club with jacuzzi, weight room and sauna. Ask for a room with a view of the Connecticut River. ~ Monarch Place, Springfield; 413-781-1010, 800-426-9004, fax 413-734-3249. MODERATE.

The **Yankee Pedlar Inn** has 40 guest rooms in five separate buildings on a busy street in Holyoke. Rooms are individually decorated in Early American decor, with period pieces and antiques, canopy and four-poster beds. The Pedlar has a Colonial-style tavern, an oyster bar and a restaurant. Although not an isolated country inn, this is a popular place for business travelers, and its location just off Route 91 makes it convenient to all parts of the Pioneer Valley. ~ 1866 Northampton Street; 413-532-9494, fax 413-536-8877. MODERATE.

Near downtown Northampton and right next to the Smith campus, the **Autumn Inn** is a simple, comfortable 30-room hostelry. Guest rooms are large, clean and individually decorated with wall-to-wall carpeting, Colonial reproductions, brass lamps, Hitchcock rockers and prints from the owner's collection. Extras include a pool and coffee shop with a large fireplace. The place has attracted a regular clientele for its location and attention to detail. ~ 259 Elm Street; 413-584-7660, fax 413-586-4808. DELUXE.

The **Hotel Northampton** has undergone a facelift, converting a once semiseedy, middle-aged downtown hotel into something with a touch of class. There are 77 rooms here, including some with canopy beds and jacuzzis. The lobby is nicely decorated in a Colonial motif, and the hotel has become a favorite for Smith College parents for its accommodations and its proximity to the campus. Reservations advised. ~ 36 King Street, Northampton; 413-584-3100, 800-547-3529, fax 413-584-9455. MODERATE TO DELUXE.

Standing in the center of Amherst, the **Lord Jeffrey Inn** has been a fixture in this college town for decades. Many of its 50 rooms are decorated with antiques, and some overlook the lovely town common. The inn has the sedate feel of an Ivy League faculty club, with an elegant dining room and tavern, as well as several cozy public sitting rooms, comfortable arm chairs and a fireplace. It's located within walking distance of the shopping area and Amherst College. ~ 30 Boltwood Avenue; 413-253-2576, 800-742-0358, fax 413-256-6152. MODERATE TO DELUXE.

HIDDEN ► The Allen House is a wonderful Victorian inn (just five rooms, all with private baths) that opened in 1991. The owners painstakingly restored it to its original form, earning it the Historic Preservation Award from the Amherst Historical Commission. It's set on three wooded acres within walking distance of town. A big country breakfast and afternoon tea are included in the price of the room. ~ 599 Main Street, Amherst; 413-253-5000. MODERATE.

The Campus Center Hotel offers 116 rooms in standard low-cost hotel decor in a concrete highrise on the University of Massachusetts campus. The ambience is nothing special, but the hotel is convenient for visitors to the university, and the view of the Holyoke range and the campus is great. ~ University of Massachusetts, Amherst; 413-549-6000, fax 413-545-1210. MODERATE.

One of the few elegant old country inns in the northern Pioneer Valley, the century-old Deerfield Inn stands along a lovely, tree-lined street in Historic Deerfield. Its 23 rooms are decorated in antiques and Graeff fabric wallpaper. There's a comfortable sitting room with a fireplace to enjoy predinner drinks, and a good restaurant. The regular clientele from Boston and New York enjoy the ambience as well as the services of innkeepers Karl and Jane Sabo, themselves urban refugees. Breakfast and afternoon tea are included. ~ 81 Old Main Street; 413-774-5587, fax 413-773-8712. ULTRA-DELUXE.

Berkshire and Greater Springfield Bed and Breakfast is a reservation service that matches travelers with private homes and small country inns in the Pioneer Valley. ~ P.O. Box 211, Williamsburg, MA 01096; 413-268-7244. BUDGET TO ULTRA-DELUXE.

✔ CHECK THESE OUT—UNIQUE LODGING

- *Moderate:* Discover **The Allen House**, a painstakingly restored Victorian set on three wooded acres within walking distance of Amherst. *page 354*
- *Moderate to deluxe:* Turn in at the **Historic Merrell Inn**, where guests have been stopping since 1794. *page 367*
- *Deluxe:* Retreat to a 225-year-old tavern turned B & B at **River Bend Farm**, situated not far from Williams College campus. *page 366*
- *Deluxe to ultra-deluxe:* Conjure up images of a bygone era at the elegant **Red Lion Inn**, one of the few remaining wood hotels in America. *page 367*

Budget: under $50 Moderate: $50–$90 Deluxe: $90–$120 Ultra-deluxe: over $120

What the Pioneer Valley lacks in fancy eateries it makes up for with
a solid roster of good, moderately priced restaurants, including a
number of ethnic and vegetarian spots.

DINING

In downtown Springfield, **Tilly's** is a good choice for lunch or dinner, with an eclectic assortment of sandwiches, burgers, salads,
quiches and pasta. In the old days, this would have been called a "fern
bar," with a brick interior and a nice bar. The place used to be an old
hotel. Closed Sunday. ~ 1390 Main Street; 413-732-3613. BUDGET.

The **Yankee Pedlar Inn** offers breakfast, lunch and dinner. Traditional New England fare is served here, including clam chowder,
chicken pot pie, corned beef and cabbage, a large selection of seafood,
as well as dishes like seafood alfredo and grilled chicken teriyaki. The
dining room is a handsome Colonial-style scene, with working fireplaces and wood-planked walls. ~ 1866 Northampton Street, Holyoke; 413-532-9494. MODERATE TO DELUXE.

Joe's Café is a quintessential dive, with peeling paint and great
Italian food: eggplant parmigiana, spaghetti and a marvelous vegetarian pizza primavera. Mingle with the locals and college students
over pitchers of beer, and try to figure out exactly what that mural on
the wall means. Joe's is an oasis in an area fast succumbing to culinary gentrification. ~ 33 Market Street, Northampton; 413-584-
3168. BUDGET TO MODERATE.

At the other end of the Italian food spectrum is **Spoleto**, a local
favorite. This place is a real find, with imaginative Italian dishes at
reasonable prices. Dishes include a sublime chicken rollatini, homemade pasta served with shrimp, scallops, mussels and calamari, vegetarian lasagna and veal scaloppine. Desserts are homemade, and the
espresso is strong. ~ 50 Main Street, Northampton; 413-586-6313.
MODERATE.

Paul and Elizabeth's has a local following for its natural food
lunches and dinners. You might be tempted by their salads—hummus,
tabouli, spinach and egg—good soups, fish broiled with tamari, a vegetable and seafood tempura, sandwiches and pasta. Decor is light and
airy; some nights the place can be bursting with vegetarian baby
boomers and their vegetarian babies, but the staff always keeps its
cool. ~ Thorne's Market, 150 Main Street, Northampton; 413-584-
4832. BUDGET TO MODERATE.

Classe Café looks like your average coffee shop, with big plate
windows and cramped tables, but its menu includes a variety of
well-prepared vegetarian dishes, like hummus and homemade soups,
in addition to the usual burgers, shakes and salads. Popular with the
college crowd, it has a lively people-watching scene. ~ 168 North
Pleasant Street, Amherst; 413-253-2291. BUDGET.

Judie's is an Amherst dining institution, noted for its sun-room
view of the comings and goings of downtown Amherst, its chic clientele and wonderful desserts. The cuisine here is "nouvelle à la Judie"

and includes some unusual dishes like paella and a chicken breast salad stuffed into an oversized popover. Desserts include chocolate truffle fudge cake and fried bananas and ice cream. ~ 51 North Pleasant Street; 413-253-3491. BUDGET TO MODERATE.

The dining room at the **Lord Jeffrey Inn** is a good choice for a more formal meal (though in Amherst, a college town, *formal* means anything except jeans). It's a big Colonial-style room with a fireplace; tables are lit by oil lamps. Menu items include such dishes as grilled salmon filet, grilled New York sirloin and chicken prepared in a variety of ways, plus some house specialties, including a wonderful lemon-and-dill cured salmon as an appetizer and a Mediterranean vegetable pasta dish. There's a pianist on Friday and Saturday nights and at Sunday brunch. ~ 30 Boltwood Avenue; 413-253-2576. MODERATE TO DELUXE.

SHOPPING   **Shops at Baystate West** includes 50 department, specialty food, gift and clothing stores. ~ 1500 Main Street, Springfield; 413-733-2171.

Holyoke Mall at Ingleside has over 150 specialty and department stores, including **J. C. Penney** (413-536-3963), **Filene's Basement** (413-536-2777) and **Lord & Taylor's** (413-534-5800). ~ Exit 15, Route 91, Holyoke.

Thorne's Market is an old department store renovated into five floors of shops and boutiques, including a record store, bead store, clothing stores and toy shops, as well as a natural-foods restaurant. ~ 150 Main Street, Northampton; 413-584-5582.

A favorite Sunday excursion for locals, **Yankee Candle**, with its assortment of hundreds of hand-dipped candles, gifts and a remarkable Christmas shop with ornaments and toys from around the world. A bakery and café offer light lunches, and self-guided tours of the candlemaking plant are available. ~ Routes 5 and 10, South Deerfield; 413-665-8306.

The Pioneer Valley is especially noted for the large number of craftspeople who make their home here, and their presence is reflected in several fine shops in Northampton and beyond. A few worth looking into include:

In Northampton visit the **Pinch Pottery and the Ferrin Gallery**. ~ 179 Main Street; 413-586-4509.

In Shelburne Falls, check out the **Salmon Falls Artisans Showroom** ~ 1 Ashfield Street; 413-625-9833.

The town of Leverett offers **Leverett Crafts and Arts**. ~ Montague Road; 413-548-9070.

A list of members in the **Pioneer Valley Antique Dealers Association**, which guarantees authenticity of merchandise, is available by sending a SASE to them. ~ c/o Donald Schimke, Secretary, Hadley Place, Hadley, MA 01035.

Concerts, entertainment and sporting events are held regularly at the **NIGHTLIFE** **Springfield Civic Center and Symphony Hall**. ~ 1277 Main Street, Springfield; 413-787-6610.

Stagewest, Springfield's resident theater company, presents comedies and dramas during its season from September to May. ~ 1 Columbus Center; 413-781-2340.

The Paramount Performing Arts Center is an old theater restored to its 1929 grandeur. From September to late May, a variety of popular artists and comedians perform. ~ 1700 Main Street, Springfield; 413-734-5706.

For a wide array of folk, blues, African, Caribbean and Celtic music nightly in a coffeehouse setting check out the **Iron Horse Music Hall**. There's a good dancefloor and wide selection of imported beers at this intimate spot. Cover. ~ 20 Center Street, Northampton; 413-584-0610.

The Fine Arts Center at the University of Massachusetts offers concerts, plays, lectures and dance events year-round. ~ Amherst; 413-545-2511.

SKINNER STATE PARK 🏃🏇🏛 Located high atop the Holyoke **BEACHES** Range, this park offers a view of the Connecticut River that is remi- **& PARKS** niscent of Thomas Cole's painting *The Oxbow*, depicting an ancient bend in the river. Here the Summit House, a Victorian-style hotel built in 1851, has been restored as a visitors center. Birdwatchers can view hawk migrations in the park in mid-April and mid-September. There are horseback riding trails but no stables. Picnic area, restrooms; day-use fee on weekends and holidays, $3. ~ On Route 47 in Hadley; 413-586-0350.

▲ Nearby, at Daughters of the American Revolution State Forest (Route 112, Goshen; 413-268-7098), there are 50 tent/RV sites (no hookups); $12 per night (reservations available, two-night minimum).

MOUNT SUGARLOAF RESERVATION Jutting up out of the Connecticut River Valley farmland like a huge monument to nature, Mount Sugarloaf shows a red sandstone face and varied natural life. This forested, 652-acre reservation overlooks the Connecticut River from on high and is a foliage season favorite. Picnic areas, restrooms and lookout tower. Closed in winter. ~ Off Route 116 in Deerfield; 413-665-2928.

MOHAWK TRAIL STATE FOREST 🏃🏛 ⛵ One of the state's well-kept secrets, this forest covers over 6000 acres spread along the Deerfield and Cold Rivers. The old Indian Trail used by Mohawks to travel from upstate New York to the Pioneer Valley is etched into the woods here, and open fields and meadows lead down to the river. Fish for trout on the Deerfield River and take a dip in a sheltered, sandy pool off the Cold River, or in the more exciting "whirlies," small waterfalls downstream. This park has a regular camping clientele because of its size and the number of activities available. Picnic areas, showers, restrooms; groceries nearby in Greenfield, Shelburne Falls and Charlemont. ~ On Route 2 three miles west of Charlemont; 413-339-5504.

▲ There are 56 tent/RV sites (no hookups), $6 per night.

The Happy Valley

▼▼▼▼▼▼▼▼▼▼▼▼

To its many inhabitants of alternative sexual orientations, the Pioneer Valley is fondly referred to as "The Happy Valley." A scenic rural retreat with fine inns and restaurants, the Pioneer Valley is a relaxing vacation spot. With the second-largest lesbian population in the country (after the San Francisco Bay Area) and a sizable population of gay men, the Valley offers a rural version of the gay-friendly atmosphere found in such cities as New York or San Francisco.

A number of the Valley's happy denizens are spread out along quiet backroads and in the outskirts of towns, enjoying the peace of the country; many of the gay establishments, consequently, are also widely dispersed throughout the area. Northampton (or "Noho" to locals) serves as the pulse of the Valley's gay scene. It's here that you'll find the concentration of gay clubs, restaurants and inns. You can pick up a copy of *The Metroline*, a free bi-monthly, at local cafés. ~ 860-570-0825. Or you can get the Noho-based periodical, *The Lesbian Calendar,* at area bookstores for an update on local happenings. ~ 413-586-5514.

In addition to the places listed here, the Happy Valley's five colleges—especially Smith and the University of Massachusetts—sponsor gay dances and events just about every weekend. *The Five College Bulletin* (available in campus buildings and at bus-stop racks) is a good resource, or you can check flyers on campus to find out what's happening.

LODGING

The lesbian-run **Tin Roof Bed & Breakfast** offers three comfortably furnished guest rooms, with a shared bath, in a 1909 New England farmhouse. In the living room you'll find games, videos, a lesbian library and the resident cat. Set on two acres, the inn boasts a large yard and a beautiful garden. ~ P.O. Box 296, Hadley, MA 01035; 413-586-8665. BUDGET TO MODERATE.

On the outskirts of town, the **Old Red Schoolhouse** provides a peaceful retreat. This Colonial-style building was the first schoolhouse in the area when it was built in the early 19th-century. The entire inn, a suite with three guest rooms, a living room and a fully stocked kitchen, is available for one to six people. The decor is a combination of country antiques and art deco. One room has a fireplace, and the bathroom boasts a big, old clawfoot tub. Most of the guests are gay or lesbian. ~ 67 Park Street, Northampton; DELUXE.

In a row of old brick buildings in downtown East Hampton, the **Lesbian Towers** is right in the middle of things. You'll find a variety of large guest rooms, as well as suites with fully equipped kitchens. The rooms have a floral theme (lilac, lavender-rose and rosebud) and feature antique furniture and art deco decor. ~ 89 Main Street; 413-584-1228. MODERATE TO DELUXE.

Set on seven wooded acres only a few miles away from Northampton, **Innamorata** is a large Colonial home that has three spacious guest rooms with shared baths. Each room is decorated in a floral design and furnished with antique writing tables and sitting chairs. A sunporch wraps around one side of the house, and the cozy living room features a fireplace. The clientele is predominantly lesbian. ~ 47 Main Street, Goshen; 413-268-0300. MODERATE.

For gourmet vegetarian food, try lesbian-owned **Bela**. A lively, casual eatery with local art on the walls, Bela features an eclectic variety of healthful entrées. This is a popular spot with the gay crowd. ~ 68 Masonic Street, Northampton; 413-586-8011. BUDGET TO MODERATE.

DINING

The happening **Haymarket Cafe** serves coffee, tea and pastries and is always crowded with gays, lesbians and other alternative thinkers. ~ 185 Main Street, Northampton; 413-586-9969. BUDGET.

Named after the inventor of the graham cracker, Dr. Sylvester Graham, **Sylvester's Restaurant** is popular among both gays and straights. One dining area sports a decor that is 19th-century brick with a tin roof. The other is modern and airy with lots of windows. Lunch entrées include soups, salads and sandwiches. Steaks, seafood and pasta fill out the dinner menu. ~ 111 Pleasant Street, Northampton; 413-586-5343. BUDGET TO MODERATE.

Healthful, organic food is the focus at **The Copper Angel Cafe**. Choose between vegetarian, poultry and seafood dishes at this small, cozy restaurant decorated with heavenly creatures. For lunch, get a soup, salad or sandwich. For dinner try one of the seafood entrées such as pepper-seared scallops with basil-braised asparagus. Closed Tuesday from May through October; closed Monday and Tuesday from November through April. ~ 2 State Street, Shelburne Falls; 413-625-2727. MODERATE.

One of the area's best bookstores, **Northampton Pride & Joy** carries a wide range of literature, poetry and history, as well as one of the best selections of feminist and lesbian titles. ~ 20 Crafts Avenue; 413-585-0683.

SHOPPING

You'll find the **Food For Thought** bookstore well stocked with gay/lesbian and progressive political material. ~ 106 North Pleasant Street, Amherst; 413-253-5432.

Pearl Street Night Club features local and nationally known rock, jazz, blues, reggae and funk performers in an art deco–style nightclub. Wednesday is gay/lesbian night. Cover. ~ 10 Pearl Street, Northampton; 413-584-7771.

NIGHTLIFE

The Grotto offers live music on Thursday and Saturday, a gay/lesbian disco on Friday, open mike on Wednesday and blues on Monday. Cover. ~ 25 West Street, Northampton; 413-586-6900.

Wednesday is gay/lesbian night at the industrial-looking **Club Metro**. The club features dance music on Friday and Saturday; Sunday is salsa night. Cover. ~ 492 North Pleasant Street, Northampton; 413-582-9898.

The Berkshires

The lay of the land is different in the Berkshires. It's more rural than the Pioneer Valley and central Massachusetts, with more broad, open valleys and stretches of farmland and forest. There are three kinds of towns here: the old mill towns like Dalton and Great Barrington, which have their own red-brick, utilitarian beauty; small country towns like New Ashford and Monterey, with tree-lined greens, a general store or two and a white church; and the tourist towns like Lenox and Stockbridge, whose identities are closely tied to a plethora of cultural activities. Despite the tourism and second-home building boom of the 1980s, the area is still remarkably rural, and you can find yourself in a Lenox traffic jam one minute, and a few minutes later on the open road with nothing but lush green scenery around you.

The Berkshires have a noteworthy cultural heritage as well. For years, the hills drew authors, poets and artists for their natural beauty and remoteness. The rich followed. At the turn of the century, the area was nicknamed the "inland Newport" for the large number of wealthy families who built their ornate "cottages" (actually, they were 20-odd-room mansions!) here as summer retreats.

SIGHTS

The gateway to the northern Berkshires, the city of **North Adams** was once a thriving manufacturing center of textiles and electrical components. Today, the old mills lie idle, and North Adams is a bit down-at-the-heels. The city may be on the comeback trail, however, thanks to the construction of the **Massachusetts Museum of Contemporary Art**. The town hopes to turn a 28-building abandoned mill complex into the world's largest contemporary art museum (scheduled to open in Fall 1997). The complex is listed in the National Historic Register. ~ 87 Marshall Street, North Adams; 413-664-4481.

Natural Bridge State Park is the site of the only natural marble bridge in North America, formed by the raging waters of melting glaciers millions of years ago. Also interesting to look at are the many carvings done by quarrymen and visitors, many dating back to the 1800s. Open Memorial Day through Columbus Day. Admission. ~ Route 8, North Adams; 413-663-6392.

Traveling into downtown North Adams, you'll pass huge mills—monuments to bygone days. **Western Gateway Heritage State Park** has a fascinating exhibit on the construction of the four-and-three-

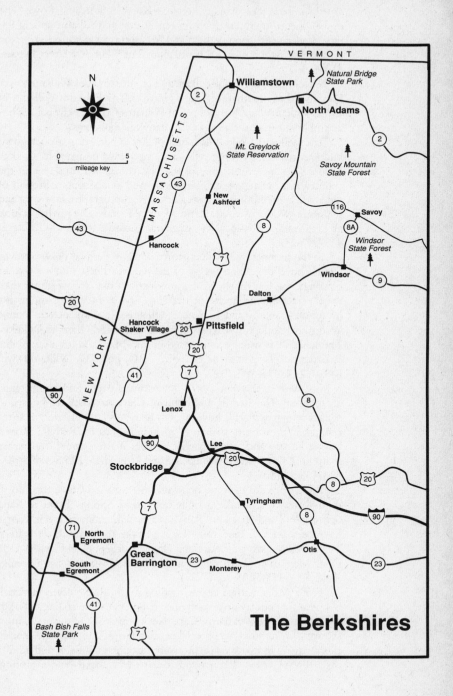

The Berkshires

fourths-mile Hoosac Tunnel between North Adams and Rowe. The tunnel opened up rail traffic between Boston and Albany, and, at the time of its construction in the mid-19th century, was considered to be an engineering wonder. ~ Off of Route 8 at 9 Furnace Street Bypass; 413-663-8059.

West on Route 2 is the college and culture town of Williamstown. Established as the town of "West Hoosuck" by Ephraim Williams in 1750, Williamstown is the home of **Williams College**. The college has a rambling, classical campus with many fine buildings.

The **Williams College Museum of Art** is housed in an octagonal building inspired by Monticello and a new wing designed by Charles Moore. The museum is one of the best college art museums in the country, with changing exhibitions as well as a strong collection of older and contemporary watercolors, oils, photographs, fabric art and sculpture. Works by Charles and Maurice Prendergast provide a look at 19th-century seaside New England. Closed Monday. ~ Route 2; 413-597-2429.

In the summer, the **Williamstown Theatre Festival** draws crowds from around the country. One of the nation's finest summer theater offerings, the festival showcases productions that are weightier than the average summer stock, such as *The Legend of Oedipus* and works by Anton Chekhov and Tennessee Williams. Regulars include Joanne Woodward and Paul Newman, Dianne Wiest and Olympia Dukakis. The schedule is usually announced in mid-May, and it's a good idea to order tickets as early as possible. ~ P.O. Box 517, Williamstown, MA 01267; 413-597-3399.

Just west of the center of Williamstown, you'll find another fine art museum. The **Sterling and Francine Clark Art Institute**, housed in a classical white marble building, has an extensive collection of 19th-century impressionist paintings, including ones by Renoir, Monet, Degas, Pisarro and Sisley, as well as older masters and 17th-century sculptures, prints and drawings. Closed Monday. ~ 225 South Street; 413-458-9545.

For a cool dip in some naturally therapeutic waters, turn north onto Route 7 and take a right onto Sand Springs Road to **Sand Springs Pool and Spa**. This place has a casual, family feel to it. People have been coming here since 1762 to take the natural, 74 waters. There are also two whirlpools, an Olympic-size pool and a baby pool. Open Memorial Day through Labor Day. Admission. ~ Sand Springs Road, 413-458-5205.

From Williamstown center heading south, Route 43 to Hancock is a pleasant country drive with open countryside and rolling hills dotted with tumbledown barns. **Caretaker Farm** is one of the area's most successful community-supported organic farms, and owners Sam and Elizabeth Smith invite visitors to walk through their fields and admire their diverse crops. It's a good idea to call ahead before visiting.

Closed Saturday afternoon, Sunday and November through April. ~
Route 43, Williamstown; 413-458-4309.

Stay on Route 43 long enough and you'll end up in Stephentown,
New York. But just before the state line, you'll come to a sign that
reads "Hancock Village." Turn right, and about a mile up on the right
is the **Babcock Barn Home,** home of Richard W. Babcock. He's ◄ *HIDDEN*
known around the country as "Mr. Barn" for his work restoring what
he calls "roots barns," built by first-generation immigrants to
America. The museum is an informal place, with three old barns, the
centerpiece of which is a giant, 200-year-old cider press, set up in a
300-year-old Dutch barn. Babcock is a talkative New England resource, a man who is passionate about preserving part of the region's
heritage. Call ahead to make sure he's there. ~ 413-738-5051.

If you love the furniture and crafts of the Shakers, you may also
enjoy learning more about how they lived, with a visit to **Hancock
Shaker Village.** Restored in the 1960s, the Shaker settlement at Hancock was the third of 18 communities to be established by the followers of Mother Ann Lee in the early 19th century. At its height in
the 1840s, the population in Hancock reached 250 members, divided
into six groups called "families." The Shaker economy was built on
agriculture, including the growing, processing and selling of medici-
nal herbs and seeds, as well as the crafting of furniture for which they
have become so well known. The guides stationed in the buildings are
an excellent source of information on the Shaker way of life. Crafts
demonstrations take place on a regular basis in many buildings, and
the village's round stone barn, originally built in 1826, is a real sight
to behold. For horticulturalists there are daily tours, occasional workshops and special dinners. Open April through November. (Note:
Visitors coming from the north on Route 7 should be aware that
Hancock Shaker Village cannot be reached through the town of Hancock. Keep heading south toward Pittsfield and take Route 20 west.)
Admission. ~ Route 20, five miles west of Pittsfield; 413-443-0188.

With a population of about 50,000, **Pittsfield** is the largest city in
Berkshire County, but it's not the most attractive. One exception to
Pittsfield's otherwise dull demeanor is the **Berkshire Museum.**
Established in 1903 by Zenas Crane, a member of the Crane paper
family, the museum has 18 galleries of permanent and changing exhibitions, including works by a number of Hudson River School
painters and early American portraits by Bierstadt, Copley and Peale.
There are also classic and modern sculptures as well as an aquarium
with a touch tank. Open daily in July and August; closed Monday the
rest of the year. Admission. ~ Route 7, Pittsfield; 413-443-7171.

"The **Lenox and Stockbridge** region is Berkshire in its best dress
suit and evening gown," wrote the authors of a Federal Writers
Project book on the Berkshires in 1939. The writers were no doubt
assessing the remnants of the so-called "Gilded Age" in the days be-

fore income taxes, when the Vanderbilts, Carnegies, Roosevelts and others frolicked at their famous "Berkshire Cottages."

These estates, with their ornate architecture, elaborate furnishings and lovely gardens hold an allure even for the staunchest of socialists. For your viewing pleasure are 20 to 25 summer mansions from the time when Lenox was known as the "Inland Newport." Among these estates are:

The Mount was the home of Pulitzer Prize–winning author Edith Wharton from 1902 to 1911. Wharton, in her day a recognized expert on interior design, designed the interior as well as the gardens. The white American Classical mansion has marble floors and fireplaces, elaborate molding and plaster ceilings, and beautiful grounds. During the summer, Shakespeare and Company at the Mount performs the Bard's plays as well as plays based on Wharton's books and on episodes of her life. Open Tuesday through Sunday from May through October; open daily in July and August. Admission. ~ Plunkett Street, Lenox; 413-637-1899.

Chesterwood is a Colonial Revival mansion that served as the summer estate of Daniel Chester French, sculptor of *The Minuteman* and the Lincoln Memorial. French traveled widely, and his home is decorated with a remarkable collection of European and American furnishings, antiques and sculptures gathered in his travels. The grounds feature country gardens and woodland walks, and his studio houses the small-gauge railroad track that French used to move his sculptures into the natural light for viewing. The plaster casts of the Lincoln statue were made here and, as you'll see, still dominate the interior. Closed November 1 to April 30. Admission. ~ Off of Route 183, Stockbridge; 413-298-3579.

Naumkeag, designed by Stanford White, was built in 1885 for Joseph Choate, the ambassador to England. The stately home remains an excellent example of turn-of-the-century design, in its architecture as well as its landscaping and furnishings. Though it is not the largest of the mansions, Naumkeag's collection of antiques and porcelain from the Far East make it worth a visit. And, like those of the other cottages, the gardens and grounds are magnificent. Closed Monday. Closed Columbus Day until Memorial Day. Admission. ~ Prospect Hill Road, Stockbridge; 413-298-3239.

Route 7 south of Lenox takes you through another piece of lovely farmland, where you'll get a sense of just how rural this area actually is. Before too long you'll come to the town of **Stockbridge**, a pretty, if increasingly glossy small town whose tree-lined main street is dominated by small shops and the rambling wooden Red Lion Inn. Stockbridge has been immortalized in popular culture in two very different ways: as the setting for Arlo Guthrie's song "Alice's Restaurant" (now La Fête Chez Vous) and as the subject of works by its most famous former resident, artist Norman Rockwell.

Stockbridge center is worth a stroll, with many shops and small galleries. One of the more interesting ones is the **Image Gallery,** owned and run by photojournalist Clemens Kalischer. Closed Sunday and Monday. ~ Main Street; 413-298-5500.

The home of poet William Cullen Bryant, **Great Barrington** is a departure from the country-style villages of Stockbridge and Lenox. Its funky downtown looks as though it came straight out of an old Jimmy Stewart movie.

For a pretty country drive, take Route 23 east from Great Barrington to Monterey, and head north to the town of Tyringham.

The **Tyringham Gallery,** featuring contemporary paintings, sculpture and ceramics, is in a fairytale-like cottage built in the 1930s by sculptor Sir Henry Kitson. The place could only be described as magical, with an undulating, thatched roof, large, jutting stones built into its walls and a sculpture garden with a lily pond and nature trail. Closed Columbus Day until Memorial Day. Admission. ~ Tyringham Road; 413-243-3260.

For further information on the Berkshires, contact the **Berkshire Hills Conference Visitors Bureau.** ~ Berkshire Common, West Street, Pittsfield; 413-443-9186.

LODGING

This area offers a larger selection of elegant accommodations and smaller bed and breakfasts. Restrictions are common here, however, and some of the room rate cards are as complicated as life insurance policies. In a nutshell: rates are highest (and they do get high!) on weekends in summer and fall; and most places close to Lenox require a two-night minimum stay on weekends during Tanglewood season, from mid-June through early September.

Budget lodging is virtually impossible to find in the Berkshires. One budgetary strategy is to make a home base in towns slightly away from the often-crowded and expensive Lenox-Stockbridge area. To the north, Williamstown offers a wider price range of motels and inns, with fewer restrictions. Just south of Stockbridge, the small towns of

---

NORMAN ROCKWELL AMERICANA

Though there are "Norman Rockwell museums" in other places around New England, the **Norman Rockwell Museum** is the only collection of original paintings authorized by the Rockwell family. The museum houses the largest collection of Rockwell art in existence, including selections from his *Saturday Evening Post* covers, early drawings for *St. Nicholas* magazine, portraits and advertising works and the famous Four Freedoms and Main Street at Christmas. Admission. ~ Route 183, Stockbridge; 413-298-4100.

South Egremont, Sheffield and Great Barrington offer many historic and pretty inns and bed and breakfasts.

A resort built around a country-inn motif, **The Orchards** offers 47 rooms individually decorated in English antiques and fancy bedspreads, some with fireplaces, refrigerators and marble-floored bathrooms. The ambience here is one of quiet elegance, despite the inn's incongruous proximity to the Route 2 commercial strip. Tea is served each afternoon in the graciously appointed lobby, and guests get a chocolate chip cookie with their turned-down beds each evening. Pool, sauna, concierge service and restaurant all on the premises. ~ Route 2, Williamstown; 413-458-9611, 800-225-1517, fax 413-458-3273. ULTRA-DELUXE.

The **Maple Terrace Motel** is a budget-conscious traveler's find. The 17 rooms are clean with standard motel decor, but the Maple Terrace, set back from the street, is a bit quieter than others along the highway. Behind the motel is an open field, with a spacious swimming pool, picnic tables, swings and several large weeping willow trees. This is a good place for families, within walking distance of the Williamstown Theater Festival, shopping and restaurants. ~ 555 Main Street, Route 2, Williamstown; 413-458-8101. MODERATE.

HIDDEN ►   **River Bend Farm** is a historic bed and breakfast set in a 225-year-old tavern built by Colonel Benjamin Simonds, one of the founders of Williamstown. The place has been meticulously restored and has shared baths and five rooms, each individually decorated in Colonial-style antiques. Its location makes it convenient to the Williams College campus. Gourmet breakfast. ~ 643 Simonds Road, Williamstown; 413-458-3121, 800-418-2057. DELUXE.

The **Canyon Ranch in the Berkshires** is an East Coast version of a famous Tucson fitness resort. It's housed at the 120-acre estate called Bellefontaine, one of the most ornate of the original Berkshire "cottages" and a replica of the French Petit Trianon built by Louis XV. The 120-room resort is geared for busy city folk looking for a bit of down time away from it all. There's a full fitness program, gourmet "spa cuisine," indoor and outdoor pools, walking trails and gardens. ~ Bellefontaine, Kemble Street, Lenox; 413-637-4100, 800-326-7080, fax 413-637-0057. ULTRA-DELUXE.

A very homey Berkshire cottage, **Garden Gables Inn** is a lovely white clapboard house built in 1780. Though it is located within walking distance of downtown Lenox, the inn is quiet and relaxed, with nice gardens and a swimming pool. The inn's 18 rooms are individually decorated in a mix of styles, and all have private baths; some have jacuzzis or fireplaces, others balconies with a view of the pool. The inn has many regular long-term visitors. Full breakfast is offered in a small dining room. ~ 141 Main Street, Lenox; 413-637-0193, fax 413-637-4554. DELUXE TO ULTRA-DELUXE.

The **Village Inn** is a 200-year-old hostelry with 32 rooms, all with private baths. All rooms are furnished with country antiques, some with working fireplaces and four-poster beds. This Federal-style building has served as an inn since 1775, and the innkeepers have restored and modernized the building without destroying its integrity. The low-beamed tavern downstairs offers a full bar. This place has a comfortable, homey feel despite its size and is conveniently located in the center of Lenox. ~ 16 Church Street, Lenox; 413-637-0020, 800-253-0917, fax 413-637-9756. DELUXE TO ULTRA-DELUXE.

Red Lion Inn is a New England classic. Built originally in 1773 as a stagecoach stop, the inn was destroyed by fire and rebuilt in 1897. Today, the rambling wooden structure is one of the few remaining old wood hotels in the country. An icon of the Berkshires, the Red Lion serves as the centerpiece of Stockbridge Center. The lobby-parlor, with its fireplace, comfortable old couches and rich Oriental rugs, is always full of visitors and diners. And there may be no finer place to enjoy a summer afternoon drink than from a rocking chair on the front porch. There are 109 rooms, including some suites with parlors, decorated with antiques and reproductions. Though it offers modern amenities, like an outdoor pool, the Red Lion is an elegant old lady of a place that conjures up images of a bygone era. ~ Main Street, Stockbridge; 413-298-5545, fax 413-298-5130. DELUXE TO ULTRA-DELUXE.

The Historic Merrell Inn wears its age well, having welcomed guests since 1794, when it was the next-to-last stop on a busy stagecoach route between northwestern Connecticut and the Berkshires. Original furnishings, such as the wooden birdcage bar in the dining room, the only complete and unmodified one of its kind in the country, adorn the inn. The nine guest rooms are luxurious and, for the most part, quite large, although a few of the bathrooms are small but adequate. All beds have canopies, and several of the rooms have working fireplaces. The owners continually search for antique furnishings that complement the inn's historic past. Take a look at the book in the dining room that records the names of the inn's visitors and their horses on the corresponding date in the early 19th century. ~ 1565 Pleasant Street, South Lee; 413-243-1794, 800-243-1794. MODERATE TO DELUXE.

◄ *HIDDEN*

For a bed and breakfast that focuses on informal hospitality—the innkeeper calls it a "chintz-free zone"—spend a night or two at **Race Brook Lodge** in the southwestern corner of Massachusetts. It's a restored barn with a variety of rooms (all with private bath). It also has suites, which are perfect for a small group. The country decor—quilts, understated stenciling and hooked rugs on plank floors—allows the beauty of the building to speak for itself. Take a walk from the lodge to the Race Brook waterfall, then up to the Appalachian Trail. Or poke around in the nearby antique shops: Sheffield is a mecca for antiquing fiends from all over New England. ~ 864 Under Mountain Road/Route 41, Sheffield; 413-229-2916, fax 413-229-6629. MODERATE TO DELUXE.

The **Egremont Inn** is a cozy country inn with 20 rooms decorated in 19th-century furnishings. A feeling of subdued elegance is conveyed by a long white porch where guests enjoy coffee and brunch during summer months. A Colonial-era tavern with a low, beamed ceiling adds to the ambience. The Egremont Inn has a full dining room, as well as a pool and tennis courts. Modified American plan offered on weekends, ultra-deluxe; bed and breakfast Sunday through Thursday. ~ Old Sheffield Road, South Egremont; 413-528-2111, 800-528-1780, fax 413-528-3284. MODERATE TO DELUXE.

Located in a 200-year-old New England home, the **Weathervane Inn** has ten rooms, all with private baths, plus a swimming pool and a fine dining room. This is a comfortable, informal place with a regular clientele. Modified American plan offered on weekends; bed and breakfast Sunday through Thursday. ~ Route 23, South Egremont; 413-528-9580, fax 413-528-1713. DELUXE TO ULTRA-DELUXE.

Berkshire Motor Inn offers proximity to southern Berkshire attractions in a motel setting, with indoor pool and sauna. For those who like to stay in places with televisions and no innkeepers to talk to, this is one of the few motels in the region. ~ 372 Main Street, Great Barrington; 413-528-3150. MODERATE TO DELUXE.

The Turning Point offers a nonsmoking environment in a handsome, 200-year-old brick inn that served as a stagecoach stop in the 19th century. Innkeepers Irving and Jamie Yost emphasize a healthy country ambience and offer vegetarian and whole-grain breakfasts, as well as fruit and herbal teas. The inn has six rooms and a two-bedroom ultra-deluxe-priced cottage, with lovely grounds and hiking trails through the surrounding woods and fields. ~ Route 23, Great Barrington; 413-528-4777. MODERATE TO DELUXE.

Berkshire and Greater Springfield Bed and Breakfast can match you up with private homes and small country inns in the Berkshire area. ~ P.O. Box 211, Williamsburg, MA 01096; 413-268-7244. BUDGET TO ULTRA-DELUXE.

DINING

There are many restaurants to choose from in the Berkshires, roughly divided into two classes: the expensive, fancy places that draw weekenders and visitors, and the places where locals eat, which are generally less expensive, casual and strong on all-American, meat-and-potatoes menus.

HIDDEN ►

Diner fans will adore **Miss Adams Diner**, a 1949 Worcester lunch car being restored to its original condition. Here the owners serve traditional diner breakfasts and lunches, along with some special touches, like hummus salads, cold blueberry soup and buckwheat flapjacks. Great homemade pies! Closed Monday. ~ 53 Park Street, Adams; 413-743-5300. BUDGET.

The **Cobble Café** dishes up meals to the locals, including the luminaries who drop by each summer to work at the Williamstown

Theatre Festival. The walls are adorned with artwork from local talent. Fare includes traditional breakfast plates and lunch items such as chicken *quesadillas* and Mediterranean salad. Dinner is more elaborate, with a creative American-cuisine menu that changes seasonally. ~ 27 Spring Street, Williamstown; 413-458-5930. MODERATE.

Church Street Café offers an eclectic lunch and dinner menu in a pleasant outdoor café or indoor setting in the heart of Lenox's shopping district. Lunch features sandwiches and burgers, as well as more exotic fare like Louisiana gumbo, tabouli salad and bean quesadillas; dinner features Thai beef salad, Jamaican "jerked" chicken and red chile pasta with corn, peppers, cilantro and jalapeños. Closed Sunday and Monday from Columbus Day to Memorial Day. ~ 65 Church Street, Lenox; 413-637-2745. MODERATE TO DELUXE.

Eating philosophies collide at **Cheesecake Charlie's and Wholesome Harold's**. Divided in two, the wholesome side of the establishment houses a health-food café that serves fare such as tofu salads and organic turkey and vegetable pâté sandwiches. Over on the decadent side is a bakery that sells a grand assortment of rich, creamy and butter-heavy pastries as well as (how'd you guess?) cheesecake. ~ 60 Main Street, Lenox; 413-637-3411. MODERATE TO DELUXE.

Gateways Restaurant is one of the most highly acclaimed dining spots in Lenox. The restaurant is located on the first floor of the small and elegant Gateways Inn, built in 1912 as the summer mansion of Harley Procter of Procter and Gamble. The entranceway is graced with a sweeping mahogany staircase, rich tapestries and beautiful flower arrangements. Gateways offers southern Italian cuisine such as *orecchiette con braciole* ("little ears" pasta and veal stuffed with parmesan, garlic and parsley), osso buco served with risotto and rack of

---

✔ **CHECK THESE OUT—UNIQUE DINING**

- *Budget:* Sink into a seat at **Miss Adams Diner**, a restored 1949 Worcester lunch car serving great homemade pies. *page 368*
- *Budget to moderate:* Try to figure out the meaning of the mural on the wall as you dine with locals at **Joe's Café**, a quintessential dive serving robust Italian food. *page 355*
- *Moderate to deluxe:* Rearrange your schedule to make a stop at the **Salem Cross Inn**, where meats are roasted over a fieldstone open pit as they were in the 1700s. *page 344*
- *Ultra-deluxe:* Imagine yourself in 19th-century Italy at **Wheatleigh**, a palazzo built for a countess that now serves French cuisine—jackets for men preferred, please. *page 370*

Budget: under $8 Moderate: $8–$16 Deluxe: $16–$24 Ultra-deluxe: over $24

lamb *provinciale.* ~ 51 Walker Street; 413-637-2532. MODERATE TO DELUXE.

Wheatleigh is a restaurant of some renown, within walking distance of Tanglewood. It's a special spot, known for fine food and formal service, located in a restored 19th-century Italian palazzo built for a countess. The decor recalls the splendor of the Gilded Age, with a fireplace and crystal chandeliers. Wheatleigh serves contemporary French cuisine in five-course, *prix-fixe* meals, and the menu includes such imaginative items as red snapper with sauce Genovoise and roast pheasant with fresh white truffles. Reservations required; jackets for men are preferred. Closed Tuesday from Labor Day until Memorial Day. ~ Hawthorne Road, Lenox; 413-637-0610. ULTRA-DELUXE.

The **Red Lion Inn** has a menu that combines traditional New England fare like roast turkey and prime rib with such Continental dishes as shrimp scampi. You can choose the Colonial-style formal dining room, with pink-and-rose wallpaper and Norman Rockwell prints on the walls, and fresh flowers on the table. Or try the more casual tavern, with its publike atmosphere, wide-plank floorboards and beamed ceiling. In good weather, meals are served in the courtyard. ~ Main Street, Stockbridge; 413-298-5545. DELUXE TO ULTRA-DELUXE.

Once an old blacksmith's shop, and yes, even an old mill, **The Old Mill** is now one of the nicer restaurants in the southern Berkshires. The menu includes grilled salmon filet with orange fennel salsa and veal chop with morel sauce, in addition to chicken, steaks and chops. The building itself is a handsome one, set on a river, with large beams, rough wood paneling and old tools decorating the interior walls. Closed Monday November through May. ~ Route 23, South Egremont; 413-528-1421. DELUXE.

Right on Main Street in Great Barrington is **La Tomate**, a French bistro with black-and-white photos of Parisian scenes adorning its walls. Expect terrific Provençal dishes such as bouillabaisse, *tarte á l'oignons*, and *mousse au chocolat.* ~ 293 Main Street; 413-528-3003. MODERATE.

The **Castle Street Café** is a lively little bistro known for its creative pastas and grilled fish dishes. It's a handsome spot with an exposed brick wall. There's a small bar in the back. Closed Tuesday. ~ 10 Castle Street, Great Barrington; 413-528-5244. MODERATE TO DELUXE.

SHOPPING   Serious antique hunters head to the southern Berkshires and the towns of Egremont, South Egremont and Sheffield. There are dozens of shops in this corner of the state, featuring pieces from early American to European to deco to plain old junk. One of the better shops is **Bird Cage Antiques** for antique furnishings, jewelry and silver. ~ Route 23, in the South Egremont Post Office building; 413-528-3556.

For 18th and 19th century formal antique furniture and decorative accessories, stop by **Darr Antiques and Interiors**. ~ 28 South Main Street, Sheffield; 413-229-7773.

Or check out **Centuryhurst Berkshire Antique Gallery** for old American clocks, Wedgwood and a large collection of Wallace Nutting photographs. Forget the bargains here, however; the area's proximity to New York City money has raised the antique ante substantially. ~ Main Street, Sheffield; 413-229-8131.

During the summer **The Orchards** features soft rock by a piano and guitar duo in its pub. ~ Route 2, Williamstown; 413-458-9611.

NIGHTLIFE

Lenox is home to **Tanglewood,** where the Boston Symphony Orchestra performs through the summer months. For program and ticket information call 617-266-1492 (between October and June) or 413-637-1600 (between June and September). ~ Route 183.

The **Berkshire Performing Arts Theater** is a 1200-seat concert hall featuring jazz, country, rock and folk performers as well as comedy acts. Open in summer only. ~ 70 Kemble Street, Lenox; 413-637-4718.

Shakespeare and Company offers theatrical performances during the May through October season. ~ The Mount, Lenox; 413-637-3353.

Jacob's Pillow Dance Festival produces summer dance performances featuring companies from a variety of distant lands, including Cambodia, Indonesia and India. Open late June through August. ~ George Carter Road, Becket; 413-243-0745.

In Stockbridge the **Lion's Den** regularly showcases folk music with occasional bluegrass, blues and jazz. ~ Red Lion Inn, Main Street; 413-298-5545.

SAVOY MOUNTAIN STATE FOREST

BEACHES & PARKS

Nearly 11,000 acres, this popular retreat bordering on the Berkshire hills is favored by families. North and South ponds offer fishing and swimming, and campsites are in an old apple orchard. The park has miles of hiking trails, including a route to Tannery Falls. The dramatic set of cascading waterfalls that once powered small mills there is now one of the prettiest spots in western Massachusetts. There's good trout fishing in North Pond, and trout and bass are found in Burnett and Bogg ponds. North Pond and South Pond have swimming beaches. Non-motorized boats are allowed. Picnic areas, restrooms, nature center; groceries are in North Adams; parking fee, $2. Closed mid-October to mid-May. ~ Off Routes 2 and 116 in Savoy; 413-663-8469.

▲ There are 45 tent/RV sites (no hookups); $6 per night; information, 413-664-9567. There are also cabins available that sleep up to four people ($8 per night); reservations are required and are taken six months in advance.

Text continued on page 374.

The Sounds of Music in Rural Massachusetts

It's said that New England has only two seasons, July and winter. That's not exactly true, of course, but folks here do try to pack as much as possible into the fleeting times of good weather. Case in point: the large number of concerts and music festivals held in this area during summer and autumn, many spreading out under the warm, open skies. In central and western Massachusetts, visitors have some rich choices when it comes to music, from Cuban jazz under the stars to chamber music in a church.

The undisputed king of the music festivals in this region, and perhaps in the whole country, takes place at **Tanglewood**, the 210-acre Lenox summer home of the Boston Symphony Orchestra. ~ Before mid-June, contact Symphony Hall, Boston, MA 02115; 617-266-1492. After mid-June, contact West Street, Lenox, MA 01240; 413-637-1600.

Tanglewood takes its name from a story by Nathaniel Hawthorne, and, with its tall and stately pine trees, rolling lawns and nearby mountains, the place is renowned for its physical beauty as well as the quality of the musicians and composers who perform there. These have included Leonard Bernstein, John Williams, Yo-Yo Ma, Itzhak Perlman and jazz performers like Ella Fitzgerald and Ray Charles.

Weekend symphony concerts are held Friday through Sunday in July and August, and chamber music concerts take place most Thursdays and other selected weeknights. Saturday morning rehearsals are open to the public (admission), providing an opportunity to see music-making in a more relaxed setting.

Seating is available in the Shed, a covered, open-air theater, or, more reasonably, on the lawn. The tradition on the lawn is to bring a blanket or lawn chairs and an elaborate picnic lunch or dinner, complete with candelabra and champagne.

Tanglewood is just one of many music series and festivals in this region, offering all types of music in some spectacular settings. A sampling of some others:

South Mountain Concerts, a chamber music series running from August to October, takes place in the acoustically superb, 400-seat South Mountain Concert Hall, built in 1918 and listed in the National Historic Register. ~ Box 23, Pittsfield; 413-442-2106.

Stockbridge Summer Music Series includes light opera, classical music, cabaret and jazz concerts performed in a turn-of-the-century mansion (Seven Hills Country Inn). A dinner is served on the estate's rolling lawn before the performance. ~ 148 Summer Street, Lanesboro, MA 01237; 413-443-1138.

Mohawk Trail Concerts offers summer and fall chamber music concerts in the intimate setting of a charming old white clapboard Federated church on the Mohawk Trail in Charlemont. ~ P.O. Box 75, Shelburne Falls, MA 01370; 413-625-9511.

Bright Moments Jazz Festival is one of Amherst's biggest summer assets, featuring Caribbean, Afro-pop and jazz concerts on the lawn by the campus pond on Thursday nights in July.

Although it's always a good idea to reserve tickets ahead of time for most of these events, last-minute seats are generally available. Check out the local newspapers for concert dates and times, and bring a sweater for those summer evenings that can turn cool once the sun goes down. ~ University of Massachusetts; 413-545-2511.

WINDSOR STATE FOREST 🏃 🏊 🚣 This spot is known for the spectacular Windsor Jambs, a half-mile-long series of waterfalls that travel through sheer granite cliff gorges of up to 100 feet. There are many old roads and trails for hiking and a good 100-foot sandy beach on a dammed-up spot on the Westfield River. There's good trout fishing in the West Branch of the Westfield River. This is a popular place for families with small children. Open Memorial Day through Labor Day. Picnic areas, restrooms; groceries are nearby in Adams; day-use fee, $2. ~ On River Road off Route 9 in Windsor; 413-684-0948, in summer; 413-442-8928, in winter.

▲ There are 25 sites recommended for tents only; $4 per night.

MOUNT GREYLOCK STATE RESERVATION 🏃 🚵 🏕 🚣 If you have time for a visit to only one park on your tour of the area, this is the one to see. This 11,000-acre reserve is atop the state's highest mountain. Immortalized by Thoreau, Hawthorne and Melville, Mount Greylock is noted for the number of rare species of bird and plant life, and the views in all directions are truly breathtaking. Hiking trails—including a stretch of the Appalachian Trail—and nordic ski trails are plentiful. Picnic areas, restrooms; Bascom Lodge (413-743-1591) has a snack bar and offers evening camp dinners by reservation. ~ Off Route 7 in Lanesboro or off Route 2 in North Adams; 413-499-4262.

▲ There are 35 sites; $4 per night.

MT. WASHINGTON STATE FOREST 🏃 🚵 🏇 🏕 🎣 🚣 This 5000-acre expanse stands on the New York–Connecticut–Massachusetts border. The forest spreads out over mountainous, densely wooded land, and there's a feeling of isolation and solitude here. Even during daylight, watch for deer as you drive into the area; they seem to be everywhere. **Bash Bish Falls State Park**, within the state forest, is home to Bash Bish Falls, featuring 80-foot drops and cascading pools, along with the serene view of farmland. You can also angle for trout in brooks and streams. All this provides a great escape from the sometimes-maddening crowds of Stockbridge and Lenox. Non-motorized boats only. Picnic areas, restrooms; groceries in Great Barrington and Egremont. ~ Off Route 41 in Mount Washington; 413-528-0330.

▲ There are 15 primitive, hike-in sites; no fee.

▼▼▼▼▼▼▼▼▼▼▼▼▼

Outdoor Adventures

The large number of lakes, ponds and rivers in this region provide ample opportunities for canoers and kayakers.

CANOEING AND KAYAKING

CENTRAL MASSACHUSETTS In central Massachusetts, canoe, kayak and rowboat rentals are available at **Fin and Feather Sports**. ~ Route 140, Upton; 508-529-3901.

PIONEER VALLEY In the Pioneer Valley, **Zoar Outdoors** offers raft trips, canoe rentals and canoe and kayak instruction on the Deerfield River. ~ Mohawk Trail, Charlemont; 413-339-4010. Canoe rentals are also available at **Barton Cove Nature and Camping Area** ~ Route 2, Gill; 413-863-9300.

THE BERKSHIRES In the Berkshires try **Berkshire Outfitters**. ~ Route 8, Adams; 413-743-5900.

A fishing license is required for all freshwater fishing in Massachusetts.

FISHING

PIONEER VALLEY In Northampton, visit **Pioneer Sporting Center**. ~ 104 Damon Road; 413-584-9944. Rod and reel aficionados may also want to visit **Thomas and Thomas Rod Makers**. ~ 22 3rd Street, Turners Falls; 413-863-9727.

THE BERKSHIRES Fishing gear is available at **Dave's Sporting Goods**. ~ 1164 North Street, Pittsfield; 413-442-2960. You can also try **Pittsfield Sporting Goods**. ~ 180 North Street, Pittsfield; 413-443-6078.

The downhill ski areas in this region are tame compared to their sisters to the north, but lift lines are often shorter, the ambience less pretentious and the lift tickets cheaper. These are also good places to take the family.

SKIING

PIONEER VALLEY In Princeton, you can hit the slopes at **Wachusett Mountain**. ~ 499 Mountain Road, off Route 140; 508-464-5101. In Holyoke visit **Mount Tom**. ~ Route 5; 413-536-0516. In Charlemont, there's **Berkshire East**. ~ Mohawk Trail; 413-339-6617.

You can also find good cross-country skiing in this area. For wide, well-groomed trails, try **Northfield Mountain**. ~ Route 63, Northfield; 413-659-3714. For a more rustic ski on narrower trails through the woods, try **Stump Sprouts Ski Touring Center and Guest Lodge**. ~ West Hill Road, Hawley; 413-339-4265. Also try any of the region's state parks, most of which offer good trails, groomed by the ubiquitous (and noisy) skimobile crowd.

THE BERKSHIRES In New Ashford, try the runs of **Brodie Mountain Ski Area**. ~ Route 7; 413-443-4752. In Hancock test the slopes at **Jiminy Peak, the Mountain Resort**. ~ Corey Road; 413-738-5500. In Great Barrington there's **Butternut Basin**. ~ Route 23; 413-528-2000.

Those who prefer cross-country skiing will find some wonderful spots here, from open farmland to quiet, wooded state parks.

The wide open spaces offer several good golfing spots in the region.

GOLF

CENTRAL MASSACHUSETTS You can tee off at **Crumpin-Fox Club**. ~ Parmenter Road, Bernardston; 413-648-9101. In Worcester try **Green Hill Golf Course**. ~ Marsh Avenue; 508-852-0913.

THE BERKSHIRE In South Williamstown visit **Waubeeka Golf Links**. ~ Routes 7 and 43; 413-458-5869. In Lanesboro there's **Skyline Country Club**. ~ 405 South Main Street, Route 7; 413-445-5584.

BICYCLING Steep mountains in western Massachusetts make bicycle traveling between regions difficult, but once you're settled in, bicycling is a great way to explore the country backroads.

PIONEER VALLEY In the Pioneer Valley, the Amherst-Northampton area offers some fairly flat and easy rides. The **Northampton Bicycle Path** begins at the end of State Street and ends up two-and-three-tenths miles later in Look Park. Several local bicycle groups also offer weekend day-trips, including the **Franklin Hampshire Freewheelers**. Schedules of the group's trips and events are available in local bike shops. ~ 413-527-4877.

THE BERKSHIRES Brooks Country Cycling and Hiking Tours offers weekend tours that include inn accommodations in the Lenox-Stockbridge area. ~ 140 West 83rd Street, New York, NY 10024; 212-874-5151.

Bike Rentals In the Berkshires, **Valley Bicycles** rents mountain and hybrid bikes. ~ 319 Main Street, Amherst; 413-256-0880. In the Pioneer Valley, **The Spoke** has one-, three- and ten-speeds by the day, weekend, week and month. ~ 618 Main Street, Williamstown; 413-458-3456. **Plaine's Bike Golf Ski** rents bikes by the day, week and month. ~ 55 West Housatonic Street, Pittsfield; 413-499-0294.

HIKING There's no better way to experience the natural beauty of the hills and mountains of this region than on your own two feet, particularly during fall foliage season, when the highways can seem like parking lots. Hiking opportunities abound at any of the region's state parks and conservation areas.

Some private companies offer tours geared to the serious hiker. **New England Hiking Holidays** offers hiking tours of the Berkshires as well as other New England locales. ~ P.O. Box 1648, North Conway, NH 03860; 603-356-9696. Nature photographer and tracker **Paul Rezendes** combines hiking tours with nature photography and animal tracking workshops. ~ Bearsden Road, Star Route, South Royalston, MA 01331; 508-249-8810.

CENTRAL MASSACHUSETTS The **Mid State Trail** (91 miles) travels from Mount Watatic at the New Hampshire state border through Worcester County to the Rhode Island border. The trail offers a mixed bag of central Massachusetts scenery, traveling along old cart roads, through forests and across open fields. You can pick up stretches of the trail in several spots in the Worcester area, including Douglas State Forest in Douglas and Rutland State Park in Rutland.

Wachusett Mountain State Reservation offers a comprehensive network of 18 trails (total 17 miles) through nearly 2800 acres, with some steep going in parts. Trails take you through hardwood forests of oak and maple, past stands of mountain laurel, spring wildflowers, ponds and meadows. You may catch a view of some wildlife on the mountain, and this area offers some good trails for fall foliage vistas. ~ 508-464-2987.

PIONEER VALLEY   The **Big River Trail** (.5 mile) at Laughing Brook Education Center and Wildlife Sanctuary (Hampden; 413-566-8034) takes you along the Laughing Brook (named by author Thornton Burgess, a one-time resident), across a bridge to the Scantic River and along a boardwalk through a red maple swamp. Burgess' home, the oldest residence in Hampden, may be toured during the summer.

At Arcadia Wildlife Sanctuary in Easthampton, the **Fern Trail** (1 mile) takes you past many different types of ferns and includes an observation tower for birdwatching. It is one of many self-guided trails that wind through some 650 acres of forests on an ancient oxbow of the Connecticut River.

The **Enfield Lookout Trail** (3 miles) at Quabbin Park leads up to the Enfield Overlook, from which you can spot eagles in the winter months. The trail is part of a 22-mile network that takes you through the largest piece of wilderness land in the state.

Located at Northfield Mountain Recreation and Environmental Center (413-659-3714), the **Hidden Quarry Nature Trail** (1 mile) offers a minicourse in the geology and natural history of the upper Pioneer Valley. The trail winds past the ancient beds of Lake Hitchcock, as well as porcupine dens, wooded wildflowers and stands of eastern white pine.

THE BERKSHIRES   **Pike's Pond Trail** (.5 mile) at Pleasant Valley Wildlife Sanctuary in Lenox takes you through fields and forest and ends up near beaver habitats on the pond and nearby Yokun Brook. Other trails at the sanctuary run past meadows, a hemlock gorge and a hummingbird garden.

One of the Berkshires' better-known hiking spots is Bartholomew's Cobble, a rocky-topped hill named after 18th-century farmer George Bartholomew. The **Bailey Trail** (1 mile) at the Cobble is a large

✔ **CHECK THESE OUT—UNIQUE OUTDOOR ADVENTURES**

- Cross-country ski while taking in the views from **Mount Greylock State Reservation,** a mountain reserve immortalized by Thoreau, Hawthorne and Melville. *page 374*
- Angle for trout in small brooks and streams or take in the cascading waterfalls in the **Mount Washington State Forest.** *page 374*
- Trek through hardwood forests and fields of wildflowers, on the hiking trails of **Wachusett Mountain State Reservation.** *page 376*
- View summer hawk migrations along the Connecticut River from high atop the Holyoke Range at **Skinner State Park.** *page 357*

loop that leads into the **Sparrow Trail** (1 mile). It's a gentle walk along the flood plain of the Housatonic River, through silver maple groves and rich deciduous woods and past an old oxbow. The Cobble offers wonderful views of the Housatonic Valley and, in late April and early May, a beautiful array of wildflowers.

▼▼▼▼▼▼▼▼▼▼

Transportation

CAR

This area is easily accessible from **Route 90**, the **Massachusetts Turnpike**, which runs the entire length of the state's southern half and has exits at Worcester, Sturbridge, Springfield and Stockbridge.

From Boston, **Route 2** offers a scenic highway route to the famed Mohawk Trail and the northern portions of central and western Massachusetts.

AIR

Many people fly into Boston's **Logan International Airport** (see Chapter Four). The area is also served by **Bradley International Airport** in Windsor Locks, Connecticut (see Chapter Two), near Hartford, and **Worcester Municipal Airport**, a smaller but increasingly popular alternative to Logan, which is serviced by Continental Express and USAir Express. Those who are combining a trip to the Berkshires with a visit to Vermont may want to use **Albany County Airport** in Albany, New York.

Peter Pan Bus Lines (413-781-3320) provides regular shuttles between Bradley International and the Springfield Bus Terminal at 1780 Main Street.

There's no public transportation to or from the airport. **Worcester Airport Limousine** provides door-to-door van and minibus shuttle service between the airport and points in Worcester County, including Sturbridge. ~ 508-756-4834.

Taxis serving the Worcester airport include **Yellow Cab** (508-754-3211), **Arrow Cab** (508-756-5184) and **Red Cab** (508-752-5601).

BUS

All long distance bus lines operate from terminals at 75 Madison Street, Worcester, and 1780 Main Street, Springfield.

Greyhound Bus Lines (800-231-2222) links Worcester and Springfield with the Berkshires, Boston and New York City. **Peter Pan Bus Lines** (800-343-9999) provides transportation to Boston; points west, including Springfield, Amherst, Northampton, the Berkshires and Albany; and points south, including Hartford and New York City. **Bonanza Bus Lines, Inc.** (413-781-3320) connects Springfield with the Berkshires, Albany and Providence, Rhode Island. **Vermont Transit Lines** (413-781-1500) connects Springfield with points north: Northampton, Vermont, New Hampshire and Canada.

TRAIN

Amtrak serves the Worcester area from New York City and Albany. The *Montrealer* leaves New York City each day with stops in Amherst, and there are several trains daily between Springfield and New

York's Pennsylvania Station. ~ 45 Shrewsbury Street, Worcester; 66 Lyman Street, Springfield; 800-872-7245.

From the Worcester airport, you can rent a car from **Avis Rent A Car** (800-331-1212), **Hertz Rent A Car** (800-694-3131) or **National Interrent** (800-328-4567).

CAR RENTALS

In central Massachusetts, **Worcester Regional Transit Authority** has bus service to local destinations within Worcester County. ~ 508-791-2389. In the Pioneer Valley, **Pioneer Valley Transit Authority** offers frequent service throughout greater Springfield, Holyoke, Northampton and Amherst. ~ 413-781-7882. During the school year, the free **Five-College Bus Service** links the campuses of the University of Massachusetts, Smith College, Mount Holyoke College, Amherst College and Hampshire College. ~ 413-545-0056. **Greenfield Montague Transportation Area** provides bus service throughout greater Greenfield, South Deerfield, Montague and Turners Falls. ~ 413-773-9478.

PUBLIC TRANSIT

In the Berkshires, **Berkshire Regional Transit Authority** links Pittsfield with Williamstown, North Adams, Lenox, Lee, Stockbridge and Great Barrington. ~ 413-499-2782.

EIGHT

Vermont

Vermont offers a soothing dose of old-fashioned Americana, a carefully tended piece of pastoral utopia that's down-home, uphill and intrinsically genuine. Here, dreams are lived, farms are cultivated and children are raised the traditional ways. Vermonters are at peace with their land—and it shows.

Its candid beauty is unpretentious and beguiling, a patchwork of slumbering red barns, tangled country roads and old covered bridges riveted against a backdrop of emerald mountains that twist through the heart of the state. Forming the backbone of Vermont's terrain, those towering Green Mountains—New England's oldest range—burst forth some five billion years ago when the earth's crust trembled and buckled.

Though only 9528 square miles in size, Vermont explodes with soul-gripping tableaux—alpine ridges and surging rivers, sporadic flatlands and miles of untamed wilderness. Skinny at the bottom and wide on top, this New England wedge spans an easy 151 miles in length and ranges in width from 41 miles at the Massachusetts border to 90 miles at the Canadian line.

But more than just a spot to behold, Vermont is a place to *be*. For its magic persists not only in its glorious scenery but also in its illustrious history and fastidious Yankee ideals and uncomplicated mode of existence.

Vermont may be the only landlocked New England state (a detail many Vermonters remain quite touchy about), but travelers need only scan the shores of vast Lake Champlain to find a coastline whose beauty parallels any Atlantic Ocean vista.

It was, in fact, that extraordinary lake that seduced the state's first European explorers back in 1609. Frenchman Samuel de Champlain, accompanied by native Algonquian Indians, who told great tales of mysterious waters, led an expedition from Canada and instantly claimed the lake (modestly naming it for himself) and surrounding lands for France.

During the next two centuries, the French, British and Dutch grappled to control the waterway, the sixth largest freshwater lake in the United States. The scrap was finally settled during the War of 1812, when an American naval fleet won a battle off Valcour Island.

Vermont found itself entangled in a different kind of tug-of-war during the mid-1700s, when its territory was claimed by both New York and New Hampshire. England eventually ruled in favor of New York, prompting settlers who had come from New Hampshire to organize a Vermont military force known as the Green Mountain Boys. This troupe, led by Ethan Allen, harassed New York landholders and went on to defeat the British in several decisive American Revolution battles, including the Battle of Bennington.

A flamboyant patriot determined to conquer any who attempted to steal his precious state, Allen vowed to preserve the independence of Vermont or "retire with my hardy Green Mountain boys into the caverns of the mountains and make war on all mankind."

The state supposedly earned its moniker from those cavernous Green Mountains when, in 1763, the Reverend Samuel Peters ascended Killington Peak and proclaimed his beautiful surroundings *Vert Mont*, French for Green Mountain.

Though New Hampshire inevitably surrendered its claims to Vermont, New York persisted. In July of 1777, Vermonters called a convention in the town of Windsor, drew up a constitution and declared their independence.

Drafted by 72 delegates who met for seven arduous days in a town tavern, the constitution prohibited slavery and was the first to establish suffrage for all men. According to local lore, the Windsor document was nearly abandoned by the delegates, who were about to dash off to fight advancing British forces at the state's west border when a fierce storm arose and prevented their leaving.

Despite pleas to the Continental Congress for recognition as a state, Vermont was forced to remain an independent republic for 14 years because of boundary disputes with New York. Finally, in 1791, both sides acquiesced and Vermont became the 14th state.

Early 19th-century Vermont was a land of milk and honey, where cows outnumbered people and people took to fashioning grand Victorian estates and lobbying for abolition. But prosperous times turned tumultuous during the Civil War, as half of Vermont's young men headed for the battlefield. When it was all over, Vermont had lost a larger percentage of its men than any other state. The four-year war caused population and economic devastation that affected the state for more than 40 years.

Tourism eventually helped set things straight during the early 1900s, when word got out that Vermont was "The Switzerland of North America." Well-to-do New Yorkers set up fancy summer estates, developers threw up dozens of roadside attractions and interstate highways helped fuel the influx. Suddenly, the land boom was on.

By the 1950s, yet another new breed of visitors—the kind with skis—arrived en masse. Much to the dismay of firmly rooted Vermonters, dozens of ski runs were carved in the mountainsides, and resorts were planted where dense forests once thrived.

Today, ski resort areas remain the only real tokens of full-scale development in Vermont, often called the most rural state in the nation. Yankee conservatism has spawned a rigorous array of zoning and antipollution laws meant to stave off mass growth. Vermonters' sentiments toward development were summed up by former Governor Thomas P. Salmon in 1973 when he declared: "Vermont is not for sale."

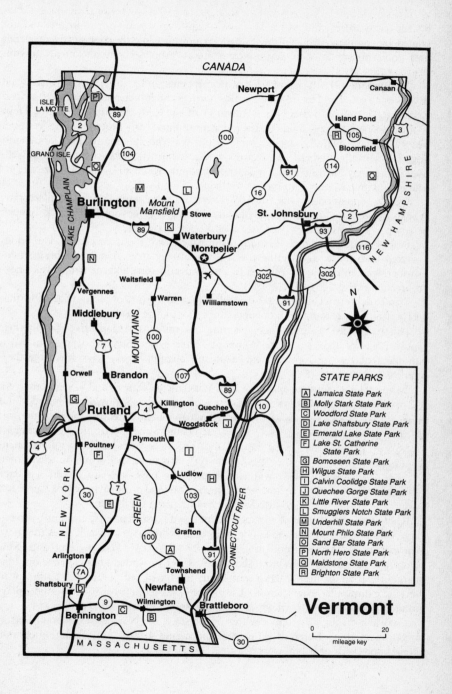

CANADA

Newport

Canaan

ISLE LA MOTTE

Island Pond

Bloomfield

GRAND ISLE

Burlington

Mount Mansfield

Stowe

St. Johnsbury

Waterbury

Montpelier

Waitsfield

Warren

Williamstown

Vergennes

Middlebury

Orwell

Brandon

Killington

Quechee

Rutland

Woodstock

Poultney

Plymouth

Ludlow

Grafton

Arlington

Shaftsbury

Townshend

Newfane

Bennington

Wilmington

Brattleboro

MASSACHUSETTS

LAKE CHAMPLAIN

GREEN MOUNTAINS

CONNECTICUT RIVER

NEW YORK

NEW HAMPSHIRE

N

STATE PARKS

A Jamaica State Park
B Molly Stark State Park
C Woodford State Park
D Lake Shaftsbury State Park
E Emerald Lake State Park
F Lake St. Catherine State Park
G Bomoseen State Park
H Wilgus State Park
I Calvin Coolidge State Park
J Quechee Gorge State Park
K Little River State Park
L Smugglers Notch State Park
M Underhill State Park
N Mount Philo State Park
O Sand Bar State Park
P North Hero State Park
Q Maidstone State Park
R Brighton State Park

Vermont

0   20

mileage key

Forests still cover 78 percent of the state, and a 1960s law banning all roadside billboards has worked wonders for Vermont's highways, which remain pristine and untainted by commercialism. In the 1980s, Vermont became the first state to prohibit automobile air conditioners that use chlorofluorocarbons, chemicals known to damage the ozone layer.

Through the years, Vermont's feisty independence and great beauty have attracted dozens of national and international artists, writers and folk heroes, including Norman Rockwell, Dorothy Canfield Fisher, Robert Frost and Rudyard Kipling, to name a few.

Today's new artisans follow in the footsteps of those early protagonists of Vermont history, fleeing America's big cities for a simpler existence among the quiet mountains. Together with the die-hard Republicans, patriotic farmers, leftover hippies and well-heeled elite, they form a curious, independent populace, united by their laissez-faire attitudes and unwavering devotion to free living.

With a population just over 560,000, Vermont is the nation's third smallest state, though its exquisite forested mountains and shimmering lakes and rivers pack as much beauty per square mile as any of the other 49.

Best of all, the terrain reveals four distinct faces as the seasons change. Fall brings a sacred occurrence, and during the season—usually from mid-September to mid-October—the entire state is covered by resplendent colors, and the temperature hovers around a crisp 50° to 60°.

Winter delivers a Currier and Ives backdrop, with carpets of plush white snow that weave through the country and temperatures that plunge toward 0°.

Waterfalls thaw and gush forth in spring, and millions of maple trees give up their candied sap for that wonderful Vermont maple syrup. Summer is pure green, a panorama of verdant forests, lucid lakes and blissful, breezy days when the thermometer reads about 75°.

Vermont's enchantment exists not only in its fanciful seasons and scenery but in the 242 small towns that comprise the essence of this state. Sprinkled on hillsides and straddling mountain streams, these quaint villages often cling to the social values of times past and harbor historic legacies and colorful personalities. Their very structures spell tradition: each town will almost certainly have a Main Street, a village square, a general store and a cemetery where you're apt to discover tombstones from the 1700s.

Nearly half a million people flock to Vermont to witness the fall foliage.

Then, too, each region of the state maintains its own separate, intriguing personality. Southern Vermont is a mingling of forests, ski resorts and small cities that have seen strong influences from neighboring New York, Massachusetts and New Hampshire. In central Vermont, "The Marble City" of Rutland has churned out tons of smooth stone for more than a century, its marble-plated buildings a testament to this vital industry. Nearby Woodstock is the state's center of prosperity, a summer playground of majestic estates, trendy shops and restaurants and total gentility.

Crawling through the upper center of the state, the Northern Mountain Region thrives as an alpine haven of ski centers and maple sugarhouses, obscure mountain hamlets and fields of wildflowers.

Gorgeous Lake Champlain wanders along the western border, edged by New York's Adirondack Mountains and Vermont's fertile Champlain Valley, and supports the state's largest city. Burlington—home to a mere 40,000 people—is a dynamic port and culture center whose well-groomed cityscapes and obvious lack of pollution make it a splendid place to tarry.

The Northeast Kingdom is undoubtedly Vermont's last stand, a 2000-square-mile piece of rural wonderland snuggled against Canada and New Hampshire. Here, craggy peaks hover above dozens of glacier-dug lakes, evergreen spires ache toward the clouds and man and nature exist together simply and peacefully.

But of all Vermont's jewels, perhaps none is so extraordinary as its people. Amiable, generous and always interested, Vermonters know how to make a person feel right at home.

In fact, visiting Vermont is a lot like coming home: Once you're there, you feel like you've always belonged. Once you leave, you'll yearn to go back.

▼▼▼▼▼▼▼▼▼▼▼▼▼

Southern Vermont

Edged by New York, Massachusetts and New Hampshire, this southerly precinct serves predominately as a gateway for skiers, weekenders and other seekers of pleasure and solace. Here, spun into one fine geographical web, are all the components that typify the state of Vermont—wooded mountain corridors, lazy farmlands, bucolic villages and a cornucopia of history.

Two of Vermont's largest cities, Brattleboro and Bennington, anchor the state corners and bring culture, politics and manufacturing into the region. In between are several towns that were founded in the 18th century as frontier outposts.

SIGHTS

Nestled nicely between the Connecticut River and a string of western mountain ledges, **Brattleboro** debuted as a sparse colony in 1724, making it Vermont's first permanent settlement. Today, Brattleboro owes its importance to health care and educational centers, as well as wholesale distribution facilities.

The **Visitors Information Booth** in Brattleboro stocks loads of maps and can help with itineraries. ~ Putney Road; 802-257-1112. The **Brattleboro Chamber of Commerce** is also very helpful. ~ 180 Main Street; 802-254-4565.

Every proper 1800s Brattleboro home simply *had* to have a parlor organ, and a few of those relics still remain at the **Brattleboro Museum and Art Center**. Located in a 1915 native stone railroad station, the museum has eight beautiful wood Estey organs, manufactured locally by the thousands until the plant shut down in the 1960s. You'll also encounter dynamic rotating exhibits of visual arts as well as historical programs. Closed Monday. Admission. ~ Main and Vernon streets; 802-257-0124.

Back in 1892, Rudyard Kipling put down roots just north of Brattleboro in the village of Dummerston. Here, in an odd, ship-shaped house called **Naulakha,** he lived for four years with his wife, Vermont native Carrie Balestier, and penned *Captains Courageous* and two *Jungle Books.* Now available for weeklong rentals, the dwelling is set back from the road and cloaked in tall trees. ~ Kipling Road, two miles north of Black Mountain Road.

To experience the rural rhythms of this state, head north on Route 30 to **Newfane.** Settled in 1774, this beguiling village is a paradigm of Vermont culture, showcasing 40 exquisite buildings that harken back to the 1700s. White clapboard houses mingle with graceful maple and elm trees and vast green. The grand **Windham County Courthouse** (802-365-4257), a Greek Revival design with enormous pillars, edges the green and is the village focal point. Closed Saturday and Sunday. Across the green rests the **Old Newfane Inn** (802-365-4427), a venerable 1787 Colonial building trimmed in white lattice porches and chimneys.

A drive northward on Route 30 and then Route 35 will put you smack in the middle of back country, a piece of terrain laced with mountain brooks and meandering meadows, occasional farms and one-room schoolhouses.

If you're like Ulysses S. Grant and Oliver Wendell Holmes, you'll make a pit stop in Grafton at the **Old Tavern at Grafton,** an 1801 Colonial-style inn that's filled with marvelous antiques and Old World character. Once a popular stagecoach layover, the tavern also hosted the likes of Ralph Waldo Emerson and Rudyard Kipling. ~ Route 121 near junction with Route 35; 802-843-2231

Some say **Grafton** got its name in a bidding contest—won with $5 and a flask of rum—back in 1791, though the village owes its existence to sheep farming (15,000 grazed here during the 1800s). Grafton now boasts two covered bridges, 650 residents and a network of well-preserved white frame buildings.

✔ CHECK THESE OUT—UNIQUE SIGHTS

- Keep an eye out for bears and moose as you explore the brilliant fall foliage along Route 9 in the **Green Mountain National Forest.** *page 396*
- Board a covered wagon to tour **Shelburne Farms,** a Vanderbilt home with grounds designed by Central Park's architect. *page 421*
- Indulge your curiosity—and, of course, your salivating taste buds—at **Ben & Jerry's Ice Cream Factory Tours** in Waterbury. *page 410*
- Satisfy your sweet tooth for good at the **Maple Grove Farms of Vermont,** the world's oldest and largest maple candy factory. *page 427*

Exquisite views await back along Route 9, to the west of Brattleboro, where the road climbs 2350 feet to the top of **Hogback Mountain**. This captivating plateau, surrounded with lofty spires of spruce and fir trees, affords a 100-mile panorama across New Hampshire and Massachusetts' Berkshires.

Tucked in the basement of the Vermont Country Market, the **Luman Nelson Museum of New England Wildlife** offers a walk on the ◄ HIDDEN wild side. This bizarre grotto, "stuffed" with thousands of familiar and unusual birds and animals, represents the lifetime work of taxidermist and naturalist Luman Nelson. The winged collection alone is staggering: more than 1000 different bird species are there, including a large eagle and owl collection and the extinct passenger pigeon and heath hen. Even stranger, though, are the albino deer and skunks. ~ Route 9, Marlboro; 802-464-5494.

Continue through this forested mountain wonderland, traveling west on Route 9, and you'll descend into the town of **Wilmington**. Long a juncture between Brattleboro and western Bennington, this bucolic town of 1800 swells to 15,000 during winter when skiers pack nearby **Haystack Mountain** and **Mount Snow**. Of course, summer activities abound, too, and you can learn about these and other leisure pursuits at the **Mount Snow/Haystack Region Chamber of Commerce**. ~ Route 9 (Main Street), Wilmington; 802-464-8092.

Heading west toward Bennington, Route 9 cuts through the broad, verdant expanse of the **Green Mountain National Forest**. This sinuous, heady trail explodes with brilliant color during fall foliage season, though the views border on amazing the rest of the year, too. Keep an eye out for bears, coyotes and moose, which roam the area frequently.

You can see it before you get to Bennington, an intimidating limestone obelisk looming over the city like some celestial figure. The 306-foot **Bennington Battle Monument**, the region's geographical frame of reference, pays tribute to the 1777 Battle of Bennington, a decisive conflict during the American Revolution. Though American general John Stark organized his troops and supplies here in Bennington, the battle was actually waged five miles away on a New York hill. Open from mid-April until the end of October. Admission. ~ 15 Monument Circle, Old Bennington; 802-447-0550.

Bennington is Vermont's southwesternmost city and the first town chartered in the state, though residents didn't arrive until 12 years later in 1761 because of fierce raids during the French and Indian War. Suffused with culture and Revolutionary War history, the city is flanked by the Green Mountains and the Taconic range, a setting that's nothing short of spectacular.

The downtown area is pretty but naturally quite commercialized, so you'll want to spend most of your time in **Old Bennington**. Draped across a hill on the city's west quadrant, this pristine borough harbors marvelous expressions of early American history. Here you'll find more than 80 well-preserved 18th- and 19th-century buildings, comprising a sort-of outdoor museum.

Before you start exploring, pick up a walking tour map from the **Bennington Area Chamber of Commerce.** ~ Route 7; 802-447-3311.

American history becomes an enthralling experience at the **Bennington Museum.** This vine-covered, 1855 building—one of New England's finest museums —evokes America's past with Civil War and American Revolution artifacts, 18th- and 19th-century furnishings and paintings, a rare collection of blown glass and a New England genealogical library packed with 3000 volumes. Admission. ~ West Main Street, Bennington; 802-447-1571.

Housed in a separate wing of the museum is the frame schoolhouse, moved from Eagle Bridge, New York, that Grandma Moses attended as a child. This structure displays the largest public collection of her paintings and working utensils in North America. The spirit of this remarkable woman—who began painting at age 76—shines through in her paintings of New England rural cheer, in her portraits and photographs, and in her tilt-top painting table, shawl and apron.

West on Main Street rests Vermont's Colonial shrine, the **Old First Church,** erected in 1806 and now a much-photographed sight. Nestled on the green in Old Bennington, the simple white building has columns formed with single pine trees, arched Romanesque windows and well-preserved pine box pews. In this state of tradition, some of today's church members are descendants of the original founders. ~ Monument Avenue, Bennington; 802-447-1223.

Beside the church on a shady knoll, symmetrical rows of granite comprise the **Old Burying Ground,** where you can stroll peacefully among tombstones dating back to the 1700s. Many epitaphs are intriguing, ruminations of early settlers and soldiers who toiled here under a more difficult life, but perhaps the most reflective endures on the grave of poet Robert Frost: "I had a lover's quarrel with the world."

Head north from Old Bennington on Fairview Street, cross one of three quaint covered bridges, and you'll arrive at **Bennington College.** A medley of Colonial designs, the campus lazes peacefully across 550 acres on a pretty hill overlooking mountains and valleys. ~ Route 67A; 802-442-5401.

Since its founding in 1929, the tiny liberal arts school has initiated some of the country's most progressive teaching styles, employing accomplished (and oftentimes renowned) artists, writers and musicians to act as both teachers and colleagues to students. Among the more famous who have graced these halls are dancer and choreographer Martha Graham and author Bernard De Voto. Rigorous scholastic and artistic exercises students must endure are often referred to as "The Bennington Experience."

Perhaps the most intriguing sight on campus is **Jennings Hall,** a grand three-story structure carved of solid granite. Built in the mid-

1800s, the building was home to the Frederic B. Jennings family, who donated their estate to the college.

The cozy pastoral spirit and thoughtful personalities of **Arlington**, 16 miles north of Bennington off Route 7A, remain preserved on *Saturday Evening Post* covers, sketched by Norman Rockwell when he lived here during the 1940s and early 1950s. Rockwell's farm and studio are now the **Inn on Covered Bridge Green**, a scenic resting place nestled among apple orchards and dairy farms. ~ River Road at Covered Bridge Road, four and a half miles west of Route 7A, West Arlington; 802-375-9489.

◄ *HIDDEN*

You can chat with some of the local people Rockwell painted if you stop by the **Norman Rockwell Exhibition**, a 19th-century church where several hundred *Saturday Evening Post* covers, illustrations and prints are displayed. Admission. ~ Route 7A, Arlington; 802-375-6423.

Meander north on Route 7A to Sunderland, then head west on **Skyline Drive** toll road for a hair-raising, five-mile trek to the top of **Mount Equinox**. At 3816 feet up, the panorama is inspiring, the air brisk and the feeling serene.

On the way down the mountain, stop at the **Southern Vermont Art Center** for a tryst with culture and nature. A beautiful late-1800s Georgian mansion holds ten galleries and over 700 artworks, chiefly contemporary paintings, graphic art and photography. Set on 375 acres of forest and pastureland, the center also boasts a performing arts pavilion for outdoor concerts, an extensive botany trail and a sculpture garden sprinkled with wildflowers. Open late May through late October. Admission. ~ West Road, Manchester; 802-362-1405.

Avid fishers—and even nonanglers—will get a kick out of the **American Museum of Fly Fishing**. Peruse more than 30,000 flies and 1000 rods and reels, tracing the history of this intriguing sport. You'll see what Dwight Eisenhower, Daniel Webster and Ernest Hemingway used to snag a fish, along with artifacts from famous rod-makers like Thomas and Orvis. A real treat for anyone fishing for fun. Closed on weekends from November to May. Admission. ~ Route 7A, Manchester Village; 802-362-3300.

Just a stone's throw southward on Route 7A lies **Manchester**, which made its imprint last century as a thriving summer resort town and this century as a nucleus for designer outlet stores. But its main claim to fame is a former resident, Robert Todd Lincoln, eldest son of Abraham Lincoln, who built a Georgian Revival mansion here in 1905 and called it **Hildene**.

Possibly one of New England's finest historic scenes, Hildene offers a glimmer of the gilded, intriguing life of Robert Lincoln, an attorney, minister to Great Britain and U.S. Cabinet member. Laid against 412 acres of beautiful formal gardens, evergreen trees and nature trails, the 24-room mansion is extremely well-preserved and filled with original furnishings and possessions including a grand 1908 Aeolian pipe organ once played by the Lincoln women. Open from mid-May to the end of October. Admission. ~ Route 7A, Manchester Village; 802-362-1788.

LODGING

Art deco in Vermont? Just check out **The Latchis Hotel,** a 1938 deco charmer in the heart of downtown. This four-story find sparkles in bright terrazzo floors and curved chrome designs and boasts 30 guest rooms in soft pastels offset by black lacquer furniture and some restored 1930s pieces. The best part is that many rooms peek a view at the Connecticut River. There's also a movie theater on the premises. ~ 50 Main Street, Brattleboro; 802-254-6300, fax 802-254-6304. MODERATE.

Something about the **Old Newfane Inn** makes you instantly feel as though you've come home. Perhaps it's the lazy wraparound porch with rocking chairs, the warm parlors with brick hearths or the wonderful old general store across the street. It could be the eight rooms, decorated without pretension in rich woods and country wallpapers, or the massive maple trees that stand across the front lawn. Whatever the reason, the magic is there—and has been since this venerable country inn opened way back in 1787. ~ Route 30, Newfane; 802-365-4427, 800-789-4427. DELUXE.

The sophisticated serenity of the **Four Columns Inn** has long drawn celebrities (Mick Jagger and Michael Jackson among them) seeking a quiet reprieve from life's fast lane. Set amidst 150 forested acres, the 19th-century Greek Revival inn sports a swimming pool enveloped in flowers and a cobblestone path that wends across brooks and meadows. Its trademark is four majestic columns that stand astride the loggia—a marvelous place to mellow out and listen to birds chirp. The 15 guest rooms offer wide plank floors, lace curtains and a mix of canopy and four-poster beds. Two suites are also available. ~ 230 West Street, Newfane; 802-365-7713, 800-787-6633. DELUXE TO ULTRA-DELUXE.

The Old Tavern is possibly the most renowned spot in Grafton, and rightly so, since guest rooms are scattered in ten different historic buildings across town. The main house is an 1801 Colonial design brimming with lovely antiques, original pine floors and pewter and brass. Formerly a popular stagecoach stop, the tavern boasts a notable guest list that included Ulysses S. Grant and Ralph Waldo Emerson. Houses might feature braided rugs, Victorian furnishings and full kitchen. ~ Routes 35 and 121; 802-843-2231, 800-843-1801. DELUXE TO ULTRA-DELUXE.

HIDDEN ►   If you want to escape from absolutely everything, consider **The Hermitage Inn.** This 18th-century farmhouse is a hidden treasure tucked down a piece of paved road and nestled against a rushing brook. The owner's love of hunting is evidenced by the English setters that roam the 24 acres, as well as hundreds of antique decoys found throughout the inn. There is even a court for clay pigeon shooting. Twenty-nine rooms—many with working fireplaces—are adorned in hunting motif and feature four-poster beds. Breakfast and dinner at the inn's exceptional gourmet restaurant are included in the price. ~ Coldbrook Road, Wilmington; 802-464-3511, fax 802-464-2688. ULTRA-DELUXE.

Skiers seeking close proximity to the slopes should check out **Mount Snow Resort Lodge**, a lodge and a cluster of condominium buildings at the base of Mount Snow. There are 240 accommodations, ranging from hotel rooms to modern, apartment-style condos. Many rooms offer slope-to-front-door skiing, as well as use of tennis courts and pools. ~ 89 Mountain Road; 802-464-7788. MODERATE.

Thirteen miles west of Wilmington, the **Greenwood Lodge American Youth Hostel** lolls peacefully in a picturesque wooded glen. Rustic but tidy, the mountain lodge has 20 beds in four rooms, some of them available for private use. There's a fireplace and community kitchen, plus fishing ponds, canoeing, great cross-country skiing and 20 wooded campsites. Open from May through October. ~ Route 9, adjacent to Prospect Ski Mountain, Woodford; 802-442-2547. BUDGET.

A gorgeous Victorian mansion cloaked in a sea of trees, the **South Shire Inn** is positively dazzling. The first floor is a series of parlors and sitting rooms suffused with mahogany woods, etched-glass doors, high carved ceilings and a knockout spiral staircase. Upstairs, nine guest accommodations are equipped for indulgence, with Queen Anne beds, eyelet quilts, window sofas and jacuzzi tubs. For a bit of nostalgia, read through the century-old guest diary, which contains wonderful anecdotes. ~ 124 Elm Street, Bennington; 802-447-3839, fax 802-442-3547. DELUXE TO ULTRA-DELUXE.

✔ CHECK THESE OUT—UNIQUE LODGING

- *Budget to moderate:* Brave the washboard road leading past grazing cows and over a covered bridge to the whitewashed **Heermansmith Farm**. *page 429*
- *Moderate:* Experience curved-chrome designs and 1930s restored furniture at downtown Brattleboro's sleek art deco **Latchis Hotel**. *page 390*
- *Deluxe to ultra-deluxe:* Surround yourself with apple orchards and farms at Norman Rockwell's 1792 timber house, **The Inn on Covered Bridge Green**. *page 392*
- *Ultra-deluxe:* Practice your yodeling at the **Trapp Family Lodge**, a onetime singing camp venue for Maria Von Trapp of *The Sound of Music* fame. *page 412*

Budget: under $50 Moderate: $50–$90 Deluxe: $90–$120 Ultra-deluxe: over $120

For homey in-town accommodations, consider the **Molly Stark Inn**, an 1890 Victorian house that's been carefully restored by an enthusiastic and artistic innkeeper. The six bedrooms are small but charming, featuring hardwood floors, clawfoot bathtubs, lace curtains, antique patchwork quilts, ceiling fans and wall stencils. There's also a wraparound front porch and nifty antique wood-burning stove in the living room. A very private saltbox-style guest cottage with a cathedral ceiling and skylight, and a jacuzzi is also available. A full gourmet breakfast is included. ~ 1067 East Main Street, Bennington; 802-442-9631, 800-356-3076, fax 802-442-5224. MODERATE TO DELUXE.

HIDDEN ►

"Who is there, I wonder, who doesn't want to escape from the speed and rudeness of today's living . . . ?" When Norman Rockwell penned those words, he likely had in mind his secluded farmhouse in West Arlington. Today, the 1792 timber house is **The Inn on Covered Bridge Green**, a beguiling bed and breakfast offering a glimmer of the rural cheer that Rockwell's paintings so cleverly depicted. The scenic Battenkill River runs in front of the five-acre grounds, surrounded in all directions by apple orchards and tranquil horse and dairy farms. There are four bedrooms (one of which is a two-bedroom suite) set off by broad pine floors and provincial antiques, and a tennis court that Rockwell built. ~ River Road, 4.5 miles west of Route 7A; 802-375-9489, 800-726-9480, fax 802-375-1208. DELUXE TO ULTRA-DELUXE.

Ethan Allen and his Green Mountain Boys checked in **The Equinox** once for a little rest and relaxation. It was the late 1700s, and the hotel was *the* place to stay. Two centuries later, the place still draws history-makers, as well as anyone seeking indulgent surroundings. A main four-story building, fronted by Greek Revival columns, features 163 guest rooms graced with Vermont pine floors and furniture and adorned with Victorian accents. An adjoining building offers one- and two-bedroom suites with fully stocked kitchens and elegant country decor. There are indoor and outdoor pools, a country club, 18-hole championship golf course, spa, tennis courts and several restaurants. All set on 350 acres etched with cross-country ski trails. Who could ask for more? ~ Route 7A, Manchester Village; 802-362-4700, 800-362-4747, fax 802-362-4861. ULTRA-DELUXE.

For close proximity to Manchester's factory outlet stores, consider **Barnstead Innstead**. Built in 1830, the post-and-beam hay barn has been nicely converted with all its charm intact. Fourteen tidy bedrooms are eclectically outfitted with old-time furniture and wall-to-wall carpets, and there's a heated pool out back. ~ Route 30; 802-362-1619, 800-331-1619. MODERATE.

DINING

The diminutive venue of **T. J. Buckley's** is the last place you'd expect to find some of the city's finest gourmet fare. But here it is, served in an adorable Worcester diner with eclectic decor and only eight tables.

Four entrées are offered nightly on an ever-changing menu. Selections might include seared striped bass with fresh horseradish, chicken breast with baby mustard greens, and jumbo shrimp and littleneck clams served in a porcini mushroom stock prepared with carmelized Vidalia onions and raspberry vinegar. Closed Monday. ~ 132 Elliot Street, Brattleboro; 802-257-4922. DELUXE.

Climb a battered flight of stairs to the second-floor roost of **The Common Ground,** a venerable mecca of ethnic and organic creations. Formerly a mid-1800s fire station, the eatery has dusty plank and brick floors and a glass solarium overlooking the downtown hubbub. The open kitchen, a jumble of pots and chefs, is where all the vegetarian goodies get whipped up. Try the cashew burger, seaweed salad and homemade ginger ale. Closed Tuesday. ~ 25 Elliot Street, Brattleboro; 802-257-0855. BUDGET.

Things take on a subdued pace at **Peter Havens,** a tiny but sophisticated eatery obscured beneath streetside awnings. Continental fare focuses on fresh seafood, including curried shrimp, sea scallops Provençal and grilled swordfish with geneva butter. Linen tablecloths, original artwork and only ten tables make this a cozy spot for two. Closed Sunday and Monday. ~ 32 Elliot Street, Brattleboro; 802-257-3333. MODERATE TO DELUXE.

◀ HIDDEN

A majestic country establishment built in 1787, the **Old Newfane Inn** possesses quite an impressive restaurant. The surroundings are pure Vermont: dark pine floors, high beamed ceilings and brick walls sprinkled with beautiful antiques. The bill of fare includes an array of highbrow delights such as smoked goose pâté and frogs' legs Provençal. Dinner only. Closed Monday. ~ Route 30 on the village green, Newfane; 802-365-4427. DELUXE.

Charm and elegance embrace at the **Four Columns Inn** restaurant, renowned across the region for its exceptional native cuisine. Built in 1839 of hand-hewn timbers, the Colonial-style inn exhibits four

---

✔ **CHECK THESE OUT—UNIQUE DINING**

- *Budget to moderate:* Climb up a rickety flight of stairs for excellent Mexican food at **Julio's,** a downtown niche with colorful Mexican prints and blankets on the walls. *page 416*
- *Moderate:* Gaze at a vista stretching 100 miles from the downhome **Skyline Restaurant,** perched on 2000-foot Hogback Mountain. *page 394*
- *Deluxe:* Quaff your dinner drink from beautiful stemware created by glassblower Simon Pearce at **Simon Pearce Restaurant.** *page 405*
- *Deluxe to ultra-deluxe:* Take your pick from over 40,000 bottles of wine at **The Hermitage,** where antique duck decoys line the walls. *page 394*

Budget: under $8 Moderate: $8–$16 Deluxe: $16–$24 Ultra-deluxe: over $24

grand columns across its loggia. Inside, candlelit tables are arranged cozily around a brick fireplace accented by windows draped in lace sheers. Try the grilled duck breast with berry sauce; curried shrimp with warm greens and pineapple yogurt salad; and the steamy New England bouillabaisse. Closed Tuesday. ~ 230 West Street, Newfane; 802-365-7713. DELUXE.

The Old Tavern imparts a warm formality that reveals its rich heritage. Indeed, the inn's handsome pine floors and beam ceilings, which date back to the late 1700s, have seen the likes of Oliver Wendell Holmes and Henry David Thoreau. Two lavish dining rooms are decorated with antiques and American portraits, while a sunny greenhouse affords picturesque views of gardens. The menu focuses on local fare such as Green Mountain lamb, smoked pork loin and New England salmon. ~ Intersection of Townshend Road and Route 121, Grafton; 802-843-2231. MODERATE TO DELUXE.

A down-home eatery with spectacular views, the **Skyline Restaurant** is a great place to while away the morning. Perched 2000 feet up on Hogback Mountain, the Skyline offers simple decor and a vista that stretches more than 100 miles. Breakfast is the highlight, with goodies like banana and coconut griddlecakes smothered in (what else?) Vermont maple syrup, bountiful omelettes and steamy oatmeal. For dinner, try pan-fried trout or sugar-cured ham. ~ Route 9, Marlboro; 802-464-5535. MODERATE.

HIDDEN ▶

Tucked down a washboard road on the mountainside, **The Hermitage** is a tribute to gracious country dining. Fashioned in cool blue and cream tones, the three dining rooms are graced with picture windows, large hearths and hundreds of antique decoys collected by an owner who loves bird hunting. There's more evidence of his passion on the menu, which often features partridge, quail, pheasant, duck and venison. The owner has also garnered national recognition for his wine collection, which exceeds 40,000 bottles. An exceptional dining choice. Dinner is served nightly and there is a Sunday brunch. ~ Coldbrook Road, Wilmington; 802-464-3511. MODERATE TO ULTRA-DELUXE.

You find plenty of local color at **Poncho's Wreck**, a pub-style eatery with nautical decor and stained-glass windows. The food is dependably good and ranges from Mexican fare and smoked meats to seafood. The mood is casual but festive, particularly during ski season. ~ South Main Street, Wilmington; 802-464-9320. MODERATE.

An old timey coffee shop, **Geanneli's** is a downtown tradition. Waitresses in green shirts scurry across green carpet, doling out hearty breakfasts and solid country cooking. There's also a counter where plenty of local chatting gets done. The menu features liver and onions, fried chicken, grilled ham steak and voluminous homemade pies. ~ 520 Main Street, Bennington; 802-442-9778. BUDGET.

When it comes to fabulous views, it's tough to surpass the **Publyk House Restaurant**. This remodeled 1940s barn is the perfect place to gaze upon Bennington's battle monument and beautiful Mount Anthony. Carved wood doors, stained-glass windows and loads of greenery make for aesthetic surroundings. Expect interesting American-style fare including poultry, seafood and steak dishes. ~ Route 7A, Bennington; 802-442-8301. MODERATE TO DELUXE.

During the mid-1940s, Norman Rockwell took a fancy to the **Quality Restaurant**. Chances are you will, too. This downtown tradition, which has long served as the local socializing nest, reeks of character. Polished wood floors saunter up to a worn pine bar where Rockwell used to read the daily paper. Along a wall hangs an inspiring print of *War News*, in which the artist captured the bar's essence during World War II. Breakfast, lunch and dinner are all-American affairs, from blueberry pancakes to burgers to smoked salmon alfredo. ~ Route 7A, Manchester; 802-362-9839. MODERATE.

SHOPPING

For the most part, Vermont shops are down-home and unpretentious, a smattering of country gift marts, antique nooks and epicure emporiums with locally made cheeses and maple syrup. To assist with shopping excursions, the **Vermont Travel Division** has excellent brochures on where to find antiques, designer outlets, cheese and Christmas trees (in case you brought the car). ~ 134 State Street, Montpelier, VT 05602; 802-828-3236.

Pick up your designer clothes with discount price tags at **Sam's Army and Navy Department Store**, a downtown institution housed in a ruddy brick building. ~ 74 Main Street, Brattleboro; 802-254-2933.

Little people will adore **Jeannie Mac**, which sells 100% cotton clothes for tots made exclusively in Vermont. ~ Route 30, Townshend; 802-365-7040.

The fun and funky selections at **Bartleby's Books & Music** reflect the owner's love of fiction, history, Vermont, cooking, rock-and-roll and classical music. ~ North Main Street, Wilmington; 802-464-5425.

Mountain Jeanery, once an 1800s blacksmith's shop, caters to thrift shop fans with an assortment of army/navy gear and new and vintage women's clothing. ~ Route 9, Wilmington; 802-464-5818.

You can dress like Marilyn Monroe (or Madonna—take your pick) after a visit to **The Next Store**, a vintage clothing mart with elbow-length lace gloves, rhinestone sunglasses and Victorian and art deco jewelry. ~ Route 9, Wilmington; 802-464-5818.

Now and Then Books has a top-notch collection of used and out-of-print books. ~ 439 Main Street, Bennington; 802-447-1470.

The outstanding **Bennington Museum Shop** features Grandma Moses prints, Fenton glass, salt-glazed pottery and works by local artisans. ~ West Main Street, Bennington; 802-447-1571.

A tad futuristic, **Panache** is equipped with contemporary women's clothing, gifts and accessories such as neon sashes, Indonesian and Pacific jewelry and wild art stationery. ~ 434 Main Street, Bennington; 802-442-8859.

NIGHTLIFE   A marvelous neighborhood bar with a vast draft beer selection including their own brewed on the premises, **McNeill's Brewery** features recorded jazz and contemporary music. ~ 90 Elliot Street, Brattleboro; 802-254-2553.

Locals go underground at **Mole's Eye Café**, a noisy, crowded nook with booths and occasional blues and rock bands. Weekend cover; closed Sunday. ~ Main and High streets, Brattleboro; 802-257-0771.

Deacon's Den, near Wilmington, is a wood and glass tavern where skiers stop off for a cold brew. There's live rock-and-roll and blues on weekends during winter. Cover depending on the entertainment. ~ Route 100, West Dover; 802-464-9361.

Smack in the middle of ski action, **The Snow Barn** draws huge winter crowds with live rock-and-roll. Cover. ~ South Access Road, Mount Snow; 802-464-3333.

One of the most prestigious thespian groups in Vermont, **Oldcastle Theater Company** stages dramas, comedies and musicals in their new arts center. ~ Performing in the regional Bennington Center for the Arts, Route 9 and Gypsy Lane, Bennington; 802-447-0564.

Lilly's, a worn sports bar with dusty wood floors and outdoor volleyball action, has canned and live music on weekends, everything from country to contemporary rock. Cover Thursday through Saturday. ~ 135 Depot Street, Bennington; 802-447-2139.

BEACHES & PARKS   **GREEN MOUNTAIN NATIONAL FOREST** 🏃 🚲 🐴 🏕 🚣 ⛵
This colossal tract of greenery constitutes the spine of Vermont, uniting over 350,000 acres that slice through the center of the state. Technically, it's divvied into two big chunks, starting at the Massachusetts border and climbing to the town of Wallingford, then picking up again in Mendon and heading northward to Bristol. Dense, verdant and pristine, the forest provides asylum for thousands of animals and birds, including black bears, coyotes, moose, white-tailed deer, wild turkeys, raptors and endangered peregrine falcons. You can spot these intriguing inhabitants by exploring miles of nature trails and canoeing the waters.

The trees themselves are no less enthralling, those great sweeps of maple, beech and birch, intermingled with black cherry, white ash, balsam firs and occasional hemlock forests. Rivers gush forth from the mountains, giving rise to imaginative waterfalls and tiny, pebble-studded brooks perfect for wading. Swimming is excellent at several spots, including **Hapgood Pond** and **Grout Pond**, a developed but rustic site in Stratton on Kelley Stand Road, six miles west of Route

HIDDEN ►

100. There's excellent fishing from 440 miles of rivers and tributaries. Anglers ply the Otter Creek for brook trout and the White, Deerfield and nearby Battenkill and West rivers for rainbow and brown trout. To see everything the park offers would take several weeks, though there are several choice spots perfect for an afternoon rendezvous. Non-motorized boats only. Picnic areas, restrooms, nature trails and ranger stations are dispersed throughout the forest. ~ Route 7 scales the west side of the forest, while Route 100 borders the east side. In between, Routes 73, 125, 9, 11 and 30 slice through the middle. Along these roads are all 32 access points for trails, waterfalls, ponds, rivers and campgrounds. Before you go, contact the Green Mountain National Forest (231 North Main Street, Rutland, VT 05701-2417; 802-747-6700) about maps and information on the huge forest network.

▲ Several good campsites exist, in five developed campgrounds; four accommodate RVs (no hookups). Most sites are on a first-come, first-served basis and are $5 per night; reserved sites (Hapgood Pond only) are $10 per night. Try Hapgood Pond, on Hapgood Road in Peru, five miles from the intersection of Routes 11 and 30; and Moosa-lamoo, a developed campground on Ripton-Goshen Road, 3.2 miles from Route 125 and one mile east of Ripton. Some campgrounds are open all year, but lose their water in winter; others close for winter. Call for information.

FORT DUMMER STATE PARK 🏃 Stashed along some sylvan back roads,   ◄ HIDDEN
this 217-acre, heavily forested park is named after the first white set-tlement in Vermont, established in 1724. There's a small shaded clear-ing for picnicking and a mile of nature trails that ramble through ever-greens to views of the Connecticut River and peeks at the Vermont Yankee Power Plant. Picnic tables, restrooms and playground. ~ From Routes 91 and 5 in Brattleboro, take Route 5 south one-tenth of a mile to Fairground Road, then head east one-half mile to Main Street. Go south on Main Street—which turns into Old Guilford Road—for one mile. The park is near the dead end; 802-254-2610.

▲ Camping is permitted at 61 wooded sites, including ten lean-tos, with showers and fireplaces but no hookups. Rates are $10 per night for tent/RV sites, $14 per night for lean-tos.

TOWNSHEND STATE PARK 🏃 ⚓ 🚣 Resting amidst a slew of craggy green mountains, this fine park spans 856 acres and borders the scenic West River. For delightful views, take a hardy hike 1680 feet up to the top of Bald Mountain; for sunbathing and swimming, take a one-mile trek down to **Townshend Dam Recreation Area**, where an 1800-foot thread of tawny sand stretches lazily along the river. Try by the dam for brook trout, walleye and smallmouth bass. You'll also find nice nature trails near the dam. Picnic tables, restrooms. Open from Memorial Day through Columbus Day. ~ On Town Road, three miles south of Route 30 near Townshend; 802-365-7500.

▲ Permitted at 34 campsites (eight for RVs) with fireplaces and showers but no hookups. Rates are $10 per night for tent sites, $14 per night for lean-tos.

LIVING MEMORIAL PARK 🏃 🏊 As municipal parks go, this one is tops. Blanketing 53 acres of gentle hills, this shady sanctuary teems with recreational opportunities, including a swimming pool and ice skating rink, ski hill with T-bar lift, outdoor tennis courts, an indoor rink for rollerblading and inline hockey and an expansive playground with some state-of-the-art equipment. Families love this place, and it's one of the few parks that manages to be packed (or even open) year-round. Picnic pavilions, lifeguards, two snack bars, softball fields, tennis and basketball courts, ski trails. ~ On Route 9 a quarter of a mile west of Route 91, near Brattleboro; 802-254-6700.

MOLLY STARK STATE PARK 🥾 Magnificent stands of maple and birch blanket this pristine area, marked by lots of beavers, deer and rabbits. There's a broad clearing that affords cool picnicking and a one-and-a-half-hour roundtrip hike to the summit of Mount Olga. Once you're there, climb the abandoned fire tower and be rewarded with a view into New Hampshire. Picnic tables, shelters; day-use fee, $1.50; stores are located two miles west on Route 9 in Wilmington. Open from late May to early October. ~ On Route 9, about four miles east of Wilmington; 802-464-5460.

▲ There are 34 sites, including ten lean-tos, with showers and fireplaces (no hookups); $10 per night for tent sites, $14 per night for lean-tos.

JAMAICA STATE PARK 🥾 🏊 🎣 🚣 The arrow-straight, wide, rocky West River plows right through this beautiful park, creating a cool, 689-acre playground for outdoor lovers. A short cord of gravel forms a semibeach against the river, where you can swim or roll up your pants legs and explore. You can also cast a rod for walleye, trout and panfish. But the best part is a trail along an old railroad bed that leads to the Ball Mountain Dam, a monstrous structure that's unleashed twice a year for popular canoe and kayak races. There's also a wooded trail leading up to Hamilton Falls, where eons of torrential water flow have formed curious miniature bathtubs among slippery rocks. Restrooms, picnic tables, playground; stores one-half mile south on Route 30 or north on Route 100; open from late April to early October; day-use fee, $3. ~ Off Route 30 in Jamaica; 802-874-4600.

▲ Excellent, with 46 tent sites ($12 per night) and 16 lean-tos ($16 per night), with showers and fireplaces but no hookups. Some sites accommodate RVs.

WOODFORD STATE PARK 🥾 🏊 🎣 🚣 Certainly one of the most picturesque parcels in the state, this 400-acre mountain woodland teems with wildflowers and all sorts of wildlife, from moose, deer and bear to very active beavers. Much of the activity centers around Adams Reservoir, dotted with small boats and canoes and rimmed by a small beach with coarse grey sand. You can swim, though the water can be murky at times. When the reservoir is stocked, the trout are biting. At 2400 feet up, the setting is cool and serene. Picnic areas, boat and canoe rentals, nature trail; store is located one-half mile east on Route 9; day-use fee, $3. Open from mid-May to early October. ~ Ten miles east of Bennington on Route 9; 802-447-7169.

▲ Some of the most extensive in the state, with 102 sites, including 20 lean-tos, with fireplaces and hot showers. A third of the sites accommodate RVs (no hookups). Rates are $12 per night for tents, $16 per night for lean-tos.

LAKE SHAFTSBURY STATE PARK Situated along a fine, clear lake, this park possesses 101 acres sprinkled with evergreens and maple trees, nature trails and those industrious beavers. Locals fancy the 600-foot beach of fine, ginger-colored sand that allows great sunbathing and swimming. You can fish along parts of shore or from boats for bass and rainbow trout. Picnic areas, boat and canoe rentals; stores are nearby in Arlington; day-use fee, $3. Open from mid-May to Labor Day. ~ On Route 7A in Shaftsbury; 802-375-9978.

EMERALD LAKE STATE PARK True to its name, this body of water glistens with a green glow and is so clear you can see much of its sandy bottom. A choice thread of tawny sand forms a popular beach, while nature trails crisscross the hillside terrain. Here you'll also find some of the tallest (more than 100-foot) maple trees in Vermont. In the lake you can cast a rod for panfish, smallmouth bass and northern pike. Playground, restrooms, canoe and boat rentals; day-use fee, $1.50. Open from Memorial Day through the Columbus Day weekend. ~ On Route 7 in Dorset; 802-362-1655.

▲ Permitted in 105 sites, including 36 lean-tos, with showers and fireplaces but no hookups. Lean-tos are $16 per night; all other sites are $12 per night.

Central Vermont

Sprawled across the lower waist of the state are a diverse lot of mining cities, picturesque mountain hamlets, ski areas and affluent riverside towns. Driving through this fertile area, you'll encounter a variety of lifestyles and people—fifth-generation farmers, descendants of European immigrants, small-time merchants and established aristocrats.

On the region's west side, Rutland and nearby villages are pocked with marble quarries that have churned the wheels of industry for two centuries. Eastward, Woodstock is a meld of tree-lined streets and gracious 19th-century architecture that owes its affluence and elegance to a line of wealthy partisans, including Laurance S. Rockefeller and railroad magnate Frederick Billings. Beyond Woodstock rambles the lazy Connecticut River, a natural divider between Vermont and New Hampshire.

SIGHTS

HIDDEN ►

HIDDEN ►

Just south of Rutland and off Route 7 is a mandatory side trip (via a few dirt roads) to **Shrewsbury** (North Shrewsbury Road, about eight miles east of Route 7), a quiescent village of 800 that seems buried at the end of the world.

The **Meadowsweet Herb Farm** is a joyous feast for the senses, a skein of luxuriant gardens and greenhouses radiating brilliant flowers and redolent herbs. You get "free sniffs" of herbs, plus a wonderful shop filled with potpourri, spices and dried-flower arrangements. Pack a lunch and picnic by the pond under the apple trees. Open to the public from May to October. ~ 729 Mount Holly Road; 802-492-3565.

Northward lies **Rutland**, which earned the name "Marble City" during the mid-1800s when local marble mining exploded, though it was also the state's largest railroad junction. This commercial city—Vermont's second largest with 20,000 people—bears a handful of marble-plated buildings, but much of its marble was used for more than 250,000 headstones at Arlington National Cemetery in Virginia as well as the Lincoln Memorial in Washington, D.C., and the U.S. Supreme Court.

The **Rutland Region Chamber of Commerce** will assist with sightseeing in the area. ~ 256 North Main Street, Rutland; 802-773-2747.

The marble bridge, sidewalks and high school are a testament to more than a century of serious quarrying in nearby **Proctor**, where you can check out the **Vermont Marble Company Exhibit**, a series of intriguing marble displays with history to boot. Admission. ~ 61 Main Street; 802-459-3311.

A short (and very worthwhile) trip north on Route 7 will bring you to the town of **Brandon**, where you'll find one of the state's best expressions of 19th-century architecture. This fertile farming town, lined with serene, shady streets, was chartered in 1761 and was the birthplace of Stephen A. Douglas, the famous Illinois debater who lost the 1860 presidential race to Abe Lincoln. Excellent walking-tour maps are available at the **Brandon Area Chamber of Commerce**. ~ Central Square; 802-247-6401.

A sensational drive along Route 73, **Brandon Gap** cuts through precipitous mountains and miles of forest and gurgling brooks. While you're there, why not take a hiking or biking tour of the area? You can book reservations at the **Churchill House Inn**. The inn also offers flyfishing tours, as well as wildflower and bird watching walks. ~ Route 73 East; 802-247-3300.

East of Rutland, **Killington** and **Pico** constitute the state's largest and perhaps most popular ski area, though the resort scene seems quite contrived when compared to the genuine quaintness of surrounding villages (as most any native Vermonter will quickly point out).

From Killington, go east on Route 4 to Route 100 South, then it's just a few miles to **Plymouth Notch**. This gloriously remote mountain hamlet harbors the **Calvin Coolidge Homestead**, where the 30th president was born and spent most of his life. The entire scene is quite striking, a thread of well-preserved white clapboard and stone buildings and gravel lanes set against stalwart trees and mountain peaks. There's a one-room schoolhouse, a general store operated by Coolidge's father, the 1924 Summer White House with all its original furnishings and the home where, following President Harding's sudden death, he took his 2:47 a.m. presidential oath. There is also a restaurant on the premises. Closed mid-October through mid-May. Admission. ~ Route 100A; 802-672-3773.

A short drive east on Route 4 transforms you from bucolic byroads to overt affluence and centuries of prosperity in **Woodstock**. Superb red brick and white clapboard buildings skirt the beautiful oval green, fashionable shops and restaurants line side streets and a chalkboard called the **Woodstock Town Crier** (Central and Elm streets) provides the scoop on local goings on.

For more detailed information, stop by the **Woodstock Area Chamber of Commerce**. ~ 18 Central Street; 802-457-3555.

While some Vermonters bash Woodstock as bombastic, the community's attempts to preserve the natural surroundings shine through any pretentions that may exist. Power lines are hidden from sight, thanks to donations from resident Laurance Rockefeller, and rural beauty has been preserved at **Billings Farm and Museum**.

A railroad magnate and Rockefeller's grandfather-in-law, Frederick Billings established the farm in 1890, planted 10,000 trees and waged wars for agrarian protection. Today, exhibits take you through those early days of sidehill plows, corn planters and "nooning" (lunching) in the fields, providing an interesting reflection on 19th-century farming. You can even watch the cows being milked every afternoon. Open seven days a week from May through October; open weekends only in November and December; closed January through May. Admission. ~ Route 12, Woodstock; 802-457-2355.

Picturesque and subtly beguiling, neighboring **Quechee** lolls across the banks of the Ottauquechee River and claims a large concentration of resort estates. These grand mansions and sprawling country villas serve as summer homes for members of society's upper echelons and as eye-pleasing spectacles for passersby.

Vermont supposedly acquired its name on top of **Killington Peak**, the state's second largest summit, in 1763 when the Reverend Samuel Peters ascended on horseback and proclaimed the area *Vert Mont*, French for green mountain.

Even more inspiring than the resort estates is **Quechee Gorge**, a mammoth rocky chasm chiseled by the Ottauquechee River. Maple and fir trees skate down the rocky walls of the 165-foot-deep gorge, carved by glaciers during the Ice Age. It's a mile walk to the bottom, but the trek is scenic, cool and rewarding. ~ Route 4, ten miles north of Routes 89 and 91.

LODGING There's plenty of room in the apartmentlike suites at **Best Western Hogge Penny Inn,** a modern hostelry just outside downtown. Set at the foot of the mountains, the medley of two-story frame buildings is accented by generous landscaping and a broad swimming pool. Expect one- and two-bedroom suites with vaulted ceilings, sectional couches, distinctive windows and kitchens with modern appliances. Motel rooms available. ~ Route 4, Rutland; phone/fax 802-773-3200, 800-828-3334. DELUXE TO ULTRA-DELUXE.

Nestled on a bank of rolling hills between Rutland and Killington, **The Vermont Inn** is a congenial 1840 farmhouse trimmed in chimneys and red-and-white awnings. The whole place is terribly cozy, a timeless structure of rubbed pine floors, cherrywood furniture and wallpaper with pictures of country flowers. Bedrooms follow suit with homespun accents such as eyelet quilts, lace curtains and brass four-poster beds. Breakfast and dinner are included. ~ Route 4, Mendon; 802-775-0708, 800-541-7795. ULTRA-DELUXE.

The Grey Bonnet Inn mixes new and old with 40 modern rooms decorated in 1800s country motif and accompanied by amenities such as indoor and outdoor pools, tennis courts and an exercise room. Outside the two-story building wood shingles scale the walls and balconies, while inside the lobby is an intimate affair donned in carved wood beams, antique spinning wheels and a stately grandfather clock. Cross-country ski through the lodge's 25 acres, or take on Killington's slopes two miles away. The inn is closed from Columbus Day to Thanksgiving and from April to July. Winter rates include breakfast and dinner. ~ Route 100 North, Killington; 802-775-2537, 800-342-2086, fax 802-775-3371. DELUXE TO ULTRA-DELUXE.

Daniel Boone would have felt right at home in the **Inn at Long Trail**, a woodsy resting place with big country throw rugs, rustic furniture, pine tree pillars and a fieldstone fireplace. Six fireplace suites are heaped with rough-hewn wood furniture, and 16 smaller rooms feature private baths and cozy decor. But what ole' Dan would have liked best is the "relaxation room" fitted with a huge redwood hot tub. The inn is closed for a month after ski season, usually from late April to June. ~ Route 4, Killington; 802-775-7181, 800-325-2540. MODERATE TO ULTRA-DELUXE.

Ski zealots will want to plant themselves at the **Mountain Green Ski and Golf Resort,** a maze of 216 alpine-style condominiums skirting the foot of Killington Peak. Here, convenience and amenities are stressed: lifts are within walking distance, and so are the heated outdoor pool, hot tub and health club. Accommodations range from studios to four-bedroom suites, all with fireplaces and modern designs such as vaulted ceilings and carpeting. ~ Killington Road, Killington Village; 802-422-3000, 800-336-7754, fax 802-422-2328. DELUXE TO ULTRA-DELUXE.

About 16 miles north of Rutland, the lovely town of Brandon is a labyrinth of beautiful historic buildings, shade-giving maple trees and fine-trimmed lawns. Stashed away high in the mountains above Brandon, the **Churchill House Inn** is a fetching 1871 farmhouse known best to cross-country skiers and hikers. Three stories tall and fashioned in the Federal style, the inn features cozy sitting rooms with early American furniture and Vermont casting stoves, as well as homey bedrooms adorned with pine plank floors and rocking chairs. Closed from late October to the middle of December; also closed in April. Rates include homecooked breakfasts and gourmet dinners. ~ Route 73 East, Brandon; 802-247-3078, fax 802-247-6851. ULTRA-DELUXE.

◄ *HIDDEN*

The quintessence of Old World luxury exists at **The Canterbury House,** an elegant 1880 Victorian townhouse within walking distance of Woodstock's best sights and activities. Eight bedrooms are named after the *Canterbury Tales* (there's a Parson's Tale and Monk's Tale) and decorated with refinement: antique spool and brass beds, pedestal sinks and old-fashioned clawfoot tubs. ~ 43 Pleasant Street, Woodstock; 802-457-3077, 800-390-3077. MODERATE TO ULTRA-DELUXE.

Perhaps no other Vermont inn has received so much acclaim as the **Woodstock Inn & Resort,** partly because of all the luminaries who frequent the place. The other part is that it's just plain wonderful to look at and, of course, *be* at. Nestled against the village green, the grand, Colonial-style estate sports a ten-foot stone fireplace in its lobby and a country-style motif of braided rugs, rough-hewn beams and columns and artwork from the Rockefeller collection. Most of the 143 rooms are furnished rather simply, but extensive amenities include a huge sports center, golf course and ski touring center. ~ Route 4, Woodstock; 802-457-1100, 800-448-7900, fax 802-457-6699. ULTRA-DELUXE.

Run by a couple who fulfilled their dream of running away from their high-pressure New York City lives, the 27-room **Kedron Valley Inn** is a haven for other well-heeled escapees who need a shot of gentrified country life. Antique quilts adorn the guest rooms and common areas, and several rooms have furniture that has been handed down through the owners' families. Depending on the season, guests may stroll around the 15 acres, take a walk to nearby Woodstock, ski at one of the many nearby resorts, swim in the inn's enormous swimming pond or laze away a few hours on the front porch. Closed in April and the ten days immediately preceding Thanksgiving. ~ Route 106, South Woodstock; 802-457-1473, fax 802-457-4469. DELUXE TO ULTRA-DELUXE.

The Parker House Inn is a meticulously renovated Victorian mansion with seven generously proportioned guest rooms (all with private bath) that are furnished with period antiques. One room has a marble fireplace and an impressive iron and brass bed; another looks out over the Ottauquechee River. Once the home of Senator Joseph Parker, this 1857 home is now a National Historic Site. Be sure to inspect the painstakingly preserved original stenciling on the plaster walls in the entrance hall. The restaurant features local game and produce, and

◄ *HIDDEN*

guests may dine on the porch during warmer weather. Full breakfast included. ~ 16 Main Street, Quechee; 802-295-6077. DELUXE.

A sprawling 1793 farm that was home to Vermont's first lieutenant governor, **The Quechee Inn** radiates a spirit of untamed romanticism. Furry teddy bears cuddle in rocking chairs next to a brick hearth in the living room, while 24 bedrooms are embellished with satin-and-lace comforters and hints of sweet-smelling potpourri. Outside, a rolling green lawn dotted with tulip beds and willow trees surrounds a scenic lake. Breakfast and dinner are included. ~ Clubhouse Road, Quechee; 802-295-3133, 800-235-3133, fax 802-295-6587. ULTRA-DELUXE.

DINING

The surrounding Green Mountains make a perfect setting for the Austrian-style **Countryman's Pleasure**. Delicate pine chairs, pink draperies and straw wreaths create a soothing effect, reminiscent of the majestic Alps. The impressive menu boasts roast duck with raspberry sauce and veal medallions with fiddleheads (a Vermont specialty) and Jarlsberg. ~ Off Route 4 East on Town Line Road, Mendon; 802-773-7141. MODERATE TO DELUXE.

Just north of Rutland, **Swadi's Steak and Seafood** enjoys a long-standing reputation for serving thick, juicy, aged beef and fresh, no-nonsense seafood. The menu also features cajun-style entrées, as well as nightly blackboard specials. Wood tables and chairs, dim lighting and a blazing fire make for a venerable Vermont atmosphere. ~ Route 7, Pittsford; 802-773-8124. MODERATE.

For a bit of mountain funkiness, drop in to **Mother Shapiro's**, a joint that promises "Hot Food Till Last Call." Portions are large and range from kosher breakfasts and meat loaf to seafood salad and chicken soup. Popular with the après-ski set. ~ Killington Access Road, Killington; 802-422-9933. MODERATE.

Beautifully prepared, innovative cuisine has garnered **Hemingway's** quite a reputation around these parts. Everything is fresh and scrupulously served among elegant surroundings of white tablecloths and crystal. There's lobster and corn chowder with vanilla, sauté of pheasant with wild mushrooms and grilled striped bass with spring vegetables. The desserts are true works of art. Closed Monday and Tuesday. ~ Route 4, Killington; 802-422-3886. ULTRA-DELUXE.

Spooner's is a straightforward kind of place that serves New York steak and mud pie. Situated in an old barn, the eatery bears a long brass bar, multiple archways and picture windows framing a pretty courtyard. Pickings are basic American, from burgers to sole. ~ Route 4, Woodstock; 802-457-4022. MODERATE TO DELUXE.

It began as a modest greenhouse that later took on a soda fountain. Now **Bentley's** is the local noshing post, an uptown eatery decked in Oriental rugs, lace curtains and fringed lampshades. You can show up in casual or dressy attire and feast on treats such as scampi pescatore, gourmet chili and fresh pasta. ~ 3 Elm Street, Woodstock; 802-457-3232. MODERATE TO DELUXE.

Simon Pearce Restaurant affords an unusual blend of sophisticated cuisine and artistic talent. Quechee glassblower Simon Pearce—who's quite well known around New England —has fashioned beautiful stemware and globes that rest on formal tablecloths. His creative Continental cuisine menu is a perfect accompaniment, highlighted by roast duck with mango chutney and sesame-crusted tuna with noodle cakes. The brick building—a story in itself—was an 1830s mill that produced the country's largest supply of wool flannel. ~ Main Street, Quechee; 802-295-1470. DELUXE.

SHOPPING
◄ *HIDDEN*

Chocolate peppermint, pineapple sage and lemon-scented marigold herbs create some fine smells (and tastes) at **Meadowsweet Herb Farm**, where several greenhouses and gardens make for merry shopping. They also sell wreaths, seasonings and packaged herb seeds. ~ 729 Mount Holly Road, Shrewsbury; 802-492-3565.

Christmas is a year-round affair at **The Christmas Tree Barn**, a voluminous 1800s barn with every imaginable holiday item, plus potpourri, dried flower arrangements, oils and antiques. ~ 48-B Cold River Road, North Clarendon; 802-775-4585.

For unusual hand-crafted items, check out **Truly Unique Gift Shop**. Also available are various Vermont food products. ~ Route 4 East, Rutland; 802-773-7742.

Woodstock's wealthy set fosters quite a posh shopping nest, centered downtown where strolling is very pleasurable. The **Vermont Workshop**, in an 1826 house, has an impressive cache of gifts, furniture and needlepoint kits. ~ 73 Central Street; 802-457-1400. Great kitchen treasures await at **F. H. Gillingham & Sons**, where you can pick up picnic baskets, costly wines and froufrou cooking devices. ~ 16 Elm Street; 802-457-2100. Indulge your eyes and nose together at **Primrose Garden**, a venerable assortment of fragrant potpourri and silk flowers, candelabras and blown glass. ~ 26 Central Street; 802-457-4049.

Vermont-style paraphernalia, from maple products and cheese to wicker baskets and country cookbooks, are all jammed under one big red roof at the vast **Timber Village**. ~ Route 4 West, Quechee; 802-295-1550.

NIGHTLIFE

The Other Room, a local watering hole with real character, features karaoke singing and the occasional band. ~ Mother Shapiro's Restaurant, Killington Access Road, Killington; 802-422-9933.

During ski season, skiers jam into the **Pickle Barrel**, where you'll find late-night rock, a huge dancefloor and a barnlike environment. Closed May through September. ~ Killington Access Road, Killington; 802-422-3035.

The heart of trendiness, **Bentley's** is (and has been, forever) the town noshing spot, decked in lace curtains, antique lamps, Oriental rugs and one long, polished bar. Tunes are snazzy, leaning toward jazz and classical. There's dancing on Friday and Saturday nights, live entertainment Thursday and Sunday evenings. ~ 3 Elm Street, Woodstock; 802-457-3232.

BEACHES & PARKS

GREEN MOUNTAIN NATIONAL FOREST See "Beaches & Parks" in the Southern Vermont section.

LAKE ST. CATHERINE STATE PARK With a three-mile shoreline, St. Catherine is one of Vermont's largest and most beautiful lakes. The 117-acre park borders only part of the lake, but its 250-foot beach draws large crowds, particularly on weekends. Swimming in the lake is exceptional and there are great opportunities to catch rainbow and lake trout, smelt, yellow perch, northern pike, bullhead and smallmouth and largemouth bass. There's also a trail where you're apt to see deer, raccoons and rabbits. Picnic areas, playground, concession stand; boat rentals and ramp; stores are nearby in Poultney; day-use fee, $1.50. Open from just before Memorial Day through the Columbus Day weekend. ~ On Route 30, three miles south of Poultney; 802-287-9158.

▲ There are 51 tent/RV sites ($12 a night) with hot showers, fireplaces and ten lean-tos ($16 a night); no hookups.

BOMOSEEN STATE PARK This vast area harbors Vermont's largest lake, the 2379-acre Lake Bomoseen, along with an incredible stretch of forest sprinkled with dormant slate quarries. The park itself spans 365 acres and contains yet another large freshwater body called Glen Lake. There's a nice long tawny beach on Bomoseen, plenty of surrounding nature trails, plus a visiting naturalist who conducts bird and wildflower walks and other programs. Swimming is good only in Lake Bomoseen, but fishing is exceptional in both lakes, with possibilities for panfish, yellow perch and bass. Picnic areas, snack bar, boat and canoe rentals. ~ Along Route 4 (also West Shore Road) about four miles north of Hydeville; 802-265-4242, 802-483-2001 (January–May).

▲ Permitted in 66 sites with hot showers, fireplaces and ten lean-tos but no hookups. Rates are $12 per night for tent/RV sites and $16 per night for lean-tos.

CALVIN COOLIDGE STATE PARK The 30th president spent most of his life in this incredibly scenic, remote swath of forest, which spans 17,949 acres and now serves as a nucleus for hiking, fishing (trout and panfish), snowmobiling and relaxation. The dusky Black River and gurgling Broad Brook—great for wading and stone collecting—cut through dense, cool pine stands. Trails will lead you to magnificent views atop Shrewsbury and Killington Peaks. Picnic tables, restrooms, hiking and nature trails, extensive snowmobile network; historic Calvin Coolidge Homestead only two miles away; day-use fee, $3. Open from late May to the middle of October. ~ In Plymouth on Route 100A, two miles north of the intersection with Route 100; 802-672-3612.

▲ There are 25 tent/RV sites ($10 per night) and 35 lean-tos ($14 per night), with hot showers and fireplaces but no hookups.

CAMP PLYMOUTH STATE PARK 🏃 🚣 🏊 🛶 ⛵ There's gold in them there hills—at least in this park. Believe it or not, this 300-acre wooded spread attracts a sprinkling of gold diggers, who wade ankle-deep and pan the silty bottom of the Buffalo Brook. Of course, no one has struck it rich lately, but who cares? This hilly park's other claim to fame is shimmering Echo Lake, which possesses a very pretty but small slice of cinnamon-colored sand. You can swim or try for smelt, trout, bass and yellow perch. Picnic tables, playground, restrooms, snack bar, volleyball, nature trails, rental boats; day-use fee, $3. Four cabins are available for rentals. The park is open from Memorial Day to Labor Day. ~ Off Route 100 just north of Ludlow in the town of Plymouth; 802-228-2025.

WILGUS STATE PARK 🏃 🛶 ⛵ This 100-acre park draws life from the very wide, very fertile Connecticut River. Most of the area is heavily wooded, but a small clearing allows for cool picnicking and nice views across the river to New Hampshire. There's no beach, but an opening in the steep river banks makes way for canoes. The strong currents discourage swimming. Picnic areas, restrooms, playground, canoe rentals, nature trails; day-use fee, $3. Open from May to the middle of October. ~ On Route 5 south of Ascutney; 802-674-5422.

▲ There are 29 campsites with nine lean-tos, including hot showers and fireplaces. Tent/RV sites are $11 per night and lean-tos are $15 per night.

QUECHEE GORGE STATE PARK 🏃 ⛵ This is one of the most visited parks in Vermont, and rightly so, since it provides access to the geological phenomenon called Quechee Gorge. Carved by glaciers during the Ice Age, the 165-foot gorge provides a cool, scenic milieu along the Ottauquechee River. Quite large, the 612-acre park mostly skirts calmer, flatter parts of the river and provides asylum for plenty of white-tailed deer. For anglers, this area is trout land. Picnic tables, restrooms, top-notch nature trails; stores nearby, west on Route 4. Open from Memorial Day to Columbus Day. ~ On Route 4 three miles west of Exit 189 in Quechee, six miles from White River Junction; 802-295-2990.

▲ There are 48 tent/RV sites ($11 per night) and six lean-tos ($15 per night), with hot showers and fireplaces but no hookups.

Northern Mountain Region

Interminable forests of maple trees, or "sugarbushes," have earned this region its image—along with a handsome maple syrup industry. Indeed, the entire region evokes a sense of ultimate Vermont charm, a place crisscrossed with valley farms and corn fields, winding country roads, hidden swimming holes and the whizzing Mad River that inspires virtually every part of local life.

Most of the tranquil villages here can trace their roots to the early 1800s (some even further back), making them a delight to visit and investigate. Tiny, endearing Montpelier, the state capital, was established way back in 1805 after Vermont's legislature roamed for almost 30 years. Austria-like Stowe, its great alpine peaks forming a sea of green, harkens back to 1833 when it was a crossroads for travelers on horseback.

While longtime Vermonters surely appreciate the region's idyllic aura, it's the flatlanders—natives of New York, Massachusetts or any other place that's not Vermont—who have lately sought out the serenity of these vertical reaches. Typically owners of small businesses or bed and breakfasts, these "immigrants" have left the so-called good life in big cities for what they say is a better life among Vermont's Green Mountains.

SIGHTS

Though the Sugarbush ski resort area churns up the most activity, the real local beauty lies in **Warren** (off Route 100 east of Lincoln Gap Road) and **Waitsfield** (northward along Route 100), a pair of pastoral towns with covered bridges, general stores and friendly, down-home folks.

The region's alpine setting and excellent thermal currents make it a splendid place for **gliding**, also known as **soaring**. Ride the air currents 5000 feet up and secure a bird's-eye view of farmlands and mountaintop beaver ponds. Flights are offered at the **Warren–Sugarbush Airport**, where a pilot will take one or two passengers for rides lasting 15 to 30 minutes. Rides are offered from mid-May to the end of October only. ~ Airport Road off Route 100; 802-496-2290.

East on Route 89 lies **Montpelier**. With a population of only 8500, Montpelier is the smallest state capital in the nation, though its grand old buildings and manicured cityscapes may well be the country's most charming.

To direct you around town—and the state—the **Vermont Travel Division** provides an impressive array of information on sights as well as history, culture and the economy. ~ 134 State Street; 802-828-3236, 800-837-6668.

The **State House**, with its gold-leaf dome resting dramatically against the evergreens of Hubbard Park, easily takes center stage. Modeled after the Greek temple of Theseus, the 1838 granite granddaddy sports a statue of Ceres, Roman goddess of agriculture. Take a free tour (mid-July to mid-October only), or wander around and muse over the Civil War murals, Victorian decor and quotations by Theodore Roosevelt, Ethan Allen and other national legends. Open Saturday in summer; closed on weekends the rest of the year. ~ 115 State Street; 802-828-2228.

Across the street, the **State Agriculture Building** commands a look with its red brick facade, fancy turrets and arched, convex windows. ~ 116 State Street; 802-828-2416.

Don't miss the fine exhibits at **The Vermont Museum**, housed in the old red brick Pavilion Hotel, built in 1876. There's an impressive collection of fine and decorative arts, farm and industrial equipment and memorabilia that imaginatively traces the state's history (exhibits change during the year). Admission ~ 109 State Street; 802-828-2291.

Montpelier's sister city is **Barre**, though no two siblings could be less alike. Barre is the rough-and-tumble one of the pair, a working-class town put on the map by the granite industry. During the late 1800s, thousands of European and Canadian immigrant stoneworkers flocked to town, making Barre quite a bustling place and along the way producing frequent labor disputes and strong movements toward socialism.

Today, this self-proclaimed Granite Capital of the World harbors the largest monumental granite quarry in the world, known as **The Rock of Ages**. This colossal stony pit, which plunges more than 485 feet down and spans 50 acres, is strewn with mining equipment and boulders. Open from March through Christmas, weather permitting. Admission charged for tours. ~ Main Street, off Route 14, Graniteville; 802-476-3115.

Some of the granite found its final resting place at the **Hope Cemetery**, a fascinating collection of memorial art. The delicate engravings of granite craftsmen (often designed for their deceased brethren) survive on everything from small headstones and ornate monuments to giant mausoleums. There are scrolls, hearts, religious sculptures and even a large soccer ball. ~ Merchant Street, Barre.

Remember those two crazy guys named Ben and Jerry who hit the big time with an ice cream recipe? Here's where you'll find them,

SMUGGLERS NOTCH

Perhaps the area's ultimate nature encounter occurs at **Smugglers Notch** (Mountain Road), a slender, sensational pass through the mountains with dramatic sheets of silver rock on either side. Used as a secret passage between Canada and the U.S. during the War of 1812, the notch harbors dozens of intriguing rock formations (check out the singing bird and elephant head) and a rock crevasse where the summer temperature hovers around 49. Keep an eye out for rock climbers who navigate the cliffs and rappel down.

smack in the middle of Vermont rural country, at **Ben & Jerry's Ice Cream Factory Tours**. The factory—the state's number one tourist attraction—is a lesson in American free enterprise. You'll see the creamy stuff being made, get free samples and learn about two guys who haven't let success stand in the way of having fun. Ben and Jerry are revered around this state, and not surprisingly, since one out of ten Vermont families owns stock in their ice cream corporation. Tours are offered seven days a week, but no ice cream is made on Sunday and holidays. Admission. ~ Route 100 North, Waterbury; 802-244-5641.

Another fun stopover is the **Cold Hollow Cider Mill,** an old barn that houses a small apple cider mill and a vast country gift shop. You can watch the apple presses at work year-round. ~ Route 100, Waterbury; 802-244-8771.

Northward along Route 100 lies picturesque, alpine **Stowe,** a country town augmented by a bustling ski resort area and set against a deep green necklace of mountains.

The busy "downtown" area, situated at the crossroads of Route 100 and Mountain Road, is a pleasing meld of 19th-century buildings and contemporary marts and restaurants. All the ski action awaits up Mountain Road, a seven-mile jog lined with hotels and inns, shops, pubs and eateries of every culinary calling.

Vermont's highest peak, **Mount Mansfield,** looms 4393 feet above the town and presents an incredible backdrop, its craggy profile resembling the silhouette of a human face. In the summer, you can take an **auto toll road** or **gondola ride** to the summit. Admission. ~ Mountain Road; 802-253-7311. You can also navigate a sled down the thrilling **alpine slide.** Admission. ~ Mountain Road; 802-253-7311.

The Stowe Land Trust was established during the 1980s by a group of Stowe citizens who are dedicated to preserving the rural quality of life in and around this picturesque mountain village. One of the trust's conservation projects is the **Wiessner Woods,** 80 acres of woods, streams, and meadows that overlook the Stowe valley from Edson Hill. If you keep your eyes open and your conversation quiet, you're likely to see partridge, thrush, falcons, and perhaps even an owl. From Mountain Road, turn right onto Edson Hill Road (3.5 miles from the village). Pass the entrance to the Stowehof Inn. Take the next drive on the right. Park on the left in the marked parking area. From here follow signs to the Wiessner Woods trailhead.

Several decades after the film *The Sound of Music* was released, Stowe visitors still keep asking the same question: how do we get to the **Trapp Family Lodge?** Certainly much of the town's appeal is bound to the history and beauty of this place, built as a singing camp during the 1940s by Maria Von Trapp and her family. The baroness chose the spot because she said it resembled her beloved Austrian Alps. The Tyrolean-style buildings of the lodge sit high on a mountain, surrounded by 2000 acres of forest, ponds and pasture. Alpine ridges extend as far as the eye can see. During the summer, popular

Sunday concerts are held in an adjacent meadow. Though Maria died in 1987, her family still runs the lodge. ~ 42 Trapp Hill Road off Mountain Road; 802-253-8511.

There's no sign for **Bingham Falls** (off Mountain Road, about 100 yards north of The Lodge resort), but you won't want to miss this pristine look at nature's handiwork. A rocky footpath winds one-quarter mile through the evergreen forest, culminating at a scenic gorge where rushing, gurgling water swirls around large boulders. A great swimming hole, if you don't mind chilly waters.

◄ *HIDDEN*

The closest proximity to downhill skiing can be found at **Sugarbush Village Condominiums**, where you can choose from 200 condos (many ski-in and ski-out) sprinkled about the base of Sugarbush South. Most accommodations are modern apartment-style, though they vary widely from small studios and loft apartments to townhouses and four-bedroom condominiums. ~ Sugarbush Access Road, Sugarbush Village; 802-583-3000, 800-451-4326, fax 802-583-2373. DELUXE TO ULTRA-DELUXE.

LODGING

Set on a lovely hill, enveloped by terraced lawns, cobbled paths and winding streams, **Sugarbush Inn** is the plushest hostelry near the ski slopes. Inside the vanilla clapboard inn is a lobby done in dark, polished woods and rich blues, and 46 guest rooms adorned with country wallpapers, handloomed rugs and reproduction antiques. The Terrace restaurant, with its brick floors, French doors and mountain views, is a marvelous place for breakfast. An extensive health club, a golf course and 11 tennis courts make this the best resort choice in Sugarbush. ~ Sugarbush Access Road, Warren; 802-583-2301, 800-537-8427, fax 802-583-3209. DELUXE TO ULTRA-DELUXE.

You can get a true feel for Vermonters and their lifestyles if you stay at **Lareau Farm**, a picturesque 67-acre spread hugging the Mad River. The owners are convivial and genuine, ready to show you their farming methods, local customs and all the town crazies. The 1832 farmhouse is quintessential New England: big gracious rooms with wide-plank floors, a living room with a fireplace, a fabulous gazebo-style porch overlooking the mountains and 13 very comfortable bedrooms with antique beds and plush quilts made by the owners. Don't miss the winter sleigh rides. ~ Route 100, Waitsfield; 802-496-4949, 800-833-0766. MODERATE TO DELUXE.

Call it pastoral luxury or rural fancy, but the **1824 House Inn** is the place to indulge while soaking up the country. Set on more than 22 scenic acres in the Mad River Valley, this two-story gabled farmhouse is awash with beautiful antiques, Oriental rugs, French doors and a distinct air of elegance and precise design. There are seven bright and airy bedrooms with feather beds done in different themes, plus a gracious dining room where guests get treated to fresh garden omelettes, huevos rancheros and fruit-filled baked pancakes. ~ Route 100, Waitsfield; 802-496-7555, 800-426-3986. DELUXE.

The most eloquent place to stay in the state capital is **The Inn at Montpelier,** a pair of stately antebellum buildings that breathe history. There are high ceilings and beautiful Victorian furnishings, ten fireplaces and an enormous wraparound porch dotted with hanging plants and fan-back chairs. Lavishly decorated, the 19 guest rooms feature mirrored armoires, Queen Anne and teak poster beds and polished pedestal sinks. Well worth the price. ~ 147 Main Street; 802-223-2727, fax 802-223-0722. DELUXE.

The prow-like roofline of **The Stowehof Inn and Resort** is deceptive: there's nothing remotely marinelike about this large, luxurious hotel. Perched on a hillside that overlooks the dips and swells of the Stowe valley, the Stowehof's generous spaces are attentively fitted out, with comfortable chairs in the lounge area and extra-thick drapes on the bedroom windows for guests to block out the bright morning light. Room decor varies: when you call for a reservation, ask about the range of rooms available during your visit (and unless you really want one, request a room without a mirrored wall). Although most travelers associate the Stowe area with winter sports, the Stowehof is a true four-season resort: in addition to the miles of cross-country trails and sleigh rides available right from the hotel during the winter, a swimming pool, four tennis courts, and stables and riding lessons are available for guests' use during warmer weather. Breakfast included. ~ 434 Edson Hill Road, Stowe; 802-253-9722, 800-932-7136, fax, 802-253-7513. MODERATE TO DELUXE.

Butternut is one of those inns that tries to be homey and elegant at the same time—and pulls it off swimmingly. Wrought with dozens of beautiful country American antiques, the three-story lodge is nearly a museum. There's more refinement outside, where twinkling lights meander through evergreens, and a gazebo overlooks a swimming pool and perennial gardens. There are also four miles of lighted cross-country skiing trails. The fireside breakfasts, cozy game room and warmly decorated bedrooms suggest quite a snug lodging experience. A full country breakfast is included. ~ Mountain Road, Stowe; 802-253-4277, 800-328-8837. DELUXE TO ULTRA-DELUXE.

One of the best bargains in the area is **The Siebeness,** a straightforward country inn with comfy bedrooms. Count on a homelike setting with two floors of rooms adorned simply but tastefully in heavy wood antiques, downy, hand-stitched quilts and wall stenciling. There's a large pool and a hidden mountain stream out back, plus bountiful breakfasts that are extra special. ~ Mountain Road, Stowe; 802-253-8942, 800-426-9001, fax 802-253-9232. MODERATE.

Endless waves of mountains and evergreen valleys create a milieu that's nothing short of sensational at the **Trapp Family Lodge.** This peaceful, 2000-acre slice of nirvana was set up as a 1940s singing camp by Maria Von Trapp. Tyrolean in style, the enchanting buildings have flowerpots that brim with kaleidoscopic colors and 93 guest rooms simply adorned in dark woods and muted colors and featuring modern amenities. You can't miss the scenic pond, two swimming pools edged with lawn, greenhouse and gardens—and many more sightseers than guests. Breakfast and dinner are included. ~ 42 Trapp Hill Road, Stowe; 802-253-8511, 800-826-7000, fax 802-253-5740. ULTRA-DELUXE.

A serene French Provincial manor obscured down a winding mountain road, **Edson Hill Manor** offers 225 acres of solitude amid majestic surroundings. Featuring brick walls, hewn-wood ceilings and Oriental rugs, the main house offers nine spacious rooms—five with beautiful fireplaces—while a carriage house contains 16 guest rooms. You'll also find a terraced swimming pool, riding stables, nature trails and plenty of cross-country skiing possibilities. ~ Edson Hill Road off Mountain Road, Stowe; 802-253-7371, 800-621-0284, fax 802-253-4036. DELUXE TO ULTRA-DELUXE.

DINING

This is ski country, and most restaurants cater to those tired skiers with hearty appetites. Oftentimes, you'll find a cauldron of soup steaming over a blazing hearth and cushy chairs for snuggling.

The refinement and understated elegance of **The Common Man** has earned it a solid culinary reputation across Vermont. Situated in a 19th-century barn, the place is simply romantic. Pretty chandeliers hang from high beam ceilings, while well-spaced tables hug a large stone hearth. The cuisine is *très* gourmet, with an accent on native offerings. There's *faisan rôti* (Vermont pheasant), Vermont veal sweetbreads and *caneton* normandy (roasted duckling with apple glaze). Closed Monday. ~ German Flats Road, Warren; 802-583-2800. MODERATE TO DELUXE.

◄ HIDDEN

Two miles down an unmarked dirt road rests the **Dinersoar Restaurant,** a splendid spot to observe all the local airplane activity. Nestled on the top of a teeny building called the Warren-Sugarbush Airport, the Dinersoar affords exhilarating views of the surrounding Green Mountains and valleys. A diligent young owner serves inexpensive breakfasts, soups and deli fare, along with delicious baked desserts. It's a great place to hang loose. Closed from October to Memorial Day. ~ Sugarbush Airport, Airport Road, Warren; 802-496-8831. BUDGET.

A charming 1850s inn and restaurant, the **Millbrook Inn and Restaurant** truly captures the flavor of Vermont. The decor is warm and inviting, with wide-plank floors, country antiques and paintings of local life. A congenial couple act as manager and chef, serving hand-rolled pastas and very special pies. Entrées include two fresh fish specials every day, an "innkeeper's choice" of roast meat, *badami rogan josh* (lamb) and shrimp curry. Closed April, May and November. Open seven days a week in winter and closed Tuesdays in summer. ~ Route 17, Waitsfield; 802-496-2405. MODERATE.

Text continued on page 416.

Vermont
Maple Syrup

It begins quite subtly during the first hint of spring: a tiny sprig of green sprouts, a bird chirps gaily and the sap inside a maple tree breaks free from its icy chamber and trickles ever so gently toward the warm ground.

Squirrels, rabbits and other forest dwellers scurry to lap up the sweet elixir, a welcome indulgence after a long, frigid winter. Along comes another mountain inhabitant, a farmer, who pierces the maple trunk with a plastic tap, drawing the sticky sap into a clear plastic tube. He does this hundreds, perhaps thousands of times, tapping trees and connecting them with little tubes until their sap trickles harmoniously down the mountain.

And so it goes. Each spring, millions of Vermont maple trees surrender their gooey, candied essence for the sake of that sought-after substance known as maple syrup. Called "sugarbushes" or "maple orchards," these grand stands of trees blanket the mountains with their stalwart trunks and burgeoning canopies of delicate toothed leaves.

Vermont is the country's largest supplier of maple syrup, producing an annual average of half a million gallons. Though the harvesting processes are fairly simple, they've changed quite a bit since Native Americans cooked sap over an open fire back in the 1500s.

Today, most farmers use the plastic tubes, drawing sap by gravity or with a vacuum system, but some still opt for the time-honored metal bucket system. In this method, sap drips from trees into large buckets, which are carted on sleds down the mountains.

Back at the sugarhouse, sap is boiled all day (and sometimes all night) in huge metal pans until it's reduced to a smooth syrup. It takes an average of 40 gallons of sap to net one gallon of syrup.

All the cooking takes place in hundreds of wooden sugarhouses—characterized by vented roofs to help steam escape—that dot verdant mountains and valleys. You can peek in on all the action by visiting large syrup mills, but for the most rewarding experience, stop in on a family-owned operation. Here, cordial folks will bring you up to snuff on the sweet stuff as well as share their lifestyles and family histories.

You'll discover small, family-owned farms all over the state, and while many display a small sign that says "Maple Syrup," others have no sign (these you can find out about at the local general store). More than 100 large and small operations are listed in *Maple Sugarhouses Open to the Public*, a dandy, free brochure published by the Vermont Department of Agriculture (116 State Street, Drawer 20, Montpelier, VT 05620; 802-828-2416). Listings are by county and town and provide information on number of taps, size of sugarhouses, methods of operation and tours.

The **New England Maple Museum** promises "The Sweetest Story Ever Told" if you visit its displays of maple sugar nostalgia. A great place to bone up on syrup history, the museum stocks old artifacts like wooden buckets and taps and horse-drawn sleds used for toting sap. The best part, though, is the free syrup tasting. Admission. ~ Route 7, Pittsford; 802-483-9414.

Or, immerse yourself in syrupy activities at the **Vermont Maple Festival**, held each April in St. Albans, north of Burlington. Feast on pancakes smothered in syrup, take in the fiddlers' contest and savor the honeyed flavor of assorted syrup varieties. ~ Contact the Vermont Maple Festival Council, Box 255, St. Albans, VT 05478; 802-524-5800.

Plan to visit from late February (southern areas) through mid-April (northern areas). The choicest syrup, a fancy golden extract, is harvested first. As the season progresses, syrup turns a medium amber, then a dark amber and finally a bitter, murky consistency that's seldom edible.

Of course, the finer things in life always cost more, and such is the case with maple syrup. Usually double and triple the price of blended syrups, the real stuff can cost you from 40 to 60 cents per ounce.

But be forewarned. Those accustomed to blended syrup shall unwittingly be seduced by the pure maple kind, a victim of their own newly enlightened taste buds. Syrupoholics say it's sort of like switching from jug wine to fine wine: once you've tasted the good stuff, it's impossible to go back.

Many of Vermont's restaurateurs grow their own produce and herbs, and such is the case at **Tucker Hill Lodge**. The menu features northern Italian cuisine served in a Mediterranean-style setting of Italian paintings and pottery. Start off with an antipasta dish, then try the wood-oven pizza, the freshly made pasta or one of the veal or fish dishes. ~ Route 17, Waitsfield; 802-496-3983. MODERATE TO DELUXE.

In Montpelier, the New England Culinary Institute operates three restaurants where you'll discover very vogue cuisine. The most up-scale is the **Chef's Table**, which serves innovative and classical American cuisine in an intimate setting. The red walls, antique oil paintings and low lighting create a Baroque effect and a romantic atmosphere. The seasonal menu changes daily and features gourmet dishes such as warm goat cheese Napoleon and hickory-smoked duck. Dinner only. ~ 118 Main Street; 802-229-9202. MODERATE TO DELUXE.

For more casual surroundings, visit the Culinary Institute's **Main Street Grill & Bar** downstairs. This casual bistro offers hearty fare amidst eclectic country decor. Try the portabello mushroom sandwich or the herbed roast chicken with garlic mashed potatoes. The outdoor patio is open in the summer. ~ 118 Main Street; 802-223-3188. MODERATE.

At **La Brioche Bakery and Café**, also run by the Institute, you can pick up puffy croissants, gourmet cookies, napoleons and other baked goodies. ~ 89 Main Street; 802-229-0443. BUDGET.

The glistening gold-plated dome of the state capitol peeks through the windows of the **Horn of the Moon Café**, a bohemian habitat with bamboo shades and scuffed wooden floors. Politicians like to hobnob over the vegetarian inventory of imaginative soups, salads and desserts. Try the chapati salad with tahini dressing. Closed Monday. ~ 8 Langdon Street, Montpelier; 802-223-2895. BUDGET TO MODERATE.

HIDDEN ▶

For top-notch Mexican fare, check out **Julio's**. This serene downtown niche, stashed up a rickety flight of stairs, offers up basic south-of-the-border entrées plus interesting selections such as Mexican pizzas and egg rolls. There's a shiny oak bar, brick archways and walls

BREAKFAST BRIGHT AND EARLY

To experience the true flavor of **McCarthy's**, get there just after dawn when local farmers arrive dressed in overalls and straw hats. This congenial breakfast and lunch café offers friendly service, huge portions and great prices. You'll find apple and blueberry pancakes with hot Vermont syrup, country eggs Benedict, sticky buns and pumpkin bread. Surroundings are modern and airy with Irish country touches. ~ Mountain Road, Stowe; 802-253-8626. BUDGET.

covered with Mexican prints and blankets. ~ 44 Main Street, Montpelier; 802-229-9348. BUDGET TO MODERATE.

Jack's Backyard is a popular town rendezvous with real flair. The two-story, ranch-style eatery is flanked by wagon wheels and exhibits walls smothered in old license plates and farm tools. Popcorn is divvied up in tin pails for those with "drinking" appetites, but most opt for the potpourri of stacked sandwiches, chili, crêpes and salads. Closed Sunday. ~ 9 Maple Avenue, Barre; 802-479-9134. BUDGET TO MODERATE.

The beautiful **Trapp Family Lodge** boasts one of the area's most renowned dining rooms. Situated in a marvelous mountain setting, the restaurant is simple yet elegant, with picture windows, draped hanging plants and light oak tables. The food is gourmet with Austrian touches. Try the *zwiebelrostbraten* (Viennese onion steak) or *kassler ritpchen* (braised smoked pork loin with sauerkraut and potato pancakes). The menu is *prix-fixe*, with a five-course meal. ~ 42 Trapp Hill Road, Stowe; 802-253-8511. ULTRA-DELUXE.

Culinary aficionados won't want to miss **Isle de France**, a classic French restaurant with all the trimmings. The decor is terribly Parisian, accented by provincial furniture, impressionist paintings, huge, ornate mirrors and well-spaced tables designed for romance. The deluxe-priced menu is an assortment of fresh seafood, steak, poultry, sweet-breads and frogs' legs, all draped in a variety of heady sauces and beautifully served. But here's the real scoop: dine in the cozy lounge and those same entrées are about half price. ~ Mountain Road, Stowe; 802-253-7751. MODERATE TO DELUXE.

SHOPPING

Absolutely don't miss **The Warren Store**, a former stagecoach inn that's like Grandpa's general store. The place starts with a jumble of fresh farm produce, jams, homemade honey and baskets, continues with a wonderful bakery, then finishes upstairs with clothing, jewelry and leather goods. ~ Main Street, Warren; 802-496-3864.

The **Blue Toad** is a florist with a twist: It carries candles, soaps and doll boxes from Russia, Poland and other countries. ~ Route 100, Waitsfield; 802-496-2567.

Even if you leave empty-handed, don't miss a trip to **The Store**, a bi-level, cook's fantasy world of gourmet gadgets galore. They also feature accessories for the home, and American, English and Irish antiques. ~ Route 100, Waitsfield; 802-496-4465.

More than 50,000 books crowd **The Yankee Paperback Exchange**, where you'll find everything from old classics and out-of-print gems to volumes on religion, cooking and lifestyles. ~ 11 Langdon Street, Montpelier; 802-223-3239.

Candles, incense, hammered jewelry and offbeat reading material are featured in an eclectic bazaar called **The Mystic Trader**. ~ 23 Langdon Street, Montpelier; 802-229-9220.

Everything Cows possesses bovine treasures such as cow ties and T-shirts, moo lights and clocks and "udder" necessities. ~ Main Street, Stowe; 802-253-8779.

HIDDEN ►

Beautiful hand-wrought jewelry, made by over 30 local artisans, awaits in an underground nook called **The Silver Den**. ~ Main Street, Stowe; 802-253-8787.

Women won't need to vacillate at **Decisions, Decisions**, where they can choose among beautiful sleepwear, lingerie and snug winter items. ~ 1813 Mountain Road, unit 2, Stowe; 802-253-4183.

NIGHTLIFE

The Blue Tooth is an after-the-slopes place to hang loose and listen to live contemporary music. Cover. ~ Mountain Access Road, Warren; 802-583-2656.

Local theater in Vermont tends to be high quality, and such is the case at **Valley Players Community Theater**, which focuses on drama and comedy performed in a 200-seat, two-story, brick building. ~ Route 100, Waitsfield; for information call the Sugarbush Chamber of Commerce at 802-496-3409.

The dancefloor is small and tables scarce, but the disco at the **Backroom Saloon** may be the hottest spot around during ski season. They also feature weekend DJs and occasional live bands on Wednesday nights. ~ Sugarbush Village; 802-583-2600.

Politicians rub elbows at **The Thrush**, a tiny watering hole with framed old photos and occasional live folk music. ~ 107 State Street, Montpelier; 802-223-2030.

Tattered carpets lie before a worn pine bar at **Charlie O's**, a pool hall with live rhythm-and-blues on the weekend and a sound system that cranks. ~ Main Street, Montpelier; 802-223-6820.

For live jazz on the weekends, head to the **Main Street Grill & Bar**. This comfortable basement bar has exposed flagstone walls, original artwork and one of the state's largest collections of wine, beer, and liquor. ~ 118 Main Street, Montpelier; 802-223-3188.

For a relaxing time, head to **The Pub at Stowe**, an authentic English pub with Tudor decor. ~ 311 Mountain Road, Stowe; 802-253-8669.

The Matterhorn, Bamboo Bar and Oasis Grill, a voluminous rock-and-roll bar perched near the base of Mt. Mansfield, hosts big-name rock groups during the ski season. Cover. ~ Mountain Road, Stowe; 802-253-8198.

BEACHES & PARKS

GREEN MOUNTAIN NATIONAL FOREST See "Beaches & Parks" in the Southern Vermont section.

LITTLE RIVER STATE PARK 🏃 ⚓ 🚣 A dense, bushy area lying within Mount Mansfield State Forest, this park spans 12,000 acres of maple, birch and fir forests and a big manmade body of water called the Waterbury Reservoir. There are three beaches—two in a wooded camping area and one in a large picnic clearing—comprised of silver, silty sand. Nature lovers will revel in the excellent gridwork of trails. Swimming and fishing (for perch, rainbow trout, and small and big-mouth bass) are good all over the reservoir. Picnic tables, restrooms, playground, boat rentals and ramp; day-use fee, $1.50. Open from mid-May to mid-October. ~ From the junction of Routes 100 and 2, take Route 2 one and one-half miles west to Little River Road and go north for three and one-half miles; 802-244-7103.

▲ There are 101 sites with hot showers, fireplaces and 20 lean-tos. Fees are $12 per night for tent/RV sites (no hookups); $16 per night for lean-tos.

GROTON STATE FOREST 🚶 ⛱ 🛶 🛥 🚣 This 25,625-acre wonderland nurtures several natural jewels. Fishing is good at the campgrounds, but the best place in the forest is **Seyon Fly Fishing Area** (802-584-3829), just off Route 302 three miles west of Groton, where you'll find a trout pond, rental canoes and overnight lodges.

At **Ricker**, you'll find fireplaces, picnic tables, boat rentals, playground, showers. ~ On Route 232, three miles northwest of Route 302; 802-584-3821.

At the picturesque **Boulder Beach**, bulky rocks dot a coarse, cream-tinted sand that edges Lake Groton. Small boats laze across the water, surrounded by mighty stands of evergreen trees. Swimming is excellent along a calm, shallow shelf at Boulder Beach. Picnic areas, restrooms, boat rentals, snack bar, pavilion; day-use fee, $1.50. ~ From Groton, go two miles west on Route 302, then six miles northwest on Route 232, then two mile east on Boulder Beach Road; 802-584-3823.

Facilities at **Stillwater** include picnic tables, fireplaces, boat rentals, dock, boat launch, playground and showers. ~ From Groton, go two miles west on Route 302, then six miles northwest on Route 232, then one mile east on Boulder Beach Road; 802-584-3822.

The **Groton Nature Center** houses interesting displays of plant and animal life. Restrooms, nature walks, films. ~ One mile west of Boulder Beach on Boulder Beach Road; 802-584-3827

One of the most popular forest activities is the hike to the summit of **Owl's Head Mountain**, where incredible views stretch across Camel's Hump Forest. Picnic tables, primitive toilets; information. ~ On Route 232, eight and a half miles northwest of Route 302; 802-584-3820.

New Discovery Campground (on Osmore Pond) offers a scenic clearing for picnicking. Picnic tables, restrooms, pavilions; stores nearby in Groton. ~ On Route 232, nine and a half miles northwest of Route 302; 802-584-3820.

All areas are open from the week before Memorial Day to Labor Day except Stillwater, which is open until Columbus Day.

▲ Groton Forest has five camping areas, including primitive, group and developed campgrounds. All of the above-mentioned areas have camping except Boulder Beach, which is day-use only. Rates are $10 to $12 per night for tents, $14 to $16 per night for lean-tos. RVs are welcome; no hookups.

SMUGGLERS NOTCH STATE PARK 🏃 Wedged at the apex of two stony, sheer mountains, Smugglers Notch offers idyllic surroundings of rock ledges and formations, fern grottos and damp caves for exploring. The park itself comprises 25 acres of shady, brookside picnic grounds, but you can walk to many choice sights outside the park grounds, including frigid Big Springs pool and the 6000-ton King Rock that broke from the mountain in 1910. Check out the great elephant head formation just above King Rock. Picnic tables, restrooms and hiking trails. Open from mid-May to the middle of October. ~ On Route 108 (Mountain Road) in Stowe, about eight miles north of Route 100 junction; 802-253-4014.

▲ Small area with 24 tent/RV sites ($11 per night) and 14 lean-tos ($15 per night); hot showers and fireplaces but no hookups.

HIDDEN ► **UNDERHILL STATE PARK** 🏃 Remote and rustic, this pretty park lies in the midst of back country, smothered in maple and birch trees and filled with moose, bear, deer, rabbits and raccoons. It covers 150 acres of mountain terrain and features three popular trails that ascend the western flank of Mount Mansfield. The park also holds rare, federally protected alpine tundra, which can only be viewed from specific trails. To get here, you'll have to tackle four miles of steep gravel road—but it's well worth it. A picnic shelter, restrooms; day-use fee, $1.50 for adults, $1 for children. The park is open from Memorial Day to Columbus Day. ~ From the town of Essex Junction, go nine miles east on Route 15, then four miles east on Pleasant Valley Road, then three miles east on gravel Mountain Road (there's a sign at this point); 802-899-3022.

▲ There's a small primitive area with 11 tent sites ($11 per night) and six lean-tos ($15 per night).

▼▼▼▼▼▼▼▼▼▼▼
Champlain Valley
A great big meeting of mountains, water and islands, the Champlain Valley is a prosperous, breathtaking region that ambles leisurely along Vermont's northwestern edge. Lake Champlain, the area's frame of reference, stretches 130 glistening miles and divides Vermont's flat, irregular lakefront border from New York's Adirondack Mountains. Back in 1609, French explorer Samuel de Champlain discovered the lake, named it for himself and laid the groundwork for its flourishing maritime history. Champlain Valley is also home to Vermont's most populated city, Burlington, which was founded in 1763.

SIGHTS   The state's most popular attraction lies in this region. Just south of Burlington, the **Shelburne Museum** is really a *collection* of buildings—37 to be exact. It takes two days to tackle this amazing 45-acre trek through Vermont and New England history. There's something for everyone here, from the 220-foot sidewheel steamboat and toy shop to the round barn, 1890 slate jail and 1786 sawmill. Kids and adults will love the circus building with its carousel ride and remarkable 500-foot miniature circus parade that took 30 years to complete. A 168-foot covered bridge, built in 1845 and moved to the museum from Cambridge, Vermont, is the United States' only remaining two-lane bridge with a footpath. If snipes, loons and yellowlegs are your bag, stop in the wildfowl decoy museum, where an eye-popping 1000 specimens line the walls. A marvelous place to muse, the hat and fragrance house has hat boxes, costumes, perfumes and lace dating back to the early 1800s. You'll also find the state's largest collection of fine art, divided among several buildings. Admission, good for two days. ~ Route 7, Shelburne; 802-985-3346.

Board a covered wagon for a tour of **Shelburne Farms,** a vast land empire that gives new meaning to the term "pastoral aristocracy." Sprawled across 1400 acres along Lake Champlain, the estate was designed back in the 1800s for Dr. William Seward Webb and wife Lila Vanderbilt, whose 45-room Queen Anne Revival farmhouse is still one of the largest in Vermont. The beautiful grounds—a series of free-flowing perennials, statues and fountains—were designed by Frederick Law Olmsted, architect of New York City's Central Park. There are extensive walking trails, scenic picnic sites and a children's farmyard. Closed from mid-October to late May. ~ Admission. Bay and Harbor roads, off Route 7, Shelburne; 802-985-8686.

Five miles south of the Shelburne Museum is the **Vermont Wildflower Farm,** which produces more wildflower seeds than any other flower farm in the eastern United States. If you're not allergic to pollen, take an hour or so to wander along the paths that cross the six acres. The stupendous array of flowers are thoughtfully labeled with plaques describing the plants' provenance and, often, relating legends about the mystical powers attributed to them. Open from early May through October. ~ Route 7, Shelburne; 802-425-3500.

Just north of Shelburne, skirting the lake and reigning over the valley, is Vermont's Queen City, **Burlington.** With a population of 40,000, it's the state's largest city but one that manages to maintain an intimate milieu. Burlington's remarkable alliance of mountain and water vistas were lauded by none other than Charles Dickens when he landed here back in the mid-1800s. Today, art centers, innovative theater, a university and four colleges add to the cultural mix of this spirited, youthful metropolis. In the last couple of years, the waterfront area has flourished. A community boathouse provides boat rentals and a seven-mile path has been created along the lake shore for bikers, joggers and walkers. Restaurants and shopping abound, making the lakefront a very pleasant place for a stroll.

In fact, nearly half of Burlington's population is made up of college students, many of whom attend the statuesque hilltop campus of the **University of Vermont**. ~ Off University Place and Colchester Avenue; 802-656-3480.

The university's **Robert Hull Fleming Museum**, a grand Colonial Revival building, houses an excellent collection of European and American paintings, decorative artworks and costumes, and ethnographic objects from around the world. Closed Monday. ~ Colchester Avenue; 802-656-0750.

Keep your eyes peeled for "Champ," Lake Champlain's own Loch Ness Monster, whose bulky outline and distinct humps were first sighted by Samuel de Champlain and recorded in his ship's log.

To help get you started in the area, stop by the **Lake Champlain Regional Chamber of Commerce**. ~ 209 Battery Street; 802-863-3489.

The city's best side exists, naturally, on glittering Lake Champlain. Stroll along **Lake and Battery streets** and peer across the water to New York's Adirondack Mountains, then take a two-hour roundtrip **ferry** from Burlington over to Port Kent, New York while absorbing all the scintillating views. ~ Ferry: King Street Dock, King and Battery streets; 802-864-9804.

Most of the day and nighttime activity occurs on **Church Street Marketplace**, a thriving pedestrian mall jammed with outdoor cafés, trendy shops, strolling musicians and magicians and graced with 19th-century architecture. The effect is European, to say the least. ~ Church Street between Main and Pearl streets.

Northward, the **Champlain Islands** comprise Vermont's own "seacoast," a virgin outpost of apple orchards and dairy farms, rustic lakeside retreats and shores lined with anglers casting their nets. Though today there's a causeway linking these isles to Burlington, 19th-century residents had to make do with small skiffs and winter weather, when a frozen lake afforded the best access to the mainland. Route 2 traces a 30-mile path over water and land through this quiescent, largely undeveloped archipelago.

Revolutionary War veteran Jedediah Hyde, Jr., built a log cabin on the largest island, Grand Isle, back in 1783. Today the **Hyde Log Cabin** is thought to be the oldest log cabin in the country, a one-room alcove of rough-hewn beams held together by clay and straw. Amazingly, some of the original furniture and farm tools remain intact. ~ Route 2.

Up on Isle La Motte, 19th-century stone houses and a meandering rocky coastline form quite a beautiful tableau. The **St. Anne Shrine** denotes the site of Fort St. Anne—Vermont's earliest settlement—built in 1666 by Captain Pierre La Motte. ~ Off Route 129.

LODGING   Near the southern end of the Champlain Valley lies the vibrant college town of Middlebury. Here, the **Swift House Inn** reposes among enormous elm and maple trees and broods with New England history. The 1814 main house, a Federal-style building that was home to former Vermont Governor John W. Stewart, has ten rooms with poster beds and some marble fireplaces. An 1876 Victorian carriage house offers six cozy rooms with fireplaces and whirlpool tubs, while the gatehouse features five rooms with a mixture of reproductions and antiques. ~ Route 7 and Stewart Lane; 802-388-9925, fax 802-388-9927. MODERATE TO ULTRA-DELUXE.

Occupying a choice 700 acres along Lake Champlain, the **Basin Harbor Club** has been a prime waterside getaway since 1886. Sprinkled along the lake banks and peeking across to New York's Adirondack Mountains are 38 rooms and 77 cottages with simple, lodge-style furnishings. This self-contained retreat, open from mid-May through mid-October, boasts an 18-hole golf course, swimming pool, tennis courts, top-notch restaurant and airstrip. ~ Basin Harbor Road off Route 22A, Vergennes; 802-475-2311, 800-622-4000, fax 802-475-2545. ULTRA-DELUXE.

Perhaps the most distinguished lodging address in all the Champlain Valley is the **Shelburne House**. Formerly home to Lila Vanderbilt Webb, the 1899 brick manor has all the Vanderbilt trimmings: incredible Lake Champlain and mountain vistas, 24 guest rooms with opulent Queen Anne Revival furnishings and 1400 acres of lovely farmlands sprinkled with 19th-century buildings. Settle in, soak up the history of this fascinating place and pretend you'll never have to leave. Closed mid-October to mid-May. ~ Harbor and Bay roads, off Route 7, Shelburne; 802-985-8498. DELUXE TO ULTRA-DELUXE.

Burlington, Vermont's largest city, offers little in the way of homey bed and breakfasts and quaint inns but does have a smattering of motor lodges, motels and hotels.

At the **Sheraton Burlington Inn,** you will find 309 spacious rooms with contemporary furnishings, marble vanities and mountain views (though in the distance), as well as a health club with a removable glass atrium over the pool. There is also a large interior courtyard and a sundeck. ~ 870 Williston Road; 802-862-6576, 800-677-6576, fax 802-865-6670. DELUXE TO ULTRA-DELUXE.

On the northeast side of town, the **Days Inn** is a no-nonsense place where you can swipe a clean, modern-style room with a moderate price. The three-story design is generic motel, though the decor is a notch above, with cushy couches, designer draperies and cedar siding. Suites are more expensive. ~ 23 College Parkway, Burlington; 802-655-0900, 800-329-7466, fax 802-655-6851. MODERATE TO DELUXE.

DINING

Woody's perches on the bank of Otter Creek in the middle of pretty Middlebury. The restaurant is three stories high, with floor-to-ceiling windows that make even the rainiest day seem bright to indoor diners. During warm weather, try to get a table on the outdoor deck. Fresh ingredients star in most dishes: the homemade soups are especially good. Some of our favorites include fajitas, caesar salad with grilled chicken and cheddar cheese soup. Closed on Tuesday from November through April. ~ 5 Bakery Lane; 802-388-4182. BUDGET TO MODERATE.

Burlington is Vermont's largest city and its restaurant capital, so not surprisingly, you'll find a medley of choice dining establishments. Some of the best can be found on Church Street's four-block Marketplace, a brick-lined pedestrian mall packed with outdoor cafés and college students.

A rare Vermont sushi bar is part of the **Marketplace at Sakura**, a simple but cheery restaurant with a tatami room and small wooden tables that peek out over the street. The sushi and sashimi are fresh and served on wooden trays with pretty designs. If you prefer a hot Japanese meal, opt for the *yakitori* (broiled chicken on skewers) or *gyoza* (meat dumplings) or select from the host of teriyaki and tempura entrées. ~ 2 Church Street, Burlington; 802-863-1988. MODERATE TO DELUXE.

The place for fresh New England seafood is the **Ice House**, a restored harborside building with a venerable seafaring aura. There's a wharf and ferry station a stone's throw away. Specialties include grilled swordfish and salmon, Maine lobster and a shrimp, calamari and sea scallop combination. The place is draped in wood and stone and features an outdoor deck. ~ 171 Battery Street, Burlington; 802-864-1800. MODERATE TO DELUXE.

Waterworks is a typical yuppie-style bistro with one very special attraction: water. The enclosed terrace here affords a sweeping view of the Winooski River, where waves of water rush and swirl across huge boulders, creating quite a commotion and a sublime dining environment. The cuisine is reliable and includes an assortment of chicken, seafood and steak dishes, as well as sandwiches. Inside, you'll find red brick walls, high ceilings and large windows for good water views. ~ The Champlain Mill, Winooski; 802-655-2044. MODERATE.

SHOPPING
HIDDEN ▶

It nearly takes a miracle to find **Authentica African Imports**, but once you're there, it's worth it. More than just a shop, this place offers a look at African styles and customs, with jewelry from West and East African nations, rugs made of camel hair and goat skin, Mali blankets, Ethiopian rugs, Zulu clay pots, fertility statues from Malawi and much more. ~ Greenbush Road about one mile north of Ferry Road, Charlotte; 802-425-3137.

Stroll Burlington's four-block **Church Street Marketplace** and you'll be rewarded with a bevy of fine, trendy shops. ~ Church Street between Main and Pearl streets.

Forests find their ways into clocks, toys and furniture at **The Symmetree Company**. ~ 89 Church Street; 802-658-1441.

NIGHTLIFE

The hottest night scene pulses in Burlington, where 16,000 college students feed a multitude of discos, progressive clubs and bebop joints.

The **Flynn Theater for the Performing Arts**, a 1400-seat art deco palace and old vaudeville house, offers a terrific lineup of international and Broadway theater and major symphony and dance. ~ 153 Main Street, Burlington; 802-863-5966.

A dark, smokey cubbyhole with a crowd predominantly in their 30s, **Nectar's** serves up top-notch live blues and rock. ~ 188 Main Street, Burlington; 802-658-4771. Upstairs at **Club Metronome** there's live music, including blues, funk, ska and hip-hop. Cover depending on the band. ~ 802-865-4563.

The place to cut a rug is **Sh-na-na's**, where a sprawling checkered dancefloor is accented by pinups of Elvis and other '50s paraphernalia. With recorded music from the '50s through the '90s, this joint is often packed. Cover Friday and Saturday. ~ 101 North Main Street, Burlington; 802-865-2596.

Sweetwaters is undeniably the area's upscale meeting place, where patrons linger around a shiny bar and watch all the street activity through large glass windows. ~ Church and Collins Street, Burlington; 802-864-9800.

Late-nighters flock to **The Vermont Pub and Brewery**, a spacious but cozy brew house with brick walls, archways, mirrors and hanging plants. There's usually live acoustic music on Thursday, Friday and Saturday. ~ 144 College Street, Burlington; 802-865-0500.

The only gay bar for miles, **Pearl's** offers dancing Thursday through Sunday, an 18-and-over juice bar on Wednesday, and cabaret on Sunday. The crowd is mostly gay. Cover. ~ 135 Pearl Street, Burlington; 802-863-2343.

The ever-popular **Sneakers Bar & Grill** is a down-and-dirty pub with a lineup of jazz and bluegrass. Cover charge. ~ 36 Main Street, Winooski; 802-655-9081.

MOUNT PHILO STATE PARK 🏃 Resting right on top of Mount Philo, this park rewards those who tackle its very steep but paved road with astonishing panoramas. From here, you can peer across Lake Champlain into New York's Adirondacks and farther. A total of 163 acres, most of the park is vertical and forested. There is a nice picnic area, and the park's hiking trails are splendid. Picnic tables; store one mile south on Route 7; day-use fee, minimum $1.50. Open from a week before Memorial Day to Columbus Day. ~ Off Route 7, six miles north of Route 22A near North Ferrisburg; 802-425-2390.

▲ There are 13 tent sites ($10 per night) and three lean-tos ($14 per night), with hot showers and fireplaces (firewood is for sale).

SAND BAR STATE PARK One of the flattest areas in the state, this ever-popular locale borders Lake Champlain and a waterfowl refuge. Families and college students crowd the coarse, mocha-colored sand and grassy areas lining the lake, while windsurfers and sailboats whiz along just offshore. The views across the lake of the Adirondack Mountains are exceptional. The water is waist-deep at

BEACHES & PARKS

least 100 yards out, and is popular with swimmers. Picnic facilities, bathhouse, volleyball courts, boat and windsurfing rentals, snack bar; day-use fee, minimum $1.50. Open from Memorial Day to Labor Day. ~ On Route 2 in Milton, three miles west of Route 89; 802-893-2825

NORTH HERO STATE PARK From its perch on a thickly wooded peninsula, this 400-acre park captures a prominent view of Lake Champlain and glances backward on North Hero Island. Though it actually borders two miles of lake, the only real accessible shore is a small but pretty shale beach at the peninsula's tip, a secluded spot favored by Canadians and local sailboaters. Swimming is good, but you must wade out past a rim of slippery rocks. Immense Lake Champlain provides superb fishing opportunities, from bass and pike to perch, walleye and pickerel. Picnic tables, restrooms, playground, rowboat and canoe rentals and boat ramp; store four miles southwest on Route 2; day-use fee, $1.50. Open from Memorial Day to Labor Day. ~ From Alburg, go ten miles south on Route 2 and cross the bridge to North Hero Island. Take an immediate left onto Bridge Road. Follow Bridge Road two miles to Lakeview Drive and take a left onto Lakeview. Go one mile on Lakeview, and the entrance will be on your left; 802-372-8727.

▲ Permitted at 117 sites with hot showers and fireplaces but no hookups. Rates are $11 per night for tent/RV sites and $15 per night for lean-tos.

▼▼▼▼▼▼▼▼▼▼▼▼▼
Northeast Kingdom

This vast rural outback could well contain the largest stretch of splendid scenery in all of Vermont. A broad land inhabited by log cutters, cattle drivers and mountain folk, it forms a fine skein of glacier-dug lakes, mellow ponds and rivers, untamed evergreen forests and abrupt alpine ridges. Fall foliage first peeks out its gorgeous head up here, snow falls early and huge bodies of water turn to compact ice.

Beginning in St. Johnsbury and extending northward to the Canadian border, the Northeast Kingdom could well be termed Vermont's last stand. Its thin population and lack of major industry perpetuate considerable unemployment (by Vermont's standards), though firmly rooted residents vow their rugged country living surpasses that in southern ski meccas any day.

SIGHTS St. Johnsbury, the region's largest city, is a quaint, mostly blue-collar town located where the Moose and Sleepers rivers flow into the Passumpsic River. The local **Northeast Kingdom Chamber of Commerce** will provide walking-tour maps and regional information. ~ 30 Western Avenue; 802-748-3678.

A perfect spot to learn about local history is the **Fairbanks Museum and Planetarium**, where exhibits are imaginative and informative. The extensive wildlife collection includes stuffed condors and owls, pythons and chamois, and monstrous polar bears and Kodiaks.

The building itself, with a barrel-vaulted ceiling and Romanesque designs of red sandstone, is marvelous. Admission. ~ Main and Prospect streets, St. Johnsbury; 802-748-2372.

Tucked in the back of a beautiful 1871 library, the **St. Johnsbury Athenaeum Art Gallery** is a step back in time. The place bills itself as "oldest unaltered art gallery in the United States," and indeed, its collection has not changed since the mid-1920s. The 100-plus paintings feature numerous American landscape scenes by Albert Bierstadt and other famed Hudson River School artists. The library, a lovely Victorian-style masterpiece, has seen minimal architectural change over the century. ~ 30 Main Street, St. Johnsbury; 802-748-8291.

◄ HIDDEN

Maple Grove Farms of Vermont house the world's oldest and largest maple candy factory. Founded in 1915 by two local women, the little farmhouse was converted into a factory in 1929. Tours take visitors through the factory, where vintage equipment from the 1930s is still in use and where large quanities of maple syrup are packaged by hand. The old sugar house now contains a maple museum, and a third building features an extensive gift shop. Admission. ~ 167 Portland Street, St. Johnsbury; 802-748-5141.

Take Route 5A north to Route 105, then backtrack south on a splendid trek revealing yet another flawless meld of mountain and water. Gaze at the hilltop homes that scope out scenic views, at the farmers bailing hay and at old frame homes with laundry draped across their porches.

Soon you'll come to the town of **Island Pond**, where bait shops, log cabins and a gas station form an earthy setting. The town green overlooks the water and was the site of the first international railroad in North America. There's also a Civil War cannon and a World War II monument.

Head toward Canada again, traveling north along Route 111, and you'll quickly feel the French vibes of our northern neighbor. Enormous **Lake Memphremagog** shares its waters (nearly equally) with Vermont and Quebec.

SWITZERLAND ON MY MIND

Travel north of St. Johnsbury on Route 5 to Route 5A and you'll arrive at what may be the state's single most stupendous vista. **Lake Willoughby**, an incredible expanse of water chiseled by glaciers, known as the "Lucerne" of the United States, shimmers peacefully beneath the craggy peaks of Mounts Pisgah and Hor. Rimmed with rocky shoreline, fine carpets of grass and inns and lakefront cabins (not too many due to the foresightedness of local leaders), the lake dispenses all the beauty the eye can handle.

Newport is a special town, resting on a procession of hills that skirt the lake and crowned by the spires of beautiful **St. Mary's Star of the Sea Church.** ~ 5 Clermont Terrace; 802-334-5066.

Downtown offers a nice array of shops and restaurants and a helpful **Chamber of Commerce Information Booth** that will load you up with information. ~ The Causeway; 802-334-7782.

There are three dirt roads that lead to the valley hamlet of **Brownington,** though the less adventurous will opt for the one that's paved. Here awaits an enchanting museum called **The Old Stone House,** built as a school dormitory in 1836 by the Reverend Alexander Twilight, the country's first black college graduate and legislator. Twenty-three rooms are filled with inspiring memorabilia that form endearing snapshots of early American life. Nearly everything here was donated by local families, including the 18th-century furniture, 19th-century military uniforms (worn by Brownington men) and a wonderful collection of 1800s newspapers. Admission. ~ Brownington Village near Orleans; 802-754-2022.

HIDDEN ►

A block from the Old Stone House is **Prospect Hill Observatory,** a wooden tower perched atop a grassy hill. Climb a short flight of stairs and be rewarded with a 360-degree panorama of rolling mountains and evergreen spires. A splendid way to remember Vermont, for sure. ~ Take a dirt road beside Brownington Congregational Church.

LODGING

A genteel Victorian house like **The Looking Glass Inn** seems so out of place at the junction of two major highways. But step inside and you'll discover an oasis of beautiful high ceilings, French windows, cherrywood banisters and Oriental rugs. A hoppin' stagecoach stop during the early 1800s (there's still a dancefloor above the garage), the Looking Glass offers four rooms with handmade quilts, antique headboards and wash basins and modern carpets; the two suites have private baths. ~ Routes 93 and 18, St. Johnsbury; 802-748-3052, 800-579-3644. MODERATE.

Children, animals, and dramatic scenery abound at the **Wildflower Inn,** part of a 500-acre estate that's a great place to spend more than one night. Accommodations vary in size: all 15 bedrooms have private bathrooms and a mix of antique and reproduction furniture; eight suites are available, and the honeymoon cottage is complete with a jacuzzi built for two. For the kids, there's a playroom with a chestful of dress-up clothes and, outdoors, a petting barn with several horses, ponies, and cows. Breakfast and dinner are included. ~ Darling Hill Road, Lyndonville; 802-626-8310, 800-627-8310, fax 802-626-3039. MODERATE TO DELUXE.

Standing by Lake Willoughby, the **Willough Vale Inn** offers spectacular views and a rustic elegance. Though built in 1987, the Colonial-style inn harkens to yesteryear with stained-wood floors, antiques and Oriental rugs. Most of the eight rooms snatch a lake view and are enhanced with simple oak and cherry furniture and country prints. ~ Route 5A, Westmore; 802-525-4123, 800-541-0588. MODERATE TO ULTRA-DELUXE.

Just getting to **Heermansmith Farm** is a joyous adventure. Truck two miles down a dusty washboard road, past the grazing cows and romping dogs, then navigate a picturesque covered bridge and you'll arrive at the prim whitewashed farmhouse. This country gem, enveloped by fields and total solitude, has been in the same family since 1807. The innkeepers are marvelous, the atmosphere congenial and the seven bedrooms very agreeable with antique beds, pitchers and basins and large closets stacked with well-thumbed paperbacks. Some of the rooms have private baths. ~ Coventry Village; 802-754-8866. BUDGET TO MODERATE.

◄ HIDDEN

The Inn on the Common is an impeccable inn in the impeccable little town of Craftsbury Common. There are a total of 16 guest rooms in three separate buildings, one of which is on the village green; the others are steps away. Several are furnished with antiques and attractive floral fabrics. At the back of the main building are formal gardens and a far-reaching view of the surrounding Northeast Kingdom countryside. Both breakfast and dinner are included in the room rate. ~ Craftsbury Common; 802-586-9619, 800-521-2233, fax 802-586-2249. ULTRA-DELUXE.

At the end of a long dirt road in the hilly Northeast Kingdom, the **Rodgers Dairy Farm** takes in a few visitors at a time. You're welcome to pitch in with the chores that are involved in keeping cows and horses. Or, if you'd rather, avoid the animals and take a walk through the pretty countryside—you'll see that this corner of Vermont is a haven for small, family-run farms like the Rodgers'. There are five guest rooms; guests share two large bathrooms. Horseback rides are available. All meals are included. Open June through November. ~ Route 3, West Glover; 802-525-6677. BUDGET.

The Inn on Trout River is a great find for travelers who find themselves in the Jay area of northern Vermont. Skiers will be especially satisfied with the flannel-sheeted queen beds, large bathrooms with claw-footed tubs, the publike bar and the substantial discount on lift tickets to Jay Peak. During the summer, visitors can take advantage of the excellent fishing in the area's many rivers and streams. Breakfast and dinner included. ~ Main Street, Montgomery Center; 802-326-4391, 800-338-7049. MODERATE TO DELUXE.

◄ HIDDEN

The women-only **Greenhope Farm** occupies a rural setting in the mountains. You won't find lace and antiques at this contemporary, six-room farmhouse, but you will find goats and horses. You can rent the horses to explore the surrounding woods and mountains. There's also swimming, canoeing and, in winter, cross-country skiing on the grounds. Advance reservations are required. ~ Route 1, East Harwick; 802-533-7772. BUDGET TO MODERATE.

DINING

Cuisine here reflects the ruggedness of the land, and, though restaurants are far apart, they're certainly worth the scenic drive.

Nestled serenely on a glacier-carved lake, the **Willough Vale Inn and Restaurant** affords some of Vermont's most scintillating views. Polished cherrywood tables, Oriental rugs and mauve and green tones lend a rustic elegance to the dining room, which overlooks captivating Lake Willoughby. The menu features rack of lamb, rock shrimp and steamed mussels. ~ Route 5A, Westmore; 802-525-4123. MODERATE TO DELUXE.

HIDDEN ►

Locals know that to dine at **Heermansmith Farm Inn**, you must make reservations several days in advance. This 1807 farmhouse, concealed two miles down a washboard road, is an absolute find—the kind of place that instantly warms your blood. It's dinner only, served in a living room graciously adorned with antique lanterns, pine bookcases, a stone hearth and picture windows overlooking rolling meadows. The menu exhibits great flair with entrées such as roast duck masked in strawberry and chambord sauce, shrimp dijonaise and pecan chicken in a raspberry-butter sauce. A place worth finding. ~ Coventry Village; 802-754-8866. MODERATE TO DELUXE.

Lemoine's, located in The Inn on Trout River, offers a varied menu for all palates—fresh fish, leg of lamb, and good homemade soups, as well as an innovative "wholesome choices menu" for guests who need to restrict their fat intake. Try to sit near the fireplace; the carved fireplace mantel is intricate and worth a closer look, as are the mouldings and wainscoting throughout the inn. ~ Main Street, Montgomery Center; 802-326-4391, 800-338-7049. MODERATE TO DELUXE.

The **Miss Newport Diner** is one of those adorable town gossip spots that serves up great breakfasts and homestyle lunches. The 1947 Worcester diner bears five booths and a row of blue-and-silver counter stools where all the socializing gets done. The breakfast menu features four pages of eggs, omelettes and pancakes—most priced under $5. For lunch, there's meat loaf and fried chicken, ham steak and fresh turkey. ~ East Main Street, Newport; 802-334-7742. BUDGET.

SHOPPING

Going fishing, perhaps? **The Great Outdoors Trading Co.** has loads of fishing gear, plus mountain bikes and skis. ~ 73 Main Street, Newport; 802-334-2831.

The Landing Clothing Company has not only men's formal attire but jeans and sportswear for both sexes. ~ 60 Main Street, Newport; 802-334-2953.

NIGHTLIFE

Other than a few motel lounges and pool halls, this remote mountain area is short on nightlife.

Have a drink by the lake at **The Eastside**. In the summer you can enjoy the views from the outdoor deck; in the winter, relax by the fire in the nautical-themed bar. ~ Lake Street, Newport; 802-334-2340.

The **Nickelodeon Café**, a smart pub with Irish decor, is a nice spot for a cold brew. On weekends there are live bands. Cover. ~ 41 Main Street, Newport; 802-334-8055.

Canada and the United States share the **Haskell Opera House**, a marvelous, ornate historic building that hosts major comedy, musicals and drama as well as symphony, jazz and ballet. A black line divides the building nationally, with two-thirds of the wooden seats in Vermont and the stage in Quebec. ~ Casswell Avenue, Derby Line; 819-876-2471—in Canada.

BEACHES & PARKS

PROUTY BEACH This popular municipal park corners the market on local views. Situated along tranquil Lake Memphremagog, Prouty preens across the water to the town of Newport, with its quaint downtown and historic church spires. A 100-foot sliver of tawny sand skirts the lake, protected by a row of weeping willows. Try from shore or on a boat for trout, salmon, pike and bass. And with tennis and basketball courts, as well as football and soccer fields, who could get bored? Picnic pavilions, restrooms; day-use fee, $3. Open from May 15 to Columbus Day. ~ On Veterans Avenue in Newport; 802-334-7951.

▲ There are four tent sites ($14 per night) and 46 RV sites ($18 per night) with water and electrical hookups. Sixteen of those sites also have sewer hookups and are $19 per night. Amenities include washers, dryers and showers as well as a dumping station for RVs.

MAIDSTONE STATE PARK Ringed with majestic mountain peaks and tucked in the middle of nowhere, this gorgeous preserve possesses a very special feature: the crystal clear, shallow Maidstone Lake. It's enough to just sit and gaze at reflections of trees in the water, but the more adventurous might choose to sunbathe on a generous stretch of cream-colored sand. People swim here, though the water is quite chilly, even in summer. Fishing is excellent for lake and rainbow trout as well as salmon. Don't be intimidated by the remoteness of this park. Once you're there, you'll be thankful you made the drive. Picnic tables, hiking trails, boat and canoe rentals. ~ From Bloomfield, go south along the Connecticut River for five miles on Route 102, then turn southwest at the State Forest Highway (it's marked). This is a gravel road that extends six miles to the park; 802-676-3930. ◀ **HIDDEN**

▲ There are 46 tent/RV sites ($12 per night) and 37 lean-tos ($16 per night); fireplaces and hot showers but no hookups.

BRIGHTON STATE PARK Even with the fiercest of competition, this has to be the prettiest park in all of Vermont. The setting is absolutely magnificent, the mood incredibly serene. Nestled along poignant Spectacle Pond, Brighton claims a sliver of crystalline tawny beach and 152 acres packed with spruce, firs, pines and many other very green, very big trees. There's also a nature museum and ◀ **HIDDEN**

plenty of forested trails that scale the billowy terrain. There's excellent fishing for trout on Island Pond, bass on Spectacle Pond. Picnic tables, restrooms, showers, fireplaces; day-use fee, $1.50. Open from mid-May through the Columbus Day weekend. ~ Off Route 105, two miles east of Island Pond; 802-723-4360.

▲ There are 63 tent/RV sites ($12 per night) and 21 lean-tos ($16 per night), but no hookups.

▼▼▼▼▼▼▼▼▼▼▼▼▼▼
Outdoor Adventures

SKIING

The thrills of downhill and cross-country skiing draw tens of thousands of enthusiasts to Vermont every year. Ski resort villages exist all over the state, offering a variety of challenges and settings that cater to families, singles and the elderly.

Before you go, send for the *Ski Vermont: Vermont Ski Area, Resort and Travel Guide* brochure from the Vermont Ski Areas Association (P.O. Box 368, Montpelier, VT 05601; 802-223-2439).

SOUTHERN VERMONT   **Haystack Mountain** is Vermont's southernmost ski resort area, with 44 trails and six lifts catering primarily to families with children. ~ Coldbrook Road, off Route 100, Wilmington; 802-464-3333.

Nearby, and owned by the same company, **Mount Snow** climbs 3600 feet up and boasts a large array of alpine villas, condos and restaurants. Here you'll find 84 trails (many quite difficult), 18 lifts and a vertical drop of 1700 feet. ~ Route 100; 802-464-3333.

CENTRAL VERMONT   The place to be in central Vermont is **Killington**, a sprawling, six-mountain network of 162 trails (including 44 black diamond and 10 double black diamond), 20 lifts and a vertical drop that plummets 3150 feet. ~ Off Routes 4 and 100; 802-773-1330.

NORTHERN MOUNTAIN REGION   **Sugarbush**, a two-mountain area with 111 trails, maintains a congenial atmosphere with its quaint shops and medley of fine restaurants and lodging. ~ Sugarbush Access Road, off Route 100, Warren; 802-583-2381.

Nearby **Stowe** harbors Vermont's highest peak, 4393-foot Mt. Mansfield, and a stunning alpine milieu with 46 trails and 10 lifts. ~ Route 108; 802-253-7311.

Several cross-country trails connect inns around Warren and Waitsfield in the Sugarbush area.

For something completely different, snow enthusiasts can try knee sliding, which involves an apparatus called a Pro-Snowbie and, presumably, a rider with sturdy knees. This newfangled sport is practiced at **East of Eden** in Eden Mills, halfway between Stowe and Jay Peak (a half-hour's drive from either). Take Route 100 to Eden Mills. Approximately 200 yards north of Frank's Market, turn onto East Hill Road. East of Eden is one mile east. ~ 120 East Hill Road, Eden Mills; 802-635-2700.

NORTHEAST KINGDOM Vermont's best-kept ski secret is **Burke Mountain,** nestled in the outposts of the Northeast Kingdom. Here you'll find excellent skiing in an uncrowded (yes, no lift lines!) place, along with 30 trails, five lifts and a nice vertical drop of 2000 feet. ~ Off Route 114, East Burke; 802-626-3305.

The varied terrain of gentle hills and fields, old carriage roads and frozen ponds—combined with an excellent gridwork of trails—attract vast numbers of cross-country skiers to Vermont. In fact, tiny Vermont boasts more nordic ski centers than any western state.

For a list of ski centers, write for the *Best of Cross-Country Skiing* guide available from Cross-Country Ski Areas of America. The $3 charge covers all postage and handling. ~ 259 Bolton Road, Hinsdale, NH 03451; 603-239-4341.

Known as the "Longest Cross-Country Ski Trail in North America," the **Catamount Trail** will stretch 280 miles across the length of Vermont when it's completed (225 miles of the trail have already been blazed). The trail offers gentle, rolling slopes for beginners and challenging terrain for the most advanced, as well as inn-to-inn routes along old logging roads. For further information on the Catamount Trail, or to order a guidebook on the trail, call 802-864-5794.

Another scenic route traverses the farmlands and forests between the **Craftsbury Nordic Center** (802-586-7767) near Craftsbury Common and the Highland Lodge in Greensboro.

Since **Jay Peak** regularly gets more natural snow than any other ski area in the northeast, you might well expect it to be packed—but it's not. The trek from any major city is a long one, and the weather can be pretty nasty up here; consequently, few New England skiers come here and lift lines are almost unheard of. Experienced skiers who are looking for a challenge should head for Jay's glade areas when the snow is deep enough. If it's not, the runs on the smaller of the two mountains are more challenging than the curving trails that descend from the tram, on the higher peak. ~ Route 242, Jay; 802-988-2611, 800-451-4449.

Sleigh rides afford wonderful opportunities to meet local folks and take in the beautiful countryside.

SLEIGHING

CENTRAL VERMONT In Wilmington, trips are offered by **Adam's Farm.** ~ Higley Hill; 802-464-3762. In Plymouth try **Hawk Inn and Mountain Resort.** ~ Route 100; 802-672-3811. In Castleton call **Pond Hill Ranch.** ~ Pond Hill Road; 802-468-2449.

NORTHERN MOUNTAIN REGION In Williamstown, **Autumn Crest Inn** offers sleigh rides. ~ Clark Road; 802-433-6627. In Stowe try the **Trapp Family Lodge.** ~ 42 Trapp Hill Road, Stowe; 802-253-8511.

NORTHEAST KINGDOM **Smuggler's Notch Riding** offers sleigh rides in the Jeffersonville area. ~ Mountain Road; 802-644-5347.

FISHING   From salmon and trout to shad and walleye, Vermont's extensive network of streams, rivers and lakes teem with a multitude of fine fishing opportunities. Winter ice fishing has become increasingly popular all over the state but particularly in the Northeast Kingdom, where northern pike, smelt and perch can be plucked from frozen lakes.

SOUTHERN VERMONT   Fishing charters are available from **Strictly Trout.** ~ Off of Route 121 just south of Saxton River Village; 802-869-3116.

CENTRAL VERMONT   Several outfits will set you up with rental boats and/or fishing equipment.

The **Vermont Fly Fishing School** offers guide service for flyfishing the rivers and streams. ~ Clubhouse Road, Quechee; 802-295-7620. In Hydeville try **Duda's Water Sports.** ~ Creek Road; 802-265-3432. In Wells there's **Sailing Winds.** ~ Route 30, Wells; 802-287-9411.

NORTHERN MOUNTAIN REGION   In this area you can call **The Fly Rod Shop.** ~ Route 100, Stowe; 802-253-7346.

CHAMPLAIN VALLEY   In Middlebury try **Yankee Charters.** ~ Route 7; 802-877-3318.

NORTHEAST KINGDOM   In North Hero there's **Charlie's Northland Lodge.** ~ Route 2; 802-372-8822.

To find out where the fish bite, contact the **Vermont Fish and Wildlife Department.** ~ Information and Education Division, 103 South Main Street, Waterbury, VT 05676; 802-241-3700.

CANOEING   Whether you're in it for sightseeing or for rugged adventure, canoeing through Vermont can be an idyllic experience.

SOUTHERN VERMONT   In Brattleboro **Connecticut River Safari** rents canoes. ~ Putney Road; 802-257-5008. You can also try **Battenkill Canoe Ltd.** ~ Route 7A between Arlington and Manchester; 802-362-2800.

CENTRAL VERMONT   In Wells call **Sailing Winds.** ~ Route 30; 802-287-9411.

NORTHERN MOUNTAIN REGION   **Clearwater Sports** rents canoes in Waitsfield. ~ Route 100; 802-496-2708.

CHAMPLAIN VALLEY   For canoe rentals in South Burlington call **South Burlington Rent All.** ~ 340 Dorset Street; 802-862-5793.

NORTHEAST KINGDOM   In North Hero call **Charlie's Northland Lodge.** ~ Route 2; 802-372-8822. In Lyndonville try **The Village Sport Shop.** ~ Route 5; 802-626-8448.

GOLF   You can tee up at numerous public courses across the state.

SOUTHERN VERMONT   In southern Vermont, try the **Sitzmark Golf Course.** ~ East Dover Road off Route 100, Wilmington; 802-464-3384. In Bennington there's **Mount Anthony Country Club.** ~ Bank Street; 802-447-7079.

CENTRAL VERMONT   In central Vermont, there's **Killington Golf Course.** ~ Killington Access Road, Killington; 802-422-6700. In Brandon try **Neshobe Golf Club.** ~ Country Club Road; 802-247-3611.

NORTHERN MOUNTAIN REGION   You'll find **Resort Sugarbush** in Warren. ~ Sugarbush Golf Course; 802-583-2301. In Stowe, there's **Stowe Country Club.** ~ Cottage Club Road off Cape Cod Road; 802-253-4893.

CHAMPLAIN VALLEY   In Shelburne Village you can tee off at **Kwiniaska Golf Club.** ~ Spear Street; 802-985-3672. In Burlington there's **Burlington Country Club.** ~ 568 South Prospect Street; 802-864-4683. **Marble Island Resort** is another top spot in the Champlain Valley. ~ 150 Marble Island Road, Mallets Bay; 802-864-6800.

NORTHEAST KINGDOM   Up in the Northeast Kingdom, head for **St. Johnsbury Country Club.** ~ Route 5, St. Johnsbury; 802-748-9894.

Tennis fans will find both outdoor and indoor courts across the state.   **TENNIS**

SOUTHERN VERMONT   Check out **Mount Anthony Country Club** in Bennington. ~ Bank Street; 802-442-2617. **Manchester Recreation Area** also has courts. ~ Off Route 30, Manchester; 802-362-1439.

CENTRAL VERMONT   In central Vermont, try **Summit Lodge.** ~ Killington Access Road, Killington; 802-422-3535. There's also **Vail Field** in Woodstock. ~ Route 106 behind the Woodstock Inn.

NORTHERN MOUNTAIN REGION   The **Bridges Resort and Racquet Club** is an excellent indoor/outdoor facility. ~ Sugarbush Access Road, Warren; 802-583-2922.

CHAMPLAIN VALLEY   **Leddy Park** has courts open to the public. ~ North Avenue, Burlington; 802-864-0123.

NORTHEAST KINGDOM   **Prouty Park** offers fine facilities in Newport. ~ Veterans Avenue; 802-334-7951.

What could be more exciting than tromping on horseback through the unspoiled Vermont countryside? Plenty of ranches will provide horses and directions to the best trails.   **RIDING STABLES**

CENTRAL VERMONT   Try **Kedron Valley Stables** in Central Vermont. ~ Route 106, South Woodstock; 802-457-1480. You can also try **Pond Hill Ranch** in Castleton. ~ Pond Hill Road; 802-468-2449. In Waitsfield **Vermont Icelandic Horse Farm** offers plenty of trails. ~ The Commons Road; 802-496-7141.

NORTHERN MOUNTAIN REGION   **Navajo Farm** offers rides in the Northern Mountain Region. ~ Route 100, Moretown; 802-496-3656.

CHAMPLAIN VALLEY   In Chittenden try **Mountain Top Stables.** ~ Mountain Top Road; 802-483-2311.

NORTHEAST KINGDOM   For horses and trails in the Northeast Kingdom call **Vermont Horse Park.** ~ Mountain Road, Jeffersonville; 802-644-5347.

BICYCLING   Vermont's mountains and abundance of back roads create a perfect environment for bicycling. To help get you started, **Vermont Bicycle Touring** offers tours with all levels of difficulty and will help build tours for groups of 12 or more. ~ Box 711, Bristol, VT 05443; 802-453-4811. In addition, the book *25 Bicycle Tours in Vermont* offers a wealth of information, including where to find emergency repairs. ~ Available from The Countryman Press and Backcountry Publications, P.O. Box 175, Woodstock, VT 05091.

NORTHERN MOUNTAIN REGION   In the **Sugarbush** area there's a 16-mile excursion along Route 100 and East Warren Road, winding through the scenic Mad River Valley and taking in the quaint towns of Warren and Waitsfield.

CHAMPLAIN VALLEY   You can take an easy but lengthy 51-mile trek through the fertile **Champlain Valley**, meandering among apple orchards and cornfields and skirting beautiful Lake Champlain. Stick to Routes 125, 17 and 23, picking up Lake Street along the lake.

Bike Rentals   In southern Vermont, try **Brattleboro Bike Shop**. ~ 178 Main Street; 802-254-8644. Bikes can be rented in the central Vermont area at **Vermont Pedal Pushers**. ~ Routes 11 and 30, Manchester; 802-362-5200. Also in Manchester, try **Green Mountain Rental**. ~ 158 North Main Street; 802-775-0101. In the Northern Mountain Region call **Clearwater Sports**. ~ Route 100, Waitsfield; 802-496-2708. For touring around the Champlain Valley, check out **Bicycle Holidays**. ~ RD3 Box 2394, Middlebury; 802-388-2453. Or you can also try **The Ski Rack Bike Shop**. ~ 81 Main Street, Burlington; 802-658-3313. Up in the Northeast Kingdom try **Village Sport Shop** for bike rentals. ~ 74 Broad Street, Lyndonville; 802-626-8448.

HIKING   With more than 700 miles of splendid hiking terrain—including 512 miles on state and national forest lands—Vermont is a hiker's nirvana. The best time to go, of course, is early summer to late fall, avoiding the spring "mud season" from mid-April to late May.

Vermont's hiking authority, **The Green Mountain Club**, can supply books, brochures and guidance on the subject, as well as information on biking, snowshoeing and nordic skiing. ~ Route 100, Rural Route 1, Box 650, Waterbury Center, VT 05677; 802-244-7037.

The longest uninterrupted trek exists on **The Long Trail** (265 miles), a primitive footpath that crawls along the crest of the Green Mountains from Massachusetts to Canada. Purists love the abundance of wildlife and foliage on this trek, which ambles through dense evergreen forests and shaded glens and alongside quiescent ponds and rivers. An inspiration for the Appalachian Trail, which links the mountains from Georgia to Maine, the Long Trail includes 175 miles of side trails and climbs as high as 4393 feet.

SOUTHERN VERMONT   **Bald Mountain Trail** (4 miles), off Route 30 in Townshend State Park, makes a loop past an alder swamp and a cascading brook and through a hemlock forest. There are some fine mountain views along the way.

A nice, short hike in southern Vermont can be found along **Harmon Hill Trail** (3.4 miles) off Route 9 east of Bennington. There's a steep then moderate climb to the summit, where views of Bennington and Mt. Antone are fabulous.

A few miles north, **Baker Peak** and **Griffith Lake Trails** (8 miles), off Route 7 near Danby, wind through brooks and streams then scale Baker Mountain for a magnificent look at the Otter Creek Valley and marble quarry on Dorset Peak.

CENTRAL VERMONT A dramatic crevice can be seen along the **Clarendon Gorge and Airport Lookout** trail (1.6 miles), which picks up off Route 103 east of Route 7 near Clarendon. A path crosses a suspension bridge over the Mill River, then ascends steadily to a nice vantage point with views of the Otter Creek Valley and Bird and Herrick mountains.

For a history lesson capped by great scenery, take the **Mt. Independence** trail (7.8 miles) past well-preserved remains of Revolutionary War fortifications built back in 1775. You'll also discover superb views of Lake Champlain, Fort Ticonderoga and surrounding valleys. The trail begins off Route 73A west of Orwell Village.

Abbey Pond Trail (5.8 miles) affords a close look at beautiful wilderness areas teeming with marsh plants, deer, rabbits, bear and other wildlife. Follow the trail from Route 53, near Forest Dale, past a series of cascades to a view of the twin peaks of Robert Frost Mountain.

The **Battell Mountain and Skylight Pond** trail (5 miles) commences at Steam Mill Clearing, a pretty meadow and former logging camp, and meanders easily up Battell Mountain, then continues to picturesque Skylight Pond. Pick up the trailhead off of Route 125 seven and a half miles east of East Middlebury.

NORTHERN MOUNTAIN REGION For a 180 view of the Champlain Valley and New York's Adirondack Mountains, opt for the **Sunset Ridge Trail** (2 miles), off Route 100 in the scenic Lincoln Gap.

✔ CHECK THESE OUT—OUTDOOR ADVENTURES

- Cast a rod for rainbow trout in one of **Green Mountain National Forest**'s 440 miles of rivers and tributaries. *page 396*
- Ride Vermont's air currents 5000 feet above the ground while **gliding** over hills and farmlands. *page 408*
- Navigate a sled down a thrilling **alpine slide** on Mount Mansfield, Vermont's highest peak. *page 410*
- Whoosh through gorgeous mountain scenery at Vermont's best-loved ski area, **Stowe**. *page 432*

Mount Mansfield is Vermont's highest peak (4393 feet) and naturally the most hiked. The easiest trek is via the **Long Trail** (4.6 miles), the most ghoulish endures along **Hell Brook Trail** (3.6 miles), a supersteep rocky climb recommended only for experienced hikers. Both trailheads begin off Route 108 in Stowe.

One of the most beautiful, secluded spots on the Long Trail is at **Devil's Gulch Trail** (8.2 miles), an interesting rock defile and fern grotto. The trailhead is along Route 118 five miles west of Eden.

CHAMPLAIN VALLEY Take a hike to Lake Champlain on the **Red Rocks Park Trails** (2.5 miles), a series of short paths through cool pine woods that lead to vantage points on the lakeshore. The park is off Queen City Park Drive west of Route 189 in South Burlington.

Open only to campers using the campgrounds, the **Grand Isle State Park Trail** (.3 mile) is short on distance but long on views. The path cuts through a lush thicket and makes a loop over a low bluff to an observation tower. You can see Lake Champlain in the distance. The park is on Route 2 one mile south of Grand Isle.

Knight Point State Park Trail (1 mile) follows Lake Champlain's shoreline through a dense hardwood forest. You'll find the trail on Route 2 in North Hero.

NORTHEAST KINGDOM **Mount Pisgah Trail** (6.9 miles) crosses this 2751-foot mountain via thick forests and wooden walkways over beaver ponds. There are exceptional views packed into this trek, including a 60-mile panorama from Lake Memphremagog and Jay Peak to beyond Camel's Hump. The trail starts along Route 5A, about six miles from West Burke.

The remote Northeast Kingdom offers some glorious hikes, including the **Wheeler Mountain Trail** (5.4 miles), which creeps through meadows and woods and across open rocks to a 2371-foot summit. Along the way, you'll catch splendid views of Mount Mansfield and Lake Willoughby. The trail picks up off Route 5 east of Barton.

▼▼▼▼▼▼▼▼▼▼

Transportation

CAR

Automobile travel is quickest (though not very scenic) on Routes 91 and 89, Vermont's two interstate highways. Route 91 cuts in from Massachusetts and follows Vermont's eastern border, while Route 89 starts at the New Hampshire line and snakes across the northern center of Vermont to Quebec.

From New York, opt for **Route 7** or **Route 4**, entering on Vermont's western edge. Though not a major highway by any means, **Route 100** is the picturesque thoroughfare slicing north-south through the center of the state.

AIR

Burlington International Airport, a small and easily accessible facility in Burlington, is the major air gateway for Vermont. Carriers serving it are Continental Airlines, Delta Airlines, Northwest Airlink, United Airlines and USAir.

Burlington Airport Ground Transportation provides service from the airport to anywhere in the state. ~ 802-863-1889.

Vermont Transit Lines provides extensive service throughout New England, with major Vermont stops at Brattleboro, Bennington, White River Junction, Rutland, Burlington, St. Johnsbury and Newport. Reservations: 802-864-6811. Brattleboro: Junction of Routes 5 and 91; 802-254-6066. Bennington: 126 Washington Avenue; 802-442-4808. White River Junction: Sykes Avenue; 802-295-3011, Rutland: 122 Merchants Row; 802-773-2774. Burlington: 135 St. Paul Street; 802-864-6811. St. Johnsbury: Railroad Street; 802-748-4000. Newport: Coventry Street; 802-334-2132.

BUS

Amtrak offers direct service from Washington, D.C., Philadelphia, New York, Connecticut and Montreal. The train stops in Vermont at White River Junction (Railroad Row), Montpelier (Montpelier Junction Road), Waterbury (Park Row) and Essex Junction Station (29 Railroad Avenue, near Burlington). ~ 800-872-7245.

TRAIN

If you arrive at Burlington International Airport, you'll find the following rental companies: **Avis Rent A Car** (800-331-1212), **Budget Rent A Car** (800-527-0700), **Hertz Rent A Car** (800-654-3131) and **National Interrent** (800-227-7368). **Thrifty Car Rental** (800-367-2277) is located near the terminal and provides free airport transfers.

CAR RENTALS

NINE

New Hampshire

New Hampshire. It's a heart-stopping collage of sculpted mountains, stony profiles, seamless country roads, expansive lakes and broad beaches. A place you yearn to clutch tightly, to safeguard and to proclaim.

That slender fragment of Yankee domain framed by Vermont, Maine and Massachusetts, New Hampshire is all this and much, much more. It is a region that seems not quite real when you first reach the state, yet you're certain you've been there before. New Hampshire's daunting landscape flirts with the imagination; its spirit roams wild around untamed timberland, wilderness expanses and riots of flowers.

Born of molten granite and giant glaciers, the state's geologic surface was but a labyrinth of smoke, dust and ice sheets some 300 million years ago. Hot rock hissed beneath the earth, forced its way up and drove the ground to buckle and split. Advancing ice sheets smoothed the rock, forming it into hills and mountains, then swiftly melted to create rivers and lakes.

Along the way, these icy torrents deposited thousands of granite chunks. All that stone gives today's New Hampshire a rugged veneer, as well as its moniker of "The Granite State." Boulders lie strewn across farmlands, jut out into the sea and loom atop mountains, their mystic profiles often evocative of some familiar face or object.

Human rumblings in this area go back at least 8000 years, when the Abenaki and Pennacook Indians roamed the lands. Members of Algonquin tribes, they fished the swift rivers, hunted forests for game and fruit and culled maple sugar from the trees. Their first European visitor, British captain Martin Pring, sailed up the Piscataqua River in 1603, though it was not until 1623 that the first settlement was founded at Odiorne Point in present-day Rye.

Several towns soon sprang up along the coast and river. Strawbery Banke, now Portsmouth, became the capital and commercial center of New Hampshire life as fishers, coopers and shipbuilders plied their trades there. In 1643, a greedy Massachusetts annexed the settlements into its Bay Colony, holding them for 36 years until England declared New Hampshire a royal province.

Thick forests, bitter winters and unforgiving earth made life difficult for those who tried to tame New Hampshire's interior. Even worse, previously friendly Indians came to resent white intrusion and exploitation, and a series of violent skirmishes ensued. In one infamous incident, Indians captured a settler named Hannah Dustin, a 39-year-old mother of 12, and took her to River Islet, near present-day Concord. During the night, Dustin killed and scalped her ten sleeping captors, escaping with her life.

In the mid-1700s, settlers struggled to cultivate the rocky soil that became bloodied by French and Indian conflicts. The French and Indian War finally settled the matter in 1763, though the subsequent American Revolution only brought more strife to a battered land.

New Hampshire entered the Revolution with a vengeance. In December 1774, when patriots received word from Paul Revere that British soldiers would soon be at Portsmouth, they stormed Fort William and Mary. Six months later, England's governor was driven from the colony.

After the war, people gave up on agriculture and turned to textile manufacturing. But an even more lucrative source of income was about to arrive: the stream of pleasure seekers who, lured by bewitching landscapes and a bevy of natural resources, started coming to New Hampshire in droves. Exclaimed one well-traveled visitor: "There is no doubt but the scenery of New Hampshire is more varied and beautiful than can be found in any other state in the Union."

Thousands of new arrivals, known as "summer people," converged on the land. Those with money built grand estates or lavish hotels, while the majority put up frame houses and white picket fences and settled on their front porches for the summer. All of a sudden, New Hampshire's first tourist industry was raging.

By the late 1800s, a different kind of industry had emerged. Virtually overnight, logging businesses penetrated the White Mountains and cleared thousands of acres of trees to feed a voracious lumber demand. Within 20 years, barren patches scarred the mountainsides and wildlife was dwindling.

It might have been the undoing of New Hampshire's precious mountains had not public outcry prompted Congress to halt the destruction. The Weeks Act of 1911 called for federal purchase of most of the state's forest lands, which today make up the 768,000-acre White Mountain National Forest.

Now forests cloak 84 percent of the state, while some 1300 lakes form pockets of beauty and intrigue. Shaped like a skinny triangle that points toward Canada, New Hampshire spans only 168 miles from top to bottom and 90 miles at its broadest point. Its 9304 square miles cover six geographic regions so disparate you might think they existed in separate states, though together they create a powerful display of nature.

The wind-whipped seacoast ambles a mere 18 miles from Massachusetts to Maine, though its dramatic jetties, swirling tidepools and generous stretches of sand pack a state-sized dose of beauty. Northern Portsmouth, one of the finest ports in New England, brims with culture and commerce and endearing remnants of history.

The Merrimack Valley crawls up the lower spine of New Hampshire, its old textile mills clinging to the shores of the Merrimack River. The valley claims its largest city, Manchester, and seat of government, Concord.

Draped across the southwest corridor are lone mountains known as monadnocks. The Monadnock Region embodies a perfect canvas of rural New England, speckled with covered bridges, weathered barns and charming country towns that seem locked in the 18th century.

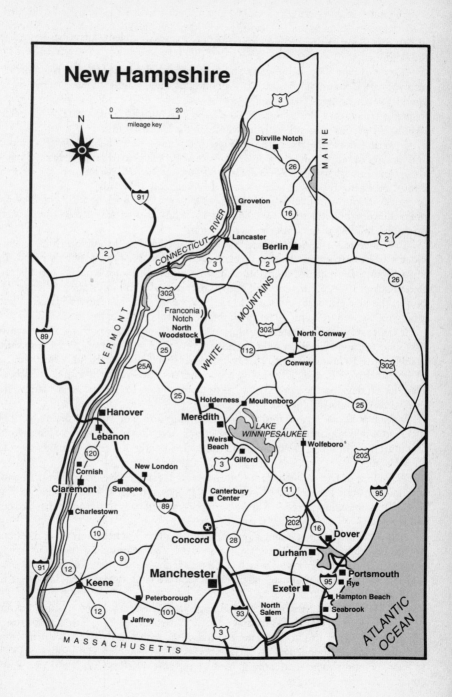

New Hampshire

The state's midwestern edge, flanked by the Connecticut River, is graced with corn-fields, subtle mountains and the culture of Dartmouth College. Nearby Lake Sunapee and its attendant sentinel, Mount Sunapee, are a year-round playground for lovers of the outdoors.

A tryst of twinkling azure water and gentle peaks, the Lakes Region is altogether captivating and soothing. A total of 273 bodies of water bundle together across New Hampshire's heartland. Their names—many were given by the Indians—conjure up romance and exotica. Lake Winnipesaukee, with 283 miles of coast and 274 habitable islands, is the sixth largest lake lying wholly in the United States.

Towering above the lakes are the White Mountains, overwhelming in appearance and massive in scope. Life slows down up here as people tend to small farms and businesses and raise their families. There are pockets of tourism, particularly ski resorts, nestled between canopies of evergreens and remote country roads.

In addition to its obvious aesthetic appeal, New Hampshire basks in the nation's political limelight every four years. Since 1915, it has secured the edge on presidential primaries, holding the first one in each election.

This claim to firstdom has yielded the tiny state considerable political clout, as candidates frequently gauge their campaigns according to New Hampshire's mood. In 1988, George Bush gained momentum after he trounced Robert Dole in New Hampshire. Back in 1976, a little-known Jimmy Carter earned credibility after a warm reception in the first primary. And since 1952, New Hampshire has chosen the candidate who would go on to be president, with the exception of Bill Clinton in 1992.

It's certain that New Hampshire aims to keep its first-primary position. Once, when Vermont mentioned it might hold elections earlier than its neighbor, New Hampshire quickly passed a law mandating that its primaries be held on the Tuesday before those of any other New England state. Wily Massachusetts once made the mistake of scheduling its primary on the same day as New Hampshire's. Indignant, New Hampshire pushed its elections up one week.

Indeed, politics is serious business in New Hampshire. The state legislature has 424 members—making it the third largest governing body in the English-speaking world (behind Great Britain's Parliament and the U.S. Congress). The state tends to vote Republican.

"Live Free or Die" is New Hampshire's motto, as every native reminds you. It's emblazoned on state license plates, on not a few homes and across some businesses. But despite this constant assertion of autonomy, the state still sees fit to restrict itself in curious ways.

Nightclubs and bars standing alone are banned; they must be connected to a restaurant, sports club, bowling alley or similar business. You can purchase hard liquor only from state-run stores, many of which dot major highways and interstates. These cobwebbed laws have been in place since Prohibition and don't seem likely to change in the near future.

For the most part, freedom to New Hampshire inhabitants means no sales tax and no personal income tax. Not surprisingly, these particular freedoms have lured throngs of people who now live in New Hampshire but work in nearby states. Miffed at the situation, Maine responded by taxing its workers who live in New Hampshire—as well as their spouses who live and work in New Hampshire. Needless to say, the two states continue a classic Yankee feud.

Today's New Hampshire is home to a new band of artists, as well as the factory workers and bankers, innkeepers and small business people who run the general stores. Its thriving tourism and aesthetic surroundings make the state a desirable place to live for its 1.1 million residents.

Despite some apparent modernization, New Hampshire still clings to its founding principles. It is a world focused on clapboard houses and slender steeples, Yankee ingenuity and memories of Pilgrims, town halls and the freedom to worship and vote.

Over the years, New Hampshire changes—yet somehow stays quite the same. Lifestyles and customs are passed on through generations firmly rooted in its granite soil. With a seashore, mountains and lakes that remain poignant and timeless, this state is a glorious place under the sun.

The Seacoast

Despite its diminutive size—only 18 miles in length—New Hampshire's seacoast is one of the state's most revered possessions. And rightly so, for its alliance of pounding surf, rocky headlands and tidepools, stately mansions and nature preserves offers a wealth of beauty and continuous intrigue.

Naturally the dramatic seaboard is a driver's paradise, which explains why it remains perpetually clogged with traffic. Warm summer breezes and sunshine draw the most crowds—particularly on weekends—though locals claim that winter snow falling on the sand is truly a sight to behold.

SIGHTS

Just north of the Massachusetts line, whiffs of salty marsh air will signify you've reached the town of **Seabrook**. Families favor this small oceanside nook for its amusement centers and pretty beaches, though the main attraction is **Seabrook Greyhound Park**. More than 1000 agile racing dogs call this fast track home, performing for bettors year-round. Admission. ~ Route 107; 603-474-3065.

Since 1976, Seabrook has received national attention because of the controversial **Seabrook Station Nuclear Power Plant**. Though citizens groups and the state of Massachusetts waged a long and costly battle to block the opening of the plant, it began operating in March 1990—three years after it was completed. The controversy continues today. For a closer look, the 1150-megawatt, $6.5 billion facility offers bus tours around the outside of its containment building, along with a ten-minute video of what's on the inside. Closed Sunday. ~ Routes 107 and 1; 603-474-9521.

Traveling northward on Route 1A, you'll notice the scenery changing from marshlands to wide open beaches as you approach the seacoast's most animated stretch of sand, **Hampton Beach**. Mobbed by hundreds of thousands of vacationers every year, this heavily developed tract is one giant pleasure center, its nucleus an oceanside promenade that reels with constant activity.

Start out by walking the promenade, a three-mile human fiesta extending along Ocean Boulevard from Dumas Avenue to Hampton Beach State Park, taking in the well-strolled boardwalk jammed with trinket and T-shirt vendors, low-slung motels and the aroma of carnival food. This is people-watching at its best, a place where a whole spectrum of humanity—drifters, beach bums and the highbrow—converges on one long slab of concrete.

There's a constant hum of cars, joggers, bicyclists and curious sightseers who stop to ponder the **New Hampshire Marine War Memorial,** a tribute to soldiers lost at sea. The granite statue features a forlorn maiden draped in rolls of stone cloth and clutching a wreath. ~ Ocean Boulevard and Nudd Avenue.

Great Boars Head, a rocky bulkhead in the ocean, projects an imposing silhouette just north of Hampton Beach. Topped with grand old mansions and seaside homes, Boars Head is particularly intriguing at sunrise, when the day's first light and the ocean mist produce a surreal portrait. ~ Ocean Boulevard and Dumas Avenue.

To help get you organized with local sightseeing, stop by the **Hampton Beach Area Chamber of Commerce,** located a couple miles west of Hampton Beach in Hampton. ~ 180 Ocean Boulevard; 603-926-8718.

A ten-minute drive west will land you in the rural respite of **Applecrest Farm Orchards,** where 20,000 apple trees and two pumpkin patches bask along the hillsides. Show up from Labor Day to mid-October and pick your own, or check out the applemart, an 1812 barn stocked with apple ciders, pies, butter, sauce and other great-smelling goodies. During the summertime, strawberries, raspberries and blueberries come ripe for pickin'. ~ Route 88 west of Interstate 95, Hampton Falls; 603-926-3721.

HIDDEN ► The best place to snag those plump, radiant raspberries is nearby **Raspberry Farm.** This 60-acre spread is a honey of a find. Wander through luxuriant patches, pluck your own berries and receive harvesting facts from the friendly owners. Don't miss the market filled with pies, tarts and jams. Closed from late October through early June. ~ Route 84 (also Kensington Road), three miles west of Route 1, Hampton Falls; 603-926-6604.

Hop back over onto Route 1A, heading north along this roving high road flanked on one side by a turgid ocean and on the other by regal New England mansions known as "Millionaire's Row" for the old-monied families who live here.

The largest tract of undeveloped coastline exists at **Odiorne Point State Park,** which wanders along two oceanfront miles and covers 327 acres. Back in 1623, New Hampshire's first white settlers landed here and found thick vegetation and whistling winds. The park includes grave sites, old stone walls, remains of a formal garden and several World War II bunkers. A visitors center, open during summer, will fill you in on local history. Admission during summer. ~ Route 1A, Rye; 603-436-7406.

From here you can peer out to sea and spy the stony profile of the **Isles of Shoals,** an archipelago that harbors great mysteries and torrid tales of pirates, treasures and wrecked ships. In 1614, Captain John Smith dubbed the isles "barren piles of rocks with a few scrub cedar," and they've seen minimal change since. Blackbeard and Captain Kidd supposedly stashed their loot among the rocky crevices, the former abandoning his wife there in 1723. Some say her spirit still roams the shores.

The isles later drew many artists and writers, including Nathaniel Hawthorne and Childe Hassam. Today, you can visit the islands via the **New Hampshire Seacoast Cruises,** which offers narrated tours seasoned with history. Closed from mid-October through early May. Admission. ~ Rye Harbor State Marina, Route 1A, Rye; 603-964-5545.

Anchoring the northern end of the seacoast, **Portsmouth,** with its rich maritime history, has long played a critical role in the state's prosperity and development. Lying at the mouth of the Piscataqua River, the city seems like some profound old sage, locked in a bygone era yet quite vibrant and progressive at the same time.

Stone sidewalks and ivy-clad brick buildings, their walls holding two centuries of memories, gather stoically along the harbor. In central downtown, known as Market Street, immaculately restored 18th- and 19th-century enclaves mingle with sleek new highrises. Young artists and professionals continue to arrive from Boston, New York and Maine, polishing the cultural patina and dynamic night scenes of this port city.

There's so much to see here, and the best place to get organized is the **Greater Portsmouth Chamber of Commerce.** Pick up the *Harbor Trail,* a resource book featuring historical facts and a map outlining several self-guided tours. ~ 500 Market Street; 603-436-1118.

Built between 1716 and 1807, the houses vary architecturally and enjoy their own special museums and personalities. At the **John Paul Jones House,** a 1758 Georgian design, you'll find a room arranged with marvelous wedding gowns worn in the 1800s as well as the oldest piano in the United States. There's also a collection of Civil War

✔ **CHECK THESE OUT—UNIQUE SIGHTS**

- Explore the original settlement of Portsmouth at **Strawbery Banke,** ten acres of rambling gardens and Colonial buildings dating from 1695. *page 448*
- Puzzle over the one of New England's most peculiar phenomena, the rocks atop Mystery Hill better known as **America's Stonehenge.** *page 458*
- Delve into the past with a look into one of America's first religious utopias, the **Canterbury Shaker Village.** *page 458*
- Uncover the secrets of Moultonboro's magical, medieval-looking **Castle in the Clouds,** which appears to be floating in air. *page 476*

guns, a nifty wooden bathtub and oars and paddles from the South Seas. Admission. ~ 43 Middle Street; 603-436-8420.

George Washington dropped by a party at the **Governor John Langdon House**. back in 1789. According to memos he later penned, George found the home quite warm and its proprietor, future New Hampshire Governor John Langdon, very hospitable. Today, beautiful wood carvings and precious period furnishings adorn the interior. Closed Monday and Tuesday and from mid-October through May. Admission. ~ 143 Pleasant Street, Portsmouth; 603-436-3205.

In January 1776, New Hampshire became the first independent American state.

One treat that goes with the Portsmouth Trail is the opportunity to meet the congenial docents (many are Portsmouth natives) who fill you with history and interesting anecdotes. Most of the trail homes close during winter and open only a few days each week the rest of the year, so call ahead.

To find out what makes Portsmouth tick, stroll southeast on Market Street down to **the docks**, where the Piscataqua River laps at the city's edge. Back in the 18th and 19th centuries, furniture makers, potters, coopers and shipbuilders gathered along the waterfront to ply their trades, while a flourishing sawmill industry provided Great Britain with thousands of ships' masts. Today, tugboats, fishing vessels and sailboats scoot across the dark waters that flow to nearby Kittery, Maine.

From here you can catch a harbor cruise or take a longer jaunt to the Isles of Shoals. **Isles of Shoals Steamship Co.** provides trips. ~ 315 Market Street, Portsmouth; 603-431-5500. You can also try **Portsmouth Harbor Cruises**. ~ 64 Ceres Street, Oar House Dock, Portsmouth; 603-436-8084.

Follow the water northwest to Marcy Street, where you'll discover Portsmouth's most prized gem, **Strawbery Banke**, site of the original settlement. Sheltered within ten acres of rambling gardens and Colonial buildings is a wonderful lesson on New England architecture through 1943 and the struggles and lifestyles of America's founders. The area gets its moniker from the profusion of berries found here in 1630 by the city's first English settlers.

Thanks to the foresight of local leaders, the banke's 42 buildings, dating from 1695 to 1954, were spared demolition in the 1950s. Every place offers some fascinating historical insight, and it takes a full day to see it all. There's the **Daniel Webster House**, where Webster and his wife, Grace, lived from 1814 to 1816 (not open to the public), as well as the boyhood home of author Thomas Bailey Aldrich, whose book *The Story of a Bad Boy* inspired Mark Twain to write *Tom Sawyer*. Admission. ~ Entrance off Marcy Street south of Court Street; 603-433-1100.

The 1766 **Pitt Tavern**, perhaps the banke's most historically significant building, was a meeting place for loyalists and then patriots. Revolutionary War strategies were devised within these walls, which now display ads from 1770s newspapers announcing those historic meetings.

Before you leave town, stop by the **North Cemetery**, purchased by the town for 50 pounds in 1753. Buried on this unassuming grassy swell are John Langdon, former New Hampshire governor and signer of the Constitution, and General William Whipple, who signed the Declaration of Independence. ~ Maplewood Avenue and Russell Street.

The coastline bustle takes on a gentler cadence as you head north of Portsmouth. **Dover**, a working class mill town with charm, was founded by fishermen during the early 1600s and remained independent until 1642, when it joined the Massachusetts Bay Colony. Route 9 trundles right through town, flanked by huge mansions sporting multiple chimneys, many built last century by wealthy mill owners.

You can mull over the town's beginnings at the **Woodman Institute**, which houses an excellent display of New Hampshire memorabilia, wildlife and natural history. ~ 182 Central Avenue, Dover; 603-742-1038.

Travel south on Route 108 to the college town of Durham, where the **University of New Hampshire** provides a restful haven for strolling. A third of the campus' 200 acres is a nature preserve, crisscrossed with walking trails and lakes perfect for winter ice skating. ~ Route 155A; 603-862-1234.

West on Route 108, **Durham Landing** recalls the venue of a bloody battle in 1694, when more than 200 Indians attacked about 100 settlers, destroying their houses and garrisons along the Oyster River.

In nearby **Exeter**, you'll find a constant drum of traffic and human motion caused by the presence of exclusive **Phillips Exeter Academy**. One of the oldest and most renowned preparatory schools in the country, the academy has aged beautifully. Founded in 1781, the school boasts lovely brick buildings that lay masked in tangled ivy and are edged by green lawns and maple trees. Through the years, its hallowed halls have seen students like Daniel Webster, historian George Bancroft and Booth Tarkington. ~ Main Street; 603-772-4311.

LODGING

A noisy sub shop is tucked in the bottom of the **Sunrise Guest House**, but with budget-priced oceanside rooms, who cares? This adorable, two-story shingled beach house sports two pilasters and has two simple but modern apartments, each with small refrigerator and private bath. Ask for the one in the back, which has a skylight and private bath. ~ 65 Ocean Boulevard, Hampton Beach; 603-929-0636.

Toward the north (and somewhat quieter) end of Hampton Beach, the **Hampton House** offers very comfortable accommodations amid contemporary surroundings. A breezy lobby edges the busy beach-front street and comforts with soothing ocean views from the floor-to-ceiling glass windows. Three floors of spacious guest rooms feature wall-to-wall carpets, modern wood furnishings and private balconies that yield some fine ocean views and people-watching opportunities. ~ 333 Ocean Boulevard; 603-926-1033, 800-458-7058. DELUXE TO ULTRA-DELUXE.

From the outside, you'd swear it's little more than a generic beach motel. But wander into the **Oceanside Hotel** and you'll enter a world of superb 19th-century Victorian designs. Handsome pine floors show off period furniture and braided rugs. Each of ten rooms (including two that face the ocean) is named after Hampton Beach settlers, with decor matching the pioneer period. ~ 365 Ocean Boulevard, Hampton Beach; 603-926-3542. DELUXE TO ULTRA-DELUXE.

The Inn at Hampton possesses all the charm and detail of a fancy bed and breakfast. The guest rooms offer such personal touches as mirrored armoires, quilted headboards and dust ruffles, vaulted pine ceilings and scents of jasmine. Among the other niceties of this family-fun inn are an indoor pool and jacuzzi, an exercise room and, of course, a congenial staff. ~ 815 Lafayette Road, Hampton; 603-926-6771, 800-423-4561, fax 603-929-2160. DELUXE.

Set off in the woods, the **Governor's B & B**, opened in 1992, is the new kid in town. This Georgian Colonial mansion, originally owned by Governor Charles Dale of New Hampshire, is within walking distance of Portsmouth's historic sites. It has four rooms furnished with antiques. ~ 32 Miller Avenue, Portsmouth; 603-431-6546, fax 603-427-0803. DELUXE.

For the charm of a country inn with the luxuries of a large hotel, consider the **Sise Inn**. Set in an 1881 Queen Anne home within walking distance of most downtown Portsmouth sights, the hostelry fea-

---

✔ **CHECK THESE OUT—UNIQUE LODGING**

- *Budget to moderate:* Ramble down a labyrinth of obscure country roads to the friendly country lodgings at **Wyman Farm**. *page 460*
- *Moderate:* Surround yourself with pines at **The Backside Inn**, an 1835 farmhouse cum caravansary located in the shadow of Mount Sunapee. *page 469*
- *Moderate to deluxe:* Park your coach at **The Inn on Newfound Lake**, a former stagecoach station and grand old summer house with an unhurried pace. *page 477*
- *Ultra-deluxe:* Experience quintessential New England lodging at **Christmas Farm Inn**, where you might think you're in a colonial village. *page 485*

Budget: under $50 Moderate: $50–$90 Deluxe: $90–$120 Ultra-deluxe: over $120

tures a lobby that soars three stories and is highlighted by pretty butternut banisters and Oriental rugs. Oversized guest rooms are suited with bay windows, four-poster beds, showers *and* tubs (some with whirlpools) and nice extras like VCRs. ~ 40 Court Street, Portsmouth; 603-433-1200, 800-267-0525. DELUXE TO ULTRA-DELUXE.

Resting on a shady knoll adjacent to a busy thoroughfare, the **Martin Hill Inn** will send you back in time. This gracious pair of 19th-century buildings, linked by a flower-lined brick path, lies awash in lovely antiques accented by bouquets of day lilies. Seven bedrooms are decorated in Williamsburg wallpaper, brass and spindle beds and clawfoot tubs. ~ 404 Islington Street, Portsmouth; 603-436-2287. MODERATE TO DELUXE.

The **Bow Street Inn** claims an unusual location: a second floor above a performing arts center in central downtown. Not to worry—all ten guest rooms are nicely soundproofed and come with accouterments like brass beds, plush carpets and ruffled curtains. A brewery during the 19th century, the ruddy brick building peers across the Piscataqua River. ~ 121 Bow Street, Portsmouth; 603-431-7760. DELUXE TO ULTRA-DELUXE.

Around 1800, Christian ship captains—anxious to separate themselves from military captains—settled in modest homes west of downtown Portsmouth. Now the **Inn at Christian Shore** harkens back to those early days with simple, Federal-style design and sunny ambience. Six bedrooms are cheerfully outfitted with floral wallpaper and antique furniture. The dining room, with its low-slung beam ceilings and large fireplace, is quite cozy. ~ 335 Maplewood Avenue; 603-431-6770. MODERATE.

Northwest of Portsmouth, the historic mill town of Dover maintains a handful of motels and one very special bed and breakfast called the **Silver Street Inn**. Built in the 1880s by well-to-do mill owners, the ornate mansion displays such Victorian indulgences as high carved ceilings, marble and slate floors, Spanish mahogany doors and Italian-tile hearths. There's a formal library and dining room and ten bedrooms ranging from simple to lavish. ~ 103 Silver Street; 603-743-3000, fax 603-749-5673. MODERATE.

DINING

Count on at least a short line at **The Old Salt Eating and Drinking Place**, a great beachfront cranny with nautical accents and plenty of cheap eats. Breakfast means apple and blueberry waffles, three-cheese omelettes and pancakes, while dinner brings hefty portions of spaghetti, meat loaf and mashed potatoes, baked chicken with cranberry sauce and other home-cooked gems. ~ 83 Ocean Boulevard, Hampton Beach; 603-926-8322. BUDGET TO MODERATE.

For superb seafood amidst some hopping beach action, try **Ashworth by the Sea**. Lobster fiends will revel in the ten different lobster entrées such as baked stuffed lobster pie, lobster à la newburg and a sinful baked stuffed lobster with extra lobster. For non-seafoodites, there's veal and chicken plus roast Vermont turkey. ~ 295 Ocean Boulevard, Hampton Beach; 603-926-6762. MODERATE TO DELUXE.

Possibly the finest seafood restaurant on New Hampshire's 18-mile coast is popular **Ron's Beach House.** Elegant yet quite relaxed, this breezy white Colonial house sits across the street from the ocean, yet the Atlantic views are marvelous from its second-floor sun porch. Small tables draped in starched cloth and perfectly folded napkins create an intimate atmosphere. The Continental menu features a generous seafood selection plus interesting chicken and beef entrées. Sunday brunch is special. ~ 965 Ocean Boulevard, Hampton Beach; 603-926-1870. MODERATE TO DELUXE.

Back in 1764, a 26-year-old grenadier named Thomas Fletcher reportedly died of fever after drinking a hot beer. Forlorn and eager for companionship, his widow turned their tiny frame home into a tavern. Today, **Widow Fletcher's Tavern** remains one of New England's supreme pubs, framed in hand-hewn wood beams and booths and wide plank floors worn to a perfect 200-year-old patina. Fare goes a step beyond standard tavern food, with entrées such as seafood linguine, prime rib stroganoff and broiled haddock, and a slew of excellent salads, sandwiches and appetizers. ~ 401 Lafayette Road, Hampton; 603-926-8800. BUDGET TO MODERATE.

HIDDEN ▶   **The Eatery** is a very special place: Here the homecooked delights are served by a local couple and their eight children. The restaurant is warm and inviting, with its oil lamps, skylights and several tables that overlook the woods and open-air dining on the deck. For lunch, there are thick chowders and stacked sandwiches; for dinner, chicken divan, cajun steak tips and scallop gratiné. Breakfasts feature home-baked breads and pancakes. ~ Behind the Inn at Hampton, 815 Lafayette Road, Hampton; 603-926-8639. MODERATE.

Paul's Carriage House provides a curious mix of Colonial and seaside ambience—and pulls it off swimmingly. The two-story casual nook rests across the street from Jenness Beach but looks like a mountain eatery. Early American wood tables and booths encircle a big hearth downstairs, while upstairs a smaller room promises great views of the beach. The Continental-style bill of fare offers gems like steak *au poivre*, roast Long Island duckling with red raspberry and onion glaze and sole Oscar with lobster and asparagus in a champagne shallot sauce. ~ 2263 Ocean Boulevard, Rye; 603-964-8251. MODERATE TO DELUXE.

The waterfront **Blue Strawberry Restaurant** is a small restaurant with a big following. The menu is *prix fixe*, offering whatever is freshest in the local seafood market that day. The restaurant offers only one or two seatings nightly, depending on the time of year, so reservations are a must. Closed Tuesday and Wednesday. ~ 29 Ceres Street, Portsmouth; 603-431-6420. DELUXE.

A departure from traditional New England fare can be found at **Porto Bello**. Here, southern and northern Italian cuisine is the order of the day. The menu changes seasonally and might include such indulgences as farfalle with crab and light cream sauce, roast rack of lamb with rosemary and stuffed calamari. It's all served in a stylish, second-floor dining room overlooking the river. Closed Sunday and Monday. ~ 67 Bow Street, Portsmouth; 603-431-2989. MODERATE TO DELUXE.

◀ *HIDDEN*

The place for sushi is **Sakura**, a small but airy downtown nook that serves up fresh nori rolls and sashimi, tempura and teriyaki dishes, and interesting appetizers like a gingered raw beef (seared outside but raw inside). The decor borders on plain, with a small sushi bar, wood tables and railings, but it's as neat as a pin. Very popular with the business set. Closed Monday. ~ 40 Pleasant Street, Portsmouth; 603-431-2721. BUDGET TO MODERATE.

The **Harbor's Edge Restaurant** captures a superb view of the harbor amidst romantic surroundings. Decked in hues of emerald and rose, the eatery conveys an air of refinement with crystal and carnation-topped linen tablecloths. Cuisine falls in the American and nouvelle categories, with seafood and mixed grill items. ~ In the Sheraton Portsmouth, 250 Market Street, Portsmouth; 603-431-2300. MODERATE TO DELUXE.

Portsmouth's famous old spaghetti house is **Rosa's**, a great family-style place that opened back in 1927. Adorned with dimly lit wood booths and old-time photographs, the restaurant serves up those heart-stopping, traditional Italian favorites like parmigianas and cacciatores, lasagna, ravioli, tortellini and thin-crusted pizza. ~ 80 State Street; 603-436-9715. BUDGET TO MODERATE.

East of Hampton Beach, the town of Exeter is home to Phillips Exeter Academy, one of the country's most renowned and oldest preparatory schools. Here, the student population sustains a happy array of quaint street cafés, one of the best being **The Loaf and Ladle**. Everything is homemade and fresh, served cafeteria-style by friendly young people. There's black bean soup and country pâté, stacked sandwiches and cheesecakes. ~ 9 Water Street; 603-778-8955. BUDGET.

SHOPPING

For shopping in Hampton Beach, you can slum it on the boardwalk, bartering with vendors for jewelry, T-shirts and endless assorted souvenirs. The main action is along **Ocean Boulevard** from Nudd Avenue to Haverhill Avenue, where you can snag everything from leather jackets and tattoos to fake photo IDs and suntans (in tanning salons, of course).

North Hampton Factory Outlet Center is your place for discounted designer effects. There's a nice variety of items, from linens, shoes and coats to lingerie, leather and ingenious kitchenware. ~ Route 1, North Hampton; 603-964-9050.

Bona fide mallaholics should head straight for **Fox Run Mall,** where over 100 stores and eateries provide quality browsing amid fashionable surroundings. ~ Fox Run Road off Spaulding Turnpike, Newington; 603-431-5911.

It's so much fun to stroll Portsmouth's colorful, funky shops that you'll likely forget you're spending money.

Spacious and entertaining, **G. Willikers!** has enough toys, stuffed animals, tiny clothes and other kiddie paraphernalia to make a tot go crazy. ~ 13 Market Street, Portsmouth; 603-436-7746.

Handmade paper ·sneakers, techno-romantic jewelry and "butt heads"—cigarettes painted with faces—are among the wonderfully crazy artwork at **Gallery 33.** ~ 111 Market Street, Portsmouth; 603-431-7403.

Another noteworthy art stop, **N. W. Barrett Gallery** proffers wood, handblown glass and other crafts by local and nationally acclaimed artists. On the second floor, there's a fine art gallery with, among other gems, museum quality ship models. ~ 53 Market Street, Portsmouth; 603-431-4262.

It's Raining Cats and Dogs is an animal lover's delight. Fake fire hydrants, doggie raincoats and cat-to-cat greeting cards are but a few of the crazy critter antics. ~ 13 Commercial Alley, Portsmouth; 603-430-9566.

HIDDEN ► The avant-garde woman shops at **Le Club Boutique,** an underground emporium of offbeat postcards, nouveau attire and bangle earrings displayed in a pinball machine. ~ 19 Market Street, Portsmouth; 603-433-4455.

NIGHTLIFE Despite its stringent liquor laws—which mandate that bars must be part of restaurants, ski lodges or similar businesses—New Hampshire manages an ample share of lively establishments.

The 1800-seat **Hampton Beach Casino Ballroom,** one of those great old big-band clubs built in the 1920s, headlines top-name rock-and-roll, jazz, country-and-western and comedy. ~ 169 Ocean Boulevard; 603-929-4100.

An under-25, high-beach-fashion crowd shows up at the **Electric Wave,** a cavernous bilevel disco with a giant dancefloor and live bands downstairs. Cover. ~ 85 Brown Avenue, Hampton Beach; 603-926-8666.

Nautical decor and contemporary tunes set the scene at **The Pelican Club.** Live music plays Fridays and Saturdays at this popular, upscale oasis. ~ At the Galley Hatch Restaurant, Route 1, Hampton; 603-926-6152.

You can dance your heart out at **Rosa's,** a swanky venue that jams with Dixieland, rock-and-roll and rhythm-and-blues. Cover. ~ 80 State Street, Portsmouth; 603-436-9715.

Have a home-brewed beer (and watch it being brewed) at **Portsmouth Brewery.** You can enjoy the "Upstairs Unplugged" acoustic music shows or opt for a laid-back evening downstairs playing pool, or board games in oversized padded booths. Occasional cover for bigger shows on weekends. ~ 56 Market Street; 603-431-1115.

Nautical in style, **Dolphin Striker** resides above an underground tavern built curiously around a spring-fed well. Feed the exotic fish that swarm the well, or relax to piped-in reggae or occasional live acoustic music. ~ 15 Bow Street, Portsmouth; 603-431-5222.

Set in a 19th-century brick brewery, the **Seacoast Repertory Theatre**, housed in the beautiful Bow Street Theatre stages Shakespearean plays and other drama, major musicals and comedy in an intimate, under-300-seat pit theater. ~ 125 Bow Street, Portsmouth; 603-433-4472.

For the most part, New Hampshire's parks are open only for the summer, usually from Memorial Day through Labor Day. During the off-season, contact the **New Hampshire Division of Parks and Recreation**. ~ Box 1856, Concord, NH 03302; 603-271-3556.

BEACHES & PARKS

HAMPTON BEACH STATE PARK 🏊 One of the most popular parks in all New Hampshire, this place boasts a quarter mile of broad pewter-colored beach flecked with smooth stones. A jetty shoots several feet into the ocean, and there's a long row of sand dunes, some of the few remaining in the state. From here, you have tremendous views northward of Great Boars Head. Cast a rod from the jetty for striped bass, cod and flounder. Gazebo with picnic tables, restrooms, bathhouse, snack bar, lifeguards; day-use fee, minimum $5. Closed mid-October through early May. ~ On Route 1A at the southern tip of Hampton Beach; 603-926-3784.

▲ There's an RV campground with 20 full hookup sites; $30 per night.

HAMPTON SEASHELL STATE PARK 🏊 This is *the* liveliest sand in New Hampshire. For six months a year, thousands jam a three-mile stretch of fine ashen grains whipped by waves and surrounded by street action. The boardwalk, with its sidewalk vendors, carnival food and trinket shops, follows the beach and creates constant activity. Despite the size of this beach, the crowds do follow a certain order: families cluster around the north end, older folks lay claim to the south tip and the skimpy-suited, let's-party group stakes out the middle near the Beach Patrol Station. Restrooms, playground, lifeguards, pavilion, amphitheater and band shell; restaurants, stores, nightclubs and motels line the boardwalk. Closed November through April. ~ In Hampton Beach along Ocean Boulevard between M Street and Great Boars Head; 603-926-6705.

NORTH BEACH 🏊 🎣 A thick seawall hides this beach from the roadway, though rough waves occasionally send salt water over the top and onto passing traffic. The narrow cord of hard-packed sand, stretching one-and-a-half-miles, is submerged during most high tides, when locals congregate atop the wall for prime wave watching. This is the most popular spot in New Hampshire to surf; it's best around Great Boars Head, a rocky bulkhead on the northern end of the beach. Restrooms; stores within walking distance. ~ In Hampton Beach along Ocean Boulevard between Great Boars Head and 19th Street; 603-926-2862.

HIDDEN ►　**PLAICE COVE BEACH** Strewn with gray boulders and pebbles, this volcaniclike beach is encased in sand as silver as gunpowder. Small but picturesque, it rests before beautiful homes and appears to be a private beach. Locals know it as one of the quietest spots around and assemble here at low tide when the sand area is widest. Seagulls hang around the north end, scurrying about seaweed patches and constant ocean sprays. Swimming is okay at low tide during summer, though water is frequently quite rough. Stores located within walking distance; information, call the Hampton Chamber of Commerce at 603-926-8718. ~ Take the unmarked footpath that starts on Route 1A, across from Ron's Beach House restaurant just north of the intersection of Route 101C in Hampton Beach. The path leads between two houses down to the beach.

NORTH HAMPTON STATE BEACH Stretching 1000 feet along the ocean, this fine sliver of mocha sand covers a short lapse between seaside neighborhoods. Families favor the park for its subdued tone and gentle waves. Lovely Little Boars Head, a rocky ocean spur, looms to the north. Restrooms, lifeguards; snack shops are across the street. ~ Along Ocean Boulevard just south of Little Boars Head in North Hampton; 603-436-9404.

SOUTH RYE BEACH This so-called "beach" consists solely of millions of silvery pebbles (bad for the back but pretty to look at) that extend about one-quarter mile. Dedicated sunbathers set up lawn chairs and wear sturdy shoes, but the real action centers around surfing. Board toters call this beach "Rye on the Rocks" and arrive en masse anytime there's a whiff of wind. Stores less than a mile away in Rye. ~ On Route 1A, south of Causeway Road in Rye.

RYE HARBOR STATE PARK Situated on Ragged Neck Peninsula, this park offers commanding views of Rye Harbor and a 200-foot jetty for prime fishing (flounder and pollack) and sightseeing. There's no beach, but a grassy lawn is flecked with trees, and you can swim in the calm cove. On a clear day, the historic Isles of Shoals hover in the distance. Picnic areas, restrooms; day-use fee, $2.50. Closed Columbus Day through Memorial Day. ~ On Route 1A at Rye Harbor Road in Rye; 603-436-5249, 603-436-1552.

WALLIS SANDS STATE BEACH Wild and scenic, Wallis Sands boasts one of the coast's choicest swaths of copper-colored sand punctuated by a dramatic jetty. On windy days, waves slash the rocks, sending sprays as high as 60 feet. Only 18 acres in size, the park features soft patches of grass and a concrete walkway that edges the beach. Get there at low tide, when the beach spans up to 800 feet. When the tide comes in, the sand shrinks back to 150 feet—the only drawback of this beautiful place. Restrooms, lifeguards, bathhouse, showers, store; day-use fee, minimum $5. ~ At Route 1A and Marsh Road in Rye; 603-436-9404.

ODIORNE POINT STATE PARK New Hampshire's first settlers landed amid these rocky headlands and marshes back in 1623. Today, the natural sanctuary accounts for 330 acres and three-fourths of a mile of shoreline—the largest undeveloped tract on the coast. You can spend days exploring all the goodies this place offers, including old grave sites and stone walls, three World War II bunkers, remains of a formal garden, five miles of trails, two ponds, fishing for bass and flounder in spring and fall, dozens of tidal pools and the Sea Coast Science Center with wildlife exhibits, bookstore and local history displays. Besides historical secrets, the park harbors a secluded beach on **Frost Point**, known along the coast as the only spot to swim in your birthday suit. There's no sand here, only grass and pebbles and total seclusion. Just north of the point, sandy shores draw larger crowds. Visitors center, restrooms, bathhouse, pavilions; day-use fee, $2.50. ~ There are two entrances on Route 1A in Rye. To get to Frost Point, park at the north entrance and take the rocky trail about one-quarter mile through the woods; 603-436-7406.

◄ HIDDEN

GREAT ISLAND COMMON Picturesque and serene, this municipal beach belongs to the tiny island of New Castle, near Portsmouth. Swampy meadows share the shoreline with hard-packed sand and several rocky beaches. There's a spacious grassy area for excellent picnicking and a series of jetties that offer interesting tide-pooling. A lighthouse hovers in the distance, occasionally sounding its foghorn. Picnic areas, restrooms, playground; stores nearby in New Castle village; day-use fee, $2.50. ~ Off Wentworth Road in New Castle; 603-431-6710.

▼▼▼▼▼▼▼▼▼▼▼▼

Merrimack Valley

For the last two centuries, towns have grown alongside the Merrimack River, their inhabitants making use of its swift waters first for fishing, then for running textile mills. Today many of New Hampshire's 1.1 million residents call the Merrimack Valley home, making the area a seat of commerce and the state government.

This industrial region takes in a string of sizable cities, including Nashua, often called a "suburb" of nearby Boston, as well as the metropolis of Manchester and the capital, Concord. Spiraling out from these cities are bedroom communities and fragments of endearing rural areas.

SIGHTS   Scenic Route 111 twists its way southwest from Exeter to one of the state's most peculiar phenomena. **America's Stonehenge**, also known as Mystery Hill, may seem to some like a big pile of rocks. To archaeologists and astronomers, who have pored over its contents for 50 years, it presents an unsolved puzzle. How old is it and where did it come from? Spread across 30 acres, the erratic stone walls and bizarre rock formations are reputed to be an astronomical site of an ancient civilization—some claim it goes back 4000 years. England's Stonehenge it's not, but it's worth a look. Admission. ~ Haverhill Road, off Route 111, North Salem; 603-893-8300.

A short drive northward will land you in **Manchester**, New Hampshire's largest city with a population of over 100,000. Get a feel for this predominantly industrial city by strolling Elm Street, the main drag, lined with tired brick buildings and coffee shops and crowded with businesspeople. The **Greater Manchester Chamber of Commerce** can point you to the best local sights. ~ 889 Elm Street; 603-666-6600.

The valley's other large city, **Concord**, is the state capital and probably best known for its Concord Coach. Drop by the **New Hampshire Historical Society Museum** for a peek at the coaches that helped connect America's East and West during the 19th century. ~ 30 Park Street; 603-225-3381.

Pick up a copy of *The Historic Downtown Concord Walking Tour*, which will direct you to the city's choicest sites. It's available at the **Greater Concord Chamber of Commerce**, which also supplies general information on Merrimack Valley. ~ 244 North Main Street, Carrigan Commons; 603-224-2508.

Locals are fond of saying the carpets are rolled up at dusk in this very conservative city, and that holds some truth. The streets do clear out around dinner time, and except for a couple of watering holes, you'll be hard-pressed to find much activity around here.

Of course, people who go to Concord looking for action will ultimately be sidetracked by the **State House**, a beautiful 1819 building coated in smooth granite and capped with a gold-plated dome. Inside this grand old edifice throbs the pulse of the city, setting the political, social and oftentimes cultural agenda for the entire state. It's the nation's oldest state house in which the legislature still occupies the original chambers. ~ 107 North Main Street; 603-271-1110.

After you've roamed the capital streets, head north for the wilds of **Canterbury Shaker Village**. Stashed way out in an agrarian sanctuary, this insightful place will hold your attention for hours. Founded in the mid-1700s by one very progressive woman named Ann Lee, the religious sect lived in self-contained villages and aspired to create a utopia. Each of Canterbury's 24 buildings reflects principles of efficiency: drawers are built into walls and wall pegs are used to eliminate floor clutter.

Exhibits display Shaker inventions, including the circular saw, clothespin and flat broom. There's also a Paul Revere bell. Shakers believed in equal rights, shared work and celibacy, the last of which may have caused their virtual disappearance in the early 1900s. From November through May the Village is only open on Friday, Saturday and Sunday. Admission. ~ 288 Shaker Road off Route 106, Canterbury; 603-783-9511.

Small chain motels are the most frequent accommodations along New Hampshire's industrial combe, though you will find a few very special inns and bed and breakfasts.

LODGING

One of the nicest chain motels, **Fairfield Inn by Marriott** mingles the new and old with its Federal-style red brick design and its many modern amenities. There's a swimming pool out back and a lobby fashioned with reproductions of Victorian antiques and framed prints of hunting scenes. You'll find more antiques in the 114 guest rooms, along with designer wallpapers and a crisp, manicured feeling. ~ 4 Amherst Road, Merrimack; 603-424-7500, 800-228-2800, fax 603-424-7500. BUDGET TO MODERATE.

Think about it this way: with rooms offering Italian marble whirlpool baths, big-screen televisions and gorgeous four-poster beds, how could you *not* adore **The Bedford Village Inn**. This vanilla-coated estate, a medley of Colonial-style buildings, barns and grain silos, is a lesson in ultra-indulgence, a place where staying in your room may well be preferred to venturing out. Wet bars, pine chests and huge bay windows are also standard accessories in the higher-end rooms, or opt for the two-bedroom apartment with a fireplace and six-foot whirlpool. ~ Village Inn Lane, Bedford; 603-472-2001, 800-852-1166, fax 603-472-2379. DELUXE TO ULTRA-DELUXE.

Accommodation choices in Manchester are generally limited to motel and hotel chains. Nicely situated downtown, the **Center of New Hampshire Holiday Inn** caters mostly to business travelers and thus features plenty of extras like an indoor pool, sauna and a restaurant.

RENAISSANCE PALACE

It's enough just to stand outside and ogle the **Currier Gallery of Art**, with its lustrous limestone facade and gorgeous mosaics that resemble a Renaissance palace. But step inside and your eyes will feast on a series of archways and carved ceilings, then trail off to a substantial collection of artworks ranging from the Romanesque and Byzantine eras to modern times. There's also a fascinating collection of blown vases and mid-1800s photography. The Currier ranks as one of the finest small museums in the country. Admission. ~ 201 Myrtle Way, Manchester; 603-669-6144.

Expect upscale motel decor in 250 rooms, including plush carpets and marble countertops. ~ 700 Elm Street; 603-625-1000, 800-465-4329, fax 603-625-4595. MODERATE TO DELUXE.

For exploring the state capital, the **Holiday Inn** provides prime proximity to downtown sights. The layout is classic motel, with a four-story, nondescript exterior and 122 comfortable rooms decorated with wall-to-wall carpets, formica dressers and headboards and standard conveniences. There's also an indoor heated pool and sauna. ~ 172 North Main Street, Concord; 603-224-9534. DELUXE.

HIDDEN ►

Standing amid acres and acres of rambling meadows and gardens and surrounded by mountain peaks, **Wyman Farm** is a place worth finding. Built back in 1783, the lovely farmhouse awaiting down a labyrinth of obscure country roads is the family homestead of one of the innkeepers. There are three suites warmly fashioned with old pine floors, sitting rooms or parlors, and Oriental or hook rugs. For a real treat, request the room with the copper tub. Full breakfast and an evening tea tray are included. To get there, take Route 106 to the Clough Pond Road exit, then turn left on Flagg Road. Go eight-tenths of a mile on Flagg Road to Wyman Road, a dirt road. ~ 22 Wyman Road, Loudon; 603-783-4467, fax 603-783-4467. BUDGET TO MODERATE.

Staying at the **Hitching Post** is like visiting Grandma's house. A gregarious Danish grandma runs the bed and breakfast, a 1787 farmhouse that's rustic yet inviting. Walk through the carriage house, strung with dozens of dusty farm tools, then climb the creaking stairs to four small bedrooms (with shared baths) outfitted in country lace curtains and early-1900s wallpaper. Wake up in the mornings to a full gourmet breakfast. ~ Routes 4 and 202, Chichester; 603-798-4951. MODERATE.

DINING

Just south of Manchester, **Hannah Jack Tavern** complements its round of warm dining rooms with marble fireplaces, stained-glass windows and New England wall murals. Locals show up for the homemade breads (the raisin nut brioche is divine), the 100-label wine list and the prime rib, cut daily at the restaurant. Hannah Jack's does something that more restaurants should do—it offers smaller portions of many entrées. ~ Daniel Webster Highway off the Everett Turnpike, Merrimack; 603-424-4171. MODERATE TO DELUXE.

In a world of Americanized Mexican restaurants, it's rare to strike authentic south-of-the-border cuisine. That, of course, is what makes **Hermanos** so very special. Here, surrounded by Aztec murals and paraphernalia, you discover hefty burritos, enchiladas, quesadillas and tostadas, served with verve and panache. The specials are interesting, too—try the *estufada* (spicy stew), Mexican pizza and *taco pastor* (soft-shelled tacos stuffed and wrapped in grilled corn tortillas). ~ 11 Hill's Avenue, Concord; 603-224-5669. BUDGET TO MODERATE.

HIDDEN ►

Tucked away in the bucolic lull of Shaker Village, **The Creamery** offers a leap back in time. Indeed, the village and its 24 buildings have changed little since the early 1800s. Dine on heavy wood tables, surrounded by simple country decor. In keeping with Shaker mandates of absolute freshness, menus utilize locally grown foods and might feature applewood-smoked pork loin with hard cider, pan-seared salmon on stewed white beans, hickory-smoked ham with spiced cherry catsup and peach oatmeal pie. From October through December and the month of April, the price includes a tour of the village or a musical program. Closed Monday through Thursday and in January, February and March. ~ 288 Shaker Road, in Shaker Museum, Canterbury; 603-783-9511. ULTRA-DELUXE.

Pompanoosuc Mills proffers contemporary and Shaker-style furnishings such as plush couches and silk arrangements and oak dressers. ~ 3 Eagle Square, Concord; 603-225-7975.

SHOPPING

It's well worth a trip into the countryside to peruse the **Gift Shop** at Canterbury Shaker Village, an 1825 carriage house stocked with cookbooks, potpourri, handmade sweaters and crafts. ~ 288 Shaker Road, Canterbury; 603-783-9511.

◄ HIDDEN

The best place to catch top-quality international and national plays is the **Palace Theatre**, an ornate, 883-seat downtown arena that also hosts musicals, ballet and concerts. ~ 80 Hanover Street, Manchester; 603-668-5588.

NIGHTLIFE

There's high-energy dancing at **High 5 Restaurant and Lounge**, which hosts nightly acts ranging from local comedy to live bands. Cover for comedy. ~ 555 Canal Street, Manchester; 603-626-0555.

Thumbs is a dim, underground gathering spot for politicians and a crowd of folks in their 20s. Live blues and rock is featured most nights. Cover. ~ Thursday's Restaurant, 6 Pleasant Street, Concord; 603-224-2626.

SILVER LAKE STATE PARK Locals mob this place on summer weekends for one reason: a very special sliver of sand. These toffee-colored granules extend 1000 feet along Silver Lake and churn up a storm of activity. The 34-acre lake itself is also quite stunning, sheltered by a cascade of grassy knolls and gracious pine trees. Picnic area, restrooms, bathhouse, play field, refreshment stand; day-use fee, $2.50. ~ On Route 122 one mile north of Hollis; 603-465-2342.

BEACHES & PARKS

PAWTUCKAWAY STATE PARK Tucked just outside the bustle of several major cities, this 5500-acre park has it all. There's 803-acre Lake Pawtuckaway with its broad mocha beaches and islands, a vast oak and hickory forest and hemlock ravine, 25 acres of wooded picnicking spots and the Pawtuckaway Mountains, surrounded by curious rock formations carved some 275 million years ago. There are extensive trails for hiking, snowmobiling and cross-country skiing. Swimming and fishing for bass are excellent here. You need to explore all three areas to get a good feel for this diverse park, so plan to spend some time. No pets are allowed. Picnic area, restrooms, snack bar, playground, rental boats, pavilion; day-use fee, $2.50. ~ Off Route 156, three and a half miles north of Route 101 in Nottingham; 603-895-3031.

▲ Horse and Big islands offer 170 tent sites, many right on the lake. Reservations are required for Horse Island. Most take RVs (no hookups); $14 to $20 per night.

BEAR BROOK STATE PARK 🏃🚲 ⚓ ⛺ ⤴ This mammoth place covers 9600 acres and offers a slew of activities. Of the park's six ponds, Catamount Pond attracts the most activity with its wide beach, ball fields and picnic facilities for 1500 people. Cool, dusky Bear Brook snakes through the park, which is dense with red and white pines. You'll also find more than 50 miles of hiking trails, a physical fitness course, snowmobile museum, nature center with a popular glass beehive, family camping museum and two archery ranges. Fishing is excellent for trout, perch, bass and pickerel in lakes and streams. Archery Pond is reserved for fly fishing. You can swim in Beaver and Catamount ponds (restricted to campers only at Beaver Pond). Picnic areas, pavilions, snack bars, restrooms and bathhouses; day-use fee, $2.50. ~ Off Route 28, five miles northeast of Hookset; 603-485-9874.

▲ Beaver Pond features 94 RV/tent sites (no hookups); $14 per night; information, 603-485-9869. The campground is open from May 20 through Columbus Day only.

WINSLOW STATE PARK 🏃 After a 1820-foot climb (via auto) up Mount Kearsarge, the park rewards with magnificent panoramas that stretch into Vermont. The park was named for Civil War admiral John Winslow, and hang glider enthusiasts occasionally hurl themselves from the summit, landing (hopefully) in a parking lot below. A steep, one-mile hike takes you to the peak—2937 feet up. Picnic area, restrooms; stores nearby in Wilmot; day-use fee, $2.50. ~ Off Route 11, three miles south of New London in Wilmot Flat. You can also take Exit 10 off Route 89 and follow the signs to Winslow State Park; 603-526-6168 or 603-927-4724.

▼▼▼▼▼▼▼▼▼▼▼▼▼

Monadnock Region

Curled along the southwest bend of New Hampshire, the Monadnock Region makes up a collage of all the virtues one associates with New England. White steepled churches and old covered bridges, itinerant country roads edged by miles of wild woods and lazy lakes, and lovable Currier and Ives towns all mesh to give this domain a warm Yankee flavor.

SIGHTS

General stores, coffee shops and old-time pharmacies line the streets of **Peterborough**, founded in 1738 and believed to be the model for Thornton Wilder's *Our Town*. It's easy to see why Wilder may have taken to this mountain hamlet, which has spawned old saltbox homes and very congenial townsfolk.

A friendly caretaker at the **Peterborough Historical Society Museum** will walk you through exhibits of the town's heritage and commercial interests, including thriving agriculture and manufacturing industries and, lately, electronics and publishing. ~ 19 Grove Street; 603-924-3235.

South on Route 202, **Jaffrey** purports to be the only Jaffrey in the world but more important is home to **Mount Monadnock**, which looms 3165 feet over the region like an astute sentinel. This imposing butte has become world famous as the most-climbed peak; myriads ascend its 30 miles of trails each year.

Henry David Thoreau and Ralph Waldo Emerson scaled Monadnock, now part of **Monadnock State Park**, where you'll also find an environmental center with historical and geological displays. (See "Beaches & Parks" section below.) Admission. ~ Off Route 124, Jaffrey; 603-532-8862.

Behind the Colonial Meeting House rests a shaded cemetery and the graves of novelist Willa Cather and Amos Fortune, an African-born slave who purchased his freedom.

Just east of the park on Route 124 you'll encounter Jaffrey's grandest manmade structure, the **Colonial Meeting House**. Its huge clock and bell tower, built in 1773, are framed by Mount Monadnock, an arousing sight for sure.

Some of Monadnock's choicest views can be had at **Cathedral of the Pines**, a wood and stone shrine built by local parents for a son who was slain in World War II. There are guided tours, offering views of the precious artifacts donated from every U.S. president and from people around the world. A piece of the Rock of Gibraltar is there, along with a hunk from the Blarney Stone. You'll also see a holy ark carved in Portugal. When these carillon bells ring, they reverberate down the mountain and make melodies for miles. Closed from November 1 through April 30. ~ Off Route 119, Rindge; 603-899-3300.

Nature has surely blessed the Monadnock Region, and nowhere is it more evident than at **Rhododendron State Park**. Arrive in mid-July and be rewarded with 16 acres smothered in fields of wild rhododendrons. There's a one-mile trail through this riot of color. (See "Beaches & Parks" section below.) ~ Rhododendron Road, off of Route 119, Fitzwilliam; 603-532-8862.

Nestled in a marvelous Currier and Ives setting, **The Birchwood Inn** oozes history and enchantment. Fashioned of deep red brick, the 1775 Federal-style building brandishes twin chimneys and lazes across from a white steepled church and a grassy hill topped with war memorials. Murals of itinerant artist Rufus Porter spread across dining room walls, while seven bedrooms exhibit different themes and eclectic decor. An "editorial room" features newsprint wallpaper, while a "music room" is arranged with musical instruments. Lose yourself in the 18th century at this place. Full breakfast is included. ~ Route 45, Temple; 603-878-3285. MODERATE.

LODGING

The ultimate New Hampshire hideaway may well be **Woodbound Inn**, a captivating retreat stashed deep in a mountain forest. Here you

◄ HIDDEN

have the trying task of choosing between several accommodations: Early American–style bedrooms housed in a 19th-century farmhouse; contemporary rooms with brass beds in the annex; or cozy lakeside cabins with fireplaces. It's easy to kick back in any of the three, or explore the inn's 165 acres thick with pines and firs. There's also a nine-hole golf course, numerous cross-country ski trails, a clay tennis court and a superb restaurant. ~ East of Route 202 on Woodbound Road, Rindge; 603-532-8341, 800-688-7770. MODERATE TO ULTRA-DELUXE.

For up-to-date motel accommodations, consider **Jack Daniel's Motor Inn**. A single, two-story building covered with wood shingles, the inn maintains 17 quite modern guest rooms with plush carpets, high-back chairs, large showers and upstairs balconies. Some rooms overlook the pretty Contoocook River. ~ Route 202, Peterborough; 603-924-7548, fax 603-924-7700. MODERATE.

The Hancock Inn radiates an ancient aura, and rightly so—it's the state's oldest continuously operating inn. Braided rugs rest atop the 1789 floor, bouquets of fragrant flowers bask on old tabletops and walls sport early-17th-century Rufus Porter murals and Moses Eaton stencils. Upstairs in 11 bedrooms, sunlight streams in through rows of windows framed with ruffled curtains, and antique chests and beds provide a cozy demeanor. Don't miss the library. ~ 33 Main Street, Hancock; 603-525-3318, 800-525-1789, fax 603-525-9301. DELUXE.

DINING

Huddled beneath the great profile of Monadnock Mountain, the **Monadnock Inn** proffers relaxed New England dining in a perfectly provincial setting. Polished oak floors set off a cozy dining room, while plastic tables and chairs are settled around a breezy screened porch that offers plenty of countryside views. For dinner, they offer rack of lamb, grilled salmon and filet mignon; for lunch, there's bay shrimp and chicken stir fry as well as sandwiches, quiche and pastas. ~ Route 124, Jaffrey Center; 603-532-7001. MODERATE TO DELUXE.

For quick, affordable Italian pies, try the **Jaffrey Pizza Barn**, a modest downtown cubbyhole with just four rows of orange formica

---

✔ CHECK THESE OUT—UNIQUE DINING

- *Budget:* Join the line at **Polly's Pancake Parlor** for her special griddle cakes smothered in maple syrup. *page 486*
- *Budget to moderate:* Mourn the loss of Thomas Fletcher at **Widow Fletcher's Tavern**, founded in 1764 and still serving up delicious vittles. *page 452*
- *Moderate to deluxe:* Dine in a splendid provincial manor on New Hampshire cuisine while enjoying the view at **The Red Hill Inn**. *page 479*
- *Ultra-deluxe:* Step back in time to the 1800s Shaker-style **Creamery**, and dine on locally grown foods served on long wooden tables. *page 460*

Budget: under $8 Moderate: $8–$16 Deluxe: $16–$24 Ultra-deluxe: over $24

booths. Thick- or thin-crusted pizzas come with a good selection of toppings (including steak and eggplant); there are hot and cold grinders, too. ~ Blake Street, Jaffrey; 603-532-8383. BUDGET TO MODERATE.

One of the toniest addresses around, the **Boiler House** captures an elegant feeling with black lacquer chairs, crisp white linens and a glass wall overlooking the Contoocook River. Formerly a 19th-century boiler room, the place has retained its now-hip exposed steel pipes. The setting is a perfect one for gastronomic encounters with blackberry braised boneless Long Island duck and cracked black pepper pork tenderloin with blue cheese sauce. Closed Monday. ~ Route 202 South, Peterborough; 603-924-9486. MODERATE TO DELUXE.

"Epicurean collage" is how owners of **Latacarta** describe their unusual but successful natural cuisine. Inspiring soups, sandwiches and entrées are prepared with imagination and a philosophy of freshness. Housed in a recycled cinema, this very popular eatery is decorated with rotating local artwork, track lighting and cane chairs. Try the pan-grilled tofu sandwich or escalopes of salmon with dill sauce. ~ 6 School Street, Peterborough; 603-924-6878. MODERATE TO DELUXE.

The Hancock Inn doles out some of the best Yankee cookin' around, dependable fare like Shaker cranberry pot roast and broiled swordfish stuffed with crabmeat, shrimp and scallops. Set in New Hampshire's oldest operating inn (circa 1789), the three dining rooms feature cultured country decor and face a rambling flower garden. ~ 33 Main Street, Hancock; 603-525-3318. MODERATE TO DELUXE.

Over in the small but bustling city of Keene, **Henry David's** packs 'em in with dressed-up American fare and greenhouse surroundings. Light streams in through skylights, giving life to the more than 1300 plants draped across ceilings and walls. Named after *the* Mr. Thoreau, the place features outstanding prime rib and soups and baked stuffed shrimp. ~ 81 Main Street; 603-352-0608. MODERATE TO DELUXE.

SHOPPING

Wanna feel better? **Maggie's Marketplace** supplies natural foods like organic corn chips and no-cholesterol ice cream, plus cookbooks. ~ 14 Main Street, Peterborough; 603-924-7671.

Your literary layover is **The Toadstool Book Shop**, a small-town shop with everything from warship catalogues and world radio handbooks to New England journals. There's a coffee shop on the premises. ~ 12 Depot Square, Peterborough; 603-924-3543.

It's mall shopping 19th-century style at **Colony Mill Marketplace**. Located in a recycled 1838 mill, the aesthetic trading center houses a medley of stores offering clothes, gifts, cards, home decor items and books. ~ West Street, Keene; 603-357-1240.

NIGHTLIFE

One of the most respected theater troupes in New England, the Peterborough Players perform at the **Hadley Barn** in a marvelous converted barn. ~ Hadley Road off Middle Hancock Road, Peterborough; 603-924-7585.

A solid local hangout, the **Copper Bar** is a chic place to bend an elbow. Depending on the bartender's mood, you'll hear taped jazz, blues or contemporary music. ~ Boiler House Restaurant, Route 202 South, Peterborough; 603-924-9486.

BEACHES & PARKS

MONADNOCK STATE PARK 🏃 The lonely, imposing peak of Mount Monadnock has long been a fixture of southwestern New Hampshire, inspiring poets and intriguing all those who cast eyes upon it. Frequently called the world's most-climbed mountain, its barren granite pinnacle has been scaled by Mark Twain, Ralph Waldo Emerson, Henry David Thoreau and thousands of others. Today, the 5000-acre park remains a hiker's mecca, crisscrossed with 40 miles of trails enriched by views of every New England state. Picnic area, restrooms, refreshment center, environmental center; day-use fee, $2.50. ~ Off Route 124, four miles west of Jaffrey; 603-532-8862.

▲ 21 tent sites are open year-round; about half accommodate RVs (no hookups); $12 per night for two, $6 for each additional person.

HIDDEN ►

CONTOOCOOK LAKE PUBLIC BEACH 🏊 It's a rare find indeed, this tiny but choice spot. Edging the shore of beautiful Contoocook Lake, a sliver of beach features glistening white sand as soft as talcum powder. During the summer, the town closes part of the road and spreads sand across it, making it a great spot for small children. Picnic areas, restrooms; stores nearby in Jaffrey. ~ From the junction of Routes 124 and 202 in Jaffrey, take Stratton Road southeast to Squantum Road. Head east on Squantum Road, and you'll soon arrive at the beach; 603-532-7863.

MILLER STATE PARK 🏃 New Hampshire's oldest state park was settled back in 1891 and named for General James Miller, a hero of the War of 1812. It rests atop the 2300-foot summit of South Pack Monadnock Mountain, a one-and-a-half-mile semivertical drive with numerous hairpin curves. Incredible vistas extend to the skyscrapers of Boston. Picnic area, primitive restrooms. ~ Off Route 101, three miles east of Peterborough; 603-924-3497.

RHODODENDRON STATE PARK 🏃 No doubt, this place is extra special. Arrive around mid-July and revel in the explosion of rhododendrons that form a pink-and-white canopy across 16 acres. A one-mile trail meanders up Little Mount Monadnock, ensuring a feast for the senses and lovely views of Mount Monadnock. Other jewels bloom here, too, including the jack-in-the-pulpit, trillium, mountain laurel and pink lady's slipper. The Wildflower Trail (.4 mile) offers views of stunning patches of wildflowers clearly marked by the Fitzwilliam Garden Club. Picnic area, restrooms; stores nearby in Fitzwilliam; day-use fee, $2.50. ~ On Rhododendron Road, off Route 12, two and a half miles north of Fitzwilliam; 603-239-8153.

The area north of the Monadnocks—edged on the west by the Connecticut River—is a long, lazy union of cornfields and hills and big tufts of wildflowers tossed against Vermont's western border. Bustling mill towns, Ivy League schools and colonial hamlets bless this quiescent region. Inland, Lake Sunapee exists as a world unto itself, stretching ten glittering miles beaded with sylvan villages and a statuesque mountain crisscrossed with ski trails. Life here is lived slowly, a welcome pace for travelers seeking bona fide tranquility.

Lake Sunapee–Dartmouth Area

SIGHTS

In the summer of 1777, General John Stark, commissioned by New Hampshire's legislature, organized a military force in **Charlestown**, the first town we visit in this area. That 1500-man troop marched westward across Vermont's border and defeated British-German forces in the famed Battle of Bennington. Now a **historical marker** (Route 12) pays homage to these local heroes.

Of course, Charlestown had its own share of skirmishes, as you'll see over at **The Fort at No. 4**, a re-creation of the great log stockade village built by pioneers in 1744. The fort suffered a three-day attack in 1747 by French and Indian forces, who were staved off by a 31-man garrison. Today, a medley of log cabins, barns, blacksmith shop and saw pit are displayed alongside original 18th-century tools. A nice trip back in time. Closed Tuesday and from mid-October through early May. Admission. ~ Route 11; 603-826-5700.

North of Charlestown, the industrial town of **Claremont** sustains a maze of centuries-old mills, weaving sheds and mansions. The folks in this blue-collar town are quite congenial. Stop by the **Claremont Chamber of Commerce** for a walking tour map of the **Historic Mill District**, which is bounded generally by Main, Spring and Central streets. ~ Moody Building in Tremont Square; 603-543-1296.

From here, the **Lake Sunapee** area presents an obvious side trip and promises panoramas of small towns, rocky coastlines, rhythmic beaches and distinguished lighthouses. Tourism has certainly hit this outdoor playground, but it's not yet overwhelming. Start by rounding the lake on Routes 11 and 103, gazing across pristine waters at the windsurfers and small boats and gentle backdrop of forest-covered Mount Sunapee.

The **M.V. Mount Sunapee II** offers narrated tours of the lake from mid-May through mid-October. Go during fall foliage season to appreciate the area at its peak. Admission. ~ Sunapee Harbor, off Route 11; 603-763-4030.

Head back east to Route 12A and the hushed town of **Cornish**, where you'll find the country's longest covered bridge. Just in sight of the cornfields, the **Cornish-Windsor Covered Bridge** arches 470 feet across the Connecticut River, linking Vermont and New Hampshire.

Built in 1866, it was the fourth at the site, the first two falling victim to raging floodwaters. An ancient sign still warns today's travelers to "Walk your horse or pay a two-dollar fine."

Cornish became a cultural mecca during the late 1800s and early 1900s when a series of noted artists, writers, poets, musicians and sculptors arrived and formed the Cornish Colony.

This mass migration was spurred by the 1885 arrival of Augustus Saint-Gaudens, one of America's foremost sculptors, whose works include the Admiral David Farragut statue in New York's Madison Square and the statue of Abraham Lincoln in Chicago's Lincoln Park.

Those artists and writers left Cornish long ago, but the **Saint-Gaudens National Historic Site** survives as a marvelous tribute to that great era. Saint-Gaudens' white brick house, his studios and beautiful formal gardens afford an endearing glimpse of a prolific life. High hedges of pine and hemlock and birch-lined paths are a testament to Saint-Gaudens affection for gardening, while originals and copies of his sculptures reveal his gift of hand. Closed from mid-October through early May. Admission. ~ Route 12A; 603-675-2175.

Novelist Winston Churchill, poets Percy MacKaye and Witter Bynner, former *New Republic* editor Herbert Croly, landscape painter Willard Metcalfe and actress Ethel Barrymore all took up residence in Cornish.

North of Cornish throbs the valley's pulse, *the* reason why thousands pour into the region, and *the* place to go at night. Ivy League **Dartmouth College** exists in the archetypical New England college town of Hanover, although many would argue it *is* the town. ~ 603-646-1110.

There's no other way to say it: this campus is absolutely beautiful. It at once impresses with masterful old buildings that seem to go on forever. Stately red brick Federal styles stand next to softer Georgian architecture, erected in the late 1700s and so unaffected by age or wars or government strife.

Dartmouth was actually started in Lebanon, Connecticut in 1755 as a school for American Indians, called Moor's Indian Charity School. A donation of 3300 Hanover acres—plus a generous sum of money from England's second Earl of Dartmouth—put the school on its current site in 1769. Its charter, dated that year, can still be found in the hallowed halls of **Baker Library**, as can celebrated murals by Mexican painter José Clemente Orozco. ~ 603-646-2560.

The Hopkins Center for the Performing Arts is a must see. The exterior of Hopkins resembles the Lincoln Center in New York City, while inside, barreled ceilings, dramatic plant sculptures and abstract art combine to make this a work of great beauty. ~ Wheelock Street; 603-646-2422.

Next door at the **Hood Museum of Art**, you'll encounter a splendid small museum with a diverse permanent collection featuring works by American and European masters such as Whistler, Eakins, Paul Revere, Picasso and Dürer. There are also excellent examples of

African, American Indian and Oceanic art, Assyrian reliefs and Chinese bronzes and ceramics. ~ Wheelock Street; 603-646-2808.

Dartmouth's distinguished life, combined with nearly 5000 students, spills over nicely into the town of Hanover. Gracious tree-lined streets, underground pubs and polished shops make the town a great place for strolling but awful for parking. For more information, stop by the **Hanover Chamber of Commerce.** ~ 37 South Main Street; 603-643-3115.

No signs even hint of **Goddard Mansion.** Pity those who bypass this camouflaged treasure, a European-style estate that exudes elegance and refinement. The expansive, ornate living rooms and parlors feature high-beamed ceilings, carved mantles and a baby grand piano. A breezy porch overlooks the manicured lawn, croquet court and tea house, and bedrooms are designed to gratify. Several rooms command views of mountains all the way to Vermont. ~ 25 Hillstead Road and Route 12, Claremont; 603-543-0603, 800-736-0603, fax 603-543-0001. MODERATE TO DELUXE.

LODGING

◀ *HIDDEN*

Lingering in the shadows of Mount Sunapee, **The Backside Inn** tenders home-style accommodations in an 1835 farmhouse-cum-inn. Resting on 120 acres, pines envelop the inn, which has ten comfortable bedrooms featuring pretty antiques and wall-to-wall carpets or stenciled wood floors. You can walk to a 49-acre pond or take the five-minute drive to sprawling Lake Sunapee. ~ Brook Road off Route 103, Sunapee; 603-863-5161. MODERATE.

Barely 12 miles from Lake Sunapee, **New London Inn** is one place that has grown beautiful with time. Built back in 1792, the three-story clapboard inn overlooking the town green and bandstand is surely the prototype of gracious New England sojourns. Spacious porches wrap around the lower floors, wood hallways lead to carpeted rooms, and beams crisscross ceilings. Thirty bedrooms have personality and flair, adorned in brass or wicker beds and lovely antique dressers and chairs. ~ 140 Main Street, New London; 603-526-2791, 800-526-2791. MODERATE TO DELUXE.

Its milieu is rural and unpretentious, but the history and intrigue of **The Chase House** is enough to liven your spirit. Within the walls of this modest 18th-century Colonial dwelling, Salmon P. Chase (as in Chase Manhattan Bank) was born and spent his early childhood. Chase was also a founder of the Republican Party and treasury secretary to Abraham Lincoln, among other things. Today, stacked firewood rests on the porch, and flower beds brighten the yard. The seven bedrooms—all with private baths—are heavy on country decor, including canopy beds and original softwood floors. Closed in November and December. ~ Route 12A, four miles north of Route 131, Cornish; 603-675-5391, 800-401-9455, fax 603-675-5010. MODERATE TO DELUXE.

◀ *HIDDEN*

Snuggled nicely against the upper Connecticut River, **The Sunset** tenders simple accommodations. The configuration is standard motel L-shape, with 18 modest but clean rooms. Expect industrial-grade carpets, formica furniture; some rooms have splendid views across the river and mountains. ~ 305 North Main Street, Route 10, West Lebanon; 603-298-8721. MODERATE.

The place to stay in Hanover is **The Hanover Inn**. For one, it's right across from (and owned by) Dartmouth College, thereby drawing all sorts of Ivy Leaguers. For another, it's one of those beautiful old buildings that absolutely commands respect. Graced in red brick and crowned by a sloping shingled roof, this granddaddy has been accommodating the rich and prestigious since the late 1700s. Four floors of guest rooms reflect early Colonial designs but throw in amenities such as cable television and air-conditioning. ~ Main and Wheelock streets; 603-643-4300, 800-443-7024, fax 603-646-3744. ULTRA-DELUXE.

A former stagecoach stop, **The Alden Country Inn** lounges under the shadows of the White Mountains and harkens back to the early 1800s with an unhurried pace and old-fashioned design. Indeed, the whole place is brimming with gorgeous antiques, from old clocks and handmade quilts to maple hutches and a pretty sleigh. There are no less than ten fireplaces, and 14 rooms and suites accented with stenciled wallpaper, wingback chairs and hooked rugs. Breakfast at the inn's excellent restaurant is included. ~ On the Common, off of Route 10, Lyme; 603-795-4404, fax 603-795-4220. DELUXE.

DINING

For standard American, family-style dining, **Dimick's** is your destination. The menu includes sandwiches—grilled chicken, tuna melt, roast beef—and entrées such as steak, pork chops, fried chicken and baked haddock. If available, ask for one of the three tables that overlook the Sugar River. ~ Lower Main Street, Claremont; 603-542-6701. BUDGET TO MODERATE.

Depending on what's in season, the **Millstone** might be serving venison, pheasant, swordfish or even Bavarian schnitzel. Fashioned as a country inn, this congenial restaurant is embellished with bow back chairs, linen tablecloths and local artwork. Freshness is the key word on this varied menu, and it keeps showing up in the seafood, game vegetables, pasta and herbs. ~ Newport Road, New London; 603-526-4201. MODERATE TO DELUXE.

HIDDEN ►

You'll swear you've reached the outer limits of the universe by the time you arrive at **Home Hill Country Inn**. Stashed five mountain miles up a wooded sinuous road, the restored mansion conceals a French restaurant with a serious following. The dining room is intimate, with plank floors and blazing hearths. A *prix-fixe* menu changes daily, offering delights such as scallops and shrimp in a sundried tomato sauce and veal in sage and crimini mushroom sauce.

Closed Sunday and Monday. ~ River Road, off Route 12A, Plainfield; 603-675-6165. ULTRA-DELUXE.

Dartmouth students love to hang loose at **Peter Christian's Tavern**, an underground habitat with great character and soul-warming grub. Zesty beef stew (some of the best anywhere) and fish chowder are definite favorites, but you can't go wrong with the spudley doright (stuffed potato) and Peter's Russian mistress (turkey sandwich with bacon, swiss and spinach). Wood beams criss-cross a low stucco ceiling, oversized mugs hang above the bar and knotty-pine booths are battered to a perfect college pub complexion. ~ 39 South Main Street, Hanover; 603-643-2345. BUDGET TO MODERATE.

It's tough to miss the big bubble windows of **Molly's Balloon**, a chic little nook that has "yuppie" written all over it. There's an expansive oak bar in the middle, enveloped by brass railings and loads of hanging plants and trendy young diners. The cuisine runs the gamut from stacked deli sandwiches, soups and salads to Mexican fajitas, baby-back ribs and pasta dishes. ~ 43 South Main Street, Hanover; 603-643-2570. MODERATE.

SHOPPING

Powerhouse Mill Arcade is like a fairyland, adorned with barreled ceilings and colored strands of light. The stores are imaginative and often feature a single theme. ~ Glen Road off of Route 12A, West Lebanon; 603-298-5236. **Artifactory**, for instance, leans toward the unusual with whimsical gifts like wizard-shaped candles and tie-dyed hats. ~ 603-298-6010. **HomeScapes** has furniture, glassware, rugs and other accessories for home styles ranging from colonial to contemporary to high-tech. ~ 603-298-6038.

If cooking is your passion, stop in **Board & Basket** for the latest kitchenware gadgets, cookbooks and gourmet foods. ~ Powerhouse Plaza, West Lebanon; 603-298-5813.

NIGHTLIFE

The historic **Claremont Opera House**, with its arched stained glass and scrolled columns, is a superb place to see regional and national opera, orchestra, ballet and musicals. ~ Main Street in Tremont Square, Claremont; 603-542-4433.

Dartmouth College nightlife sizzles on the underground circuit. Among the best below-ground pubs, **Five Olde Nugget Alley** features a long, battered maple bar, a round of maple tables and piped-in contemporary music. ~ Olde Nugget Alley, off Wheelock Street, Hanover; 603-643-5081.

Step down a flight of stairs to **Peter Christians Tavern**, a cozy establishment with high-back wood booths and a perpetual crowd of lively students. ~ 39 South Main Street, Hanover; 603-643-2345.

Dartmouth College's dazzling **Hopkins Center for Performing Arts** hosts major drama, musicals, concerts and films in two auditoriums. ~ Wheelock Street, Hanover; 603-646-2422.

BEACHES & PARKS

PILLSBURY STATE PARK 🏃 🚴 ⛵ 🛶 A 5000-acre wilderness of forests, ponds and subtle hills, Pillsbury was once a bustling village of sawmills and frame homes. Today there's no hint of that 18th-century activity as ducks, deer and other wildlife roam the moist hammocks and dense thickets. Hiking and picnicking are superb, and nine ponds provide havens for serious fishers and excellent still-water canoeing. Picnic areas, pit toilets; stores are in Washington; day-use fee, $2.50. ~ Off Route 31, four miles north of Washington; 603-863-2860.

▲ There are 38 primitive sites bordering May Pond (4 accessible by canoe only); $12 per night. Warning: treacherous for big RVs.

MOUNT SUNAPEE STATE PARK 🏃 🚴 ⛷ 🏊 🛶 This ever-popular park is more like a resort (minus the accommodations), a year-round recreation haven that caters to swimmers and sunbathers, hikers and skiers, ice fishers and sightseers. Chair lifts cruise up 2750-foot Mount Sunapee for downhill skiing and lovely views of Lake Sunapee and the surrounding alpine mountains. There's a cafeteria up here and another at the mountain's base, where you'll find a sun terrace, auditorium and exhibition trout pool. Spring-fed Lake Sunapee is renowned for trout and salmon fishing. And there's more: the 2700-acre park claims a ski school and shop, nursery and lineup of events like state craft shows, bike races and outdoor concerts. Across the street, **Sunapee State Beach** is a 900-foot ribbon of crystalline sand edging the lake. Picnic areas, restrooms, bathhouses, lifeguards, cafeterias, snack bars; day-use fee, $2.50. ~ On Route 103, three miles west of Newbury; 603-763-2356.

▼▼▼▼▼▼▼▼▼▼▼▼

The Lakes Region

Strewn across New Hampshire's heart like a strand of aquamarine beads, some 273 lakes range from sealike to pondlike. Skirted by olive hills and sheltered coves, the lakes weave about 39 towns and three cities and engender a slew of outdoor pursuits. Many of the lakes bear Indian names, including Kanasatka, Ossipee, Squam and Winnipesaukee, queen of them all.

SIGHTS

One of the westernmost—and least visited—lakes is **Newfound**, whose fine sandy shores are covered by spiraling evergreens, sand and chimney-topped cabins. It lies along Route 3A.

The town of Hebron, on the northwest corner, harbors an unexpected treasure known as **Sculptured Rocks**. This geological treat comprises dozens of undulating rocks, carved into designs by thousands of years of swift water. There's a frowning face, a seal, a camel and other interesting sculptures. ~ Sculptured Rocks Road, a gravel road off North Shore Road, just southwest of town center.

HIDDEN ►

Tucked away in North Groton you'll find a darling clapboard cottage that was the **Mary Baker Eddy Historic Home**. Eddy, an astute woman who founded the Christian Science religion and *Christian Science Monitor*, lived here from 1855 through 1860. The house has

HIDDEN ►

been nicely maintained and features her old iron pot-bellied stove and bed strung with ropes. (Tours of this structure begin at Eddy's Rumney home.) Closed from late October to May. Admission. ~ Hall's Brook Road; 603-786-9943.

Eddy left North Groton in 1860 and moved to nearby Rumney, where her **Colonial frame house** rests behind a white picket fence. ◄ *HIDDEN* Here she penned the poem "Major Anderson and Our Country" in response to the Civil War and waged her own war against slavery. The late-1700s house is adorned with relics like a banjo clock, melodian piano and unusual wall drawers used to store ammunition. Closed from late October to May. Admission. ~ Stinson Lake Road; 603-786-9943.

From here, head east though the mountains and cut over to **Squam Lake**, speckled with fishing skiffs, sailboats and loons. Antique shops, decoy stores, rustic cabins and miles of tall trees give this area a peaceful milieu, a setting that no doubt attracted makers of the movie *On Golden Pond*, parts of which were filmed here.

Get close to those crazy loons at the **Science Center of New Hampshire**, a 200-acre wildlife preserve near Squam Lake. From the trails here you can spot whitetail deer, black bears and bald eagles, visit ponds and a turtle island and view otter and raptor (bird of prey) exhibits. Kids love the hands-on nature exhibits, games and puzzles. Closed from November to May. Admission. ~ Route 113, Holderness; 603-968-7194.

South on Route 25, **Meredith** is a very lucky place. Resting on a finger of Lake Winnipesaukee, it also touches Lakes Wicwas, Waukewan, Pemigewasset and Winnisquam. The town bears a charming demeanor with cosmopolitan touches like small shopping malls, art galleries and numerous restaurants and motels.

The **Meredith Chamber of Commerce** has area sightseeing information. ~ South of Routes 3 and 25, across from the town docks; 603-279-6121.

Drawing more people than any shopping mall, **Annalee's Doll Museum** stocks every doll imaginable (and even those you can't imagine). Displays are colorful and creative, featuring animals, presidents, Indians, spiders and witches, a Christmas section that would impress Santa himself, and much more.

But more fascinating is the story of Annalee, a housewife who began making dolls at her kitchen table in the 1950s. Turned down for a loan because banks considered her business impractical, Annalee worked at home without electricity or running water and delivered dolls door-to-door from her VW Bug. Today, she's the area's largest employer. Closed from October through May. Admission. ~ Reservoir Road and Hemlock Drive, Meredith; 603-279-4144.

Lake Winnipesaukee (pronounced Win-a-peh-SAW-kee), which translates as either "the smile of the great spirit" or "smiling water in

Text continued on page 476.

The Roads
Less Traveled

They crisscross the state like a tangle of veins, concealing treasures that can be unlocked only by foraging through unfamiliar terrain. The **roads less traveled** may not be the shortest way to get there from here, but you can bet they're the most scenic. New Hampshire's byroads exist everywhere, yet they are chosen by very few. They link towns and lakes, clamber up mountains, trundle through isolated villages and navigate miles of wild forest. They sometimes lead to nowhere, but they always harbor a special prize: an 18th-century cemetery, a glistening pond or beach, a wildlife hollow or perhaps a vista to ignite your spirit.

To natives, these tireless country routes are known as "shunpikes," used to "shun" crowded main roads and highways. During fall-foliage time, shunpikes are ripe with brilliant splashes of red and gold and purple leaves that form one incredible spectacle. They undoubtedly provide the best leaf-peeping seats in the house.

You'll discover glorious back roads in all of New Hampshire's six regions: When you get tired of battling traffic on coastal Route 1A, take a jog on **Willow Avenue**, which starts just north of Little Boars Head, and relish a peaceful ride that explores grand 19th-century mansions and manicured lawns and gardens.

Few think of the seacoast in terms of fruit farms and old barns, but they're here, right along **Routes 88** and **84**. These roads twist through 1700s farmhouses and lonely stretches of pastureland, apple orchards and raspberry farms (where you can pick your own). Both begin in Hampton Falls. Take Route 88 from Route 1 to Route 101C; Route 84 starts at Route 1 and Wild Pasture Road.

New Hampshire's most populated region, the Merrimack Valley, manages to have some fine less-traveled roads. One of the best, **North Pembroke Road**, snakes through five miles of rural scenes between Route 28 near Allenstown and Route 106. It winds past a cornfield, wildflower farm, several log cabins, an old cemetery and a sap house where you can buy maple syrup.

The Monadnock Region shelters dozens of shunpikes, but perhaps the most beautiful is **Route 119**, which hovers near the Massachusetts border between Routes 202 and 10. Wend your way through the bucolic town of Rindge, then along remote Pearly Pond, where lakefront homes peek out from evergreen forests and reflect against the water. At sunset, bright orange light bands ignite the pond and make it appear to be on fire.

For unmatched views of Mount Monadnock, veer off Route 124 onto **Webb Depot Road** in Marlborough. Here you'll spy an old stone bridge and wonderfully clear vistas across open fields toward the vast summit.

Way out in the boondocks of the Lake Sunapee–Dartmouth area, **Stage Road** is one shunpike worth finding. It scouts out the soul of this fertile region, fording three brooks and a covered bridge and miles of hardwoods and idle hills. You'll find this gem between Route 120 in Meriden and Route 12A.

In the Lakes Region, seek out **West Shore Road** along the west side of Newfound Lake. A series of hairpin curves through patched tar and forest, the road frequently squeezes between the mountains and lake and dispenses unobstructed water vistas. With views of Squam Lake, **Route 113** and **Route 109** will take you past classic New England landscapes with villages, farms, and old estates in Sandwich Notch.

Scenic Drive is like a secret pass along the west brink of Lake Winnipesaukee. Prized by local residents for its peaceful, uncongested feeling, this shady bypass affords breathtaking panoramas of one of New England's most prominent lakes. It picks up just south of Weirs Beach.

In the White Mountains, **Bear Notch Road** is a cool, misty tryst with nature, a natural high of rock grottos, evergreen spires and tiny patches of blue sky. Keep your eye out for the pretty sandy cove along the Swift River, a solitary respite for those lucky enough to uncover it. The road runs from the Kancamagus Highway at Passaconaway to Route 302.

Route 116 from Jefferson to Franconia is the archetype of New England tranquility. Cows graze on grassy knolls, windmills twirl across hayfields and old farmhouses repose against the mountains. During fall foliage season, maple and elm trees flail their yellow and orange canopies across the road, truly a sight to behold.

Before you take the roads less traveled, get a good map, and when in doubt, ask for directions at a local general store. Shunpiking is primarily a summer and fall sport, since many byroads are jammed with snow the rest of the year. Don't be afraid to venture upon these foreign passages. It's virtually impossible to get lost, and if you do, there's always someone to set you straight again.

a high place," is by far the state's largest and most impressive lake, spanning 72 square miles with 283 miles of shoreline and 274 habitable islands. If you care to explore the big lake by train, show up at **Winnipesaukee Scenic Railroad** and catch the next choo-choo south to Weirs Beach. Of course, you can hop on at the Weirs Beach station (Lakeside Avenue) for the return trip. From mid-October to May, the railroad is only opened on weekends. Admission. ~ Route 3, Meredith; 603-279-5253.

At **Weirs Beach**, New Hampshire's own little Coney Island, a well-roamed boardwalk extends several blocks along Lake Winnipesaukee, sprinkled with arcades and bumper cars, pizzerias and souvenir shops. There's also a dock where you board the **M.S. Mount Washington**, a 230-foot passenger ship that glides across the lake on sightseeing excursions. Closed from November to May. ~ 603-366-5531.

Winnipesaukee's southeastern joints shelter miles of wooded estuaries and broad water vistas, and you can wind your way around on Routes 11 and 28. You'll soon land in **Wolfeboro**, a busy little town wedged between Lakes Winnipesaukee and Wentworth. The village harkens back to 1763, when Governor John Wentworth built the country's first known summer resort here.

A fine source of local and regional information is **The Lakes Region Association**. ~ Glidden Road, Center Harbor; 603-253-8555.

Scattered under some maple and elm trees, the **Clark House Historical Exhibit and Museum** is a trio of buildings that recall Wolfeboro's earlier years. There's a one-room clapboard schoolhouse built in 1805, a 1778 Cape Cod–style house with painted plank floors and marvelous antiques, and a late-1800s fire station with a shiny red fire engine. Open in July and August and by appointment the rest of the year. ~ South Main Street; 603-569-4997.

One local resident nicely catalogued Wolfeboro goings-on, and the results can be seen at the **Libby Museum**, a natural history collection with a refreshing funky flavor. Here you'll find rows of stuffed birds, fish, animals and other native wildlife, relics from the long-destroyed Governor Wentworth mansion, an early American living collection, and great Indian artifacts. Admission. ~ Route 109, Wolfeboro; 603-569-1035.

HIDDEN ▶

Tucked in a forest off the road, **Abenaki Tower** is one place you can have all to yourself. The post-and-beam tower, erected by local townsfolk, will seduce you with stirring vistas of surrounding lakes and random wooded islands. ~ Route 109 about five miles north of Wolfeboro in Melvin Village.

Castle in the Clouds is an incredible place, cloaked in secrets and almost magical in design. Fashioned as a medieval castle and tangled in vines that droop from its awnings, it sits high on a mountain and gives the illusion that it's floating. The castle's maker, shoe magnate Thomas Gustave Plant, bought 6300 acres—including seven mountains—and paid $7 million to have his dream built between 1911 and 1914.

The 16 rooms and 8 bathrooms add to the mystique with their five- and eight-sided designs, doors of English lead, an enormous skylight, fluted windows and the curious absence of any nails. Plant had 12 closets and a secret reading room seen by others only after his death. At one time, he was worth $21 million. But on the advice of friend Teddy Roosevelt, Plant invested heavily in Russian bonds during the 1930s. In 1946, he died a penniless man. Closed Monday through Friday from mid-May through mid-June; closed from November through April. Admission. ~ Off Route 171, Moultonboro; 603-476-2352.

LODGING
◄ *HIDDEN*

Along placid Newfound Lake rests a grand old summer house and former stagecoach station called **The Inn on Newfound Lake.** Here you'll discover great vistas, fabulous sunsets, friendly innkeepers and a completely unhurried pace. The 26 rooms are casually decorated and offer painted wood floors or carpets, some canopy beds and wicker chairs. During summer, there's a sandy lakefront beach across the street; during winter, the lake freezes and makes for splendid ice fishing, skating and skiing. ~ Star Route 1, Bridgewater; 603-744-9111, 800-745-7990. MODERATE TO DELUXE.

The Inn on Golden Pond took its moniker from the movie (not vice-versa), and its serene ambience does resemble the restful house depicted in the film. Stationed in a 50-acre wooded glen near Squam Lake—not on it—the graceful white clapboard house offers eight comfortable units enhanced by country decor with contemporary touches. Early American dressers and braided rugs contrast nicely with lace curtains and sleek bathrooms. Out back, a breezy lawn provides solace. ~ Route 3, Holderness; 603-968-7269. DELUXE TO ULTRA-DELUXE.

Shielded from a busy road by a string of giant rocks, the **Boulders Motel and Cottages** fits the standard motor court genre with one exception: every room claims a fabulous view of Squam Lake. There's also a small but pristine sandy beach out back, a great place to gape at passing boats. Accommodations range from 12 clean but sparse rooms to six efficiencies and three rustic cottages. Closed November through April. ~ Route 3, Holderness; 603-968-3600, 800-968-3601. MODERATE TO DELUXE.

COUNTRYSIDE CREATIVITY

The state's unswerving individualism, coupled with its bucolic settings, have enticed some of the country's most creative minds. Robert Frost, Nathaniel Hawthorne, Ralph Waldo Emerson, Thornton Wilder, sculptor Augustus Saint-Gaudens and many other talents employed New Hampshire's rural reaches as their studios.

Lake views, dreamy Colonial architecture, shops and restaurants right outside your door. Sound enticing? Then **The Inn at Mill Falls** is where you want to be. Residing in a restored turn-of-the-century mill, the spiffy resting place has 54 rooms done in rose chintz dust ruffles and draperies and designer shower curtains. A busy road is all that separates guests from Lake Winnipesaukee. ~ Route 3 in the Mills Falls Marketplace, Meredith; 603-279-7006, 800-622-6455, fax 603-279-6797. MODERATE TO ULTRA-DELUXE.

HIDDEN ▶   A short distance from the lake you'll happily discover **The Red Hill Inn**, a sublime country estate ringed with mountain vistas and a lovely herb path. Fashioned in 1904 as a summer retreat, the inn now boasts 21 rooms in the main house, two old farmhouses and an unusual stone cottage. Rich colors and period furniture spell traditional elegance. Gay-friendly. ~ Route 25B and College Road, Center Harbor; 603-279-7001, 800-573-3445, fax 603-279-7003. MODERATE TO ULTRA-DELUXE.

HIDDEN ▶   **Greystone Motel** has two very important virtues: It's hidden down a scenic, little- traveled side road, and it's right on gorgeous Lake Winnipesaukee. There are two cottage-type buildings with basic but clean accommodations and a glass solarium, though the name of the game here is boating, fishing and outstanding panoramas. ~ 132 Scenic Drive, off Route 11 in Gilford; 603-293-7377, 800-470-7377. MODERATE.

Wolfeboro's premier lodging establishment is undoubtedly **The Wolfeboro Inn**, a rambling, Cape Cod-like manor resting beside Lake Winnipesaukee. The lobby is a fusion of wood beams, stone floors and velvet high-back chairs, while 43 rooms feature modern touches of sleek oak and pine furniture and pedestal sinks. ~ 90 North Main Street; 603-569-3016, 800-451-2389, fax 603-569-5375. DELUXE TO ULTRA-DELUXE.

Wolfeboro is lucky enough to border three lakes, and you can catch views of two at **The Lake Motel**. Nestled on the picturesque corner of Lake Wentworth and Crescent Lake, the motor court takes advantage of its surroundings with an enormous lawn stretching to the shorelines. Most rooms offer water views and are aesthetically furnished with textured wall coverings and wall-to-wall carpets. ~ Route 28; 603-569-1100. MODERATE.

DINING   Diminutive, intimate and remote, **The Inn on Newfound Lake** restaurant is a marvelous spot with rough hardwood floors, tables topped
HIDDEN ▶   with fresh flowers and windows framing serene Newfound Lake. The key here is the chef, who owns the inn with his family and brings his refreshing French Belgian style into the cuisine. Touches of bacon are added to many dishes (the dandelion salad with sautéed bacon is unusual), or try the rack of lamb, veal sweetbreads with mushrooms in Madeira cream sauce, or other culinary dreams. ~ Star Route 1, Bridgewater; 603-744-9111. MODERATE TO DELUXE.

On a fancier note, **The Millworks** offers a chic mall setting where lush ferns dangle from exposed pipes and beams and sunlight streams in through pretty picture windows. The fare ranges from a basket of assorted fried seafood to grilled raspberry chicken to Maine lobster. Steaks are especially good. ~ Route 3 in the Mills Falls Marketplace, Meredith; 603-279-4116. MODERATE.

The Common Man enjoys a sterling reputation around the lakes, undoubtedly for its steadfast, uncomplicated cuisine and nostalgic surroundings. Old farm tools and classic *Life* and *Saturday Evening Post* covers are parked on the walls of the two-story brick eatery, formerly an early-1800s home. Go for the steaks (the prime rib is heady stuff) or the fresh fish and seafood. There's also chicken Oscar, pasta primavera and barbecued spareribs. ~ Main Street, Ashland; 603-968-7030. MODERATE.

A splendid provincial manor in the grand style, **The Red Hill Inn**   ◄ HIDDEN will make you forget life's worries. Set on the crown of an obscure country hill, the place has an outstanding restaurant adorned in period furniture and offering marvelous mountain views. The cuisine is unequivocally New Hampshire, sophisticated and heart-warming. Try the oven-fried rabbit, roast pheasant, chicken breast stuffed with cranberry sauce and herbed bread, or lemon pepper sea scallops. ~ Route 25B and College Road, Center Harbor; 603-279-7001. MODERATE TO DELUXE.

It's not hard to figure out why **West Lake Asian Cuisine** stays perpetually packed. Snuggled in a wooded area along Lake Wentworth, the eatery headlines over 100 different and delicious dishes that make choosing extremely difficult. You'll find seafood, poultry, beef and pork dunked in steamy sauces with garlic, chili or black beans, along with specials like mala lamb, and dragon and phoenix (whole lobster paired with chicken and scorched red peppers). Closed Monday from November through March. ~ Route 28, Wolfeboro Center; 603-569-6700. MODERATE.

The Chequers Villa is synonymous with outstanding Italian fare around the lakes, serving up a bright array of hearty, fresh dishes prepared with imagination. The place is warm and friendly, decorated in a medieval motif with stucco archways and oil lamps. Spaghetti entrées might feature a medley of seafood, tomatoes and herbs, or mounds of parmesan cheese and bacon in egg sauce. There's also lasagna blanca (layered with chicken breast, spinach and cheesey cream sauce) or linguine pollo Don Juan (with artichoke hearts and black olives). Dinner only. ~ Route 113, Tamworth; 603-323-8686. MODERATE.

Lake residents frequently mob **The Yankee Smokehouse**, a modest cinderblock joint parked on the corner of a rural intersection. Smoke trundles out the top, and an old air conditioner hums away while diners scarf down massive portions of ribs and chicken that hang off plastic plates. Also known for its sliced beef and pork and killer barbecue sauce, the smokehouse offers summer outdoor dining on picnic tables. ~ Junction of Routes 16 and 25, West Ossipee; 603-539-7427. BUDGET TO MODERATE.

SHOPPING

HIDDEN ►

Tucked in a 1700s roadside barn, **William F. Dembiec Antiques** is a gem of a place with old brass mirrors, porcelain, '50s and '60s baseball cards and other fun collectibles. ~ Routes 3 and 25, Holderness; 603-968-3178.

Mill Falls Marketplace is a pretty lakeside complex where Christmas and bath shops mingle with sports stores, candy kitchens and art galleries. ~ Route 3, Meredith. One of the largest stores here is **Country Carriage**, a purveyor of American folk art, Yankee candles and other fine New England gifts. ~ 603-279-6790.

NIGHTLIFE

Don't miss the one-man, six-piece band at **The Common Man**, a lively place featuring comfortable couches, shag lamps and dart boards. ~ The Common Man restaurant, Main Street, Ashland; 603-968-7030.

The Barnstormers, New Hampshire's oldest professional theater group, perform a variety of summer comedy, mystery and drama in an old barn. ~ Main Street off Route 113, Tamworth; 603-323-8500.

Farm tools, wagon wheels and an American flag set a rustic tone at **Chequers Villa**, a friendly, crowded nook with saucy tunes and excellent pub grub. ~ Route 113, Tamworth; 603-323-8686.

BEACHES & PARKS

HIDDEN ►

BRISTOL TOWN BEACH 🏊 There's something about a really obscure beach that warms your soul, and this pristine sandbox fits the bill. Sheltered by pine and maple trees, it stretches like powdered cinnamon along Newfound Lake and opens onto a broad expanse of very clear water. A local beach, it's packed on summer weekends. This beach is officially for residents only; however, people are rarely checked for identification. Crystal clear water and sloping sandy bottom create perfect swimming conditions. Picnic area, volleyball nets; stores are located nearby in Bristol. ~ On West Shore Road, a quarter mile west of Route 3A in Bristol.

WELLINGTON STATE PARK AND BEACH 🏊 Secluded pine coves, strings of granite boulders and a brow of chestnut sand amble around Newfound Lake at this ultra-scenic spot. Lying on a peninsula and framed by small peaks and isles of evergreens, Wellington *has* the views. The lake's white sandy bottom and gentle shores make it one of the best swimming holes in New Hampshire. Picnic area, pavilions, bathhouse, restrooms, playground, store; day-use fee, $2.50. Closed October through Memorial Day. ~ Off Route 3A, four miles north of Bristol; 603-744-2197.

WEIRS BEACH 🏊 This *is* the paradigm of summertime family vacations. It rests in an elbow of Lake Winnipesaukee and bears a half moon of amber granules bordered by grassy slopes. Though the lake views are pretty spectacular, the beach itself is nothing to write home about. Still, crowds flock here for the carnival mood stirred up by the adjacent boardwalk and amusement centers. There's also excellent fishing for lake trout and salmon. The monument called the Endicott Rock marks what used to be the most northerly point of Massachusetts before New Hampshire became a state. Picnic area, restrooms, playground; stores and restaurants across the street; parking fee, $5. Closed after Labor Day through late June. ~ Off Route 3 at Lakeside Avenue in Weirs Beach; 603-524-5046.

ELLACOYA STATE PARK AND BEACH ≈ ⌐ The only state park on Lake Winnipesaukee and one of its few parcels of public land, Ellacoya combines a 600-foot beach with birch groves and fabulous sunsets. Mocha-colored sand, flecked with pine needles and cones, weaves about the lake and courts sublime views of the Ossipee and Sandwich mountain ranges. Lake trout and salmon fishing is excellent. Picnic areas, restrooms, bathhouse; day-use fee, $2.50. Closed October through May. ~ On Route 11 in Gilford; 603-293-7821.

▲ There's an RV campground with 38 full hookups; $30 a night. Closed October through May.

White Mountains Region

A bold sweep of compelling peaks hover against New Hampshire's northern horizon. The White Mountains, which cover more than 760,000 acres, were named by 19th-century sailors for their brilliant crowns of snow framed by blue sky. Their drama—for centuries painted on landscape canvases—lies amid swift waterfalls, rocky gorges, rugged passes, granite silhouettes and one of the most stirring foliage displays in all of New England.

Towering above the region, broad Mount Washington is etched with jagged ravines and topped with rock-strewn grassy lawns. At 6288 feet, it's the highest peak east of the Mississippi and north of the Carolinas.

For the sightseer, the White Mountains ensure exploration at its height. Roads are scenic, usually remote and almost always dotted with hidden treasure. Even short distances can take a while to cover on mountain roads, so always allow extra travel time.

SIGHTS

Franconia Notch (off Route 93, Franconia) must be one of New England's seven wonders. At first glance, it is entirely overwhelming, offering dozens of natural phenomena and activities that could fill several days. A dramatic mountain gap caused by eons of glacial and river erosion, the notch lies within **Franconia Notch State Park's** 6500 acres and draws more than two million visitors annually.

Most sights can be accessed by scenic **Franconia Notch Parkway**, which *is* Route 93 for the eight-mile length of the park. The best place to start is **Park Headquarters**, which will help organize the numerous activities. ~ North end of Franconia Notch Parkway; 603-823-5563.

From the park headquarters, board the **Cannon Mountain Aerial Tramway** for a seven-minute cable car ride with panoramic views into Canada, Vermont, Maine and New York. The mountain, whose rocky profile resembles the barrels of a cannon, has the first engineered ski slopes in the United States. Admission. ~ 603-823-5563.

Here also is the trail leading to pretty **Profile Lake**, headwaters of the Pemigewasset River. Pemigewasset, Indian for "swift waters," provides a reflecting basin for the granite profile of **Old Man of the Mountains,** his gnarled eyebrows and prominent chin looming 1200 feet up and keeping watch over the notch.

The **Flume Visitors Center,** is a state-of-the-art complex with historic films and photographs of the park. It's also the entrance to The Flume (admission), a dramatic chasm that plummets 800 feet to the base of Mount Liberty. Carved before the Ice Age by the rushing waters of the Pemigewasset River, The Flume is banked in rare flowers and mosses and takes one-and-a-half hours to visit fully. Closed late October through April. ~ Franconia Notch State Park; 603-745-8391.

After you leave the park, head northward to the town of **Franconia,** a lovely mountain burg where you'll find **The Frost Place.** An old mailbox with the inscription "Frost" rests against a shady dirt lane, adjacent to the modest frame home where Robert Frost spent several years. Here he penned "Evening in a Sugar Orchard," "The Tuft of Flowers," "Mending Wall" and many other poems, gleaning inspiration from a backyard filled with sugar maples and wildflowers. A Poetry Trail winds through the area, right by the Mending Wall. Closed Tuesday; closed from October through April. Admission. ~ Off Route 116; 603-823-5510.

Sugar Hill, Franconia's sister town, is just as charming and bucolic. The Abenaki Indians once hunted in this area, which today is sprinkled with whitewashed Colonial buildings and country stores. The **Sugar Hill Historical Museum** traces local ancestry to the late 1700s and has two barns filled with farm tools, old photographs and other juicy relics. Closed from late October through May. Admission. ~ Route 117; 603-823-8142.

Work your way eastward to Route 302, a picturesque mountain trail that crawls to Crawford Notch. A nice side trip from here, **Santa's**

A BATH FIT FOR A GODDESS

South on the Parkway, turn off for a look at **The Basin.** Formed 25,000 years ago, this large pothole of whirling azure waters and smooth rock is bored 15 feet into the Pemigewasset River. It has long intrigued spectators, including Henry David Thoreau in 1839 and Samuel Eastman in 1858, the latter calling it "a luxurious and delicious bath fit for the ablutions of a goddess."

Village is a tot's fairy-tale world. The place is laid out like a fantasy-land, with gingerbread houses and miniature trains, sleigh rides, a "Rudolph-Go-Round" and "Frosty's Freezer." Open weekends only from Labor Day through Columbus Day, closed after Columbus Day through mid-June. Admission. ~ Route 2, Jefferson; 603-586-4445.

Then on to **Crawford Notch**. Moose hunter Timothy Nash discovered the pass in 1771, reporting his find to Governor John Wentworth. Nash could have a large piece of land, Wentworth said, if he took his horse through the treacherous notch. Nash and a friend got the horse through, sometimes hoisting him over ledges with ropes. In 1775, the first notch road opened.

The geographical pinnacle here is the big guy himself, **Mount Washington**. Sighted from the ocean back in 1605, the mountain soars 6288 snow-capped feet across the skyline. It's reputed to be the world's most dangerous small mountain, with wind-chill temperatures tantamount to those in Antarctica. The highest wind velocity ever recorded at a surface weather station (231 mph) was logged here.

Perhaps this fierce reputation only heightens the mountain's intrigue, as several hundred thousand people scale its slopes each year. One of the most popular ascents is on **The Mount Washington Cog Railway**, a three-hour round-trip with great vistas. Admission. ~ Route 302, Bretton Woods; 603-846-5404.

The other easy climb is via **Mount Washington Auto Road**, a considerable drive east then north from the railway. The road takes a relaxed zigzag up the northeast ridge named for Benjamin Chandler, who died of exposure on the mountain in 1856. Toll. ~ Route 16, Pinkham Notch in Gorham; 603-466-2222.

About 25 miles south, **North Conway** and **Conway** are the White Mountains' tokens of modern development. Actually it's the stretch of Route 16 *between* the two towns—jammed with outlet stores, fast-food joints, tacky tourist centers and condos—that seems so out of place in this earthy setting.

North Conway, which stays very crowded year-round, features quaint shops, restaurants and century-old buildings ringed with mountains. The **Mount Washington Valley Chamber of Commerce** is there to assist with your travels. ~ Main Street; 603-356-3171.

Smaller Conway is the gateway for the **Kancamagus Highway**, one of the most inspiring treks in the White Mountains. Officially it's pronounced Kan-ka-MAW-gus, but don't worry if you get it wrong—locals are quite used to abuse of this Indian word for "the fearless one." Cool and evergreen, the road is rimmed with shaded glens, scenic overlooks, ponds, rocky gorges and lovely waterfalls.

The top half of the White Mountains region, for the most part, still belongs to nature. This is wild country, an unremitting stretch of land peppered with jagged hills, lucid ponds and very green, very tall trees. There's only a handful of people up here, including some old-timers so firmly rooted they seem part of the very earth.

Between civilization and Canada, several geographic points do stand out. **Dixville** is known for two things: its extremely remote location and as the first town in the nation to vote in presidential elections. The town lies within **Dixville Notch**, a stunning, narrow mountain pass formed by glaciers. Mention you've been to Dixville Notch and the likely response is: "You went all the way up *there*?"

Indeed, this area truly is "at the end of the world"—New Hampshire's world, that is.

LODGING

A rustic old-time air fills the **Woodstock Inn**, a homey kind of resting place that beckons to the late 1800s. Rosy wallpaper, pine floors and lacy Victorian draperies frame the 19 rooms, many of which face the Pemigewasset River. ~ Route 3, North Woodstock; 603-745-3951, 800-321-3985, fax 603-745-3701. MODERATE.

HIDDEN ►

Wild winds whip through a slender valley, become trapped in a narrow opening and whirl backward to form what's known as a bungay jar. This explains the moniker of **The Bungay Jar**, a beautifully renovated 18th-century barn positioned at the mouth of just such a "tunnel valley." Set in a wooded mountain nest, this cozy bed and breakfast features six rooms decorated with antiques. Guests enjoy the use of a small library, sauna and living room. ~ Route 116, just south of Sugar Hill Road, Franconia; 603-823-7775, fax 603-444-0100. MODERATE TO DELUXE.

You'll enjoy taking in the view from a wicker chair on the front porch of the **Ammonoosuc Inn**, on the western edge of the White Mountains. This nine-room B & B has been a tourist destination for nearly a century; along with that porch, guests love the spacious parlor and the sunny, roomy bedrooms (all with pretty coverlets on the beds, private bathrooms and claw-foot tubs). For summer visitors, there's a nine-hole golf course, tennis courts and an outdoor pool. If you're here in the winter, the White Mountain ski areas aren't far away. Breakfast included. Closed in November. ~ Bishop Road, Lisbon; 603-838-6118. BUDGET TO MODERATE.

HIDDEN ►

Perhaps it's the dozens of nostalgic curios, or the cozy feel of the six bedrooms, or even the hardwood floors that glide so smoothly under bare feet. Regardless of the reason, **The Hilltop Inn** is sure to make you feel at home. Situated along a secluded byroad, the inn is run by an amiable couple who love to work around the house. The rates include a full breakfast. ~ Route 117, Sugar Hill; 603-823-5695, 800-770-5695, fax 603-823-5518. MODERATE TO DELUXE.

By far one of New England's grandest summer retreats, **The Mount Washington Hotel and Resort** has been displaying its magical opulence ever since 1902. Set at the foot of the Presidential Range, the imposing, red-roofed mansion rests on 2600 acres and is striking from miles away. Horse-drawn carriages meander through rolling manicured hills sprinkled with flower and rock gardens. Inside, an expansive lobby is heavy with archways, Doric columns and ornate chandeliers, and a rear porch seems to stretch for miles. The staff numbers 350, the rooms 195. Expect room decor ranging from simple to extravagant. Closed from mid-October through mid-May. Breakfast and dinner are included. ~ Route 302, Bretton Woods; 603-278-1000, 800-258-0330, fax 603-278-3457. ULTRA-DELUXE.

Accommodations may be minimal, but you'd be hard pressed to find a more scenic spot than the **Crawford Notch Youth Hostel.** Mountains and wide-open valleys surround this bucolic niche, a favorite of hikers and cross-country skiers. Lodging takes the form of three rustic cabins that sleep up to 12 people each. Kitchen facilities provided. ~ Route 302, Bretton Woods; 603-466-2727. BUDGET.

Logs stay stacked on the stone porch of **The 1785 Inn,** a gracious old house that seems to say "Do drop in." One of the oldest homesteads in Mount Washington Valley, the inn was built as a "publik house" by Revolutionary War veteran Elijah Dinsmore. These days, 17 guest rooms offer simple accommodations featuring country wallpaper, antique bed frames and ample mountain scenery. ~ Route 16, North Conway; 603-356-9025, 800-421-1785, fax 603-356-6081. MODERATE TO ULTRA-DELUXE.

If you're traveling with children, the whole family will enjoy spending a night at **Rockhouse Mountain Farm Inn,** just south of Conway. The main attraction for kids is the old red barn, where swings hang from the rafters and kittens dart across the floor. They're also welcome to make friends with the farm's chickens, geese, peacocks, ducks, pheasants, horses, cows, pigs and llamas. Parents will enjoy the main house, where there are 15 rooms, while the kids can spend the night in the bunkhouse that's available for all visiting kids to share. The farm's 450 acres boasts woods, fields, ponds and mountain trails to explore. Nearby is Crystal Lake, where you can launch a canoe, swim or laze away the day on the inn's private beach. Breakfast and dinner are included in the rates: meals incorporate fresh vegetables and fruit from the farm's gardens and eggs from the henhouse. Open mid-June through October. ~ Eaton Center; 603-447-2880. MODERATE.

The **Inn at Thorn Hill** was designed by Stanford White in 1895. The main inn and private cottages are elegantly furnished with period pieces. There are 20 rooms with private baths plus a restaurant, pub and pool. ~ Thorn Hill Road, Jackson; 603-383-4242, 800-289-8990, fax 603-383-8062. ULTRA-DELUXE.

The quintessence of New England lodging exists at the **Christmas Farm Inn,** a tranquil place tucked high in the mountains. Resembling a quaint colonial village, the inn includes a main house built in 1786, plus a cozy log cabin, 1777 saltbox and honeymoon cottage. Rooms are carefully accented with canopy beds, vaulted ceilings, whirlpool tubs and beautiful quilts. Congenial innkeepers make Christmastime here special, organizing caroling, eggnog breaks and visits from Santa. Breakfast and dinner included. ~ Route 16B, Jackson Village; 603-383-4313, 800-443-5837, fax 603-383-6495. ULTRA-DELUXE.

The Balsams Grand Resort Hotel is one of those places that makes you wonder how guests can ever bring themselves to leave. This self-contained mini-city sprawls across 15,000 acres of exquisite landscape. This is escapism at its height, a reveling in alpine ridges and thick forests and spectacular lakes and rivers. Stashed way up in New Hampshire's northern boondocks, the rambling, castlelike resort boasts 232 rooms decorated in French provincial style. There's a movie theater, 27 holes of golf, Olympic swimming pool, croquet and tennis courts, and an outstanding restaurant. The price includes three meals and the use of all facilities. ~ Route 26, Dixville Notch; 603-255-3400, 800-255-0600, fax 603-255-4221. ULTRA-DELUXE.

DINING

A popular town spot that's just plain fun, **Truants Taverne** has pull-down wall atlases, library shelves and a menu that lists "electives," "detention delights" and "prerequisites." The decor is casual wood-lined pub, the food is basic, with items such as chicken parmigiana and chimichangas. ~ Main Street, North Woodstock; 603-745-2239. BUDGET TO MODERATE.

HIDDEN ►

Stationed along a wooded mountain backroad, **Horse and Hound Inn** abounds in colonial gentility. Lofty pine beams and large hearths are accented by a hunting motif in the 1832 farmhouse. The menu includes filling fare like veal marsala, lamb chops and roast duckling. On warm summer days, opt for the breezy outdoor terrace overlooking the forest. Closed Monday and Tuesday. ~ 205 Wells Road off Route 18, Franconia; 603-823-5501. MODERATE TO DELUXE.

Polly's Pancake Parlor was little more than a backwoods diner before the "Good Morning, America" crew wandered in one day. Ever since, the place has been invaded by tourists who line up outside the 1830 red-shingled carriage shed for home-style breakfast and lunch goodies. Polly's is still out in the boondocks, but views of the countryside are special. Ditto the griddle cakes, made from whole wheat and cornmeal batters and smothered in a choice of maple syrup, maple sugar or maple spread. From mid-October to December 1, and April 1 through Mother's Day, Polly's is open on weekends only; closed from December through March. ~ Route 117, Sugar Hill; 603-823-5575. BUDGET.

The **Scottish Lion Inn and Restaurant** provides a nice change of pace with fare from the British Isles. There's a sandwich lineup for lunch, including Scottish bridie (puff pastry turnover), while dinner is strong on roasts and steaks. Hearty appetites should opt for the highland game pie (with venison, beef, hare, pheasant and goose). Surroundings are merry, with red plaid wallpaper, red tablecloths and dark brick walls. ~ Route 16, North Conway; 603-356-6381. MODERATE TO DELUXE.

The views are superb, the surroundings intimate and the cuisine sublime at **The 1785 Inn**. The restaurant, a pretty glassed-in porch that scans a broad mountain range, resides in a venerable 18th-century inn. French dishes are served with flair and understated elegance and include appetizers like cinnamon-spiced shrimp and entrées like raspberry duckling and shrimp and scallop Provençal. Breakfast and dinner. ~ Route 16, North Conway; 603-356-9025. DELUXE.

It takes a bit of searching, but you'll eventually find **The Cinnamon Tree Restaurant**. One of those charming country diners with lacy curtains and "Welcome Friends" wallpaper, "The Tree" features swivel stools that wind around a U-shaped counter. Customers belly up for breakfast and lunch eats such as chili omelettes, blueberry pancakes and burgers. ~ Pleasant Street Plaza off Pleasant Street, Conway; 603-447-5019. BUDGET.

◄ HIDDEN

Small gas lanterns flicker on linen tablecloths and beautiful valanced draperies hover across walls at the **Christmas Farm Inn**. The romantic mountain hideout purveys "French country" cuisine, exceptional dishes such as grilled lamb kebabs, sauté of trout and medallions of veal with wild mushrooms. For breakfast, there are waffles with bananas in yogurt cream and corned beef hash. ~ Route 16B, Jackson; 603-383-4313. MODERATE TO DELUXE.

Conway and North Conway extend endless shopping opportunities. Quaint, eclectic marts line Main Street in North Conway, while Route 16 between the two towns is shoulder-to-shoulder with factory outlets and novelty stores.

SHOPPING

North Country Angler combines a wildlife art gallery with loads of fly-fishing paraphernalia. This is also your spot for expert local fishing advice. ~ Route 16, North Conway; 603-356-6000.

If it's nippy out, drop by **Jack Frost** for earmuffs, colorful sweaters, leather goods and skiwear. ~ Route 16A, Jackson; 603-383-4391.

The **North Country Center for the Arts**, located in a partially rehabbed 1800s machine shop, presents musicals and stellar drama. ~ Route 112, Lincoln; 603-745-2141.

NIGHTLIFE

Arrive before 9 p.m. at **The Red Parka Pub** or you'll probably stand in line. The wildly popular après ski bar hosts rock-and-roll bands that keep things cranking. ~ Route 302, Glen; 603-383-4344.

GET IN HERE!

Mount Washington Valley's premier noshing post is **Horsefeathers**, a downtown pub with awnings that command "Get in Here!" There is an extensive menu—with a focus on seafood dishes like pan-blackened salmon and swordfish with black-bean and papaya salsa, as well as basic burgers and munchies—but the main reason you go here is to see and be seen. Get there early—lines are known to form at the drop of a "feather." ~ Main Street, North Conway; 603-356-2687. MODERATE.

Wear a kilt and a drink is on the house at **Scottish Lion Pub**, a mellow joint with brick walls, candlelit tables and piped-in classical music. ~ Scottish Lion Restaurant, Route 16, North Conway; 603-356-6381.

Horsefeathers wins hands-down as the hippest mountain restaurant and neighborhood pub, a genuine rooting place with sports decor, crazy bartenders and a rough pine bar where patrons stand three-deep. ~ Main Street, North Conway; 603-356-2687.

Looking like a low-slung barn, **Up Country Saloon** jams with rock-and-roll and mixes Tiffany lamps and greenery with pinball machines and a rambling oak bar. ~ Route 16, North Conway; 603-356-3336.

BEACHES & PARKS

WHITE MOUNTAIN NATIONAL FOREST A colossal land mass draped across northern New Hampshire, the forest is New England's largest piece of public land and one of the country's most popular forests. It's so all-encompassing that you soon realize it *is* much of New Hampshire. Its 770,000 acres (45,000 lie in Maine) gobble up several state parks and 1200 miles of hiking trails, 50 lakes and ponds, 750 miles of fishing streams and 22 campgrounds. Most of the Northeast's highest peaks call this forest home, as do whitetail deer, black bear, moose, beavers and a host of other wildlife. There are endless possibilities for trout, salmon, bass, perch and cusk in ponds, lakes and streams. Some of the best are Basin Reservoir and Russell, Sawyer and Long ponds. The state's most spectacular fall foliage displays occur here, and one of the best places to see the changing colors is along the 34-mile Kancamagus Highway from Route 302 to Route 3A. Hiking trails, including part of the Appalachian Trail, are scattered throughout the forest. Picnic areas. ~ The forest stretches more or less from Percy southward to Rumney, and from Benton eastward into Maine. Several main routes cut through, including Routes 93, 302, 16 and 2; 603-528-8721, 603-447-5448.

▲ Permitted in 23 campgrounds, including primitive and trailer camps (no hookups); RVs can go into most of the 824 sites. Fees range from $12 to $14 per night.

FRANCONIA NOTCH STATE PARK This is the flagship of New Hampshire parks, the one that everyone raves about. A truly incredible place, Franconia blankets 6500 acres, hosts more than 2 million visitors a year and boasts a dizzying array of natural and manmade wonders that make it seem like the Disney World of parklands. Flanked by rocky peaks and riddled with rivers and lakes, the park encompasses the Cannon Mountain ski area and tramway, an intriguing rock pool called the Basin, a minicanyon known as the Flume, and the famous granite profile of **Old Man of the Mountains**. Then there are sandy beaches, miles of hiking trails, swimming and fishing (especially in Echo Lake), beautiful fern grottos and some of the finest bike paths in New Hampshire. The best advice here? Plan to spend some time. (For more information, see the "White Mountains Region" sightseeing section in this chapter.) Picnic areas, restrooms, bathhouse, cafeterias and snack bars, New England Ski Museum, boat launches. ~ Located north of North Woodstock. Access all sights from Franconia Notch Parkway, which is also Route 93 for the eight-mile length of the park; 603-823-5563.

▲ Lafayette Campground (603-823-9513) has 97 sites, most accommodating RVs (no hookups), and includes showers; $14 per night. There are seven full hookups at Cannon Mountain State RV Park (603-823-5563); $24 per night.

CRAWFORD NOTCH STATE PARK 🏃 ⤙ A rugged mountain pass navigates some of the most untamed forest and rocks in New Hampshire. It forms a six-mile shear through the U-shaped Saco River Valley and harbors numerous ponds, trails and cascades, including Arethusa Falls, the highest in the state. Several log cabins commemorate the Willey Family, some of the area's first settlers who were killed in 1826 while fleeing a horrible landslide. Picnic areas, restrooms, gift shop, snack bar. Closed mid-October through mid-April. ~ Along Route 302, six miles north of Bartlett; 603-374-2272

▲ Dry River Campground features 30 tent sites (a few take RVs); $12 per night.

MOUNT WASHINGTON STATE PARK 🏃 This 59-acre park wraps around the hood of Mount Washington, the highest peak in the northeastern United States. The summit—some 6288 feet up—tingles the spine as you peer across a cosmos of mountains and forests that seem to fall off the horizon. The mountain itself has long been the subject of curiosity and wonder. Its sometimes freakish weather can change from toasty to blizzardlike (or vice versa) in a matter of minutes, and its plant life is an unusual mix of sparse lichens, shrubs and rare wildflowers. Back in 1934, it endured the highest wind velocity (231 miles per hour) ever recorded on earth. You'll find more on this uncanny butte at the Observatory Museum, parked right on the treeless, rocky crest. Restrooms, snack bar, museum, gift shop, post office. ~ On Route 16 in Pinkham Notch, off Route 302 north of Crawford Notch; 603-466-3347.

COLEMAN STATE PARK ⤙ It's safe to say that this place is virtually   ◄ HIDDEN
at the end of the planet. Purists will find the surroundings heady stuff, a coalition of thick timbers, broad mountains and sparkling lakes. Much of the activity (though there's really not much) centers around Little Diamond Pond, sprinkled with small fishing boats and surrounded by rolling hills. Picnic area, recreation building; stores located 12 miles west in Colebrook. ~ From Route 26 in Kidderville, take Diamond Pond Road north into the park; 603-237-4520.

▲ Permitted in 30 sites (most take RVs); $12 per night.

▼▼▼▼▼▼▼▼▼▼▼▼▼

Outdoor Adventures

SKIING

Both downhill and cross-country skiing are pursued with a vengeance in New Hampshire. Ski centers are sprinkled along highways and a few rural roads, while backwoods trails exist everywhere.

For ski information, write to the **New Hampshire Office of Travel and Tourism**. A wintertime report on current ski conditions is available by calling 800-258-3608 (alpine) or 800-262-6660 (cross-country). ~ Box 1856, Concord, NH 03302; 603-271-2343.

SEACOAST   Though the seacoast has no downhill facilities, you can ski through the countryside along New Hampshire's western corridor. One of the best (and least-known) cross-country spots is **Applecrest Farm Orchards**, where you can ski through hills of apple orchards. ~ Route 88, Hampton Falls; 603-926-3721. Also excellent is the **University of New Hampshire's College Woods**, a 200-acre preserve covered with wooded trails. ~ Route 4, Durham; 603-862-1234.

HIDDEN ►

HIDDEN ►

MERRIMACK VALLEY   **Pats Peak**, just outside Concord, is the largest downhill ski facility in the Merrimack Valley, offering 19 trails and seven lifts. ~ Route 114, Henniker; 603-428-3245. The valley has several cross-country ski centers, including **Pine Acres Ski Touring Center**. ~ Raymond; 603-895-2519.

MONADNOCK REGION   In the Monadnock Region, **Temple Mountain** features 17 trails and a 598-foot plunge. ~ 729 Wilton Road, Peterborough; 603-924-6949. There are plenty of cross-country locales in the region, such as **Inn at East Hill Farm**. ~ Off Route 12, Troy; 603-242-6495. There's also **Tory Pines**, which has more than 33 miles of trails. ~ Route 47, Francestown; 603-588-2000.

LAKE SUNAPEE–DARTMOUTH AREA   For skiing in the area, try **Mount Sunapee** which has 37 trails and a 1510-foot drop. ~ Route 103, Newbury; 603-763-2356. For cross-country skiing in these parts, try **Snowhill at Eastman**. ~ Off Exit 39 at intersection of Routes 89 and 10, Grantham; 603-863-6772. **Norsk Touring Center** also offers cross-country skiing. ~ Fairway Lane, off Route 11, New London; 603-526-4685.

LAKES REGION   Around the Lakes Region, **Gunstock** features 39 trails and a 1400-foot vertical drop. ~ Route 11A, Gilford; 603-293-4341. Wooded lakeside trails exist at **Red Hill Inn**. ~ Route 25B, Center Harbor; 603-279-7001. **Nordic Skier** has 20 kilometers of trails and offers lessons for all levels of skiers. ~ 19 North Main Street, Wolfeboro; 603-569-3151.

HIDDEN ►

WHITE MOUNTAINS REGION   Of course, the White Mountains Region possesses an enormous number of ski possibilities, so take your pick. Five of the largest downhill ski centers run along (and just off) the spine of Route 93. The **Waterville Valley Ski Area** is one good spot. ~ Route 49, Waterville Valley; 603-236-8311. In Lincoln, you can check out **Loon Mountain**. ~ Kancamagus Highway; 603-745-8111. In Franconia Notch State Park, there's **Cannon Mountain**. ~

Route 3; 603-823-7771. **Bretton Woods** also offers some good slopes. ~ Route 302, Bretton Woods; 603-278-5000. Cross-country ski centers also exist at Waterville, Loon and Bretton Woods.

Way up in the northern wilderness, the **Balsams** is a marvelous setting with 12 downhill runs and over 30 miles of cross-country trails. ~ Route 26, Dixville Notch; 603-255-3951.

FISHING

Aficionados of both saltwater and freshwater fishing will find a bounty of opportunities in New Hampshire. Angle for pollack, cod, mackerel and bluefish off the seacoast, or for trout, salmon, cusk, perch and bass in one of several hundred ponds and lakes.

SEACOAST Deep-sea fishing charters are offered by **Eastman's Fishing Parties**. ~ River Road, Seabrook Beach; 603-474-3461. **Al Gauron Deep Sea Fishing** also provides charters. ~ Hampton Beach State Pier on Ocean Boulevard, Hampton Beach; 603-926-2469. Or you can try **Smith & Gilmore Fishing Pier**. ~ 3A Ocean Boulevard, Hampton Beach; 603-926-3503. In Rye Harbor there's **Atlantic Fishing Fleet**. ~ Route 1A; 603-964-5220.

LAKES REGION Freshwater anglers should head for **Landlocked Fishing Guide Service**. ~ Lake Winnipesaukee, Center Harbor; 603-253-6119. Or they can try **Squam Lakes Fishing Tours**. ~ Route 3, Holderness; 603-968-7577.

For fishing-boat rentals in the Lakes Region visit **Meredith Marina**. ~ Bay Shore Drive, Meredith; 603-279-7921. In Laconia **Winni Sailboarders' School** rents boats. ~ 687 Union Avenue; 603-528-4110. In Gilford try **Fay's Boat Yard**. ~ Varney Point Road; 603-293-8000. In Weirs Beach there's **Thurston Enterprises**. ~ Route 3; 603-366-4811.

WHALE WATCHING

SEACOAST Humpbacks, finbacks, minke and other New England whales are known to put on quite a show. Whale-watching expeditions are offered by **Eastman's Fishing Parties**. ~ River Road, Seabrook Beach; 603-474-3461. In Hampton Beach, there's **Al Gauron Deep Sea Fishing**. ~ Hampton Beach State Pier, Ocean Boulevard; 603-926-2469. In Rye Harbor, **New Hampshire Seacoast Cruises** offers expeditions. ~ Route 1A; 603-964-5545. In Portsmouth, there's **Oceanic Whale Watch Expeditions**. ~ 315 Market Street; 603-431-5505.

GOLF

Golf enthusiasts will happily find an array of scenic courses in New Hampshire.

SEACOAST Along the seacoast, visit **Sagamore Hampton Golf Club**. ~ 101 North Road, North Hampton; 603-964-5341. In Rye try the **Wentworth By the Sea Golf Club**. ~ Route 1B; 603-433-5010.

MERRIMACK VALLEY In the Merrimack Valley, check out **Deeryfield Country Club**. ~ 625 Mammoth Road, Manchester; 603-669-0235. Or you can tee off at **Passaconaway Country Club**. ~ 12 Midway Avenue, Litchfield; 603-424-4653.

MONADNOCK REGION In the Monadnock Region, try **Bretwood Golf Course.** ~ East Surry Road, Keene; 603-352-7626.

LAKE SUNAPEE-DARTMOUTH AREA Claremont Country Club offers 18 holes. ~ Maple Avenue, Claremont; 603-542-9550. Or you can visit the **John H. Cain Golf Course.** ~ Unity Road, off Routes 11 and 103, Newport; 603-863-7787.

LAKES REGION Waukewan Golf Club is in the Lakes Region. ~ Waukewan Road, West Center Harbor; 603-279-6661.

WHITE MOUNTAINS REGION Up in the White Mountains, there is **Waterville Valley Sports Center.** ~ Route 49, Waterville Valley; 603-236-8371. In Bretton Woods, try **Mount Washington Hotel and Resort.** ~ Route 302; 603-278-1000.

TENNIS

SEACOAST You'll find courts at **Exeter Recreation Park.** ~ Route 108, 32 Court Street, Exeter; 603-778-0591. Public courts in Portsmouth are on the **South Mill Pond.** ~ Junkins Avenue.

MERRIMACK VALLEY In the Merrimack Valley, there's **Memorial Field.** ~ South Fruit Street, Concord; 603-225-8690.

MONADNOCK REGION Wheelock Park is in the Monadnock Region. ~ Park Avenue, Keene; 603-357-9829.

LAKE SUNAPEE-DARTMOUTH AREA Dartmouth College Athletic Complex offers courts in the Lake Sunapee–Dartmouth region. ~ Wheelock and South Park streets, Hanover; 603-646-2109.

LAKES REGION In the Lakes Region, try **Prescott Park.** ~ Route 3, Meredith; 603-279-8197. In Moultonboro there's **Moultonboro Tennis Courts.** ~ Playground Drive; 603-253-4160.

WHITE MOUNTAINS REGION Up in the White Mountains Region, you'll find **Mountain Club Fitness Center.** ~ Route 112 at Loon Mountain, Lincoln; 603-745-8111, ext. 5280. In Waterville Valley, there's **Waterville Valley Sports Center** (Route 49; 603-236-8371).

RIDING STABLES

What better way to take in New Hampshire scenery than on horseback?

MERRIMACK VALLEY In the Merrimack Valley try **Winged Spur Ranch.** ~ 24 Currier Road, Candia; 603-483-5960.

MONADNOCK REGION Over in the scenic Monadnock Region, **Honey Lane Farm** has winter wonderland and fall foliage rides for overnight guests. ~ Gold Mine Road, Dublin; 603-563-8078.

LAKE SUNAPEE-DARTMOUTH AREA Morning Mist Farm offers trail rides southeast of Lake Sunapee. ~ 15 College Hill Road, Henniker; 603-428-3889.

LAKES REGION Around the Lakes Region you'll find superb riding at **Castle in the Clouds.** ~ Route 171, Moultonboro; 603-476-2352. In the town of Hill, try **King's Western Trail Rides.** ~ Route 3A; 603-934-5740.

WHITE MOUNTAINS REGION   If you are up in the White Mountains, check out the **Nestlenook Inn and Equestrian Center**. ~ Dinsmore Road, Jackson; 603-383-0845.

This state of grand mountains, vast lakes and rocky coastline is truly a bicyclist's nirvana.

BICYCLING

SEACOAST   One of the most popular routes in all New Hampshire, the 18-mile **Atlantic Shoreline** wends along the rugged seacoast on Route 1A from Massachusetts to Portsmouth. Caution is advised during summer months, when traffic is extremely heavy.

Seven miles of rolling hills and apple orchards await along Route 88 between **Exeter and Hampton Falls**.

MERRIMACK VALLEY   In the Merrimack Valley, there's a 34-mile trek from **Milford to Concord** along Route 13, lined with old red barns, rivers and streams and superb vistas.

MONADNOCK REGION   For a picturesque, less-traveled odyssey, take Route 149 from **South Weare to Hillsboro**, in the Monadnock Region. The 12-mile excursion slices through archetypical New England villages and rambling farmlands.

◄ *HIDDEN*

LAKES REGION   With its gorgeous water and mountain views, the 62-mile loop around **Lake Winnipesaukee** is understandably a favorite of cyclists everywhere. Terrain varies from flat to very hilly, and roads can be congested during summertime. Stick to Routes 28, 109, 25B and 11.

WHITE MOUNTAINS REGION   The strong at heart will opt for a very steep ten-mile journey on Hurricane Mountain Road from **North Conway to the Maine Border**. An easier mountain route that's just as scenic, Route 16 and Side Road edge the Androscoggin River for 29 miles from **Errol to Berlin**.

Bike Rentals   Because of high liability insurance rates, bike-rental centers are scarce across New Hampshire. **Piche's** rents bikes in the Lakes Region. ~ 318 Gilford Avenue, Gilford; 603-524-2068. **Mountain Valley Bikes** rents, sells and services bikes. ~ Town Square, Waterville Valley; 603-236-4666. In Lincoln, call **Loon Mountain Bike Center**. ~ Kancamagus Highway (Route 112); 603-745-8111.

New Hampshire's gridwork of vast timberlands and lakes, wide mountains and ravines makes it a hiker's haven. Forests cover 87 percent of the state, and the White Mountain National Forest alone has over 1200 miles of trails. For information on many of these trails, contact the **White Mountain National Forest**. ~ 719 Main Street, Laconia, NH 03246; 603-528-8721.

HIKING

The Appalachian Mountain Club's **White Mountain Guide**, considered the hiker's bible, is available through the club. ~ Box 298, Gorham, NH 03581; 603-466-2721. For inn-to-inn hikes, get in touch with **New England Hiking Holidays**. ~ Box 1648, North Conway,

NH 03860; 603-356-9696; 407-778-4499 or 800-869-0949 from December through April 15.

Remember that the weather here can be highly unpredictable so you should always carry a flashlight and food essentials. Current weather and trail conditions can be checked easily by calling parks ahead of time.

SEACOAST Though you won't scale any broad peaks along the coast, you can explore some very scenic footpaths. One of the best spots to try is **Odiorne Point State Park**, where trails wander along gently curled shoreline, rocky beaches and stands of pines, oaks and wild roses.

Located a few miles inland, the **University of New Hampshire's College Woods** offers a labyrinth of nature trails that crisscross more than 200 thickly forested acres. There's also the **College Brook Ravine** trail (1 mile), which follows a brook through a 15-acre ravine and offers peeks at 155 species of plants.

MERRIMACK VALLEY In the Merrimack Valley, the **Uncanoonuc Mountain Trail** (.6 mile) cuts through a stone wall and hemlock forest and passes a small cave on the way to the summit, where views of Manchester await. To find the rather obscure trailhead, take Route 114 east from Goffstown to Mountain Road. Go south for a mile, then bear left for a mile and a half.

MONADNOCK REGION Isolated Mount Monadnock, often called "the world's most-hiked mountain," offers more than a dozen trails with all levels of difficulty. For detailed information, stop by the visitors center (off Route 124, four miles west of Jaffrey). **White Arrow Trail** (2 miles), one of the mountain's oldest footpaths, ambles across brooks, ledges and narrow gullies to the summit. It commences at the end of the mountain toll road.

Pumpelly Trail (4.5 miles) zigzags up Monadnock, following a ridge and passing a huge rectangular boulder and several glacial carvings. The trailhead starts on Old Marlboro Road off Route 101, just west of Dublin.

Hikers took the **Marlboro Trail** (2.2 miles) as early as 1850, tackling the steep nose of Monadnock's ridges to open ledges. Start on the dirt road off Route 124, west of Monadnock State Park.

The popular **White Dot Trail** (1.9 miles), a steep and rocky course, is the most direct route to the summit.

Wapack Trail (23 miles) is a popular skyline trek along the Wapack Range, running from Watatic Mountain in Ashburnham, Massachusetts across the Pack Monadnocks in New Hampshire. Filled with open ledges and beautiful views, it navigates a large spruce forest.

LAKE SUNAPEE–DARTMOUTH AREA In this region is the **Monadnock-Sunapee Greenway** (50 miles) which crawls across ridgetops between Mounts Monadnock and Sunapee. You can also scale **Mount**

Sunapee via its ski slopes (2 miles), which plow through heavy forests to gorgeous, secluded Lake Solitude and then go on to the summit.

LAKES REGION   With its marvelous union of mountains and water, the Lakes Region provides some of the most scenic hiking in New Hampshire. On the north end of Squam Lake, a pair of low-lying mountains called the Rattlesnakes feature easy treks with unparalleled views.

Old Bridle Path (.9 mile), off Route 113 near Center Sandwich, meanders along an old cart road to the summit of West Rattlesnake. **Ridge Trail** (1 mile) connects East and West Rattlesnakes, beginning northeast of the cliffs on the western mountain.

In the Red Hill area of Squam Lake, **Eagle Cliff Trail** (2.3 miles) ambles through a thicket and dense woods, scales the steep cliff and ends at the fire tower for great views from Red Hill. The trailhead is off Bean Road, 5.2 miles from the junction of Routes 25 and 25B in Center Harbor.

For excellent views of Lake Winnipesaukee, try the **Mount Shaw Trail** (3.5 miles), which travels through a hemlock forest and past several streams and brooks to an open knob. It starts at a dirt road on the north side of Route 171 west of Tuftonboro.

East Gilford Trail (2.1 miles), which begins on Wood Road off Route 11A, climbs Belknap Mountain and affords several fine outlooks over Lake Winnipesaukee.

WHITE MOUNTAINS REGION   Spectacular hiking exists everywhere in the White Mountains Region.

Offering splendid scenery, **Welch Dickey Loop Trail** (4.4 miles) follows rock outcroppings and gives the feeling that you're above the timberline. The trailhead is along the Mad River on Orris Road, off Upper Mad River Road from Route 49.

Along the beautiful Kancamagus Highway near Conway you'll find **Boulder Loop Trail** (3.1 miles), a gradual climb with panoramas

---

✔ **CHECK THESE OUT—UNIQUE OUTDOOR EXPERIENCES**

- Hike the **Appalachian Trail** through White Mountain National Forest during spectacular fall foliage displays. *pages 488, 493*
- Glide across hills of apple orchards as you cross-country ski at **Applecrest Farm Orchards,** one of New Hampshire's best-kept secrets. *page 490*
- Espy frolicking humpbacks and other New England cetacea on **whale-watching expeditions** along the coast. *page 491*
- Cycle through archetypical New England villages and farms on the 12-mile route from **South Weare to Hillsboro.** *page 493*

of Mount Chocorua and the Swift River Valley. **Sabbaday Falls Trail** (.3 mile), a spur path off the 4.9-mile **Sabbaday Brook Trail**, wanders to a series of cascades in a narrow chasm. The Brook Trail offers easy grades, numerous brook crossings and views of the falls.

The Franconia Notch area is a maze of trails for all hiking levels. **Falling Waters Trail** (3.2 miles) navigates lovely cascades and brooks, shady glens and narrow gorges, and offers great vistas of the notch. It starts at Lafayette Place.

Whitehouse Trail (.8 mile), which winds along the Pemigewasset River, makes a nice trek through Franconia Notch State Park. Pick up the trail at the Flume Visitors Center.

Bald Mountain–Artists Bluff Trail (.8 mile) makes a panoramic loop in the notch, starting at Peabody Base on Route 18. Nestled up in the mountains, **Lonesome Lake Trail** (1.6 miles) offers commanding views of surrounding peaks. It commences at the Lafayette Campground off Route 93.

Often overlooked, **Kinsman Falls Trail** (5 miles) is a stroll through verdant foliage along Cascade Brook. The trail begins at the White House Bridge in Franconia Notch State Park and ends at the Kingsman Pond Shelter.

One of the state's most popular hikes, **Tuckerman Ravine Trail** (2 miles) is a rugged cirque with bare slopes and sheer cliffs on Mount Washington. A moderately difficult path, it commences at the Appalachian Mountain Club's Pinkham Notch Camp on Route 16.

Thompson Falls Trail (.8 mile) clambers up the south side of Wildcat Brook to several cascades and views of the Presidential mountain range. The trailhead starts at Wildcat Ski Area on Route 16.

▼▼▼▼▼▼▼▼▼▼

Transportation

CAR

The fastest means of road travel are New Hampshire's interstate highways. **Route 93** scoots up the north-south center of the state, while **Route 95** cuts in from Massachusetts, follows the seacoast, then heads out into southern Maine.

On the west corridor, **Route 91** actually lies in Vermont but is used by many New Hampshire drivers as a major north–south artery.

There's no quick way to reach the state's northern wilderness, but **Route 16** and **Route 3** will take you there while skirting some spectacular scenery.

AIR

New Hampshire's air traffic flows through **Manchester Airport**, a small but quite convenient facility in Manchester. Several major carriers provide service, including Continental Airlines, Delta Airlines, United Airlines and USAir.

Boston's **Logan International Airport**, about 30 miles from New Hampshire's seacoast, is also a major air gateway for the state (see Chapter Four).

First Class Limousine transports passengers from Logan to most points in southern New Hampshire, including Nashua, Merrimack and Manchester. ~ 603-883-4807.

Concord Trailways operates a broad network across New Hampshire. Buses start from Boston's Logan Airport and stop in Manchester, Concord and smaller towns as far north as Littleton. ~ 603-228-3300, 800-639-3317.

BUS

Train travel is practically nonexistent here, though Amtrak does provide service to Vermont's White River Junction and Bellows Falls, along New Hampshire's western border. The trains make direct routes from Washington, D.C., New York and Montreal to Springfield, Massachusetts; a bus connection will then take you into Vermont. ~ 800-872-7245.

TRAIN

Arriving at Manchester Airport, you'll find the following rental companies: Avis Rent A Car (800-331-1212), Budget Rent A Car (800-527-0700), Hertz Rent A Car (800-654-3131) and National Interrent (800-227-7368). Thrifty Car Rental (800-367-2277) is located near the terminal and offers free airport transfers.

CAR RENTALS

TEN

Maine

Mention you're going to Maine and you get all sorts of envious looks. People automatically envision the Andrew Wyeth landscapes, the pine-scented woods, the candy-striped lighthouses, the huge platters of lobster and baskets of steamers. Over the years, its name has practically become synonymous with the word "vacation." License plates even read "Vacationland." Indeed, visitors can find many opportunities to vacate cluttered lives in this spectacularly scenic New England state.

Maine has the Ice Age to thank for its smashingly good looks. Massive glaciers left over 6000 lakes and ponds and 32,000 miles of rivers and streams in their wake as well as the towering peaks of Cadillac Mountain and Mt. Katahdin (the latter stretches about a mile high). The coast is made of a series of deeply cut indentations and narrow peninsulas and has more offshore islands than you can count. Measure the seaboard in a straight line and you come up with about 230 miles. Count every inch of shoreline and it's an amazing 3478 miles.

The state's name supposedly came from sailors' use of the term "main" for the mainland apart from the offshore islands. In later years, Maine was given the nickname "Pine Tree State" because nearly 90 percent of its land is covered with fragrant evergreens.

Maine's beauty, however, is not skin deep. It's home to some 1.2 million year-round residents, a startlingly small number when you consider it's as big as all of the other New England states put together. The people who live here are really what make this state so special. Real Mainers—or State-of-Mainers as the most patriotic refer to themselves—are full of pride. They're also very individualistic and don't put on any airs. They are who they are, whether you like it or not. And they're tough. While carloads of tourists and summer residents pack up and head south at the end of the summer, they prepare for the long, cold winters ahead. Many Mainers also devotedly preserve the traditions of the past. You see crafts such as wooden boatbuilding, quilting and weaving still very much alive all over the state.

The biggest concentration of the population is clustered around the harbor-perched city of Portland, the state's commercial and cultural center. Established in 1624, Portland was destroyed four times, twice by Indians in the 1600s, once by the British in 1775 and again by the great fire of 1866. Today the phoenix—the mythical Egyptian bird that rises from the ashes of destruction—is the city symbol.

A very progressive city, Portland has attracted people from across America as well as immigrants from Greece, Cambodia, Jamaica, Finland and a host of other countries. Maine's statewide residents are a mix of nationalities as well. These include Abenaki Indians whose ancestors can be traced back 2000 years and Europeans whose forefathers settled along the coast in the beginning of the 1600s.

Most historians believe that Maine was sighted by Vikings as early as the year 1000, but since no real evidence can be found, the credit of discovering the area has been passed along to others. It is believed that John Cabot saw the Maine coast on his second voyage to the New World in 1498, thereby establishing all future British claims to the land. However, the first European colony was established at the mouth of the St. Croix River in 1604 by French explorers Sieur de Monts, Pierre du Guast and Samuel de Champlain. The colony didn't last very long, however. In 1605, England's King James I included the area in the land grant given the Plymouth Colony.

The years that followed were marked by territorial struggles between the English, French and Indians. In spite of its bitterly cold winters, Maine had an abundance of natural assets to fight over, including dozens of deep-water harbors, timber-filled forests, navigable inland rivers and waters teeming with fish. The fighting eventually led to the 18th-century French and Indian Wars. After the British were victorious, what would be the State of Maine became a part of the Commonwealth of Massachusetts. Not until 1820 was Maine admitted to the union as a free state.

About 50 years later, word got out that Mount Desert Island and its then-sleepy little fishing village of Bar Harbor was an exceptionally beautiful place. Indeed, with its rock-hewn shores and sky-poking mountains, it's certainly spectacular. Before long, the island became an exclusive retreat for wealthy and powerful American families who came by steamboat and train. Folks with names like Rockefeller and Vanderbilt built sprawling summer "cottages" on bluffs overlooking the sea. They hired locals to staff these homes and the well-appointed yachts on which they hosted glamorous cocktail parties. By the turn of the century, there were over 200 magnificent mansions on Mount Desert Island. Other areas along the coast south of Bar Harbor started to become popular summering spots as well, as trains brought in the moneyed people looking to build by the sea.

These golden years did pass, however, their demise brought by the Depression and World War II. But the final blow to Bar Harbor's days of grandeur came when a fire broke out in 1947 and burned over a third of Mount Desert Island, including nearly 70 of its estates. The island was eventually rebuilt but in a less-opulent fashion. Affordable motels and hotels sprouted like mushrooms after a rain, making the area much more accessible to average tourists.

Maine's coastal beauty is still what attracts most travelers today. Dozens of little fishing villages here burst with character. Some have gone a little overboard trying to attract tourists and are a bit too gussied up. If you're interested in seeing places that haven't sprung into tourist hubs, you have to be willing to go an extra yard. Follow the little roads that turn off like stray thoughts. They may take you to a tiny village on the sea. Consider taking a boat trip out to an island you've never heard of. And go north! The coast above Mount Desert Island is still largely undiscovered.

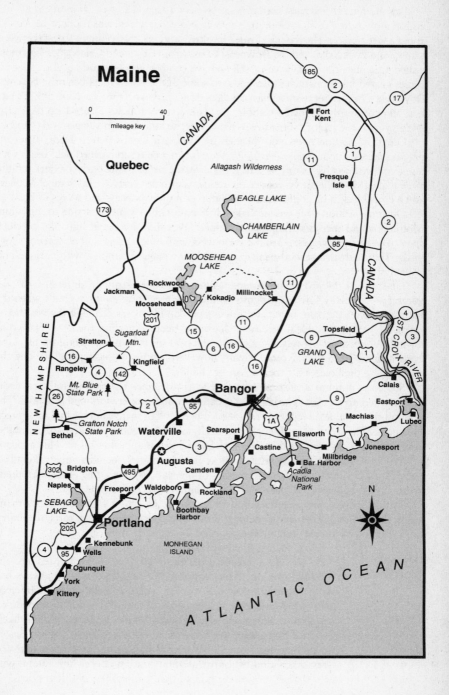

Bear in mind that Maine is enormous, so taking on a little piece at a time is all any visitor should do. We've broken it up into four areas, each of which might be seen in about a week's time. The coast is divided into two sections, the Southern Coast (between Kittery and Bucksport) and the Downeast Coast (from Castine to Calais). Maine's most visited area, the Southern Coast is well endowed with hotels, restaurants and other facilities geared for tourists. It's also home to some of the state's most beautiful beaches. Downeast Coast is not quite as busy and less developed, with the exception of Bar Harbor, an enormously popular vacation hub. This chapter follows Route 1 up the coast, taking you to the major tourist towns as well as the little-known villages and islands.

Our third section takes you through the northern woods, which Henry Thoreau praises endlessly in his book *The Maine Woods*. An area of unmatched wild beauty, it's home to the state's highest peak (Mt. Katahdin), the biggest state park (Baxter) and the largest lake (Moosehead). Its year-round residents include hearty-souled State of Mainers and a large black bear population, in addition to moose, bobcats and scores of birds.

Our final section—the western lakes and mountains—is an excursion to the White Mountains and the sprawling Indian-named lakes that are set in hills like precious gems. The woods that wrap around them teem with moose, deer and all sorts of songbirds. There are also several picture-perfect little villages crammed with antique and craft shops.

Like all the New England states, Maine has four distinctly different seasons. Summer—especially July and August—is the customary time to visit. That's when the bays swell with pleasure boats and towns open up like roses. Though the weather is predictably unpredictable (one day the harbor is bundled in mist, the next it's clear as a window), it's always lovely. Temperatures all over the state remain comfortable, hovering around 70 in the daytime. Nights, however, can get nippy, especially along the coast where the breezes off the sea can be chilling.

Some say autumn is the very best time to visit Maine. The summer-only residents have packed up and left. The partying vacationers are back at work and in school. The real full-time Mainers reappear. You're no longer one of many tourists but an appreciated guest. The weather is often phenomenally beautiful, with blue skies and sunshine. And, of course, you can see the fall colors. Spring, too, is appealing, as new life appears.

Winter brings on a whole array of snow-based activities, including great skiing, especially in the northern and western parts of the state. Maine's long and cold winters create a died-and-gone-to-heaven land for winter sports enthusiasts.

In this chapter, we introduce you to just some of Maine's attractions. In many ways, this is a very American state, but in others it feels almost like a foreign country. One visit and you'll inevitably feel compelled to return.

▼▼▼▼▼▼▼▼▼▼
Southern Coast

Many people cross the New Hampshire border into the state of Maine expecting to find what they've always pictured: postcard fishing villages with salty characters, sprawling farms, pine forests. Well, dear readers, you have to look a little to find these pictures in southern Maine. What you're most likely to notice first along the Southern Coast—besides scores of factory outlets that line Route 1—is a profusion of hotels, motels, inns and every other kind of tourist accommodation conceivable, along with clam shacks and lobster joints broadcasting their low, low prices.

This is the gateway to the Vacation State. Just about everybody passes through the narrow southern tip on their way to the big tourist hubs like Boothbay Harbor and Mount Desert Island as well as the never-heard-of-before villages and hamlets that line the coast and lie scattered around the northern and western parts of the state. Interstate 95 can get you up north much faster, but we're going to take it slow, meandering up Route 1.

Southern Maine does have an abundance of something the rest of the state can envy—sandy beaches. In fact, even though Maine boasts nearly 3500 miles of coastline, sandy beaches skirt fewer than 100 of those miles, and the majority lie below Portland. They start almost immediately around Kittery, Maine's southernmost town. As you drive along Route 1, don't hesitate to detour along shore roads and Route 1A, which lead right by the beaches.

SIGHTS

You can pull over at any time (why not, everybody else does—the traffic problem is part of the fun) to gaze out at the fury of the sea and the beach crowd. Beachgoers in this part of the world dress the gamut from string bikinis to down parkas and wool socks in August (the winds can really send chills racing through your body). If you want to take a swim, you can have your pick of beaches in Kittery, York, Cape Neddick, Ogunquit, Wells and other spots (see "Beaches & Parks" below).

These southern towns are also rife with worthwhile attractions. In **Kittery**, you might want to take a look around the **Kittery Historical and Naval Museum**. It's filled with naval relics from the Portsmouth Naval Yard and exhibits explaining the history of the Southern Coast. Closed late October through May. Admission. ~ Route 1, just north of the Route 236 Rotary; 207-439-3080.

In **York**, several historic structures have been beautifully restored. Guides take you through buildings including the **Old Schoolhouse**, the **Emerson–Wilcox House** (a tavern/family dwelling-turned-general-store-turned-tailor-shop) and the 18th-century **John Hancock Warehouse and Wharf**. Orientation and tours start at **Jefferds Tavern** on Route 1A. For more information, contact the Old York Historical Society. Closed late September through mid-June. Admission. ~ 207-363-4974.

One of the more intriguing of York's historic sights, the **Old Gaol** first opened its doors and dungeons in 1720. Today a museum, the goal gives visitors a look at its gruesome relics—cramped cells, the disciplinary pit and jailer's quarters. You'll also find displays of Indian and pioneer artifacts. ~ Route 1A, York Street.

Ogunquit, named for an Algonquin word meaning "beautiful place by the sea," is a well-known art colony. You can see some of the area's most cherished works at the **Ogunquit Museum of American Art**. Closed October through June. Admission. ~ 183 Shore Road; 207-646-4909.

If you can drag yourselves away from the beaches in **Wells,** there are some good attractions for children, including the **Wells Auto Museum,** where over 70 antique cars are displayed. Closed Columbus Day through Memorial Day. Admission. ~ Route 1; 207-646-9064.

Birdwatchers can log in some remarkable sightings at Wells' **Rachel Carson National Wildlife Refuge.** See the "Beaches & Parks" section below. ~ Off Route 9. Another public preserve is the **Wells Research Reserve.** Admission in July and August. ~ 342 Laudholm Farm Road, off Route 1; 207-646-1555.

Just north of Wells, you'll come to the Kennebunks—the commercial center of **Kennebunk** and the port town, **Kennebunkport.** Both towns were early shipbuilding and fishing settlements. The latter is now referred to as **Bush Country,** since it's home to former President Bush's summer home. The little town itself is a bit too gussied up for tourists (with prices to match), but it's a worthwhile stop nonetheless. Consider putting the car in a lot for a good part of the day and picking up a copy of the *Kennebunkport Walking Guide,* which is available at various lodgings and restaurants around town and at the **Kennebunk–Kennebunkport Chamber of Commerce.** ~ Routes 35 and 9, Kennebunk; 207-967-0857.

In summer months, there are walking tours of Kennebunkport's historical area on Wednesday morning and Friday afternoon. They start at **Nott House,** a stately Greek Revival building that dates back to 1853. Closed in the winter. Admission. ~ Maine Street, Kennebunkport; 207-967-2513.

If you want to get a glimpse of the former president's compound, take a drive along mansion-dotted **Ocean Avenue. Walker's Point** is the name of the Bush compound. It's a beautiful promontory surrounded by the horizonless waters of the Atlantic. The brown-shingled house is the centerpiece.

While you're in the neighborhood, you might want to stop at the **Seashore Trolley Museum.** Its comprehensive collection of antique electric trolley cars includes samples from around the world—Japan, Germany, Canada and Boston. And visitors can hop aboard one trolley for a four-mile journey. Closed November through April. Admission. ~ Log Cabin Road, Kennebunkport; 207-967-2712.

Back inland, you can take an architectural walking tour of Kennebunk's **National Register District.** It includes **The Brick Store Museum,** a block of restored early-19th-century commercial buildings. Admission. ~ 117 Main Street; 207-985-4802.

One of the most well-known attractions in southern Maine is the **Wedding Cake House.** As the name implies, it's a yellow house with intricate white latticework that looks like lace. A local sea captain fashioned his house after cathedrals he saw in Milan, Italy. The public is not welcome inside, however. ~ Summer Street.

As you continue north from the Kennebunks, you can either pick up Route 1 (at Kennebunk) or opt for the more scenic Route 9 from

Kennebunkport. The latter takes you past several sun-soaked beaches. When you reach the town of Scarborough, turn right onto Route 207, which leads to **Prouts Neck**. This oddly shaped peninsula juts into Saco Bay about eight miles south of Portland. Much of its coastal scenery—steep cliffs, swirling surf and dwarfish rock-clinging trees— can be seen on the canvases of American painter Winslow Homer, who lived and worked here. His studio, a converted stable overlooking the ocean, is open to the public for touring. There's also the **Prouts Neck Bird Sanctuary** at the tip, where all sorts of exotic birds have been spotted.

Portland, Maine's largest city, is the next stop. Often called "The Little San Francisco of the East," it's a lovely city of hills surrounded by water. Many of Portland's streets are lined with beautifully preserved Victorian buildings. Very progressive, the city boasts a horde of museums, galleries, shops and restaurants.

Since so many people come to Maine to get away from the urban life, they often steer clear of Portland. The very pleasant result is that you get to enjoy a city without having to skirt around all the tourist clutter. You can also see most of it on foot. Tops on our list of priorities is the **Portland Museum of Art.** Housed in a striking postmodern building designed by Henry N. Cobb of I. M. Pei's firm, it has extensive collections of Maine-based artists such as Andrew Wyeth, Edward Hopper and Winslow Homer, among other exhibits. Closed Monday from late October through late June. Admission. ~ 7 Congress Square; 207-773-2787.

Just down the street is the **Wadsworth Longfellow House,** where the poet spent his childhood. Admission. ~ 485 Congress Street; 207-772-1807.

One of the most interesting districts in the city is the **Old Port Exchange,** between Exchange and Pearl streets, on the waterfront. Here you'll see old brick and granite buildings that were erected during the early 19th century, when Portland was a major rail center and shipping port. Many now house restaurants, taverns and shops.

✔ CHECK THESE OUT—UNIQUE SIGHTS

- Walk through the tidy little coastal town of **Castine** and its pristine 18th- and 19th-century Georgian and Federalist homes. *page 525*
- Retreat to bucolic **Great Chebeague Island**, a small island accessible by ferry and perfect for a day's bike ride. *page 506*
- Hop on an excursion boat from the fishing village of Cutler to see the puffins on **Machias Seal Island.** *page 529*
- Make your way to Campobello Island and visit FDR's **summer home,** which has been maintained exactly as the family left it. *page 530*

For exploring Portland's historic districts, consider stopping by the Portland Convention and Visitors Bureau's **Visitors Information Center**. Here you can pick up self-guided walking tours of the Old Port Exchange, **Congress Street** (Portland's most important commercial street since the early 1800s), **State Street** (a wealthy residential district with large Federal-style mansions) and the **Western Promenade** (a fascinating selection of architectural styles, including high Victorian Gothic, shingle-style and Italianate mansions). ~ 305 Commercial Street; 207-772-5800.

For a wonderful view of the city and island-dotted Casco Bay, climb the 102 steps up the **Portland Observatory**. Closed from early November to late May. Admission. ~ 138 Congress Street; 207-774-5561.

For a seal's-eye view of the bay, take a guided boat tour from Commercial Street. You can contact **Casco Bay Lines**. ~ Casco Bay Ferry Terminal, Commercial and Franklin streets; 207-774-7871. Or you can try **Bay View Cruises**. ~ Fisherman's Wharf; 207-761-0496.

HIDDEN ►

For something completely different, spend a few days on **Great Chebeague Island**. One of the 365 Calendar Islands scattered across Casco Bay, Chebeague (pronounced "sha-BEEG") is a small forested island with only a few hundred hardy year-round residents. They earn their living from the sea or commute by ferry to the mainland and then on to Portland, which is approximately a half-hour's drive from the ferry parking area. Chebeague is a place for people who love to walk or bike along quiet roads. You can easily visit the island as a day trip. In Cumberland, call **Chebeague Transportation Company**. ~ 207-846-3700. In Portland, call **Casco Bay Lines**. ~ 207-774-7871.

About 20 miles north of Portland along Route 1 is the world-famous town of **Freeport**, home of the legendary **L. L. Bean**. The mall-ike shop looks just like the catalogs: it's wall-to-wall camping gear, outdoor wear and sporting equipment. Aside from Bean's, the whole town has sprouted into a factory-outlet hub. You'll find all the big-name designers (Polo–Ralph Lauren, Calvin Klein, Laura Ashley) have set up shop here. This is definitely the place to come with your Christmas lists. ~ Route 1; 207-865-4761.

A few miles down the road, Brunswick is home to **Bowdoin College**, founded in 1794. Such luminaries as Nathaniel Hawthorne and Henry Wadsworth Longfellow have walked the halls of this venerable school. ~ College Street; 207-725-3000.

On campus, the **Bowdoin College Museum of Art** showcases colonial and federal portraits, including Gilbert Stuart's *Thomas Jefferson*. Also found here are Roman and Greek artifacts as well as Winslow Homer memorabilia. Brunswick's also the spot where Harriet Beecher Stowe wrote *Uncle Tom's Cabin*, reportedly after seeing a vision. Closed Monday. ~ Walker Art Building; 207-725-3275.

The next town along the coast is **Bath**, which holds in its borders a wealth of shipbuilding history. In the days of wooden ships, nearly half the world's seacraft came from Bath's shipyards. For a journey back to that era, stop by the **Maine Maritime Museum**. From June to October, visiting vessels are docked here and open to visitors. The museum's four venues also showcase marine artifacts, a working shipyard and a lobstering exhibit. Admission. ~ 243 Washington Street; 207-443-1316.

To glimpse a retail business that's dramatically different than the Freeport scene down the coast, pull off in Woolwich (just beyond Bath) at the **Montsweagg Flea Market**. One of the state's biggest flea markets, Montsweagg features hundreds of dealers peddling everything from old postcards to used trailers. Even if you're not in the market for anything, it's worth stopping just for the shot of local color. ~ Route 1.

Wiscasset is a very worthwhile stop as you travel north on Route 1. This lovely little village of sea captain's houses and beautifully maintained old brick buildings was a very prosperous shipping port between the years of the American Revolution and the War of 1812.

Musical Wonder House has a vintage collection of antique music ◄ *HIDDEN* boxes, musical automata, victrolas, talking machines and advertising icons such as the RCA Victor dog. Owner Danilo Konvalinka plays the rare Steinway player grand pianola, the classic boxes and other instruments during the tour. The museum, located in a 30-room sea captain's house, is one of the authentic treasures of the Maine Coast. Don't miss it. Closed from late October through April. Admission. ~ 18 High Street, Wiscasset; 207-882-7163.

There's something incredibly lovable about the seaport of **Boothbay Harbor**, down a peninsula south of Wiscasset. Admittedly, it's about as overripe as a tourist town can be—and it's hit by around 500,000 visitors each summer. But Boothbay (which started life as a tiny lobstering and fishing town) definitely has a personality of its own.

If you've come to Maine for the serenity of the sea, you're best off totally skipping Boothbay. Though there are the customary seaside elements (soaring seagulls, lobster traps, bobbing buoys), this village leans more to manmade amusements. Just pause on the footbridge that stretches across the harbor and you'll hear bowling balls trundling down alleys, the ringing and dinging of pinball machines and the smack of a cue stick hitting a pool ball. The beauty of Boothbay, however, extends far beyond the footbridge. Walk into any restaurant, and you're sure to be served by a genuinely cheery college waiter or waitress whom—by the end of the meal—you'll know absolutely everything about.

Besides popping in and out of the dozens of shops and galleries that crowd around the hilly little streets, there are several ways to amuse yourselves in Boothbay. One of the very best is by taking a boat trip. Several booths down on the wharf sell tickets for anything from a one-hour sunset cruise to an all-day outing to nearby Monhegan (see the "Beaches & Parks" section in this chapter). If time is limited, at least go out on a short trip. You'll glide by tiny islands covered with spruce and fir trees, colonies of seals lounging around with their bellies up and the kinds of birds you've seen on the pages of *National Geographic*. If you're lucky, you'll spot a great blue heron standing in the water like a caryatid.

The sweet little village of **Waldoboro** is one of the next towns you'll come to as you continue up Route 1. It has several old homes and a Lutheran church that dates back to 1771. Farther out on that peninsula (following Route 220) is **Friendship**, a picturesque lobstering port. You have to go around the inlet and then out to the tip of St. George Peninsula to get to **Port Clyde**, launching site for the mail boat to Monhegan Island. You can head out to the island from here or take a boat from Boothbay Harbor. **Monhegan Island**, a mere smidgen on the map (less than two miles long and one mile wide), has been known as a popular artists and writers retreat for years. Its scenery is striking: steep cliffs thrashed by Atlantic surf and graced with pine forests and golden meadows. The lighthouse was built in 1824. The island's many hiking trails give the visitor on foot a chance to scout out its lovely terrain.

Don't miss the Maine Coast Artists Gallery, on Russell Avenue in Rockport, which showcases contemporary Maine—what else—artists. Closed Sunday and Monday from Columbus Day through Memorial Day. ~ 207-236-2875.

On your way back to Route 1, take time out to visit the picture-perfect waterfront towns of **Tenants Harbor** and **Sprucehead**. Around this point of the coast—at **Penobscot Bay**—you start to see the Maine coastline everyone has always raved about. There are startlingly beautiful islands rising abruptly out of the choppy waters with sparkling sailboats gracefully skimming the waves.

Most beautiful, though, are the tall-masted **windjammers** that are famous in this area. You can spend three to six days on one eating hearty home-cooked meals and flitting about from one gorgeous island to another. The main departure points are located in the Rockland and Camden areas. ~ For further information, contact the Maine Windjammer Association. P.O. Box 1144, Blue Hill, ME 04614; 800-807-9463.

The towns of Rockland and Camden are fishing villages that have been discovered by tourists. They are "cute" and can be counted on for restaurants, shops and inns. Some say they're too cute and have given into the pressures of pleasing tourists, therefore losing their original charms.

One worthwhile attraction in this area is the **William A. Farnsworth Library and Art Museum**, a museum dedicated to Maine's role in the history of American art, and where many Wyeth family works are displayed. Closed Monday from Columbus Day through Memorial Day. Admission. ~ 256 Main Street, Rockland; 207-596-6457.

You should also visit the **Owls Head Transportation Museum**, which houses one of the country's most impressive collections of antique planes and cars. Admission. ~ Just south of Rockland on Route 73; 207-594-4418.

As you continue up the coast, you'll come to **Searsport**, an old shipping port with stately old sea captains homes and a multitude of antique shops. Bucksport is next. That's home to the **Fort Knox State Park**, a very impressively constructed fort that was manned during the Civil and Spanish-American wars. Closed November through April. ~ Prospect, west of Bucksport on Route 1; 207-469-7719.

From there, you can take Route 15 right into **Bangor**, Maine's third-largest city and a commercial and lumbering center. Take time to stroll around the **West Market Square Historic District** (a mid-19th-century block of shops) and the **Broadway Area**, where you'll see one lumber baron's mansion after another lined up as if contestants in a beauty contest. Then, jumping from the sublime to the unusual, you can spot the huge—31-foot-tall, 3000-pound—statue of **Paul Bunyan** (Main Street), which commemorates the town's great logging past.

LODGING

Maine accommodations come in all sizes and shapes, from conventional sea-viewing motels to European-style inns. Most are concentrated along the coast, predominantly in the southern and midcoast regions. Many places are seasonal, open only during the warm-weather months, so you should call ahead if you're traveling during the late fall or winter.

You have two options at **Dockside Guest Quarters**. You can stay either in the main house (a stately 19th-century building with five guest rooms) or in one of the 17 modern shore-hugging units. If it's charm you're after, go for the main house, where rooms are individually decorated with antiques and floral fabrics. Two rooms share a bath while the other three have private baths. Choose one of the "units" for extra privacy. Though not exactly oozing with charm, they're very separate. ~ Harris Island Road, York; 207-363-2868, 800-270-1977, fax 207-363-1977. MODERATE TO ULTRA-DELUXE.

In a state rife with bed and breakfasts, **The Wild Rose of York** is a real standout. The house itself is an eye-catcher, an 1814 sea captain's house surrounded by fragrant gardens. Inside, there are three guest rooms filled with antiques and New England folk art. Breakfast is an eye opener of waffles and apricot french toast. ~ Long Sands Road, York; 207-363-2532. MODERATE.

Though right on Route 1, **Cape Neddick House** provides the kind of hospitality and homeyness you'd expect to find in the deep woods of Maine. There are five antique-furnished bedrooms in this 110-year-old farmhouse, each named after one of the New England states. You can't help but feel as if you're living back in the 1800s when you stay here. The breakfast that comes with a night's stay typically includes cinnamon popovers, strawberry scones and fresh fruit. A five-course gourmet dinner is available from fall through spring by advance reservation. ~ 1300 Route 1, Cape Neddick; 207-363-2500. MODERATE.

Walking into the **Wooden Goose Inn**, you almost feel as if you've been thrown a life preserver, rescuing you from the tourist clutter that has colonized this part of the Maine coast. The Wooden Goose, indeed, is an island of elegance in a sea of souvenir merchants. All six rooms are exquisitely furnished with antiques and Early American pieces but have modern comforts as well, such as air conditioning and wall-to-wall carpeting. The food competes for your attention, however, starting with huge breakfasts and ending with afternoon teas that blow the British teas right out of the water. Closed in July. ~ Route 1, Cape Neddick; 207-363-5673. DELUXE.

A former Catholic church, **The Haven** is now a delightful bed and breakfast lovingly operated by the La Rose family. All nine rooms have private baths, while the common areas include a lobby with a three-story cathedral ceiling. You'll find a direct view of the ocean and a beach only 200 steps away. Closed January through April. ~ Church Street, Wells; 207-646-4194. MODERATE TO ULTRA-DELUXE.

One of the most wonderful things about the **Captain Lord Mansion** is that it successfully combines impeccably good taste with true comfort. Designed by Captain Lord, a wealthy merchant and shipbuilder, it's a stunning three-story Federal-style building that dates back to 1812. Inside, it has all the hallmarks of a ship carpenter's craft, including a suspended elliptical staircase, blown-glass windows and mahogany doors with brass locks. Each of its 16 rooms has been thoughtfully decorated with period-reproduction wallpaper, exquisite antiques and four-poster beds. Most have working fireplaces; all have private baths. ~ Pleasant and Green streets, Kennebunkport; 207-967-3141, fax 207-967-3172. DELUXE TO ULTRA-DELUXE.

✔ CHECK THESE OUT—UNIQUE LODGING

- *Budget:* Angle for trout in the well-stocked pond at the rustic **Frost Pond Camps.** *page 544*
- *Moderate:* Fly, ski or take a horse to rustic **Katahdin Lake Wilderness Camps** because there are no cars out this way. *page 544*
- *Deluxe to ultra-deluxe:* Hit the hay at the 1763 **Squire Tarbox Inn**—it's a barn, but it's beautifully decorated and quite clean. *page 512*
- *Ultra-deluxe:* Play a game of croquet on the lawn before dressing for a formal dinner at Mount Desert Island's legendary **Claremont.** *page 534*

Budget: under $50 Moderate: $50–$90 Deluxe: $90–$120 Ultra-deluxe: over $120

When George Bush was president, the **Cape Arundel Inn** was *the* place to be—it overlooks the Bush family compound. But even if you couldn't care less about what was once the Summer White House, it's a good choice. Propped up on cliff-hanging Ocean Avenue, it's just one of several eye-poppingly beautiful shingle-style buildings that line the road. From the front porch and some of the 13 rooms you have a wide-angle view of Walker's Point and the Atlantic all around. Closed from October 11 through May. ~ Ocean Avenue, Kennebunkport; 207-967-2125. MODERATE TO ULTRA-DELUXE.

Back in the late 1800s when wealthy out-of-staters were flocking to Maine to build their summer houses, the **Black Point Inn** came into being. Like many of its neighbors, it's a massive shingled building complete with a front porch and far-reaching ocean views. The main house has 60 guest rooms, and there are another 20 in cottages on the grounds. Rooms are decorated very simply with white crewel bed-spreads, crisp white curtains and rock maple beds. Closed December through April. Two meals. ~ Prouts Neck; 207-883-4126, 800-258-0003. ULTRA-DELUXE.

The **Inn at Park Spring** is the type of place that doesn't have to ad-vertise. This elegantly furnished three-story Victorian rowhouse's seven rooms are usually filled with found-it-by-word-of-mouthers. Some of the rooms have ornamental fireplaces with decks or terraces. A breakfast of croissants, homemade muffins and more tops the bill. ~ 135 Spring Street, Portland; 207-774-1059, 800-437-8511. DELUXE.

The **Inn on Carleton** not only sounds like a place you'd find in London but looks like it, too. This townhouse in the Western Promenade part of town offers seven rooms lavishly decorated with Victorian antiques. ~ 46 Carleton Street, Portland; 207-775-1910, 800-639-1779. MODERATE TO DELUXE.

If you want the big-city hotel experience, try the **Radisson Eastland Hotel**. It's certainly big (203 rooms) and offers all the typi-cal metropolitan-hotel services and amenities, including a health club, ballrooms and a choice of restaurants and cocktail lounges. Rooms are conventionally furnished with wall-to-wall carpeting and soft earth tones. Many have delicious harbor views. The building itself is a landmark, originally built in 1927 as the Eastland Hotel. ~ 157 High Street, Portland; 207-775-5411, 800-333-3333, fax 207-775-2872. MODERATE TO DELUXE.

If peace and quiet in a remote country setting sounds good to you, spend a few days at **Chebeague Orchard Inn**. The 120-year-old Greek Revival home sits behind an impressive stone wall that borders a two-acre apple orchard. The five bedrooms and one apartment are com-fortably appointed and tastefully decorated. The hospitable owners are only too happy to suggest walks or bike rides (rentals are avail-able if you didn't bring your own), and guests can play a game of cro-quet or relax on the swing. A full breakfast is included. ~ Route 1, Box 453, Chebeague Island, ME 04017; 207-846-9488. MODERATE.

If you want to be near L. L. Bean and the profusion of factory outlets that have taken over the once very New England (now almost mall-like) town of Freeport, consider booking a room at the **Harraseeket Inn**. This Colonial-style inn is within walking distance of all the shops and outlets. There are 54 guest rooms, with jacuzzis and canopied beds; some even have working fireplaces. Eight of the rooms are in the lovely older section of the building dating from the 1850s. Afternoon tea is served. ~ 162 Main Street; 207-865-9377, 800-342-6423, fax 207-865-1684. ULTRA-DELUXE.

Serenely situated on Westport Island, the **Squire Tarbox Inn** offers 11 guest rooms. Four of them are located in the main Federal-style house, the others, well, er . . . they're in the barn. But don't panic— it's a lovely barn dating back to 1763. And it's spanking clean. Meals in the colonial dining room are a big part of any stay at the Squire Tarbox Inn. They usually are accompanied by goat cheese, fresh from the resident goats. Closed November through April. Breakfast and dinner. ~ Wiscasset; 207-882-7693. DELUXE TO ULTRA-DELUXE.

Though the **Boothbay Harbor Inn** is clearly a motel (and not an inn as the name leads one to believe), it does have some personality. For one thing, it's smack-dab on the water. You walk into your room, roll open the glass doors and *voilà!* The bobbing buoys, the wooden fishing boats, the screaming gulls—you feel as if you've just walked into the postcard you bought down at the desk. Don't get your hopes up about the rooms, however. They're about as generic as motel rooms get. Closed from November through April. ~ 37 Atlantic Avenue, Boothbay Harbor; 207-633-6302, 800-533-6302. MODERATE TO DELUXE.

One look at the cluttered little streets of Boothbay Harbor and you'll be happy you're staying at the **Spruce Point Inn**. It's set apart from the ongoing carnival of town, on a 100-acre peninsula at the eastern end of the harbor. There's a main inn as well as a handful of cottages and lodges scattered around the grounds. Sports are big here, with a pool, tennis courts, a putting green and some lawn games. Closed November through late May. Breakfast and dinner. ~ Atlantic Avenue, Spruce Point; 207-633-4152, 800-553-0289, fax 207-633-7138. ULTRA-DELUXE.

You can walk to the center of the village in minutes from the **Broad Bay Inn & Gallery**, a lovely Colonial house offering bed and breakfast. The five rooms are very New England with canopy beds and brightly polished antiques. Take time to stroll around the art gallery and art library, which is run by innkeeper Libby Hopkins. ~ 1014 Main Street, Waldoboro; 207-832-6668, 800-736-6769. BUDGET TO MODERATE.

Many of the most beautiful houses in the state of Maine were once sea captain's homes. Such is the case with **Cap'n Am's**, a bed and breakfast right on the water. The large, rambling Cape-style abode, originally built in the late 1700s, has a lovely wraparound porch. There are three guest rooms, two with far-reaching ocean views and all with shared baths. Closed from Columbus Day through Memorial Day. ~ Flood's Cove, Friendship; 207-832-5144. MODERATE.

For years, **The Trailing Yew** has been a favorite among artists visiting Monhegan. It's a friendly place where returning guests are welcomed as if family. Its 40 guest rooms—in a main house and some neighboring cottages—are basic, with kerosene lamps and shared baths. Meals are hearty, home-cooked and served family-style. Breakfast and dinner. ~ Monhegan Island; 207-596-0440. DELUXE.

◄ *HIDDEN*

A former sea captain's house, the 26-room **East Wind Inn** looks like something right out of Sarah Orne Jewett's *Country of the Pointed Firs*. Indeed, the author wrote the book in nearby Martinville. All of the 26 rooms are beautifully furnished with antiques and gaze out over the harbor. This view brings you the Maine coast just as you've pictured it—lobster traps piled high and wooden boats gently undulating with the tide. ~ Mechanic Street, Tenants Harbor; 207-372-6366, 800-241-8439, fax 207-372-6320. MODERATE TO DELUXE.

Choosing just one inn in Camden is like picking one chocolate out of a whole box. There are many you'll want to try. Be that as it may, you definitely won't be sorry if you stay at the **Edgecombe–Coles House**. Set back behind a tall private hedge, it's a beautifully maintained 19th-century house with half a dozen rooms. Three of them are especially blessed with views of Penobscot Bay, which sparkles like mica off in the distance. All the rooms are attractively decorated with Early American furniture, antique knickknacks and the innkeepers' collection of turn-of-the-century art. A night's stay includes breakfast on the porch with a view of the bay and bicycles free for the use of guests. ~ 64 High Street; 207-236-2336, fax 207-236-6227. DELUXE TO ULTRA-DELUXE.

An 1873 music store, the restored **Quality Inn–Phenix** has four floors of rooms decorated with reproduction mahogany antiques such as canopied beds. Located near the town's business district, the motel includes most modern amenities. ~ 20 Westmarket Square, Bangor; 207-947-3850, 207-947-0411, fax 207-947-0255. MODERATE.

The **Cape Neddick Inn and Gallery** is a local legend of sorts, having been remarkably rebuilt after a fire damaged the original landmark building. The new dining room is tastefully decorated with artworks. And though you are actually sitting in a gallery, there is a wonderful warmth to the place. The changing menu generally features lots of fish, lamb and duckling dishes accompanied by celestial sauces. Closed from February 18 through May. ~ Route 1; 207-363-2899. MODERATE TO DELUXE.

DINING

The **Cape Neddick Lobster Pound** is not just lobster and clams. It boasts an array of other dishes such as reef and beef kebab, a mix of skewered shrimp, scallops, steak and vegetables. Its setting is fairly predictable in these parts—a shingled building right on the water. Closed October through April. ~ Route 1A and Shore Road, Cape Neddick; 207-363-5471. MODERATE TO DELUXE.

Follow your noses into **Pie in the Sky Bakery** if you're looking for a snack. Baker/owners John and Nancy Stern seem to be on a never-ending roll of creating one yummy treat after another, including breads, muffins and, of course, pies. Closed January. ~ Route 1 and River Road, Cape Neddick; 207-363-2656. BUDGET.

For a quiet, elegant dinner in Ogunquit, try **Tavern at Clay Hill Farm**. It's a lovely New England restaurant located in an old farmhouse just west of the village. The menu is rather refined, with items like broiled salmon marinated in Cajun spices and rack of lamb. A dreamy pianist provides the background music throughout dinner. Closed Tuesday through Thursday in January and February. ~ 220 Clay Hill Road; 207-646-2272. MODERATE TO DELUXE.

Look for crowds outside **Barnacle Billy's**. It's your basic Maine lobster joint where you pull a number, wait to be called and then settle in for a feast. You can sit in the dining room, which has the air of a bustling fish house, or on the deck, where you can gaze out at boats while you eat. Closed October through mid-April. ~ Perkins Cove, Ogunquit; 207-646-5575. MODERATE TO DELUXE.

A good spot to grab a sandwich in Ogunquit is **Einstein's Deli**. You can sit at the counter or grab a table and order up a pastrami sandwich, a bagel or any of the other traditional deli selections. The one big difference between Einstein's and a real New York deli is the quality of the clam chowder. Here it's dense with clams and deliriously good. There's also take-out service. ~ 2 Shore Road; 207-646-5262. BUDGET.

The menu is what drew us into the **White Barn Inn**, a barn-turned-restaurant. The cuisine is somewhat of a departure from the norm in these parts; the *prix fixe* four-course dinners change seasonally and may feature irresistible dishes such as Maine lobster and sweetbreads ragout, grilled tenderloin of beef with a carmel potato custard, and grilled vegetables with tomato coulis and basil oil. All this in a lovely candlelit barn. ~ 37 Beach Street, Kennebunk Beach; 207-967-2321. ULTRA-DELUXE.

Expect perfection at the **Kennebunkport Inn**. This ultra-elegant restaurant prides itself on making sure everything is just right. The hushed Colonial dining room is a fitting background for flawlessly grilled native swordfish, traditional bouillabaisse and rack of lamb. Closed from October through April. ~ 1 Dock Square, Kennebunkport; 207-967-2621. DELUXE TO ULTRA-DELUXE.

Windows on the Water has a major-league claim to fame. Its chef—John—was one of 52 who prepared food for former President Bush's inauguration. Admittedly, the food is right up there with the best, including dishes like scallops in parchment with Arizona chili butter and grilled prosciutto-wrapped shrimp. The *spécialité de la maison* is the lobster-stuffed potato, a concoction of fresh lobster, cream and Jarlsberg cheese fitted into one half of a hot baked potato. Scrumptious! The view almost one-ups the meal, however. Diners look out at the busy little port through the arched windows or from the terrace during warm-weather months. ~ 12 Chase Hill Road, Kennebunkport; 207-967-3313. MODERATE TO DELUXE.

For some real down-to-earth Maine dining, head to **Nunan's Lobster Hut.** Here you can stuff yourselves on ultra-fresh lobster and piles of steamers and top it all off with homemade apple pie. It's a typically casual Maine restaurant, housed in a low-slung shed. Dinner only. ~ Mill Road, Cape Porpoise; 207-967-4362. MODERATE.

The **Baker's Table** is a good choice for either lunch or dinner. For lunch you'll find a good selection of homemade soups and salads. Dinner is a little more formal; there are elaborate entrées including coquilles St. Jacques and chicken Chambourd (sautéed with fresh herbs, raspberries and Chambourd liqueur). You can eat in the brick-walled interior amid paintings by local artists or—if the weather's nice—grab a table on the patio. ~ 434 Fore Street, Portland; 207-775-0303. MODERATE TO DELUXE.

To say **Green Mountain Coffee Roasters** has the best coffee in town would be an understatement of classic proportion. The selection of coffees here is nonpareil. As you walk in the door of this red brick building the aroma engulfs you—much of it coming from the enormous roaster that churns beans from around the world, producing all sorts of we'll-never-give-you-the-recipe blends. The place resembles a Parisian café, with high ceilings, black-and-white-tiled floors and a throw-the-diet-out-the-window selection of pastries. Breakfast and lunch only. ~ 15 Temple Street, Portland; 207-773-4475. BUDGET.

✔ CHECK THESE OUT—UNIQUE DINING

- *Budget to moderate:* Settle in to a lunch of fresh oysters and a crab sandwich while gazing at Castine's harbor from **Dennett's Wharf.** *page 534*
- *Moderate:* Join the breakfast line at **Andrew's Harborside Restaurant** for cinnamon rolls fresh out of the oven. *page 516*
- *Moderate to deluxe:* Dunk homemade bread into rich cheese fondue as you overlook Highland Lake at the **Tarry-A-While Restaurant.** *page 554*
- *Moderate to deluxe:* Gaze out at Kennebunkport's busy harbor while dining on Presidentially approved cuisine at **Windows on the Water.** *page 514*

Budget: under $8 Moderate: $8–$16 Deluxe: $16–$24 Ultra-deluxe: over $24

The raw bar at **David's Restaurant at the Oyster Club** draws a crowd of fanatical regulars—many of them businesspeople grabbing a bite after work. Downstairs is a whole different story. There you can settle in for a very hushed seafood dinner amid very clubby furnishings. Upstairs is budget to moderate, downstairs moderate to deluxe. ~ 164 Middle Street, Portland; 207-773-4340. BUDGET TO DELUXE.

If you want to combine dining with a bit of partying, find your way to the **Great Lost Bear**. This is one of Portland's most popular bar-cum-restaurants where you can count on getting the old standbys like chili, burgers, steaks and salads. It's located in the former Cameo Theater in Portland's tiny SoFo District (Southside Forest Avenue). ~ 540 Forest Avenue; 207-772-0300. MODERATE.

On Chebeague Island, visit the tiny **Nellie G. Café**. You can sit down for a full meal at one of the three tables, but most people order pizza or sandwiches to go. ~ South Road; 207-846-3882. BUDGET.

The owners of **Le Garage** have a good sense of humor. After all, this really is a 1920s-era garage-turned-restaurant. You'd hardly know it though, since they've gussied the place up and added on a glassed-in porch. The food is very good (predominately seafood, but lamb, steaks and chicken, too) and the value unmatchable. Closed January. ~ Water Street, Wiscasset; 207-882-5409. BUDGET TO DELUXE.

A two-story restaurant right in the pulsating heart of things, the **Black Orchid Restaurant** serves by-the-book Italian. In its dimly lit and somewhat cramped rooms, you can stuff yourselves on all the standard Mediterranean favorites such as fettucine with fresh mushrooms, lobster in Alfredo sauce and spaghetti smothered in a tomato sauce as well as a selection of local fish dishes. Save room for the *tiramisu*. Closed mid-October to mid-May. ~ 5 By-Way, Boothbay Harbor; 207-633-6659. MODERATE TO DELUXE.

Located on the wharf, the nautically-themed **J. H. Hawk Restaurant and Pub** is a testament to the owner's sailing fanaticism. There's a downstairs raw bar and a classy upstairs dining room serving a diverse menu, from fat burgers with all the trimmings to salmon en croute with lobster stuffing in puff pastry. For dessert try the heavenly chocolate hazlenut mousse. Piano music provides background delights in the evening. Closed November through April. ~ Pier 1, Boothbay Harbor; 207-633-5589. DELUXE TO ULTRA-DELUXE.

One look at the tiny yellow house called **No Anchovies** and you can't resist going in. It's super casual inside, with vinyl booths. They serve a large selection of seafood, steak, pasta and pizza. Closed from November to April. ~ 51 Townsend Avenue, Boothbay Harbor; 207--633-2130. BUDGET TO MODERATE.

In spite of its magnet-for-tourists location, **Andrew's Harborside Restaurant** attracts quite a few locals for all three meals. Lines form outside for the breakfasts, which are prefaced by large cinnamon rolls fresh out of the oven and dripping with a glassy icing. Lunch and dinner dishes are largely of the seafood variety, though you can get meat and poultry dishes as well. The restaurant is unimaginatively decorated, but the setting—inches from the water's edge—makes it enormously appealing. Closed from mid-October to mid-May. ~ 8 Bridge Street, Boothbay Harbor; 207-633-4074. MODERATE.

Tired of understated decor? Then make a beeline for the **Harbor View Tavern** where you'll find carriages hanging from the ceiling, airplanes built out of tin cans, nautical mementos, violins, trombones and enough mirrors to make a Caesar's Palace executive feel right at home. Graze on appetizers like fried mozzarella, mussels in cream or the deep-fried calamari. Then move in on scallops au gratin, sirloin or a shrimp boat. There's prime rib on weekends. Ask for a seat on the enclosed deck or open terrace and you'll enjoy a great view. ~ 1 Water Street, Thomaston; 207-354-8173. BUDGET TO MODERATE.

Any trip to Maine would not be complete without one meal at a diner. That's where you see the real characters, the perennial Mainers. One of our favorites is **Moody's Diner**. It's been passed down through the Moody family for generations. The decor is authentic dineresque. The menu is mainstream but good enough to make you want to go back several times—especially for breakfast! ~ Route 1, Waldoboro; 207-832-7468. BUDGET.

Even the most definitive, self-assured diners can't make up their mind what to order at **The Waterfront**. The dinner menu lists an inviting selection of specialties including broiled scallops. And, of course, there are lobsters and steamers to further throw you into a tizzy. The setting—right on the harbor—is unmatchable. ~ Bayview Street, Camden; 207-236-3747. MODERATE TO DELUXE.

Scooping up spoonfuls of clam chowder at **Cappy's Chowder House** is close to having a spiritual experience. But that's just the chowder. Cappy's is also famed for its seafood dishes, pasta, hamburgers—you name it. It's a pubby kind of place with nautical decor, always abuzz with both out-of-towners and salty locals. In the summer, there's a raw bar upstairs for quick meals where it's more laid-back, with booths and tables. Closed Wednesday in the winter. ~ Main Street, Camden; 207-236-2254. MODERATE.

One of the oldest family-operated restaurants in Maine (opened in 1940), **Pilot's Grill** serves up home-style American food, with an accent on local seafood as well as steaks, roast beef and lamb chops. The neat brick eatery has tables covered with linen cloths and fresh flowers. ~ 1528 Hammond Street, Bangor; 207-942-6325. MODERATE TO DELUXE.

SHOPPING

The most southern part of Maine, along Route 1, seems to be suffering—actually, prospering would be a more accurate term—from factory-outlet-and mall-itis. Discount stores are everywhere. Unless you've come specifically to scout out bargains, you might be better off

Text continued on page 520.

State of the Artists

Like all beautiful places, Maine draws artists like a magnet. Along the shore, you'll spot painters studying the colors of the sea before easels firmly rooted in the sand. Shops often display watercolors, sculpture and jewelry by local artisans. Even in rural villages, you'll find artwork as impressive as that of sophisticated urban areas and European capitals. In fact, many resident Maine artists hold national or international reputations. Some of their studios and workshops are open to the public. Here's a sampling of what you'll find.

In Portland's Old Port District lies the **Maine Potter's Market**, a cooperative gallery featuring the work of 15 local potters. ~ 376 Fore Street; 207-774-1633.

Of course, you won't want to miss the prominent **Portland Museum of Art** and its rooms filled with the work of Maine natives Wyeth, Hopper and Homer. Daily tours are available. Admission. ~ 7 Congress Square; 207-773-2787.

It may be just a barn, but that building behind the **Broad Bay Inn and Gallery** features watercolor paintings and hosts several workshops during the summer. It's open from late June until mid-October. ~ 1014 Main Street, Waldoboro Village; 207-832-6668.

The art of building wooden boats is still very much alive in the state of Maine. This is certainly evidenced at **The Artisan College**, where visitors can tour workshops and exhibits when class is in session. Closed June through August. ~ 9 Elm Street, Rockport; 207-236-6071.

Maine Coast Artists, located in a historic firehouse, is a nonprofit gallery dedicated to promoting contemporary Maine art. ~ Russell Avenue, Rockport; 207- 236-2875.

A self-taught artist, Jud Hartman has created a series of bronze sculptures depicting the Amerindians of the Northeast. You can view them at the **Jud Hartman Gallery and Sculpture Studio**, along with changing exhibits of watercolor paintings. ~ Main Street, Blue Hill; 207-374-9917 or 207-359-2544.

Works by over 30 contemporary artists are on view at the well-known **Leighton Gallery**. The exhibit changes monthly, and the grounds also feature a sculpture garden. Closed mid-October through late May. ~ Parker Point Road, Blue Hill; 207-374-5001.

A large number of artists and craftspeople live and work on Deer Isle. For starts, you'll find **Ronald Hayes Pearson's Studio/Gallery**. This is definitely a high-risk zone if you're trying not to spend money; his sterling silver and gold jewelry pieces are stunning. Closed Sunday. ~ Old Ferry Road; 207-348-2535. The **Turtle Gallery** features works by regional artists and craftspeople. In the summer, the gallery offers two- and three-week exhibitions in a wide variety of media, including watercolors, oils, glassworks, collage, sculpture and clay. ~ Main Street; 207-348-9977.

On that same serene little island, at the end of a bumpy dirt road, you'll find the **Haystack Mountain School of Crafts**. Here artists from around the world gather to produce works in metal, textiles, wood, glass, pottery and paper. The school is housed in a series of studios designed by noted architect Edward Larrabee Barnes. Works created here are not for sale at the school, but you can purchase them at various studios and galleries around the island, including the Blue Heron Gallery and Studio in Deer Isle Village. A free tour of the school is conducted twice a week. Call ahead for information. Closed October through May. ~ Route 15; 207-348-2306.

Kennedy's Studio displays watercolor and pen-and-ink pieces by New England artist Robert Kennedy. Some of his work has been applied to decorative sweatshirts and T-shirts, which can be purchased at the gallery. ~ 4 Cottage Street, Bar Harbor; 207- 288-9411.

As one Eastport artist put it, "All great places are discovered—or rediscovered—by artists." Such is the case with this former sardine canning town on the northernmost coast of Maine. Here, the painters and potters are the prominent citizens, and the works of 20 artists are on display at the **Eastport Gallery**, a brand-new, two-story gallery. ~ 69 Walker Street; 207-853-4166.

With this list in hand, visitors will surely have a great deal of Maine art to choose from or simply to browse through. But travelers in these parts will undoubtedly find worthwhile art throughout the state, sometimes where they least expect it—in a hole-in-the-wall café, perhaps. Or you might discover the next Andrew Wyeth standing right next to you on a scenic stretch of beach, touching up his canvas.

sniffing out the small shops, especially those that specialize in Maine arts and crafts. (See "State of the Artists" in this chapter.)

In York, stop by **The Old York Historical Society Museum and Gift Shop**. It offers a delightful array of traditional Maine crafts along with a large collection of Maineana books. Closed October through mid-June. ~ Route 1A and Lindsay Road; 207-363-4974.

Cape Neddick is home to **Cape Neddick Woolens,** where you'll inevitably walk out with a new sweater. There's a stunning selection of quilted-front sweaters by Michelle Moody. Open by chance or by appointment. ~ Off Route 1, near the post office; 207-363-4294.

R. Jorgensen Antiques is definitely worth stopping at, unlike some of the faux-antiques shops that have staked out prime tourist territory on the coast. There's a little bit of everything here including genuine Americana and 18th- and 19th-century antiques. Closed Wednesday. ~ Route 1, Wells; 207-646-9444.

If you're in the market for some pottery, stop by **The Good Earth**. It's filled with decorative stoneware and cooking pieces in a fascinating array of designs—all produced by local potters. Closed December 25 through May 15. ~ Dock Square, Kennebunkport; 207-967-4635.

Some very attractive wood carvings, wooden boxes and other functional wares are found at **Gerard Craft Woodproducts**. They're all skillfully handcrafted by Gerry and Linda Laberge. ~ 510 Mitchell Road, Cape Elizabeth; 207-799-3526.

In Portland, the best shopping can be found at the **Old Port Exchange**, along Fore and Exchange streets. For American crafts, make your way to **Abacus**. Over 600 of the country's craftspeople are represented here. (There are also galleries in Boothbay Harbor and Freeport.) ~ 44 Exchange Street, Portland; 207-772-4880.

The Maine Potters' Market is just as it sounds: a place to shop for clay works created by local potters. There's a wonderful selection of traditional pieces as well as some avant-garde finds. ~ 376 Fore Street, Portland; 207-774-1633.

Pick up sandwiches and other provisions at the **Island Market**, Chebeague Island's only store, where you're sure to meet the proprietor, congenial Chebeague native Ed Doughty. ~ South Road; 207-846-9997.

It's been called the preppy mecca, among other things. But love it or not, don't deny yourselves the privilege of seeing **L. L. Bean**. Today, the quality of the rugged outdoor clothes and equipment is legendary, and the store—a huge mall-like building—is open 24 hours a day, 7 days a week, 365 days a year. L. L. Bean's success comes largely from marketing the image of Maine (outdoors, fresh-air, healthy) and the Maine people (hard-working, rugged, independent). ~ Route 1, Freeport; 207-865-4761.

Right in the heart of the factory outlet town of Freeport stands the **Harrington House Museum Store**, a lovely Greek Revival house. It holds fine examples of the state's craftmanship, from handwoven baskets and wooden toys to 18th-century pieces. ~ 45 Main Street; 207-865-0477.

Pop into the Boothbay Harbor branch of **Abacus** just to take a quick look around and an hour later, you realize you're still there. It has a captivating selection of crafts by a variety of American artisans. Check out the oak bentwood rocking chairs by Paul Miller. Open May through December. ~ 8 McKown Street; 207-633-2166.

It may never have occurred to you that you needed a chowder mug. But one look at the selection of Edgecomb potters' mugs at **Hand in Hand** and you can't live without one. But that's not all. The potters' high-gloss, berry-colored pieces come in all sizes and shapes, from very attractive creamer and sugar sets to huge bowls. You'll also find a wide selection of jewelry in the store. Closed mid-October through late May. ~ McKown Street, Boothbay Harbor; 207-633-4199.

L. L. Bean was started by an avid outdoorsman who built up a mail-order business for his Maine hunting shoe.

A silver-mirrored disco ball hangs from the ceiling of **Enchantments**, casting confetti-like shadows as it twirls around. The floor is littered with colored metallic stars. This is the place to go for crystals and healing gemstones. It also has a book section that's broken into categories such as Findhorn, New Age, Astrology, Kabbalah, Runes and Fairies and Lore. ~ 16 McKown Street, Boothbay Harbor; 207-633-4992.

A delicious array of mohair, silk and cotton handwoven scarves, stoles and throws are the results of **Nancy Lubin Designs** hard work. A very worthwhile stop. ~ 13 Trim Street, Camden; 207-236-4069.

Étienne and Company specializes in fine designer jewelry. Though somewhat pricey, they're cherishable works of art. Closed Sunday. ~ 20 Main Street, Camden; 207-236-9696, 800-426-4367.

Crafts, crafts and more crafts can be found at the **Maine Gathering**. Over 80 of the state's craftspeople and artisans are shown here. ~ 13 Elm Street, Camden; 207-236-9004.

NIGHTLIFE

The **Ogunquit Playhouse**, more than 60 years old, still draws theatergoers from all over the country. It has a ten-week season every summer, usually with three musicals and two dramatic plays. ~ Route 1, Ogunquit; 207-646-5511.

Portland is where you'll find the most to do after dark in southern Maine. It's rife with cultural diversions, including the **Portland Stage Company**, which puts on about half a dozen plays per season. ~ Portland Performing Arts Center, 25-A Forest Avenue; 207-774-0465. The **Mad Horse Theatre Company** also presents a selection of plays every year. ~ 955 Forest Avenue; 207-797-3338. Another theater company is the **Portland Players**. ~ 207-799-7337. There's also the **Lyric Theater**. ~ 207-799-6509 or 207-799-1421. You can buy tickets for performances by the **Portland Symphony Orchestra**. ~ 30 Myrtle Street; 207-773-6128. You can also get tickets for the **Portland**

Concert Association. ~ Box office, 100 Fore Street; 207-772-8630. There's always something happening at the **Portland Performing Arts.** ~ Portland Performing Arts Center, 25-A Forest Avenue; 207-774-0465. Dance aficionados can try the **Ram Island Dance Company.** ~ Portland Performing Arts Center, 25-A Forest Avenue; 207-773-2562.

Portland also has quite a few thriving night spots, such as **Gritty McDuff's Brew Pub,** where you can chomp on fish and chips and down some beers brewed right on the premises. It's a rowdy spot, especially on Saturday nights, when you may have to scream your order across the copper-topped bar. ~ 396 Fore Street; 207-772-2739.

Another good pub is **Three Dollar Dewey's,** an English-style tavern that prides itself on its wide selection of draught beers and three-alarm chili. A large following of fanatical regulars really whoops it up here, knocking 'em down at long tavern tables. ~ 241 Commercial Street, Portland; 207-772-3310.

Alternative rock, world beat, reggae and African music are all performed at **Zootz.** Adorned with works from local artists, this dance club features a dancefloor on the weekends and two full bars. Cover for live shows and on weekends. ~ 31 Forest Avenue, Portland; 207-773-8187.

Raoul's Roadside Attraction features local talent and typically showcases blues. There's also a mystery theater (by reservation). Cover. ~ 865 Forest Avenue, Portland; 207-775-2494.

If you're timing is right, someone famous—like Bonnie Raitt—will be putting on a show at the **Cumberland County Civic Center.** ~ 1 Civic Center Square, Portland; 207-775-3458.

For additional entertainment suggestions in the Portland area pick up a copy of the **Casco Bay Weekly.** ~ 207-775-6601.

If you're in the Freeport area after dark, you can get in on some of **L. L. Bean's** evening workshops and clinics at the Casco Street Conference Center. They offer a vast variety of programs including an introduction to maps and compasses and instruction in outdoor photography, wilderness survival, canoeing and kayaking. Call ahead for details and reservations. ~ Casco Street; 207-865-4761 ext. 7800.

There's no entertainment at the **Broad Arrow Tavern,** but with its mahogany furniture, dinner menu and cozy fireplace overseen by a mounted moose head, the pub makes for a relaxed evening setting. ~ 162 Main Street, Freeport; 207-865-9377.

If you're interested in something more sedate, consider making reservations at the **Carousel Music Theatre,** a dinner theater offering lively cabarets. ~ Route 27, on the approach to Boothbay Harbor; 207-633-5297.

On weekends, **Gilbert's Public House** offers live bands playing rhythm-and-blues, jazz, pop and rock-and-roll as well as dancing in a maritime bar setting. Cover. ~ Sharp's Wharf, Bayview Street, Camden; 207-236-4320.

RACHEL CARSON NATIONAL WILDLIFE REFUGE 🏃 This 4600-acre preserve offers coastal access in 11 towns along a 45-mile stretch from Kittery to Cape Elizabeth. Each of ten divisions protects estuarine rivers forming a salt marsh where they meet the Atlantic. Hiking trails make it easy to explore the coast and adjacent woodlands. The Wells headquarters offers a mile-long wheelchair-accessible trail. This unit is also adjacent to Laudholm Farm, a public facility offering seven miles of trails. Picnic area and restrooms. ~ Headquarters is on Route 9 East, north of Kennebunkport; 207-646-9226.

OGUNQUIT BEACH 🏃 Driving along Route 1, you can't help but pull over and gasp at the beauty of this spacious beach. It's utterly magnificent. You see the wild ocean crashing in, waves breaking in a series of prismatic explosions. On a good day, the sky's a beautiful blue punctuated with perfect white clouds. Wide and smooth, the beach stretches for three miles and divides into three main areas. You'll find the most popular expanse at the foot of Beach Street. The Footbridge Street area, slightly less crowded, is off Ocean Street. Moody Beach, off Eldridge Street, is even less peopled. Since the water temperature rarely exceeds 60 even in July and August, not all people would say swimming is good here. However, for northern Mainers and Canadians, it's tepid. Toilets at the main beach area, restrooms at the Footbridge Beach. ~ Near Ogunquit, off Route 1; 207-646-5533.

WELLS BEACH Just north of the wave-slapped sands of Ogunquit Beach, this is similar in its natural beauty. The beach is wide and smooth and has great bodysurfing waves but, ooooooh, is the water chilly. It does, however, go a bit overboard with the tourist clutter. There are motels, cottages, condos, lobster huts and restaurants lining the beach. Toilets, playgrounds, parking area, lobster huts. ~ On Route 1 in the village of Wells Beach.

GOUCHE'S BEACH One look at this beach and you'll understand why former President Bush lives nearby and why everyone else bought summer cottages in this area. It's wildly spacious, long and wide (some fine sand areas, some shingle patches) and smashed by waves that drown out any conversation you might try to have. Add a couple of diving gulls and an invigorating breeze and what more could you possibly want? There are toilets. ~ On Beach Avenue, one and a half miles southwest of Kennebunkport; 207-967-0857.

COLONY BEACH This small sandy pocket has a marvelous air of exclusivity in spite of its Bush Country location. It's backed by huge rocks that are fun for climbing on. It's also right down the coast from Walker's Point, where former President Bush's Summer White House is located. ~ Off Ocean Avenue in Kennebunkport.

FERRY BEACH STATE PARK 🏃 Hugging the coastline, this 117-acre preserve is densely scenic. Along with patches of pines and other northern trees, there's a surprising stand of tupelo trees, which are rare at this latitude. The whole park is threaded with self-guiding trails. The beach—a sweep of white smashed by Atlantic waves—is perhaps its biggest attraction. Picnic tables, grills, toilets, changing rooms; day-use fee, $2 per person. ~ Off Route 9 on Bayview Road, between Camp Ellis and Old Orchard Beach; 207-283-0067.

HIDDEN ▶ **SCARBOROUGH BEACH PARK** 🏊 Just before following Route 207 out to Prouts Neck (a funny shaped little peninsula), you can turn off and find yourselves face to face with a gorgeous sandy beach that's backed by dunes and marshes. It's not big, and it's not heavily populated, thanks to limited parking. There are good bodysurfing waves and almost no undertow. Changing rooms, drinking water, lifeguards; day-use fee, $2 per person. ~ Take Route 207, three miles south of Route 1, from the town of Scarborough; 207-883-2416.

▲ See listing for Crescent Beach State Park, following.

CRESCENT BEACH STATE PARK 🏊 Located in Cape Elizabeth, this park is known for its sandy beach that sprawls on for a mile. It attracts lots of Portlanders, especially during summer weekends. They come to swim in the sudsy surf and to soak up rays. The beach is situated so that you're protected from the real cool Atlantic and northern breezes. Elsewhere in the park, you'll find a rocky headland, tidal pools, a freshwater marsh, a spruce and oak forest and abundant wildlife and birds. Picnic tables, grills, changing rooms with showers, playground, snack bar; day-use fee, $2 per person. ~ Along Route 77, eight miles south of Portland; 207-767-3625.

▲ There are two campgrounds near this park and Scarborough Beach Park. **Bayley's Camping Resort** has 50 tent sites and 350 RV sites (with hookups); $28 to $37 per night. ~ Route 9, Scarborough; 207-883-6043. **Wild Duck Campground** has 15 tent sites and 45 RV sites (with hookups); $12 to $16 per night; closed from mid-October through April. ~ Route 9, south of Scarborough; 207-883-4432.

WOLF'S NECK WOODS STATE PARK 🚶 🏂 You don't have to go very far from L. L. Bean's to try out your new hiking boots or cross-country skis. This 250-acre park is in Freeport, about five miles away. It's woven with well-maintained trails that offer achingly beautiful views of Casco Bay, its spruce and fir-covered islands and the coast's rocky shoreline. The park is largely covered with woods colonized by birds that belt out arias as if they were opera singers. Picnic tables, restrooms, nature programs; day-use fee, $2 per person. ~ On Wolf Neck Road, south of Freeport; 207-865-4465.

▲ Nearby **Recompence Shores** (Burnett Road, south of Freeport; 207-865-9307) has 100 tent/RV sites (seven with hookups); $12 to $17 per night.

POPHAM BEACH STATE PARK 🏊 Seemingly at the end of the world, this park offers an array of beachy pleasures. Along with a spacious sandy beach, there are tidal pools, smooth rocks to climb around on and a sand bar to explore when the tide goes out. It's right at the mouth of the Kennebec River. Bathhouses, freshwater showers, charcoal grills; day-use fee, $2 per person. ~ Off Route 209 south of Phippsburg; 207-389-1335.

▲ One half mile south of the park entrance is **Ocean View Park** (Route 9, Phippsburg; 207-389-2564), which has 50 tent/RV sites (43 with hookups); $15 to $18 per night.

REID STATE PARK 🏊 The centerpiece here is a great expanse of sand beach that stretches nearly a mile and a half and is backed by dunes and marshes. In addition to ocean swimming, there's a saltwater pond that is especially great for young children. Fortunately, the area never seems to get too crowded. Bathhouses with freshwater showers, grills, snack bar; day-use fee, $2 per person. ~ Off Route 127, 14 miles south of Woolwich; 207-371-2303.

RACHEL CARSON SALT POND PRESERVE 🏃 Named for the author of *Silent Spring*, this lovely Pemaquid Peninsula refuge offers a wide range of habitats to explore. Located a few peninsulas north of Boothbay Harbor, the one-quarter acre salt pond is encircled by rocks and home to a multitude of marine species, ducks and other waterfowl. ~ From New Harbor, follow Route 32 for about a mile and look for the entrance sign.

CAMDEN HILLS STATE PARK 🏃 A huddle of gentle hills, this park is always lovely whether bundled in mist or reflective as mica. It's laced with wooded trails that wrap around the hills like vines, offering beautiful views of Penobscot Bay, the wind-swept mountain scenery and the piney forests. Picnic area, restrooms; day-use fee, $2 per person. ~ Two miles north of Camden on Route 1; 207-236-3109.

▲ There are 112 tent/RV sites (no hookups); $11.50 to $15 a night.

Downeast Coast

Maine's Downeast Coast extends roughly from the east side of Penobscot Bay up to Calais on the Canadian border. Except in patches, it's not quite as built up as the Southern Coast. The farther north you go, the more apt you are to find hidden places and Mainers (who, up here, are called Downeasterners) who are still genuinely curious about travelers. Don't expect to find lots of restaurants, nightlife and that sort of thing. The Downeast Coast—especially in the northern parts—is worlds away from big-city life. We continue up Route 1, veering off to several villages. Our first stop is Castine, poised on the tip of a peninsula about half an hour's drive from Bucksport.

SIGHTS
◀ HIDDEN

If the state of Maine were to have a Tidy Village Award (like the Cotswolds in England), it would probably go to the village of **Castine**. The attraction here is the town itself: a community of 18th- and 19th-century Georgian and Federalist houses standing in impeccable condition. Most of these were originally erected in the mid-19th century when Castine was a prosperous shipbuilding town. Many have since been restored by people "from away" (in other words, big city folks with money to invest). Much to the objection of some natives, the town is beginning to look and feel like an open-air museum. Like most of these small coastal villages, Castine is best seen *à pied*. For information call the **Town Office**. ~ Court Street; 207-326-4502.

From Castine, it's a short, steadily scenic drive over to the village of **Blue Hill**. You'll pass storybook farmhouses, ponies with tangled manes, shiny blue coves surrounded by firs and golden meadows rippling off in every direction. Blue Hill is not for everyone. In fact, many neighboring towns consider it snobby and pretentious. Indeed, it does have a big summer-home-owning community, and you're likely to see BMWs, Mercedes Benzes and turbo-engined Saabs with New York or Massachusetts plates.

The name Blue Hill comes from the hill that looms up behind, supposedly covered with blueberry bushes. The town itself is home to 75 buildings listed on the National Historic Register. Take time out to walk around and poke in the pottery and crafts shops for which Blue Hill is well-known (see the "Shopping" section in this chapter).

If you head southwest of Blue Hill, you'll eventually cut through a corner of Little Deer Isle and then climb an arching suspension

HIDDEN ► bridge that takes you over to **Deer Isle**, a wonderful little island almost too beautiful to promote. Thanks to its seemingly end-of-the-world location, it gets only the serious Maine visitors. For a small island, it's well endowed with attractions—both manmade and natural.

Tops on our list of worthwhile stops on Deer Isle is the sweet lit-

HIDDEN ► tle town of **Stonington** at the southern tip. In a state where once-quaint fishing villages turn into Disneyesque attractions seemingly overnight, this town is a welcome relief. It has everything you've been expecting in Maine—shingled houses, lobster traps piled high, seagulls screeching above, a harbor bundled in mist—but hasn't been completely colonized by the "Kennebushport" crowd. Ask one of the locals to point you in the direction of **Ames Pond**, about a two-minute drive east from the center of town. During the summer months, the rare pink lilies in the pond bloom, turning it into a meadow of pink blossoms.

Back on Deer Isle, plan on arriving for the tour that starts at 1 p.m. at the **Haystack Mountain School of Crafts**. Dramatically situated amidst deep piney woods right on the water, the shingled buildings house artists' studios where you can observe devoted artisans skillfully manipulating clay, blowing glass or working in other media. Open in the summer only. ~ South of Deer Isle Village, turn left off Route 15, and follow signs for about seven miles; 207-348-2306.

As you drive back in the direction of the mainland, go slow where you probably missed the turnoff on the way out to **Nervous Nellie's**

Jams and Jellies, a jam and jelly kitchen surrounded by landscape sculptures by one of the owners. You're welcome to sample the jams and jellies. We took home a jar of blue-razz conserve and instantly became hooked. Thank goodness they do mail order. Closed October through May. ~ Sunshine Road, Deer Isle; 207-348-6182.

One of the nicest ways to enjoy Deer Isle is on foot or by kayak (see the "Outdoor Adventures" section at the end of this chapter). Think twice about riding bikes, though. With the narrow, shoulderless roads, it's not only dangerous, apparently the locals abhor bikers slowing down traffic.

Ever since the mid-19th century, **Mount Desert Island** has been one of Maine's most popular destinations. Once you cross the bridge connecting it to the mainland, it's easy to see why. The island (New England's second-largest) is home to **Cadillac Mountain,** at 1530 feet the highest point on the Atlantic coast of the United States. Looming all around are 16 other mountains that drop right down into the sea. Fortunately, most of the island (35,000 acres) is under the protection of **Acadia National Park,** which is threaded with miles of hiking, driving and biking trails.

Wherever your peregrinations take you, there's plenty to keep you enormously busy for at least a couple of days on Mount Desert Island. By the way, Mount Desert Island is pronounced like "dessert," the sweet course that follows a meal. It was given the name by French explorer Samuel de Champlain, who discovered the island in 1604. He named it *L'Isle des Monts Déserts* because of its bare, desertlike mountaintops.

Start by heading to **Acadia National Park's visitors center** to pick up a copy of the *Official Map and Guide to Acadia*. There's also a 15-minute introductory video and several racks of nature books. Ask for a copy of *Acadia's Beaver Log*, a park newspaper, if you're interested in finding out that week's naturalist activities. ~ Off Route 3 in Hulls Cove; 207-288-4932.

The **Park Loop Road** takes in the major sights of the park, including Frenchman Bay Overlook, a scenic lookout that faces Schoodic Peninsula; Sieur de Monts Spring, with its nature center; the Wild Gardens of Acadia, a lovely patch featuring local flowers, trees and

DAY TRIP TO ISLE AU HAUT

From the Atlantic Avenue Hardware dock in Stonington, you can catch the mail boat, *Miss Lizzie* (207-367-5193), for a day trip over to elf-sized **Isle au Haut.** Since you've come this far, you might as well not miss it. Part of Acadia National Park, it has some mapped out trails to explore and picnic areas. It's also home to a one-room schoolhouse and a general store.

shrubs; Sand Beach, made partially of the crushed shells of marine animals; the Abbe Museum of Stone Age Antiquities, showcasing prehistoric artifacts of the area's original Indian tribes; and the summit of Cadillac Mountain. The road traverses approximately 27 miles up mountains, by the sea, through forests and past ponds and lakes, taking in the park's highlights (see "Beaches & Parks" below). For a closer look at the park's multitude of attractions, consider hiking along the many foot trails or signing up for a naturalist program. There are also boat trips, fishing opportunities and places to swim. In winter, there's cross-country skiing, snowmobiling, ice fishing and winter hiking. For more information, write: Superintendent, Acadia National Park, P.O. Box 177, Bar Harbor, ME 04609.

The island's main town is **Bar Harbor**, which back in the late 1800s was a thriving resort community for very wealthy and powerful American families. They built more than 200 enormous summer homes along the sea that were just as opulent as the Newport mansions. The Depression years and two world wars really took a toll on the community, however. And finally, the Great Fire of 1947 all but wiped it out. Many of the grand old hotels and about 70 mansions were destroyed.

Bar Harbor did recover, but it emerged as a more middle-class resort. Today, during summer months, it's crawling with tourists. The main street is a tangle of T-shirt shops, motels and restaurants busy with teeny-boppers and young families. We recommend visiting the **Bar Harbor Historical Society**, which features a collection of early photographs of the town before the big fire. ~ Jesup Memorial Library, Mount Desert Street; 207-288-4245.

We also encourage a visit to the **Natural History Museum**, a small museum that showcases stuffed birds and animals from the area. Admission in summer. ~ College of the Atlantic, Route 3; 207-288-5015.

A quartet of other towns on the island—Northeast Harbor, Southwest Harbor, Seal Harbor and Somesville—are likely to appeal more to the traveler in search of hidden attractions. They're quintessential Maine fishing villages. One especially worthwhile stop to make is the **Asticou Azalea Gardens**, a lovely spot devoted to azalea and Japanese gardens. ~ Route 3, near the junction of Route 198, Northeast Harbor, 207-276-5040.

You must also stop at the **Wendell Gilley Museum** if you're interested in seeing bird carvings. Closed Monday in the summer and weekdays November through April. Admission. ~ Route 102, Southwest Harbor; 207-244-7555.

Families with children will want to stop at the **Mount Desert Oceanarium**, where you'll find plenty of hands-on exhibits, live sea animals and a touch-tank with sea snails, starfish and horseshoe crabs. Closed October through April. Admission. ~ Clark Point Road, Southwest Harbor; 207-244-7330.

Back on the mainland, in busy Ellsworth, try not to miss the **Colonel Black Mansion,** a startlingly beautiful Georgian mansion filled with furnishings and decorative pieces from the past hundred years. Closed mid-October through May. Admission. ~ 81 West Main Street; 207-667-8671.

Also worth visiting in Ellsworth is the **Stanwood Museum and Birdsacre Sanctuary,** a 130-acre nature preserve centerpieced by an old homestead that dates back to 1850. Closed in the winter. ~ Route 3; 207-667-8460.

As you work your way up the coast, you'll see less traffic, fewer commercial buildings and increasingly beautiful scenery (rolling farmlands, pine forests, glimpses of the sea). You'll also notice fewer tourists—here they're chiefly RV families and rugged outdoor sports enthusiasts en route to the dense wilderness of Baxter State Park. Your chances of meeting real, hard-working, homespun locals are much greater here than along the Southern Coast, where everyone grows up learning how to treat "people from away" properly so they'll come back. You'll find Downeasterners love to strike up a conversation with a "foreigner" and have a wonderful sense of humor.

Continue to follow Route 1, veering off whenever a road looks appealing. There are several interesting detours to watch for, including **Jonesport** and **Beals Island,** which you have to squint to find on most maps. Ask any Maine aficionado which are their favorite coastal villages and they're sure to mention this little duet of lobstering and fishing towns at the end of Route 187. The two are connected by a bridge and in people's minds—rarely do you hear someone mention one without the other. Your best bet is to park in Jonesport and wander around aimlessly. You'll find a handful of restaurants, antique stores and other salty little shops.

◄ *HIDDEN*

Back on Route 1, don't miss the **Ruggles House.** Built by a wealthy lumber dealer named Thomas Ruggles, it's a very extravagant Federal-style building with a flying staircase and meticulously carved woodwork throughout. Closed mid-October through May. ~ Columbia Falls; 207-483-4637.

Machias is one of the next towns you'll come to. It's worth pulling over and getting out to take a stroll around. An old commercial center, it now has a handful of shops and restaurants and is home to the **Maine Wild Blueberry Company,** which you can tour if you call ahead. ~ Elm Street; 207-255-8364.

Machias is supposedly an Indian word that means "bad little falls," named because of the falls that run through the middle of town, where you'll also find a nice picnicking spot. Less than 15 minutes away is **Machiasport,** another photogenic village.

At East Machias, you can either continue on Route 1 or sidetrack to Route 191, taking in the little fishing village called **Cutler.** Consider taking a trip to see the puffins on **Machias Seal Island** (from May through August) on **Captain Norton's** excursions. Admission. ~ 207-497-5933.

Next stop is **Lubec**, a once-very-active sardine-canning town. Today, it has sort of a lonely, end-of-the-world feel to it, but it's lovable nonetheless. For some background on its past, stop in at **The Old Sardine Village Museum**. Closed Monday and Tuesday and after Labor Day through June. Admission. ~ Route 189, on the approach to Lubec; 207-733-2822.

Lubec is a stepping-stone to **Campobello Island** (506-752-2997), noted as the summer home of Franklin Roosevelt's family, which is actually in New Brunswick, Canada. You don't need passports or any special papers or even toll change to cross over the bridge and spend the afternoon visiting FDR's house. From late May to October, visitors can tour **Roosevelt Campobello International Park** (506-752-2922), the 34-room "cottage" where Roosevelt spent his boyhood summers from 1905 to 1921. Start by watching the excellent 15-minute movie. Then explore the house, which has been maintained exactly as the family left it. The grounds are decorously landscaped with flower beds and woven with over eight miles of trails through piney woods and along the shore. Elsewhere on the island are 15 miles of park drives and the perfect-snapshot **Quoddy Head Lighthouse**, at the end of a long bumpy dirt road. Signs warn visitors not to venture out when the tide is coming in. It rises five feet per hour and could leave you stranded for eight hours.

> The Quoddy Head Lighthouse's claim to fame is that it's sitting on the easternmost point of the land in the continental United States.

Back in Lubec, follow South Lubec Road to the end to get to the **Quoddy Head State Park**. You've undoubtably seen this lighthouse before: the candy-striped, red-and-white tower is practically an emblem for the state of Maine. There are some hiking trails to wander along as well as benches if you feel like sitting and waiting for the sun to come up.

Route 189 will take you back out to Route 1 and up through West Pembroke, where you can detour off to see Reversing Falls (see "Beaches & Parks" below).

You might also consider taking another detour along Route 214 to **Meddybemps**. The road stretches out like a canvas over one waterslide of a hill after another, edged by wheaty fields right out of an Andrew Wyeth painting. One little hill-clinging farm has a stand of vegetables with a self-service sign. Meddybemps itself is an adorable little village with a white church, white houses and a general store. There's also a pier on Meddybemps Lake and a small beach where you can swim.

HIDDEN ►

It's worth arranging to spend a few days in **Eastport**, an intriguing port city set on Moose Island in Passamaquoddy Bay. For years, it's had a statewide reputation of being somewhat down and out, but actually it's quite charming and those who have discovered—or re-discovered—the spot keep it to themselves. At one time, Eastport was a bustling town with 18 sardine canneries. The population had reached 5300 by the turn of the century. But between 1937 and 1943, it went bust. Canneries closed, and people moved out, leaving houses standing empty. Today, grand old Federal and Victorian houses remain as testimony to its better days. The skeletal population (maybe 2000) is a combination of old-timers remaining from the town's hey-day, a thriving artist population and a small infusion of investment-seeking out-of-towners.

The best way to get acquainted with Eastport and the Eastporters is to wander along its streets. Water Street is the hub, with more empty commercial space than filled. The town has been slowly up-grading and has completed a revival of the 19th-century storefronts on the waterfront. Unfortunately, few tenants have moved in. How-ever, many say Eastport is the next frontier. The next Bar Harbor. We hope not. The star attraction is the **Eastport Gallery**, a highly re-spected and lovingly cared for showcase of local art. In addition to a changing ground-floor exhibit, upstairs you'll find an ongoing display featuring the works of 20 regional artists. Closed January through April. ~ 69 Water Street; 207-853-4166.

One way to take in a big bite of this part of the coast is to drive the **Quoddy Loop**. Also known as "The Loop," it's a network of car-ferry services linking the New Brunswick mainland with Campobello Island, Deer Island (not to be confused with Deer Isle, farther down the coast), Lubec and Eastport. The route—which eas-ily fills up a full day—is mapped out in a free pamphlet you'll find in shops and restaurants around town. You can also call 207-255-4402 for more information.

Calais (pronounced CAL-lus) is the last real stop along this stretch of coast, and actually it's set on the St. Croix River a little inland. It's a jumping-off spot for many outdoors sportspeople, since it lies near **Grand Lake,** one of Maine's most beautiful and salmon-rich lakes. While in the area, stop at the **St. Croix Island Overlook** at Red Beach. It's a view of the island on which French explorers established the first European settlement in North America north of Florida (in 1604).

Another worthwhile stop in this area is the **Moosehorn National Wildlife Refuge**. Managed by the U.S. Fish and Wildlife Service, it's the northeast end of a chain of migratory bird refuges that extend all the way up the East Coast. Two areas make up the park, the largest (16,000 acres) in Baring, north of Calais, and the other about 20 miles south near Edmunds. This is a wilderness area crisscrossed by hiking trails. ~ Calais; 207-454-3521.

If you're looking for the perfect New England inn in the perfect New England village, consider detouring off Route 1 to Castine and the

LODGING

Castine Inn. The 1898 bed-and-breakfast inn is ideally situated in town minutes from the water's edge. Its 20 antique-furnished rooms are bright, big and lovingly maintained by innkeepers Mark and Margaret Hodesh. Most have views of the sea. ~ Main Street; 207-326-4365, fax 207-326-4570. MODERATE TO DELUXE.

Poised on Castine's stately Main Street is the main building of the **Pentagoet Inn**, a large old Victorian bed and breakfast. Guests can stay either in that house or at neighboring Ten Perkins Street, a 200-year-old building where all guest rooms have country antiques. Between the two, there are 16 rooms, all with private baths. ~ 207-326-8616, 800-845-1701, fax 207-326-9382. DELUXE.

Snugly set on 48 acres, **Blue Hill Farm** seems to attract a healthy, life-loving crowd, including the occasional troop of Vermont Country Cyclers who come pedaling in on their inn-hopping tours. There are fourteen guest rooms in the farmhouse and seven in the renovated barn, all looking as though they might have been photographed for *Country Living* magazine. The highlight every morning is breakfast: fresh-out-of-the-oven breads, homemade granola, fresh fruits and various cheeses. ~ Route 15, Blue Hill; 207-374-5126. MODERATE.

The **Pilgrim's Inn** has found its way into travel and gourmet publications all over the United States and Canada. It's not surprising. Perched on a shiny millpond directly opposite Northwest Harbor, this 1793 house is impeccably maintained and run by experienced innkeepers Jean and Dud Hendrick. Rooms—a total of 13, plus a neighboring guest cottage—are simply decorated with antiques, Laura Ashley fabrics and artwork and crafts by local artists, who are numerous in these parts. Tourists and Mainers from as far as Bar Harbor come for the dinners here, which are among the best in the midcoast area. Closed mid-October through mid-May. ~ Deer Isle; 207-348-6615, fax 207-348-7769. ULTRA-DELUXE.

As one totally satiated guest said while stretching his legs in a lounge chair and peering out at the fog-bundled sea with its hooting vessels, "This may not be luxurious, but you can't beat the setting." The **Inn on the Harbor** features 13 rooms of varying sizes, most of which are smack-dab on the water with ocean views. All are furnished with antiques and some feature private decks, sitting areas and fireplaces. Stepping out on the deck that hangs over the harbor is like walking right into a painting. ~ Main Street, Stonington, Deer Isle; 207-367-2420, 800-942-2420, fax 207-367-5165. MODERATE TO DELUXE.

HIDDEN ►   Though many visitors take the mail boat out just to spend the day on Isle au Haut, you can overnight there. **The Keeper's House** is a stone lighthouse-keeper's-cottage-turned-inn that still uses kerosene and candles for its lighting. There are four large, airy and simply decorated bedrooms along with a dining room in the main cottage, a separate accommodation in the tiny Oil House with its own outdoor shower and another unit in the Wood Shed. Closed from November through April. Three meals provided. ~ Robinson's Point; 207-367-2261. ULTRA-DELUXE.

You can spend hours—no, days—roaming around the rooms of **Clefstone Manor**, which are filled with European bric-a-brac that's been collected over the years. The house is a huge, 33-room mansion built in 1894 as a summer home for James Blair, secretary of the Navy under President Lincoln. Its 16 ornately decorated guest rooms, with private baths, are named for British nobility, locations and writers. The grandly proportioned Romeo and Juliet room, with its shiny brass canopy bed, beamed ceilings, Oriental rugs and fireplace, is worth taking a peek at if you happen to be staying in one of the others. However, all are jaw-droppingly impressive. Closed November through April. ~ 92 Eden Street, Bar Harbor; 207-288-4951, 800-962-9762. ULTRA-DELUXE.

If you want to glimpse what life was like in turn-of-the-century Bar Harbor summer cottages, consider staying at the **Ledgelawn Inn**. You can have your pick of rooms in either the main house, the Carriage House or the Balanced Rock Inn on the water. There are 39 rooms, some with working fireplaces and verandas and, for a modern touch, whirlpool baths and saunas. All are handsomely decorated with beautiful antiques. Guests enjoy access to a heated oceanfront pool at the Balanced Rock Inn. Closed late November through late May. ~ 66 Mount Desert Street; 207-288-4596, 800-247-5334, fax 207-288-9968. DELUXE TO ULTRA-DELUXE.

You have to book well in advance to get a room at **The Tides**. This marvelous Greek Revival manse is propped on a carpet of lawn with a stunning view of the bay and its own beach. Classical music streams through the living room, a grand affair adorned with plush champagne carpets and a fireplace. There are just three guest rooms, each elegantly furnished with Victorian and Empire pieces. The master suite with its fireplace is the most coveted, but the other two rooms—with private balconies—are worth calling ahead for as well. The innkeepers are extra-friendly and hospitable, preparing breakfasts that look like they might grace the cover of a gourmet magazine. ~ 119 West Street, Bar Harbor; 207-288-4968. ULTRA-DELUXE.

Listed in the National Register of Historic Places, the **Manor House Inn** is yet another summer cottage that has been restored and preserved. This lovely 22-room Victorian mansion, built in the late 1800s, has 14 guest quarters, all with private baths, working fireplaces and Victorian furnishings. A full breakfast is included in the price. Closed mid-November to mid-April. ~ 106 West Street, Bar Harbor; 207-288-3759. MODERATE TO ULTRA-DELUXE.

The big old hillside farmhouse at **Seal Cove Farm** is a three-room B & B that is also a working goat farm. The herd is a pampered lot, and they repay their caretakers with fine milk that is used to produce several highly respected varieties of cheese. Guests are welcome to take part in the daily chores of a working farm that is also home to pigs, chickens, turkeys, a horse and several vegetable gardens. The rooms are simply decorated with white curtains and floral comforters. Take a walk while you're here: the seaside views from the surrounding hills are stunning. ~ P.O. Box 140, Mount Desert, Maine 04660; 207-244-7781. MODERATE.

Fortunately, some things never change. Such is the case with the **Claremont**, Mount Desert Island's oldest summer hotel (it dates to 1884). Of course, this grande dame (listed in the National Register of Historic Places) has been renovated—heavily. But it still manages to preserve the old Maine vacation traditions such as dressing for dinner (that means jacket) and socializing with fellow guests. The large, rambling, shingled building has a wide veranda lined with wicker rocking chairs. The view—of Cadillac Mountain across Somes Sound—is nonpareil. The food—lots of lobster and seafood—is unfailingly good. The rooms (a grand total of 43 units, 12 of them cottages) are homey and comfortable. On top of all that, guests can sample the many on-site sporting facilities, including clay tennis courts, badminton, water sports equipment, rowboats and croquet courts. Closed November through May. Breakfast and dinner included. ~ Claremont Road, Southwest Harbor; 207-244-5036, 800-244-5036. ULTRA DELUXE.

HIDDEN ▶   Many guests intending to spend one or two nights at the **Weston House** end up extending their stay. From what we could tell, it was the combination of the bed and breakfast itself (it feels very European) and the enormously interesting town of Eastport. There are five guest rooms and two baths on the upper level of the house, a stately old Federal built in 1810. All the rooms are thoughtfully furnished with comfortable beds along with tasteful antique pieces and little touches like fresh flowers in season. The house is within walking distance of everything. The breakfasts are unmatchable, featuring all sorts of inspired recipes. ~ 26 Boynton Street; 207-853-2907, 800-853-2907. MODERATE.

The Inn at Eastport, a former sea captain's house, has five very attractive rooms furnished with antiques. It's a good in-town base. The pièce de resistance is an outdoor hot tub with an ocean view. Also, a real rarity in these parts, the inn provides evening turndown service. ~ 13 Washington Street; 207-853-4307. BUDGET TO MODERATE.

DINING   In a little town as amphibious as Castine, it's surprising to find just one restaurant on the water. Fortunately, the food at **Dennett's Wharf,** a net-hung, bustling fish house, is just as appealing as the view of the sailboat-dotted harbor. A lunch of freshly cracked oysters followed by a grilled crab sandwich and a chilled glass mug of beer is deliriously good. Dennett's is ultracasual, with waitresses sporting jeans or miniskirts. Closed from October through April. ~ Sea Street; 207-326-9045. BUDGET TO MODERATE.

The **Castine Inn** is elegantly accoutred with wall murals depicting harbor scenes and pretty table settings. The changing menu features innovative entrées including roast pork loin with peach chutney, salmon ravioli with a tomato-saffron sauce and leek pot pie. Be sure to try the crabcakes served with a mustard sauce or any of the delicious desserts such as baked Indian pudding, crème brulée and pumpkin gingerbread. Closed mid-October through April. ~ Main Street, Castine; 207-326-4365. MODERATE TO DELUXE.

The town of Blue Hill has a very sophisticated summer crowd who spend their evenings dining well and attending chamber concerts. However, there are still only a handful of truly commendable restaurants, including **Jonathan's**, with its two lovely dining rooms. The front room is very colonial, with antique blue-and-beige walls and lots of woodwork throughout. The rear room has a more rustic feel, with exposed beams and oak tables. On the ever-changing menu, you'll find lots of seafood dishes with imaginative sauces you'll beg to have the recipe for. Jonathan's also boasts one of the coast's best wine lists. Dinner only. ~ Main Street; 207-374-5226. MODERATE TO DELUXE.

The **Left Bank Café** is a little too trendy for its own good, with its Greenwich Village coffeehouse and in-house art gallery, but it's fast becoming an institution for the local crowd. It offers lots of ethnic just-hits-the-spot dishes such as pad thai noodles, chicken *kijafa* (chicken breast with raspberry sauce) and Japanese *dashi* (seafood soup). Best of all are the bakery desserts, especially the strudel. ~ On Route 172, northern edge of Blue Hill; 207-374-2201. MODERATE.

If you can't stay at **Pilgrim's Inn,** by all means do have dinner there. Your five-course *prix-fixe* meal—served in a converted timber-beamed barn—could be a butter-soft poached salmon with beurre blanc, tenderloin with cabernet, mushroom-leek sauce or perhaps glazed roasted duck. Among the other courses, you'll find wonderful bisques, chowders, salads (largely from the garden out back), home-baked breads and write-home-about desserts. Closed mid-October to mid-May. ~ Deer Isle Village, Deer Isle; 207-348-6615. ULTRA-DELUXE.

The light of wallet but discriminating seafood eater won't find a better value than **Fisherman's Friend Restaurant**. Go when you are starving—the place prides itself on its generous servings of spanking fresh fish and seafood. The diner decor could use some gussying up, but with a platter piled high with clams, who cares? Closed November through March. ~ School Street, Stonington, Deer Isle; 207-367-2442. BUDGET TO MODERATE.

◄ HIDDEN

We sat for hours at our window seat in the **Reading Room Restaurant** at the Bar Harbor Inn, mesmerized by the view. In addition to the expansive dining room with a circular view of the bay, there's an outdoor waterfront terrace. The food is lovely, too, with specialties like fresh lobster pie and grilled mixed seafood. Closed November through March. ~ Newport Drive, Bar Harbor; 207-288-3351. DELUXE.

When driving the Park Loop Road in Acadia National Park, you couldn't ask for a better place to stop for lunch, tea or dinner than **Jordan Pond House**. Along with a mountain view, it offers Maine specialties such as lobster stew and baked haddock—in a setting of piano music warmed by the fireplace. Closed mid-October to mid-May. ~ Park Loop Road, Bar Harbor; 207-276-3316. MODERATE TO DELUXE.

Children are in their glory in the delightfully decorated **Route 66**. The owners—Fred Pooler and Susan Jackson—are antique toy collectors. Everywhere you spot old toys, tools and other gadgets, each having a story of its own. The food is good old Americana, with standard favorites like grilled steaks and boiled lobster. And there are more innovative dishes as well, including shrimp fettucine and chicken cordon bleu. Closed mid-October to mid-May. Dinner only. ~ 21 Cottage Street, Bar Harbor; 207-288-3708. MODERATE TO DELUXE.

Certain restaurants tend to get everyone's recommendation, and such is the case with **Porcupine Grill**. This jewel of a place, tucked down a residential street, offers New American dishes with a Maine twist. The chef turns out inspiring creations such as caesar salad crowned with fried shrimp and sautéed lobster and mussels. Flickering oil lamps, art deco accents and big oak tables—spread far apart—make this one venue not to miss. Closed April. Dinner only. ~ 123 Cottage Street, Bar Harbor; 207-288-3884. MODERATE TO DELUXE.

Beal's Lobster Pier is another outstanding place to stuff yourselves on clams or lobster. It's super casual, with picnic tables set outside in nice weather. They'll pack lobsters in ice to go and arrange air freight as well. Closed mid-October to mid-May. ~ Clark Point Road, Southwest Harbor; 207-244-7178. MODERATE.

If hunger strikes while you're driving north on Route 1, stop in Milbridge at **The Red Barn**, a very casual, knotty-pine-paneled spot with some counter seats, booths and separate dining rooms. It has a mainstream menu (pastas, burgers, steak, seafood) as well as some house specialties like the seafood stew, a delicious concoction of shrimp, scallops, haddock and crabmeat. ~ Main Street; 207-546-7721. MODERATE TO DELUXE.

The **Waco Diner** solves the pesky problem of wanting a shot of local color. Here you'll see all the local Eastport characters, including salty seafaring types and former sardine cannery workers. The food—standard diner fare—is nothing to get excited about, but that's not the point. You're here for the Eastport atmosphere. ~ Water Street; 207-853-4046. BUDGET TO MODERATE.

One does not live by seafood alone. Try the salsa, enchiladas, burritos or Mexican pizzas at **La Sardina Loca** the easternmost Mexican restaurant in the United States. And on those cold Maine winter nights there just can't be a better place to sip a margarita than the skylight bar. The eatery is decorated with balloons, grandfather clocks and antiques. Dinner only. ~ 28 Water Street, Eastport; 207-853-2739. BUDGET TO MODERATE.

Before taking off for the northern woods, do yourselves a favor and have a meal at **Chandler House Restaurant**. This warm and popular restaurant is well known in these parts for its prime rib and seafood dishes. All the baking is done right there. ~ 20 Chandler Street, Calais; 207-454-7922. MODERATE.

SHOPPING

Though you probably won't find any bargains in the little shops and art galleries of Castine, you can find yourselves happily occupied looking at all the truly original fashions, the nautical gifts and the New England crafts and artwork. A bookstore-cum-art gallery, the **Compass Rose** has the best postcards in town. ~ Main Street; 207-326-9366. The **McGrath Dunham Gallery** showcases New England artists from May through October. ~ Main Street; 207-326-9175. The **Water Witch** has fashions that look like works of art. ~ Main Street; 207-326-4884.

The village of Blue Hill is well known in the area for its profusion of potters and artisans. You'll find some of their works at **Rowantrees Pottery**. ~ Union Street; 207-374-5535. You can also try **Rackliffe Pottery**. ~ Route 172; 207-374-2297. **Handworks Gallery** is another good spot. ~ Main Street; 207-374-5613.

The **Blue Heron Gallery & Studio** showcases the work of the Haystack Mountain School of Crafts' faculty. Closed November through April. ~ Church Street, Deer Isle Village; 207-374-5001.

William Mor Stoneware is a good source for good-looking—and functional—stoneware and porcelain kitchen pieces. This is also the place for Oriental rugs. ~ Reach Road, Deer Isle; 207-348-2822.

Any visitor to Maine really ought to stop at **Nervous Nellie's Jams and Jellies**. Though it's actually a mail-order company, walk-in customers can sample the goods—Hot Tomato Jelly, Strawberry Rhubarb Conserve, Spicy Apple Cider Jelly just to name a few—before deciding what to buy. Closed October through May. ~ Sunshine Road, Deer Isle; 207-348-6182.

Bar Harbor is chockablock with shops, many of them purveying the standard tourist goods—T-shirts that say "Baa-Haa-Bah" (the way

LEISURE READING

Try to get your hands on the Eastport edition of the Maine magazine called *Salt* (sold in various shops in town). It has beautiful essays about the town's wonderful characters. Another publication to pick up is the *Quoddy Tides*, a bimonthly newspaper highlighting all the area's goings-on, including the new titles the Lubec Library has added. Don't laugh. Some people love this little tabloid so much, they end up getting a subscription sent to their Park Avenue apartment.

Mainers pronounce it), multicolored wind socks (a craze here) and Maineana books, calendars and cards. However, there are some worthwhile galleries and shops to make a point of finding.

Look for **MDI Workshop**, a showcase for Maine arts and crafts created by adults with disabilities. ~ Route 3; 207-288-5252. **Birdnest Gallery** has oils, watercolors and graphics by contemporary New England artists. ~ 12 Mount Desert Street; 207-288-4054. **Island Artisans** is a cooperative with works by local artists. ~ 99 Main Street; 207-288-4214. **The Lone Moose** is a good source for made-in-Maine baskets, woodwork, furniture, jewelry, crafts and clothes. ~ 78 West Street; 207-288-4229. Another interesting shop in Bar Harbor is **The Woodshop Cupolas, Inc.**, where you can buy handcrafted cupolas and weather vanes. ~ Route 102, Town Hill; 207-288-5530.

The number of shops and galleries dramatically drops off as you go north of Ellsworth on Route 1. One worth looking out for is **The Sow's Ear**, which has a sweet selection of toys, some made-in-Maine clothes, jewelry and a good collection of books about Maine. Closed Sunday. ~ 7 Water Street, Machias; 207-255-4066.

If you're interested in pottery, be sure to get to **Connie's Clay of Fundy** where you'll find museum-quality contemporary earthenware. If you're lucky, you may see the artist at work in her adjoining studio. ~ Route 1, East Machias; 207-255-4574.

Eastport is the salmon aquaculture capital of America. To sample this local specialty, stop by **Jim's Smoked Salmon.** ~ 37 Washington Street; 207-853-4831.

For a selection of regional and American Indian titles visit **Fountain Books**, housed in a former drugstore. A reminder of that bygone era—when Eleanor Roosevelt frequented the store—is the old-fashioned marble soda fountain which brings in large summer crowds. ~ 58 Water Street, Eastport; 207-853-4519.

You may not find anything to buy at **Border Crafts**, but it's worth browsing around. There are a lot of hand-sewn and knitted garments made by the "local ladies" who have lived there for decades, as well as so-called "antiques" that probably fall more aptly into the "secondhand" or "thrift" category. Like Eastport itself, this little shop is bursting with local charm. ~ Water Street, Eastport.

NIGHTLIFE   One look at Castine and it's clear: no neon-zapped discos here. Not even a sleazy bar. Most visitors plan their nights around a big, satiating seafood dinner. You can also catch a performance by **Cold Comfort Productions, Inc.** It's a summer theater group that puts on plays such as *The Glass Menagerie, South Pacific* and *Agnes of God*. ~ P.O. Box 259, Castine, ME 04421.

The big night out in Blue Hill is attending concerts at the **Kneisel Hall Chamber Music Festival.** From late June to late August, string and ensemble performances are held on Friday evenings and Sunday afternoons. ~ For information, write: P.O. Box 648, Blue Hill, ME 04614; 207-374-2811. You can also see a performance by the **Surry Opera Company**, a young but internationally respected group that performs a variety of productions in their original languages. Open May through August. ~ Blue Hill; 207-667-9551.

Lights go off early on Deer Isle and Isle au Haut, as well. In Bar Harbor, we managed to scrounge up a couple of things to do after dark. The hottest pub spot is **Geddy's**, a magnet for the young, hip and trendy. Everyone congregates to hear folk and dance music, pop or rock—whatever happens to be on that night's playbill. Closed November through mid-April. ~ 19 Main Street; 207-288-5077.

Acadia National Park offers all sorts of nocturnal diversions, including ranger-led walks that focus on "Stargazing over Sand Beach" or learning about the nightlife of a beaver. There are also slide presentations in the amphitheaters at Seawall and Blackwoods Campgrounds. Programs are listed in the daily Ranger Activity Schedule. Closed mid-October through May. ~ 207-288-3338.

Like many parts of the Maine coast, Mount Desert Island has a flourishing cultural life. Check the local papers to find out what performances are on while you're on the island. The **Acadia Repertory Theatre** puts on nearly half a dozen plays a season in the Somesville Masonic Hall. ~ Route 102, Somesville; 207-244-7260. The **Deck House Restaurant Cabaret Theatre** features outstanding summer cabaret shows in an ocean-view setting. ~ Swan's Island Ferry Road, Bass Harbor; 207-244-5044. Between mid-July and mid-August, the **Bar Harbor Music Festival** is in full swing with concerts of all strains—pops, tea, string and new composer—performed at sites around town. ~ Rodick Building, 59 Cottage Street, Bar Harbor; 207-288-5744. Also from mid-July to mid-August, there's the **Mount Desert Festival of Chamber Music**, a series of chamber concerts. ~ Neighborhood House, Main Street, Northeast Harbor; 207-276-5039. The **Arcady Music Festival** draws a big crowd with summer performances that range from small ensembles to baroque orchestras in locations throughout Bangor and Bar Harbor. ~ 207-288-3151.

Once you get north of Ellsworth, you'll find even less to do after the sun goes down. This is real Maine country, where going to the movies constitutes the big night out.

In July and August, there are a series of chamber music concerts hosted by the **Machias Bay Chamber Concerts**. ~ Centre Street Congregational Church, Machias; 207-255-3889.

In Eastport, check to see if there's anything going on at the **Eastport Arts Center**. In the summer they have a Friday night series of concerts and films that is a magnet for the intellectuals, artists and literati that have discovered the area. There is also a very active community theater that stages three or four productions each season. ~ Dana Street; 207-853-4133.

BEACHES & PARKS

ACADIA NATIONAL PARK 🧍🚴🐎🏕️🏊⛵🚣🚤🛥️⛵ One of Maine's most scenic areas, Acadia National Park encompasses a large portion of Mount Desert Island, the Schoodic Peninsula on the mainland and teeny Isle au Haut. For exploring on Mount Desert, consider driving the Park Loop Road. It hits the major highlights, including Frenchman Bay Overlook, a spectacular lookout point complete with interpretive signs pointing out the islands before you; the Wild Gardens of Acadia, a colorful wildflower garden; Champlain Mountain Overlook, another jaw-dropping view of the island-dotted Frenchman Bay area; Sand Beach, made up of the crushed shells of marine animals; and the summit of Cadillac Mountain, an above-the-clouds view of it all. The Schoodic Peninsula provides a good day-long side trip. A one-way road wraps around the peninsula, with sweeping views of Frenchman Bay, the Atlantic Ocean and the Mount Desert Mountains, while another climbs to the top of Schoodic Mountain. It takes a bit of planning to reach Isle au Haut, but once there, you can go hiking, birding and camping. To fish within the park, try Jordan Pond for salmon and lake trout; Long Pond for landlocked salmon; Eagle Lake for brook trout, salmon and lake trout; Echo Lake for brook trout and salmon; and Upper and Lower Hadlock Pond for brook trout. You can swim at Sand Beach or in freshwater Echo Lake. Information center, picnic areas, restrooms, souvenir shops. ~ The best way to approach Mount Desert Island is via Route 3 from Route 1 at Ellsworth. Isle au Haut is reached by a mail boat (207-367-5193; fee) that makes regular trips from Stonington. The Schoodic Point peninsula is farther up the coast, off Route 186; 207-288-3338.

▲ There are two campgrounds in the park, **Blackwoods** and **Seawall**. Blackwoods has 310 sites for tents and RVs (no hookups); free in winter, $14 per night in season. Seawall, open only in summer, has 212 sites for tents and RVs (no hookups); $8 to $12 per night. ~ For more information, write: Superintendent, Acadia National Park, Box 177, Bar Harbor, ME 04609.

LAMOINE STATE PARK 🏊🚣🚤⛵ Located on Frenchman Bay, Lamoine State Park offers spectacular views of the dramatic peaks of Mount Desert Island. Its own 55 acres of woods and waterfront are popular for camping and picnicking. You can fish or swim (no lifeguard) in the cold water. Picnic tables, restrooms, dock and boat launch; day-use fee, $2 per person. ~ Follow Route 184 from Ellsworth to Lamoine.

▲ There are 61 tent/RV sites (no hookups); $11 to $14 per night; information, 207-667-4778.

ROQUE BLUFFS STATE PARK 🏊⛵ Carved out of Englishman Bay, Roque Bluffs is a 300-acre park with both a saltwater and freshwater beach. There's a pebble beach on the ocean. The other beach is sandy and skirts the edge of a sheltered freshwater pond. This is a great place to fish and spot eagles. Picnic areas, changing areas, toilets, playground; day-use fee, $1 per person. Closed mid-October through Memorial Day. ~ About six miles off Route 1; turn off Route 1 just beyond Jonesboro; 207-255-3475.

COBSCOOK BAY STATE PARK 🚶🏕️🏊 An extremely scenic park, Cobscook (an Indian word that means "boiling tide") sits on the shores of Cobscook Bay, where tides can reach 24 feet. Its 888 acres are covered with spruce and fir trees and snaked by hiking and cross-country ski trails. It's also a good place to spot bald eagles. Fishing and clamming are permitted in the bay. Picnic area, restrooms; day-use fee, $2 per person. ~ On Route 1 in Dennysville.

▲ There are 106 tent/RV sites (no hookups); $12 to $15 per night; information, 207-726-4412.

QUODDY HEAD STATE PARK 🚶 Dramatically situated at the easternmost point of land in the continental United States, Quoddy Head State Park offers some magnificent views of the Atlantic Ocean and Grand Manan Island. The biggest attraction here is the red-and-white-striped lighthouse that surveys the Bay of Fundy, known for its extreme tides. Hiking trails ribbon through spruce groves; one skirts a high ledge along steep cliffs that drop into the sea. Picnic tables, fireplaces; day-use fee, $1 per person. Closed November through April. ~ From Route 1, take Route 189 to the town of Lubec and follow the signs; 207-764-2040.

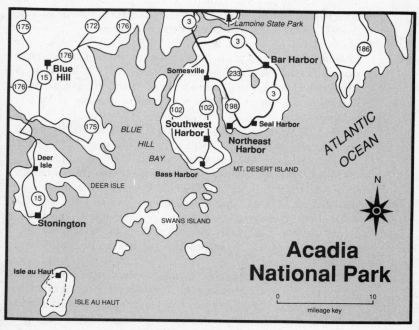

REVERSING FALLS PARK 🏃 You're not alone if you're wondering what reversing falls are. This is definitely one of those go-see-for-yourselves situations. The falls are actually a field of rapids dramatically galloping in the middle of the waterway. The Baltic scenery around it is part of a 140-acre park with hiking trails and picnic sites. Picnic tables and grills, outhouses. ~ Traveling north on Route 1, you'll pass the turn-off for Cobscook Bay State Park. Continue on for nine and a half miles and turn right at Antone's Triangle Store. Almost immediately, you'll turn right again at the red building. Follow that for three and a half miles, then turn right again. Follow for almost three miles, bearing left at the water. It's easier than it sounds, but none of these dirt roads have names.

▼▼▼▼▼▼▼▼▼▼▼▼
Northern Woods

Dense wilderness is what you'll find in this part of Maine. Thick woods that seem to go on forever. Mountains holding shiny blue lakes as if they were precious gems. Rivers roaring through canyons. The air here is invigoratingly fresh. Hiking, fishing, camping and other outdoor pastimes abound. For serious nature lovers, the northern woods provide the ultimate nirvana.

Not until you actually go to northern Maine can you understand how big the state really is. You can go for hours passing only an occasional farmhouse or two. You can't take anything for granted (such as service stations and restaurants). Once you decide to travel up there, be sure to take a good map (you'll really need one, since there's often nobody to bail you out of jams). Your best bet is to pick a destination for the day and take your time getting there.

SIGHTS

Continuing on from Calais, you can stay on Route 1, which turns from a coastal road into an inland route and can be taken to **Aroostook County**, where lakes and forests reign. **Presque Isle** is the hub up in this region and also the commercial center of Maine's potato country.

We will, however, head for the Baxter State Park and the northern lakes area in the central northern part of the state. It'll take several hours to get to **Millinocket** (pronounced the proper Maine way, it's Mill-a-NORK-it), and there's not much in between. You can finally leave Route 1 at Topsfield, turning onto Route 6 East and following the network of roads that eventually get you into the heart of Millinocket, where even one of the main streets is dirt. This town's biggest claim to fame is very big indeed. Being the home of Bowater Inc., it is one of the largest producers of newsprint in the United States.

Don't get your hopes up for anything more, though. Look at it as a good place to stock up on supplies and gas before heading off to the wilderness areas. In fact, do yourselves a favor and stop by the **Baxter State Park Headquarters** for some detailed maps. Closed April and mid-October through November. Millinocket is also a popular take-off point for canoe trips to the Allagash Wilderness Waterway. This 95-mile passage comprises 200,000 acres of interconnected lakes and rivers than run from Telos Lake to the Canadian border. Before attempting to canoe the waterway, one should have some experience (see "Beaches & Parks" below). ~ 64 Balsam Drive; 207-723-5140.

You'll find the main entrance to **Baxter State Park** about 20 miles north of Millinocket. Sprawling majestically over 200,000 acres, this largest of Maine's parks is awe-inspiring. It was a gift to the state in 1931 by Percival Baxter, who, while serving as a legislator and as governor of Maine, urged creation of a park around Mt. Katahdin. Rebuffed, the governor bought the land with his own capital and deeded to the state of Maine the land "to be forever left in its natural, wild state." Closed mid-October to mid-May.

The centerpiece is, indisputably, **Mt. Katahdin**. At 5267 feet, it's the highest peak in Maine. It's also the northern terminus for the **Appalachian Trail**. Open mid-May to mid-October, the park has 45 other peaks and over 175 miles of well-marked trails. You can drive around the perimeter in less than three hours. (See "Beaches & Parks" below.)

As you continue west of the park, you'll come to **Ripogenus Dam**, where the mighty waters of several interconnected lakes are halted and washed out the other side in a narrow river that races triumphantly through a deep gorge. This is the departure point for several whitewater rafting trips. It's also the turnoff for those driving into the Allagash Wilderness Waterway.

Moosehead Lake is 40 miles long and 20 miles wide—the biggest of Maine's countless lakes.

A dirt road takes you south of Ripogenus Dam to **Kokadjo**, an adorable little complex of camps and a general store that was built as the headquarters for a lumber company in the early 1900s.

Continue south, stopping at **Lily Bay** (see "Beaches & Parks" section below) and **Greenville**, a major New England seaplane base. You can stuff yourselves on local steamboat history at the latter's **Moosehead Marine Museum**, which displays local memorabilia as well as the restored steamship Katahdin, now a floating museum. Closed mid-October to late May. Admission. ~ Greenville; 207-695-2716.

From there, drive up the western coast of **Moosehead Lake** to the waterfront towns of Moosehead (a lumberman's depot and departure point for wilderness excursions) and Rockwood. The whole area is mesmerizingly beautiful, with mountains looming all around and evergreens perfectly reflected in the lake. It's very common to see moose in these parts.

Moosehead Lake is the center for the state's wilderness sports and the source of the Kennebec River. For more information, contact the **Moosehead Lake Chamber of Commerce**. ~ Main Street, Greenville, ME 04441; 207-695-2702.

LODGING

Before setting out into the wilderness of Baxter State Park, you can fuel up for a night by staying at **Pamola Lodge**. It's just as it sounds, a basic motor lodge with 30 generic motel rooms and efficiencies. ~ 973 Central Street, Millinocket; 207-723-9746. BUDGET.

Like a little nest hidden up in the trees, **Pray's Cottages & General Store** is a homey spot tucked away in the thick woods. It's the take-off point for many bear-hunting groups and whitewater rafters, as well as a civilization-stopover for rugged campers desiring some hot water and electricity for a change. There are four one-bedroom efficiency units in a ranch-style building, two separate three-bedroom cottages and two duplexes. All are practically furnished with the kind of things you might have used to decorate your first apartment, but they're comfortable nonetheless. They also have all the modern kitchen conveniences. The general store is the hub of activity here, which is at its best around 6 a.m. during bear-hunting season, when the hunters congregate to swap eyebrow-raising stories before heading out again. ~ Ripogenus Dam; 207-723-8880. BUDGET.

Anglers are the biggest fans of **Frost Pond Camps**. It's a group of ten campsites and eight rustically furnished housekeeping cabins set on Frost Pond, which is loaded with trout. It's also a great place for canoe groups, families and hunters (in the fall). Closed December through April. ~ Three miles beyond Ripogenus Dam near Baxter State Park; 207-695-2821. BUDGET.

HIDDEN ►

The scenery around **Katahdin Lake Wilderness Camps** is gaspingly beautiful. There are ten log cabins (two to seven people can stay in each one) and a main lodge propped up on a bluff overlooking a lake. Each cabin is rustically furnished with the basic essentials (including kerosene lamps and a supply of firewood); some have gas stoves. There's no auto access to the camps, so you must arrange to be met by the owner with pack horses, or fly in from Millinocket Lake. In the winter, the facility is open only to cross-country skiers. ~ 3.5 miles off Roaring Brook Road; 207-723-4050. MODERATE.

Remotely situated within the Allagash Wilderness Waterway (50 miles north of Millinocket), **Nugent's Chamberlain Lake Camps** is a collection of eight rustic log cabins. The best way to reach them is to fly in (contact Folsom's Air Service, 207-695-2821). Otherwise, it's a five-mile boat (or snowmobile) trip up Chamberlain Lake. This is a year-round sporting camp with fishing, canoeing, nordic skiing and snowmobiling. ~ Greenville; 207-944-5991. BUDGET TO MODERATE.

Try to get one of the two rooms that has a fireplace at the **Greenville Inn**. But if you can't, don't worry. All ten guest rooms at this former lumber baron's home are wonderful. There are antiques scattered throughout the bed and breakfast, and in the common rooms cherrywood and mahogany panels warm up all the corners. Best of all are the views of Moosehead Lake and the encircling mountains from the porch and the dining room. ~ Norris Street, Greenville; 207-695-2206. MODERATE TO DELUXE.

You can stay right in Chesuncook, a 19th-century lumberman's village that's on the National Register of Historic Places, at the **Chesuncook Lake House.** It's a beautifully maintained 1864 farmhouse with six gas-lit rooms at ultra-deluxe rates (also equipped with electricity) and three separate cabins for a moderate price. To reach it, you can be picked up by boat at Cushing's Landing or fly in. Three meals a day are included. ~ Route 76, Greenville; 207-745-5330. MODERATE TO ULTRA-DELUXE.

◄ *HIDDEN*

If images of a palace and castles run through your head when you hear about **Chalet Moosehead,** forget them. It's just a motel with a bizarre name. It's ideally situated, however, overlooking Moosehead Lake. The "chalet" is also a very inexpensive way to settle into the area, with eight efficiencies, seven standard rooms and two cabins as well as a slew of diversions to keep you happily occupied (including a private beach with a dock and free use of canoes). ~ On Moosehead Lake, off Routes 6 and 15, Greenville; 207-695-2950. MODERATE.

Poised on the shores of Moosehead Lake, **The Birches** is a string of 17 log cabins privately spaced out in a grove of birch trees. All of them have porches and wood-burning stoves or fireplaces; some have kitchens. There's a main lodge with an open-timbered dining room where the fare is wholesome and good. Major pastimes include hiking, fishing, swimming, canoeing and boating. There's also tennis and golf nearby. In winter, there's over 25 miles of cross-country trails. ~ Two miles from Rockwood; 207-534-7305. MODERATE.

Gazing over at Mt. Kineo on Moosehead Lake are the **Rockwood Cottages.** Eight cottages come with fully equipped kitchens, baths with showers, barbecue areas and screened porches. There's a long list of activities to enjoy, including fishing, hunting, whitewater rafting, seaplane rides, tennis and hiking. Come winter, there's ice fishing, snowmobiling and both alpine and cross-country skiing. ~ Rockwood; 207-534-7725. MODERATE.

Maynards in Maine is one of Moosehead Lake's oldest established sporting camps. The centerpiece of it all is a grand old lodge filled with memorabilia from earlier hunting trips (such as stuffed fish and moose heads) and comfortable sofas and chairs that date back to the early 1900s. The dining room is always abuzz with outdoor lovers who congregate for three hearty meals a day. The camp has 12 cabins, with one to three bedrooms and full baths. Closed December through April. ~ Rockwood; 207-534-7703. DELUXE.

There are just six units at **Sundown Cabins,** so be sure to reserve yours early. Located on Moosehead Lake, these one-to-three bedroom kitchenette units are ideally located for water sports and fishing. ~ Route 15, Rockwood; 207-534-7357. MODERATE TO DELUXE.

DINING

In this neck of the woods, you'll find most meals are included in the price at camps and lodges. They're often served family-style and consist of good solid home cooking. But there are a handful of restaurants you might want to try.

We were a little turned off when we saw the waitress/chef/cashier/store manager spray the grill with some aerosol and squeeze cheese out of a tube to make our grilled cheese at **Pray's General Store**. But hey, what can you say about a meal for under five bucks? And good luck finding another place to eat out in these woods. ~ Ripogenus Dam; 207-723-8880. BUDGET.

One of the most elegant meals you can have in the northern woods

HIDDEN ▶

is at the **Greenville Inn**. In its graciously decorated dining room, there's a good selection of Continental dishes, all enhanced by festive sauces created by an adept kitchen. Delicious homemade popovers accompany every meal. Closed November through April. Dinner only. ~ Norris Street, Greenville; 207-695-2206. MODERATE TO DELUXE.

If you're in the mood for a hamburger, lobster roll or a big bowl of chili, make your way to **Flatlander's Pub**. They serve heaping platters of Americana. It's a casual spot, attracting plain folks and backpacker types. ~ Pritham Avenue, Greenville; 207-695-3373. BUDGET TO MODERATE.

The barn-shaped **Cabbage Patch** is known for its lobster and sirloin tip dinner. This establishment also boasts a big salad bar, steaks and, for those larger than average appetites, gingerbread and brownie sundaes. The interior features a giant moosehead. Dinner only. ~ Routes 6 and 15, Greenville Junction; 207-695-3314. MODERATE.

Kelley's Landing is a great diner-style spot for breakfast. It opens at 7 a.m. and has a traditional American menu. ~ Greenville Junction; 207-695-4438. BUDGET TO MODERATE.

SHOPPING

There's not much in the way of shopping in the northern woods, unless you're into hunting gear and camouflage hats. But here's a place you might want to pull up to. **The Indian Store** is filled with baskets, pottery and other Indian-inspired items. ~ Main Street, Greenville; 207-695-3348.

BEACHES & PARKS

BAXTER STATE PARK 🏃 🏊 ⛵ Maine's grande dame of parks, this 200,000-acre wilderness preserve is magnificent. There are over 75 miles of hiking trails that take you through pine forests, by rivers of rapids, alongside blue lakes and up mountains—including Mt. Katahdin (5267 feet), the highest in Maine. Katahdin is the northern terminus for the Appalachian Trail. Wildlife and birds are abundant here, as are a phenomenal variety of trees and plants. You can fish or swim (if you can stand the cold) in the park's streams and lakes. Once you're in the park, there's no food, fuel or supplies. Stock up in Millinocket. Closed mid-October through November. ~ You can't miss this place. Look at any map, it's that huge green area in the central north section. The easiest approach is from Millinocket. Park headquarters, 207-723-5140.

▲ There are hundreds of sites in ten campgrounds. Among these are 72 lean-to sites, 80 tent sites and 21 cabins; prices range from $6 to $17 per night per person. Permit and reservations are required; write: Reservation Clerk, Baxter State Park, 64 Balsam Drive, Millinocket, ME 04462; 207-723-5140.

AROOSTOOK STATE PARK Maine's northernmost park, Aroostook covers more than 600 thickly wooded acres on the shores of Echo Lake. It's an outdoor lover's paradise, with hiking and cross-country trails and secluded glassy coves for swimming. There's good trout fishing on Echo Lake. Picnic sites, paddleboat and canoe rentals, boat launch; day-use fee, $1 per person. ~ Off Route 1, just south of Presque Isle; 207-768-8341.

◄ HIDDEN

▲ There are 30 tent/RV sites (no hookups); $8 to $10 per night.

ALLAGASH WILDERNESS WATERWAY Stretching for 95 miles from Telos Lake (north of Ripogenus Dam) to the far north near Fort Kent, this famous corridor of lakes and rivers is most well known for its flatwater/whitewater canoe trips. It's quite beautiful and known as "God's Country." The strip also boasts good fishing waters and snowmobiling in winter. You can swim the clear lakes as well. If you plan to canoe, it's necessary to register. Write the Maine Department of Conservation, Bureau of Parks and Recreation, State House Station #22, Augusta, ME 04333. ~ Most of the Allagash Wilderness outfitters are in Allagash Village. If you're on your own, a good put-in point is Chamberlain Thoroughfare at the junction of Chamberlain and Telos lakes. You'll find rangers at Allagash Lake, Chamberlain Thoroughfare, Eagle Lake, Churchill Dam, Long Lake Thoroughfare and the Michaud Farm; 207-287-3821.

▲ There are 100 sites for tents only; $4 to $5 per night.

LILY BAY STATE PARK This is a beautiful wilderness area on the shores of 40-mile-long Moosehead Lake. The lake really does sparkle and is framed by evergreen forests and mountains that look like waves plastered against the sky. There is a hiking trail, but most of the activity revolves around the water—swimming, fishing or boating. Moosehead Lake is well known for its brook trout, salmon and lake trout. During the winter, snowmobiling and skiing takes over. Two boat launches with berths; day-use fee, $1 per person. ~ About eight miles north of Greenville on the eastern shore of Moosehead Lake.

▲ There are 92 tent/RV sites (no hookups); $12 to $16 per night. For more information, call 207-695-2700.

▼▼▼▼▼▼▼▼▼▼
Western Lakes and Mountains

Stretching along the New Hampshire border right up to Quebec, the western lakes and mountains of Maine are unusually scenic. This area is home to dozens of lakes (in the Rangeley area alone there are about 40) and mountains (including Sugarloaf). The southern reaches—Waterford, Bridgton and the Sebago Lake area—are within easy reach of Portland and other coastal destinations, and they attract lots of visitors, especially during the summer months. The northern parts such as Bethel and Rangeley take a bit longer to get to and feel as if they're worlds away. These areas tend to attract skiers in winter and wilderness-seeking vacationers in summer.

SIGHTS

The star winter attraction in the western region is **Sugarloaf/USA**, the state's second highest mountain and its biggest ski mountain (see the "Outdoor Adventures" section at the end of this chapter). At the top, you'll find New England's largest self-contained ski village, complete with hotels, restaurants, shops and a church. Below is **Carrabassett Valley**, home to the Carrabassett Valley Ski Touring Center, an enormous network of cross-country trails. The town of **Kingfield**, at the southern entrance to the Carrabassett Valley, was founded in 1816. It has a fine collection of shops, restaurants and inns.

Year-round, however, inland Maine is becoming more and more popular, especially the **Rangeley Lakes** region. Like the northern woods, this whole western area is almost solid wilderness punctuated with an occasional town (by town, we often mean a post office, a church and a general store). Moose, bear, wildflowers that look as strange as their Latin names, and birds who know a good thing when they spot one, are the most abundant residents. Some of the biggest lakes have names that are almost impossible to pronounce, but go ahead, try. They're Mooselookmeguntic, Kennebago, Aziscohos, Cupsuptic and Umbagog. Okay, we'll throw in a few easy ones: Rangeley and Richardson. They're all busy with boaters and anglers in summer months. And scattered along the shores are small camps with rustic log cabins hidden behind thick pine trees or in birch groves.

The town of **Rangeley** is evolving fast. Too fast, according to some old-timers. Seemingly overnight, it has gone from a sleepy backwoods town to an up-and-coming tourist center. Besides the little town of Oquossoc down the road, it's really the only place where you'll find restaurants, a handful of shops, gas stations and, of course, ice cream parlors. The truth is, however, that Rangeley can't hold a candle to the real tourist towns on the coast. It's still a little town in the middle of the woods, no matter how many out-of-state license plates you count.

Rangeley does have some wonderful attributes on top of being one of the only signs of civilization for miles. It's *right* on the water. The silky ripples of Rangeley Lake practically slosh up onto the main street. It also has a landmark **library** (in the middle of town) that according to one resident, "still smells the way it used to in the '40s."

As you move south of the Rangeley Lakes region, you come to the **Bethel** area, which is in the Oxford Hills, not far from the **White Mountain National Forest** on the New Hampshire border. Bethel itself is a lovely 19th-century village with a meticulously maintained green and stately old houses. Come winter, Bethel is a thriving cross-country skiing area.

One of the town's highlights is the **Moses Mason Museum**, a restored Federal-style house displaying period furnishings and local historic exhibits. Admission. ~ 14 Broad Street; 207-824-2908. The **Gould Academy** is a very widely respected prep school. ~ 207-824-7700. The **Broad Street Historic District** is lined with historic homes.

The area south of Bethel (including Waterford, Bridgton and the towns near Sebago Lake) is loved mostly for its profusion of lakes and rivers (see "Beaches & Parks" below). In fact, from the summit of **Pleasant Mountain,** you can see about 50 lakes. These include crystal-clear **Sebago Lake,** Maine's second largest, popular with fishers and city folk from nearby Portland.

In addition to water sports galore, the area is rife with *terra firma* attractions, including the **Sabbathday Lake Shaker Community and Museum,** a complete Shaker settlement and one of the oldest in the United States. Closed from mid-October through April. Admission. ~ Route 26, New Gloucester; 207-926-4597.

The **Jones Museum of Glass and Ceramics** displays over 7000 works in glass and ceramic. Closed mid-November to mid-May. Admission. ~ Off Route 107, Douglas Hill; 207-787-3370.

LODGING

There are over 300 condominium units available through **Sugarloaf Mountain Corporation**. Each has its advantages. Some are close to the lifts, others to the restaurants and shops. They range from very modern accommodations with all sorts of new conveniences to ones that are older but more affordable. Some are bare-bones hotel rooms, others full-fledged homes. ~ Sugarloaf Mountain; 207-237-2000, 800-843-5623, fax 207-237-3052.

Nearby is the **Sugarloaf Mountain Hotel,** a six-story building with one- to three-bedroom suites. ~ 207-237-2222, 800-527-9879, fax 207-237-2874. DELUXE TO ULTRA-DELUXE.

TRAINS AND TIMBER

About 18 miles from Rangeley is the town of Phillips where you'll find the **Phillips Historical Society**. There's an interesting collection of pictures from the area's early days when a narrow-gauge railroad connected nearby lumbering communities. Ask about the summertime rides on the Sandy River– Rangeley Lakes Railroad. ~ Pleasant Street; 207-639-2881 or 207-639-3352.

You can stay near the Sugarloaf area at the **Widow's Walk**, an exceptionally friendly inn that attracts lots of skiers in winter and nature lovers in summer. Listed on the National Register of Historic Places, it's a beautiful Victorian house that was built in the late 1890s. There are six guest rooms, all with shared baths and basic New England furnishings. Full breakfast included. ~ Route 27, Stratton; 207-246-6901. BUDGET.

Fanatical skiers on a budget have a choice of bare-bones motels to choose from in this area, including **White Wolf Inn**, which actually is quite homey in spite of its generic looks. The ten rooms are ultra-basic but can accommodate between two and five guests. It's great for a pack of friends. ~ Route 27, Main Street, Stratton; 207-246-2922. BUDGET.

About 17 miles south of Sugarloaf Mountain stands **The Herbert**, an alternative to the mountain condos. It's a grand old hotel with 33 tastefully decorated guest rooms—all with combo jacuzzi/steambaths in the bathrooms. The main lobby area offers a warm reprieve, and it's often filled with rosy-cheeked skiers who don't feel guilty about taking an afternoon off from the slopes to sit in front of the fireplace and listen to piano music. Continental breakfast. ~ Main Street, Kingfield; 207-265-2000, 800-843-4372. MODERATE TO DELUXE.

Named after Amos Winter, the founder of the Sugarloaf ski area, the **Inn on Winter's Hill** is a Georgian Revival mansion with 20 charming antique-filled rooms in the main house and connecting barn. Registered as a National Historic Property, the Inn's lavishly decorated common rooms look as if they should be roped off like a museum, but actually they're very comfortable. Additional amenities include a pool, hot tub and tennis court. ~ Kingfield; 207-265-5421, 800-233-9687, fax 207-265-5424. MODERATE TO ULTRA-DELUXE.

The **Sugarloafer's Ski Dorm** is just as it sounds: a basic dorm. It was designed especially for ski groups and has six separate dormitories that accommodate 10 to 40 people. Closed May through October. Breakfast and dinner included. ~ Kingfield; 207-265-2041. MODERATE TO DELUXE.

Right on the water in Rangeley, the **Rangeley Inn and Motor Lodge** is a town landmark. The older building—erected back in the railway and lake steamer days—is a three-story shingled structure with 36 remodeled guest rooms. There's also a newer motel wing with 15 rooms, some offering fireplaces or wood-burning stoves, waterbeds and whirlpool baths. ~ Main Street; 207-864-3341, 800-666-3687. MODERATE TO DELUXE.

Magnificently situated on a hill overlooking Rangeley Lake and surrounded by an 18-hole golf course, the **Country Club Inn** is a grand old summer resort built by a wealthy sportsman back in the 1920s. The living room is lavishly endowed with two immense fireplaces that face each other. The 20 rooms are nothing to get excited about though. They're rather ordinary for this extraordinary setting.

Breakfast included; guests can choose to have dinner included. Closed mid-October through late December. ~ Country Club Road, Rangeley; 207-864-3831. DELUXE TO ULTRA-DELUXE.

Sunset Point Cottages could be in Sweden. As the name implies, ◀ HIDDEN
Sunset Point is a sprig of land jutting into spectacularly scenic Mooselookmeguntic Lake. It's colonized by a quintet of housekeeping cottages (with one, two or three bedrooms), all inches from the water's edge. Though satisfyingly rugged (wood burning stoves, gas lights), the place provides real plumbing and hot showers (!) in one common bathhouse. Closed October through May. ~ On Mooselookmeguntic Lake, outside of Rangeley; 207-864-5387. MODERATE.

Bald Mountain Camps are the woods of Maine just as you pictured them. They're right on Mooselookmeguntic Lake, surrounded by hundreds of miles of dense wilderness. Guests stay in small cabins (there are 15, all with fireplaces) that are warm and homey. No fancy furnishings here—you never have to worry about the kids spilling things. Meals are taken in the log dining room, which is always alive with vacationers who come back to their same cabin year after year. Three meals included. Closed October through mid-May. ~ Bald Mountain Road, Oquossoc; 207-864-3671. ULTRA-DELUXE.

If you've never experienced a real Maine lodge, consider staying at the **Kawanhee Inn**. It has the works: exposed timber beams, an immense stone fireplace, woodsy smelling rooms. Guests can stay in one of ten rooms with basic furnishings in the main lodge or settle into a cabin (each accommodates two to seven people). All 12 cabins have their own fireplaces and screened-in porches. The setting is lovely—on a hill overlooking Lake Webb—and guests can use the small beach and boats. ~ Weld; 207-585-2000. MODERATE TO DELUXE.

A lovely old Victorian house surrounded by five piney acres, **The Douglass Place** is beautifully situated in the small mountain town of Bethel. There are four guest rooms, all attractively furnished with antiques. Guests are welcome to use the common rooms as well, including the game room (with a piano, pool table and ping-pong table), living rooms, den and screened-in gazebo. Continental breakfast included. ~ Bethel; 207-824-2229. MODERATE.

The **Bethel Inn and Country Club** is a large resort-type place that has everything. By everything, we mean 137 rooms (all with their own telephones, televisions and bathrooms), a well-respected dining room and an array of sporting options including golf, tennis, fishing, swimming, exercise rooms, sauna and cross-country skiing in winter. A huge, sprawling yellow building right on the town's common, it's impossible to miss. The individual rooms are decorated in a ho-hum style with all the modern comforts. The common rooms are formally attired in antiques. Breakfast and dinner are included. ~ On the Common, Bethel; 207-824-2175, 800-654-0125, fax 207-824-2233. ULTRA-DELUXE.

Within walking distance of the town's shops and restaurants, L'Auberge is the kind of place you fall in love with and then hesitate to tell even your best friends about. Formerly a barn, it has seven guest rooms simply but elegantly furnished with country antiques. Guests are free to roam about the common rooms, which include a living room with a hearth, baby grand piano and the kind of chairs and couches you sink into. During the winter months, you can cross-country ski right from the door. Breakfast is included. ~ Mill Hill Road, Bethel; 207-824-2774, 800-760-2774, fax 207-824-2774. MODERATE TO DELUXE.

In South Casco, you can visit Nathaniel Hawthorne's Boyhood Home on Hawthorne Road, where the 19th-century author spent his early years.

Gazing out onto the village green of North Waterford is the Olde Rowley Inn, a beautifully maintained place that dates back to 1790. The seven guest rooms are all warmly furnished with floral prints and country antiques. There are also three dining rooms, an antique shop and a network of cross-country ski trails. Breakfast is included. ~ Route 35; 207-583-4143, 800-700-0560, fax 207-583-2413. MODERATE TO ULTRA-DELUXE.

The Noble House offers nine guest rooms in a turn-of-the-century Queen Anne. Set on a hill, this bed and breakfast is comfortably furnished with antiques. Some of the rooms and suites come with whirlpool baths and porches. You're welcome to play the baby grand piano or the pump organ. Explore the inn's private lake frontage with a canoe or foot-pedal boat, or just watch the sunset from the comfort of your own hammock. Closed November through mid-May. ~ 37 Highland Road, Bridgton; 207-647-3733, 800-476-9218. MODERATE TO DELUXE.

Surrounded by 34 lakeside acres, the Tarry-A-While Resort is a grand old summer hotel with 11 main-house rooms and another 17 in a quartet of cottages that punctuate the grounds. The innkeepers pride themselves on their unending hospitality. You almost feel as if you're guests in a private home. There's an array of diversions nearby, including water sports (two beaches plus canoes, rowboats, motorboats, sailboats and windsurfers), tennis and golf. Closed mid-October through late May. ~ Highland Ridge Road, on Highland Lake, Bridgton; 207-647-2522, fax 207-647-5512. DELUXE.

DINING

For a quick but satiating meal between ski runs, try Gepetto's. You can warm up with a bowl of seafood chowder or a thick slice of pizza or settle in for fresh chicken and seafood dishes. From its windowed walls (it's the greenhouse style) you can sit and watch skiers schussing down the mountain. Dinner only. Closed Sunday. ~ Village West at Sugarloaf; 207-237-2192. MODERATE.

Julia's, an ornate dining room at The Inn at Winter's Hill, is as romantic and handsomely decorated as the rest of the historic building it occupies. The restaurant offers intriguing cuisine like lobster and shrimp with stuffed pasta in cream sauce along with breathtaking mountain views. ~ School Street, Kingfield; 207-265-5421. ULTRA-DELUXE.

The area's most highly regarded restaurant is **One Stanley Avenue**. It's housed in a Queen Anne–style Victorian building and offers classic regional cuisine (maple cider chicken, saged rabbit with raspberry sauce). Desserts can be counted on to elicit oohs and aahs. Open in the winter only. ~ 1 Stanley Avenue, Kingfield; 207-265-5541. MODERATE TO DELUXE.

The blue-and-peach-colored, antique-filled dining room is so pretty you'll want to linger for hours at **The Herbert**. A lovely spot for dinner, the changing menu offers a host of American dishes. ~ Main Street, Kingfield; 207-265-2000. MODERATE.

The food at the **Country Club Inn** is almost upstaged by the view. From your table you can look out over Rangeley Lake, often as smooth as glass and interrupted only by a lone canoe. All around loom mountains that seem to change colors as often as you change courses. Fortunately, the food holds its own, with a selection of traditional American dishes along with some French recipes. Closed mid-October through late December. ~ Routes 4 and 16, Rangeley; 207-864-3831. MODERATE.

When locals want to celebrate birthdays or anniversaries, they usually go to the **Rangeley Inn**. It has a formal, turn-of-the-century dining room where you can feast on French or American specialties. Closed November through April. ~ Main Street, Rangeley; 207-864-3341. MODERATE TO DELUXE.

If you just don't feel like cooking in your housekeeping cottage yet you're not in the mood to dress up for dinner out, pull up to the **Red Onion**. It's your basic pizza and subs kind of place that's crammed with locals and tourists alike. Don't be surprised if you have to wait a few minutes for a table to free up. Deck dining in summer months. ~ Main Street, Rangeley; 207-864-5022. BUDGET TO MODERATE.

If you're not staying at the **Bethel Inn**, at least treat yourselves to dinner there. The fare at this lovely country resort is traditional New England served in the formal dining room (with views of the golf course and hills), in the Mill Brook Tavern downstairs or on the screened-in veranda during the summer. ~ On the Common, Bethel; 207-824-2175. MODERATE TO DELUXE.

You can't help but fall in love with **Mother's**. It's a gingerbread house with wood stoves, crammed bookshelves and all sorts of eclectic adornments filling five dining areas. Lunches are simple and light (soups, salads, sandwiches), while dinners include a selection of seafood, pasta and chicken dishes. Closed November through May. ~ Upper Main Street, Bethel; 207-824-2589. BUDGET TO MODERATE.

The Old Rowley Inn boasts four-star candlelit dining. There are stenciled walls, pumpkin and pine floors, lace curtains, a fireplace and period antiques that take you back to 1790 when this restaurant was a stagecoach stop. You'll find the American-Austrian menu is influenced by the *chef de cuisine's* travels through the Pacific and Asia. ~ Route 35, North Waterford; 207-583-4143. MODERATE TO DELUXE.

If you get a craving for New American cuisine while hiking around these alpine hills, you're in luck. The **Tarry-A-While Restaurant** in the Tarry-A-While Resort serves such entrées as chicken *tortella*, a sautéed chicken breast filled with goat cheese, asparagus and sundried tomatoes in a rosemary and port wine demiglaze. While you take turns dunking homemade bread in the rich fondue, you can peer out at Highland Lake. Closed from Columbus Day through Memorial Day. ~ Bridgton; 207-647-2522. MODERATE TO DELUXE.

True gourmands find their way to the **Oxford House Inn**, a 1913 house that faces the White Mountains. It has a lovely repertoire of dishes including salmon Pommery and grilled pork tenderloin. During the summer, cocktails are served on the piazza. ~ Main Street, Fryeburg; 207-935-3442. DELUXE.

SHOPPING   If you lose your ski hat or mittens, head straight for **Keenan Auction Company**, where you can find all sorts of great bargains. ~ Main Street, Kingfield; 207-265-2011.

Lively patterned ski sweaters are the forte of **Patricia Buck's**. But she also sells hats and mittens as well as books and cards. ~ Main Street, Kingfield; 207-265-2101; also in the Alpine Village at Sugarloaf.

The **Yarn Barn School** sells everything from supplies for spinners, weavers, knitters and basket makers to beautiful final products. Closed November through late May. ~ Route 4, on Rangeley Lake, Oquossoc; 207-864-5917.

Bonnema Potters specialize in lamps, but they also have a beautiful assortment of functional stoneware pieces and porcelain pottery. Ask about seconds. ~ Main Street, Bethel; 207-824-2821.

In Bridgton, over 50 Maine craftspeople have also joined together to form the **Society of Southern Maine Craftsmen, Stone Soup Artisans**, where their works are sold. ~ 88 Main Street; 207-647-5984.

In addition to artwork and crafts, Bridgton is a good place to shop for antiques. Its **Wales & Hamblen Antique Center** purveys the goods of more than 30 dealers. Closed late October through Memorial Day. ~ 134 Main Street; 207-647-3840.

The **United Society of Shakers** sells reproduction Shaker furniture, herbs, tea and handcrafted items. Closed late October through mid-May. ~ Route 26, New Gloucester; 207-926-4597.

NIGHTLIFE   Nightlife in this area is also limited. In many towns, you're lucky if there's even a movie theater.

However, if you're in the Rangeley Lakes Region, you might be able to see a performance sponsored by **Rangeley Friends of the Arts**. They're put on throughout July and August at local churches, lodges and the high school. Contact the chamber of commerce for this year's program. ~ P.O. Box 317, Rangeley, ME 04970; 207-864-5364.

The **Sebago-Long Lake Region Chamber Music Festival** is a series of concerts held in July and August. Call for information. ~ Deetrees Theatre, Harrison; 207-583-4533.

RANGELEY LAKE STATE PARK This is unadulterated wilderness. Pine trees point to the sky, while white birch are perfectly reflected in the glassy lake. Moose are seen here frequently. The park covers 1000 acres, taking in lots of forest and the southern rim of Rangeley Lake. Anglers love to try for trout and land-locked salmon. People that know about the Rangeley Lake State Park usually keep it to themselves. Picnic sites, bathhouse, children's play area, boat launch; day-use fee, $2 per person. ~ Off Route 17 on South Shore Drive, south of Oquossoc.

▲ There are 50 tent/RV sites (no hookups); $12 to $16 per night. Information, 207-864-3858.

MOUNT BLUE STATE PARK A 5000-acre park that encompasses Mount Blue and Webb Lake, Mount Blue offers one jaw-droppingly beautiful vista (mountains, lakes, more mountains) after another. There are plenty of hiking trails, as well as boating opportunities on Webb Lake. The lake also has good fishing for bass, perch, trout and salmon. The park offers guided nature walks. Picnic area, bathhouse, amphitheater and recreation hall, canoes for rent; day-use fee, $2 per person. ~ Off Route 156 in Weld.

▲ There are 136 tent/RV sites (no hookups); $10 to $13 per night. Information, 207-585-2347.

GRAFTON NOTCH STATE PARK Over on the Maine–New Hampshire border, between Upton and Newry, is Grafton Notch. The 2000-mile Appalachian Trail passes through it on the way to its northern terminus, Mt. Katahdin. Throughout the park, you'll see waterfalls, caves and beautiful mountain scenery (it's at the end of the Mahoosuc Range). Picnic tables, grills, toilets, water pump; day-use fee, $2 per person. ~ On Route 26, 16 miles north of Bethel; 207-824-2912.

▲ Nearby, Stoney Brook (Route 2, six miles from Bethel; 207-824-2836) offers 30 tent/RV sites with hookups; $14 to $16 per night.

SEBAGO LAKE STATE PARK Some days, this gigantic lake shines like one huge sheet of aluminum foil. You'll find the water deliciously clear (it's Portland's main water supply). Many people come just for the day to swim and play on and off the sandy beaches. Some stay at the campsites that are spread out along the shores and in the woods on the northern end. You can fish for salmon and togue. Picnic sites with tables and grills, bathhouses, playgrounds, amphitheater, lifeguards; day-use fee, $2 per person. ~ Off Route 302, between Naples and South Casco; 207-693-6613.

▲ There are 250 RV/tent sites (no hookups); $12 to $16 per night.

▼▼▼▼▼▼▼▼▼▼▼▼▼▼
Outdoor Adventures

In a state where the sea, lakes and rivers sparkle like diamonds, you couldn't ask for a better way to explore than in a canoe.

CANOEING

SOUTHERN COAST You can rent canoes from **Sally Mountain Cabins.** ~ Off Route 201, Jackson; 207-668-5621. **Maine Sport** also rents canoes. ~ Route 1, Rockport; 207-236-8797. In Bar Harbor you can try **Acadia Bike & Canoe/Coastal Kayaking.** ~ 48 Cottage Street; 207-288-5483.

DOWNEAST COAST In Southwest Harbor you can rent canoes at Mansell Boat Rental. ~ Main Street; 207-244-5625.

NORTHERN WOODS Up north in Millinocket, call **Katahdin Outfitters.** ~ 207-723-5700. You can also try **Allagash Wilderness Outfitters.** ~ 207-723-6622 or 207-695-2821. On Moosehead Lake, contact the **Wilderness Expeditions.** ~ Rockwood; 207-534-2242.

WESTERN LAKES AND MOUNTAINS In western Maine, try **Saco River Canoe & Kayak.** ~ 188 Main Street, Fryeburg; 207-935-2369. In Rangeley go to the **Rangeley Region Sport Shop.** ~ Main Street; 207-864-5615.

SPORT-FISHING

Opportunities to get out on deep-sea fishing boats abound on Maine's coast.

SOUTHERN COAST In York you can contact **Seabury Charters** (York Harbor; 207-363-5675). In Ogunquit try the **Ugly Anne.** ~ 207-646-7202. In Portland there's the **Devil's Den**, with Captain Harry Adams. ~ DiMillo's Marina; 207-761-4466. In Boothbay Harbor call **Bingo Cruises.** ~ Tugboat Inn; 207-882-9309.

DOWNEAST COAST In Southwest Harbor contact **Masako Queen.** ~ 207-288-5927.

GOLF

The central part of the coast is where you'll find Maine's largest concentration of golf courses.

SOUTHERN COAST In Bar Harbor you can visit **Kebo Valley Golf Club.** ~ Eagle Lake Road; 207-288-3000. Or you can try **Bar Harbor Golf Course.** ~ Junction of Routes 3 and 204, Trenton; 207-667-7505. On Deer Isle you'll want to try **Island Country Club.** ~ Route 15A, Sunset; 207-348-2379. In Hancock swing by **White Birches Golf Course.** ~ Thorsen Road; 207-667-3621.

DOWNEAST COAST In Castine head for the green at **Castine Golf Club.** ~ Battle Avenue; 207-326-8844. In Southwest Harbor try the **Causeway Club.** ~ Fernald Point Road; 207-244-3780. In Northeast Harbor visit the **Northeast Harbor Golf Club.** ~ Sargent Drive; 207-276-5335. In Calais you can try the **St. Croix Country Club.** ~ River Street; 207-454-8875. In Winter Harbor there's **Grindstone Neck Golf Course.** ~ Grindstone Avenue; 207-963-7760.

You'll find every kind of sailboat imaginable in Maine's waters, from simple Sunfish to tall-masted windjammers.

SAILING

SOUTHERN COAST   In Saco you can call **Saco Bay Sailing.** ~ Beach Avenue; 207-283-1624. In West Boothbay Harbor contact **Holladay Marine.** ~ 207-633-4767. In Rockland, try **Schooner Captains.** ~ 207-594-8007. In Rockport call **The Timberwind.** ~ Rockport Harbor; 207-236-3639. If you're near Belfast contact **Chance Along Sailing Center.** ~ 207-338-1833. In Northeast Harbor there's **Great Harbor Charters.** ~ 207-276-5352. In Bar Harbor try **Golden Anchor Sloop.** ~ Golden Anchor Pier; 207-288-9505. Sailing lessons are offered by the **Camden Yacht Club Sailing Program.** ~ Bayview Street, Camden; 207-236-4575.

Gliding through Maine's miles and miles of pine-scented cross-country trails on skis is a beautiful way to experience the essence of the state's winters.

CROSS-COUNTRY SKIING

NORTHERN WOODS   **Currier's Flying Service** offers fly-in touring trips. ~ Greenville; 207-695-2778. Or you can contact **Birches Ski Touring Center.** ~ Rockwood; 207-534-7305. A great center around here is the **Moosehead Nordic Center.** (Route 16 at Indian Hill; Greenville; 207-695-2870).

WESTERN LAKES AND MOUNTAINS   In Kingfield try the **Sugarloaf Touring Center.** ~ Carrabassett Valley; 207-237-2000. In Rangeley, there's the **Ski Nordic Touring Center at Saddleback.** ~ 207-864-5671. In Bethel call **Bethel Inn and Country Club.** ~ Bethel; 207-824-2175. Or you can try the **Sunday River Cross Country Ski Center.** ~ Bethel; 207-824-2410.

SOUTHERN COAST   In this region you can hit the slopes at **Camden Snow Bowl.** ~ Barnestown Road, Camden; 207-236-3438.

DOWNHILL SKIING

WESTERN LAKES AND MOUNTAINS   Maine's downhill skiing revolves largely around **Sugarloaf/USA,** which is the biggest ski mountain in New England. ~ Carrabassett Valley, Kingfield; 207-237-2000. However, **Saddleback Mountain** is another mountain to check out. ~ Rangeley; 207-864-3380. You can also hit the slopes at **Sunday River Skiway.** ~ Bethel; 207-824-2187. Or you can try **Shawnee Peak at Pleasant Mountain.** ~ Bridgton; 207-647-8444.

NORTHERN WOODS   The northern woods are laced with choppy-water rivers. For a wild ride try **Eastern River Expeditions.** ~ Greenville; 207-695-2411. In Rockwood call **Wilderness Rafting Expeditions.** ~ 207-534-2242. You can also brave the waters with **Northern Outdoors, Inc.** ~ The Forks; 207-663-4466. Or you can try **Crab Apple White Water.** ~ The Forks; 207-663-2218.

WHITE-WATER RAFTING

BICYCLING   One of the best ways to see the coast is by pedaling along it. You can pick a spot—any spot—and start riding. Just watch out for summer traffic.

SOUTHERN COAST   A lovely 22-mile loop on Cape Elizabeth, just south of Portland, starts and finishes at the **Scarborough Public Library** on Route 207. It winds through Scarborough Marsh, by several beaches (including Scarborough Beach and Crescent Beach State Park) and through Lights State Park and Prouts Neck Bird Sanctuary.

The **Boothbay Harbor** area is a lot more manageable on two wheels than four. From Boothbay Harbor itself, try pedaling east to East Boothbay and then south to Ocean Point (about 14 miles round-trip). Or do the loop around Southport Island (about 16 miles starting and finishing in Boothbay Harbor).

DOWNEAST COAST   On Deer Isle, there are several bicycling possibilities. From the center of the village, you can ride through silent woods out to the Haystack Mountain School of Crafts (seven miles one way) or to the little lobstering village of Stonington (six and a half miles one way). Or take your bikes over on the mail boat to Isle au Haut and ride along the sea for a couple of miles.

There are over 50 miles of carriage paths on **Mount Desert Island** to cycle on. One of the most exhilarating trips is the 28-mile **Acadia National Park Loop** (the car route with detours). The steep ascent of Cadillac Mountain is not for everyone though.

NORTHERN WOODS   There are also some pleasant inland trips as well, though distances tend to be long and—if you're in the western region—hilly or mountainous. A stunningly beautiful trip for big-time bicyclers can be had up at **Baxter State Park**. It's about 46 miles, between Ripogenus Dam and Spencer Cove. You pass waterfalls, whitewater rivers and miles of majestically beautiful forest and you can see Mt. Katahdin looming on the horizon.

Bike Rentals   There are a number of Southern Coast rental stores. In Kennebunkport, try **Cape-able Bike Shop**. ~ Townhouse Corners; 207-967-4382. In Rockport, you can rent bikes at **Maine Sport**. ~ Route 1; 207-236-8797. Bikes for rent in Boothbay Harbor can be found at **Tidal Transit**. ~ By the Footbridge; 207-633-7140. To rent bikes in Bar Harbor, contact **Acadia Bike & Canoe/Coastal Kayaking**. ~ 48 Cottage Street; 207-288-5483. At Moosehead Lake in the Northern Woods bikes are available at **The Birches**. ~ Birches Road; 207-534-7305.

HIKING   **SOUTHERN COAST**   The **Fore River Trail** (1 mile) goes through the heart of Portland's Fore River Sanctuary. It's an easy walk weaving through woods and marshes to a 30-foot-high waterfall. Several other trails veer off the main loop.

The whole of Monhegan Island is prime hiking territory, but if time is limited, at least try to follow **Cliff Trail** (about 2 miles). It takes you through the most densely scenic part of the island, over the dramatic headlands and coves that make up the eastern shore. You'll probably spend about half the day following it, but the views (plunging cliffs, deeply indented coves, open sea) are worth it.

The hike to the top of **Bald Rock Mountain** (1 mile round-trip) in Camden Hills State Park rewards trekkers with glorious views of Penobscot Bay, Blue Hill, the rugged peaks of Mount Desert Island and the islands anchored offshore. It's a fairly easy climb that passes through forests ablaze with wildflowers. To reach the trailhead take Route 1 north of Camden to Lincolnville Beach. Turn left on Route 173 and take another left when you reach Young Town Road. The trailhead is near a fire road (Bald Rock Road).

DOWNEAST COAST   Duck Harbor Mountain (1 mile) is a delightful   ◀ *HIDDEN* short hike on Isle au Haut. From its peak, you can see much of the island itself, which is covered largely with dense stands of spruce and fir, marshlands, streams and ponds and some spectacular cliffs.

From atop **Blue Hill** (2 miles round-trip) you won't be able to take your eyes off the view. Like a painting, the peaks of Mount Desert Island and the sailboat-dotted waters of the Blue Hill Bay spread out before you. On a clear day, you can see the villages of Penobscot and Castine and the Camden Hills. The trail itself passes through thick spruce and fir forests. To reach it, turn west on the Mountain Road opposite the entrance to the Blue Hill Fairgrounds and you'll see the trailhead about a mile down on the right.

Acadia National Park has an enormous network of hiking trails that attract hikers and rock-climbers from around the world. The Visitors Center has an information sheet, profiling many of the trails, which range in difficulty from very easy paths to strenuous hikes.

The **North Ridge of Cadillac Mountain** (4.4 miles) in Acadia Park is a moderate trail with some steep grades and level stretches. By and large, though, it's a gradual ascent with exhilarating views of the island-dotted bays, coastline and clouds—below you.

✔ CHECK THESE OUT—UNIQUE OUTDOOR EXPERIENCES

- Follow the wooded trails of **Camden Hills State Park** through pine forests to windswept views of Penobscit Bay. *page 525*
  - Drop your canoe into the lakes and rivers of the **Allagash Wilderness Waterway** for a terrific flatwater/whitewater trip. *pages 547, 556*
    - Tackle the moguls at **Sugarloaf/USA**, the largest ski mountain in New England. *pages 548, 557*
      - Cycle beside waterfalls, whitewater rivers and miles of majestic mountain forests in **Baxter State Park**. *page 558*

If you feel up to it, consider climbing **Acadia Mountain** (2.5 miles), also in Acadia National Park. It's fairly strenuous but offers achingly beautiful views of the mountains, the offshore islands (from the top they look like croutons floating in soup) and Somes Sounds, the only fjord of the eastern U.S. seaboard.

Another good, though strenuous hike inside Acadia National Park is **Beachcroft Trail** (1.6 miles), whose trailhead is along Route 3 at the northern end of the Tarn. The trail takes you up—steeply—the side of an ice-carved valley where you can read the glacial record.

Beech Mountain (1.3 miles) over in Southwest Harbor is our personal favorite. As you ascend, the land seems to fall off all around you, revealing increasingly magnificent views of the sea and islands. There's a fire tower at the summit if you really want to stuff yourselves on gorgeous scenery.

NORTHERN WOODS   Baxter State Park's **Owl Trail** (3 miles) begins gradually, passing through woods and by streams. However, it does get steep in patches, taking you through bouldery cliff areas. If you've got the physical fortitude, it's worth it. From the wind-slapped summit, you can see the lakes and streams that wash through this startlingly beautiful chunk of Maine. To reach the Owl Trail, start off on the Hunt Trail at the Katahdin Stream Campground. You'll see blue markers indicating where the Owl Trail turns off.

One of the most spectacular routes to Baxter Peak is the **Cathedral Trail** (1.8 miles). It is very steep and rocky, though, so be forewarned. Its name comes from the cathedrals you'll see—huge outcroppings of vertical rock slabs. To return, pick up either the **Dudley Trail** or **Knife Edge Trail**, which are not as treacherously steep and easier to descend. All three trails begin and end at the Chimney Pond Campground in Baxter State Park.

Along the Allagash Waterway at Umsaskis Lake begins the trail up **Priestly Mountain** (7 miles round-trip). From the fire tower that crowns its peak (about 1900 feet), you'll have far-reaching views of the whole water-webbed Allagash area. To reach the trail, leave your canoes at the park ranger's camp about halfway down the western shore. You'll see a sign.

Two trails lead to the summit of **Mount Kineo**, which rises dramatically from the middle of Moosehead Lake. **The Indian Trail** (1 mile) is the tougher of the two, taking you along steep cliffs. The **Bridle Trail** (1 mile) is easier but not half as beautiful. Either way you choose, the views from the bald summit make your heart throb. To reach the mountain, you have to boat in. There are motorboats for rent along the Moose River and in Rockwood, on the western shore of Moosehead Lake as well as shuttle boats departing every other hour from Kineo House.

If you take just one hike while in New England, let it be at **Gulf Hagas** (10 miles round-trip), otherwise known as "Maine's Grand Canyon." This area is perhaps the most scenic in the state, taking in the three-mile canyon, five major waterfalls and 40-foot-high vertical walls. The only catch is finding this place. It's east of Greenville and west of Katahdin Iron Works. Your best bet is to consult *The Maine Atlas*, where it's clearly indicated. If you're game for a hunt, follow these directions: From Routes 6 and 15 in Greenville take a right on Pleasant Street and follow it for two miles. Pleasant takes a sharp right and then turns into a dirt road; follow it for ten miles, and you'll come to Hedgehog Check Point gate. The attendant will guide you from there.

The **Sally Trail** (6 miles round-trip) winds its way up Sally Mountain through forests of birch hardwoods and fir trees. From the summit, you can see island-dotted Attean Pond and other mountains that loom up all around. To reach the trail, drive two miles south from Jackman on Route 201 to Attean Road. Turn right and follow the road for about two miles to the Attean Lake Resort. The trail starts near the lake landing, by the railroad tracks.

WESTERN LAKES AND MOUNTAINS   A good "starter" mountain in the Rangeley Lakes Area is **Bald Mountain** (2 miles round-trip), where the trail gradually ascends through hardwood forests. From the top you can see portions of Mooselookmeguntic Lake and nearby lakes. You'll also see the Kennebago Mountains to the north, the Azis cohos and Deer Mountains to the west and Saddleback Mountain to the east. To reach the trailhead, follow Route 4 from the Oquossoc Post Office for a mile and take a sharp left onto Bald Mountain Road.

The somewhat tricky trail up **Little Jackson Mountain** (6.5 miles) climbs above the timberline through pretty woods and patches of blueberry and cranberry bushes. The view of the Weld area from the summit is worth the hike. To get there, follow the unmarked road that heads west out of Weld Corner. Stay on it until you see a cemetery. Just beyond that, turn right onto the bumpy dirt road.

Step Falls (1 mile) is a long, dramatic string of cascades and icy pools. During summer months (even late August), take along your bathing suits for a dip in the thrilling nature water slide. The falls are located off Route 26, about 15 miles northwest of Bethel. There's no sign, but you'll see cars parked at the trailhead.

A simple walk recommended for young families is the trail to the summit of **Sabattus Mountain** (1.5 miles round-trip), which passes through silent woods on gentle inclines. At the top, there are wide-angle views of the mountains. To reach the trail, follow Route 5 to just north of Center Lovell; turn right on the dirt road. When you come to a fork, stay right. Continue on past a white house to the parking area.

▼▼▼▼▼▼▼▼▼▼

Transportation

CAR

The most common way to enter Maine is from the south, on Route 95, the interstate. It's the fastest way to reach Portland, Augusta and Bangor. It's also the quickest way to get to most of the coastal resort areas between the border of New Hampshire and Mount Desert Island, and to the edge of the northern woods.

An alternative to Route 95 is **Route 1**, which roughly runs along the coast from Kittery to Calais. At Calais, it turns north and follows the Canadian border all the way up to Fort Kent in the state's northern reaches. A word of caution: Route 1 is notoriously slow, especially in the south in the summer months, when tourists are traveling and stopping at the scores of factory outlets that line it. It's also hilly in parts (especially in the north), which makes passing quite dangerous.

You can easily reach towns in the southern half of the state on the well-maintained webwork of roads that cover it. The north is a bit more difficult, however. There are times when you may have to go north, south, north, south just to get from a western town to an eastern town. Fortunately, the scenery in these parts more than compensates. One more note about the north. Once you get north and west of Millinocket, you'll spend most of your time on dirt roads. Some are downright rough and rugged. And some are private and require permits.

AIR

There are two major airports in the state: the **Portland International Jetport** and the **Bangor International Airport.**

Portland is served by Continental Airlines, Delta Air Lines, United Airlines and USAir plus several regional airlines. Flying into Bangor are Delta Air Lines and United Airlines, as well as regional air carriers.

At both, you'll find plenty of taxis to take you into town. In Portland, you can bus in with the **Metro Bus Company** (207-774-0351). There are also small airports in Auburn/Lewiston, Augusta, Bar Harbor, Frenchville, Presque Isle, Rockland and Waterville—all serviced by either Continental Express or Valley Airlines.

FERRY

From Nova Scotia, Canada, you can ferry to Portland on one of the **Prince of Fundy Cruises**. Arrivals and departures are from 468 Commercial Street near Million Dollar Bridge. ~ 207-775-5616.

BUS

Greyhound Bus Lines cruises up Route 1, stopping in Brunswick, Bath, Wiscasset, New Castle, Waldoboro, Thomaston, Rockland, Camden and Belfast. ~ Corner of St. John and Congress streets, Portland; 207-772-6587, 800-231-2222.

CAR RENTALS

Unless you're planning to stay put in one hotel or in one city for the duration of your trip, you'll most likely need a car in Maine.

At the Portland and Bangor airports, you'll find **Avis Rent A Car** (800-331-1212), **Budget Rent A Car** (800-527-0700), **Hertz Rent A Car** (800-654-3131), **National Interrent** (800-328-4567) and **Thrifty Car Rental** (800-367-2277).

For getting around Portland on your own, there's a very good bus system called the **Metro**. It has regularly scheduled routes throughout the greater Portland area. ~ 207-774-0351.

Several taxi companies serve the Portland International Jetport, including **Town Taxi Co.** (207-773-1711). In Bangor, try **Barons** (207-945-5671) or **Checker** (207-942-5581).

Hundreds of boat companies along the Maine coast offer excursions that range from one-hour cocktail cruises to day-long whale-watching expeditions to week-long cruises on historic windjammers. You'll find the biggest concentrations of such companies in Kennebunkport, Boothbay Harbor, Rockland and Rockport, and on Mount Desert Island. Keep in mind that these are generally offered only in the summer months. Here are a few to try:

In Kennebunkport, go whale watching on the 65-foot **Nautilus**, which leaves from the Arundel Shipyard. ~ Route 9; 207-967-5595.

Second Chance Cruiselines offers a scenic lobster cruise that glides by George Bush's summer home and past lolling harbor seals. The captain even provides a lobster-trapping demonstration. ~ 207-967-5507, 800-767-2628.

Cap'n Fish Boat Trips is just one of many excursion companies competing for your attention on the Boothbay Harbor wharf. They offer sunset cruises and nature-viewing trips that spot seals, exotic birds and whatever else decides to fly or swim by. ~ Pier 1, Boothbay Harbor; 207-633-3244.

Penobscot Bay is where you'll find Maine's tall-masted windjammers. You can spend three days or a week sailing on one, staying in comfortable cabins and eating like royalty. Contact the **Maine Windjammer Association** for a complete listing of all the possibilities. ~ P.O. Box 317, Rockport, ME 04856; 207-374-2293.

For a scenic cruise to the legendary artist colony of Monhegan Island, head south from Thomaston to Port Clyde and board the **Laura B.** or the **Elizabeth Ann**. The cruises lead past seabird rookeries to idyllic Monhegan Island. Here you'll learn the fascinating story of renaissance man Rockwell Kent and see the summer home of artist Jamie Wyeth. ~ 207-372-8848.

From Stonington, the **Miss Lizzie**, Isle au Haut's mail boat, doubles as a sightseeing cruise boat. Ninety-minute cruises depart from the Atlantic Avenue Dock (207-367-5193). **Palmer Day IV** also departs from Stonington and offers cruises around the waters of Penobscot Bay.

On Mount Desert Island, there are a number of boating possibilities, including whale watching with **Acadian Whale Watcher**. ~ Bar Harbor; 207-288-9776. There's also nature-viewing with **Sea Princess Naturalist Cruises**. ~ Northeast Harbor; 207-276-5352.

Lodging Index

Edgecombe-Coles House, 513
The Edgewater, 325
Edson Hill Manor, 413
Egremont Inn, 368
1824 House Inn, 411
Eliot and Pickett Houses, 186
Eliot Suite Hotel, 193
The Elms, 48
The Equinox, 392

Fairbanks Inn, 255
Fairfield Inn by Marriott, 459
Florence Frances', 200
Four Chimneys Inn, 243
Four Columns Inn, 390
Four Seasons Hotel, 175
463 Beacon Street Guest House, 193
Frost Pond Camps, 544

Garden Gables Inn, 366
Garden Park Motel, 47
General Thurston House, 119
George Fuller House, 311
Goddard Mansion, 469
Goodwin Hotel, 70
Governor's B & B, 450
Greenhope Farm, 429
Greenville Inn, 544–45
Greenwood Lodge American Youth
  Hostel, 391
Greenwood's Gate, 59
The Grey Bonnet Inn, 402
Greystone Motel, 478
Griswold Inn, 84

Hampton House, 449–50
The Hancock Inn, 464
The Hanover Inn, 470
Harbor View Hotel, 274
Harbor Walk, 261
Harraseeket Inn, 512
Harvard Manor House, 215
The Haven, 510
The Hawthorne Hotel (Salem), 308
Hawthorne Inn (Concord), 230
Heermansmith Farm, 429
The Herbert, 550
Heritage House, 255
The Hermitage Inn, 390–91
Hillside Motel, 69
The Hilltop Inn, 484
The Historic Merrell Inn, 367
Hitching Post, 460
Holden Inn, 249
Holiday Inn (Concord), 460
Holiday Inn Express (East Haven), 77
The Homestead Inn, 47
Hopkins Inn, 57–58

Horizons Inn, 262
Hostelling International—Martha's
  Vineyard, 275
Hotel Duncan, 77
Hotel Manisses, 119
Hotel Méridien, 175
Hotel Northampton, 353
Hyatt Regency Cambridge, 216

Inn Among Friends, 260
The Inn at Castle Hill, 129
The Inn at Chapel West, 76
Inn at Christian Shore, 451
The Inn at Eastport, 534
The Inn at Fernbrook, 262
The Inn at Hampton, 450
Inn at Harvard, 215
Inn at Long Trail, 402
The Inn at Longshore, 47
The Inn at Mill Falls, 478
The Inn at Montpelier, 412
The Inn at Mystic, 91
Inn at Park Spring, 511
Inn at Thorn Hill, 485
Inn at Watch Hill, 117–18
Inn at Woodstock Hill, 97
Inn on Carleton, 511
The Inn on Cove Hill, 309–10
The Inn on Covered Bridge Green, 392
The Inn on Golden Pond, 477
The Inn on Lake Waramaug, 58
The Inn on Newfound Lake, 477
The Inn on the Common, 429
Inn on the Harbor, 532
The Inn on Trout River, 429
Inn on Winter's Hill, 550
Innamorata, 359
Inntowne Inn, 130
Irving House, 215–16
Isaiah Clark House, 243
Ivy Lodge, 130

Jack Daniel's Motor Inn, 464
Jared Coffin House, 284
John Carver Inn, 324–25
John Jeffries House, 187

Katahdin Lake Wilderness Camps, 544
Kawanhee Inn, 551
Kedron Valley Inn, 403
The Keeper's House, 532–33
King's Inn, 97

The Lake Motel, 478
Lambert's Cove Country Inn, 275
Lantana House, 311
The Larchwood Inn, 119
Lareau Farm, 411

Dining Index

Index

Area chapters are Boston, Cape Cod and the Islands, Central and Western Massachusetts, Connecticut, Maine, Massachusetts Coast, New Hampshire, Rhode Island and Vermont.

Notes

Notes

HIDDEN GUIDES

Adventure travel or a relaxing vacation?—"Hidden" guidebooks are the only travel books in the business to provide detailed information on both. Aimed at environmentally aware travelers, our motto is "Adventure Travel Plus." These books combine details on unique hotels, restaurants and sightseeing with information on camping, sports and hiking for the outdoor enthusiast.

THE NEW KEY GUIDES

Based on the concept of ecotourism, The New Key Guides are dedicated to the preservation of Central America's rare and endangered species, architecture and archaeology. Filled with helpful tips, they give travelers everything they need to know about these exotic destinations.

ULTIMATE FAMILY GUIDES

These innovative guides present the best and most unique features of a family destination. Quality is the keynote. In addition to thoroughly covering each destination, they feature short articles and one-line "teasers" that are both fun and informative.

Order Form

Ulysses Press books are available at bookstores everywhere. If any of the following titles are unavailable at your local bookstore, ask the bookseller to order them. Or you can order them directly from Ulysses Press (P.O. Box 3440, Berkeley, CA 94703; 510-601-8301, 800-377-2542).

HIDDEN GUIDEBOOKS

____ Hidden Boston and Cape Cod, $9.95

____ Hidden Carolinas, $15.95

____ Hidden Coast of California, $15.95

____ Hidden Colorado, $12.95

____ Hidden Florida, $14.95

____ Hidden Florida Keys and
Everglades, $9.95

____ Hidden Hawaii, $15.95

____ Hidden Idaho, $13.95

____ Hidden Maui, $12.95

____ Hidden New England, $16.95

____ Hidden Oregon, $12.95

____ Hidden Pacific Northwest, $16.95

____ Hidden Rockies, $16.95

____ Hidden San Francisco and
Northern California, $15.95

____ Hidden Southern California, $15.95

____ Hidden Southwest, $16.95

THE NEW KEY GUIDEBOOKS

____ The New Key to Belize, $14.95

____ The New Key to Cancún and
the Yucatán, $13.95

____ The New Key to Costa Rica, $15.95

____ The New Key to Ecuador and
the Galápagos, $15.95

____ The New Key to Guatemala, $14.95

ULTIMATE FAMILY GUIDEBOOKS

____ Disneyland and Beyond, $11.95

____ Disney World and Beyond, $12.95

Mark the book(s) you're ordering and enter the total cost here ⟹ [   ]

California residents add 8% sales tax here ⟹ [   ]

Shipping, check box for your preferred method and enter cost here ⟹ [   ]

❑ BOOK RATE   **FREE! FREE! FREE!**

❑ PRIORITY MAIL $3.00 First book, $1.00/each additional book

❑ UPS 2-DAY AIR $7.00 First book, $1.00/each additional book

[   ]

Billing, enter total amount due here and check method of payment ⟹

❑ CHECK   ❑ MONEY ORDER

❑ VISA/MASTERCARD _____

NAME _____ PHONE _____

ADDRESS _____,

_____

CITY _____ STATE _____ ZIP _____

MONEY-BACK GUARANTEE ON DIRECT ORDERS PLACED THROUGH ULYSSES PRESS.

ABOUT THE AUTHORS & ILLUSTRATOR

SUSAN FAREWELL, a graduate of Boston University, contributed the chapter on Maine. She has written about New England for newlyweds (*Bride's*), young parents (*Child*) and Japanese travelers (*Gulliver*). Farewell is the author of *How to Make a Living as a Travel Writer*, *Quick Escapes From New York City* and several other travel books.

STACY RITZ is the author of *Disney World and Beyond: The Ultimate Family Guidebook*, *The New Key to Belize* and *Hidden Carolinas*, as well as co-author of *Hidden Florida*. Formerly a staff writer for *The Tampa Tribune*, she has also written for the *Washington Post*, *Fort Lauderdale Sun-Sentinel*, *Miami Herald*, *Parents* and *Bride's*.

PATRICIA MANDELL, author of the introductory and Boston chapters, has lived on Boston's South Shore for over a decade. She belongs to the American Society of Journalists and Authors and has published in the *Christian Science Monitor*, *New England Monthly*, *Miami Herald* and *Denver Post*.

RYAN VOLLMER, who penned the Massachusetts Coast chapter, is a freelance writer based in New York. She is the author of *Affordable Spas and Fitness Resorts* (Ventana Press) and has written for the *New York Times*, *Rolling Stone*, *New York Daily News*, *San Francisco Chronicle*, *Self*, *Psychology Today* and *Woman's Day*.

ALBERTA EISEMAN, author of the Connecticut chapter, is a regular contributor to the Travel and Connecticut sections of the *New York Times*. She has written for the *International Herald Tribune*, *Connecticut Magazine*, *Historic Preservation*, and penned many books for children and young adults.

B. J. ROCHE, author of the chapter on Central and Western Massachusetts, is a graduate of the University of Massachusetts at Amherst where she now teaches journalism. Roche is a regular contributor to the *Boston Globe* and has written for the *Washington Post*, *Los Angeles Times*, *Chicago Tribune* and *Travel & Leisure*.

BRENDA FINE, who wrote the Rhode Island chapter, is a member of the Society of American Travel Writers. She is co-author of *The Women's Travel Guide*. Her articles have appeared in the *New York Daily News*, *Ladies' Home Journal*, *Endless Vacation*, *Diversion* and the *New York Post*.

TIM CARROLL, the illustrator for *Hidden New England*, has illustrated several Ulysses Press guidebooks, including *Hidden Florida* and *Hidden Southern California*. His artwork has appeared in *Esquire*, *GQ*, the *Boston Globe*, *San Francisco Focus*, *Premiere* magazine, the *New York Times* and the *Washington Post*. He has also done animation for Nickelodeon.

PRAISE FOR
THE CLASSIC PARKER NOVELS

"Westlake's ability to construct an action story filled with unforeseen twists and quadruple-crosses is unparalleled."
—*San Francisco Chronicle*

"The neo-hero: the ruthless, unrepentant, single-minded operator in a humorless and amoral world....No one depicts this scene with greater clarity than Richard Stark."
—*New York Times*

"Donald Westlake's Parker novels are among the small number of books I read over and over. Forget all that crap you've been telling yourself about War and Peace and Proust—these are the books you'll want on that desert island."
—Lawrence Block

"Grittily and chillingly noir...[Westlake] succeeds in demonstrating his total mastery of crime fiction."
—*Booklist*

"As Donald E. Westlake or Richard Stark, this crime novelist gives the best lines to the bad guys."
—*TIME*

"The real thrill is seeing Parker back in action again...If you're new to Stark's work, think of all the comic Dortmunder capers he's written under his real name— Donald E. Westlake—but with as baleful an absence of humor as in *The Ax*."
—*Kirkus Reviews*

more . . .

The Mourner

ALSO BY RICHARD STARK

The Hunter {Payback}
The Man with the Getaway Face
The Outfit
The Mourner
The Score
The Jugger
The Seventh
The Handle
The Damsel
The Rare Coin Score
The Green Eagle Score
The Dame
The Black Ice Score
The Sour Lemon Score
Deadly Edge
The Blackbird
Slayground
Lemons Never Lie
Plunder Squad
Butcher's Moon
Comeback
Backflash
Flashfire

RICHARD STARK

The Mourner

Published by Warner Books

A Time Warner Company

Warner Books Edition
Copyright © 1963 by Richard Stark
All rights reserved.

This Warner Books, Inc. edition is published by arrangement with Avon Books

 Mysterious Press books are published by Warner Books, Inc., 1271 Avenue of the Americas, New York, NY 10020.

Visit our Web site at www.twbookmark.com.

For information on Time Warner Trade Publishing's online publishing program, visit www.ipublish.com.

 A Time Warner Company

Printed in the United States of America
First Trade Printing: September 2001
10 9 8 7 6 5 4 3 2 1

Library of Congress Cataloging-in-Publication Data

Stark, Richard.
   The mourner / Richard Stark.—Warner Books ed.
      p. cm.
   ISBN 0-446-67772-8
   1. Parker (Fictitious character)—Fiction. 2. Criminals—Fiction. I. Title.

PS3573.E9 M6 2001
813'.54—dc21   2001031586

ONE

1

When the guy with asthma finally came in from the fire escape, Parker rabbit-punched him and took his gun away. The asthmatic hit the carpet, but there'd been another one out there, and he landed on Parker's back like a duffel bag with arms. Parker fell turning, so that the duffel bag would be on the bottom, but it didn't quite work out that way. They landed sideways, joltingly, and the gun skittered away into the darkness.

There was no light in the room at all. The window was a paler rectangle sliced out of blackness. Parker and the duffel bag wrestled around on the floor a few minutes, neither getting an advantage because the duffel bag wouldn't give up his first hold but just clung to Parker's back. Then the asthmatic got his wind and balance back and joined in, trying to kick Parker's head loose. Parker knew the room even in the dark, since he'd lived there the last week, so he rolled over to where he knew there wasn't any furniture. The asthmatic, coming after him, fell over a chair.

Parker rolled to where the wall should be, bumped into it, and climbed up it till he was on his feet, the duffel bag still clinging to his back. The duffel bag's legs were around Parker's hips, and his left arm was around Parker's chest. His right hand kept hitting the side of Parker's head.

Parker moved out to the middle of the room, and then ran backward at the wall. The second time he did it, the duffel bag fell off. Across the room, the asthmatic was still bouncing back and forth amid the furniture. Parker went over that way, got the asthmatic silhouetted against the pale rectangle of the window, and clipped him. The asthmatic went down, hitting furniture on the way.

Parker waited a few seconds, holding his breath, but he couldn't hear anybody moving, so he went over and shut and locked the window, pulled the venetian blinds, and switched on the table lamp beside the bed.

The room was a mess. One bed had been turned at a forty-five-degree angle to the wall, and the mattress was half-pulled off the other one. The dresser was shoved out of position so it was blocking the closet door, and the wastebasket lay on its side in the middle of the floor with a big dent in it. All four chairs were knocked over. One of them had both wooden arms broken.

Parker walked through the mess to see what he'd landed.

Fifteen minutes ago it had started, with Parker lying clothed on the bed in the darkness, thinking about one thing and another, and waiting for Handy to come back. That was after eleven o'clock, so Handy was late already. The lights were off because Parker liked it that way, and the window was open because November nights in Washington, D.C., are cool but pleasant. Then through the window had come the faint clatter of somebody mounting the fire escape, four flights below at street level. Parker had got off the bed and listened at the window. The somebody came up the fire escape about as quiet as the Second World War but trying to be quieter, and stopped at Parker's floor. Somebody with asthma. It was all so amateurish, Parker couldn't take it seriously, which is why the second one surprised him. He'd waited, and the guy with asthma had waited outside—probably to make sure there wasn't anybody home in Parker's room—and then finally he came in and it all had started.

The nice thing about a hotel. Nobody questions any noise that lasts less than ten minutes.

They were both out, the duffel bag on his face and the asthmatic on his back. Parker looked them over one at a time, and then frisked them.

The asthmatic was short, scrubby, wrinkled as a prune, and fifty or more, with the withered look of a wino. He was wearing baggy gray pants, a flannel shirt that had once been plaid but had now faded down to a gray like the pants, and a dark-blue double-breasted suit coat with all but one button missing and the shoulder padding sagging down into the arms. He had white wool socks on and brown oxfords with holes in the soles.

Parker went through his pockets. In the right-hand coat pocket he found a boy-scout knife with all the attachments—a screwdriver, nail file, corkscrew, everything but a useful blade—and in the left-hand pocket a hotel key. The board attached to the key was marked: HOTEL REGAL 27. In the shirt pocket was a crumpled pack of Camels and in the left-hand pants pocket forty-seven cents in change. From the hip pocket he took a bedraggled old child's wallet of imitation alligator skin, with a two-color picture of a cowboy on a bucking bronco on one side and a horseshoe on the other. Inside the wallet was a hundred dollars in new tens and four dollars in old singles, plus half a dozen movie-theater ticket stubs, a long, narrow photo of a burlesque dancer named Fury Feline, clipped from a newspaper, and a Social Security card and membership card in Local 802, International Alliance of Chefs and Kitchen Helpers. The Social Security card and the union card were made to James F. Wilcoxen.

That was all. Parker left Wilcoxen and went over to the duffel bag, who had started to move. He had long, straight, limp hair, dry blond in color, and Parker grabbed a handful of it and slapped his head against the floor. He stopped moving. Parker rolled him over.

This one was just as short, and maybe even thinner, but about twenty years younger, with the face of a ferret. He was dressed all in black. Black shoes and socks, black pegged trousers, black wool-knit sweater. He had long, thin fingers and narrow feet.

Parker searched him. Under the black sweater was a blue cotton shirt, and in the pocket was a pair of sunglasses. The right-hand pants pocket contained fifty-six cents in change and a key to room 29 in Hotel Regal; the left, a roll of bills—one hundred dollars in new tens. Left hip pocket, a Beretta Jaguar .22, with the three-and-a-half-inch barrel. Right hip pocket, a wallet containing seven dollars, plus a bunch of dog-eared clippings about the various arrests of Donald Scorbi on suspicion of this and that, mostly assault or drunk and disorderly, with one narcotics possession. The wallet also disgorged a laminated reduced photostat of a Navy discharge—general discharge, for medical reasons—with the same name on it, Donald Scorbi.

Parker kept the two stacks of new tens and the Beretta, but put everything else back in Scorbi's and Wilcoxen's pockets. Then he used their shoelaces to tie their hands behind them, and their belts to secure their ankles together. Scorbi started to come out of it again and he had to be put back to sleep, but Wilcoxen was still out, wheezing through his open mouth.

Parker looked them over, and decided to keep Wilcoxen. He used a washcloth and face towel to gag Scorbi, then dragged him into the bathroom and dumped him in the tub. He closed the door and searched around the room for the other gun, the one he'd taken from Wilcoxen early in the scuffle.

It was under the dresser, a Smith & Wesson Terrier, five-shot .32. Parker took it and the Beretta and stowed them away in his suitcase. His watch said eleven-thirty-five, which made Handy over half an hour late, so something had gone wrong.

Parker straightened the room and Wilcoxen still hadn't come out of it. Parker dragged him over to the wall, propped him up in a sitting position, and pinched him awake. Wilcoxen came out of it complaining, groaning and thrashing his head around and keeping his eyes tight shut. There was a sour smell of wine on his breath. His face was all wrinkled gray leather except for two bright red circles on his cheeks, like a clown's makeup.

Parker said, "Open your eyes, Jimmy."

Wilcoxen stopped complaining and opened his eyes. They were a wet, washed-out blue, like an overexposed color photo. He took a while getting them to focus on Parker's face, and then the red blotches on his cheeks got suddenly redder, or the rest of the face paler.

Parker said, "Good," then straightened up and went away across the room to the nearest chair. He brought it over and sat down and kicked Wilcoxen conversationally in the ribs. "We'll talk."

Wilcoxen's lips were wet. He shook his head and blinked a lot.

Parker said, "I got a partner. You had a partner. Scorbi."

Wilcoxen looked around and didn't see Scorbi.

"Your partner wouldn't tell me about my partner. I threw him back out the window."

Wilcoxen's eyes got bigger. He stared at Parker and waited, but Parker didn't have anything else to say. The silence got thicker, and Wilcoxen squirmed a lot. His feet jiggled, and he licked his lips and kept blinking. Parker sat looking at him, waiting, but Wilcoxen's eyes kept darting all over the place.

Finally, he asked, "What you want from me?"

Parker shook his head and kicked him again. "Wrong answer."

"I don't know no partner. Honest to Christ."

"What *do* you know?"

"I got a hundred bucks. Donny and me both. Go to the Wynant Hotel, first fire escape in the alley, fifth floor. If there's nobody home, take everything there. Suitcases and like that."

"And if there's somebody home?"

"Don't do nothing. Come back and report."

"Back where?"

Wilcoxen's blinking was getting worse. His eyes were closed more than they were open. "Listen," he said. "It's just a job, you know? A hundred bucks. Nobody hurt, just pick up some suitcases. Anybody woulda took it."

Parker shook his head. He didn't care about that. "Back where?" he asked.

"Howison Tavern. On E Street, down by Fourth Precinct."

"Who do you see?"

Wilcoxen frowned, and the blinking settled down a little. "I don't know," he said. "He just told us go in there and sit down. If we got the stuff, somebody would come by, pick it up. If not, somebody would come by, get the report."

"What time you supposed to be there?"

"By one o'clock."

"Which E Street?"

"Huh? Oh, Southeast."

"Who gave you the job?"

"The job? Listen, I got pins and needles in my hands."

Parker looked at his watch. Quarter to twelve. He had an hour and fifteen minutes. "I'm in a hurry, Jimmy," he said.

"How come you know my name?"

Parker kicked him in the ribs again, not hard, just as a reminder.

"I'm giving you the straight story. I ain't going to lie for a hundred bucks. You didn't have to throw Donny out no window."

"Who gave you the job?"

"Oh, uh—a guy named Angel. He's a heavy, he hangs out around North Capitol Street, up behind the station. Donny and me, we was in a movie on D Street, and when we come out Angel grabs onto us and gives us the offer."

"Is Angel going to be at the Howison Tavern?"

"He says no. He says somebody will come by, don't worry, he'll recognize us. We should sit in a booth and drink beer. Schlitz."

"Where do I find this Angel?"

"I don't know. Honest to Christ. Hangin' around someplace, up around behind the station. In around there, you know."

It was no good. Parker thought it over, chewing his lip. The meeting couldn't be faked, so there was no way to start a trail from there. And it would take more than an hour and a quarter to find somebody named Angel hanging around the Union Station area somewhere. If Handy was still alive, he'd be alive till one o'clock. Then, when Scorbi and Wilcoxen didn't show up, whoever had Handy would know there was trouble. The easiest thing would be dump Handy.

So it had to be done from the other direction, through the girl.

Parker nodded to himself. "All right, Jimmy," he said. "You can go. Roll over so I can untie you."

"You mean it? Honest to Christ?"

"Hurry, Jimmy."

Wilcoxen scramble away from the wall and flopped over on his stomach.

"You're all right, honest to Christ you are. You know it wasn't nothing personal. There wasn't even supposed to be nobody here, just suitcases and like that. We ain't torpedoes or nothing."

"I know," Parker said. He untied Wilcoxen's hands and stepped back. "Undo your ankles yourself."

Wilcoxen had trouble making his hands work. While he was loosening the belt from around his ankles and putting his shoelaces back in his shoes, Parker got the Terrier out of the suitcase, and held it casually where Wilcoxen could see it. He left the Beretta where it was; he didn't like .22's much.

When Wilcoxen got to his feet, Parker said, "Scorbi's in the bathroom. Go untie him."

Wilcoxen suddenly smiled, beaming from ear to ear. "I knew you didn't throw Donny out no window," he said. He hurried over and opened the bathroom door. "Donny! He's lettin' us go, Donny!"

After a while Scorbi came out, walking lame like

Wilcoxen. He looked sullen, not joining in Wilcoxen's happiness. Parker said, "Out the way you came in."

"What about our dough?" Scorbi asked.

"Hurry," Parker said.

"Come on, Donny," said Wilcoxen. He tugged at Scorbi's sleeve. "Come on, let's go."

"Our rods and our dough."

Parker said, "Go on, Jimmy. Either he follows you or he don't."

Wilcoxen hurried over and climbed out the window onto the fire escape. Scorbi hung back a second, but then he shrugged and went out the window. The two of them started down the fire escape, making even more noise than they had coming up.

Parker stowed the Terrier away inside his coat and picked up the phone. When the operator came on, he made his voice high-pitched and nervous. "There's somebody on the fire escape! Get the police! Hurry! They're going down the fire escape!"

He hung up while the operator was still asking questions, switched off the light, and left the room. He took the elevator down and crossed the lobby and went outside. A prowl car was parked down to the left, with the red light flashing. Hotels get fast service.

Parker stood on the sidewalk, and a couple of minutes later two cops came out of the alley alongside the hotel, pushing Scorbi and Wilcoxen in front of them. So that was that. Because the Scorbis and Wilcoxens never talk to the law, it couldn't get back to Parker. So, no matter how good a story they thought up, they'd miss that one-o'clock meeting, and whoever had Handy wouldn't be warned. It was better even than keeping them tied up in the bathroom.

Parker turned and walked the other way. A block later he hailed a cab.

2

It was just over the Maryland line, in Silver Spring, a squat, faded apartment building called Sligo Towers. Built of dark brick aged even darker, the bricks widely separated by the plaster, it looked like an old Thirties standing set left over on the Universal back lot. Thirties-like imitations of Gay Nineties gaslights, containing twenty-five-watt bulbs, flanked the arched entrance to the courtyard.

The courtyard was just concrete, but pink coloring had been added before it set. It was bounded on three sides by the building, rising eight stories and sprouting air conditioners here and there like acne. On the fourth side was a double arch with a concrete pillar, separating courtyard from sidewalk. Beyond, dark cars slept at the curb, hoods mutely reflecting the street light from down the block. A car purred by, without pausing.

Parker turned the far corner and came striding toward the Sligo Towers. He wore a gray suit and a figured shirt, the suit coat open despite the night chill. He looked like a businessman, in a tough business. He could have been a liquor salesman in a dry state, or the automobile-company vice-president who takes away the dealerships, or maybe the business manager of one of the unions with the big buildings downtown around the Capitol. He could have been a hard, lean businessman coming home from a late night at the office.

He turned at the double arch and went into the court-yard, his shoes with the rubber soles and heels making no sound on the pink concrete. There were walls on three sides of him, all around the courtyard, with a door in each wall. Each was marked with a letter so rococo it looked like a drawing of an ivy-covered window.

He didn't know which door. Slowing down would spoil the effect, stopping would tip any watcher that he was a stranger here. He kept on toward "B," the door straight ahead. Three brick-lined pink concrete steps led up, and then the door was metal, painted to look like wood. It was a double door, and inside there was a metal bar like those found on the doors of schools and theaters. A half flight of metal stairs painted red led up to a hall-way running at right angles. There was no interior door, which was a surprise. With no trouble at all, he was al-ready in the building.

Facing the stairs, on the wall, was a double row of brass mailboxes, with name plates. Parker read the names, but didn't find the one he wanted. He looked to right and left, and in both directions the hallway ended short at apartment doors, so the three sections of the building weren't connected at this level. They would be, in the basement. He went back down the half flight to a longer hallway, this one walled with rough plaster and dimly lit. He turned left.

At the end, the hallway made a right angle to the left. Parker followed it, came to another flight of stairs, and went up. He was now in section A, and the name he wanted was under the fifth mailbox from the left on the bottom row. Miss Clara Stoper. Apartment 26.

There were four apartments to a floor, so 26 would be on the seventh floor. The elevator was to the right of the mailboxes. Parker got out at the seventh floor. Apartment 26 was to the left. Parker moved down that way and listened at the door, but could hear nothing. There was a thin crack between the bottom of the door and the floor, but no light showed through.

Parker rang the bell. There was no peephole in the door, so he waited where he was, in front of the door. Nothing happened for a while, so he rang the bell again. Then he saw light under the door, and a bolt clicked.

He frowned, trying to remember the name Handy was using with her. Pete Castle, that was it.

The door opened a few inches, held by a chain from opening any farther. A chain like that can't keep anyone out; it only serves as an irritation. Beyond was a sleepy-eyed girl's face. She was sleepy-eyed and holding a robe closed at her throat, but her hairdo was in perfect shape without a net.

"Who is it? What do you want?" she said, the voice a good imitation of sleepy blurriness.

But the hairdo had given it away. Parker didn't have to ask questions after all. His right foot went out and wedged in the doorway, so the door couldn't be closed. His right hand reached through and grabbed a handful of hair on the top of her head. He slammed her forehead against the edge of the door. Her hands started to come up toward his wrist, and her mouth was opening wide to shout, so he did it again. The third time, she became a dead weight and collapsed straight downward, leaving several strands of hair in his fist.

It took two high, flat kicks with his heel to pop the chain loose from the doorpost. The door swung open, and beyond the lighted foyer and the dark living room was a bright doorway. The silhouette of a fat man appeared in it and Parker dove for the rug, stabbing into his pocket for the Terrier. The fat man fired over his head. Parker rolled into a wall and came up with the Terrier in his hand. The bright doorway was empty. Parker moved quickly, slamming the hall door and flicking off the foyer light.

The fat man had the same idea. There wasn't any bright doorway any more. The whole apartment was dark.

The fat man knew this place, and Parker didn't. The fat man could sit and wait, and Parker couldn't take the time. The fat man could stay where he was and listen, shoot at the first sound, or just wait for Parker to go away.

In the dark, Parker found the unconscious girl. He dragged her into the living room and knelt beside her on one knee. In a conversational voice he said, "Fat man. Listen to me, fat man. You fired one shot. The light sleepers around here are awake now; they think it was a truck making a backfire. You turn on a light, fat man, and you come out here where I can see you, or I make more noises. I can scream like a woman, and then very slow I can empty this pistol into your girl. Too many backfires, fat man. Somebody will call the police. Before I'm finished, somebody will call the police. Then I wipe the gun clean and put it down on the floor and beat it. No fingerprints of mine here, fat man. Nothing to connect me. But your fingerprints are everywhere. And somebody'll connect you up with this woman."

Silence.

"Now, fat man. The next thing I do is scream like a woman."

"Wait."

It was a soft voice, and from the left somewhere. Not in the room.

"Hurry."

"I will not turn on the lights," said the voice. It had a faint accent, something Middle European. "But it is possible we can talk."

"Not in the dark."

"You must be reasonable. We will effect a compromise."

"Name it."

"You want something here, quite obviously, else you wouldn't have come. Yet I don't know you. I cannot imagine what it is you want. Your reactions and movements are hardly those of a burglar or a rapist. Either you have come to murder me, at the behest of the opposition, or you are here seeking information of some sort. If murder is your purpose, it would hardly be sensible for me to show myself. If what you want is information, we can discuss it just as profitably in the dark."

While the fat man was talking, Parker was crawling toward the sound of his voice, moving cautiously across the carpet on hands and knees. When the voice stopped, Parker stopped. He turned his head away, so he wouldn't sound any closer. "I'm here for information. Where's Pete Castle?"

"Ah!" The fat man seemed pleased to have the mystery cleared up. "He *did* have associates."

"Where is he?"

"Reposing in a safe place, I assure you. And relatively unharmed. I would suggest, by the way, that you come no closer. You are now nearly to the doorway, and I pride myself on my shooting. If you clear that doorway, and then are foolish enough to speak, it will take me no more than one backfire to dispose of you."

"Why warn me?"

"Curiosity, just curiosity. The same motive that impelled me to have your friend taken away to where he could be questioned at leisure. Our operation is of a complexity and a delicacy. Your friend's presence became, quite naturally, of concern to us. We had to know whether his goal coincided with our own. Now I discover that there are two of you, perhaps more. You might tell me just what it is you want with Kapor. If our purposes are the same, it is possible we could come to an agreement."

"All I want is Pete Castle. You'll tell me where to find him, or I'll start making that noise——"

A body suddenly fell on him, grappling with him, and the girl's voice shrilled in his ear, "I've got him, Mr. Menlo! I've got him, I've got him!"

Parker struggled with her, hampered by the darkness, and over her shouting he heard the pounding of running feet. He flung her off at the last in time to catch a glimpse of the hall door opening, and the back of the fat man. Parker headed that way, but the girl got him around the ankles, dropping him again. He kicked free, made it to the hallway, and heard the clatter of taps on metal stairs. The fat man was already halfway down.

Parker ran back into the apartment, switching on lights as he went. The girl was slowly and groggily getting to her feet. Her robe was disarranged, and beneath it she was fully dressed except for shoes. Parker ran past her to the first window he found, in the kitchen, but it faced the rear of the building. So did the bedroom window. No window faced the courtyard.

Parker came back to the living room. The girl was on her feet but weaving, moving at a snail's pace toward the door. Parker came after her, grabbed her by a shoulder, flung her back into the living room. The chain attachment on the front door was broken but the bolt still worked. Parker shot it, and went back to the living room.

The girl was no more than half-conscious. She'd been battered once too often in the last five minutes. She was standing in the middle of the room, frowning and squinting as though not sure what was going on. Parker took hold of her arm and steered her into the kitchen.

She moved with no complaint, repeating under her breath, "Mr. Menlo? Mr. Menlo?"

Parker sat her on a kitchen chair and slapped her face to get her attention. "Where have they got Pete Castle?"

She frowned up at him, and then rationality came back to her and her face hardened. "You can just go to hell."

Parker shook his head in irritation. He hated this kind of thing, hurting people to make them talk. It was messy and time-consuming and there ought to be a better way. But there wasn't.

He found twine in a kitchen drawer, and tied her to the chair, and gagged her. She fought it, but not successfully. He left her right hand free and put paper and pencil on the table.

"Write the address when you're ready," he said. Then he reached for the kitchen matches.

3

There was a delivery truck out front, a small, dark panel truck with the name KELSON FURNITURE on the sides. It was way after one o'clock, but two men in white coveralls were carrying a rolled-up rug out of the dark bungalow.

This was in Cheverly, off Landover Road. Parker crouched in the back seat of the cab, watching them through the windshield. They were half a block ahead, and on the other side of the street. Just the two men in white coveralls and the rolled-up rug. No fat man.

Parker said, "Douse your lights."

It was a lady cab driver, a small, middle-aged black woman with a wild red hat. She glared over her shoulder at him. "What was that?"

Parker found a twenty and shoved it at her, wishing he had the Pontiac. But Handy had taken that with him. Parker said, "I want you to put out your lights. Then follow that delivery truck over there when it takes off."

She now looked baffled, but just as suspicious. "Is this some kind of gag, mister?"

"No gag."

"We're not supposed to do nothing like that."

"Just take the twenty."

"How I know you ain't a cop? Or a inspector or something?"

"Do I look like a cop?"

"Some cops, yeah."

"All right," Parker said. "We'll do it the hard way." He dropped the twenty in her lap and showed her the Terrier.

The gun she could understand. She doused the lights. "If you got robbery or rapery on your mind, big man," she said, "you just forget it."

"All you do is follow that delivery truck. Get ready now."

"Sure. They got a body in that rug." She thought she was being scornful.

"That's right," Parker answered.

"Huh?"

The delivery truck started away from the curb. Parker said, "Give them a block. Keep the lights off till I say so. You can see by the street lights."

"If I get stopped by a cop——"

"Don't worry about it."

The cab, with its headlights off, trailed the taillights of the delivery truck out to Landover Road, where the truck turned back toward the city. As soon as it had made the turn and was out of sight, Parker said, "Put your lights on now."

The truck barreled along ahead of them, and didn't seem aware it was being followed. There was no circling of blocks, or speeding up and slowing down, to check for a possible tail. The truck just ran on over to Bladensburg road and down into the city. In the Trinidad section it made a right turn. Parker said, "Keep back a block and a half unless they turn."

Ahead, the truck turned in at a driveway. This was a commercial section, shut down tight. Parker said, "Turn at the corner here. Don't go past where they turned in. Now go half a block and stop."

He had another twenty ready when the cab stopped. He tossed it to her. "This one's to forget to call the cops."

She shrugged and shook her head. "I sure hope you got your money's worth," she said. She sounded doubtful.

Parker hurried back around the corner, and down the block toward where the truck had turned in. There was no reason to hurry, except he wanted to know what the hell was going on.

One thing he knew now—Handy was still alive. If

Handy were dead, they'd either have left him there or driven the body further away from town. But he was alive, because they still wanted to know what he was up to, and they'd just moved him so they could question him some more. The fat man had hurried away, then set up this new place to bring Handy and called his friends to get Handy out of there. If Parker had taken three minutes longer getting the answers out of the girl, he'd have missed the move completely.

Whether Handy was alive or dead wasn't the important part. The important part was who these people were and what they wanted. If they were after the mourner too, it would complicate things.

Parker came to the driveway. It was blacktop and narrow, hemmed in on both sides by brick walls. The one on the right was a garage and on the left was a dry cleaner's. From the front, both looked dark and empty.

Parker moved cautiously down the driveway and found the truck at the end, against another wall. The truck doors were open, and the rug was gone.

Both side walls contained metal doors back here. Parker tried the one leading to the garage first, and it was unlocked. He stepped through into darkness, and listened. A dim murmur of voices came from his right and above. He moved that way, skirting first a workbench and then some machinery, and ahead of him saw a dim light. The ceiling was high, and a row of offices was built out from the rear wall, with a wooden staircase going up. The light was spilling down from one of the offices.

Parker moved forward, and then saw a cigarette glow for a second ahead of him. There was somebody sitting at the foot of the stairs.

Parker moved in slowly, staying back under the stairs, which had been built hastily, without risers. Parker held the Terrier by the barrel, reached through between two of the stairs, and put the guard out with the gun butt. He slumped, and slid off the stairs to the floor.

Parker came around and checked him, and he was out. The voices were still murmuring upstairs, without a break. He went up the stairs, the butt of the Terrier in his hand now, and followed the sound of the voices.

There was a walkway outside the offices, with the office wall on one side and a wooden railing on the other. The wall was paneling halfway up, and glass the rest of the way. The light was coming through the glass down toward the other end of the walkway. Parker moved that way, and edged close enough to look in through the glass.

It was just a small office, with pale-green filing cabinets and pale-green partitions. There was a desk, and three chairs, and the usual office furniture, with a big calendar on the back wall showing a trout leaping in a mountain stream.

They had Handy sitting on the floor, his back against the wall under the calendar. He was tied with a lot of white clothesline, but not gagged. There was blood on his face, and his clothes were messed up. The two men in the white coveralls were with him, talking to him. Handy's eyes were shut, but from his posture he was probably awake. Or mostly awake.

Parker couldn't quite hear what they were saying. And he was surprised that the fat man wasn't there with them. But the way the fat man could run, he maybe never got too close to the action. He just stayed back by a telephone somewhere where he could be the general.

Parker turned back and retraced his steps. There was only one door leading into the offices, but each had connecting doors. Parker stepped into one from the walkway and moved along through three other dark offices, opening and closing doors as he went without a sound. Then he was at the partition, standing in front of the inner door to the lighted office, and he could hear now.

". . . but now we've got plenty of time. We've got all night, you know that? That partner of yours is plenty good, catching on so quick, but how's he gonna find you here? Even if he gets anything out of Clara, so what? Off he goes to the house in Cheverly, right? And there's the dead end."

The other one said, "Or maybe you got another partner. How many of you in this thing, Pete? Just the two of you? Or maybe three, four? What do you say, Pete?"

There was silence, and then a thud, and the first voice said, "Take it easy, boy. You want to put him out again?"

"All he has to do is be civil, that's all. Just answer a polite question, that's all."

"I tell you what, we'll go over it for him again. Maybe he's just a slow study."

"Let me take my pliers to his fingers. He'll be a real quick study."

"No, Mr. Menlo said don't mess him up too bad till we find out what the score is."

"You *got* to mess him up. Look at him."

"I figure he'll listen to reason. Isn't that right, Pete? You know we can't do nothing drastic to you, but Pete boy, we got all night. Like, I could just take your hair like this, and just real gentle rap your head on the wall, see? Boom. And then again. Boom. See? The first time ain't so bad. The second time's a little worse. Now the third time. Boom. See? What do you think, Pete? Maybe forty times? We got all night, Pete."

"So boom him and get it over."

"Now wait a minute, let me talk to him. We got interrupted before; let me talk to him. Pete, listen to me. We don't want so much. We ain't greedy, Pete. But just listen. We're getting this operation set up, getting everything ready, and all of a sudden you come into the middle of it. You make a play for Clara, so pretty soon Clara's got it figured what you're after is to get into Kapor's house. You're working on something and we're working on something. Now, all we want to know, Pete—is it the same something? What do you want in Kapor's house, Pete? And how many of you are in it? That's all we want to know. What the hell, Pete, we were here first. I mean, fair's fair, right? Boom, Pete. Boom. Isn't fair fair, Pete? Boom, Pete."

There was no sense listening to any more. They wouldn't be saying more about themselves. There was Clara, and fat man, Menlo, and these two, plus the one downstairs and maybe the one named Angel. Maybe some others too. They were all after something that Kapor had, just as Parker was, and if they, like Parker, were after the mourner, they wouldn't be volunteering that information to Handy. So Parker opened the door and went into the light, gun first. "Freeze."

Nobody ever does. The two of them spun around, shock-eyed, and Handy opened tired eyes and grinned.

"Untie him," Parker said.

The conversational one did it, while the one with the impatient pliers stood there and glowered. Then Parker had the one with the impatient pliers use the same ropes to tie up the conversational one. Parker only wanted to take one with him, and he had decided to take Pliers because in his experience the people who were the most anxious to use torture were also the ones most anxious to talk instead of being tortured themselves. Parker had been forced to ask questions the hard way twice already tonight. It hadn't been bad with Wilcoxen, but with the woman, Clara, it had been very bad, because she was stubborn and Parker was in a hurry.

Handy couldn't walk; his legs were numb from being tied so tight for so long. Parker had Pliers carry Handy, and the three of them left the office and went downstairs and out to the truck. Parker got the ignition key, and then arranged the three of them. There was no partition between the seats and the load area, so Handy lay in back with the Browning .380 automatic Parker had taken away from the conversational one upstairs. From there he could keep an eye on Pliers, in front. Parker drove.

He backed the truck down the driveway to the street, but for a second he didn't know where to go. They hadn't set up any place private yet, because the job wasn't that close to being ready, and the hotel room wouldn't be any good for questioning Pliers. Then Parker remembered the bungalow where they'd been holding Handy. Why not? If any place in the District was guaranteed empty right now, it was that bungalow.

They drove in silence. Parker had his questions, but he wanted the proper atmosphere in which to ask them.

And among them, he was wondering if Harrow had been dumb enough to send two teams after the same ball. Could the fat man and his friends be working for Harrow too? That would be stupid, and dangerous, for everybody.

But Harrow wasn't all that smart. . . .

4

That was two months ago.

For eighteen years, Parker had lived the way he wanted, to a pattern he liked. He was a heavy gun, in on one or two institutional robberies a year—a bank, or a payroll, or an armored car—just often enough to keep the finances fat, and the rest of the time he lived in resort hotels on either coast, with a cover that would satisfy even the income-tax beagles. Then, because of a snafu in one job, he'd got fouled up with the syndicate.* He'd thought he'd got that straightened out—he'd even picked up a new face from a plastic surgeon†—and then, two months before in Miami, a syndicate heavy had tried for him, in his own hotel room, late at night. There'd

*The Hunter
†The Man With the Getaway Face

34

been a girl in the bed with him named Bett Harrow, and when the syndicate heavy died, Bett had taken off with the gun that had helped kill him. The gun could be traced to Parker's cover name, Charles Willis, and that was bad. There was a lot of money and time and preparation tied up in that cover.

Bett had let him know he could have the gun back for a price, but he'd told her she had to wait while he got the syndicate off his back. He'd got in touch with Handy McKay, who'd worked with him on other jobs in the past, and this time the syndicate question was settled for good.‡ Then Parker went back to Miami with Handy to find out what Bett Harrow wanted.

But it wasn't Bett who wanted anything, it was her father. Parker set up the meeting, but left Handy out of it. It might be useful sometime if neither Bett nor her father knew anything about Handy.

The Harrows came to Parker's hotel room at one-thirty in the afternoon. They knocked on the door and when Parker opened it there was Bett, tall and slender and blonde, with vicious good looks, and next to her an older man, short and stocky and gray-haired. He had no tan at all, and the suit he was wearing was too heavy for Miami Beach, so he'd obviously just arrived in town. He was looking uncomfortable and carrying a book under his arm.

‡The Outfit

Bett said, "Can we come in, Chuck?"

He motioned them in. Bett came in first, and her father followed, clutching the book protectively to his chest. It was a large, slender book with a red binding and a picture on the cover of some people in a balloon.

"Dad, this isn't Chuck Willis, but he says he is." Bett was enjoying herself. It was the kind of scene she liked, which was one of the reasons she was living on alimony.

Ralph Harrow was fifty-three, the principal stockholder of the Commauck Aircraft Company. He owned 27 percent of that company's outstanding shares. And he was additionally a large stockholder in three airlines and one insurance company. He was also a member of the board of each of the five companies thus represented in his stock portfolio. He had been born to money, and had multiplied his inheritance. A staff of attorneys saw to it that nothing he did was technically illegal, and they earned their money.

He came into the room showing an unusual apprehension, and responded to his daughter's introductions with a brief, wary nod. "This is my daughter's idea, uh, Willis," he said. "I assure you, coercion is not my normal, uh, my normal policy."

"You haven't coerced me yet," Parker had answered. "First you got to tell me what you want."

Harrow licked his lips and glanced at his daughter,

but she was no help. "To begin with, I'd like you to read a brief article in this magazine."

He said magazine, but it was obviously the book he meant. He held it up, and Parker saw above the picture a title: *Horizon*. And below the picture a date: September, 1958. So it was a magazine that looked like a book.

Harrow opened the magazine-book, muttering to himself, "Page sixty-two." He found the page and extended the open book.

Parker shrugged, not taking the book. "Just tell me what you want."

If it had been just the father he'd been dealing with, he'd squeeze the gun out of him now and throw him away. But the daughter was tougher stuff.

Harrow was looking pained, as though he had indigestion. "It would really be quicker if you'd read this first," he said.

"Go on, Chuck," Bett said. "It's short."

"Just two pages," Harrow added.

Parker said, "You read it, didn't you?"

"Well . . . yes."

"So you can tell me about it."

Parker turned away from the book and went over to sit at the writing desk, turning the chair around to face the room.

Bett was still smiling. She settled luxuriantly on the

bed, catlike, and said, "You might as well do it his way, Dad. I don't think Chuck's a reader."

"Well, but . . ." Harrow was confused and unhappy; this wasn't the way he'd planned things.

Parker had had enough waiting around. "Either get to the point or get out," he said.

Bett said softly, "And go to the police?"

"If you want. I don't give a damn."

Bett laughed, and looked challengingly at her father. Harrow sighed. "Very well. It would have been easier if you'd . . . but very well. This article concerns a group of eighty-two statuettes in a monument at Dijon, in France." He turned the book around so Parker could see. "You see the title? 'The Missing Mourners of Dijon,' by Fernand Auberjonois."

"You want me to steal a statue," Parker said, and Bett laughed again.

"I want you to understand the background." Harrow answered unhappily. "It is important that you understand the background."

"Why?"

"Dear Dad's a romantic," said Bett, with honeyed venom in her smile.

Parker shrugged. He didn't care what the Harrow family thought of each other.

"These statuettes, eighty-two of them, were made for the tomb of John the Fearless and Philip the Good,

Dukes of Burgundy," Harrow said. "John was murdered in 1419, but not before ordering the tomb to be built. Philip was his son, and survived till 1467, when he—"

"The statues," Parker said.

"Yes. The statues. They are sixteen inches high, made of alabaster, and were placed in niches at the base of the two memorials. No two of them are precisely alike, and they all express an attitude of mourning. Every possible variation on mourning, both true and false. There are monks, priests, choirboys—Well. At any rate, they are priceless. And at the time of the French Revolution, many of them were stolen or lost. At the present time, seventy-four of the statuettes are still in Dijon; some were always there, others have been found and returned. Of the remaining eight, one is owned by a private collector in France, two by a private collector in this country, in Ohio, and two are in the Cleveland Museum. The other three mourners are still missing."

He closed the book, but kept his finger in the place. "That's what this article would have told you," he said, "and just as quickly as I have told it to you."

Parker waited, controlling his impatience. None of this was necessary. Harrow wanted a statue stolen, that was the point. If the job looked easy enough, and if the price was right, he might do it. Otherwise, no. All this talk was a waste of time.

But Harrow wasn't finished yet. "Now, for you to understand what I want, and why I want it, you must understand something about me."

"Why?"

Bett said, "Let him, Chuck. It's the only way he knows how to talk."

"Elizabeth, please."

"Get on with it," Parker said.

"Very well. Very well. I, Mr. Willis, am in a very small and special way a collector of medieval statuary. I say in a special way. My collection is small, but if I do say so myself it's excellent. I have at present only eight pieces. This is because my criteria are very high indeed. Each piece must be unique, must be one of a kind, must have no counterpart anywhere in the world. Each must be valued so highly as to be for all practical purposes priceless. And each must have an unusual and fascinating history. My daughter is right, Mr. Willis—I am a romantic. I am fascinated by each piece in my collection, by its creation and by its history. You understand this collection is for my own satisfaction, and not on display."

Bett laughed and said, "Because they were all stolen."

"Not so!" Harrow looked indignantly at his daughter. "Every piece was paid for, and handsomely too."

"But the *fascinating history*," she said, mocking the words. "It always includes a theft or two, doesn't it?"

"That is not at *all* my concern. I myself have—"

"Shut up," said Parker.

They stopped their bickering at once, and looked at him startled. "You want me to steal one of these statues, right? From a museum?"

"Good heavens, no!" Harrow seemed honestly shocked. "In the first place, Willis, all the statuettes mentioned in this article are far too easily traceable. They're *unique*, you see, each a separate and distinct figure. Here, look." He came forward, opening the book again, shoving it under Parker's nose. "Here are pictures of some of them. See? They're all different."

Five of the statuettes were pictured, and Parker looked at them, nodding. Five sad, robed, weeping mournful little people, in five different postures of grief.

"Besides," added Harrow, "besides, none of these has the kind of history I mean, the sort of background I want for the pieces in my collection."

Parker shoved the book away. "What then?"

"Let me tell you." Harrow stood in front of him, suddenly beaming, a glint of excitement in his eyes. "You remember, three of the mourners are still missing? No one knows where they are. But I've located one of them!"

"And that's the one you want me to get?"

"Yes. Yes. Now, the way it—"

"Sit down. You're making me nervous."

"Oh, of course. I'm sorry. Yes, of course."

Harrow retreated, and sat poised on the edge of the chair by the door. Parker's tone had drained some of the excitement out of him, and he went on more normally. "The way I happened to discover this mourner was rather odd. My company, about three years ago, received a small order for cargo planes from Klastrava. Six planes, I believe. You know the country?"

"Never heard of it."

"I'm not surprised. It's one of the smallest of the Slavic nations, north of Czechoslovakia. For all I know it was a part of Poland at one time; most of those countries were. The point is, it's a nation on the other side of the iron curtain, so of course we were somewhat startled to get this order from them. The satellite nations are encouraged to deal with the Soviet Union, you know."

"No news reports," Parker answered. "Just tell the story."

"I'm trying to give you the background."

Harrow was beginning to get petulant. Parker shrugged. Over on the bed, Bett was smiling dreamily at the ceiling.

"It's turned out," said Harrow, plunging on with his story, "that this was one of the de-Stalinization periods and Klastrava was taking advantage of the milder climate to do some of its purchasing in the more competitively priced Western market. Needless to say, we never sold them any more planes, but in the process of that sale I met a gentleman named Kapor, from the Klastravian embassy. What Kapor's normal duties are I don't know, but at the time he was handling the negotiations for the sale of the planes. I met him, as I say, and we discovered we had quite a bit in common—"

This set the daughter to laughing again, and Harrow glared at her. Then, before Parker could say anything to hurry him along, he went quickly back to his story. "At any rate, he was a house guest in my home two or three times, and once or twice when I was in Washington he invited me to stay with him. And it turned out that he too has a small collection of statuary, but of no particular value. However, his collection did include an alabaster figure of a weeping monk, approximately sixteen inches high."

Harrow smiled broadly, and rubbed his hands together. "I suspected what it must be at once, and learned that Kapor had no idea that it was anything more than an interesting piece of early-fifteenth-century statuary. I also discovered where he'd bought it. I made discreet inquiries, and gradually pieced together this little monk's history, working backward, or course, to its original home in Dijon."

"I don't need all that," Parker interrupted. Harrow seemed ready to play the romantic all week.

"Let him go, Chuck," Bett said. "He's just bubbling over to tell you all about it."

"The information cost me quite a bit," Harrow added defensively. "At one point, I even had to hire a French private investigator to check on a piece of information for me."

Parker shrugged.

"At any rate," said Harrow, hurrying now in an attempt to keep Parker from interrupting, "this particular statue was one of those looted in 1795, when revolutionaries desecrated the tomb. Who stole it I have no idea, but it did turn up in Quebec as a result of the Rebellion of 1837. Economic reprisals against one Jacques Rommelle, a follower of Louis Joseph Papineau, forced him to sell most of his possessions and move to Nova Scotia. Among the household goods sold was this small alabaster statuette. Rommelle had a knack for aligning himself with the wrong people. He'd left France for Canada in 1795, primarily because he was one of the strongest supporters of Robespierre. It's possible Rommelle personally stole the statue from Dijon, but unlikely, because he'd lived most of his life in Rennes, which is in Brittany, on the other side of France. I think it more likely that the original looter was killed during the Terror, and that Rommelle was the second owner."

He paused, cleared his throat, rubbed his hands together briskly, and smiled. "There's such a fascination in this," he said. "At any rate, Rommelle sold the statue in 1838, to a dealer named Smythe. Smythe didn't manage to resell it, and when he died in 1852, his business was inherited by a grandson who had emigrated to the United States and was at the time living in Atlanta. The grandson sold most of what he'd inherited but he did hold on to a few items he liked, among them the statue of the weeping monk, but it was stolen by a Captain Goodebloode, a Union cavalry officer in 1864, when General Sherman's army captured the city. Captain Goodebloode brought the statue to Boston, where it remained in the family till 1932, when the Goodebloode finances were depleted by the depression, and the contents of the ancestral house were sold at auction. A Miss Cannel purchased the statue in Boston and brought it home to Wittburg, a small town in upstate New York, where, for some reason best known to herself, she was attempting to set up a museum. If she'd had the wit to hire a professional curator, of course, the game would have been up right then, but this was a one-woman museum, and Miss Cannel apparently had more money than sense. At any rate, the statue went into the museum and when Miss Cannel died in 1953, the entire contents of the museum were sold to various dealers. One of them, in 1955, sold the statuette to Lepas Kapor. Finis."

Harrow looked back and forth from Parker to his daughter, beaming and happy. "A fascinating history," he said, dwelling on the words, "a fascinating history. A bloody revolution, a somewhat less bloody rebellion, a civil war, an economic crash—all have touched this small statue and influenced its destiny. It has traveled from France to Canada to Atlanta to Boston and to a provincial upstate New York town. Now it is in Washington. It has been stolen at least twice, and possibly three times, and now it is to be stolen again. A fascinating, fascinating history."

"Yeah," said Parker. He lit a cigarette and threw the match toward an ashtray. "The point is, you want me to get it for you."

"Exactly. I will give you, of course, full particulars—"

"What's in it for me?"

"What? Oh." Harrow looked puzzled for a second, but now he smiled radiantly. "Of course, you expect to be paid. You'll get the gun, for one thing, and a certain sum of money."

"What sum?"

Harrow sucked on his cheek, studying Parker's face. Finally, he said, "Five thousand dollars. In cash."

"No."

Harrow raised his eyebrows. "No? Mr. Willis, I consider the gun to be the major item of payment. Any cash would be in the nature of a bonus."

"Fifty thousand," Parker said.

"Good God! You aren't serious?"

Parker shrugged, and waited.

"Mr. Willis, I could *buy* the statuette for little more than that. I've told you, the present owner has no idea—"

"You can't buy it at all," Parker said, "or you would."

"Well." Harrow pursed his lips, glanced with an aggrieved look at his daughter, sucked on his cheek again, drummed his fingers on the book in his lap. "I'll go to ten thousand, Mr. Willis. Absolutely my top offer. Believe me, the statuette is worth no more than that to me."

"I'm not bargaining," Parker replied. "Fifty thousand or get out."

"And shall we go to the police, Mr. Willis? Shall we go to the police?"

Parker got to his feet, went over to the closet, and took out a suitcase. He opened it on the bed and turned to the dresser.

Harrow said, "Very well. Twenty-five. Half now, and the balance when you get the statuette."

Parker opened the top dresser drawer and began transferring shirts to the suitcase.

Harrow watched him a minute longer, and Bett watched them both. The father was frowning, the daughter smiling.

"Thirty-five."

Parker started on the second drawer.

"Damn it, man, we have the gun!"

Bett said, "Give up, Dad, he won't change his mind."

"Ridiculous," Harrow said. "Absurd. We have him over a barrel." He frowned in petulance at Parker. "All right. All right, stop that asinine packing, you're not fooling anyone."

Parker started on the third drawer.

"I said you could stop packing. Fifty thousand. Agreed."

Parker paused. "In advance," he said. "The fifty thousand now, the gun after I get the statue."

"Half now."

"I told you I don't bargain."

Harrow shook his head angrily. "All right. The money now, the gun afterward."

Parker left the suitcase and went back to the chair by the writing table. "All right," he said. "Come over here. Bring your chair. I want this Kapor's address. You've been in his house, I want as detailed a ground plan as you can give me. I want to know what room the statue is kept in, and if he's got more than one there I want a detailed description of the one I'm after. I want to know how many people are in the household, and what you know about the habits of each of them."

It took a while. Harrow wasn't an observant man, and his memory had to be prodded every step of the way. It took half an hour to get even an incomplete ground plan, with half the interior still terra incognita. As for the people living there, there was Lepas Kapor himself, and some servants. Harrow didn't know how many, or if any of them lived in. Kapor was unmarried, but Harrow thought that occasionally a woman stayed in the house overnight.

When Parker finally had everything from Harrow he was likely to get, Harrow was put on the send for the fifty thousand. Bett wanted to stick around for bed games, but Parker wasn't in the mood. He was never in the mood before a job, always in the mood right after.

After they'd gone, Parker went down to the bar and got Handy. Together they went over the ground plan and the sketchy information they had, and the next day, after Harrow had turned over the attaché case full of cash and Parker had checked it in the hotel safe, they took off for Washington.

Kapor lived in a sprawling colonial brick house with white trim off Garfield, four blocks from the Klastrava embassy. A five-foot hedge surrounded the property. The two-car garage was behind the house, like an afterthought. A gravel driveway led in from the street through a break in the hedge, made a left turn at the front door, and then continued on around to the garage.

Parker and Handy took turns three days and nights

watching the house, and by then they'd filled in some of the holes in Harrow's information.

There were five servants, but only one slept in. The chauffeur did not sleep in, nor did the gardener-handyman, the cook, or the maid. The butler-valet-bodyguard did sleep in. His room was on the second floor front, right corner. Kapor's room was in the back somewhere.

The house was not in an isolated neighborhood. Also, because it held an important man attached to the embassy of a country generally considered unfriendly to the United States, it was given unusually complete police surveillance. Prowl cars passed at frequent and erratic intervals day and night. There was also the possibility that the FBI or some other government agency was watching the house. It didn't look like an easy house to break into undisturbed.

Handy suggested the old tried-and-true maid ploy. Meet the maid, gain her confidence, and eventually get a chance to make an impression of the keys in her purse. With the keys, a bold frontal attack—walk straight up to the door at a relatively early hour of the night, unlock it, and go on in.

Because it was Handy's idea, and because he had a more pleasant personality, he went after the maid. He was in his early forties, tall and strong-faced, like a lean Vermont sheriff. The maid, Clara Stoper, was about thirty and good-looking in a harsh sort of way. She spent her Monday and Thursday nights in a bar on Wisconsin Avenue, and it was there that Handy made the meet. That was a week ago, and tonight he'd been going to her apartment, where he was sure he would be able to get his hands on the keys. She'd already given him a ten-thirty deadline, so he'd told Parker he'd be back by eleven. But eleven o'clock had passed and he hadn't shown up, and then the two amateur bums had come up the fire escape and gradually all hell had broken loose. So if Harrow had sent this second group after that goddamn statue, Harrow was in trouble.

Two

1

Parker left the truck a block from the bungalow, and said to Handy, "Can you keep him tight?"

"No trouble." Handy was sitting up now, and looked in better shape. He held the .380 loosely in his lap, his eye on Pliers. "He won't go anywhere."

"You guys are wasting your time," Pliers said. He looked surly and belligerent, but not very tough.

Parker got out of the truck and walked to the bungalow. It was still dark. All the houses around here were dark, and even the street lights seemed dimmed, because of the trees along the sidewalks, which cut off some of the light. Parker was the only thing moving on either sidewalk and there were no cars in sight.

There was a driveway next to the bungalow, but no garage. The driveway was just a double dirt track. Parker used it to go around to the rear. The kitchen door was locked, but it jimmied quickly and quietly. Parker stepped inside.

The house had four rooms. Living room, kitchen, two bedrooms, and a bath. Without turning on any lights, Parker moved through them and found them all empty. He went out the front door and walked back to the truck. He started it and drove to the bungalow, up the driveway, and around to the back yard. "Hold him a minute more," he said to Handy, and got out of the truck again. He went into the house and turned on the kitchen light. Enough light spilled out the rear window so he could switch off the truck lights.

Handy could walk now, but stiffly. The three of them went into the bungalow, and while Handy covered Pliers with the .380, Parker frisked him. Back at the garage he'd only gone over him for hardware; now he was emptying everything out of the man's pockets. Under the white coverall Pliers was wearing brown slacks and a green flannel shirt.

His goods gradually stacked up on the kitchen table. A wallet, a pack of Marlboros in the box, a Zippo lighter with some sort of Army insignia on one side, a pair of pliers with electrician's tape on the handles, a screwdriver, a switchblade knife, a small flat black address book, an inhaler, and a tin packet of aspirin. The wallet contained thirty-three dollars, two pictures of a girl in a bathing suit, a picture of Pliers himself in a bathing suit, and a lot of cards—Army discharge, driver's license, chauffeur's license, membership card in a Teamsters local, membership card in a gym—all made out to Walter Ambridge of Baltimore.

Finished with the wallet, Parker dropped it on the table. "All right, Wally, sit down."

"I'm called Walter." Pliers said it truculently, and he didn't sit down.

Parker hit him just above the belt. The wind whooshed out of him and he sagged. Parker pushed his shoulder slightly, to guide him, and he sat down. Handy was leaning against the refrigerator, still casually holding the .380.

Parker sat down in the other kitchen chair and rested his hands on the table. "All right, Wally," he said. "Who's Menlo?"

"Up yours."

Parker shook his head and picked up the pliers. He extended them toward Handy. "Take off his left thumbnail."

Ambridge came out of the chair roaring. They had to hit him hard enough to stun him before they could get him to sit down again. Parker waited until comprehension came back into Ambridge's eyes, and then he said, "Do we have to tie you up in the chair, Wally? Do we have to hurt you? I've been doing nothing but ask ques-

57

tions all night long. I don't like that. You answer in a hurry, Wally."

Ambridge glared harder than ever, to cover the fact he was frightened. He said, "You birds are in trouble, you know that? You didn't get cleared or nothing."

"Cleared? What the hell are you talking about?"

"With the Outfit, Goddamn it. You don't make any play around here without you clear it with the Outfit first. What the hell are you, amateurs?"

"Well, I'll be damned," said Parker. He knew what Ambridge was talking about, but he was surprised. He knew the Outfit—it was what the syndicate was calling itself that year—didn't like action in its territories without its approval, and he knew there were people in his line of work who never took on a job without letting the Outfit know about it first. But Parker himself would never work on a job that had been tipped to the Outfit, and he didn't know why anybody else did. The Outfit always wanted a piece, 5 or 10 per cent, for giving its permission, and permission was all it ever gave. Whatever local fix the Outfit had was no good for the transients if their deal went sour.

"So Menlo cleared this job with the Outfit. Which are you with, Menlo or the syndicate?"

"Outfit. I'm with the Outfit, on loan. Menlo didn't have no sidemen of his own."

Handy said, "He still doesn't have any worth a damn.

These guys had me for three hours and didn't get me to say one word."

"Nobody knew you had a partner." Ambridge sounded resentful, as though Handy hadn't played fair.

"Now we get to the question again," Parker said. He picked up the pliers and held them loosely in both hands. "Who is Menlo, and what's he after?"

"It don't make no difference," Ambridge said. "I can tell you and it don't make no difference at all. You guys have had it anyway. You ought to know better. You can't buck the Outfit."

Handy laughed then, because Parker had bucked the Outfit twice in the last year and hadn't done too badly either time. And when it came to operating without Outfit permission, Parker and Handy and most of the people they knew had been doing it for years.

Ambridge looked at Handy the way a patriot looks at somebody who forgets to take off his hat when the flag goes by. "You'll get yours," he said.

"Quit stalling," Parker replied.

Ambridge shrugged. "I'll tell you. It don't make no difference. This guy Menlo came around—" He looked suddenly startled, and stared at their faces. "Wait a minute," he said. "Are you guys Commies?"

Handy laughed again. "Not us, bo. We're capitalists from way back."

"Who is Menlo?" Parker was getting tired asking the same question and he was holding the pliers tighter now.

"Menlo's a defector." Ambridge said it the way a man says a good word he just recently learned. "He's from one of the Commie countries. They sent him over here to do a job for them, but he's copping out. He says this Kapor's heavy, and it's all got to be in the house, so we're taking it away from him."

"How heavy?"

"Maybe a hundred G."

Handy whistled low, but Parker said, "Crap. In cash? Where'd he get all that?"

"Don't ask me. This Menlo made a contract and talked to Mc—talked to the boss here, and the boss figured it's worth the chance for a fifty-fifty split. Menlo's got the goods, the Outfit's got the manpower. It don't make no difference, what I tell you; you can't buck the Outfit."

Maybe if he said it often enough, about his talking not making a difference, he'd start to believe it himself. Better than believing he'd been scared into it with nothing but threats.

Which meant he was probably telling the truth. The fat man, Menlo, had convinced the Outfit that Kapor's house was full of money. But where was an embassy aide from a small and unfriendly country likely to pick up a hundred thousand dollars? Either Menlo was pulling a fast one, giving the Outfit a tale in return for some muscle, or there was more to this Kapor than Harrow knew about.

The next one to see was Menlo. Parker asked, "Where's Menlo now?"

Ambridge shook his head. "I don't know. He's got the wind up, on account of you guys. He was going to stick at Clara's place, but he won't be there now."

"Don't get cute, Wally. You were supposed to get in touch with him after Handy talked. Where?"

"He didn't say. That's the straight goods, I swear to God. He just called us here and said take that guy to the garage, that he'd get in touch with us later."

Handy shifted his position against the refrigerator. "He'll be going deep now. We left the other two breathing back there."

"That's all right. Wally knows where he'd go."

"How the hell would I know?"

"He'll go where the rest of you can find him. He wants his muscle close to him. Where is it, Wally?"

"I don't know. That's the straight—"

Parker lifted the pliers again. "First we tie you," he said. "Then we take your fingernails off. Then we take your teeth out."

"What you want from me? I don't know where he is." Ambridge was sweating now, his forehead slick under the fluorescent light. "I been telling you what you want, what the hell do you think?"

"I think you're afraid of somebody finding out you let us know where to find Menlo. I think you're afraid of these pliers too. Which you afraid of most, Wally?"

"I don't *know* where he is!"

Parker turned his head to Handy. "Take a look in the drawers. People usually keep twine around. We'll have to tie him down this time."

"Wait—wait a second. Wait now, just wait a second." Ambridge was a big man, but he was fluttering now like a little man. "I mean, maybe I—"

"Don't make up any addresses, Wally. You'll give us the address and we'll keep you on ice here till we check it out, and if Menlo isn't there we'll come back and talk to you again."

"I can't be *sure* he's there! For Christ's sake, maybe he—"

"Take a chance."

"Well . . ." Ambridge wiped his palm across his forehead, and it came away wet. He looked at his wet hand with a sort of dull surprise. "I'm a coward. I'm nothing but a coward."

Handy took pity on him. "The information didn't come from you. It'll never get back to your boss."

"What good am I?" Ambridge asked himself.

It was dangerous. They'd had to push him, but there was always the chance with somebody like Ambridge, a bluffer, that you'd push him too hard and he'd be forced to look at himself and see the truth. You take a coward, and you force him to look at himself and see that he *is* a coward, he's liable all of a sudden to not give a damn anymore, to get fatalistic and despairing. If he gets to that point, all of a sudden nothing will work on him anymore, no threats no punishment. He'll just sit there and take it, thinking he deserves it anyway, thinking he's dead anyway so what difference does it make?

Ambridge was on the edge of that, and Parker could see it. A few more seconds, and Ambridge would be unreachable. Parker reached out and slapped him across the face, open-handed, a contemptuous slap, and said with scorn, "Hurry it up, punk. You're wasting my time."

It was enough. The slap didn't hurt, but it stung. So did the words, and the tone behind them. It was enough to snap Ambridge out of his introspection. He threw up the old defenses again, came back with the bluff as strong as ever. He glared at Parker and started up out of the chair. Parker and Handy had to work a little to get him to sit down again, then Parker said, "You started to give us the address. Now give."

It was the old Ambridge who answered. "You think it makes any difference? You think you can just walk in and take him? You think he's alone? You go after him and you're both dead."

"Let us worry about that."

"You'll worry about it. There's a house in Bethesda, on

Bradley Boulevard. Menlo's got the borrow of it from the Outfit till the job's done. We were supposed to call him there after we found out what your partner was up to. Go on out there, get your heads blown off. I only wish I could be there to watch."

They had him write the address down, and then they tied him and left him in a closet. They never did remember to go back.

2

On that block was a row of two-family houses, built before the war. The one they wanted was on the corner. What the Outfit used it for normally they didn't know, but right now Menlo was living in the downstairs flat, and the upstairs flat, according to Ambridge, was empty.

They'd stopped off on the way to get rid of the truck and pick up their own car, where Handy had left it earlier in the evening. The car was a Pontiac, two years old. It was hot, but not on the East coast, and the papers on it were a good imitation of the real thing.

Handy was driving, and a block from the address he took his foot off the accelerator. The car slowed. There were taillights ahead. A car was double-parked in front of the house they wanted, lights on and motor running.

"Go on past," Parker said. "Then around the block."

Parker looked the car over on the way by. It was a

black Continental. The man at the wheel wore a chauffeur's cap and was reading the *Star*. The car carried New York plates, and they started DPL. Diplomat. Beyond the car was the house, the ground floor all lit up, the upper story dark.

It was almost three o'clock in the morning. The Continental out front with diplomat plates at three in the morning wasn't a good sign. Parker said, "Hurry around the block. Park on the cross street."

"I'm ahead of you," Handy answer. "What did that guy say Menlo was? A defector?"

"Yeah."

They left the Pontiac half a block from Bradley, on the side street that flanked the house they wanted. This way they could get to the back door without tipping the chauffeur in the Continental.

There was a white picket fence separating the back yard from the sidewalk, with a white picket gate. The gate opened with no trouble and no squeaking, and they went across the slate walk to the stoop and up onto the back porch. The kitchen door stood wide open, and the storm door was closed but not locked. The kitchen was empty, but casting bright, wide swatches of light out through the window and doorway.

Handy's touch with doors was the lightest. The storm door never made a sound. They stood on linoleum with a black-and-white diamond design, and listened. The re-

frigerator hummed, and on a different note the circular
fluorescent light in the ceiling also hummed. The rest of
the house was silent. Bright and silent.

An open door to the right led to a bedroom, but with
no bed in it. The ceiling light was on—two seventy-five-
watt-bulbs unshielded—and in the glare the bedroom
was a bleak cubicle full of unmarked cardboard cartons,
stacked along the walls. The venetian blinds were down
across both windows.

A hall led off the kitchen. Midway along it was a brace
of doorways facing each other. The one on the left opened
onto the bathroom, gleaming with white tile and white
porcelain and white enamel, with a brightly burning
white fluorescent tube over the mirror above the sink.
The doorway on the right led to another bedroom, this
one containing a bed. This too was garishly lit, and
looked like a whore's crib. A double bed dominated the
room, covered by a cheap tan spread, and without pillows. A scarred dresser stood on the opposite wall, and
the bed was flanked on one side by a black kitchen chair
and on the other by a small wooden table containing
nothing but a chipped ashtray.

At the end of the hall was a dining room, lit by a rococo ceiling fixture of rose-tinted glass. The cream-and-
tan wallpaper was a faded pattern of ivy and Grecian
columns. Centered beneath the light was a poker table,
round and covered with green felt, with eight wells

around the outer edge for the players' money and drinks. Eight chairs crouched around the table, on a faded Oriental rug. There was no other furniture in the room.

The third bedroom, off the dining room, was apparently the one Menlo was using, for there was clothing draped on the chair, hairbrush and cufflinks and other things on the dresser, and an expensive-looking alarm clock on the night table.

A wide archway led from dining room to living room, which was furnished in an old-fashioned way, in dark colors and heavy overstuffed furniture.

Every light in the house was on, and the Continental still waited out front, though all the rooms were empty.

Handy caught Parker's eye, and pointed at the floor. Parker nodded. Still moving cautiously and silently, they went back to the kitchen. The first door they tried opened onto the pantry, but the second showed cellar stairs angling away to the left. Light came up from below, and the sound of someone talking, softly and conversationally. And there was another sound, a steady scraping and chuffing, slow and rhythmic.

Handy already had the .380 out. Parker unlimbered the Terrier, and led the way down. The stairs angled sharply to the left, and then went straight down the rest of the way, toward the rear wall of the house, so that most of the basement was behind Parker as he came down. He came halfway, then crouching on the stairs, ducked his head under the banister and looked back at the rest of the cellar.

Three hundred-watt bulbs were spaced along under the I-beam that ran down the middle of the ceiling. All were unshielded, and all were lit, throwing the dirt-floored cellar in stark, almost shadowless, relief. An old coal furnace hulked on one side, with its squat oil converter crouched in front of it. Several barrels of trash were standing alongside two deep metal sinks.

Down at the other end, the fat man was digging his own grave, while three men surrounding him, watching. Two of the three stood silently, pistols in their hands. The third had brought a kitchen chair down with him— or had someone bring it down for him—and was sitting comfortably on it, his back to Parker. He seemed nattily dressed, and he was the one doing the talking, a steady soft flow of easy conversation, a monologue almost, in a language Parker didn't recognize. It was guttural, but not in a Germanic way.

Handy had seen too. He grinned and motioned for them to go back upstairs, but Parker shook his head. Handy looked puzzled and leaned forward to whisper. "They're getting rid of the competition. Why not let them?"

Parker whispered back, "If there's more than a statue in Kapor's house, I want to know what it is and where to find it. The fat man knows."

Handy shrugged. "I'll take the one on the left."

They leaned out on different sides of the staircase, showing only their heads and gun hands. The shots roared out in that confined space like cauvette blowing up.

Before the two gunmen had hit the ground, the talkative one was out his chair, spinning around, a flat white automatic coming out from under his coat. Parker and Handy both fired again, and the automatic sailed into the air as he toppled backward into the grave Menlo had only half dug.

Menlo, again moving faster than any fat man should, threw himself off to the side and rolled over against the side wall. But when there weren't any more shots, he got to his feet cautiously. His white shirt was a sweaty, dirty mess, his black trousers rumpled and baggy. He was barefoot, and his face and hands were also covered with dirt. He stood peering toward the stairs until Parker and Handy moved toward him, and then suddenly he smiled. "Ah!" he said. "How glad I am I did not pause to kill you at poor Clara's."

"Let's go," Parker said.

"So soon? But I have not yet expressed my appreciation. You have saved my life!"

"We'll talk later, what do you say?" Handy added.

Menlo looked around at the three scattered bodies.

"There is much in what you say," he said. "Have you dealt with the chauffeur?"

"We won't have to. Come on."

"Most certainly."

Parker went first, and then Menlo, with Handy last. They filed upstairs to the kitchen, and as Parker reached for the storm door, Menlo said, "Please! Would you take me away in such a condition?"

"You can wash up later," Handy said.

"But my shoes! My coat! My personal possessions!"

"Come on," said Parker.

"Let him get his stuff," Handy said. "What the hell?"

"You watch him, then."

"Sure."

Parker waited in the kitchen. They were gone two minutes by the kitchen clock, and when they came back Menlo was wearing shoes and a topcoat. The topcoat was too tight for him, making him look like somebody on a Russian reviewing stand. He was carrying a black attaché case covered with good leather.

Parker pointed at it. "What's in there?"

"I checked it," Handy said. "Just clothes and a flask."

"And a toothbrush," Menlo added. His face was still dirty, and when he smiled he looked like the fat boy in a silent movie comedy. "I am most proud of my teeth."

"Let's go."

They went out the back way and down the block to

their car. Parker got behind the wheel, and Handy and Menlo sat in back. "Where do we go from here?" Handy asked.

"Back to the hotel."

"What if they come looking there again?"

Parker shook his head. "The only ones who looked were Menlo's people. And Menlo doesn't have people any more. Do you, Menlo?"

Menlo smiled again, with mock wistfulness, and spread dirty hands. "Only you," he replied. "My two newly found friends."

Parker started the car. When they crossed the intersection, the Continental was still waiting out front—the lights on, the motor running, the chauffeur deeply immersed in the *Star*.

3

Bett Harrow stretched lazily and got up off the bed. "It's about time you came home. Three-thirty in the morning. Who are these nice people? And what happened to that man's face?"

Parker said, "Get the hell out of here."

"Daddy sent me for a progress report, sweetie. All that money spent and not one word from you. He got nervous. Fifty thousand dollars is fifty thousand dollars."

"An axiom, my dear," said Menlo, smiling and advancing, his hand extended. "You have stated what is possibly the ultimate truth. I am Auguste Menlo, yours to command." She gave him her hand, smiling, and he bent low over it, kissing it.

"Sit down, fat man, and shut your face," Parker said. "Bett, tell your father I'll see him when I'm done. Now get out of here."

Menlo shrugged prettily, smiling his quixotic smile. He had a way of moving as though he were making fun of his weight. "I must obey," he said to Bett. "Your friend has just saved my life. The least I owe him is obedience."

He sat down on the chair with the broken arm, crossed his ankles, and discovered the damage. "I had expected better from American hotels," he said, frowning.

Bett strolled casually toward the door, detouring slightly to cross close to Parker. "I know you must have important things to discuss," she said. "We can talk later." She moistened her lips, and her eyes gleamed. "My room is just down the hall. Five-twelve. It was the closest I could get to you, Parker. Don't take too long. You never know what I might do if you upset me." She went on out.

Menlo kissed his fingertips in appreciation, and made a small salute toward the closed door. "A beautiful creature," he said. "A magnificent woman."

Parker lit a cigarette and pulled a chair over close to Menlo. "That isn't what we'll talk about."

"No, of course. I quite understand."

"That's good."

"Might I have a cigarette?"

Handy came over and gave him one, and a light to go with it. Menlo made a production out of how much he liked the cigarette, blowing smoke at the ceiling. "Ah! One of the few things for which America will be remembered. If you have ever smoked European cigarettes, you must know what I mean."

Handy was still standing next to Menlo. He leaned down now, and said, "Listen to me, friend. My partner's a very impatient man. Besides, he's sore about her being here. You keep horsing around, he'll take it out on you."

"I am most sorry." Menlo sat forward at once, uncrossing his ankles, sitting at attention, an expression of concern on his face. "It is my way, Mr.—"

"Parker."

"Parker. Yes. It is only my way, Mr. Parker. I mean no offense by it, I assure you. I will come most directly to the point."

"That's good," Parker said.

Menlo smiled. "Yes, that's good. And the point, Mr. Parker, is: Why did you save my life?" He looked brightly from Parker to Handy, and back again. "Eh? Isn't that interesting? Why did you save my life?"

Handy said, "Go a little faster, huh? Quit repeating yourself."

"Yes, of course. But the question, you see, the question has many aspects. It is prismatic. With such a question, one can see around corners. With such a question, one can receive many other answers. For example—I am trying to hurry, I most honestly am—for instance, when I became aware of you, Mr. Castle—Mr. Castle?"

Handy shrugged. "It'll do."

"Of course. When I became aware of you, I said to myself, is this coincidence? Could you possibly be interested in the same goal toward which *I* was directing myself? Thus I had you summoned for questioning, and thus the additional events which have transpired. But now you and Mr. Parker have saved my life, and all at once the answer is clear. Your goal is *not* the same as mine. Or at least it was not, until tonight. Did you save my life for humanitarian reasons? Hardly. There could be only one other reason. To keep me alive until such time as you would know what I already know. Which means that for all your threatening statements and glowering expressions, you cannot risk having me dead."

"Nobody said anything about having you dead," Parker said.

"I must explain," said Menlo. He smiled again, pleased with himself. "Becuase of my occupation these past fifteen years, I have been equipped for instant self-annihilation. One of my teeth is false; it contains a capsule. Should I bite down hard in a certain way—a rather awkward way, to avoid doing so unintentionally—I would break that capsule. Should that happen, my breath would smell pleasingly of almonds, and I would very soon be dead. That is what Spannick was talking to me about tonight, in the cellar, while I was digging my own grave. He was suggesting to me that I save the state the price of a bullet. But where there is life, as your proverb so succinctly puts it, there is hope. In this case, well-founded hope." He smiled some more. His teeth gleamed.

"If we try to hurry you," Parker said, "you'll kill yourself. Is that it?"

"If you try to hurry me in too physical and violent a fashion, yes. I have an extremely low pain threshold. The price of high intelligence and self-indulgence. Ah, this is really a most excellent cigarette." Menlo leaned back again in the chair, and recrossed his ankles. "I will now tell you the facts. In my own way. And at my own rate of speed. If you find yourself becoming too impatient, Mr. Parker, you might perhaps spend your time instead with that charming lady who was earlier here. Your associate could rapidly and succinctly tell you the highlights later."

Parker shook his head, got to his feet, and went over to lie down on the bed. The world was full of people who never did anything but talk. "Any time you feel like it," he said.

"You are most gracious." Menlo took a deep breath, thought for a second to organize his thoughts, and began talking. "Our mutual target, Lepas Kapor, has for the past eight years been one of our most important liaison agents with our espionage network in this country. As an aide at the embassy of such a small and insignificant nation as Klastrava, he was far less likely to come under the scrutiny and suspicion of American counterintelligence. His duties have been twofold. First, he transmits information from the network to the Soviet Union. Second, he furnishes funds to pay for the network's continued existence, to cover the cost of bribes and payoffs and so on. Just recently, we discovered that Kapor has systematically been cheating us ever since getting this assignment. His method is simplicity itself. Say a particular document cost one thousand dollars to obtain. In his report he would state that it cost fifteen hundred dollars, and the overage he would merely transfer to his own pockets. How much he has accrued for himself in this way we can only guess, but the estimate is that he has stolen more than ten thousand dollars a year for eight years. Perhaps in all, one hundred thousand dollars."

Menlo looked smilingly at Handy, and then at Parker. "Interesting? Yes. Of course it is. And even more interesting is the question, what has he done with this money? Has he spent it? Hardly. An obscure aide in an obscure embassy? If he were to live beyond his means, it would be noticed at once. Shall he bank it? Considering the political orientation of Klastrava and the passion for voluminous records among bankers, this too seems hardly the answer. Nor can he invest it. He can, in fact, do nothing with it so long as he remains in his present post. He can only secrete it, somewhere in his own house, against the day when he will suddenly disappear. He intends to retire, of course, in some out-of-the-way place. South America perhaps, or Mexico. Or it is entirely possible that he will remain in the United States, in Vermont or Oregon or Nebraska. A man with a hundred thousand dollars can arrange to disappear almost anywhere."

Handy interrupted. "How do you know for sure it's in cash, and that it's in his house? Maybe he's got it buried out in the country someplace."

"Ah, wait. I'm coming to that. Please be patient."

Parker sat up and lit a fresh cigarette. For half of a hundred thousand dollars, he could make himself be patient.

"Now comes my own entry into the story," Menlo continued. "I am, in a way, a policeman. Not precisely the sort you two have undoubtedly encountered at one time or another in your careers. My occupation has no true counterpart in your country, except unofficially, among the members of some stern-jawed American society or the more belligerent American Legion posts. My duties are, in a way, religious, with an analogy drawn from the Spanish Inquisition. I am an inquisitor, a seeker of heretics, of those whose heresies are against the state. It was felt that a man of my background and unquestioned loyalty would be best suited to the task of punishing Lepas Kapor and of regaining the embezzled funds. It was decided not to trust this delicate task to our espionage organization; news of this impending doom might perhaps somehow reach the ears of our suspect. And so, for the first time in my life, I left my native land—armed with a valid passport and a map to a cache containing one hundred thousand American dollars!"

Menlo threw his head back and laughed, a full booming laugh of delight. "It was *wonderful!* The opportunity of a lifetime!" Then his laughter subsided and he leaned forward confidentially. "Do you know what my pension would be, were I to live to the retirement age of sixty-seven? In American money, it would be—let me see— approximately five hundred and thirty dollars a year. And yet they expected me to find this hidden cache of *one hundred thousand dollars* in American money, and *bring it back!*"

He shook his head. "I am not a fool. My dear friends, you will discover that about me. I am most shockingly overweight, and far too self-indulgent, but you will find that I am not a fool."

"So you figured to take the money and run?" Handy asked.

"Would you not? Of course. Let me tell you what I did. Laboriously, I managed to contact members of the American underworld. I was then introduced to an organization which calls itself the Outfit. It claims to exert total control over crime within the areas of its control but having met you two, it is only natural that I begin

to doubt this claim. Nevertheless, I met with these people, and I discussed the situation with them. It was
agreed that they would furnish me assistants and protection from local law-enforcement agencies, and—what do
they call that? Protection from local law-enforcement
agencies."

"The fix," Handy said.

"Yes! The fix is in. That's what it was. I was delighted
with the phrase. The French are so pleased with their
criminal argot, but I assure you the Americans in this re-
gard have nothing to be ashamed of. The fix is in."

"Get on with it," Parker said.

"You have no interest in your native idiom? A pity. As
I was saying, I met with these people, and we came to a
financial agreement which of course I had no intention of
honoring. And thus the operation was set in motion. We
moved most cautiously, I assure you, not wanting to
flush our bird prematurely from the nest. What had led
to the discovery of Kapor's ingeniousness in the first
place were some small slight indications that he might
be planning to make a sudden move, to defect or disappear. There is a large amount of money due to pass
through his hands very shortly, and we were convinced
he was waiting only for its arrival before making his own
departure. Unavoidable delays have kept that money
from reaching him thus far, so he still rests upon his
perch, awaiting my pleasure."

"How close were you?" Parker asked.

"We had intended to enter the house this coming Friday. Kapor will be at an official dinner most of the evening, and we intended to be in the house already upon his return."

Menlo shifted his bulk in the chair and looked with an innocent smile at Parker. "This plan could still be effected," he went on. "Without the minions of the Outfit, of course. I doubt that they were ever really happy with the operation. They disliked the thought of being connected even indirectly with international politics, but the harvest was too tempting to be missed. Now, because of all the trouble you two caused tonight, they have abandoned the plan completely. Spannick informed me of this with great pleasure tonight, while watching me dig. The Outfit recalled those who had helped me, and recouped its losses by selling to Spannick the information that I had intended in my own turn to stead the money. So the Outfit is no longer concerned with Kapor. Spannick is dead, and if I know that egotistical idiot, he would not have made any report on me until he had already done me in. He always preferred telling his superiors about a problem only after he had already solved it. Which means that Kapor has been left to us."

Parker studied the fat man's face. "Us?"

"But of course. You have business of your own with Kapor, though I confess I cannot imagine what it is. In addition, you would no doubt like to share in that hundred thousand dollars. I need assistance, which you can give me. You need to know the location of the money, which I can give you."

"You know where it is?"

"The exact spot. I must say, it is exceedingly well hidden. I hardly think you could find it without me."

"How come you know where it is?" Handy asked.

"Clara told me. She had weeks to look for it, and eventually she found it. Poor Clara."

Menlo smiled again, his ingenuous smile. "I forgot to tell you. I returned to Clara's apartment tonight, Mr. Parker, after you had left. You had mistreated the poor girl most terribly. The only humane thing I could do was end her misery."

He beamed.

Parker stubbed his cigarette. "I didn't ask her enough questions," he said.

"You are hardly to be blamed. You must have thought of her as only a pawn in our game. How could you know she was the key?"

"So you want to team up with us?"

"It seems most logical, does it not? My information, your experience. And we will, of course, split evenly. Half for me, half for you."

The fat man wouldn't be getting any of it, but Parker,

for appearance's sake, made a complaint. "That's no even split. A third for each of us."

Menlo spread his hands and smiled. "If you insist. I am not greedy, I assure you."

So the fat man was planning a double-cross too, Parker thought, and asked, "You still want to do it Friday?"

"That strikes me as the best time, yes. By the way, could you possibly tell me what it is that you two are concerned with in Kapor's house? That lovely girl mentioned the sum of fifty thousand dollars."

"Kapor's got a statue, supposed to be one of the lost statues from some tomb in France. A collector gave us fifty thousand to steal it from him."

"One of the mourners of Dijon?" Menlo smiled in surprise. "I have read of them, of course. How romantic! And a collector, you say? That charming girl's father, no doubt. I would most like to meet him."

"Maybe I can arrange it," Parker said.

4

Her full name was Elizabeth Ruth Harrow Conway. She was, as the fat man had said, a magnificent female, twenty-nine years old, and with honey hair made to gleam in candlelight. She had the hollow-cheeked aristocratic face that comes of generations of breeding and inbreeding, and the tall, lush, well-proportioned body of a stripper crossed with a Channel swimmer. She was rich now, and had been all her life, living currently on a combination of alimony from her ex-husband and atonement gifts from her father. She was well-sexed, with an occasional liking for self-cruelty, and she kept her hotel-room door unlocked.

Parker came in and closed the door and stood there looking at her. "Whose idea was this? Yours or your father's?"

She was in bed, with the covers up to her neck, and

two pillows under her head. She smiled languorously and stretched, her body moving lazily under the blanket. "It was mine, Chuck, don't you know that? But Daddy thinks it was his."

"Either you take off, or there's no job."

"Now, don't threaten me like that, Chuck. Be nice." She slid one arm out from under the covers and patted the bed next to her hip. "Come sit down beside me and we'll talk."

He shook his head. "Forget it."

"Be nice, Chuck," she murmured. "Be nice to me, and I'll go away first thing in the morning. If you still want me to."

That would have been a solution, but he rejected it without bothering to think about it. This was the way he always was before a job. He lived to a pattern. Immediately after a job he was a satyr, inexhaustible and insatiable. Then gradually it would taper off, and by the time the next job was in preparation he was a total celibate. When a job was being set up, he could only think of one thing. Bett's offer slid past him as though it had never been made. It simply didn't interest him.

"You'll go away first thing in the morning, or the deal's off," he said. "And you won't come back. I'll see you after I give your father the statue."

"Maybe I won't feel like it then."

He shrugged.

She was still trying to be coy and seductive, but the edges were getting ragged. "What if I decide not to be an obedient little girl, Chuck?"

"Your father's out fifty grand."

Her languorous smile all at once turned sour, and she popped to a sitting position, her face twisted in a frown of anger. The sheet and blanket fell to her waist. She was nude and her breasts were heavy but firm, and tanned as golden as the rest of her. She said, bite in her voice, "What's the matter with you, Chuck? This is little Bett, remember? We're not exactly strangers."

It was true. For most of two weeks they'd shared the same bedroom, though they'd seen each other only twice since.

"I've got other things to think about," Parker said.

"You want to be careful, Chuck," she said. Her voice was hard as a stone. "You want to be very careful with me."

"I'll see you when the job is done."

"I'm not so sure. And just a minute, don't leave yet. We've got more to talk about."

He kept his hand on the doorknob. "Such as?"

"Such as those other two men. The one that looks like you, only more pleasant, and the funny fat one. You didn't say anything to Daddy about working with anybody else."

"How I work is my business. Don't be here in the morning."

She was going to say something else; but he didn't give her a chance.

The other two were already asleep when Parker got back to his room. Menlo was staying here tonight, sleeping on the floor, and the three of them would move to another location tomorrow. Parker stepped over Menlo, stripped, and got into bed. He fell asleep the way he always did, completely and immediately.

He was a light sleeper. Normal predictable sounds—traffic outside a window, a radio playing that had been playing when he'd gone to sleep—didn't disturb him, but any unusual noise would have him completely awake at once. So when Menlo got up from the floor and crept cautiously toward the door, Parker came awake. He lay unmoving on the bed, watching Menlo through slitted eyes. Menlo took the time to pick up his suit coat and tie and shoes, but nothing else. He went out, the shoes in his hand, the coat and tie over his arm.

There was no point stopping him. Parker went back to sleep.

He awoke again when Menlo returned. The fat man was once again carrying shoes and coat and tie, but now he was carrying his shirt as well, and in the faint light from the window Parker could see that he was smiling to himself. So Bett had got what she'd come for after all. He wondered if Menlo had.

5

"**G**o," said Handy. He thumbed the stopwatch; it read just about nine o'clock.

Parker edged the Pontiac away from the curb in front of Kapor's house. Moving with the traffic, they went straight over Garfield to Massachusetts Avenue, and then turned right on Wisconsin. That took them through Georgetown and on north out of the city into Chevy Chase, and then Bethesda. It was a commercial road all the way, with more traffic than Parker liked on a getaway route, but it was the quickest, shortest way.

Menlo, sitting on the backseat like a renegade Buddha, watched with interest. At one point he said, "I still don't see why this is necessary. Kapor will hardly be in a position to notify the authorities."

Parker was busy driving, so Handy explained. "You say the Outfit's given up on this job, and maybe they did and maybe they didn't. You claim Spannick was the only one of your old crowd that knew what you were up to, and maybe he was and maybe he wasn't. We're going through the play the same night you planned, because it's a good setup. Besides, now that Clara's dead there's nobody inside to let us know when the next good time is. But we're running it an hour earlier than you figured just in case there is still somebody interested in you or Kapor's hundred grand. And we're working out the best route for the same reason."

"Then why go only so far as the motel? Why not continue on our way as rapidly as possible? We might go to Baltimore, for instance, and come to rest there."

Handy turned farther around in the seat, so he could talk full-face with Menlo. "Listen. If what we wanted was to get a confession out of Kapor, we'd let you handle it all the way. That's what you're a pro at; we'd follow anything you said. But what we're doing is breaking into Kapor's house and grabbing his goods, and that's what *we're* pros at. So you just let us do it, O.K."

"My dear friend," said Menlo, looking concerned, "please not to misjudge me. I mean no distrust of your abilities. You are most certainly professionals at your craft, and I appreciate this. It is in a spirit of curiosity only that I ask these questions. I would like to learn more." This was all said too earnestly to be sarcasm;

Menlo was perched forward on the seat, his hands pressed to his chest in a gesture of honesty.

Parker would have just told him to keep his mouth shut and watch and learn, but Handy didn't mind talking. "All right," he said, "I'll explain it to you. There's three ways to handle the getaway. You can do like you said, just take off and keep going, maybe a couple hundred miles. Or you can just go two blocks and hole up there till the heat's off. Or you can go a few miles and hole up and wait four or five hours and *then* take off and go your couple hundred miles. Now, if you do the first, take off and keep going, you're on the road all the time you're the most hot, and that's the way to get yourself picked up fast. If you hole up real close and stay there a week or two, you're right where the most cops are doing the most looking, and that's the way to get picked up six or seven days after the job, when you go out for more groceries. But if you hole up nearby for a few hours, you throw everybody off stride. If the law is after you and they've thrown up roadblocks, they stay up for a few hours and then the cops figure you either got through quick or you're holed up, and they take the roadblocks down. See what I mean? Right after the job is when they do their looking on the roads, and later is when they do their looking in town. So right after the job is when we stay in town, and later on is when we're on the roads. It's a feint, like in basketball. You *go*, but you don't go, and *then* you go."

Menlo nodded happily. "Yes, I follow. I can see where that would be the method most difficult for the authorities to counteract. But in this case, we need have no fear of authorities. Kapor will feel his loss most deeply, of course, but he will not contact the police."

"Not Kapor, no. But suppose some servant sees it first, that somebody's broken in, and calls the cops before he tells his boss? So whether Kapor likes it or not, the law will be in on it. Or maybe the Outfit is still hot for that money, and they'll show up at nine-thirty, the way you originally figured. They find out the swag is gone, the Outfit's after us. Or maybe it's your old group, friend's of Spannick's. We do it the safe way, the reliable way, and we never get jugged."

Menlo smiled with a touch of sadness. "I must say you remove the romance most utterly from all this. I had been seeing myself in quite dramatic terms. The defecting policeman, meting out poetic justice to the embezzler by depriving him of his ill-gotten gains, then disappearing again, quite forever, an enigma to all who seek him. But now I find I am merely a participant in a dreary and pedestrian series of quite normal activities—opening doors, driving automobiles, sitting in motel rooms." He shrugged and spread his hands.

Parker slowed the car. The motel was just ahead—the

Town Motel. They'd picked it because it was on the right side of the road, and because it was built in a U shape, on a slope down from the road, so that parked cars could not be seen from the street.

Parker made the turn, drove down into the court, and parked. Handy thumbed the watch and read it. "Just over eighteen minutes."

"Not good," Parker said.

"It's the fastest way," Handy told him.

They'd spent most of the afternoon trying various suburbs and motels, and this one had been the quickest by far. So now they had run it again at the same time of night they would be coming over it Friday. It was Wednesday, and they could expect a little more traffic on Friday, but they'd still done well. The traffic had been heavy, with the majority of the drivers—like the majority of all eastern drivers—spending the majority of their time in the passing lane. Parker had driven mostly in the right-hand lane, and had made better time than any other car on the road.

Still, he wasn't satisfied. "What if we holed up right at Kapor's house, until maybe two or three in the morning? Menlo, will Kapor be coming home alone?"

"Alas, no. Kapor is notoriously a party giver. A select group of friends, perhaps fifteen or twenty, will probably return with him from the dinner. This is always his habit, and I see no reason to expect that it will differ on Friday."

Parker shrugged. It wasn't good. Eighteen minutes on the road; with Friday's traffic, probably twenty or more. Their direction would be obvious before they were six blocks from Kapor's house. Twenty minutes was plenty of time to set up a block in front of them. He shook his head. "Let's go inside and study the map."

They clambered out of the car, Menlo with difficulty, and went up the stairs to their second-level rooms. Parker and Handy had a double, Menlo a single, three rooms down the hall.

In the room, Menlo settled in the most comfortable chair, while Handy stretched out on his bed. Parker got out the Washington-area map and studied it, frowning. "We could go over to a parallel street, but coming back's no good. The lights along the road out there give maximum red to the side streets. We'd just sit there, half a minute or more."

"Then we work a switch," Handy said. "Use another car on the job, and stash the Pontiac along the way."

"That's better. Adds more time, but it's better. Who knows about the Pontiac?"

Handy considered. "Nobody," he said. "Clara knew, that's all. Menlo's boys grabbed me in Clara's place." He looked over at Menlo. "Were they following us?"

"No, no. They waited at poor Clara's apartment for you to arrive."

"O.K. So the Pontiac's clean."

Parker folded the road map and put it away. He turned to Menlo. "Next question. What tools do we want?"

"I beg your pardon?"

"Tools, tools. The dough isn't just sitting out on a coffee table, is it?"

Menlo's smile was faintly surprised. "My dear friend, you most certainly don't expect me to tell you where to find it. My usefulness would then be at its end, would it not? You have been so kind as to include me only because of this one piece of information I have and you do not."

"I'm not asking you where it is. I'm asking you what do we need to get at it. Like if it's buried under concrete we need a pick, and maybe a couple caps of dynamite. Or if it's in a safe, we need a drill and a set of pullers for the combination or maybe some nitro, depending on what kind of safe it is."

"Ah, I see. The professional mind at work once again. But there is no difficulty, I assure you. No special tools will be required other than our own efficient hands."

Parker nodded. "All right. What size bag do we want? How big a bundle?"

"Well, I have not as yet seen this cash in actuality, only in my imagination. But from the manner of its secretion, let us say, I would suppose a container approximately the size of your suitcase would be more than sufficient."

"I'll get another one tomorrow, just like it." Parker got to his feet and lit a cigarette, pacing back and forth across the room. "Once more, to be sure. Kapor's leaving the house at five o'clock. The chauffeur's driving him, and will wait for him until the dinner is over. His bodyguard's going with him too. The cook will fix stuff for the party later on, but she'll be out of there by six, and so will the gardener. Kapor won't be back before ten, and maybe later. Between six and ten nobody's home."

"Most precisely."

From the bed, Handy said, "We like to be precise."

"What about this party after ten o'clock? No servants?" Parker asked.

"Oh, no. It will not be that sort of party. Morgan, Kapor's bodyguard, will serve as bartender. No other servants will be needed."

"There's no burglar alarms in the house?"

"Clara was quite certain on that point."

"All right." Parker sat down on his own bed, flicked ashes into the nearest ashtray. "So now we wait two days."

6

Handy was driving. They were working the side streets, back and forth, Handy sitting casual at the wheel and Parker beside him, studying the parked cars. Menlo was back at the motel.

It was seven-thirty Friday night, and already dark. The occasional major streets they crossed were full of slow-moving traffic, people heading downtown for a night out or uptown for a weekend out of town. The side streets were quiet, with few moving cars and only an occasional pedestrian.

They'd been looking for twenty minutes, and finally Parker said, "There it is."

Handy saw it too. He stopped the car.

Parker got out and closed the door, and Handy drove the Pontiac away. Parker crossed the street and strolled down toward the car.

It was a Cadillac, gleaming black, four or five years old. Being in this neighborhood, it had to be on its second owner by now, or maybe third. Still, whoever owned it kept it clean. It wouldn't look out of place turning into Kapor's driveway.

The street was empty. There were no faces in any of the house windows that Parker could see. He stopped next to the Cadillac and tried both doors. He was in luck; the rear one was unlocked. It was the rear door that people forgot most often. He hadn't needed the luck. He could have got into the Cadillac in thirty seconds even if it had been locked, but this way he didn't have to break the side vent. He opened the rear door slightly, reached around and pulled the front lock button by the front window. Then he shut the rear door, opened the front, and got in.

He lay down on the seat and took out a pencil flash. He studied the underpart of the dashboard and found he would have to remove a small, flat plate. He put the flash away, got out a small screwdriver and, working by feel, removed the three screws that held the plate in place. Then he used the flash again, for ten seconds, and that was it. He sat up, slid over behind the wheel, and took a jumper wire out of his pocket, with sticky electric tape at both ends. He unreeled part of the tape and then, working by feel once more, reached down under the dashboard and put the jumper on. The starter caught, and slipped, and caught again, and then the engine was purring. He put the automatic transmission in Drive, and pulled away.

On Wisconsin Avenue there was a movie theater, and there was a supermarket, and a blacktop parking lot between them. In the daytime the supermarket customers used the lot, and at night the movie customers used it. Parker drove there, parked the Cadillac so there was a space on his left, stalled the car, and removed the jumper wire. Then he got out and opened the hood. He stood looking down for a minute, and then went to work. It was now twenty minutes to eight.

Handy and Menlo showed up in the Pontiac on schedule, at ten minutes to eight. They parked in the slot next to the Cadillac, and got out. Parker was just finishing. He closed the hood and said, "All ready."

"Once again," Menlo said, looking at the Cadillac with distrust, "I can only reassure myself with the knowledge that you are professionals in this type of activity. The idea of driving to a robbery in an automobile just recently stolen would never have occurred to me. Having occurred to me, it would terrify me so completely I would reject it."

"This car won't be hot for a couple of hours. By then we'll be done with it," Handy said.

"I trust your judgment implicitly," Menlo assured him, "having seen you in action against those poor specimens supplied me by the Outfit. I have every confidence in you."

"That's good. Get in the car," Parker said.

"Most certainly."

Menlo got in the back again, and Parker and Handy up front. There was now a new set of wires by the steering shaft, ending in a small oblong fixture with a pushbutton. This was the new starter. Parker tested it out, and it worked fine. He backed the Cadillac out of its parking slot and drove it slowly out onto Wisconsin Avenue.

Kapor's house, when they got there, was in darkness, the way it was supposed to be. Parker spun the wheel and the Cadillac entered the driveway. The tires crunched on the gravel. The Cadillac looked right at home here as Parker tooled it around behind the house and left it in front of the garage, hidden from the street by the house.

It was eight-thirty. They were right on schedule.

There were two back doors to choose from and they picked the one that Clara had reported led to the kitchen. Handy went to work on it. He was very good with doors. It opened almost immediately.

They went in, and Parker turned on the pencil flash. From Clara, through Menlo, they now had a good ground plan of the house. His voice soft, Parker asked, "All right, Menlo. What room do we want?"

"We'll get your statuette first," Menlo said. "I have a

desire to see it. This bit of romanticism you will not deprive me of."

Parker shrugged. It didn't make any difference. He crossed the kitchen and opened the door on the other side, which led to the rear staircase, the servants' stairs.

The staircase ended on a squarish room, with a large table along one wall. On the other side was a doorless entranceway, leading to an L-shaped hall. Parker opened the third door on the left, and because this room faced the rear of the house, he switched on the light.

It was a long and narrow room, with a dark-red paper covering the walls. The lighting was soft, furnished by fluorescent tubes in troughs spaced along the upper walls, and a rich green carpet covered the entire floor.

It resembled a room in a museum. Glass-topped cases contained coins, resting on green velvet, and on squarish pedestals of varying height were statues of varying styles—of plaster, bronze, terra cotta, alabaster, wood—none over three feet tall. Around the walls fancy swords were hung, and a tall, narrow, glass-doored bookcase at one end of the room was half full of ancient-looking volumes. Most of them were thick and squat, with peeling bindings.

"It is all garbage," Menlo said, with something like contempt in his voice. "Kapor is indiscriminate in his artistic affections. He buys because a particular item is for sale, not because it adds anything artistically. Look at this gibberish! What a confusion of styles and periods. What would Kapor do with a hundred thousand dollars, if he were allowed to retain it? Create an entire house of monstrosities such as this? Such tastelessness deserves no hundred thousand dollars!"

He moved deeper into the room, frowning. "There are good pieces here," he said. "A few, but only a few. There's a Gardner over there, one of the better moderns. But in such surroundings, how can anything reveal its true value? Ah! Here is your mourner!"

It stood in a corner, near the bookcase, on a low pedestal nearly hidden from view. White, small, alone, bent by grief, the mourner stood, his face turned away. A young monk, soft-faced, his cowl back to reveal his clipped hair, his hands slender and long-fingered, the toes of his right foot peeking out from under his rough white robe. His eyes stared at the floor, large, full of sorrow. His left arm was bent, the hand up alongside his cheek, palm outward and shielding his face. His right hand, the fingers straight, almost taut, cupped his left elbow, the forearm across his midsection. The broad sleeve had slipped down his left forearm, showing a thin and delicate wrist. His whole body was twisted to the left, and bent slightly forward, as though grief had instantaneously aged him. It was as if he grieved for every mournful thing that had ever happened in the world, from one end of time to the other.

"I see," said Menlo softly, gazing at the mourner. He reached out gently and picked the statue up, turning it in his hands carefully. "Yes, I see. I understand your Mr. Harrow's craving. Yes, I do understand."

"Now the dough," said Parker. To him the statue was merely sixteen inches of alabaster, for the delivery of which he had already been paid in full.

"Of course. Most certainly." Menlo's old smile popped back into place. He walked over and handed the statuette to Parker. "As you so ably expressed it, now the dough."

He turned, looking around the room and murmuring to himself, "Apollo, Apollo—" Then he snapped his fingers. "Ah! There!" He moved through the clutter of statues, a fat man weaving lithely, and stopped at a gray figure of a nude young man seated on a tree stump.

Parker and Handy followed him, Handy carrying the suitcase. Menlo patted the statue's shoulder with pudgy fingers and smiled happily at Parker. "You see? A most ingenious solution. You have a figure of speech for this, I believe. One cannot see the forest for the trees. In this case, one cannot see the tree for the forest."

"In there? In the statue?" Parker asked.

"Most certainly! Watch." Menlo put his hands on the statue's head, and twisted. There was a grating sound, and the head came off in his hands. "Hollow," he said. "The young Apollo and his tree trunk, packed with money."

He stuck his hand down inside and brought out a batch of greenbacks. "You see?"

"All right. Let's pack it," Parker said. Handy opened the suitcase and as Menlo brought forth handful after handful of bills, Parker and Handy stowed it all inside.

The bills were all loose. There were hundreds and fifties and twenties, handful after handful, and gradually they filled the suitcase. They made no attempt to count, just stowed it away, quickly and silently.

When the suitcase was full, there were still some bills left over. "Alas, I misjudged," said Menlo, smiling at the double handful of bills he held. "Who would have thought a small statue could have held so much?"

He stuffed the bills into his own pockets, and suddenly his right hand emerged holding a derringer, a Hi Standard twin-tubed .22. It packed hardly any power at all, but at this close range it could do the job as well as anything.

Menlo's smile was now broad and cherubic. "And now, my dear professionals," he said, "I am most afraid we must part company. You have been of such excellent assistance to me, I truly wish I could at least repay you with your lives. But you have already demonstrated once your ability in tracking your quarry, and I should prefer not to spend the rest of my life looking over my shoulder. I hope you appreciate that."

Parker and Handy both moved, each in opposite directions, but Menlo in his own way was also a professional. His face tightened as he fired twice, and both were hits. Handy slammed into the wall, and collapsed in a crumpled heap. Parker flailed backward, arms pinwheeling, scattering statues, as he crashed into a pedestal.

Menlo paused a moment, but bodies lay still, and the derringer was empty. He gathered up the suitcase and statuette and hurried from the room, a round lithe fat man in a black suit, the suitcase hanging at the end of one short arm, the small white statuette tucked under the other.

The last thing he did before he left was switch off the lights.

THREE

1

Auguste Menlo was forty-seven years of age, five feet six inches tall, weight two hundred thirty-four pounds. His title was Inspector, his occupation that of spy on his fellow citizens. During the Second World War, when he was much younger, no taller, but quite a bit thinner, he had been active in the anti-Nazi underground movement in Klastrava, spending the last fifteen months of the war living in the mountains with a guerrilla band, every member of which had a price on his head, set by the Nazis.

An underground movement is primarily a destructive social force, and only secondarily a constructive political force. Whatever political ideology is present invariably reflects the political ideology of whichever outside nation supplies its matériel. Because of Klastrava's geographical location, that outside nation was the Soviet

Union. The support originally came, for the most part, from the United States through Lend-Lease, but this was never mentioned by the Russians, who were not born yesterday.

Klastravian soil was liberated from the Nazis by the Red Army. The collaborationist puppet government of wartime having been summarily done away with, was replaced by men from the wartime resistance movement, and their political orientation was reinforced by the presence of the Red Army. Klastrava was quietly and efficiently absorbed, and shortly became one of the Soviet Union's smallest but least troublesome satellites.

Before the war, Auguste Menlo had had no particular trade, being a young man content to be supported by his doctor father. During the war, and particularly during the last fifteen months of it, he had learned a trade, though his trade at first glance seemed to have no peacetime application. Then, in early 1947, through resistance comrades, he received an appointment to the National Police. At last Auguste Menlo had found his true vocation. He did his work well, and with enthusiasm, and his promotions came rapidly.

In any religion, it is the priest who is likely to ask the most pertinent questions; and if there are flaws in the religious structure, it is the priest, being closest to it and most learned in it, who is most likely to discover them. And Auguste Menlo became, in a way, a priest of Communism. In a quite literal way, he became a confessor; in the silent and private rooms of stone beneath the ground he listened to the halting confessions of the wrong in heart. Over the years, Auguste Menlo came upon the flaws that bothered no one else, and patched them as best he could, and efficiently went on about his business.

Till someone waved a hundred thousand dollars in front of his face. One hundred thousand dollars American.

Auguste knew instantly what he was going to do, the very second he was informed of his assignment. He knew it as though he had known all his life, as though his entire career had been only a preparation for this great moment when he would come into one hundred thousand dollars American. The circumstances were too perfectly joined for there to be an alternative.

Auguste Menlo had been chosen for the job in the first place because he had such a perfect record, without a blemish of any kind. He had been married, since 1949, to a plump, practical woman, a good housekeeper and an efficient mother to his two teenage daughters. So far as the record showed—and the record was exhaustive—he had never once been unfaithful to his wife, any more than he had ever been derelict in his duty to the state. He was the logical and inevitable choice.

There is a kind of man who is perfectly honest so long as the plunger is small. This kind of man has chosen his

life and finds it rewarding, so he will not risk it for anything less rewarding. And while Menlo had long since
lost interest in his Anna, the occasional woman who became available seemed to him hardly much of an im-
provement, certainly not worth the risk of losing his
comfortable home. Nor were the financial temptations
that cropped up along his official path worth the comfort
and security he already enjoyed. As time went by, his
reputation grew and so did the trust it inspired. Who
better to trust with one hundred thousand dollars, four
thousand miles from home?

There is no way for officialdom to protect itself from
such a man. Can a man be mistrusted for being *too*
honest?

So Auguste Menlo was informed of his mission and
given his round-trip jetliner ticket to the United States.
Outwardly, it was the same sober and industrious Auguste Menlo who walked out of the Ministry that day,
was driven home, packed his suitcase, and kissed the
leathery cheek of his wife good-bye. But inside he was a
totally different man. On the train to Budapest, where he
would make connections with the plane for the West, he
allowed himself, concealed by a newspaper, the first outward indication of his feelings. A broad and delighted
smile, as infectious as a giggle, spread over his face. It
made him look like a depraved and aging cherub.

The first plane took him from Budapest to Frankfurt

am Main, that foggy valley in the middle of Germany so ill-suited to the landing and taking off of airplanes. But they landed without incident, and an hour later he boarded the jet that would take him in six hours non-stop to Washington National Airport, an ocean and a continent away. A world away.

The stewardess was slender, in Western fashion, with pale-blue skirt taut over pert and girdled rump. Menlo feasted upon her, his eyes bright, almost feverish, his mouth frozen in a delighted smile. It was a foolish and dangerous way to behave. Had the Ministry chosen to keep him under surveillance—But the Ministry's trust was complete, and only the stewardess noticed the funny, happy fat man with the glazed eyes. She merely thought he was full of vodka, and hoped he wouldn't be sick. He wasn't.

In Washington, sanity returned to him. He boarded the airport bus and rode to the G Street terminal, and in the course of that ride he regained control of himself. Until he actually had the money, he must be circumspect. He must be cautious.

His hotel reservation had already been made for him. He checked in, bathed luxuriously in steaming hot water, and rose from the tub a bright pink, round and flushed and happy. He donned fresh clothing, and paid his courtesy call to Spannick.

Spannick, of course, did not know the fat man's mission. No one knew what it was, save for Menlo himself and three men back home, all in the Ministry. But Spannick did know Menlo, and was cordial and deferential to the point of nausea, for who knew what the Inspector's quest might be? Spannick tried to pump him, to find out at least that it was not to liquidate himself that Inspector Menlo had traveled all this distance. But Menlo evaded his questions. The meeting was brief; Spannick offered whatever assistance Menlo desired, and Menlo declined the offer with expressions of gratitude. Once this was over he was on his own.

His orders had been specific. His primary mission was to deal with Kapor; remove him, and in such a way that there would be no troublesome questions from local police. The secondary task was to recover, if possible, all or part of the misappropriated funds. If they could not be located, too bad; the important thing was to deal with Kapor.

Those were his orders, but for Menlo the emphasis was all wrong. He didn't particularly care what happened to Kapor; let him live to a ripe old age if he wished. But as to the money—that was the primary mission.

Had he intended to follow orders, he could have done so singlehanded, with little or no difficulty. But he recognized his limitations. He knew that to get his hands on Kapor's money he was going to need experienced and professional help. Like policemen everywhere he had often diverted himself by reading American detective novels, and so had a fairly clear picture of American crime, at least as it was described in fiction. It was all organized together, like an American corporation. So Menlo began by looking for someplace to gamble.

Four taxi drivers and two doormen responded to his questions with blank looks, but the fifth cabby admitted to knowing such a place, and was willing to take Menlo there for ten dollars. Menlo paid. He was driven across the Arlington Memorial Bridge and down into Virginia, and deposited at a place that called itself Long Ridge Inn. It seemed to be an old colonial house. Menlo entered, armed with the cab driver's instructions, and found himself in what seemed a perfectly legitimate restaurant, with a softly lit bar beyond an archway to the right.

The cab driver was gone, with Menlo's ten dollars. Menlo was suddenly convinced that he had been played for a sucker. He very nearly turned around and left without saying a word to anyone, but the headwaiter was already there, armed with a stack of outsize menus. Feeling like an idiot, Menlo repeated what the cab driver had told him: "I'm looking for the action."

The headwaiter, without a flicker of expression, replied, "Up the stairway at the end of the bar, sir. And good luck to you."

So that was how he made his contact with the Outfit.

The people he talked to at Long Ridge Inn were not of the sort he needed, but he told a circumlocutious story and they assured him he would be contacted once his story had been "checked out." He left his name, and the name of the hotel where he was staying, and went on back to Washington.

Three days in the hotel room. He was living on the Ministry's miserly expense budget, and so could have distracted himself with nothing more exciting than a motion picture. But he didn't even go out for that, afraid he would miss the contact. He stayed in his room, ordering his meals from room service, and stared forlornly at the telephone. Finally, at one o'clock in the morning of the fourth day, it rang and a voice told him to leave the hotel and walk slowly west.

He was met by a Cadillac with gland trouble, huge and rounded and with drawn curtains at the side windows. It rolled along beside him for a few seconds as he walked, and then a voice from its black interior called him by name. He entered the Cadillac, feeling a moment of irrational fright, and for the next two hours was driven hither and yon about the city, while he talked with the two men in the backseat.

He intended, of course, to ask for help in getting the money, then to pull a double-cross. He didn't want any percentage of one hundred thousand dollars, he wanted it all—one hundred thousand dollars. But the two men in the Cadillac seemed so confident, so competent, and so sinister, that he was no longer sure his original plan would work. He told them the story, and they agreed to join him in the venture, offering him 10 per cent of the take for supplying the information. He smiled, in mock surprise and mock bashfulness, and told them he had been planning to offer *them* 10 per cent for performing the physical labor. They ordered the chauffeur to stop the Cadillac, and ordered Menlo to get out.

Menlo opened the car door, and then paused to remind them he had told them everything except the name of the man who now possessed the hundred thousand dollars. He told them that if he must handle the whole thing himself he would, though he had hoped for a more sensible and businesslike attitude from any American organization, whichever side of the law it happened to be on. They said they just might be able to see their way clear to letting him have a quarter of the loot, so he shut the door, sat back, and smiled. Then the bargaining got under way in earnest.

Because he found them so impressive that he was no longer sure he would be able to get away with the whole boodle, he bargained tenaciously and well, and when he emerged from the car he had the fat end of a sixty-forty split. He also had the uneasy conviction that the Outfit really intended to try for 100 per cent. Ah, well. Though the members of the Outfit were impressive in their grim stolidity, Menlo was the product of fifteen years of Communist bureaucratic intrigue, and he thought he might be able to handle himself adequately in this situation.

His assistants came to see him the following day, and slowly the operation took shape. He revealed Kapor's name, no longer having any choice, and it turned out the Outfit had an indirect connection with a maid in Kapor's home named Clara Stoper. The connection was made more direct, and when Clara was offered a 10-per cent cut she would never receive she became a willing and eager member of the group. Events progressed without a ripple until the unexpected and somewhat frightening appearance of Handy McKay, who began playing up to Clara in a manner that was definitely suspicious.

Could someone else be after the money? Could there have been a leak back at the Ministry? Could there have been a leak among the higher echelon of the Outfit? There was too much uncertainty here and that was dangerous. Menlo gave the order that Handy be taken and questioned, and from that point events barreled onward like a plane in a tailspin. Menlo had shifted this way and that, always retaining his balance by the narrowest margin, and when the dust settled, there had been a total realignment. The Outfit was no longer a part of the scheme. Spannick was dead, and Menlo's bridges were burned; he could no longer change his plans and go home now, even if he wanted to. So Menlo found himself in an uneasy alliance with the two newcomers, Parker and McKay.

Menlo had much to be thankful to Parker and McKay for. They had, initially, saved his life. They had additionally simplified the actual mechanics of the robbery, far more so than the Outfit's plan. And also they had, indirectly, reintroduced the fat man to sex.

Bett Harrow. So long, so lean, so firm! So active and eager a participant! This was what he had been looking forward to while gaping at the airline stewardess, this was what he had been thinking of whenever the hundred thousand dollars recrossed his mind. Bett Harrow.

He had waited that night till he was sure that Parker and McKay were asleep, and then he had risen from his bed on the floor. He carried his shoes and his jacket and necktie out to the hall, and there donned them, smoothing his somewhat oily hair into place with his fingers and running thumb and forefinger down his trousers crease.

He knocked softly at the door of room 512 and after a few seconds he heard a bed creak and then her soft call: "It's unlocked."

He went in. The table lamp beside the bed offered the only light, amber and intimate. She was lying supine on the bed, the covers outlining her incredibly long body, her face framed by the blonde hair on her pillow. She looked up at him with surprise. "Oh, it's you."

"You expected our friend again?" The prospect of

Parker coming down the hallway now did not please him.

"That son of a bitch!" She seemed very angry with Parker. "Get me a cigarette, will you? Over on the dresser there."

"Most certainly. I will, if I may, join you."

"Be my guest."

The tendency to goggle and giggle, as it had on the jetliner, was growing stronger and stronger. He fought it away, retaining an urbane and practiced exterior as he carried her cigarettes over to the bed and leaned over to offer her a light. Her eyes were hazel, and deep, and knowing, and they gazed up unblinking into his own. He held her gaze, and smiled pleasantly.

"Thanks," she said, and blew smoke, but not toward his face. She patted the bed next to her mounding hip. "Sit down."

"You are most kind." His weight sagged the mattress, and she slid just slightly toward him.

"What are you to Parker?" she asked suddenly.

"Ah," he said. "How coincidental. Much the same question I had in mind to ask you, though of course since you are a lady, I would have phrased it somewhat differently."

"Parker's a pain in the ass," she said. "Sorry if I shocked you."

She had. Women at home did not speak in such a manner. He smiled to cover the instant of shock. "Precision in all things, my dear. And that phrase has admirable precision. My name, which our mutual friend neglected to tell you, is Auguste Menlo."

"You told me yourself, remember?"

"Ah, yes, so I did."

"What are you so nervous about?"

"I am most sorry. I hadn't realized I was."

"Parker won't be back, if that's it," she replied.

That was, of course, part of it.

He said, "As to Parker, my own connection with him is most transitory, and for convenience only."

"I could say the same thing," she said bitterly. "I'd like to push the bastard off a cliff."

"Dear lady, how rapidly we have come to a meeting of minds."

She didn't get it at first. She frowned slightly at him as she sorted out the words, and then all at once she responded to his smile with a dazzling smile of her own. "I'm Bett Harrow," she said.

"I am charmed." And he meant it. He leaned forward to stub his cigarette in an ashtray. "Parker has told me of the statuette."

"I didn't know Parker ever told anybody anything."

"He is not a blabbermouth, no. But he did tell me of the statuette. It was, you might say, a mutual sharing of confidences. My own is irrelevant at the moment, really. We might speak of it another time, perhaps."

To have a woman like this, and in her company to spend one hundred thousand dollars. What a glorious dream! What a more glorious reality! "If I understand aright, your father has paid for this statuette in advance? Fifty thousand dollars?"

"Cash in advance," she replied. "We've got something else Parker wants too. He gets that later.

"Anything of, uh, value?"

"Not to anybody else."

"Ah. Alas. My dear, I would like to ask you a hypothetical question."

"He would," she said.

"I beg your pardon?"

"My father would pay again. If Parker didn't have the statue, and you did, and you wanted to sell, he'd pay again."

"Another fifty thousand?"

"He might not go that high. But you could probably get twenty-five."

Menlo shrugged. "I am not greedy."

"I bet you're not."

He leaned over closer to her. "Another question, my dear."

"What this time?"

"In my country," he said, "women go to bed wearing

great white sacks made of cotton. In the United States what do women wear when they go to bed?"

"Depends on the woman."

"Well, you, for instance?"

"Skin."

"Skin? You mean, no garment at all?"

"That's exactly what I mean."

"Incredible," he said.

"You don't believe me?" There was a mock challenge in her eyes, and her hands gripped the top edge of the covers.

"If you endeavor to prove that statement to me," he replied, "I wish you to be warned that I can take no responsibility for whatever might transpire thereafter."

"Is that right?" She flicked her arms, and the covers shot back, baring her to the knee.

He'd never undressed so quickly in his life. One sock was still half on when he lumbered into the bed, looming over her like a dirigible. Her hazel eyes darkened, her body seemed to grow firmer and more taut, and all at once he found himself in congress with a panther. He said a lot of things in his native tongue, until he no longer had breath to spare on talk, and from then on he merely clung.

When it was over, and they'd smoked a cigarette together and talked a bit more, he got up and began to get dressed. "I will see you in Miami. Very soon, I hope. And with the statuette."

"You'll remember the hotel?"

"It is imprinted firmly upon my memory." He took one last cigarette from her pack, and lit it. "It might be best were you to leave in the morning, as Parker requested. He is taciturn and unpredictable, and I would want nothing to go wrong."

"All right," she answered.

"Until Miami, then."

"I'll be seeing you."

He returned to Parker's room and fell into pleasantly exhausted sleep, garlanded with sweet dreams. . . .

Watching Parker and Handy at work, those last two days, he had grown more and more impressed with the way they handled themselves. He had originally planned to remain with them throughout the robbery and the getaway, letting them handle all the details, and double-crossing them only after the operation was completed. But as the time grew shorter, he revised his plans and decided to do away with them before they left Kapor's house. Through some careful and judicious questioning, he had learned enough about the getaway route and the theories behind it to be able to handle it alone when the time came. But still, he was in a strange country and involved in an operation that was unfamiliar to him, besides being aligned with a pair of the most lupine of wolves. That last day, Friday, his nervousness and excitement grew and grew until he was afraid he would explode. It was more and more difficult to hold himself in check as the day wore on toward night.

They had not found the derringer stowed away beneath the false bottom of his leather toilet kit. It was more of a toy than a gun, especially in comparison with the weapons that Parker and McKay carried, but it was small enough and light enough to be safely hidden and it held two bullets. If he was careful, that should be sufficient.

Friday evening, when Parker and Handy left to steal the second car, he transferred the derringer to his coat pocket, hoping they would not think to search him again before entering Kapor's house.

McKay came back at the appointed time, and Menlo carried the empty suitcase they'd bought that day out to the car. He climbed in, saying, "Have you had a good fortune?"

"Good enough."

McKay, too, had his moments of taciturnity.

From this point, when he actually entered the automobile and sat down next to McKay, until the operation was complete, he was in such a state of high excitement that he scarcely knew his name. The operation went like clockwork, and the delight bubbled up in him, mixed deliciously with terror, in a heady combination that was almost like a drug. They drove to the house in the stolen Cadillac, they entered, they found the room containing Kapor's pitiful collection of bric-a-brac. And there for the first time Menlo saw the white mourner. In his state of heightened sensibilities he saw the mourner as being deeply meaningful and symbolic; in some convoluted way it expressed to him the end of mourning. Now at last all was within his grasp.

The head came off the Apollo, just as Clara had said it would, and inside was the money. It wasn't really money to him yet—when he thought of money, he still thought of his native currency—but he knew he would have no difficulty in getting used to these unfamiliar green bills, with their Presidents and public buildings. The money poured out of the hollow Apollo, filling the suitcase and more, like a cornucopia. In excitement and dread and anticipation and pleasure so intermingled and intense that he came very close to fainting, he stuffed into his pockets the fingers caressing the crisp green bills, and then pulled his hand from his right pocket again, the fingers now gripping instead the small deadly black derringer.

Both tried to escape him, flinging themselves about, knocking statues down, but the excitement ended at his wrist. His hand was calm and steady. He fired twice, and each went down. They *had* to go down. In one lightning bolt of time, Auguste Menlo had become invincible. His finger twitched twice; his adversaries ceased to exist. Their husks, their empty shells, lay broken at his feet.

He stowed the derringer back in his pocket, hearing the crisp crinkle of the bills again, and hurried over to pick up the spoils. The statuette under his left arm, the suitcase—heavier now, much heavier—hanging from his right hand. He was flushed, feverish, victorious. He didn't even remember turning the light off on his way out.

2

Menlo was dreaming.

First, there was a beach. There were great round beach umbrellas, and crowds of people swimming and splashing in the shallow water. Women wearing wool bathing suits and big floppy hats shading their eyes looked out over the water, and men and other women lay face down on blankets, sunbathing. There was a steady roar of sound, shouting and splashing and laughing, ebbing and flowing like the waves that trickled up the flat beach and down again. And children running, people hurrying this way and that. But it was all muted, all slowed down. The shouting and splashing sounded far off as if under water, and all the running and scurrying was like a moving picture run in slow motion.

A woman came walking toward Menlo across the beach. She was tall and golden and blonde and slender, with pleasing fullnesses where they should be, and she was totally nude. But no one else paid any attention. She came closer and closer to him, smiling with a smile that offered everything, and he recognized her but he couldn't remember her name. He stared at her, trying to remember, and wondering why no one at the beach was alarmed by her nudity. Then the sun got into his eyes, making them sting and water, and he closed them for relief. When he opened them again, the woman was closer, but now she was wearing Parker's face.

"No!" Menlo screamed, and in a sudden great gout of flame and smoke she disappeared. He looked out over the water, and a huge ship with tremendous white sails was racing toward him, bombarding the beach. The gouts of flame and smoke roared up all around him. People were screaming, and running every which way.

He dropped to his knees and began scrabbling in the sand, digging a hole to hide in, when a voice said, "Why not just clamp down hard on the capsule, my friend and save all that digging?"

He looked up, there was Spannick, sitting on a kitchen chair, and smiling at him. The kitchen chair was very slowly sinking into the sand under Spannick's weight.

"You're dead," he shouted, and Spannick's face changed to Parker's. He closed his eyes, knowing he was doomed. He opened them again, and he was in a motel room with one green wall and one white wall and one yellow wall and one wall of glass covered by draperies of the three colors all combined, and he was alone.

He sat up, and slowly the realization came to him that this was truth, that he was awake and the nightmare was over. His elbows were trembling, and his mouth hung open. He tried to close it, but his jaw immediately fell slack again. He tried again, and it fell slack again. He kept trying, sitting mounded in the middle of the bed like a squat pink fish, his elbows trembling and his mouth closing and falling open, closing and falling open. But reality was returning to him, and in a minute he got up from the bed and stood in the middle of the room. He was naked, in honor of the United States and Bett Harrow.

Nightmares did come to him from time to time, particularly when he had been working too hard, or an assignment was unusually difficult, like the purging of an old friend. He knew nightmares, and he knew what to do about them, how to pull their teeth and lay them to rest. The trick was to go over the nightmare detail by detail, remembering it as fully and completely as possible, discovering what part of his past experience had produced each distortion.

Still shaky, he lit a cigarette, and discovered that even American cigarettes taste foul immediately after one wakes up. Still, it should help calm his nerves. He made a face, and dragged deep.

The nightmare then. First, the beach. That was easy. It was one of the tourist beaches on the Caspian Sea; he had never been there, but he had seen such beaches in motion pictures. And in this instance it was meant to symbolize Miami Beach, which he had never seen, even in films.

The nude woman. Bett Harrow, of course. Odd he couldn't remember her name in the dream. Perhaps that meant she was not an individual to him. She, and the airline stewardess, and all the women in the American magazines were simply an erotic goal, with interchangeable bodies and faces and names. One would do as well as another. He was somewhat surprised and pleased to find his subconscious so smug about his interlude with Bett Harrow.

Next, Parker's face. It had cropped up twice, each time attached to another's body. He had met the Harrow woman through Parker, of course, but with Parker's face on Spannick's body as well, there had to be a different answer.

It could be that Parker had no body anymore, Menlo having murdered it. Was some essence of Parker after him, seeking vengeance? Friends of Parker? It was hard to imagine the man *having* any friends. Besides, even if he did, what did they know of Menlo? Nothing. Only the Harrow woman, and she was already aware that he intended to kill Parker, and approved. So the double ap-

pearance of Parker's face was simply an oversensitive reaction of having eliminated such a formidable opponent.

Next, the ship with the white sails. He had to think
about that for a few minutes, pacing back and forth in
front of the bed, and at last it came to him. Jenny's song,
from *Dreigroschenoper*. The pirate ship. He had been in
mortal danger from the pirates—first the Outfit, and
later Parker and McKay—and this was simply a recording of that fact. And the same was true of Spannick's appearance, saying exactly what he had said in the cellar
that night.

He understood the dream now, and its terror was
washed away. He went over to the nightstand, picked up
his watch, and saw that it was ten minutes to four. He
had slept six hours, having fallen deeply asleep immediately after returning here from Kapor's house, feeling
after the high-pitched excitement of the robbery and
killings a lethargy unlike any drowsiness or exhaustion
he had ever know before. So he had slept, purging his
mind of all residual terrors through his nightmare, and
now he was rested and calm.

It was time to be going. According to the getaway the-
ory explained to him by McKay, now was the time to get
started.

He showered, calm and relaxed, taking his time. He
dressed in fresh clothing from the skin out, packed his

suitcase, gathered up the other suitcase, with all the money in it, and tiptoed out of the motel room.

The Pontiac was there, waiting. He stowed both suitcases on the back seat, got behind the wheel, and took the road map from the glove compartment.

He wanted to travel south from here, but he was north of the city. Northeast. Was there any way to skirt the city to the east? He studied the unfamiliar map, following thin lines of roads with the tip of one stubby finger, and finally found a way to get over to the Capital Beltway. That would take him south into Virginia, where he could pick up a route numbered 350 which would take him to a route numbered 1, which ran all the way down the coast to Miami.

He laid the map on the seat beside him, and started the engine. He was not used to so large and soft an automobile, and he drove cautiously at first, barely touching the accelerator as he brought the car up the slope to the street. He underestimated and made far too wide a right turn, but Wisconsin Avenue at this point was four lanes wide, and at this hour in the morning there was no other car in sight anyway.

His progress at first was agonizingly slow. The automobile was unfamiliar to him, as were the street signs. The standard pictographic signs common throughout Europe were not used here. Instead of the usual white background and red frame and black pictorial silhouette, there were dull yellow diamonds, some bearing words and some deformed arrows. Stop signs were red octagons with the word STOP in white, unless they were yellow octagons with the word *STOP* in black. It was confusing, and a little frightening. He couldn't afford to have an accident now, not with one hundred thousand dollars in a suitcase on the back seat.

By the time he finally got to the Capital Beltway he was perspiring freely, despite the November chill, and there was a pain in his head from creasing his brow and squinting through the windshield.

But the Capital Beltway was a superhighway, like the German Autobahn. Menlo relaxed at once, sat back more comfortably, held the steering wheel less tightly. He also pressed more firmly on the accelerator. The car, bulky and soft as a heavyweight boxer out of condition, was nevertheless an eager sprinter. The car roared down the empty highway, as dawn slowly spread over the sky to his left. He was on his way.

3

He didn't hear the siren at first. He was trying to decide whether or not to stop in this little town for something to eat, and though the wailing filled his ears, at first he didn't connect it with himself at all.

He was just across the border between North and South Carolina, and it was one o'clock in the afternoon. He had been driving steadily for eight hours. This automobile was the most comfortable he'd ever driven, but eight hours' driving in any car has to be tiring. All the way across North Carolina he'd been telling himself to stop, but the desire to increase the distance between himself and Washington had up till now been stronger than his need for food and rest. He had stopped only once, to fill the automobile's gas tank and empty his bladder. That had been over three hours ago.

It seemed like a pleasant little town, this one, small

and somnolent. Except for the sunshine and the warmth, it could be a sleepy valley town in Klastrava. Sunshine and warmth. He had never in his life till now had enough sunshine and warmth. Klastrava was a mountainous country, in the heart of the Carpathians, and in mountainous lands the human settlements are always in the valleys. In mountainous lands the rain falls always in the valleys and mists and fogs lay there always. The summers are hazy, humid, muggy, the winters heavy with bronchial dampness.

Sunshine and warmth. And beautiful women. And one hundred thousand dollars.

He was far enough away now from Washington. It was safe to stop in this little town. Ahead on the right, a sign hung out from a building that looked like a railroad car. It read DINER. He had decided to stop here, and that was when he heard the siren.

He looked in his rearview mirror. The road was straight all the way through the little town, and almost empty. Behind him, two blocks away and coming on fast, was an automobile with a revolving red light on top.

Police.

He thought they'd caught up with him. He thought for one panic-stricken instant, that somehow they had traced him. The police authorities had learned about the robbery and the killings, and they had traced him in some inexplicable fashion. They had caught up with him.

The problem was, he didn't have the background to understand what was happening. In all of Klastrava there isn't one single solitary speed trap. There isn't enough tourism to support one.

He thought: *Run? Outrace him?*

No good. The police car would be even faster than the one Menlo was driving. Besides, his reading of crime fiction had told him what to expect ahead. Roadblocks. Parker and McKay had talked about roadblocks too, so they were not entirely fictional. In his own work, at home, he had occasionally found the need to order roadblocks set up and trains searched, even the borders closed.

Could they, in this country, close the borders between states?

The police car had caught up with him, was now beside him. An angry-looking, wrinkle-faced old man in a cowboy hat waved to him to pull over to the curb and stop.

One man? One wrinkle-faced old man? This couldn't be connected with what had happened in Washington. They would consider him, as the wording went, armed and dangerous. They would send more than one wrinkle-faced old man to apprehend him, if they were after him for what had happened in Washington.

He obeyed the old man's hand, and pulled to a stop at the curb, wondering what it could be all about. There might be some sort of border checkpoint where he was supposed to stop and hadn't, or some such thing. He would have to wait and see, find out what the old man wanted. If worst came to worst, the derringer was reloaded and in his coat pocket.

The police car nosed in at an angle in front of him, its rear jutting out into the traffic lane in the approved method, to keep him from driving suddenly off as soon as the old man got out of his car. Menlo rolled down the window on his side, and waited.

The old man came back toward him, walking with an odd bowlegged rolling gait, as though it was a horse he'd just climbed down from instead of an automobile. He was wearing black boots and dark-blue breeches several sizes too large, which sported a yellow stripe up each seam. His dark-blue uniform coat looked like the jackets worn by Army officers in the First World War. A light-blue shirt, with a dark-blue tie, and a tan cowboy hat completed him. A broad black belt, studded with shiny cartridges, encircled his pudgy waist. A heavy black holster sat on his right hip.

He came over, and stood glaring in a Menlo. "You in a hurry, bud?"

Menlo blinked. Police at home were always polite and courteous on the surface, whatever happened afterward.

He didn't know what to say. He just stared at the angry old man.

The old man said, "The posted speed limit in this village, in case you was in too much of a hurry to read the sign back there at the city line, happens to be twenty miles an hour. I just clocked you at thirty-two miles per hour, on our main street. I don't see no fire nowhere."

Menlo understood only half of it, and that half he didn't believe. "*Twenty* miles an hour?" He'd been going through cities and towns with thirty-mile-an-hour speed limits—and occasionally twenty five—all day long.

"That's what the sign said, bud," the old man said.

"I saw no sign," Menlo protested.

"It's there. Let's have your license and registration."

Impossible. He had neither.

The whole situation was ludicrous; all his high spirits and pleasant anticipations drained out of him. The United States was no different from Klastrava; no different from any other nation in the world. Mighty undertakings were blocked by petty bureaucratic insignificancies.

"Snap it up, bud. I ain't got all day."

There was no driver's license in his pocket, no automobile registration. He had only two things there: a wad of money, and the derringer. He thought quickly, trying to decide which to use.

The money. The money first. If that failed, then the derringer.

Menlo reached into his pocket, peeled one bill free, and handed it to the old man. The old man looked at it, frowned suddenly like a thundercloud. "What's this?"

It was a fifty-dollar bill.

"My license and registration," Menlo replied. He smiled tentatively.

The old man squinted, studying the bill, and then Menlo's face. He peered into the back seat, then looked the car over, front to back. "Now, what in hell have we got hold of here?" Then, with a surprisingly fast motion, his right hand snapped back, flipped open the holster flap, and dragged out an old .38-caliber Colt Police Positive Special. He took a quick step back away from the Pontiac. "Now you get on outa there, bud. You move slow and easy."

Menlo's hand started to inch toward the derringer, but the old man's trigger finger was white-knuckled with strain. The barrel of the pistol aimed at Menlo's head seemed as big as the entrance to a railroad tunnel. Meekly, cursing himself for a fool, Menlo clambered out of the Pontiac.

The old man said, "Fat one, ain't you? Turn around. Lean up against your car with your hands over your head."

Menlo did as he was told, knowing the posture the old man wanted. It was standard procedure the world around. Leaning forward off balance, the hands higher than the head, supporting the weight of the body. The position of the suspect when the police officer wants to search him for weapons. Which meant that now the derringer was to be taken from him.

How long would it be before this wretched old man took it into his head to open the two suitcases on the backseat?

And all this for driving thirty-two miles an hour on an empty street.

The old man was muttering. "I thought you was one for the judge, but now I ain't so sure. Might just be there's a poster out on you."

The old man began to pat him, searching him. The first thing he came to was the wallet in Menlo's hip pocket. He removed it, and stepped back. Menlo heard him whistle softly when he opened it; it contained money, nearly a thousand dollars in hundreds and fifties.

"Well, well, well," the old man said. "What do you know about that?" There was a pause and then a different tone. "Now, what the hell is this?"

Menlo wondered too. It hadn't, whatever it was, sounded like something the old man was pleased over. Menlo wondered where the people were. The sun was shining brightly, and this was the main street. Two cars had already gone by since he'd been stopped, both angling wide around them without stopping. But no crowd had gathered on the sidewalk. He couldn't understand it.

He didn't know that in a speed-trap town, motorists often get angry at policemen and policemen usually retaliate with a little extra humiliation such as a frisking, that in any such town, no matter how dreary, the sight of a policeman frisking a tourist is old stuff.

The old man kept mumbling to himself, and then all at once he shouted. "A Commie! A goddamn Commie!"

Then Menlo realized what the old man had found. He hadn't bothered to remove his official identification cards, and these were what the old man had been mumbling over, trying to decipher the foreign printing, until finally some sign or symbol had given the game away.

"Well, well, *well!*" cried the old man, growing excitement in his voice. "I guess maybe it's the Federal Bureau of Investigation that'd like you, bud. A big-shot Commie, no license or registration, carrying around bribe money. I guess the Federal Bureau of Investigation won't mind seeing you one bit. So you just march, bud. Get on away from that car you stole, and march. To your right. The jail's just a block away. I'll come get your car and baggage after I got you locked up good."

Menlo marched ahead of him down the street to the jail, a one-story frame structure with a blank façade, save for one small barred window and a door that had *Police Headquarters* lettered in gold on the glass.

Within, it looked like a set for a Western movie. There was a central corridor, with an office on the right containing, among other things, a rolltop desk. The door on the left was shut, and the old man had Menlo continue straight on down past it to the end, to a barred door.

It was while the old man was unlocking the door that he took his eyes off Menlo for just a second. It was then that Menlo sneaked the derringer from his pocket and fired both bullets in the old man's head.

First, he took back his wallet. Then he removed the Police Positive from the holster and tucked it inside his belt, on the left side, butt forward, where it was well concealed but he could get at it quickly. Finally, he dragged the old man's body through the barred doorway around to the other side of a desk to delay its discovery. The cells were back here, but they faced the other way. In one of them someone, probably a Negro, was singing softly and mournfully to himself about nothing in particular.

Menlo was feeling very strange. Until this moment all of his activities had been directed against the criminal elements of society, the outlaws. Kapor. The Outfit. Parker and McKay. He had been betraying his Ministry, true, but that hadn't bothered him particularly. His activity against the state had been, in a way, indirect, a sin of omission rather than commission: he was simply not returning with the money. But now he had shot down a police officer in the performance of his duty. Suddenly the break with his past was total, complete, irrevocable, much broader and deeper than he had ever imagined. Tendrils of fear began tugging at his mind and making his knees unreliable.

He had to be strong. He had made his choice, and so far he had triumphed. Whatever the obstacles, he must continue to prevail. The rules were changed now, and so was he.

He was puffing from exertion by the time he'd finished. He closed the barred door again, paused to catch his breath, and forced himself to walk casually and unconcernedly out of the building. He would not be eating lunch at the diner just ahead. He would not be eating lunch at all today.

The next major city, according to the map, was Columbia, South Carolina. He could risk driving the car that far, but there he would abandon it. He would travel the rest of the way to Miami by train. It was unlikely there would be a plane.

He got into the Pontiac, feeling the bulge of the pistol against his left side as he sat down. He started the engine, backed the car, shifted, avoided the angle-parked police car, and drove sedately out of town at twenty miles an hour.

4

It looked like a wedding cake. Menlo peered out at it from the cab's rear seat, his eyes squinting somewhat from the brightness. It was Sunday, and the sun shone bright on the Sunways Hotel, pink and white, with a great white fountain out front that looked like marzipan. The splashing water made a cool sound.

"I hate this lousy town," said the cab driver, waiting to take his turn at the canopied entrance.

Menlo, who did not answer, was glad of the delay. It gave him an opportunity to study the place, get used to it a little.

Everything was new, everything was different. Menlo's confidence had been shaken by the incident in the little South Carolina town, and in the back of his mind there was the growing suspicion that he wasn't going to make it. This was a whole new world in which he had no experience. He had no papers, no satisfactory explanation of who he was or where he came from. He had no real idea even where he was going.

There were too many things he hadn't thought of, too many things he couldn't foresee. Even in the mechanics of everyday living he was hampered by the fact that he was so brand new to the United States, and nothing here corresponded exactly with its counterpart in Klastrava. The trains he'd been on—he'd had to change twice—were unlike those at home; only one class of carriage—an open, uncompartmented, third-class type, but with up-holstered seats of a first-class style. There had been no ticket booth at the entrance to the platform; tickets were taken by uniformed conductors on the train itself. From the important difference of language and currency down to the appearance and customs of restaurants, everything was subtly and jarringly strange. He had to feel his way, groping from one situation to the next, certain that everyone he met must know that he was a foreigner. In Klastrava a foreigner as obvious as he would have been under official surveillance long before this. He knew the United States was much more lax but he couldn't just blunder along this way forever, carrying a suitcase full of unexplainable money and hoping for the best.

The currency was beginning to seem more real to him now, and he was beginning to understand why he'd had so much trouble with the old man. Most Americans were suspicious of fifty-dollar bills. He had managed with some difficulty to spend three of them, getting smaller bills in change, and he was using small bills and coins now, hoping they would last until he'd figured out what to do with the rest of the money. He realized, belatedly, that if he'd offered the old man a ten-dollar bill instead of fifty, there might have been no trouble.

It all depended on whether or not he was given time to get his bearings. He needed it, and at least in the beginning he was going to need assistance. Which meant Bett Harrow, and the statue. Bett Harrow could help him if she chose, and the mourner should put him in the debt of Bett Harrow's rich and influential father. That was all he needed.

His taxi finally reached the canopy, and the rear door was jerked open. The cab driver was paid and tipped as was the doorman. A bellboy carried his suitcases—the one on the left contained the money, the one on the right the mourner wrapped in clothing—to the desk and he too was tipped. The respectful but haughty clerk looked him in the eye. "Your name, sir?"

Name?

In panic, Menlo heard himself saying "Parker. Auguste Parker."

Why did they want his name, before he'd so much as asked for a room? And why had he said Parker? On the way over from the railroad station he had invented an alias to use in signing the hotel register, but the abruptness of the question had thrown the name right out of his mind. So he had blurted out Parker's without thinking, adding his own first name, and in the back of his mind the suspicion that he was going to fail loomed just a little larger.

The clerk had a drawer full of five-by-seven file cards. He looked at several and frowned. "I don't seem to find your reservation, Mr. Parker."

Menlo was not that much of a traveler. His infrequent jaunts in the past had always been in an official capacity; such problems as hotel reservations had always been taken care of by the Ministry. Coming to the United States, he had been checked into a Washington hotel by the Klastravian embassy officials.

But now he was traveling on his own, and he was doing things all wrong. "I don't have a reservation. I only want a—"

"No reservation?" The clerk seemed unable to believe it for a second or two. Then a sudden frost hit him. "I'm terribly sorry, but we're quite full up. You might try one of the hotels downtown; perhaps they could help you."

Menlo and his suitcases were shunted aside. The fat man's face reddened with anger, but there was nothing he could do. He was no longer Inspector Menlo. He was now merely a hunted refugee, alone and uncertain. Even a hotel clerk could treat him disdainfully with impunity.

After a minute he went back to the desk again, and caught the attention of the clerk. "Elizabeth Harrow," he asked, "what room?"

The clerk looked. "Twelve twenty-three."

"And I may call from where?"

"House telephones to your left, sir."

The minute he reached for his suitcases a bellboy materialized, but he shook his head angrily and the bellboy went away. There was a point at which hesitancy and confusion could no longer be borne, when what was needed was a sharp, sudden show of aggressive certainty. He had pussyfooted long enough; it was not his style. He would put up with it no longer.

He even took offense at the bored tone with which the switchboard operator responded. His own voice was authoritative and brisk as he gave Bett Harrow's room number. But there was no response; she was apparently not in her room.

He slammed the receiver down with annoyance, turned, caught the bellboy's eye. The boy hurried over, and Menlo pointed imperiously at his suitcases.

"I wish to check this luggage. Are there facilities?"

"Yes, sir. Right over there by—"

"You may take the luggage, and bring me the claim check."

"Yes, sir."

He lit a cigarette. He had discovered a brand that

combined the superior American tobacco with an adaptation of the Russian cardboard mouthpiece. There was an annoying wad of cotton or some foreign substance wedged down into the cardboard tube, but it didn't alter the taste much. It would do.

When the boy returned with a square of numbered red plastic, Menlo tipped him a quarter and asked for the restaurant. The boy pointed it out, and Menlo marched resolutely through the wide doorway. He had come into the hotel looking soft and fat and slump-shouldered, but now he was his normal self again, carrying his bulk with lithe dignity.

He had steak, an American specialty. His table was next to a huge glass window overlooking the beach, and as he ate he watched the hotel guests there. A few were swimming, but most were merely walking about aimlessly or lying on pneumatic mattresses. A depressing number of the women, all in bright-colored bathing suits, were stout and middle-aged and ugly, but here and there was a tall and beautiful one, and these he watched with pleasure and a feeling of anticipation.

He ate a leisurely meal, and lingered at the table afterward to smoke a cigarette over a third cup of coffee. It was mid-afternoon, a slack time in the restaurant, so no effort was made to hurry him. When at last he paid his check, he took a chance and proffered one of the fifty-dollar bills. He was terrified of running short of the smaller bills again, and surely here a fifty-dollar bill wouldn't seem unusual. The waiter didn't seem to react at all, but took the bill and soon returned with a little tray full of change. In this country, he noted, a waiter's tip was not automatically added on to the bill—at home it was a standard 10 per cent—but was left to the discretion of the diner. To be on the safe side he left a 15 per cent tip instead of 10, and strolled back out to the lobby.

Menlo crossed to the house phones and called Bett Harrow's room again, and this time she was there. "Good afternoon, my dear, this is Auguste."

He hoped she would recognize him by the first name alone. He didn't want to mention his full name, in case the switchboard operator was listening in.

There was the briefest of hesitations. "Well, I'll be damned. You did it."

"You expected less?"

"Where are you?"

"In the lobby. I would like to talk to you."

"Come on up."

"Thank you."

There was a bank of elevators across the way. He went over and was swooped up to the twelfth floor, where the corridor was uneasily reminiscent of Dr. Caligari's cabinet, the walls and ceiling painted in bright primary colors, the carpeting wine red. He found the door marked 1223 and knocked.

She opened the door almost immediately, smiling at him in amusement. "Come in, come in. Tell me all about it."

"In due time. It is more than pleasant to see you again."

She was wearing form-fitting plaid slacks and a pale-blue halter. Her feet were bare, and the toenails were painted bright red. This struck him as ludicrous—it was as though she were wearing a flowing mustache—but he refrained from any comment. Still, it was unfortunate; the golden American goddess with scarlet toes. A bit of the glamour was destroyed for him forever. Inside her shoes, had the airline stewardess too had scarlet toes? Sad.

She closed the door behind him. The room looked like a more expensive version of the motel room in Washington. There was the same cheap bright-plastic look to everything.

"To tell you the truth," she said, as they both sat down, "I didn't expect to see you again. I thought Chuck would eat you up."

"Chuck? Ah, yes. Parker, you mean."

She shrugged. "He calls himself Chuck Willis sometimes. That's the way I think of him."

"Under any name," he replied, smiling, "he did not eat me up. As you can see."

"I hope you didn't leave him alive anywhere," she said, "I think he'd be a bad man to have for an enemy."

"We need have no fears in that respect."

She shook her head in slow amazement. "There's more to you than meets the eye, Auguste. Auguste? Don't you have a better name than that?"

"I am most sorry. Only the one name."

"It's too ridiculous to call you Auguste. And you're no Augie."

"A minor problem," he said, feeling annoyance that she should find his name ridiculous. "I suggest we table it for the moment. I have the statue."

"I just can't get it through my head. You really did kill Chuck and take the statue? What about the other one, that friend of Chuck's?"

"Both of them. It is a closed issue. The past has no lasting fascination for me. It is the immediate future which now concerns me. I should like to meet your father."

"I know, you want to sell him the statue. Twenty-five thousand?"

"Perhaps not. Possibly there is something he can do for me that would be more valuable."

"Like what?" She seemed at once more alert.

He considered his words carefully. "In a sense," he said, "I am in this nation illegally. My visa was for a short time only, and good only in Washington. It is my intention to remain in this country, therefore I will need papers. Your father is a well-to-do and influential man. It is not impossible that among his contacts is someone who can furnish me with the appropriate forged papers."

"I don't know if he can help you. If he can, is that all you want?"

"One small matter in addition. I have in my possession a rather substantial sum of cash, American. I would prefer not to carry this around with me. Your father perhaps could aid me in placing it in a bank or some other safe repository?"

"How much is a large sum?"

"I have not counted it as yet, but I believe it is approximately one hundred thousand dollars."

Her eyes widened. "My God! Did you take that away from Chuck too?"

"If you mean was it his money—no, it was not."

"All right. Anything else?"

"One more small matter. I had no reservation, and cannot obtain a room here."

"I'll see what I can do."

She went to the phone, spoke to someone at length and finally hung up. She turned to Menlo. "All set. It's on the wrong side of the hotel—no view of the ocean—but it's a room. You can pick the key up downstairs. I told them your name was John Auguste, is that all right?"

"Perfectly."

"My father isn't in Miami now, but I will call him. He

should be able to get here by tomorrow. I'll let you explain to him exactly what you want. I'll just tell him Chuck Willis is dead, and that someone else has the statue and wants to sell it."

"Very good." Menlo got to his feet. "I do thank you."

"Where are you going?" She seemed displeased. "You're all business now, is that it?"

"I have been traveling, dear lady. I should like to shower, to rest, and to don fresh clothing. I had intended to ask you to dine with me this evening, to allow me to make some small gesture of appreciation for your assistance."

"You're a strange man," she said.

"Is eight o'clock acceptable?"

"Why not?"

He bowed. "I shall see you then."

She walked him to the door and even barefoot she was a good two inches taller than he. She opened the door and stood holding the knob. "You didn't even try to kiss me."

Menlo was surprised. It was true that she had granted him her favors in the hotel in Washington, but he had thought then that it was only because Parker had rejected her. Could it be that she actually found him attractive? He was shorter than she, and unfortunately overweight, and possibly twenty years her senior.

But it couldn't be the money; she was already rich.

Surprised, not quite sure what to make of her, he said,

"You must forgive me. I have been, as I say, traveling. I am somewhat weary. And also, I must confess, my mind has been occupied with my own predicament. This evening, I trust you will find me more gallant."

"This evening," she replied, "you can tell me all about how you got the upper hand with Chuck. That I've got to hear."

"I will tell all. Until this evening, then."

He bowed his way out and took the elevator back down to the lobby. He didn't approach the same clerk, but another one, giving the name Bett Harrow had invented for him. John Auguste. It would do as well as any. The clerk handed him the key, and a bellboy went to reclaim his luggage.

He had intended to bathe first, but once the bellboy had left the room he found his curiosity could wait no longer. How much exactly *did* he have in the suitcase?

When he opened it on the bed, loose bills spilled out on all sides. Hundreds, fifties, some twenties. With a flutter in his chest, as though he were standing too close to the edge of a cliff and looking over, he sat down on the bed and began to count. His weight depressed the mattress, tilting the suitcase, and another little shower of bills fluttered to the bedspread.

He made a little game out of it. First, he separated the bills into three piles, by denomination. Then, beginning with the hundreds, he sorted them into stacks, twenty-five bills in each.

Seven hundred fifty-three hundreds.

Four hundred twenty-two fifties.

And one hundred seventy-four twenties.

Nine-nine thousand, eight hundred eighty dollars. $99,880.00. Nine nine comma eight eight zero decimal zero zero. In the currency of his native land, three million, one hundred ninety-six thousand, one hundred sixty koter.

Oh, and more. In his wallet was eight hundred and fifty-three dollars. In his coat pocket, five hundred more. He had spent, coming down, he estimated approximately a hundred dollars.

Grand total: One hundred and one thousand, three hundred and thirty-three dollars!

He sang gaily in the shower. In English.

5

He was awakened the next afternoon on the beach by a funereal man in black who asked if he was Mr. John Auguste.

He opened his eyes, but immediately closed them again, against the glare of the sun. He had seen only the funereal man in black, in silhouette, bending over him, blotting out part of the sky.

Mr. John Auguste? Some mistake. I am Auguste Menlo. The similarity of—

No!

He sat bolt upright, not sure for a second whether he'd actually said the words aloud or merely thought them. But the funereal man in black was still standing there, bowed, patient, waiting for an answer. With the riot of colors on the beach, he looked like someone's odd idea of a joke.

Menlo said, "Yes, I am John Auguste."

"You are wanted on the house phone, sir. By the blue entrance, phone number three."

"Thank you."

The funereal man in black went away. He was wearing highly shined black oxfords, which sank into the sand at every step. He walked slowly and cautiously because of this, and looked like the Angel of Death. Menlo got up from the pneumatic mattress and followed him.

It was Monday afternoon, a little before three, and the hotel beach was jammed. All of yesterday's check-ins were already there, plus the layovers from the week before. Menlo had to cut a meandering path through them to get to the phone.

He was wearing maroon boxer-style bathing trunks. He looked ridiculous, and knew it, but he also realized he looked no more ridiculous than half the other men on the beach. His flesh had reddened from exposure to the sun, and it was just as well he'd been awakened. A little longer, and he would have had a painful burn. Tomorrow he would have to get some of that suntan lotion he smelled everywhere on the beach.

Already he was beginning to feel at home. Sunshine and warmth. A pneumatic mattress to lie on, and occasional beautiful girls in skimpy white bathing suits to ogle. Plus, of course, the one beautiful girl to go to bed with. After last night with Bett Harrow, this day of sleep and warmth and contentment was more than a luxury; it was a necessity. There was a twenty-year difference between them, and by approximately one o'clock that morning it had begun to show.

He smiled to himself, plodding through the sand toward the hotel. What a way to exercise the weight away, eh? Sweat it away by day beneath the hot sun, sweat it away by night beneath the cool sheets.

To the left of the blue entrance were the telephones, a row of five mounted on the wall, with soundproof barriers between them, sticking out like blinkers on a horse. Menlo went to number three and picked up the receiver. "Auguste here."

"This is Ralph Harrow."

"Ah! Mr. Harrow!"

"I'm told you have something to show me. If it's convenient, you could bring it up now. Top floor, suite D."

Bring it? Not quite so soon, Menlo thought. "Ah, I am sorry. It isn't, ah, completely ready to be shown; not quite yet. But perhaps I could come and discuss the situation with you? In one hour?"

There was the briefest of pauses, and then Harrow replied, "That's fine. One hour."

"I look forward to meeting you," Menlo said, but Harrow had hung up. Menlo returned the receiver to its hook and smiled at it. *Bring* the statue? Did Harrow have some idea he could get the statue by trickery, and not pay for it?

A depressing thought occurred to him. *That* might be why the daughter had been so free with her charms. To lull his suspicions, to dull his wits.

But would a father, even in the United States, use his daughter in such fashion?

He wished he knew for sure what Bett Harrow saw in him. He was not young or handsome, he was only rich. But she was rich too.

He couldn't understand it. He was grateful for it and he would not refuse it, but he couldn't understand it.

He left the telephones and went through the blue entrance—a slate walk flanked by cool green ponds full of tiny fish and screened on both sides by tall board fences painted blue—and entered the rear of the hotel. There was a bank of three elevators here, for the convenience of the swimmers and sunbathers. Menlo rode up to the seventh floor, and then walked the endless corridors to his room.

His black suit had been returned, beautifully cleaned and pressed. His freshly laundered shirts had come back, and the new socks and underwear he had bought in the hotel shop that morning along with the maroon bathing trunks were put away in the dresser drawer. He took a shower and dressed, checked the locked suitcase full of money in the closet, which had not been tampered with, and left the room. He went to the nearer bank of elevators, and when the elevator arrived, said, "Top floor."

"Yes, sir."

When he got off, he asked directions to suite D, and was told to bear to his right. He did so. The halls up here were done in pastel shades, much less violent than in the plebeian quarters below, much more restful. He walked a considerable distance before finally seeing a door of any kind, which was marked "C." After a turning he came to suite D.

A middle-aged gentleman who could have been nothing but an American businessman—or perhaps a Swiss businessman, or a Scandinavian businessman, but at any rate a capitalist businessman—opened the door to Menlo's knock. "Mr. Menlo?"

"The name is Auguste, for the moment. John Auguste. You are Ralph Harrow?"

"Yes. Come in."

The daughter, down on the twelfth floor, had a two-room suite. How many rooms this one contained was anyone's guess. Harrow led the way down the foyer into a large sitting room. Directly ahead, through French doors, was a terrace. Doors in both side walls were open, leading into other parts of the suite.

"Sit down," said Harrow. "Drink?"

"Perhaps, Scotch. And plain water."

"Right you are."

The long sofa in the middle of the room was white leather. The marble-topped coffee table in front of it was covered by a number of American magazines, tastefully laid out in a diagonal row, so that the name of each magazine showed. Menlo sat down on the sofa, feeling the whoosh of air leaving the cushion, and looked around. He would have to get a suite like this for himself soon. Once everything had been straightened out.

Harrow brought his Scotch and water, along with a drink for himself in his other hand. He sat down at the opposite end of the sofa. "My daughter tells me you took the statue away from Willis."

"In a manner of speaking." Menlo smiled. "Actually he never did have possession of it."

"Then you're an amazing man. Willis didn't strike me as the kind of man you could take things from. Well. But that's not why you're here. You realize I paid for the statue once, don't you?"

"So I understand."

"Fifty thousand. Willis must have had that on him too. You mean to say you didn't get it?"

"No, I did not. An oversight, possibly."

"Bett tells me you have money. Quite a bit of it. In cash."

"From another source entirely, I assure you."

Harrow waved that aside. "The point is, I've already

paid for the damn thing. I don't like the idea of paying twice."

"Your daughter didn't explain my terms?"

"No, she didn't."

Menlo outlined them quickly; a safe place for his money, the necessary papers to explain himself should it ever become necessary. "And one last thing," he said. "One of my teeth is capped, and within the cap is a tiny capsule containing poison. I don't believe—"

"Poison!"

"Yes. I don't be—"

"What on earth for?"

"In my former job it was thought I might find it necessary to take my own life under certain conditions. I somehow do not believe that will ever be necessary now."

"Good God, man, poison! What happens when you eat?"

"In normal activity of the jaw, the capsule cannot be broken. But what I would like, if possible, is to have some dental surgeon remove it. If you could obtain for me a dentist who would not ask a lot of questions, I would be most grateful, most grateful."

"I think that could be arranged," Harrow said, nodding. "I'll speak to my own dentist about it. He's a good man; I've known him for years."

"Excellent. And the other items?"

"No problem at all. We'll get you the papers first, and

then dispose of the funds. Some you'll want to invest, no doubt, and the balance you'll want handy for living expenses. No problem."

"Very good."

"But now," Harrow said, "I have my terms."

"Ah?"

Harrow's eyes, all at once, were shining. He leaned forward. "Before we go any farther," he said, "I want to hear the details. I want to know exactly how you managed to get the statue away from Willis, and I want to know what on earth your job was that you had to go around with a capsule full of poison in your mouth."

Menlo smiled. "I see." He had forgotten this essential fact about Ralph Harrow; the man was a romantic. It was the first thing that he had learned about Harrow, from hearing Parker and Bett talk about him back in Washington. On business matters Harrow was a total realist, but within was a strong streak of romanticism. It was the romantic, not the businessman, who had paid fifty thousand dollars for the mourner. "I will be most happy to tell all," Menlo said.

"Let me refresh that drink first."

"Thank you so much."

Menlo told it all then, from the time he had first received the assignment until he had arrived in Miami, deleting from the story only the sexual encounters with Bett Harrow and the murderous encounter with the old policeman. He talked also about his role as Inspector in Klastrava, and this led Harrow to question him about various high points in his fifteen-year career, and about his life as a guerrilla in the latter stages of World War II. Nearly an hour went by, and Harrow was still asking questions, Menlo still talking. Harrow seemed fascinated, and Menlo, like most people, enjoyed having a good audience.

But finally it was finished. Harrow thanked him for spending so much of his time in telling the story, assuring him again that everything he'd asked for would be supplied. "Now, Mr. Menlo—or should I say Inspector Menlo, eh?—now I do want to see the mourner. The statuette. Could you bring it?"

Menlo considered briefly, but he no longer had any doubts. Harrow could be trusted. He finished his drink, got to his feet. "I shall get it at once."

"Thank you. I'll be waiting."

Menlo rode the elevator back down to the seventh floor, and got the mourner out of his other suitcase. He wrapped the little statuette in one of the white bath towels from the bathroom, and brought it back upstairs under his arm. The elevator operator looked at it oddly, but didn't say anything.

He knocked again, and once again Harrow came to the door. "You were very quick. Is that it?"

"Yes, this is it," Menlo said, and bowed.

Harrow took the bundle and immediately began to unwrap it. "Go on in," he said. "Go on in." He pushed the door closed behind Menlo, and continued to stand in the foyer, unwrapping the statue.

Menlo walked past him into the sitting room and there was Parker sitting on the white sofa, a gun in his hand. Menlo took one shocked look at Parker's face and acted without hesitation: he twisted his jaw hard to the right, and bit down.

FOUR

1

Menlo had been too excited, back there in Kapor's house, too excited to think about checking the bodies and making sure the two of them were dead. And a derringer with .22 rim-fire cartridges isn't very much of a gun. . . .

Parker awoke to darkness, with something burning his side. He was lying on his back on a lot of rocks with an invisible flame searing his side. He moved, and the rocks made noises under him, scraping together, and then memory imploded into his mind.

They'd underestimated the fat bastard. They'd figured him to wait till they were clear of the house, maybe even clear of the city, and he'd second-guessed them. He'd dragged that crazy little gun out from somewhere, and now he was gone with the money and the mourner, and here Parker was lying on broken pieces of statues with a burning in his side.

He rolled over to the right because the pain was on the left side, and got his knees under him, then stabbed out with his hands till they hit a pedestal. Slowly he climbed up the pedestal till he was standing on his feet. He was weak and dizzy, and when he took a step it was bad footing because of all the broken pieces of statue everywhere on the carpet. He made it to a wall, and then felt his way along the wall to the end and made the turn, bumping into the bookcase. Now he knew where he was. He kept going around the wall till he got to the door and found the light switch. He flicked the light on.

Everything was a mess. The room was a mess, broken statues and tipped-over pedestals everywhere, the mourner and the suitcase both gone. His side was a mess, shirt and trousers cold and sticky with blood. And Handy, sprawled over there like a dummy dumped off a cliff, was an even worse mess. From the look of the blood on him, and his dead-white face, he was gun-shot.

Parker went over, still very shaky on his feet, and dropped to his knees beside him. Handy was still breathing, very slow and shallow. Both guns were still here, the .380 and the Terrier, lying on the floor among the broken statues. The fat bastard had been in a big hurry.

It was a good thing. If he'd taken his time, he might have done the job right.

Never underestimate the power of a smooth-talking amateur.

Parker gathered up the Terrier, got back on his feet, and lurched over to the door. He opened it, and saw light. Down at the far end of the hall there was a staircase—the front staircase, not the one they'd come up—and light was coming up from there. And, dimly, party noises.

Parker looked at his watch. Twenty to twelve. He'd been out for over three hours. Kapor was home, the party was going on.

He thought it out, came to a decision, and sat down on the floor next to the door. He kept the door slightly open, so he could hear when the party ended, be warned if anybody came upstairs.

When he pulled his shirt out of his trousers, so he could look at the wound, the pain suddenly intensified, almost blacking him out again. A kind of green darkness closed in all around him, like a camera lens closing. He leaned his back against the wall and breathed deeply until the green darkness went away. Then he looked at the wound.

The bullet had plowed a deep furrow in the flesh along his side, just above the belt. His whole side was discolored, gray and purplish and black, and sensitive to the touch, like a charley horse. The furrowed flesh was ragged, and smeared with dried blood. Fresh blood still oozed sluggishly from the wound. As far as he could tell, the bullet wasn't in him, but had scored his side and kept on going.

So he'd come out better than Handy. All he had was a pain in the side. It wouldn't even disable him badly, once a doctor had seen to it.

He looked at his watch again. Ten to twelve. The party was still going on. To his right he could hear the shallow, labored breathing of Handy. If the party lasted too long, Handy wouldn't make it.

His left arm was stiffening up. The fingers wouldn't work right. He transferred the Terrier to his left hand, so he could get out a cigarette, and the hand wouldn't hold onto the gun. It fell to the carpet. Parker cursed under his breath, and left it there. He lit a cigarette, and leaned his head back against the wall, and sat there with the cigarette in his mouth, listening to the party noises and Handy's uneven breathing. His feet were out in front of him, and his arms were hanging at his sides, the hands resting palm up on the floor. A pins-and-needles feeling kept running up and down his left side and down his left arm. His fingers on that side felt like sausages, thick and unresponsive.

The seconds limped by, dragging sacks, forming into long lines. Every line took forever to form, and then was only one more minute. Parker lit a fresh cigarette off the butt of the old one. Then that cigarette was smoked down, and he lit another fresh one. And again.

They were happy as hell downstairs.

This was six. Six times in his life he'd been shot. And this was the second time he'd been left for dead. The first time, it had been a heavier slug, and well aimed, but it had hit his belt buckle instead of his stomach, and he'd managed to crawl away from that one with only the loss of appetite for a while. In England, in forty-four, an MP had winged him when he'd taken a truckful of stolen tires through a roadblock. And three other times it had happened. He was almost as shot up as Tom Mix.

He tried to lift his left arm so he could look at his watch, but the arm felt as though it had been injected full of lead. He reached over with his right hand and grabbed his left wrist and lifted. It was a quarter after one. The sweep-second hand was in no hurry; the other two hands were just painted on.

They were too happy down there. Why the hell didn't they go home?

What if Kapor decided to show somebody all his pretty statues?

Parker grimaced, and reached over with his right hand to pick up the Terrier. He held it in his lap, and smoked, and waited. Whenever he finished a cigarette, he butted it against the wall board. There weren't any ashtrays handy.

Handy sounded like he was snoring. Blood in his

throat, probably. So maybe he wouldn't make it, and the fat bastard would be batting five hundred.

It was getting quieter downstairs. He lifted his hand again to look at his watch, and it was twenty to two. He felt as though he'd been sitting here for days. The burning had lessened in his side, and so had the pins and needles. Now there was a dull numbness, with a low throbbing pain behind it.

Quieter and quieter. He reached up and, grabbing the doorknob, pulled himself upright. The green darkness closed in again, and he waited, leaning against the wall next to the doorway, until slowly it faded away again. The cigarettes hadn't helped; they'd just made him more lightheaded.

When he could take a chance on walking, he went through the doorway and lurched across to the opposite wall, so he could lean his right side against it. He moved along, more slowly than he wanted, until he got to the head of the stairs. He peered around the edge of the wall, and he was looking down at the big front hall, with a parquet floor. The front door was open, and people were leaving. Kapor was smiling and nodding, and telling them all good-bye. They were speaking a lot of different languages, French and German and some others. Nobody was speaking English.

It took them a long while to clear out. Two or three loud-mouthed women in furs took the longest. Then the front door closed at last, and only Kapor and his butler-bodyguard were left standing in the hall.

Kapor said something, and the bodyguard bowed and went away. They were both wearing formal dress, like waiters. Kapor yawned, patting his mouth with the back of his hand. Then he took out a flat gold cigarette case and took his time lighting a cigarette. When he finally had it going, he turned around and started up the stairs.

He was short and slender and a dandy, with a hawk face and ferret eyes. His hands and face were so pale they looked as though they'd been dusted with flour. He didn't see Parker until he was all the way to the top of the stairs. When he saw Parker, and the gun, he opened his mouth wide without making any sound.

Parker said, "Keep it soft. Walk ahead of me to the trophy room."

"The what?"

"The statues," Parker said.

Sudden alarm showed on Kapor's face, and then was wiped away again. "What are you doing here?"

"We'll talk. In the trophy room."

"Shall I shout for help?"

"You won't shout twice. Move."

Kapor hesitated, thinking it over, but his eyes kept flicking past Parker toward the room where the statues were. He wanted to know if the money was still in the

Apollo. He shrugged and walked past Parker down the hall.

"Move slow."

Kapor glanced back at him. "I see you've been wounded."

"Just move slow and steady."

Parker braced himself, and then staggered over to the opposite wall. He wanted to keep his right side as a support.

Kapor walked into the room first, and stopped short in the doorway staring at the wreckage. Then he saw the Apollo, with its head off. "What has hap—"

"That's right," Parker told him. "It's gone."

Parker followed him in, and closed the door. He leaned his back against it. He would have liked to sit down on the floor again, but it would have been wrong psychologically.

Then Kapor saw Handy lying there, breath still bubbling faintly in and out of him. "Is he the one who shot you?"

"No. You ever hear of Menlo?"

"Auguste Menlo?" Kapor looked surprised, and then frightened, and then artificially surprised. "What would the Inspector have to do with this?"

"We're going to make a deal, Kapor."

"We are? I don't know yet what you're talking about."

"The hundred grand is gone. Go take a look in the statue. It's gone."

"I can see that."

"I can get you half of it back."

"Half?"

"That's better than none."

Kapor glanced at Handy. "He's dying," he said.

"If he dies, the deal's off."

"What deal? Say what you've got to say."

"I can tell you things you want to know. And I can get you half the dough back. That's what I do for you. What you do for me—you get a doctor who won't make a police report on bullet wounds. In your job, you must know a doctor like that."

Kapor nodded briefly. His eyes were wary.

"You also take care of my partner. Keep him here till he's on his feet. When he's well enough to travel, I give you your dough back."

"How do I know you can get it back?"

"I know who's got it, and where he's going."

"You seem sure."

"I am sure. He's too greedy not to go there."

"Whatever that may mean. This other point. You said you could tell me something I might want to know. What would that be?"

"Is it a deal?"

"How do I know, until I've heard what you have to tell me?"

"Forget that part. That's bonus. For half the dough back, is it a deal?"

Kapor shrugged, and looked at Handy. "I think he will die anyway. Then you won't get me the money."

"So make up your mind quick. The sooner he sees a doctor, the better."

"If he is going to die, and I get no money, why should I deal with you?"

"It's worth the chance."

"Possibly."

"Definitely. You don't have a week to think it over."

"Very true. All right, it's a deal."

"I want a doctor. Fast. For him, to keep him alive. And for me, to tape me up so I can travel. If I can't travel, I can't get you your dough back."

"Now, what do you have to tell me that I want to know?"

"After the doctor gets here. Where do I find a bed?"

"I see." Kapor smiled thinly. "There is no trust wasted between us, eh? Am I permitted to know a name by which I may call you?"

"Pick one you like."

"Of course. You may use the bedroom directly across the hall. As to your friend, I do not think we should move him without medical advice."

"That's right."

Parker slid over until he was clear of the door, then opened it and went out to the hallway. He angled over to the opposite doorway, shoved the door open, found the light switch. He didn't see anything else in the room at all, only the bed. He went over and dropped down onto it and rolled over onto his back. He kept the gun in his hand. He closed his eyes, because the ceiling light made them burn, but he wouldn't let himself lose consciousness.

After a while, he heard a movement and opened his eyes. Kapor had come in. "I've called the doctor. I'll have him look at your friend first, of course." Kapor switched on a table lamp beside the bed, then went over and turned off the ceiling light. "That will be more restful," he said. "When you see the doctor, it might be best to tell him nothing."

"Don't worry."

"I seem to have much to worry about. But I will try to take your advice."

He left, and Parker lay there, gripping the gun and holding to consciousness. The green darkness closed down around him again, leaving only one small opening in the center. He lay that way, suspended, not awake and not asleep, until the doctor came in.

The doctor was a stocky man with a brown mustache.

He looked angry. He didn't say anything at first, then he said, "Put that damn gun away."

Parker said, "No."

"No? Then take your finger off the trigger. I'm going to hurt you, and I don't want to get shot for it."

Parker's right hand was now sluggish too. He had trouble making the fingers open, but they finally did, and the gun fell. He couldn't find it again, but he knew it was on the bed somewhere.

"Don't scream now, for God's sake." Then the doctor did something painful to Parker's left side.

It woke him up. He went from the green darkness through complete awareness to a blazing red darkness on the other side. The pain subsided, and he slid softly back into the green. Then the doctor was at him again, and it was red again. He kept alternating between the two, but he didn't scream.

The doctor, or somebody, had stripped him, and rolled him over this way and that. He felt total awareness just beyond his grasp, as though any second he might be perfectly all right, his old self again. But he could never quite make it that last fraction of an inch; he just kept shuttling back and forth.

It went on and on, and there were times when he was out completely. Then, from very far away, he heard the doctor say, "You'll live. You'll be stiff in the morning, but you'll live."

He tried to answer, but it wouldn't work. He was falling down into the green again. The green got darker and darker, and then it was black, and then it wasn't anything.

2

After breakfast, he smoked a Russian cigarette. It was about three times as long as a cigarette ought to be, but most of it was a hollow cardboard tube. By the time the smoke got from the tobacco to his mouth, it tasted exactly like cardboard tube.

The maid had said nothing to him when she'd brought the tray, and she was just as uncommunicative when she came to take it away again. It hadn't taken Kapor long to replace Clara Stoper, and it hadn't taken the replacement long to learn to be a dummy.

After she took the tray, Parker stubbed out the Russian cigarette and tried getting out of bed. Practically his whole torso was taped, giving him a tight, corseted feeling, and his left arm still felt heavier and more sluggish than usual. He felt faint twinges in his left side when he swung his legs over, a minute of dizziness when he got to his feet, and his whole body was stiff, as though he'd been given a workover by experts. He took a step away from the bed, and then stopped when he saw the two suitcases standing there at the foot of the bed. One belonged to him, the other belonged to Handy.

He was still standing there looking at them when the door opened and Kapor came in "Ah! You're up and about. Very good."

Parker was wearing only shorts and bandages. "What happened to my suit?" he asked.

"All of your clothing was burned last night, except for your socks and shoes, there at the foot of the bed. The suit and shirt were ruined."

"Where'd the luggage come from?"

"Your motel room, of course. I found the key in your pocket, and sent someone there this morning to check you out. You seem to carry identification under several different names. I assume none of the names is accurate."

"You went through my stuff?"

"Of course," Kapor shrugged. "Could you expect anything else? Perhaps you'd better sit down for a while."

Parker thought the same thing. He sank down on the edge of the bed. "What about my partner?"

"The doctor is with him now. He says he can't tell one way or the other until the bullet is removed, and it couldn't be last night because your friend was in shock.

The doctor returned this morning. He is doing what he can to ready your friend for the operation."

"All right."

"He is a good man, I assure you. If your friend's life can be saved, he will save it."

"That's good."

"And now," Kapor said, "perhaps it is time we talked."

"I want some clothes on first."

"Of course. I apologize. I confess I've been thinking more about my own loss than of yours. Which bag is yours?"

Parker pointed. "That one."

Kapor lifted it and put it on the bed. "Do you feel capable of walking?"

"Yes."

"Then, when you are ready, you'll find me downstairs. Down the front staircase, and to your left."

"All right. Wait. Where's my gun?"

"Both guns are in the top dresser drawer. I put them there to avoid alarming the help."

"O.K."

Kapor smiled thinly, bowed, and left the room.

Parker dressed slowly, hampered by his stiffness and weakness. He needed a shave, and wanted to wash his face, but that could wait. He went out to the hall and downstairs, feeling better the more he moved. He turned left at the foot of the stairs and through a tall doorway into a large sitting room with a bar at the far end. Kapor was there, mixing himself something complicated, with sugar. He looked over. "Ah, there you are. Would you care for a drink?"

"Bourbon."

"Medicinally. Of course."

Kapor brought him a glass, waved him to a leather armchair, and sat down in another facing him. "Now," he said, "if you think the time has come, I am willing to listen."

"Menlo was sent here by his Ministry. They're onto you, skimming the cream off the dough you handle. They figure you've stolen around a hundred G by now."

Kapor's smile disappeared, and his eyes narrowed. "The Ministry seems to have chosen an odd way to handle the situation."

"They sent Menlo here to rub you out, quick and quiet. Find the money if he could, but mainly get rid of you. They did it that way, because any other way it might have leaked. There's a big wad of cash due here soon, and they figured you were waiting for that before you took off."

"More perspicacity than I had expected," Kapor said, grim-faced.

"They've been holding it up on purpose, to keep you here till Menlo could get to you."

"How charming." Kapor unsheathed his gold cigarette case. "Cigarette?"

"Thanks."

Kapor lit them both. "I still don't understand what happened last night. What connection have you with Auguste Menlo?"

"He'd decided to take the dough himself."

"Auguste Menlo? Incredible. He has a reputation for honesty that passes belief."

"He was never offered a hundred G before."

"Ah, so." Kapor's thin-lipped smile flashed again. "We are all human after all, eh?"

"We were in it with him. There's a lot more to it than that, but that's the way it winds up. We were in it with him. Also, a guy named Spannick got killed when he tipped to what Menlo was up to."

"Ahh! I'd heard of his death, of course. He was at some unlikely address—But go on."

"Menlo found out where you'd stashed the dough."

"How?"

"Your maid, Clara Stoper."

"I see. She hasn't been here the last few days."

"She's dead."

"So much violence going on, all around me, and I never knew. And I was its target all along. It's a frightening thought. So you came here last night and Menlo double-crossed you."

"That's it."

"And now you say you know where to find him?"

"Right."

"How?"

"That's my business."

"Ah. Of course." Kapor settled back in his chair, smoking and gazing thoughtfully over Parker's head. "If I want any of my money at all, I suppose I had best go along with you."

"That's right."

"I imagine you plan to kill Menlo?"

"Yes."

"Please do a better job on him than he did on you."

"Don't worry."

"Not about that, no. But about this other matter. How long do I have before the Ministry decides to send someone else?"

"I don't know."

"Are they aware of Menlo's change of heart?"

"I don't think so. Spannick found out, but he's dead. Menlo claimed Spannick wouldn't have reported to them until he'd taken care of things."

"That sounds logical. Spannick was the ultimate egotist. But how did he find out in the first place? If he did, won't others?"

"No. It was an earlier double-cross, before my partner and I came in on it."

"It sounds so complex. I have the feeling I've heard barely a quarter of the story."

Parker shrugged. "You heard all of your part."

"Yes. Economy in all things. I assume Menlo has left Washington?"

"Yes."

"Do you feel strong enough to travel?"

"I think so."

"Will you want anyone with you? I can offer you one or two willing helpers."

"I can handle it myself."

"Yes, I suppose you can. Very well, then. Can I make any sort of travel reservations for you?"

"Yes. The first plane I can get to Miami."

"Miami! He's spending my money already, is he?"

"Yes."

Kapor squinted again, gazing over Parker's shoulder. "Now, I wonder," he said. "You tell me Menlo is in Miami. I wonder—"

"Forget it. Miami is a big town. I know *where* in Miami; you don't. I know who he's going to contact."

Kapor smiled sadly. "You are perfectly correct. I fear I must be satisfied with my fifty per cent. Now, one last question. How long will this take? It is now Saturday. Neither of us can be certain how long the Ministry will remain patient."

"Three or four days at the most. But what about my partner?"

"Ah, yes. If I disappear, what becomes of him? You won't return before Monday, I take it?"

"I doubt it," Parker answered.

"I will talk to the doctor. If he agrees, I will have your friend moved to a private rest home on Monday. I shall expect you to pay the bill, of course, out of your half of my money."

"It isn't your money either," Parker reminded him.

Kapor laughed. "The doctrine of private property," he said. "Don't you know that's against my religion? Nevertheless, I should prefer that you take care of the expenses of your friend's confinement."

"I'll take care of it."

"Excellent. I shall now call the airport and make your reservation. When the time comes you will be driven out to the airport in my personal car."

"Great."

"Do you want to see your friend now?"

"Is he awake?"

"No, I'm sorry to say he is still unconscious."

"Then never mind."

"Whatever you say." Kapor got to his feet. "If there's anything you need," he said, "do not hesitate to ask."

"I won't."

3

Parker moved across the crowded lobby, keeping his left elbow stuck out to protect his side, and pushed through to the desk. He signaled, and when one of the clerks came he said, "Ralph Harrow. He checked in yet?"

"Just one moment, sir." The clerk checked, and then came back. "He doesn't seem to be expected sir."

So Menlo wasn't here yet. That either meant he was driving down or he was holed up somewhere for a few days. Unless Parker had figured him wrong completely. But that didn't make any sense. Menlo had gone after Bett, to get the details of the job Parker was doing for her father. He had taken the statue. It didn't make sense any way but one; Menlo was coming down here to peddle the mourner to Harrow, probably in return for Harrow giving him some sort of a cover.

The only thing to do was wait. "Tell Freedman that

Charles Willis is here without a reservation and could use a room."

"Mr. Freedman, sir?"

"He's your boss."

"Yes, sir, I know. One moment, please."

It took more than a moment, but when the clerk came back he was affable, and Parker all of a sudden had a reservation. He let a bellboy take his suitcase and lead him up to a room on the fifth floor overlooking the beach. He tipped the boy, and then sat down in the chair by the window to rest and look out at the ocean. He was still shaky.

It was a little before noon, Sunday. He hadn't been able to get a seat on a plane out of Washington till this morning, so he'd had another night's sleep at Kapor's. The bullet was out of Handy now and the doctor thought he might even live. He'd complained about the idea of moving him, but finally agreed to it, if Handy was treated like a thin-skinned egg. So tomorrow an ambulance would take Handy to a private rest home.

It was just as well. If Kapor's bosses got tired of waiting and went in to finish him, they might decide to make a clean sweep and finish everybody in the house.

Parker had felt a lot better this morning, but the hours sitting on the plane had drained him, and now he was feeling stiff and shaky again. The wound was itching under the bandages, and there was one spot in the small of his back where the tape had got bunched up that was particularly bugging him.

After a while he got up from the chair, stripped, and looked at himself in the mirror on the closet door. His side was still discolored and bruised, but it was generally less angry looking. The tape wasn't as white and clean as it had been when it had first been put on, and it wasn't holding him as securely.

He'd had the cab stop at a drugstore on the way in from the airport, so there was now a supply of bandages and tape in his suitcase. He stripped off the old bandage, wincing as the tape tore hair from his chest, and unwound the gauze that was taped around his torso until he finally got down to the wound itself. It had pretty well scabbed over, and in this area too the coloring had gone down, though it was still pretty dark. He flexed his left arm, raising it and lowering it, and watching the flesh as it moved on his side. He could feel the strain against the edges of the wound, but in a way it helped ease the itching.

He took a shower then, favoring his left side and not letting the spray beat on it directly. The hot shower, and the stiffness, made him sleepy. He dried himself, having trouble with his left side because the skin was too tender to touch, and then he put on a fresh bandage and lay down on the bed. It was almost noon, and only a sliver of gold angled through the broad window. Parker drowsily watched the sliver narrowing, and then he fell asleep.

When he awoke, the room was darker. He forgot the wound at first and started to get out of bed at his usual speed, but a wrenching pain in his side stopped him. After that he was more cautious.

He looked out the window, and now a fat dark shadow, shaped like an elongated outline of the hotel, lay across the beach. His watch told him it was a little after three, and his stomach told him it was time to eat. He dressed and took the elevator down to the lobby.

The restaurant was across and to the left. He started that way, and then suddenly turned aside and walked over to the magazine counter. He picked up a magazine and leafed through it, glancing back, watching Menlo coming out of the restaurant.

The fat bastard looked very pleased with himself.

Not yet. It wouldn't do any good to brace him yet. Not till he knew for sure where the suitcase was.

He watched Menlo go over to one of the house phones. Menlo talked for a minute or two, and then walked to the elevators. As soon as the elevator door closed, Parker put the magazine down and went over to the desk to ask again if Ralph Harrow had showed up or was expected. The answer was still negative. So Menlo had just connected with Bett.

Parker went around to the door marked MANAGER,

J. A. FREEDMAN, and went on in. There was a new girl in the outer office, as usual, so he told her to tell Freedman Charles Willis wanted to see him. She spoke into the intercom and a minute later told him he could go in.

Freedman was barrel-shaped, five feet five inches tall. He was totally bald, with a bull neck and a bullet head. He looked hard all over, except the face, which was made of globs of Silly Putty plus horn-rimmed glasses. He came around the desk, the globs of Silly Putty settled into a smile, his hands outstretched. "Mr. Willis! So happy I could find you a room."

"It's good to be back," Parker said. His voice was softer than usual, his face more pleasant. After all these years, he fell automatically back into the Willis role.

They talked about inconsequentialities for a few minutes, long enough to satisfy the aura of friendship Freedman liked to maintain with his regular guests, and then Parker said, "There's one more favor you can do me. A small one."

"Anything I can do."

"Ralph Harrow should be checking in in a day or two. Let me know when he makes a reservation, will you?"

"Ah! You know Mr. Harrow?"

"We're old friends."

"A charming man, charming."

"Yes, he is. You'll let me know then?"

"Of course."

"I'd like to surprise him. Just tell me when he's due in, and which his suite will be."

"Certainly, Mr. Willis. I'll be more than happy to."

There was a little more talk, and then Parker left. He went up to his room and lay down on the bed to wait. He had forgotten about his hunger.

4

Parker heard them come in, father and daughter. Two bellboys came in with them, carrying the luggage, and Harrow and his daughter didn't say anything to one another till the bellboys left.

Freedman had given him half an hour's warning. Over the years Parker had cultivated two or three hotel employees, in case he ever needed them, and one of them had let him into the suite. He was now in the small dining room to the right of the sitting room; it was the least likely room for either Harrow or Bett to come into. If they did he could duck into the kitchen.

The connecting door was open, and he stood behind it, listening. Bett filled her father in on Menlo, explaining that Parker was dead and Menlo had the statue but was not likely to be too demanding about price. Menlo was in the country illegally, and apparently merely wanted

Harrow to help him establish a safe background for himself and also to arrange for a safe place for a large amount
of cash he had with him.

"How can *I* help him establish a background? I don't
know anything about that sort of thing," Harrow said.

"What difference does that make?" she said. "Promise
him anything. Once you've got the statue, what do you
care? What can he do to you?"

"That's too dangerous, Elizabeth."

"I don't see why. You promise to help him, he gives
you the statue, and you tell him it might take a few days
and then call the FBI. You give them the anonymous tip
that there's an undesirable alien staying here without papers. They take him away and that's the end of it. Menlo
can't ever prove you were the one who turned him in, and
he can't ever make any trouble for you. He doesn't have
anything on you."

"I don't know. . . ."

But Bett kept talking, persuading him, and finally he
came around. She gave him the name Menlo was using—
John Auguste—and his room number. Harrow put in a
call and waited a minute, then hung up. "He left word at
the desk that he'd be out on the beach. They'll page
him."

"I'd better get out of here then."

"I'll call you after it's over."

"You want me to call the FBI, don't you?"

His voice was weak. "If you would."

"Don't worry, Daddy. Bett will take care of everything."

In a few minutes the phone in the next room rang, and Harrow spoke briefly to Menlo, who said he'd be up in an hour. Parker settled down to wait.

Menlo finally arrived, and sat down to discuss terms with Harrow. It was just as Bett had said, plus some nonsense about a dentist. Harrow agreed to everything, and it should have been over then, but all at once Harrow started asking questions about Menlo's past and Menlo had to tell him his whole life story before they were finished.

Parker, waiting in the dining room, smothered his irritation, cursing Harrow for a fool. He came close to bursting in and settling it right there, but there were two other things that had to be settled first. He had to talk to Harrow, and he had to be sure where the money was. The money and the mourner would be in the same place. When Harrow put Menlo on the send for the mourner, Parker would find out where he went from the elevator operator, and that's where he would later find the money. So he held back, controlling his impatience.

Menlo finally did leave, and the moment he was gone Parker walked into the living room.

Harrow turned, saw him, and dropped his drink. "My God!"

"Keep it low," Parker said.

"He—he said you were dead." Harrow pointed foolishly at the door. "He said you were dead."

"He thought I was. He still thinks so. Sit down, Harrow. Take a minute, get used to the idea."

"My God," Harrow said again. He went over and sat down on the white leather sofa. He pressed his left hand to his chest. "You shouldn't do that. My heart isn't all that strong."

"You want a drink?" Parker asked.

"Scotch. I think. Yes, plain Scotch."

"On the rocks?"

"Yes. It doesn't matter."

Parker made the drink, and one for himself, and came back to the sofa. He handed one glass to Harrow, and Harrow swallowed half the Scotch in one gulp. Then he breathed deeply for a few seconds, and after that he settled down. He settled down so much he looked up at Parker and said, "You're alive, but you don't have the mourner. He has it."

"You really want to go through all that garbage with the FBI? What makes you think Menlo couldn't wriggle out of it? He's a big man back home; that wasn't crap he was feeding you. He tells his boss he got the money but couldn't get Kapor because his plans got fouled up, that he was in Miami holing up until he could get back to Washington to try again. They'll swallow it, they've got no reason not to trust him. So then he's free, and there's a whole espionage apparatus he can turn around and aim at you. You call the FBI on him, and he'll make you dead. Menlo's no boy to play with."

Harrow pursed his lips, and chewed his cheeks, and stared into what was left of his drink. "You could be right."

"So instead you leave Menlo to me. He gives you the statue, then I take care of him. And he won't be coming back to bother you or anybody else."

"And what do you want for this?"

"Just the gun, same as before."

"I don't have it here."

"You better get it quick. If Bett gave you some fancy ideas about crossing me too, forget it. Menlo didn't even manage to kill my partner. He's in a private rest home in Washington, and if he doesn't hear from me at the same time every day, he'll know you made trouble for me. Then he makes trouble for you."

"From a hospital bed?"

"He won't be in it forever."

Harrow thought that one over. Finally he said, "All right. The gun is in the hotel safe. I'll have it sent up."

"After we take care of Menlo. We don't want any bellboys coming in at the wrong time."

"No. You're right."

There was a soft rapping at the door. Harrow looked startled, and Parker said, "That's him now."

"So quickly?"

"Don't let it throw you. Just go out there and let him in. Get the statue away from him before he sees me, so he doesn't get a chance to try and break it or something."

"The statue!" Harrow hurriedly got to his feet. "The statue," he muttered, and went out through the doorway into the foyer. Parker, still seated on the sofa, heard him say, "You were very quick. Is that it?"

Then Menlo's voice, "Yes, this is it."

"Go on in," Harrow said. His voice was shaking, and Parker shook his head in disgust. "Go on in."

But Menlo didn't tip. He came on in through the foyer doorway, and stood stock still when he saw Parker sitting there. The blood drained from his face, and then all of a sudden he did something peculiar with his face, twisting his mouth around. Then he pitched over forward onto the carpet.

Harrow came in, clutching the mourner to his chest. "What did you do?"

"Nothing." Parker got to his feet. "The goddam fool. The poison."

"Poison? You mean, in his tooth?"

"Yeah." Parker knelt beside him. "He's dead all right."

"For God's sake, man, how do we explain this?"

"We don't. We stash him away in a closet or something. Tonight, around midnight, pour some booze over him and drop him off the terrace. Who's to know what floor the poor drunk fell from? Bett will be here to corroborate your story. He didn't fall from here."

"I couldn't do that!" Harrow was staring at Menlo's body with horror.

"Bett can. All right, call down for the gun now."

"But—"

"Call for the gun! Stop worrying about Menlo."

Harrow made the call, his voice trembling, while Parker dragged the body out onto the terrace into a corner where it couldn't be seen from inside the suite. He heard Harrow ask that the package that was being held for him in the safe be brought up to the suite.

They waited in silence. Harrow seemed more shaken by Menlo's death than Parker would ever have guessed. He kept working on the Scotch bottle.

After a while a bellboy came with a small package wrapped in brown paper. Harrow tipped him and sent him on his way, while Parker opened it. The gun was inside all right. Parker stowed it away inside his jacket. "Phone Bett. Tell her to come up here but don't say that I'm here."

After he'd made the call, Harrow said, "She said she'd be at least half an hour."

"That's all right. I'll be back by then."

Parker went out to the elevators. He pushed the button, and when the elevator on the left arrived, he asked the operator, "Did you take a fat man down from here about fifteen minutes ago?"

"Not me."

Parker pushed a ten into his hand. "Forget I even asked."

"Yes, sir!"

The elevator went back down, and Parker pushed the button again. The other elevator came up this time, and Parker asked the same question, with another ten in his hand.

"Yes, sir, I did. Just about fifteen minutes ago," the operator answered.

"What floor did he get off?"

"Seven. Then he came right back up here, a few minutes later."

"Wait here a minute. I want to get this ten's brother."

"I'm with you, sir."

Parker went back to suite D. Harrow wasn't in the living room. Parker found him in the bedroom, lying on his back, his left hand palm up over his eyes and his right hand holding a glass half full of Scotch.

Parker left him there for a minute, went out to the terrace, and rifled Menlo's pockets. He found the room key, and went to the bedroom. "Harrow," he said. "Get up from there. I'm going to want privacy when I talk to your daughter. You take off for a while."

Harrow sat up. He looked ashen, but he was busy gathering shreds of dignity around him. "That's not the proper tone of voice."

"Come on, I've got an elevator waiting."

"You've got an elevator waiting?" Harrow seemed bemused by the idea. He got to his feet, took the mourner up from the bed, and put it in a closet and locked the closet door, then pocketed the key and followed Parker out of the suite.

The elevator was still there, the operator patient. Parker slipped the two tens into the operator's hand and said, "This gentleman is going all the way down to the lobby. I'm getting off at seven."

"Yes, sir."

They were silent on the way down. Parker got off at the seventh floor, found room 706, and unlocked the door. The suitcase was in plain sight, in the closet, the same one they'd bought to carry the money in originally. It was locked, but a suitcase lock can be picked with a piece of spaghetti. Parker opened it, saw that it was still full of bills, and closed it again. He went out, located the emergency staircase, and went down to his room on the fifth floor. He stashed the suitcase, went back up to the seventh floor, and rang for the elevator.

It was the same one that had taken him down, and the operator smiled as he got aboard. They were old friends now; twenty dollars old. On the way up, the operator asked if he had any idea about a horse at Hialeah that could make the twenty grow. Parker told him that wasn't his sport.

He went back into suite D, this time locking the door, and returned the key to room 706 to Menlo's pocket. Then he sat down.

Bett knocked at the door ten minutes later. He went over and opened it, and she stared at him. "Come on in, Bett," he said.

She came in, not saying anything, just staring at him. She was wearing pink slacks and a white shirt and Japanese sandals.

"Come over here, Bett." He took her elbow and guided her through the sitting room and out onto the terrace. He pointed.

She looked. She whispered, "Menlo."

"How was he, Bett? In the rack, I mean?"

"You killed him," she said in a whisper.

"Better than that. Menlo killed himself. He did a better job than he did on me."

"He swore you were dead. He described how he did it. How could he get the statue away from you if you weren't dead?"

Parker went back into the sitting room, and she followed him. "You want a drink, Bett?"

"Please."

"You know where the bar is. I want bourbon."

She hesitated, and then went over and got the drinks. She brought him his bourbon and he took a sip. She couldn't take her eyes off him.

"You like the strong ones," he said. "That's the way it is, isn't it? You don't care what they look like, or what they smell like, or if they're any good in the rack or not. You just want the strong ones. Menlo was going to double-cross me, so that made him strong and you took him into your bed in Washington. Then he came down here and told you how he'd really killed Parker, and that made him the strongest of all. You have a good night, last night, Bett?"

"Screw you," she said.

He finished the bourbon and put the glass down. "I'm leaving tonight," he said, "and after that we're finished. You can't be trusted. You like to watch violence too much. But we've got hours yet before I take off."

"How did you do it, Parker? Chuck, how did you do it?" she whispered.

"Menlo's dead," he said, "and I'm alive. I've got the dough he tried to take off with. I delivered the mourner to your father. And I got the gun from him. Yeah, I got the gun. So who's the strongest now, Bett?"

He could feel it coursing through him, like electricity, strong enough to blot the twinges in his side, to make him forget any stiffness or soreness in his body. The job was over, and it was always like this after a job. A satyr, inexhaustible and insatiable. He was twelve feet tall.

He walked toward the bedroom. "This way, Bett," he said. "We've got five or six hours yet."

She followed him through the doorway, and shut the door behind her.

5

Kapor himself answered the door. It was colder than ever in Washington, after having been in Florida for a few days. Parker came in, carrying the suitcase, and set it down on the parquet floor. He unbuttoned his topcoat and Kapor said, "I take it you were successful."

"In the suitcase there. There was a hundred and twenty dollars less than a hundred grand when I got to it. There's sixty dollars less than fifty grand in that suitcase."

"I will accept your bookkeeping," Kapor replied. "May I offer you a drink?"

"Just give me the address where they've got my partner."

"Ah, yes. I believe I have one of their business cards."

Parker waited in the hallway while Kapor went into the living room. He came back a moment later carrying the card, and handed it to Parker. The place was called Twin Maples, and it was out in Bethesda. Written on the card in pencil was the name Robert Morris.

"Your friend had three driver's licenses in his wallet," Kapor explained. "I chose that one. So that's the name he was admitted under."

"O.K." Parker put the card in his pocket.

"Such a shame," Kapor said, "to be leaving this way. I am going tonight."

"Any rumbles yet?" Parker didn't give a damn one way or the other, but Kapor seemed to feel like talking.

"Not yet, but one never knows. I had hoped to leave in a leisurely fashion, and in style. My books and coins and statues would be packed, various personal possessions crated, and I would remove myself to a safe place surrounded by my possessions. But I must travel fast, and light. I have less than half the money I'd expected to be taking with me and I must leave everything I love behind. Still, I have my life and my health, and this portion of my money which you have returned to me. I shall have a head start on those who most certainly will be coming after me, so I cannot complain too much."

"I'm glad it's all worked out for you," Parker said, reaching for the doorknob.

"I'm leaving the United States, of course, at least temporarily. But perhaps we will meet again eventually, and perhaps someday I shall be able to repay you for what you have done for me."

"Maybe so."

"Good-bye, whatever your name is."

"Good-bye, Kapor."

Parker went back out into the cold and walked down the drive to the cab. He'd had the driver wait. It was another black woman in a crazy hat. Washington cabs were full of them, driving like snowbirds looking for the Man.

Parker got in, took the card from his pocket, and read off the address. The woman driver nodded and the cab shot away from the curb.

On the way, Parker wondered what Handy was thinking about right now. It was a funny thing, but Handy had been going to quit. There were a lot of them like Handy in the racket; one more job, for a stake, and then they'd quit. Handy had been quitting after one more job for years.

But this time, it had seemed like he really meant it. He'd bought himself a diner near an Air Force base at Presque Isle, Maine, and he was planning to short-order it himself. He'd even bought a legitimate car from a legitimate dealer and got legitimate plates for it. It was as though he was off the kinky forever.

Parker had the feeling that this time maybe Handy would be going to Presque Isle, Maine, for good and all.

The rest home was a big old brick building, with more than two maples surrounding it. It looked as though it had been somebody's estate once, but the neighborhood hadn't retained its high tone, so they'd sold out to somebody who wanted to start a rest home. Most of the patients would be alcoholics drying out or subpoena subjects hiding out. And in the middle of them, Handy McKay.

Parker paid the cab and went inside. A professional-looking nurse was sitting at a small desk in the front hallway and Parker asked her if he could visit Robert Morris. She asked him to wait, and he sat down on the wooden bench across from the desk and idly picked up a copy of *Time*. In a moment an overly bluff and hearty man came out and shook Parker's hand overly long and said he was Dr. Wellman. He asked Parker if he was a friend of Mr. Morris's and Parker said yes. The doctor asked if he knew about Mr. Morris's bad stomach condition, and Parker said only that he'd heard there'd been an operation to remove something. The doctor smiled and nodded and said yes, and the patient was coming along just fine, and that he would personally show Parker up to his friend's room.

There was a tiny elevator, an afterthought that obviously hadn't been there originally, and Parker and the doctor crowded into it and went up to the second floor. Handy's room was at the end of the hall. The doctor stayed just long enough to make sure that Handy actually did recognize Parker and had no objection to his being there, and then he withdrew, closing the door.

Handy looked pale, but he was conscious and grinning. "How are things?"

"Taken care of. Everything. I had to make a fifty per cent cut with Kapor, but the rest is safe."

"Good."

"You're going to Presque Isle, Maine?"

"You guessed it. The worst that's gonna happen to me from now on is grease burns."

Parker nodded. He dragged a chair over near the bed and sat down. "How much longer?"

"They say I can get up and start walking in a week or so. Then I'm supposed to stay here another two or three weeks after that but I don't think I will. The story the nurses have is I'm some clown who shot himself by accident, and since I wasn't supposed to have a gun, no permit or something, that's why I'm here instead of a hospital. Not breaking the law all the way, just bending it a little."

"I'm going down to Galveston for a while. When you're ready to pull out of here, give me a call. I'll send you your share. You've got to pay for this place yourself."

"I know, they told me. I'll still have enough left over for what I want."

"You know the place I stay in Galveston?"

"Sure."

"O.K." Parker got to his feet. "Give me a call, huh?"

"You bet."

Parker went to the door. He was reaching for the knob when Handy called out to him.

He turned.

"What about Kapor?"

"He's clearing out tonight. He's free and clear, I guess."

"No trouble from him?"

"No. He got half back, and that's all he cared about."

"What did he say about the mourner?"

Parker thought for a second, and then he laughed. "He didn't even know," he said. "He never even noticed it was gone."